Revisioning, Renewing, and
Rediscovering the Triune Center

Revisioning, Renewing, and Rediscovering the Triune Center

Essays in Honor of Stanley J. Grenz

Edited by
DEREK J. TIDBALL
BRIAN S. HARRIS
and
JASON S. SEXTON

With a Foreword by Roger E. Olson

CASCADE Books • Eugene, Oregon

REVISIONING, RENEWING, AND REDISCOVERING THE TRIUNE CENTER
Essays in Honor of Stanley J. Grenz

Copyright © 2014 Wipf and Stock Publishers. All rights reserved. Except for brief quotations in critical publications or reviews, no part of this book may be reproduced in any manner without prior written permission from the publisher. Write: Permissions, Wipf and Stock Publishers, 199 W. 8th Ave., Suite 3, Eugene, OR 97401.

Cascade Books
An Imprint of Wipf and Stock Publishers
199 W. 8th Ave., Suite 3
Eugene, OR 97401

www.wipfandstock.com

ISBN 13: 978-1-61097-314-4

Cataloguing-in-Publication data:

Revisioning, renewing, and rediscovering the triune center : essays in honor of Stanley J. Grenz / edited Derek J. Tidball, Brian S. Harris, and Jason S. Sexton ; with a foreword by Roger E. Olson.

xxi + 450 pp. ; 23 cm. Includes bibliographical references.

ISBN 13: 978-1-61097-314-4

1. Grenz, Stanley J. (Stanley James), 1950–2005. 2. Evangelicalism. 3. Theology. I. Tidball, Derek. II. Harris, Brian S. III. Sexton, Jason S. IV. Olson, Roger E. V. Title.

BR118 T533 2014

Manufactured in the U.S.A.   09/15/2014

Materials designated *JRA* are from the Stanley Grenz Fonds in the Archives and Special Collections of The John Richard Allison Library, Regent College, Vancouver, BC. All materials used by permission and with grateful thanks to Rich Matiachuk.

Scripture taken from the Holy Bible, NEW INTERNATIONAL VERSION®. Copyright © 1973, 1978, 1984 by Biblica, Inc. All rights reserved worldwide. Used by permission.

New Revised Standard Version Bible, copyright 1989, Division of Christian Education of the National Council of the Churches of Christ in the United States of America. Used by permission. All rights reserved.

For

Edna Grenz

and

the next generation of evangelical theologians

Contents

Contributors   xi
Foreword by Roger E. Olson   xiii
Preface   xvii

Introduction

1   Stanley J. Grenz: A Theological Biography
    —*Brian S. Harris, Jason S. Sexton,* and *Jay T. Smith*   3

Section One: Trinity

2   Three (or More) Ways of Triangulating Theology: On the Very Idea of a Trinitarian System
    —*Kevin J. Vanhoozer*   31

3   Good News for All People: Trinity, Plurality, and Mission
    —*John R. Franke*   59

4   Uncreated and Created Perichoretic Relations
    —*Kurt Anders Richardson*   79

Section Two: Community

5   The Church Local and Universal: Catholic and Baptist Perspectives on *Koinonia* Ecclesiology
    —*Paul S. Fiddes*   97

6   Should We "Welcome" and "Affirm"? Reflecting on Evangelical Responses to Human Sexuality
    —*Stephen R. Holmes*   121

7   Divine Hospitality and Communion: A Trinitarian Theology of Equality, Justice, and Human Flourishing
    —*Veli-Matti Kärkkäinen*   135

Section Three: Eschatology

8   Aesthetics of the Kingdom: Apocalypsis, Eschatos, and Vision for Christian Mission—*Jonathan R. Wilson*   157

9   Kerygmatic Hope: Another Look at Karl Barth's Resistance to Universalism—*David Guretzki*   175

10 "Living as Jesus Did": Practicing an Embodied Future in the Present—*Cherith Fee Nordling*   195

Section Four: Scripture

11 Triangulation in the Psalms of Lament
    —*Ellen T. Charry*   217

12 Renewing a Doctrine of Scripture
    —*A. T. B. McGowan*   236

13 On (Still) Taking St. Paul Seriously: The Hermeneutical Function of Sin and Vice in Scriptural Interpretation
    —*Mark Alan Bowald*   258

Section Five: Tradition

14 A Tale of Two Pietist Theologians: Friedrich Schleiermacher and Stanley Grenz
    —*Glen G. Scorgie and Phil C. Zylla*   283

15 Lost in an Epistemological Maze
    —*William J. Abraham*   303

16 The *Corpus Theologicum* of the Church and Presumptive Authority—*Gregg R. Allison*   319

Section Six: Culture

17 Church Matters—*Stanley Hauerwas*   343

18 Theology After Pandora: The Real Scandal of the Evangelical Mind (and Culture)—*F. LeRon Shults*   361

19 Revelation, Community, and Culture: A Dramatic Inquiry —*David S. Cunningham*   382

Section Seven: Conclusion

20 Evangelical Theology After Grenz: Evangelical Theology and Global Evangelicalism—*Derek J. Tidball*   407

Memorial Sermon—*Bruce Milne*   433

Select Bibliography of the Works of Stanley J. Grenz   441

Subject Index   451
Scripture Index   455

Contributors

WILLIAM J. ABRAHAM, Albert Cook Outler Professor of Wesley Studies and Althshuler Distinguished Teaching Professor at Perkins School of Theology, Southern Methodist University.

GREGG R. ALLISON, Professor of Christian Theology at The Southern Baptist Theological Seminary.

MARK ALAN BOWALD, Associate Professor of Religion and Theology at Redeemer University College.

ELLEN T. CHARRY, Margaret W. Harmon Professor of Systematic Theology at Princeton Theological Seminary.

DAVID S. CUNNINGHAM, Professor of Religion and Director of the CrossRoads Project at Hope College.

PAUL S. FIDDES, Professor of Systematic Theology at the University of Oxford and Director of Research at Regent's Park College, Oxford.

JOHN R. FRANKE, Executive Director and Professor of Missional Theology, Yellowstone Theological Institute; Professor of Religious Studies and Missiology, Evangelische Theologische Faculteit, Leuven.

DAVID GURETZKI, Professor of Theology, Church and Public Life at Briercrest College and Seminary.

BRIAN S. HARRIS, Principal and Head of Department of Ministry and Practice at Vose Seminary, Perth, a member college of the Australian College of Theology.

STANLEY HAUERWAS, Gilbert T. Rowe Professor Emeritus of Divinity and Law at Duke Divinity School, Duke University.

STEPHEN R. HOLMES, Senior Lecturer in Systematic Theology at the University of St. Andrews.

VELI-MATTI KÄRKKÄINEN, Professor of Systematic Theology at Fuller Theological Seminary and Docent of Ecumenics at the University of Helsinki, Finland

A. T. B. MCGOWAN, Minister of Inverness East Church of Scotland, Professor of Theology at the University of the Highlands and Islands, and Honorary Professor in Reformed Doctrine at the University of Aberdeen.

BRUCE MILNE, author, Former Pastor of First Baptist Church, Vancouver, BC.

CHERITH FEE NORDLING, Associate Professor of Theology at Northern Seminary.

ROGER E. OLSON, Foy Valentine Professor of Christian Theology and Ethics at George W. Truett Theological Seminary, Baylor University.

KURT ANDERS RICHARDSON, Associate Professor at the Graduate Institute of Applied Linguistics.

GLEN G. SCORGIE, Professor of Theology at Bethel Seminary San Diego.

JASON S. SEXTON, Research Associate at the Center for Religion and Civic Culture, University of Southern California.

F. LERON SHULTS, Professor of Theology and Philosophy at University of Agder, Norway.

JAY T. SMITH, Bridger Professor of Theology and Ethics, Yellowstone Theological Institute.

DEREK J. TIDBALL, Former Principal of London School of Theology and Visiting Scholar at Spurgeon's College.

KEVIN J. VANHOOZER, Research Professor of Systematic Theology at Trinity Evangelical Divinity School.

JONATHAN R. WILSON, Pioneer McDonald Professor of Theology at Carey Theological College.

PHIL C. ZYLLA, Academic Dean of McMaster Divinity College.

Foreword

STANLEY GRENZ WAS A man on a mission. He was a complex combination of humility and ambition. He would be bemused by such an all-star collection of essays in his honor. He resisted all labels except "evangelical," "Baptist," and, of course, "Christian."

Those are the facts about my late friend Stan that readers of this *Festschrift* should know as they plunge into it.

You would be justified in asking how I know these and other truths about Stan. Stan was one of my closest friends for about twenty-five years. I was one of his closest friends. We were almost like brothers. We challenged and supported each other, not only professionally but also personally. We wrote two books together and planned more projects together that never happened, although some of my writings and some of his were at least partly the results of suggestions from the other.

One of my most vivid and enduring memories of Stan is from the numerous times we roomed together at professional society meetings. Stan would come back to the room from a day of delivering and hearing papers and interacting with publishers, editors, acquaintances, and friends. I was usually almost asleep. He would keep me awake until 2:00 AM talking about his projects, evangelical theology, his joys and disappointments, our families, our careers and . . . what I should write. I say "one memory" because all these times blur together in my memory now.

Stan's and my last communication was an email exchange about an evangelical seminary president we both wanted on "our side" (what I call postconservative or progressive evangelicalism). The president had chided Stan and me, upbraiding us publicly for talking about "new light" that God always has to give forth from his Word. This was a terrible disappointment to us as we considered him one of us and wanted his support. We had both reached out to him with poor results. Stan's last words to me were (paraphrasing) "We're pietists; he's not. There's the difference."

I can take credit for one thing about Stan's theology. I helped him rediscover and embrace his pietist roots. Toward the end he did publicly accept that label and proudly called himself a "pietist with a PhD" (meaning not anti-intellectual). To Stan and me being pietist meant having an irenic spirit toward all fellow evangelicals and a "large tent" view of evangelicalism. But this identity, and Stan's mission to turn evangelical theology back to its pietist roots, resulted in criticisms and rejections that grieved him more than me. He was optimistic about its reception; I never was.

As I said, Stan was a man with a mission. That mission was twofold. First, he wanted to help young, disillusioned evangelicals on the brink of discarding their evangelical identities to rediscover and embrace it. He wanted to redefine "evangelical" away from fundamentalism and scholastic orthodoxy, while maintaining a healthy appreciation for trinitarian theology and conversional spirituality. Second, he wanted to turn the tide of what we both considered a new fundamentalism among evangelical scholars. That's why he joined a large, conservative evangelical theology group and stayed in it long after it became clear that it was moving in a different direction, away from his vision of evangelicalism. Together we planned a new theological society that would become a "home" for progressive (what I called "post-conservative") evangelical scholars. But he died before it came to fruition. His death took the wind out of my sails—at least for a time.

On a personal level, Stan was a complex combination of humility and ambition. People who knew him well, as I did, knew his heart. He had no delusions of grandeur; he knew very well his own faults, flaws, and failings. He was as interested in helping younger scholars get published and find teaching positions as he was in publishing and climbing the ladder of success himself (if not more). His own vision of "success" was influence, not fame. Some people who did not know Stan well thought he was overly ambitious and even at times proud. Because I knew him so well, I could not see that side of him. I never did. But both of us knew some regarded him that way or at least tried to portray him as such. That hurt him deeply but did not keep him from pursuing his mission.

Stan would look at the all-star "cast" of this *Festschrift* in his honor and be bemused but at the same time very pleased. One of my memories of Stan is his reaction to a well-known theologian's public expression of admiration for Stan's "project." That night, as we reviewed the day in our hotel room, he said to me, with a very pleased expression, "I didn't know I had a project!" Other people were aware of his theological project before he was! I recall how bemused and pleased he was when he heard that students were planning to write dissertations about his theology. Stan's very sincere reaction to this *Festschrift* would be "I don't think I deserve it, but I'll gladly accept it anyway."

Stan wanted to be, if not all things to all people, as much to everyone as possible. He knew his "world" was evangelicalism, yet he wanted also to enter the "mainline," but as an evangelical. As the same time, he wanted to reach out to fundamentalists, and he befriended any who reached back. Because he desired to be influential in many "camps" and "parties" of the Christian academy he eschewed most labels. I well remember telling him over dinner at an AAR meeting "Stan, you're an Arminian." His response was "I know, but don't tell anyone." When I finally convinced him that my meaning of "postconservative evangelical" fit him to a "tee" his response was that he'd prefer not to wear that or any other label beyond "evangelical," "Baptist," and "Christian." Only toward the end did he joyfully embrace "pietist." But he was a pietist in the very best sense of the word.

Roger E. Olson

Preface

FEW THEOLOGIANS WERE SHAPING conversations in North American Evangelical theology like Stanley Grenz. Certainly Canada's primary contribution to late twentieth-century Protestant theology, he was easily one of the turn of the century's leading English-speaking evangelical theologians. During a time when evangelicalism was significantly influencing matters in the public square,[1] and as evangelical theology was coming of age in the wider academic world, Stanley Grenz stood out among his peers. This was seen especially by his commitment to serving the church with whatever abilities he had. His abilities, his gifts, showed up in the form of his writings. It is therefore only fitting that a gift seeking to honor him—just ahead of what would have occasioned his 65th birthday, and nearly ten years since we lost such a significant figure—would also take the form of a written tribute.

While no longer with us, this *Festschrift* is a collection of essays by an international cast of scholars, offered in his honor. Some of these contributors had very close friendships with Stan Grenz, while others were influenced by his work in significant ways. Yet all stood in deep appreciation and admiration for his single contribution to evangelical theology.

Grenz's academic interests covered an array of issues in his own day, from the span of the traditional systematic corpus to contemporary theology, to critical ethical issues, to popular culture and wider intellectual movements. The present volume sets out to address a number of important matters related to contemporary theology, all which represent matters Grenz was concerned with and which he contributed to, and some which have developed significantly over the past decade.

Many of the contributors chose to engage Grenz's work substantially. While not required by the editors, this was the practice largely adopted throughout, with essays quite suitably honoring their friend and colleague. Notwithstanding substantial direct engagement with Grenz's considerable corpus (work that has been offered elsewhere), the kind of engagement with

---

1. It will be remembered that Grenz was at his peak prowess during the first half of the second Bush presidency.

Grenz's writings conducted in this volume shows just how far ahead of the curve he was in his own day.

Yet the main purpose of this volume was to produce a collection of essays by first-rate scholars that not only would honor Grenz, but that would consist of essays he'd be eager *to read*. In this way, we chose to structure the volume around the big issues that his work revolved around—namely, his *motifs* and *sources* for theology. He saw three key themes in evangelical theology: Trinity, community, eschatology; and he understood theology as drawing from three primary sources, in this order: Scripture, tradition, and culture. Accompanied with essays by the editors as book ends, first exploring Grenz's intellectual journey (ch. 1) and then reflecting on evangelical theology *after* Stanley Grenz (ch. 20), this volume gathers three essays under each of the six key areas of Grenz's theology. And we suspect Grenz would have been delighted by each of the contributions as they've come in.

The essays here represent a range of perspectives: from Trinitarian and evangelical to so called post-evangelical, and far beyond—where few have boldly gone. Some of the authors offer almost playful interjections into their arguments, posing how Grenz's work might have been appropriated for their arguments and proposals, and perhaps what Grenz might have thought of them or how he may have responded to this or that.

Perhaps the most provocative piece, by LeRon Shults, would have disheartened Grenz significantly at various points, and yet raises a number of important issues that the next generation of evangelicals will surely have to wrestle with, which Grenz would have welcomed, even as he would have done LeRon in this volume. Shults's appropriation of *Avatar* (hearkening Grenz's use of cultural modalities) makes one wonder, on the other hand, what Grenz might have thought of Spike Jonze's recent Los Angeles-based film *Her*, and how humans are relating to technology with increasing sophistication, with implications for both sex ethics and theological anthropology, areas that considerably energized Grenz. Yet in the midst of cultural trends and innovations, his steady concern was with how theology might best serve the church "in formulating its message in a manner that can speak within the historical-social context," or "speak *to* culture," without being swallowed up by it.[2] In these ways, Grenz never granted culture the weight of "being the normative standard determining the nature of the gospel message itself, but as a conversation partner that as theologians we must take seriously in

---

2. Stanley J. Grenz, *Revisioning Evangelical Theology* (Downers Grove, IL: InterVarsity, 1993), 99, 106–8 (italics in original); cp. Stanley J. Grenz and John R. Franke, *Beyond Foundationalism: Shaping Theology in a Postmodern Context* (Louisville: Westminster John Knox), 151, 159.

our constructive articulations of the 'faith once delivered.'"³ Culture then provided Grenz the essential conceptual tools to "assist the church in expressing its world view in current thought-forms and in addressing current problems and outlooks."⁴

Some of the essays here set forth efforts from those working in close continuity with Grenz's proposal: see Vanhoozer's argument on the nature of a truly *Trinitarian* theology (ch. 2); or Steve Holmes on sexuality and ascesis (ch. 6); or Paul Fiddes on *koinonia* ecclesiology (ch. 5); or Andrew McGowan on a reformed doctrine of Scripture (ch. 12). Other essays buttress Grenz's work by freshly addressing issues related to Grenz's proposal which it seems Grenz had not developed as fully as he might have, including here Gregg Allison on the quality of doctrines that remain in the tradition (ch. 16), and Billy Abraham on challenges to Grenz's epistemology (ch. 15). Weighing into major issues in the wider world of contemporary theology are Richardson on perichoretic relations (ch. 4), Jonathan Wilson with a fresh contribution on the "apocalyptic" conversation (ch. 8), David Guretzki on Barth and universalism (ch. 9), and Stanley Hauerwas, naturally, on the church's political theology (ch. 17). Veli-Matti Kärkkäinen (ch. 7) and Grenz's co-author John Franke (ch. 3) offer essays related to the church's mission today in a globalized world, a situation wherein Grenz was eager to serve.⁵

This volume is far from uniform in its views of Grenz's contribution, agenda, and emphases—even the editors hardly agree on how to read him! But such is the nature of evangelical theology, often a matter of emphasis. However, no extraordinary effort was taken to hide these conflicted readings: whether Grenz was conservative or post-conservative; or whether his method gave too much weight to culture (Abraham, ch. 15); or where he fit in the wider evangelical world (ch. 1; and Scorgie and Zylla, ch. 14). Among the especially creative pieces by Vanhoozer, Wilson, Kärkkäinen, Guretzki, and others, are the essays by David Cunningham, which develops his own "dramatic" reading of theology and the role of the church in the world (ch. 19), and the essay by Mark Bowald on appropriating a theology of sin in the process of interpreting Scripture (ch. 13), a subject (*Theological Interpretation of Scripture*) that Grenz was very interested in.⁶

---

3. Grenz, "Fideistic Revelationalism: Donald Bloesch's Antirationalist Theological Method," in *Evangelical Theology in Transition: Theologians in Dialogue with Donald Bloesch*, edited by Elmer M. Colyer (Downers Grove, IL: InterVarsity, 1999), 57.

4. Grenz, *Theology for the Community of God*, 2nd ed. (Grand Rapids: Eerdmans, 2000), 19–20.

5. See comments on the occasion of his 2002 move to Baylor, ch. 1, [insert page no.]

6. See his, "Community, Interpretative," in *Dictionary for Theological Interpretation*

Beyond all these, there are two essays that stand out significantly in this collection. First, Cherith Fee Nordling's essay on living in light of the resurrected life (ch. 10) bears unique significance, both as a theme in Grenz's writing and because Grenz has gone on ahead of us in glory. Also of particular significance is the moving essay on the lament psalms by Professor Ellen Charry (ch. 11), which piece especially embodies the true spirit of evangelical theology in its attentiveness to the realities and grain of Scripture. Ahead of her work in the Brazos theological commentary series, she pens a theological-exegetical essay consistent with the strong and careful way that Grenz sought to read Scripture,[7] and which he was accustomed to sitting under, as evidenced by the powerful exposition from the Rev. Dr. Bruce Milne[8] at the conclusion of this volume. Charry even appropriates Grenz's pneumatological principle from the outset, highlighting his commitment to Scripture's authority in the life of the church, and also raising questions (as the psalmist did) of lamentation in our present, broken world where things are not as they should be.

Along with the vastly appropriate foreword from Grenz's longtime friend, Professor Olson, some of the essays contain more personal notes that don't always find their way into *Festschrifts*, at least traditionally. And yet the editors here feel that these could not be more appropriate, especially those from Cherith Fee Nordling at the close of her essay and especially the special contribution from Stan Grenz's memorial service, delivered by Stan's pastor, Bruce Milne.

Contributors to this book consist of those friends of Stanley Grenz who were influenced and remain indebted to his contribution to evangelical scholarship. And we now submit these essays in honor of Stanley J. Grenz, with special thanks to Robin Parry for believing in the project and, with us, wanting to honor our colleague with this volume. It's hard to believe it's been ten years since his death; most of today's younger generation will have much less familiarity with his contribution than the older generation of today's middler and senior scholars. And so it's also for them that we offer up this collection, in order that "a future generation . . . may praise the Lord" (Ps 102:18) as our brother Stanley Grenz faithfully did in his labors. None

---

of the Bible (2005).

7. Seen Grenz's theological exegesis of Scripture in *Social God* (2001) and the posthumously published, *Named God*; and also that he was eager to prepare a ms. from sermons on Rom 1–3 and 1 Peter.

8. Bruce Milne, a scholar in a class all his own with a PhD from New College under T. F. Torrance, has sold well over half a million copies of his books, globally, from the 1970s to the present.

of these efforts, of course, were perfect, but they were offered by a truly exceptional evangelical scholar, who was far ahead of most of us.

The Editors
Lent, 2014

Introduction

1

Stanley J. Grenz

A Theological Biography

BRIAN S. HARRIS, JASON S. SEXTON, *and* JAY T. SMITH

Stanley J. Grenz's Life, Career, and Ministry

STANLEY JAMES GRENZ WAS born 7 January 1950, in Alpena, Michigan to Richard and Clara Grenz. The youngest of three siblings, Grenz grew up in the home of a North American (German) Baptist pastor and moved several times, from Michigan to the Dakotas, to Montana, and Colorado. Grenz's childhood, far from that of the pastor's kid sometimes caricatured in popular media, was "imbued with a warm hearted piety."[1] While his writings show few references to the spirituality of his childhood, the importance of his rearing in a close knit, pietistically-oriented Baptist family is obvious to those who knew him. Richard and Clara Grenz sought to provide a home and family life for their children that was permeated by a deeply devotional and conversionist spirituality that marked the German Baptist heritage.

After completing high school, Grenz attended the University of Colorado in Boulder with the intention of pursuing a career as a nuclear physicist. His mind was sharp enough and his grades high enough to make such a career possible, yet ultimately a call to ministry experienced in 1971 forced a change in direction. During this time, Grenz's study at the University of

---

1. See his "Concerns of a Pietist with a Ph.D."

Colorado took a turn from physics to philosophy and he came under the influence of Ed Miller, a professor of philosophy at the university. Miller fondly recalls his time with Grenz and the cultivation of a relationship that would grow deeply during the balance of Grenz's life, later yielding a collaborative book project. He recounts the decision he made to bequeath Karl Barth's personal sitting chair to Grenz, but Grenz died before being able to take possession of it.[2]

While at the University of Colorado, Grenz toured with a North American Baptist sponsored musical group, "God's Volunteers," where he met Edna Sturhahn, whom he would marry in December 1971. In his 13 March 2005 eulogy, Brian McLaren emphasized Grenz's deep love for Edna and his deeply spiritual way of life. McLaren's reflection is worth repeating in its entirety:

> One topic of conversation I especially remember from that afternoon—Stan's love for his wife. At that point, I hadn't met Edna yet, but Stan talked with enthusiasm about how gifted she was, and how much he wanted to support her in her own ministry and leadership in the years ahead. When I met Edna a year or two later, I was immediately impressed by her gentleness, depth, class, and courage, and I could see why Stan didn't see her as his gracious companion only, but also as his colleague and partner in ministry.[3]

Grenz's loving relationship to his wife was generally indicative of his passion for his family, church, vocation, and colleagues. After graduation in 1973 from the University of Colorado (Phi Beta Kappa), Grenz earned the Master of Divinity in 1976 at the Conservative Baptist Theological Seminary (later becoming Denver Seminary). While in Denver, his love of Scripture and passion for theological method were developed under the influence of his professor Gordon Lewis and President Vernon Grounds. As he approached graduation from seminary, Grenz's advisor at the University of Colorado, Ed Miller, introduced him to Wolfhart Pannenberg in October 1975 during Panneberg's U.S. speaking tour. This meeting and consequent study with Pannenberg would establish Grenz's theological trajectory in significant ways.

Stan and Edna moved to Munich in 1976 in order for Stan to pursue doctoral studies with Pannenberg. Their son Joel was born in Munich, 20 August 1978. Pannenberg encouraged Grenz, as he did all of his students, to study an aspect of his own theological interest and trajectory. At

---

2. Miller, "Barth's Chair."
3. McLaren, "Foreword," in *Renewing the Center*, 2nd ed., 7.

this time Pannenberg was working on ecclesiology, and so for his research Grenz chose to study the theology and ecclesiology of Isaac Backus, the North-American Puritan and Baptist theologian, which work was later published by Mercer University Press.[4] More importantly, Grenz's personal relationship with his *doktorvater* and scholarly engagement with Pannenberg's thought brought about something of a renaissance in his own thinking that would establish his trajectory. This engagement with Pannenberg was to critically shape Grenz's understanding of theological methodology, the Trinity, anthropology, pneumatology, Christology, and eschatology. Indeed the convergence of Grenz's pietistic Baptist theological sensibilities with Pannenberg's rigorous theological project has been identified by some as proposing a postconservative paradigm for evangelical theology,[5] while virtually all have acknowledged the creativity of his project for the sake of serving the church in meaningful and imaginative ways.

In June 1980 Grenz graduated from the University of Munich. But he returned to Canada earlier in order to take up a brief stint as pastor of Rowandale Baptist Church in Winnipeg, MB, from January 1979 to June 1981, during which time his daughter Corina was born, 28 December 1979. While in Winnipeg he also taught adjunct theology courses for The University of Winnipeg and at Providence Theological Seminary (formerly Winnipeg Theological Seminary) from 1980–81, after which time Grenz began his career as a professor of theology at the North American Baptist Theological Seminary in Sioux Falls, South Dakota. He taught in Sioux Falls from 1981–90 as Professor of Systematic Theology and Ethics. Following a year-long sabbatical in Munich as a Fulbright Scholar (1987–88), Grenz published the proceeds as a book on Pannenberg's systematic theology with Oxford University Press in 1990.[6] Grenz's analysis of this work reveals at many points the manner in which he would later adopt and adapt his mentor's work into his own.[7] Following his nine-year tenure at North American Baptist Theological Seminary, Grenz accepted an appointment to Carey Theological College and Regent College in Vancouver, BC as Pioneer McDonald Professor of Baptist Heritage, Theology and Ethics. Grenz's initial twelve years in Vancouver (1990–2002) would inaugurate his prolific writing career—effectively a research post that allowed him to cultivate his rigorous publication agenda and regular speaking regimen at other academic

4. Grenz, *Isaac Backus—Puritan and Baptist*.

5. Olson, *Journey of Modern Theology*, 640–48, who acknowledges that Grenz never used the term for himself or his own work; such a claim about Grenz's work as postconservative is highly contestable.

6. Grenz, *Reason for Hope*.

7. Sexton, *Trinitarian Theology*, chs. 2–3.

institutions, events, and churches. During this period, Grenz penned fourteen books, and for a portion of it held an affiliate appointment at Northern Baptist Seminary in Lombard, Illinois as Professor of Theology and Ethics (1996–99). In 1999 he received a Henry Luce III Fellowship in the theology program, the first scholar from a Canadian institution to receive the award, which enabled the completion of the first installment of his Matrix in Christian Theology series with Westminster John Knox.

Things changed with an appointment in 2002 as Distinguished Professor of Theology at Baylor University and the George W. Truett Theological Seminary in Waco, Texas, where Grenz's career was prepared to transition to a different league of academic engagement. Here his responsibilities were primarily to teach at Truett Seminary and work with Baylor's department of religion and its doctoral program.[8] The move to Baylor included a 1–1 teaching load (on occasion 2–1) where, as Distinguished Professor, Grenz was directly under Provost Donald Schmeltekopf. Grenz understood his duties as best serving Baylor "by pursuing my scholarly endeavors, that is, by writing books and essays, as well as by representing Baylor at conferences and speaking engagements of various kinds both in the USA and elsewhere in the world."[9] Grenz understood himself as becoming a world theologian in service to the global church. This was, of course, consistent with his work with the global Baptist World Alliance, which had been ongoing since the early 1980s and was where he came to know other leaders in the wider Baptist world, like Oxford academic Professor Paul Fiddes and the notable British evangelical figure, Derek Tidball. During the 2002–3 academic year, however, while working through issues of relocation, there was a change in the provost's office and David Lyle Jeffrey became provost-elect. It became clear to Grenz, prompted from a 23 February 2003 lunch with Jeffrey and follow up email the next day, that Jeffrey did not share the same vision Grenz thought had been earlier agreed. Rather, there had been a shift in the understanding of his role toward a more "Waco-based, campus-centered, and curricular or programmically oriented" vision, where teaching would be at the "heart of our task together" as Baylor faculty.[10]

Amidst these significant challenges that seemed to have been either misunderstandings or plain shifts in agreement and emphasis for Grenz's

---

8. Fogleman, "Renowned Theologian."

9. Letter dated 12 June 2002 in files in "MyPosition" folder, in "Baylor2002–2002" folder, available as electronic file at the *JRA*.

10. See file "BaylorSituation," last saved 15 Mar. 2003 and "Musings.move" in files from "MyPosition" folder, in "Baylor2002–2002" folder, available as electronic file at the *JRA*. See other files in this electronic folder chronicling Grenz's struggle during this time to make sense of the challenging situation.

role, which he labelled "those tumultuous weeks in early 2003,"[11] he began to reconsider whether Waco was the best place for him. Through much soul-searching, it became clear that Edna was not able to find a position in Waco where she could meaningfully exercise her gifts vocationally, as she had earlier in her role as Director of Ministry and Worship at First Baptist Church, Vancouver. Through the developments that took place, Stan and Edna understood what seemed to be signs from God that they were to remain in Vancouver, even if so doing meant giving up the post at Baylor. So while professionally located at Baylor for a year, Grenz's appointment here didn't last beyond the one year and so never became established. On 31 May 2003, Grenz entered into a letter of understanding with Carey Theological College to officially return to the faculty of Carey Theological College on 1 August 2003, once again serving as Pioneer McDonald Professor of Theology.

Grenz did not resume the earlier duties he held at Regent College with his joint appointment at Carey *and* Regent College, but did receive a second appointment as Professor of Theology at the Mars Hill Graduate School (now Seattle School of Theology and Psychology) in Seattle. In this period, from 2003 until his passing in 2005, Grenz spoke widely in academic and church settings, and he continued his research agenda at Carey. From 2003 until his passing in 2005, Grenz published an additional six articles, along with multiple contributions to edited volumes, and then two more books. At his passing, he had only just completed a manuscript draft twenty-four hours earlier, with corrections and additions posthumously made by his teaching assistant, Jay Smith.

Exemplary as a theologian, Grenz was committed to the life of the church and to training his students to be ministers in the church. Many of his colleagues and friends were especially encouraged that a theologian of Grenz's stature would also sing and play his guitar and trumpet in church worship services. Of course, Grenz's profound love for the church was evidenced much earlier in his career in his service as a youth minister and pastor, having been ordained to pastoral ministry on 13 June 1976, the same year he graduated from seminary. It should come to no one's surprise that Stan's love for God would not only be on display in worship, but also in the classroom. He would frequently bring his guitar to the classroom and lead students in a brief moment of prayer and worship through song before the class would start. In light of this, it should not be surprising that one of Grenz's last published articles was on the topic of doxology.[12]

---

11. Grenz, *Rediscovering the Triune God*, xii.
12. Grenz, "Celebrating Eternity."

At the time he passed away in the early morning of 12 March 2005, twenty-four hours after suffering a massive brain hemorrhage, Stan Grenz had authored, co-authored, or edited twenty-eight books, and over one hundred articles, essays, and reviews, covering a wide-range of theological subjects. Writing came naturally to him, and colleagues at Carey recount how during dull moments in faculty meetings he would continue writing and editing his latest work, occasionally pausing to contribute to the discussion.[13] Publishers would also occasionally joke how Grenz would construct a book proposal while walking down the aisle of an academic society meeting. His insatiable desire to learn more about the church and the shape of the explication of its Trinitarian faith, in order to help the church more effectively bring the gospel into the culture of his day, was what drove Stan Grenz's life and work. And he was always eager to contribute and stand on whatever platform the Lord gave him.

Surveying Grenz's Work

The remainder of the present essay attempts to provide a selective survey of Grenz's work chronologically. The goal is to articulate the major themes and emphases in Grenz's theology as well as the progression of his thought. It is, however, appropriate to begin with some general comments on Grenz's writing.

A Wide Audience

Grenz constantly wrote with different target audiences in mind.[14] Several of his texts are intentionally a synthesis of the work of others, a genre at which he excelled.[15] Grenz wore different hats, reflecting his broad and diverse

---

13. Personal conversations between Brian Harris and Carey faculty, July 2006.

14. E.g., he reworked *Theology for the Community* (1994) into *Created for Community* (1996), and then into *What Christians Really Believe—and Why* (1998), calling these his "theological 'trilogy'" (*Renewing the Center*, 2d ed., 16). The later vols. summarize key points of the seminary-level text, distilled for undergraduates and ordinary lay people, respectively. *Theology for the Community* was due to be revised in 2012, once Grenz finished his explorative Matrix series, ahead of a larger three-volume Systematic Theology schedule to commence in 2013 (Grenz, "Writing Projects," under e-file, "WritingDeadlines.wpd" from the *JRA*, updated 22 Feb. 2005). So he saw continuity and coherence in his work, labored toward this end, as highlighted in his eagerness to revise and the natural ease displayed in his revisions.

15. E.g., *Reason for Hope*; *Millennial Maze*; *Rediscovering the Triune God*; *Twentieth-Century Theology*.

interests. It is easy to imagine Grenz the professor carefully collating material into a format suitable for a seminary text.[16] Wearing his hat as ethicist and pastor, Grenz wrote on civil religion, abortion, prayer, women in ministry, the millennium, hell, spirituality, and pastoral misconduct.[17] A special focus was in the realm of sexual ethics, this interest also extending to the question of homosexuality.[18] He wrote an introductory overview of Christian belief, an apologetic for studying theology, and short dictionaries both on theological terms and also on ethics.[19] As a Baptist theologian, some of his work is aimed at a specifically Baptist readership,[20] flowing from his initial doctoral research.[21] Several of his books are coauthored, perhaps reflecting his conviction that theology is not only for the community of God, but should flow from that community working together.[22] All his work, even when aimed at a wider readership, is carefully written and demonstrates significant theological reflection.

Given these broad parameters, one might ask what themes emerge from an analysis of Grenz's work?

The Initial Doctoral Impetus

The first stream is a series of publications that flow from his doctoral studies focusing on either the subject of his doctoral dissertation, Isaac Backus, or the work of his doctoral mentor, Wolfhart Pannenberg.

16. E.g., *Moral Quest*; *Rediscovering the Triune God*.

17. "Listen America!" (1982); "Abortion" (1984); *Prayer: The Cry for the Kingdom* (1988); "Secular Saints" (1990); *Millennial Maze*; "When the Pastor Fails" (1995); "Anticipating God's New Community" (1995); "Is Hell Forever?" (1998); "God's Business" (1999); "Postmodern Canada" (2000); "Concerns of a Pietist" (2002); *Betrayal of Trust* (1995); *Women in the Church* (1995); "Belonging to God" (1999); "Hopeful Pessimist" (2000).

18. *Aids* (1990); "What Is Sex For?" (1987); "The Purpose of Sex" (1990); "When the Pastor Fails" (1995); *Sexual Ethics* (1990, rev. 1997); *Welcoming But Not Affirming* (1998).

19. *What Christians Really Believe—and Why*; *Created for Community*; *Pocket Dictionary of Theological Terms* (1999); *Who Needs Theology?* (1996); *Pocket Dictionary of Ethics* (2003).

20. *Baptist Congregation* (1985); "Maintaining the Balanced Life" (1991); "Conversing in Christian Style" (2000); "Baptism and the Lord's Supper" (2003).

21. "Church and State" (1983); *Isaac Backus—Puritan and Baptist* (1983); "Isaac Backus and the English Baptist Tradition" (1984); "Isaac Backus" (1986); "Isaac Backus," in *Baptist Theologians* (1990).

22. *Betrayal of Trust*; *Beyond Foundationalism* (2001); *Pocket Dictionary of Theological Terms*; *Women in the Church*; *Twentieth Century Theology*; *Who Needs Theology?*; *Pocket Dictionary of Ethics*; and *Aids*.

Backus was instrumental in redefining the nature of the Baptist movement in eighteenth-century New England. Several of Grenz's earlier publications focus on Backus's legacy to Baptist life and thought and highlight his contribution to the struggle for the separation of church and state.[23]

Backus's separation of the spheres of church and state and his delineation of the roles to be reserved for the church, find echoes in Grenz's emphasis on theology being done by and for the community of faith. Neither Grenz nor Backus see this separation as being inherently escapist, but as ensuring that the church has integrity when called to exercise a prophetic role in society.[24] Grenz is also impressed by Backus's view that conversion involves entering into a covenant relationship with both God and the church, and sees it as a "needed corrective for much Baptist thinking that builds largely on the individualism of the Baptist heritage while ignoring the corporate dimension . . . ."[25] Grenz's own conviction on the centrality of the community finds an early expression in this passage. Although Backus does not feature prominently in Grenz's later theological construction, he serves as an inspirational figure for Grenz. Thus, in his preface to *Renewing the Center* Grenz writes, "This volume seeks to follow in the spirit of people like Backus and offer a hopeful appraisal of evangelical theology in the time of upheaval in which we are living."[26]

With Wolfhart Pannenberg as Grenz's doctoral mentor, it is not surprising that Grenz made a careful analysis and evaluation of Pannenberg's theology.[27] The choice of Pannenberg as his doctoral mentor is significant.[28]

---

23. "Church and State"; *Isaac Backus—Puritan and Baptist*; "Isaac Backus and the English Baptist Tradition"; "Isaac Backus: Eighteenth-Century Light"; "Isaac Backus" in *Baptist Theologians*.

24. See Grenz's approving summary of Backus's position that "all human laws and all political systems be continually subjected to scrutiny in the light of God's coming rule. In this task, the religious community must play a major role, becoming the prophetic reminder that political systems are not final, in view of God's final rule" ("Church and State," 89).

25. "Isaac Backus," in *Baptist Theologians*, 115–16.

26. Later Grenz wrote, "Evangelicals today can do no better than be admonished by, draw inspiration from, and follow after the examples of Edwards, Backus, and a host of other Evangelical luminaries" (*Renewing the Center* [2000], 7, 23).

27. "Pannenberg and Marxism" (1987); "Reasonable Christianity" (1988); "Wolfhart Pannenberg's Quest for Ultimate Truth" (1988); "Commitment and Dialogue" (1989); *Reason for Hope* (1990); "Pannenberg and Evangelical Theology" (1991); "Wolfhart Pannenberg: Reason, Hope and Transcendence" (1991); "The Irrelevancy of Theology" (1992).

28. The compliment of being accepted as a doctoral student by Pannenberg is also significant. Grenz was the second student from the USA to complete a doctorate under Pannenberg (*Reason for Hope* [1990], vii).

Though a noted theologian, Pannenberg has not traditionally been classified as an evangelical. Grenz's willingness to step outside of classical evangelical theology was an early indicator of his inclusive spirit, while in turn he has helped make the thinking of Pannenberg both more accessible and acceptable to evangelical theology.[29]

Grenz's emphasis on eschatology, which he suggested in 2000 should be theology's orienting motif, has clear links with Pannenberg's thought. This is particularly seen in his emphasis on eschatological realism.[30] However, there are interesting discontinuities. Grenz recognizes the value of science, but does not share Pannenberg's enthusiasm for the scientific method and is deeply conscious of its missiological limitations in trying to communicate with those shaped by a postmodern ethos. In an article that largely defends Pannenberg's theological method, he describes as "problematic . . . Pannenberg's apparent thorough-going rationalism and hard-nosed rejection of any attempt to base theological conclusions on a faith decision that has not been through the fire of rational reflection and challenged by alternative viewpoints."[31] Grenz, however, readily acknowledges that this rationalism is linked to Pannenberg's understanding of himself as a "theologian called to serve the church in the public marketplace of ideas."[32] By contrast, Grenz writes his theology "for the community of God."[33] This is a

---

29. Especially remarkable was Pannenberg's cooperation in allowing Grenz to publish a summary of Pannenberg's *Systematische Theologie*, when the German version of the full project was still underway and any hope of an English translation was years off. With only the first of the three volumes published in German, Grenz utilized material from Pannenberg's lectures in Munich to anticipate the thrust of the remaining two volumes. In the foreword to the book, Pannenberg notes that he thought the method "touched me as a typically American desire to be always ahead of time," while he went on to confirm that "concerning the overall synthesis of my theology, it provides a correct picture" (*Reason for Hope* [1990], ix).

30. While Grenz viewed Pannenberg's theology as consistent with several of the main trajectories of Christian theology, he maintained that Pannenberg moved beyond classical theology in his conviction that truth is not found in the unchanging essences behind the flow of time, but that truth is "essentially historical and ultimately eschatological" ("Wolfhart Pannenberg: Reason, Hope and Transcendence," 77). For a detailed exposition of features Grenz adopted and adapted from Pannenberg's methodology and theology, see Sexton, *Trinitarian Theology*, 19–66.

31. "Wolfhart Pannenberg: Reason, Hope and Transcendence," 86. Grenz was aware of another side to Pannenberg, and wrote of his mentor's first encounter with Christ when, as a teenager walking through the woods, Pannenberg had an experience of feeling himself flooded or elevated by a sea of light. Grenz noted that "Over the ensuing years this experience has become the basis for Pannenberg's keen sense of calling" (ibid., 74).

32. Ibid., 86.

33. Grenz saw theology as "a second-order discipline pursued 'from within.' The

significant difference from Pannenberg. Grenz notes that Pannenberg sees theology as a public discipline and consciously opts for this to combat what Pannenberg perceives to be the widespread privatization of religious belief.[34] An apologetic motivation thus undergirds Pannenberg's approach. There is a little irony of an evangelical theologian, such as Grenz, opting for an in-house approach to theology while the supposedly less evangelical Pannenberg opts for a method apparently more readily disposed to the German university curriculum and the wider public.[35]

Revisioning Evangelical Theology for Renewal

While Grenz's doctoral work provides a helpful focus for his earlier work, his overall theological contribution is probably better understood under the broad theme of *Revisioning Evangelical Theology*, to cite the title of his 1993 publication, which in its subtitle articulates Grenz's hope to articulate *A Fresh Agenda for the 21st Century*.

As early as in 1985 Grenz had indicated an interest in a theological agenda suited to the needs of the future. In a rarely cited article "A Theology for the Future,"[36] after analyzing six challenges likely to have a global impact, Grenz thinks through their likely implication for future theological construction and argues, "This theology cannot be merely a recounting of the doctrinal orthodoxies of the past, couched in discarded cosmologies. Rather, it must include a model of reality which can encompass future scientific breakthroughs."[37] We could argue that the 1985 Grenz appears to be encapsulated in a modern mindset. Enthusing about a theology for the future he writes of a future transforming "model of reality" (singular) encompassing "scientific breakthroughs." However, his later theological agenda remains true to the six defining characteristics he suggests will be important for a theology for the future, namely that it:

---

enterprise is a critical, reflective activity that presupposes the beliefs and practices of the Christian community" (*Revisioning*, 75).

34. *Reason for Hope* (1990), 8.

35. It is not that Grenz did not wish to be missional, but his strategy was different. Like Backus, Grenz believed that a renewed church will impact the world. Thus, citing Edwards and Backus as "surely correct," Grenz wrote that they "perceptively saw within the momentous changes transpiring in their day the Holy Spirit at work bringing renewal to the church and the world. And they were convinced that the time had come for the church to awaken so that Christ's followers might fulfil their mission to the world" (*Renewing the Center* [2000], 23).

36. "A Theology for the Future" (1985).

37. Ibid., 261.

1. be first and foremost a *biblical* theology. Of interest is his emphasis that this will be reflected in a theology that promotes reconciliation and counters fragmentation, and is in opposition to any theology which relegates any segment of humanity to second-class status in the church.[38] A passion for social justice shines through in the early Grenz, a passion which, while not absent, in his later writing is not as obvious.

2. demand and foster change at both an individual and societal level.[39]

3. be ecumenical. Grenz clarifies that by ecumenical he means a theology "which represents the whole church." In addition, he suggests that it will be "a theology for the whole world," and laments that "Human theologies easily become culture bound,"[40] an interestingly cautious comment on culture, given that he was later to embrace it as the "embedding context" for theology.[41]

4. be holistic. In this section we find the first hints of the theme of "community" that unites so much of Grenz's later writing. It comes across in statements such as, "reconciliation is horizontal as well as vertical, dealing with the individual in community, as well as the individual before God. To be a Christian, it suggests, means to be a Christian in relationship with others."[42]

5. be life affirming.

6. be oriented to the future. He writes, "Futurist theology . . . brings a vision of a coming glorious kingdom, which vision ought to shape the present."[43] Again we find hints of the later Grenz who in *Beyond Foundationalism* describes eschatology as theology's orienting motif and develops the importance of this theme in depth.[44]

If someone unfamiliar with the work of Grenz were to ask where to begin their reading of him, a sensible starting point would be his 1993 publication, *Revisioning Evangelical Theology*. At around 200 pages, it is of necessity not a closely argued work, but it meets Grenz's aim of providing an overview of the big building blocks in evangelical theology, which he considered to be in need of reformulation or to be understood from a slightly different

---

38. Ibid., 262–63.
39. Ibid., 263.
40. Ibid., 263–64.
41. *Beyond Foundationalism*, 130.
42. Grenz, "A Theology for the Future," 265.
43. Ibid., 266.
44. *Beyond Foundationalism*, 239–73.

perspective. *Revisioning Evangelical Theology* is a call for a shift in ethos, and in his later work Grenz consistently returned to the themes it articulates. While he developed them in greater depth, he did not significantly shift from the positions that he adopted in this seminal text. He thought of it as his programmatic work, and it shaped his agenda until his untimely death in 2005.

Revisioning Evangelical Theology identifies seven areas in need of revisioning, dealt with sequentially in the book's seven chapters, namely,

1. Evangelical identity
2. Evangelical spirituality
3. The theological task
4. Sources for theology
5. Evangelical views of biblical authority
6. The integrative motif for theology
7. Evangelical understandings of the church

In chapter 1, the quest for a revisioned evangelical identity begins. Grenz explores evangelicalism's roots, and suggests three streams as especially formative, the first phase shaped by the Reformation, the second by Puritanism and Pietism, and the third, the post-fundamentalist card-carrying evangelicalism that arose after the Second World War, ushering in neo-evangelicalism.

Grenz is aware that discussions about evangelicalism's historic origins often reflect partisan interests. His concern is to ensure that the stream of Pietism receives adequate attention.[45] One of his goals is to demonstrate the validity of Donald Dayton's characterization of evangelicalism's ethos as being its "convertive piety."[46] Grenz stresses that though doctrine was important in the development of evangelicalism, it was not the sole driver.[47]

---

45. It can be argued that Grenz's own bias is clear here. By insisting that Pietism and revivalism are key parts of the story of evangelicalism, he established a base from which to justify the experiential focus onto evangelical theology. Those who place greater emphasis on evangelicalism's links to the reformed movement are less convinced. In addition, Grenz's summary of the third stage of the movement, the post-World War II neo-evangelicalism, reflected a strong North American bias. E.g., he paid no attention to British evangelicals and the role played by thinkers such as C. S. Lewis, Martyn Lloyd-Jones, and John Stott. To be fair, his goal was not to provide a comprehensive history of the movement. He was far more thorough in his later work, *Renewing the Center*. A helpful study of differences between American and British evangelicalism is made in Noll, Bebbington, Rawlyk, *Evangelicalism*.

46. *Revisioning*, 23.

47. Randall suggests that the overriding theme of evangelicalism "is a personal

Grenz believes that the "card carrying" doctrine-believing trajectory of the post-fundamentalist period represents but one dimension of the broader evangelical movement.[48] To revision evangelical theology he considers it important to embrace the movement's broader history and argues strongly for the inclusion of those branches with an ethos of "convertive piety."

Grenz then becomes controversial, giving a significant role to experience next to doctrinal formulation.[49] He argues that the evangelical ethos is more readily "sensed" than described theologically. In doing this, Grenz effectively opts for a sociological or psychological grouping that correlates with a doctrinal one.[50] As an alternative, he believes that evangelicalism's roots in Pietism serve as a key characteristic. He thus departs from the so-called post-fundamentalist stress on doctrine as the definer of evangelical identity. For Grenz, it is not that Scripture or doctrine are unimportant, but that religious experience and encounter comes first in the Christian life. His first characteristic of a revisioned evangelicalism is that its identity is tied to those able to claim a certain "experiential piety cradled in a theology,"[51] which denotes the abiding strength of theology's significance.

In chapter 2 Grenz proposes a new understanding of what constitutes evangelical spirituality. He argues that spirituality should be understood in terms of a balanced life, with an emphasis on both individual and corporate elements of faith. This vision is based on his understanding of what it means to participate in the life of the God who is triune. The chapter moves in a few directions. Reacting against what he sees as evangelicalism's overemphasis on doctrinal orthodoxy in the second half of the twentieth century, Grenz suggests that the early intent of Pietism was to reform life, not doctrine.

Acknowledging that it would be presumptuous to imply that the quest for spirituality is only the concern of the evangelical wing of the church,

---

relationship with Jesus," but he extends this by suggesting that it is "also a spirituality of ordinary people" which can be understood by examining the sentiments expressed in the hymn, "What a Friend we have in Jesus" (*What a Friend We Have in Jesus*).

48. *Revisioning*, 27.

49. Ibid., 30–31.

50. One should not overlook how radical a departure this is. To suggest a revisioned theology on the basis of something "sensed," rather than described theologically, could easily be dismissed as "liberal" subjectivity. Grenz does not at this point sufficiently deal with the complex issue of what to do when one "senses" a shared experience and identity, and yet believes very differently. The subjective/objective divide is probably not as easily side-stepped as Grenz suggests. True, Grenz acknowledges the importance of doctrinal belief, but what does it mean for experience to come first when there are significant doctrinal differences? Does the shared experience override the difference, or is there a point where the difference is so great that it negates the experience?

51. *Revisioning*, 35.

Grenz asks whether an evangelical spirituality is different from any other version, and if so, what constitutes a genuinely *evangelical* spirituality. At this point Grenz still thinks of evangelicalism as a "boundaried set," with marks that delineate those who are in and those who are out. In later writings he suggests it is more helpful to think of evangelicalism as a "centered" rather than a "boundaried" set, with the center being a conversion narrative of encounter with Jesus.[52] The trajectory can move in different directions from this common center.

Chapter 3 calls for a revisioning of the theological task. Rather than devising propositions about doctrine, Grenz suggests that the theological task be seen as a discipline serving the community of faith by helping it to reflect on its faith commitment and helping it to understand its identity conferring message. This assists the community to live ethically in the context in which it finds itself.

This domesticating of the theological task has its critics. Tracy, for example, writes of the three publics of the theologian as society, the academy, and the church.[53] One could argue that Grenz's approach is unnecessarily reductionistic, though it is important to note that Grenz's concern is that in spite of the evangelical emphasis on spirituality, the theological task is usually viewed in cognitive terms as a sterile academic study of the revelation given in the Bible. He suggests that influenced by the propositionalism of the "Princeton theologians," evangelicals have often elevated biblical summarization to being the central task of theology.[54]

In the fourth chapter, Grenz addresses the need to rethink the sources for theological construction, and suggests that three should be in a dynamic trialogue, namely the Bible, tradition, and culture. Most of the chapter unpacks the reasons for his choice of these three, and he and John Franke later developed this argument more fully in their coauthored, *Beyond Foundationalism* (2001), which Grenz developed himself in *Renewing the Center* (2000).

Grenz is aware that most evangelicals would cite Scripture as the key source for theology. However, while Grenz does not want to discount the

---

52. "Die Begrenzte Gemeinschaft ("the Boundaried People")" (2002). He borrowed the concepts of boundaried and centered sets from Paul Hiebert, who explored the meaning of Christian conversion and used set theory to outline a typology of different ways in which the term "Christian" can be understood (*Anthropological Reflections on Missiological Issues*).

53. Tracy, *Analogical Imagination*, 3–46.

54. While Grenz's characterization of the Old Princeton theologians as being scholastic rationalists is not uncommon, it is controversial. An example of an alternate reading of their contribution is found in Helseth, "'Re-Imaging' the Princeton Mind."

importance of Scripture as the primary norm and supreme authority for theological reflection, he is convinced that evangelicals need to look for a new way of appropriating biblical authority. His justification for Scripture as a key theological source is largely pragmatic—the Bible is the book shaping the faith community and its tradition, providing sufficient justification for its authoritative employment in the life of the community.[55]

On the one hand, this is highly satisfactory, but on the other, it reduces the force of appeals that might be made to Scripture in naïve and potentially hermeneutically dubious ways. If the Bible is simply the book of the church rather than a divinely inspired book, appeals to its permanent and ongoing authority become tentative. Following this, Scripture is understood primarily as part of the church's tradition. It is a source for theology because tradition is a source for theological construction. If the faith community were to modify its tradition and pay attention to another text, there would be no compelling reason to continue to be guided by Scripture.[56] It is therefore not surprising that Grenz's view of Scripture has been contested by several evangelicals, D. A. Carson's quip being perhaps most cited: "With the best will in the world, I cannot see how Grenz's approach to Scripture can be called 'evangelical' in any useful sense."[57] Not that Grenz would deny the inspiration of Scripture—indeed, he links its discussion closely to pneumatology, and unpacks this in chapter 5 of his theology text. Perhaps he is just being a little provocative, and wants to make a point that he believes was receiving insufficient attention.

Grenz believes that theological construction flows best out of the conversation between the sources of Scripture, tradition, and culture. The question begging to be asked is what choices should be made when sources seem to conflict. For much of the church's history, the biblical kerygma has been at odds with contemporary culture. The role of culture as a source for theology needs careful definition. Grenz does not say that the belief system of each cultural context needs to be woven into the belief of the faith community. In the first instance the concern is that the biblical kerygma is both explained and lived out in such a way that it is meaningful to each cultural context. Part of the meaning will flow from living in the realm of contrast

---

55. *Revisioning*, 93–94.

56. In addition, if the Bible is simply the book of the church, it may be authoritative for the faith community, but there is no obvious reason why those outside that community should feel obligated to follow its teaching. To restrict the sphere of the Bible's relevance to that of the faith community has significant missiological implications and limitations. It is not clear that Grenz had thought these through. See, Strange, "Not Ashamed!"

57. Carson, *Gagging*, 481.

and providing an alternate understanding of ethical living in light of ultimate [eschatological] reality.

Chapter 5 is also controversial as Grenz proposes a revised understanding of biblical authority. He is concerned that biblical authority is often understood in a static sense, and argues that it should be responsive to the illumination of the Spirit, especially when illumination is communally mediated. His stress on the link between the Spirit and the Bible, a major Baptist distinctive,[58] finds some practical outworking. Grenz for example suggests that in the writing of systematic theology, instead of bibliology being part of prolegomena, Scripture be discussed under pneumatology—the Bible as the book of the Spirit. He also suggests linking the themes of Spirit, Scripture, church, and eschatology more closely.[59] The structure of his one-volume theology text, *Theology for the Community of God*, reflects these convictions.

Grenz begins chapter 6 by noting that most theologians order their thinking around a key integrating motif—the kingdom of God being a common choice in the twentieth century. Grenz is not convinced that this motif is sufficiently content filled, and argues that it be exchanged for that of community.[60] To the extent that all God's work in the world is directed toward creating community, he suggests that this theme best serves as the integrating motif for theology.[61]

In the closing chapter of *Revisioning Evangelical Theology*, Grenz develops what he calls a "process model" of the church to rectify evangelicalism's inadequate ecclesiology. The model argues that the church must be shaped by what it is destined to become. This requires adopting eschatology as an orienting motif for theology. He writes, "The link of the church to the reign of God means that ecclesiology has an unavoidable future reference. And this eschatological orientation ought to shape our understanding of the doctrine of the church."[62] He springboards from this insight to suggest an eschatological process model for the church. The church's task is to actualize in the present, as a sign of the future eschatological reality, the glorious

---

58. See significance of the coinherence of Spirit and Word in Yarnell, *Formation of Doctrine*, 82–90.

59. *Revisioning*, 115.

60. For the evolution of the kingdom theme in Grenz's thought, see Sexton, *Trinitarian Theology*, 146–48.

61. For a negative reaction to Grenz's proposal, see Moore, "Leftward to Scofield." Note also the major revision and expansion of the earlier (with Grenz) *Twentieth Century Theology* in Olson, *Journey of Modern Theology*, which completely dropped the kingdom theme from having any real significance in his account of modern theology.

62. *Revisioning*, 183.

fellowship that will come into fullness at the consummation of history. In short then, the church does not draw her identity from her current practice, but from her future. Grenz links this to his proposed integrating motif for theology: community. Simply looking to eschatology does not answer the question of the nature of the eschatological reality the church tries to model. Grenz suggests that a revisioned eschatology must therefore add the motif of community, for, "The church is the community of love, called to reflect the nature of triune God,"[63] and confirms the reality of this present world. It does this, while standing in the present at communion, and looking back at the Lord's work on our behalf, as well as forward toward his coming return.

Theology for the Community

In 1994, a year after the appearance of *Revisioning Evangelical Theology*, Grenz's systematic theology, *Theology for the Community of God*, was published.[64] It allowed him to implement some of the proposals made in *Revisioning Evangelical Theology*. In particular, he develops the "community" theme—more specifically, the eschatological community—as the integrating motif for theology.

It was perhaps fortuitous that *Theology for the Community of God* was first published in the same year as Wayne Grudem's *Systematic Theology*. Grudem's work is an example of the propositional approach to theology that Grenz wishes to move beyond, and Grenz's "revisioned" approach is highlighted when compared to Grudem. The "anti-liberalism apologetic" that characterizes the tone of many evangelical offerings is absent in Grenz. His work shows significant engagement with the both the historical and sociological contexts.[65] Most notable is that the work is theme driven, Grenz very consistently making use of his integrating theme of "community" to draw and hold the work together, a theme he understood as deeply Trinitarian.[66]

The work starts fairly traditionally with an examination of the questions of God's existence, and which God to believe in. What is a little surprising (from an evangelical perspective) is the delay in discussing the doctrine of Scripture, which does not appear until chapter 14 in the section on

---

63. Ibid., 184.

64. Grenz had originally planned to write a one-volume systematic theology first, but was persuaded by InterVarsity Press to precede it by a text exploring an agenda for the future of evangelical theology (ibid., 11).

65. This is in fairly stark contrast to Grudem who, as his title suggests, is adamant that the role of systematic theology is to outline biblical doctrine, and at the expense of serious engagement with the social-cultural context.

66. Sexton, *Trinitarian Theology*, 16.

pneumatology.[67] By discussing the doctrine of Scripture within the theme of pneumatology, Grenz expresses his conviction that the Bible should be seen as the Spirit's book. In this way he provides scope for an emphasis not only on the inspiration of the Bible, but also on its illumination by the Spirit. This allows for greater interaction with the historical-cultural context in which the church finds itself.[68]

Grenz's indebtedness to Pannenberg is apparent in the book. A refrain is that the community of God should be shaped by its eschatological expectations. It is the future rather than the past that serves as our reference point. Thus even when discussing creation Grenz points to the importance of the eschaton, writing that "we must give primacy to the future eschaton, and not the primordial past, as the ultimate point of creation."[69]

Also of interest is Grenz's treatment of the question of the *imago Dei*. This is an area of special focus in Grenz's later writing.[70] Following Pannenberg, Grenz initially approaches the question from an anthropological perspective under the theme of humanity's "openness to the world."[71] Later in the work he discusses a dynamic understanding of the image of God whereby, "The image of God is a reality toward which we are moving. It is what we are en route to becoming."[72] He then spells out the link to eschatology:

> The divine image is the goal or destiny that God intends for his creatures. Hence it is a future reality that is present now only as a foretaste, or only in the form of our human potential. Consequently, the focus of the idea is neither anthropology nor Christology, but eschatology. The image of God will one day be borne by resurrected humans in the new creation.[73]

The publication of *Theology for the Community of God* can be seen as the completion of stage one in Grenz's journey as a theologian. After exploring on a fairly wide canvas in his early years, in *Revisioning Evangelical Theology* he outlines his agenda for evangelical theology, and in *Theology for the Community of God* he allows that agenda to shape his approach to the usual topics addressed in an overview of systematic theology. His later

67. *Theology for the Community* (1994), 494.
68. Ibid., 510.
69. Ibid., 146.
70. It is dealt with very fully in what is arguably Grenz's most notable scholarly work, *Social God*.
71. *Theology for the Community* (1994), 169.
72. Ibid., 224.
73. Ibid.

work can be seen as an expansion on the themes raised, and also his defense of his work in the face of the controversy that it caused in some sectors of evangelicalism.

It should be observed that while Grenz's move to locate a doctrine of Scripture under pneumatology in his theology text was critically received by evangelicals, not least seen in the oft-repeated comment by Don Carson above, but also by Roger Nicole at the 1995 meeting of the Evangelical Theological Society, where Grenz's book was under review. One attendee described the event this way:

> I still vividly recall an ETS presentation in which [Roger Nicole] stood behind a lectern, facing Stan Grenz who was seated in the first row, a bit lower than the platform on which Nicole was standing, and Nicole was wagging an angry finger at Stan, wondering how in the world anyone could write a systematic theology and not address the doctrine of Scripture for hundreds of pages. Stan graciously let that tirade go.[74]

Yet Nicole was also quick to repair whatever damage may have occurred, both with a warm handshake to Grenz the morning after the panel and a personal 1995 Christmas card, which "deeply touched" Grenz.[75] The note in Nicole's Christmas card read as follows:

> Dear Brother Grenz,
>
> I fear that I may have appeared overly critical of your book at the recent ETS meeting. I do want you to know that there is no personal hostility in this, only a real apprehension that the evangelical stance may be watered down. What is novel in the book has probably not been derived from community, as you claim, but rather from Pannenberg and others who are rejecting the truly evangelical approach of ETS and ICBI.
>
> The reviews of Morrison and Williams, particularly the latter with his insistence on "rationalistic *loci*" were more out of line than your production and this seemed to demand a sharp castigation. As for Pinnock, he is so far off anyway that I cannot get ruffled by anything he says or writes.

This indication of a slightly modified response than what one might have derived from the ETS meeting suggests that the creativity and

---

74. Personal email to Jason Sexton (14 Dec. 2010).

75. Letter from Grenz to Roger Robert Nicole, dated 19 Feb. 1996 (available in Box 29-file 2 of the *JRA*).

imaginative evangelical theology (conservative, even, by some accounts)[76] that Grenz pursued was one that perhaps the evangelical community just wasn't ready for. And perhaps some of Grenz's "concern to articulate the age-old gospel of Jesus Christ in the context of the new generation" to whom he was called to minister were largely misunderstood, perhaps because the range of conservative evangelicals were not concerned about missiological issues in the present world. Grenz stated, "In seeking to be faithful to my calling, my theological constructions may not match at every point the constructions [Nicole had] sought to advance. But . . . such differences do not mean that we [i.e., he and Nicole] are not seeking to accomplish the same goals."[77]

Another oft-perceived strong critic of Grenz wrote him a letter during a Spring 1996 sabbatical at Tyndale House, Cambridge, offering this:

> I am sorry if I offended you: that was certainly not my intent. You have been one of the first of contemporary Evangelicals to wrestle seriously with . . . postmodernism. But sometimes the first people into a set of questions will be modified by those who are a little later on the scene. . . . I would like to think we can prove mutually correcting.
>
> After all, I spend more time in [my book] gently disagreeing with John Stott, an old and revered friend, than with you. . . .
>
> So please do not take umbrage. If I have misrepresented you in any way, I shall try to make corrections if the work goes to another edition[;] . . . as far as I can see at the moment, I did not mis-read you: you were not merely describing him, but describing him in such a way that some things in Schleiermacher were valued rather more than I thought they should be. But none of this suggests for a moment that I want to depreciate your work in general, or wish to think of you as other than a colleague on the same "team."[78]

But attempts to address concerns about his work within the evangelical world did not always shield him from all critique, especially in the moment

---

76. See evidence for this: Sexton, *Trinitarian Theology*, 175–82.

77. Letter from Grenz to Nicole, 19 Feb. 1996.

78. Letter written to Grenz, 29 Apr. 1996 (available in Box 29-file 2 of the *JRA*). See Grenz's response letter dated 14 May 1996, reiterating appreciation for willingness to revisit the appraisal of his work: "I'm sure you can understand my dismay when I read that in your estimation my doctrine of Scripture didn't seem 'Evangelical.' Perhaps we will have opportunity to discuss this theological matter at some future time. Until then I am put at ease to learn that you do indeed count me as a colleague and as one who is on the same team."

that Broadman and Holman dropped his *Theology for the Community of God*, the best-selling systematic theology text they'd ever had, from their list in 2000, which was immediately republished by Eerdmans. One cannot pretend that there were not complicated issues involved, especially with the original commissioning editor of the book, David Dockery, who had left for Southern Seminary, but then again departed from that institution shortly after Albert Mohler became president in 1993. In 1995, Grenz put in print his egalitarian views on women in ministry,[79] which seems to be what led Paige Patterson to withdraw his earlier endorsement from Grenz's theology book and the subsequent discontinuation of its publication with Broadman and Holman at a time when the Southern Baptists were working to add a position on the complementarian view of women in ministry to their Baptist Faith and Message.[80]

Grenz continued his methodological work, producing a short survey volume on postmodernism[81] that as of February 2005 was his second best-selling book (over forty thousand copies sold) behind the dictionary of theological terms. He also finished a volume giving a theological account of a Christian ethic,[82] and one on homosexuality.[83] These efforts (largely articulating conservative positions), along with the critique of his earlier work and battles he found himself embroiled in,[84] provided impetus for the further development of his ideas with the publications of *Renewing the Center* (2000) and *Beyond Foundationalism* (2001). At important points, both books largely argued the same thing related to issues around theological methodology, and they were stronger explications of *Revisioning Evangelical Theology*, yielding more explicitly Trinitarian features.

---

79. "Anticipating God's New Community"; and Grenz and Kjesbo, *Women in the Church*.

80. Perhaps some of the disposition towards Grenz at this time—reinforced later from additional critical engagement with a supposed non-foundationalist epistemology in his methodology, which bred deeper suspicion about his work—is seen in the careless speculation of an editor at one of Grenz's earlier publishing houses: "My suspicion was that the medical condition that took his life had something to do with some of his later thinking . . . ." (private email exchange 4 Feb. 2010).

81. *Primer* (1996).

82. *Moral Quest* (1997).

83. *Welcoming But Not Affirming* (1998).

84. Veteran editor Dan Reid said that when InterVarsity Press acquired *Revisioning* they had no idea at the time or upon publication that the book would be controversial (personal conversation, 17 Jan. 2014).

Rediscovering the Triune Center

The unfortunate title of *Beyond Foundationalism* gave the impression to many that Grenz had indeed embraced a postmodern anti-foundationalist epistemology, which others set out to quickly dismantle in various ways.[85] Unperceived, the reality was that Grenz's methodology was largely representative of a soft or chastened foundationalism[86] the real creativity of his project was in its explicitly Trinitarian shape. Much of this seems to have been bypassed, especially by those critical of his project. This is, of course, the dominant theme he picked up from Pannenberg and the feature with which he sought to construct his theology and the epistemology of theology that his explication of the "age-old gospel of Jesus Christ" would yield.[87] Incidentally, these Trinitarian sketches were not without challenges, as even he and coauthor, John Franke, disagreed on the kind of model of the Trinity that would be represented in their jointly-authored chapter on the Trinity in *Beyond Foundationalism*, with Grenz holding trenchantly to an Augustinian understanding of the doctrine of the Trinity and Franke more interested in more fashionable readings of the Cappadocians advocated by Zizioulas and others. Ultimately they found enough middle ground in Richard of St. Victor to write the chapter together.

However, Grenz began his own effort with the first explorative contribution to The Matrix series, *The Social God and the Relational Self* (2001), commencing a Trinitarian understanding of the *imago Dei* concept as a means of accessing the triune transcendent base of all things.[88] And yet before his explorative volume on theology proper,[89] he deemed it important to offer a "prequel" to that volume which would assist him in "viewing all aspects of Christian doctrine in a Trinitarian light," and in this way holding fast "the fundamental Christian conviction that God, who is the ultimate topic of theology, is triune."[90] This prequel became *Rediscovering the Triune*

---

85. See relevant essays in Erickson, *Reclaiming the Center*.

86. See discussion in Harris, *Theological Method of Stanley J. Grenz*, 156–79.

87. See Sexton, *Trinitarian Theology*, 182–88 and *passim*. Oddly, even from his 2013 plenary address at the national meeting of the ETS, Don Carson still associated Grenz's view with that of John Franke and a communitarian-driven hermeneutic. This, of course, failed again to recognize the fashionable [communitarian or "social"] model of the Trinity that Grenz was working with in his pre-2004 publications. For a charting of movement in Grenz's doctrine of the Trinity, see Sexton, "Beyond Social Trinitarianism." The ongoing failure to acknowledge the nuanced, inchoate yet explicitly *Trinitarian* grounding of Grenz's understanding the interpretive community is unfortunate.

88. For more on this, see Sexton, *Trinitarian Theology*, chs. 6–7

89. Grenz, *Named God*.

90. Grenz, *Social God*, x.

God and would mark the beginning of a shifting trajectory in Grenz's understanding of Trinitarian doctrine.[91] Yet still some found it (and still find it) difficult to see what Stan Grenz was attempting to do, especially those who have either abandoned (conservative) evangelical theology or else those who think it cannot be largely improved upon. In this way, his aim was to reach deep into the core of the Christian theological tradition and help resource evangelical theology with such a reality.

An ambitious approach to resourcing evangelical theology meant he needed to be in a strategic position. On the heels of the Baylor position, Grenz was invited by Ronald Thiemann on January 11, 2005 to apply for the McDonald Family Professorship in Evangelical Theology at Harvard Divinity School. From years prior, Grenz had a burgeoning friendship with Francis Fiorenza, who he'd corresponded with repeatedly about the possibility of a position at Harvard, and had participated in a conference at Harvard on evangelicalism in March 2001. The terms of the Alonzo McDonald chair were ambiguous, but according to a letter Peter Heltzel wrote to Grenz, 9 March 2001, the same day Grenz lectured on "People of One Book," McDonald was looking for somebody with "evangelical piety," and Grenz represented the "systematic theologian" among those other candidates under strong consideration for the position. According to Francis Fiorenza, Grenz was "a top candidate for this [new] position," and while generating considerable discussion among the members of the search committee, "his death meant a rethinking of the finalists."[92]

We have clues as to why Grenz wanted to be at Harvard. We know why he desired to be at Baylor, in order to work with graduate students and continue his research agenda seeking to serve the global church. From various correspondences available in the Grenz archives, we are sure that he was eager to supervise doctoral students, something he labored to bring together at Carey Theological College during Spring 2002, but which ultimately did not receive accreditation. This ambition, while eager to engage in the wider theological (and cultural)[93] discussions, was ultimately to serve the life of the church in holistic ways. The following quote captures this especially well:

91. Sexton, "Beyond Social Trinitarianism."

92. Personal email correspondence between Sexton and Fiorenza, 15 July 2009, used by permission.

93. In his letter to the Harvard search committee, he stated this: "I plan to draw together my interest in culture and the commitment to the renewal of trinitarian theology—a theme that together with 'community' has emerged in the last several years as central to my theological thinking—to produce a trinitarian theology of culture" (p. 3 of letter dated 13 Jan. 2005, available as an electronic file at the *JRA*).

The evangelical piety, which was passed on to me by my parents, not only underlies my scholarly work, it also informs the manner that I approach all of life. I want to be known as a person who does not only speak about the faith, but also seeks to live it. Consequently, my goal in all that I do is to seek to glorify God, to follow what I sense to be God's calling on my life in a manner that honors God. The evangelical ethos has also instilled in me a deep commitment to the church in its local expression. My wife and I are active members of a vibrant, multi-generational, multi-ethnic, internationally-oriented congregation located in the downtown core of Vancouver, where she serves on the pastoral team as Minister of Worship. Prior to launching my academic career I also served in pastoral ministry. The pastoral impulse and relational orientation that I gained thereby has continued to inform all that I do as a theological educator. In fact, I believe that this combination of scholarly competence and ministry perspective may well be one of the greatest strengths that I bring to the theological educational endeavor. And I am optimistic that this ability to blend the scholarly with the pastoral-relational, in turn, would provide a valuable—and valued—dimension to my work at Harvard.

Thank you again for honoring me by inviting my application for the Alonzo McDonald Professorship of Evangelical Theological Studies. May you sense the presence of the Holy Spirit in your deliberations, and may God grant you divine wisdom and discernment during the search process.[94]

While it is impossible to conjecture with any level of certainty what the legacy of the vocation of Stanley Grenz might have left to the church had he had another decade or more to continue his work, and especially if he had carried it out at such a place as Harvard Divinity School, such effort would surely have left us a lot. Even so, there has been a resurgent interest in the nature and shape of Grenz's theology that has come about as we approach a decade since his death and what would have been his sixty-fifth birthday. While there are various interpretations of Grenz's work—and this volume has no grand ambitions to settle any of these matters—it is a joy to see more sensible engagement with what he wrote. Stanley Grenz's was an imaginative yet deeply biblical evangelical theologian. His contribution was made at a time when evangelical theology was maturing, and his scholarship aided this process considerably. It is now up to the many evangelical scholars impacted by his work and its contribution to evangelicalism to continue his notable legacy.

94. Ibid.

Bibliography

For the works of Stanley J. Grenz, please see the bibliography at the end of this book.

Carson, D. A. *The Gagging of God: Christianity Confronts Pluralism*. Grand Rapids: Zondervan, 1996.
Grudem, Wayne. *Systematic Theology: An Introduction to Biblical Doctrine*. Grand Rapids: Zondervan, 1994.
Erickson, Millard J., Paul Kjoss Helseth, Justin Taylor, eds. *Reclaiming the Center: Confronting Evangelical Accommodation in Postmodern Times*. Wheaton, IL: Crossway, 2004.
Fogleman, Lori Scott. "Renowned Theologian and Author to Join Baylor's Truett Seminary as Distinguished Professor of Theology," 18 July 2002, http://www.baylor.edu/mediacommunications/news.php?action=story&story=4121.
Harris, Brian S. *The Theological Method of Stanley J. Grenz: Constructing Evangelical Theology from Scripture, Tradition, and Culture*. Lewiston, NY: Mellen, 2011.
Helseth, Paul Kjoss. "'Re-Imaging' the Princeton Mind: Postconservative Evangelicalism, Old Princeton, and the Rise of Neo-Fundamentalism." *Journal of the Evangelical Theological Society* 45/3 (2002) 427–50.
Hiebert, Paul G. *Anthropological Reflections on Missiological Issues*. Grand Rapids: Baker, 1994.
Moore, Russell D. "Leftward to Scofield: The Eclipse of the Kingdom in Post-Conservative Evangelical Theology." *Journal of the Evangelical Theological Society* 47/3 (2004) 423–40.
Noll, Mark A., David W. Bebbington, and George A. Rawlyk, eds. *Evangelicalism: Comparative Studies of Popular Protestantism in North America, the British Isles, and Beyond, 1700–1990*. Oxford: Oxford University Press, 1994.
Olson, Roger E. *The Journey of Modern Theology: From Reconstruction to Deconstruction*. Downers Grove, IL: InterVarsity, 2013.
Randall, Ian. *What a Friend We Have in Jesus: The Evangelical Tradition*. London: Darton, Longman and Todd, 2005.
Sexton, Jason S. "Beyond Social Trinitarianism: The Baptist, Trinitarian Innovation of Stanley J. Grenz." *Baptist Quarterly* 44/8 (October 2012) 473–86.
———. *The Trinitarian Theology of Stanley J. Grenz*. London: T. & T. Clark, 2013.
Strange, Dan. "Not Ashamed! The Sufficiency of Scripture for Public Theology." *Themelios* 36/2 (2011) 238–60.
Tracy, David. *The Analogical Imagination: Christian Theology and the Culture of Pluralism*. London: SCM, 1981.
Yarnell, Malcolm B., III. *The Formation of Christian Doctrine*. Nashville: Broadman and Holman, 2007.

Part One

TRINITY

2

Three (or More) Ways of Triangulating Theology

On the Very Idea of a Trinitarian System

Kevin J. Vanhoozer

Introduction: Varieties of Trinitarian Theology

In the waning years of the twentieth century, church historians looked back in wonder at having witnessed not one but two surprising turns of theological events, or rather, two remarkable *returns*: the second coming, as it were, of the doctrine of the Trinity, and the rebounding of the fortunes of systematic theology. Some observers speak of a "renaissance" or "resurgence" of Trinitarian and systematic theology.[1] This purported rebirth prompts the following question: are they related—identical, or perhaps fraternal twins— or did they simply happen to be born under the same centurial sign? Stated more pointedly: do the two events belong together, in which case we could say that what has occurred is the return of *Trinitarian systematic* theology?

Stan Grenz would surely have appreciated the question. After all, "re-" was Stan's favorite prefix, if his book titles are any indication: *Revisioning Evangelical Theology*, *Renewing the Center*, and *Rediscovering the Triune God*. In this last book, Grenz says that the rebirth of Trinitarian theology is

---

1. Schwöbel, "Introduction: The Renaissance of Trinitarian Theology"; Sexton, "State of the Evangelical Trinitarian Resurgence."

"one of the most far-reaching theological developments of the [twentieth] century."[2] It is therefore entirely fitting that the present volume is entitled *Revisioning, Renewing, and Rediscovering the Triune Center.*

The purpose of the present essay is to explore further what effect the adjective qualifiers "Trinitarian" and "systematic" have upon the project they purport to modify: theology. What is Trinitarian theology and in what way could it be systematic? Stan was asking similar questions. Indeed, one of the last public lectures he delivered, at the Assemblies of God Theological Seminary in Springfield, Missouri, just a few scant weeks before his untimely death, was on the topic "What Does It Mean to be Trinitarians?" The answer I give will eventually diverge from Stan's, but there is a considerable amount of convergence as well, which raises the following question: Are Trinitarian theologies more like Tolstoy's happy families that are all alike, or do they resemble unhappy families, each of which is unhappy (i.e., Trinitarian) in its own way?

It may be helpful provisionally to identify not two but three types of families on the spectrum of Trinitarian theology. On the one end of the spectrum is what we could call "weak" Trinitarianism. By "weak," I am referring to theologies that affirm Nicene orthodoxy yet nevertheless treat the Trinity as simply one doctrine among many others. Karl Rahner, who along with Karl Barth was responsible for restoring the doctrine of the Trinity to contemporary theology's front burner, bemoaned the frequency with which treatments of the doctrine occupy "a rather isolated position in the total dogmatic system."[3] All too often, when the section on the Trinity is concluded, the subject is never brought up again. Weak Trinitarian theologies are thus orthodox theologies in which the doctrine of the triune God tends to be notionally present in one's theological system yet operationally non-functioning.[4]

On the other end of the spectrum is what we might call "radical" Trinitarianism. Radical Trinitarian theologies bear two distinguishing characteristics. First, they tend to equate or identify God with the historical interactions of Father, Son, and Spirit in the history of Jesus Christ. Stated differently: radical Trinitarians begin *and end* with the *threeness* of the economic Trinity, that is, the temporal and salvific missions of the Father's Son and Spirit, instead of the *mono* of theism.[5] The second mark of radical Trini-

2. Grenz, *Rediscovering the Triune God*, 1.
3. Rahner, *The Trinity*, 14.
4. Rahner lamented that even confessing Christians "are, in their practical life, almost mere 'monotheists'" (ibid.,10).
5. Accordingly, radical Trinitarians are typically "radicalizers" of Rahner's Rule, for whom the immanent Trinity (God in himself) *is* the economic Trinity (God in his

tarianism is the tendency to make a certain construal of the divine threeness the transcendental ground of Christian understanding and practice in general. As a result, creation itself, and in particular human beings as bearers of God's image, metaphysics, and ethics alike, become as it were vestiges of the Trinity. Such Trinitarian theologians only appear to be radical; in fact, they are *reductionists*. They tend to distill the rich complexity of the Trinity into a single principle, elevating one particular vestige into something like a root metaphor or controlling image. For example, some ground the "turn to relationality" in ontology and a theological anthropology informed by a notion of the relationality of Father, Son, and Spirit.[6]

In contrast both to a "weak" Trinitarianism, where the doctrine merely idles, and a "radical" Trinitarianism that seeks to distill its essence, a "strong" Trinitarianism provides something of a middle position. A theology is strongly Trinitarian if the doctrine of the Trinity is what provides a system of theology with its overarching coherence, though not necessarily by elevating a single vestige or principle, as in the reductionist version. Rather, a strong Trinitarianism employs the doctrine as a "perspective [that] illumines each of systematic theology's traditional loci."[7] In Robert Jenson's words, the doctrine of the Trinity "is not a separate puzzle to be solved but the framework within which all theology's puzzles are to be solved."[8] This seems to be what Grenz had in mind in the aforementioned lecture, where he deals with doctrinal and practical implications of the doctrine of the Trinity. To the extent that this Trinitarian influence is across the board, we may therefore speak of a Trinitarian systematics.

Three words of caution are in order before we proceed any further. First, the dividing line between weak, strong, and radical-reductionist Trinitarian theologies is not always clear. As we shall see, it is not always self-evident where to place a given theologian on our spectrum. Second, not all strong Trinitarian theologies are strong in the same way. Third, these labels—weak, strong, radical-reductionist—are meant primarily to be descriptive rather than evaluative. Whether it is better to be "strong" than "weak" or "radical-reductionist" in one's Trinitarian theology is something that I cannot fully defend here, though I will give some reasons for preferring to be "strongly" Trinitarian.

---

world mission) and vice versa (Sanders, *The Image of the Immanent Trinity*, 160–62).

6. Shults, *Reforming the Doctrine of God*, 163. For a fuller analysis and critique of the relational turn in Trinitarian theology, which includes process, feminist, and "open" theists, see my *Remythologizing*, 112–74.

7. Metzger, "Introduction: What Difference Does the Trinity Make?" 6.

8. Jenson, "Karl Barth," 31.

The goal in the present essay is relatively modest. It is to reflect further, in dialogue with Grenz and others, on what revisioning, renewing, and rediscovering the triune center might mean, especially for the future of evangelical systematic theology in particular. To that end, we begin with a brief historical survey of representative figures from ancient, medieval, and modern theology in order to ascertain just how strong traditional Trinitarian theology has been. I turn next to a review, equally brief, of certain theologians who could be considered broadly evangelical. The question here concerns the extent to which a special focus on the gospel either *means* or even *requires* a strong Trinitarianism. Finally, I turn to examine three evangelical theologians—John Frame, Stan Grenz, and me—whose work evidences a consistent triangulating dynamic that draws, in important though different ways, on the doctrine of the Trinity. In particular, I explore, in dialogue with Grenz, how a strong Trinitarianism enables us rightly to relate Word, Spirit, and church, and hence to answer the question, "Who is Jesus Christ for us today?"[9]

On the Very Idea of a Trinitarian System: A (Very) Brief History

The first coming of Trinitarian theology happened in the fourth century, at Nicaea, where improbably enough, Latin and Greek theologians agreed that the Son was *homoousion* ("of the same being") with the Father, and later, at Constantinople, that the Spirit is to be worshipped together with the Father and the Son.[10] The signal contribution of patristic theology was to recognize the distinction of the three divine persons and yet maintain that the external works of the Trinity (e.g., creation, redemption) are indivisible: *opera trinitatis ad extra indivisa sunt*. Gregory of Nyssa expresses well how what God does is one with three aspects: "Every operation which extends from God to the creation . . . has its origin from the Father, proceeds through the Son, and reaches its completion by the Holy Spirit."[11]

---

9. This latter question is appropriate, since the original impetus for the doctrine of the Trinity at Nicaea was the Christian confession that Jesus is Lord, the exemplification not only of perfect creaturehood but also of perfect deity.

10. Ayres notes that, though the term *homoousios* is not used in connection with the Spirit, the emphasis on the common worship of the Spirit "inexorably leads to the conclusion that the Spirit is of equal ontological status with the Father and the Son" (*Nicaea and its Legacy*, 258).

11. Gregory of Nyssa, "An Answer to Ablabius," 262.

In his magisterial examination of the emergence of "Pro-Nicene" theology, Lewis Ayres touches on the idea of a Trinitarian system, only to back away from the notion, and this for two reasons. First, he takes issue with the way modern theologians typically narrate the lead-up to Nicaea, according to which the West emphasized the oneness of God and the East the threeness. It is often difficult to say where theologies "begin," either with "the One God" or "the Triune God." Ayres suggests that questions about where one's system begins are really about what is of deepest concern to a theologian. For the pro-Nicene party, being Trinitarian meant being concerned with "the union of the irreducible persons in the simple and unitary Godhead."[12]

Second, and more seriously, Ayres doubts whether modern so-called Trinitarian systematic theologies are truly "Pro-Nicene." It is one thing for modern Trinitarians to adopt the Nicene *Creed*, quite another to adopt the *culture* that produced it. By "culture," Ayres is thinking in particular of the way in which the fourth-century fathers read and contemplated Scripture to determine what counts as authoritative. According to Ayres, the culture of modern Protestant systematics is largely inimical to patristic methods and principles of biblical interpretation.[13] The Pro-Nicene fathers read Scripture as a creedal community with a view to deepening their understanding of and participation in the life of the triune God. Ayres also protests the tendency of modern systematic theology to look to some philosophical schema to give unity to various doctrines rather than understanding this coherence "as lying in the unity of God's mysterious [triune] action."[14]

Thomas Aquinas is often cited as one who, even before modernity, allowed his Trinitarian theology to "fall" into Greek philosophy. Karl Rahner fingers Aquinas as the first who wrote the treatise "on the One God" independently of, and prior to the treatise "on the Triune God."[15] Questions 2–26 of Thomas's *Summa Theologiae* deal with the existence and perfections of God. Questions 27–43 then deal with the persons, relations, processions, and missions of the Father, Son, and Spirit. The order is not inconsequential: according to Rahner, to begin examining the perfections of the divine nature is to begin with metaphysics rather than revelation and redemption. A less than charitable reading of Aquinas might even go so far as to suggest that he presents the Trinity as an additional divine attribute. Modern theologians frequently make Thomas the primary exhibit in their case against classical

---

12. Ayres, *Nicaea and its Legacy*, 301.

13. Ayres takes the sixteenth-century tendency to summarize the basic doctrinal loci of Scripture to be "an important point of departure in the development of modern Protestant systematics" (ibid., 393 n.14).

14. Ibid., 423.

15. Rahner, *The Trinity*, 15–21.

theism's alleged tendency to speak of God apart from God's revelation in Jesus Christ.

Recently, however, the Thomistic tide has turned thanks to fresh analyses of Aquinas's Trinitarian theology.[16] Gilles Emery represents the best of this new breed of scholarship. Emery corrects Rahner's (mis)reading of the significance of the way in which Aquinas structures his doctrine of God. The first part of the *Summa Theologiae* is *not* divided into a treatise on *De Deo Uno* followed by a treatise on *De Deo Trino*. On the contrary, the whole section deals with what can be known of God through revelation. Aquinas does not begin with philosophy and top it off with theology; rather, the distinction is "between what is common to the three persons and what is proper to each."[17]

Is Thomas's a "strong" Trinitarianism? Emery thinks so. After all, Aquinas explicitly says that the knowledge of the three persons is necessary not only for the right idea of creation, but more importantly so that we "may think rightly concerning the salvation of the human race."[18] Thomas interprets the eternal processions in the immanent Trinity—the begetting of the Son and the procession of the Spirit—as the Word and Love of God that are complete within the Godhead yet freely directed outward, towards the world, in creation and salvation: "With the doctrine of the Word and of Love, Trinitarian theology thus establishes the theological foundations of divine action in its entirety."[19]

That Thomas does not sequester the Trinity in his doctrine of God is confirmed by his discussion of the image of God in human being, a theme that came to loom large in Grenz's work as well. Articles 5 through 8 of Question 93 are especially interesting. The fifth article asks, "Whether the image of God is in man according to the Trinity of persons?" The brief answer is yes: to image God is to both imitate the divine nature and represent the divine persons, especially Word and Spirit, inasmuch as they are related to the God's own capacities of knowing and loving.[20]

Aquinas is more strongly Trinitarian, then, than he appears at first glance. A number of contemporary theologians nevertheless insist that they have "recovered" the doctrine from its exile in modern theology, represented supremely by Friedrich Schleiermacher's relegating the Trinity to

16. Levering, *Scripture and Metaphysics*.
17. Emery, "The Doctrine of the Trinity," 50.
18. Aquinas, *Summa Theologiae* 1 Q. 32 art. 2 ad. 3.
19. Emery, "Doctrine of the Trinity," 59. For a fuller treatment, see Emery, *Trinitarian Theology of Thomas Aquinas*.
20. For a further development of this theme, see Merriell, *To the Image of the Trinity*, ch. 5.

the appendix of his systematic theology, *The Christian Faith*. Here, clearly, is an example of a theologian who treats "the one God"—or rather, our consciousness of being dependent upon a higher unitary power—before "the triune God." Actually, the situation here too is more complicated than it appears at first glance. For though "the divine Trinity" comes at the very end of Schleiermacher's work, the end is a conclusion, not an appendix, and has for its thesis the claim "*All that is essential in this Second Aspect of the Second Part of our exposition* [i.e., Schleiermacher's explication of the consciousness of grace] *is also posited in what is essential in the doctrine of the Trinity.*"[21] The Trinity is for Schleiermacher a way of showing that the various doctrines that articulate the Christian consciousness of grace are not unrelated but connected.[22]

The situation is reversed with Karl Barth, who places the doctrine of the Trinity at the very beginning of his *Church Dogmatics*, deriving as it does from his analysis of the Word of God. Systematic theology is the attempt to set forth in speech not religious feelings (*pace* Schleiermacher) but divine revelation, which for Barth is nothing other than God's self-communicating activity in Jesus Christ, the one Word of God. In this Word, God (Father) reveals himself (Son) through himself (Spirit). God truly is as he reveals himself to be in Jesus Christ. Indeed, Barth even uses the term "system" in relation to the divine decree to elect (i.e., determine) himself to be for humanity in Jesus Christ and humanity in Jesus Christ.[23] "System" here means not product but process, something like the procedure a gambler uses in placing his or her bets. Of course, the "bet" in Barth's case is the wager of faith. Barth wagers everything on the premise that God has determined to be who he is, and human beings to be what they are, in Jesus Christ, and that this triune self-determination (to be God-with-us and God-for-us in Christ through the Spirit) conditions everything else that can be said about God and his relation to the world: "In Barth's theology, Trinitarianism stops being a rarefied riddle and becomes instead the hermeneutical key for opening up questions in all theological loci."[24]

---

21. Schleiermacher, *Christian Faith*, 738.
22. Holmes, *Quest for the Trinity*, 186–90.
23. Barth, *CD*, II/2, 8.
24. Sanders, *Image of the Immanent Trinity*, 51–52.

Trinitarian Theology and the Gospel: Five Broadly Evangelical Case Studies

If the doctrine of the Trinity is indeed the hermeneutical key to the kingdom of systematic theology, have evangelical theologians made use of it and, if so, how? B. B. Warfield's 1915 essay "The Biblical Doctrine of the Trinity" is as good a place as any to start, not least because it antedates the so-called renaissance of Trinitarian theology in the twentieth century spear-headed by Barth. Warfield devotes the bulk of his article to demonstrating the biblical grounds of the doctrine. It is not a biblical term but a biblical truth. We will not find it on the surface of Scripture but implied in its deeper meaning. Nor is it an isolated teaching. On the contrary, Warfield insists that the New Testament in particular "is Trinitarian to the core; all its teachings are built on the assumption of the Trinity."[25] He looks not to proof texts but proof deeds: the incarnation of the Son and the outpouring of the Spirit. It follows that the revelation of the Trinity was the inevitable effect of the accomplishment of redemption. The gospel just *is* Trinitarian, for the good news is that the Father has reached out with both hands—Son and Spirit—in order to lift us up to himself. Hence, says Warfield, "the doctrine of the Trinity and the doctrine of redemption, historically, stand or fall together."[26] If evangelicals are gospel people, then they must be Trinity people too.

Herman Bavinck represents another kind of Trinitarian theology that antedates Barth's revival, though the significance of his work has not always been appreciated. Whereas Warfield connects the Trinity to the plan of salvation, Bavinck makes it into a virtual worldview: "The Christian mind remains unsatisfied until all of existence is referred back to the triune God, and until the confession of God's Trinity functions at the center of our thought and life."[27] Bavinck goes further than Warfield by linking the Trinity not only to redemption but also to creation: "If God were not triune, creation would not be possible."[28] And because creation is a triune work, Bavinck fully expects to see analogies between the world and its Maker. Specifically,

---

25. Warfield, "Biblical Doctrine of the Trinity," 32.

26. Ibid., 56. Sanders makes this point eloquently in his *The Deep Things of God*: "the Trinity is the gospel . . . the good news of salvation is that God . . . has become for us the adoptive Father, the incarnate Son, and the outpoured Holy Spirit" (165).

27. Bavinck, *Reformed Dogmatics* 2:330. John Bolt comments "the fundamental theme that shapes Bavinck's entire theology is the trinitarian idea that grace restores nature" ("Editor's Introduction," 18).

28. Ibid., 420. Bavinck holds that God communicates himself "absolutely" to the Son in the process of eternal generation, which is the basis of his "relative" communication of himself (and his image) to creation.

he sees an "organic" unity in diversity in both creation and Creator.[29] Yet he is unwilling to "prove" the doctrine on the basis of these *vestigia Trinitatis* precisely because of the discontinuities: "Creatures exist in time and space, exist side by side and do not interpenetrate each other."[30] While all creatures display certain "vestiges" of the Trinity, only human beings are the *image* of God. Like Aquinas, Bavinck thinks that this means that we have been created in a *Trinitarian* image, though he is reluctant to follow Augustine and identify the threeness with the psychological faculties of memory, will, and understanding. We image the triune God not by virtue of this or that faculty or function, but rather by being an organism that displays not so much one-in-threeness, but unity-in-diversity.

Donald Bloesch's seven volume *Christian Foundations* represents yet another way of being Trinitarian. He is a pivotal figure in our account because he draws on Barth, entitles his initial volume with the promising Trinitarian rubric *Word and Spirit*, and elicits comments from other Trinitarian theologians that figure in my account.[31] Grenz rightly identifies Bloesch's "antirationalism" as deriving from his concern not to domesticate God's word by restating revelation in a system of doctrinal propositions. Revelation is an event whereby the living Word, in its unity with Scripture and church proclamation, "is brought home to us by the Spirit in the awakening of faith."[32] Despite the emphasis on Word and Spirit in the opening book, however, Bloesch's *Christian Foundation* series does not appear to be as strongly Trinitarian as that of Warfield or Bavinck. Torrance makes this clear in his study of the third volume of the series, *God the Almighty*, where he praises Bloesch for understanding God's power in the light of the gospel rather than some metaphysical notion of omnipotent causality. Yet he laments Bloesch's decision not to discuss the mystery of the Trinity until chapter 7, well after the discussion on revelation, transcendence and immanence, and the divine attributes. "I could have wished," says Torrance, "[that Bloesch] had given an account of the doctrine of the Holy Trinity not just 'as the apex and goal of theology' but as *the ultimate ground and all-determining structure of Christian theology*."[33]

---

29. Cf. Eglinton's claim that "Trinity *ad intra* leads to organism *ad extra*" (*Trinity and Organism*, 81).

30. Bavinck, *Reformed Dogmatics*, 2:331.

31. Grenz and T. F. Torrance interact with Bloesch's theological method and doctrine of God respectively in Colyer, *Evangelical Theology in Transition*.

32. Bloesch, *Theology of Word and Spirit*, 14.

33. Torrance, "Bloesch's Doctrine of God," 140.

Torrance's own massive body of work is devoted largely to showing that the Trinity is "the ground and grammar" of Christian theology.[34] Torrance resembles Barth in beginning with God's revelation in Christ but lays greater stress on the importance of theology being *scientific*. Science, theology included, investigates each kind of reality *kata physin*—"according to its nature." It follows that the method by which we come to know a particular reality is at least partly determined by the nature of what it is we want to know. To know God as he really is, according to his distinct nature, is, for Torrance, to know him as Father, Son, and Spirit. The concept of *homoousios* ("of the same being") in particular is central because it defines the pattern by which God gives himself to be known and enjoyed in Jesus Christ and thus connects the economic and immanent Trinity.[35] Through participation in the worship of the church, we begin to indwell the Trinitarian pattern of our salvation, and hence progress from knowing God as he is in the economy to knowing God as he is in himself, in his personal "onto-relations."

Indeed, everything in Torrance's theology eventually refers back to Trinitarian onto-relations: relations that are so basic they define what a reality *is*, its essential being.[36] In Torrance's hands, the *homoousion* becomes a way of grasping the God-world relationship itself, for that relationship too is defined by the history of Jesus Christ. A scientific theology attempts to bring the inherent rationality and relationality of reality to light, and it does so by thinking about the universe "as ultimately integrated from above through the creative bearing upon it of the Trinitarian relations in God Himself."[37] We come to know God only as God brings us into communion with him in the inner relations of his triune being as Father, Son, and Spirit through our union with Christ.

Torrance's Trinitarian faith is anything but weak. The Trinity is the key to understanding God, ourselves, and the relationship between God and ourselves.[38] Consider how Trinitarian theology colors theological anthropology. For Torrance, we know what persons are first and foremost from pondering the onto-relations in the Godhead. We do not first decide what persons are and then say there are three of them in the Godhead. On the

---

34. Of the many relevant works that could be mentioned, the most important are *The Trinitarian Faith* and *The Christian Doctrine of God*.

35. McGrath suggests that *homoousios* is the "cornerstone" of Torrance's theology (*T. F. Torrance*, 167).

36. See Colyer, *How to Read T. F. Torrance*, 55–56.

37. Torrance, *Christian Theology and Scientific Culture*, 38.

38. The doctrine of the Trinity is for Torrance "*the* central doctrine around which all other Christian doctrines gravitate and become comprehensible" (Molnar, *Thomas F. Torrance*, 31).

contrary, we examine the way God has revealed himself to be, and we come to understand that the relations between persons are part of what persons are: "That is the trinitarian source of the concept of person in human thought."[39]

Our final case study, Miroslav Volf, illustrates the increasing tendency in contemporary theology to look to the Trinity not only as the source for our concept of person, but also for the concept of persons-in-relation: *community*. Volf draws upon Jürgen Moltmann's social view of the Trinity, as well as John Zizioulas's claim that the very being of God is communion, to argue that the church is a community created in the image of the triune God. Volf thus provides a concrete example of what it might mean to be Trinitarian in one's ecclesiology if one takes one's bearings from the divine threeness rather than oneness: "ecclesial communion should correspond to trinitarian communion."[40] Like the Trinity, the church is a plurality of persons united in "perichoretic" fellowship in which each person is who he is only in relation to the other two.[41] It follows for Volf that "the Trinity is our social program" (to cite the title of his seminal essay). Volf argues for a non-hierarchical understanding of God's triune life, marked by symmetrical reciprocity, and thus for an egalitarian ecclesiology. For neither hierarchy nor subordination are conceivable "within a community of perfect love between persons who share all the divine attributes."[42] The church is an egalitarian community that anticipates God's new creation, where God will be all in all.

Is Volf's Trinitarian ecclesiology "strong" or "radical-reductionist"? Is the operative principle the Trinity as such or a particular construal of triune being? This is a subtle query. The Trinitarian principle to which Volf appeals—*egalitarian relationality*—is something of an abstraction, similar to Elizabeth Johnson's similar appeal, from the perspective of feminist theology, to triune relationality: "The Trinity as pure relationality . . . epitomizes the connectedness of all that exists in the universe."[43] However, other Trinitarian theologians, like Zizioulas, who also appeal to the Trinity,

---

39. Torrance, "Bloesch's Doctrine of God," 145. The elevation of "onto-relations" into such prominence does raise the worrying possibility that even Torrance's Trinitarian radicalism lists towards its own kind of reductionism.

40. Volf, *After Our Likeness*, 191.

41. Perichoresis means that each divine person is "coinherent" with or "interpenetrates" the other two, and is the reason why there can be three persons in the Godhead without there being three gods. Recall Bavinck's demurral above: "Creatures exist in time and space, exist side by side and do not interpenetrate each other" (*Reformed Dogmatics*, 2:331).

42. Volf, *After Our Likeness*, 271. For a thoroughgoing analysis of this use of the doctrine of the Trinity, see Bidwell, *Church as the Image of the Trinity*.

43. Johnson, *She Who Is*, 222.

develop their ecclesiologies in more hierarchical directions that purport to correspond to the relations of origin that characterize the Godhead (e.g., the Father "begets" the Son). The perplexed observer of such disparate appeals to the nature of the triune communion may well ask: Will the real Trinity please stand up?

Not every appeal to the Trinity is warranted. Indeed, I have elsewhere criticized too ready an appeal to Trinitarian notions like perichoresis as a paradigmatic form for human personhood or society. I call the tendency to apply categories that belong properly to the doctrine of the Trinity to things other than the Godhead "illegitimate Trinitarian transfer."[44] This is precisely Mark Husbands's concern about Volf's call to make the Trinity our social program. Husbands finds no biblical support for the idea that we are to think of human personhood in perichoretic terms, and urges us to resist the temptation to project our own social, cultural, or political concerns onto God. Indeed, a proper Trinitarian theology—one consistent with Scripture and tradition—"must preserve an ontological distinction between God and humanity in order to maintain an order consistent with their distinct natures."[45] It is especially in light of Moltmann and other who are tempted to view the God-world relationship in terms of perichoresis that we must keep in mind the difference between sound Trinitarian theology and illegitimate Trinitarian transfer.[46]

Trinitarian Triangulation: Prolegomena to Any Future (Evangelical) Systematics

Fred Sanders is right to remind us why evangelicals of all people should be Trinitarian: the doctrine of the Trinity inherently belongs to the gospel itself, he says, because "Christian salvation comes from the Trinity, happens through the Trinity, and brings us home to the Trinity."[47] Can one ever have too much of a good (i.e., gospel) thing? As we have seen, some contemporary theologians are radically reductionist in their use of apparently Trinitarian principles (e.g., perichoresis). How then should evangelicals, or anyone else for that matter, be Trinitarian theologians? In this last section we turn to examine three evangelical theologians—John Frame, Stan

---

44. Vanhoozer, *Remythologizing Theology*, 150.

45. Husbands, "The Trinity is *Not* Our Social Program," 121.

46. Moltmann posits the "mutual perichoresis" of God and world, thus threatening the Creator/creature distinction (*The Coming of God*, 327).

47. Sanders, *Deep Things of God*, 10.

Grenz, and me—whose work evidences a consistent triangulating dynamic that draws, in important though different ways, upon the doctrine of the Trinity. By "triangulate," I refer to the process whereby one determines one's location, and orientation, with reference to three different points. The goal of this triangulating exercise is to discern the best way forward for Trinitarian theology that is neither weak nor reductionist, but rather strong and biblically sound, a way forward that will consistently direct the community of God in the way of Jesus Christ.

John Frame: Multiperspectival Triangulation (Three Perspectives)

John Frame, one of evangelicalism's premier theologians, is not as well-known as he deserves to be, perhaps because he has labored largely in conservative Reformed vineyards. For years he has been doing theology both faithfully (i.e., in accordance with the Scriptures) and creatively with a "multiperspectival" method that deepens our understanding and appreciation of what it means to confess God as covenant Lord. His theology is multiperspectival in two senses. In a broad sense, this means that humans, unlike God, are finite, able to see things from one perspective at a time. We need to learn to view things from the perspectives of others as well, and ultimately this is a matter of benefiting from God's perspectives "which includes all truth from all possible perspectives, as God reveals this in Scripture."[48] In a narrow sense, however, he works with a pervasive pattern of threefold distinctions that he believes are ultimately based in the Trinity.[49]

Is Frame's triperspectivalism an example of weak, strong, or radical-reductionist Trinitarianism? It is not a simple question. Despite the various triads that pervade his work, "The Triune God" is the sixth and final part of Frame's doctrine of God.[50] Of course, positioning alone is not necessarily indicative of a doctrine's importance, as we saw in examining both Aquinas and Schleiermacher. The theme that enjoys pride of place in Frame's theology is that of *covenant Lordship*. Frame associates the three perspectives on covenant Lordship—control, authority, and presence—not with the three divine persons but with lordship attributes. It is therefore not entirely clear how they are "based" on the Trinity, though Frame thinks that the three perspectives, like the persons of the Trinity, imply and interpenetrate one

48. Frame and Sandlin, "Reflections of a Lifetime Theologian," 82.
49. Frame, "Primer on Perspectivalism" (2008).
50. Frame, *Doctrine of God*, an order repeated in his more recent *Systematic Theology*.

another (perichoresis!) "God's Trinitarian existence means that his attributes are not only personal, but interpersonal."[51]

Frame's doctrine of the Trinity itself is unremarkable in its orthodoxy. He devotes separate chapters to "God, Three in One," "The Three are God," and "Father, Son, and Spirit," and is especially concerned with providing biblical support for each of these topics. The one feature that is exceptional is his fascination with various triads. For example, in his chapter "God, Three in One" he includes a section on "Triads in the Old Testament," where he comments, "There is something mysteriously captivating to the human mind about the number three."[52] Frame is struck by the way the Aaronic benediction in Num 6:24–26 anticipates the explicitly Trinitarian apostolic benediction of 2 Cor 13:14. He also mentions the "linguistic model of the Trinity," where the Father is the speaker, the Son the word, and the Spirit the breath that conveys the word to hearers.[53]

In an appendix to his *Doctrine of God*, Frame lists more than a hundred triads from Scripture, philosophy, language, nature, culture, and mathematics that "reflect or illumine the Trinity in some way."[54] Frame distinguishes the psychological and social *models* of the Trinity from Trinitarian *analogies* that are often viewed as evidences or vestiges of the Trinity in the created world, adding that he knows of nothing in Scripture "that rules out the possibility of *vestigia trinitatis*."[55] The Trinity is thus the archetypal triad, though Frame admits that he is "not sure how all this is related to the doctrine of the Trinity, but I would be surprised if there were no significant connection at all."[56] Appropriately enough, there seems to be three ways of accounting for this significant connection.

First, in a manner somewhat reminiscent of Bavinck, the Trinity is the archetypal solution to the ancient problem of "the one and the many." Frame derives this idea from Cornelius Van Til, who viewed the whole created order, in its unity-in-diversity, as a *vestigium trinitatis*: "The universe is both one and many because God is also one and many."[57] It therefore follows that neither universals, nor particulars, nor relationships are uniquely ultimate; rather, they are equally ultimate. This first explanation of how the

---

51. Frame, *Systematic Theology*, 39. Frame is careful to add that the persons of the Trinity are really persons, "more than perspectives, but not less" ("Primer on Perspectivalism").

52. Frame, *Doctrine of God*, 634.

53. Ibid., 636.

54. Ibid., 743–50.

55. Ibid., 726.

56. Ibid., 634.

57. Ibid., 729.

Trinity serves as the archetypal triad most resembles *philosophical* theology. However, Frame resists basing his theology on anything but a biblical basis. He eschews Hegel's triadic approach (thesis-antithesis-synthesis) to logic and ontology because "it is far from that of Scripture."[58]

The second way in which Frame roots his triadic approach in the Trinity is via *biblical* theology, in particular, in Geerhardus Vos's approach to the history of God's dealings with creation.[59] Frame notes that the persons of the Trinity "correspond roughly to the three main events of the biblical story: creation (in which the emphasis on the Father), redemption accomplished (the Son's incarnation, perfect life, atonement, and resurrection), and redemption applied (the Spirit's application to our hearts of the Son's redemptive work)."[60] This way of putting it suggests a third, more *systematic* theological way of grounding Frame's covenant Lordship triperspectivalism in the doctrine of the Trinity. Because each of the divine persons is involved in everything that another divine person does (here we may recall the patristic principle *opera trinitatis ad extra indivisa sunt*), we could say that each divine person offers a "perspective" on the being-in-act of God. Here, finally, is a properly theological grounding for Frame's triadic approach: the Father plans/authorizes; the Son executes/controls; the Spirit applies/makes present.[61] Whereas Barth explicitly derives the Trinity from his analysis of revelation, however, Frame's Trinitarian credentials are less obvious, arising implicitly out of an analysis of God's covenant lordship. Yet again, it seems easier to set out the weak-strong-reductionist spectrum of Trinitarian theology than to locate particular theologians somewhere along it.

Stanley Grenz: Methodological Triangulation (Three Motifs; Three Sources/Norms)

Stan Grenz was a prolific author who, in his several attempts to revision, recenter, renew, revitalize, and re-everything evangelical theology, demonstrated a distinct triangulating tendency. In a series of constructive works, from the 1993 *Revisioning Evangelical Theology* to his 2001 *Beyond Foundationalism*, Grenz consistently deployed two sets of methodological triads: three motifs and three sources/norms. While I cannot do justice to Grenz's

58. Ibid..
59. Poythress, "Multiperspectivalism and the Reformed Faith," 179.
60. Frame, *Doctrine of God*, 727.
61. Frame comments: "all the covenantal triads I have employed in the Theology of Lordship books arise out of the unity and complexity of God's Trinitarian being" (*Doctrine of God*, 728).

corpus in a few paragraphs, by examining these two triads I hope at least to shed some light on the sense in which he could be said to have produced a Trinitarian system of theology.[62]

The best place to begin inquiring into the nature of Grenz's system is his early one-volume systematic theology: *Theology for the Community of God*. The title, taken in isolation, is ambiguous: is theology for the community that God creates (i.e., the church) or the community that God is (i.e., Father, Son, and Spirit)? Grenz quickly makes it clear, however, that he means the former. Indeed, in the preface itself he calls attention to "community" as the distinctive integrative motif around which his whole system revolves. Theology describes the faith—the mosaic of belief—of the Christian community and its place in God's plan for creation, a plan for "the establishment of community."[63]

Community is Grenz's "integrative motif"—"a systematic theology's central organizing feature."[64] In his earliest formulation, he describes the integrative motif as "the theme around which [theology] is structured."[65] Subsequently, he came to distinguish the integrative from the structural motif, which he associated with the Trinity. It is telling, however, that he identifies the central idea in light of which all other theological concepts are understood with *community* rather than the Trinity.[66] Perhaps this is because he saw community as the *meaning* of the Trinity: "God is the social Trinity, the community of love."[67]

In his mature works, Grenz made the Trinity the first of his three motifs that characterize Christian theology: the Trinity is the structural motif, community the integrative motif, and eschatology the orienting motif.[68] What is a "motif"? While I cannot be sure, I suspect that Grenz is using "motif" to identify authentic Christian theology, parallel to the way the Reformers used "marks" to identify authentic Christian churches. A motif

---

62. I am purposely bracketing out the question of Grenz's inclination towards a postmodern, postfoundationlist epistemology. I have dealt with this elsewhere (see my "On the Very Idea of a Theological System").

63. Grenz, *Theology for the Community*, xxxi.

64. Ibid., 20.

65. Ibid.

66. Though, to be fair, the structure of even this early systematic theology broadly follows the three articles of the Apostles' Creed, so the Trinity is never far from the center of his thought (Grenz, *Theology for the Community*, 24–25).

67. Grenz, *Theology for the Community*, 72.

68. The following statement is typical of his mature position: "All truly Christian local theologies are trinitarian in content, communitarian in focus, and eschatological in orientation" (*Beyond Foundationalism*, 166).

is not a mandate for a specific method of doing theology, but a certain *manner*. What is a *structural* motif? It is a way of saying that one mark of genuine Christian theology is its triune subject matter, a subject matter that bears on every tile in the Christian belief-mosaic.

The three motifs, taken together, comprise what we may term the "material principle" of his Trinitarian theology, though Grenz does not phrase it in precisely these terms. (I shall suggest below that the three sources/norms likewise constitute the "formal principle" of his Trinitarian theology).[69] Significantly, all three motifs focus on what Grenz takes to be the subject matter of Christian theology, namely, *how the communitarian God is establishing an even greater community, comprised of renewed persons from every nation, tribe, people, and language* (Rev 7:9). Grenz's orienting motif—eschatology—does not add new content but addresses the fate of the integrative motif: the church, as *believing* community. The church "is nothing less than a shared participation . . . in the perichoretic community of Trinitarian persons."[70] The church is "basic" for Grenz because (1) it is the goal of the triune God's activity in the world and (2) it is our participation in the faith community that calls forth theological reflection. In Grenz's view, that "all Christian theology is communitarian" is true in both a material and formal sense.

We can illustrate just how pervasive Grenz's communitarian material theme is by examining his understanding of the *imago Dei*. The image of God is an integrative theme inasmuch as it spans the narrative of creation, redemption, and consummation: the suspense in the biblical story arises from the question, "Will God fulfill the design for which he created humanity?" Having established that God, as triune, is essentially relational (i.e., a divine community of love), Grenz specifies the design—God's intent for humanity—as mirroring the divine nature: "humans express the relational dynamic of the God whose representation we are called to be."[71] Indeed, he goes so far as to suggest that the divine image "is fully present only in

---

69. For a further examination of Grenz's Trinitarian theology, and in particular its indebtedness to Pannenberg, see Sexton, *Trinitarian Theology*, chs. 2–3.

70. Grenz, "Ecclesiology," 268.

71. Grenz, *Theology for the Community*, 179. An additional reason Grenz gives for stressing relationality is its resonance with the present (postmodern) cultural moment, in particular, its rejection of autonomous individualism. Grenz cites this resonance with contemporary culture as a reason for being Trinitarian (*Beyond Foundationalism*, 172). But what if communitarianism falls out of cultural favor? I discuss further culture's role in theological method below.

relationships, that is, in 'community.'"[72] In short: Trinitarian theology entails relational anthropology.[73]

We turn now to the formal principle of Grenz's theology, namely, the "trialogue" he conducts between the biblical message (Scripture), the theological heritage (tradition), and contemporary context (culture). Here, too, Grenz displays a consistent emphasis on what he calls "the threefold norm of theology."[74] Unfortunately, Grenz consistently elides the distinction between "sources" and "norms." There are many sources (i.e., places, persons, and books from which we get ideas and information about God, the world, and humanity), but it makes little sense to say that they all are also norms (i.e., standards of theological discourse). Where then is the locus of theological authority? I think Grenz would say that authority lies in the triune God speaking in *and through* the Scriptures.

Indeed, Grenz's material and formal triads converge in the notion of *the Spirit's speaking to build an eschatological community*. The Spirit uses Scripture, tradition, and culture alike to construct a new world—"a holy nation, God's own people" (1 Pet 2:9), whose identity is formed by the story of Jesus Christ and the new covenant. In short: building a new community is the material principle of Grenz's Trinitarian theology, the Spirit's speaking in and through Scripture, tradition, and culture is its formal principle. Elsewhere I have criticized the way in which Grenz conceives the Word-Spirit relationship.[75] I do not have time to rehearse those arguments here. I do want to examine the extent to which Grenz's account of the Spirit's speaking is or is not biblical and Trinitarian.

To be sure, Grenz affirms the Bible as the "primary voice" in the theological conversation and "norming norm" of theology.[76] It enjoys this role because the Spirit uses its message as a means to bring about the social construction of reality, namely, a new reconciled community. The purpose of the Spirit's speaking is not primarily revelation (reality-depicting knowledge) so much as sanctification (reality-making piety). It is a matter of *reforming*

72. *Beyond Foundationalism*, 200. Grenz's claim prompts two related questions: (1) what is the basis for ascribing human dignity to individuals rather than communities? (2) did Jesus embody the image of God even when he was "despised and rejected by men" (Isa 53:3), or when he was on the cross, forsaken by the Father (Mark 15:34)?

73. Grenz launched his multi-volume Matrix of Christian Theology series with *Social God*. For an extended analysis of Grenz's attempt to make the *imago Dei* the means through which the doctrine of the Trinity was to inform the entire theological matrix, see Sexton, "*Imago Dei* Once Again," 187–206.

74. *Theology for the Community*, 16–20; "Articulating the Christian Belief-Mosaic," 124–29; *Beyond Foundationalism*, chs. 3–5.

75. See my "On the Very Idea of a Theological System," 125–82.

76. Grenz, "Articulating," 124; *Beyond Foundationalism*, 57.

(another "re-"!) the people of God. The objectivity in which Grenz believes is not "the world as it is" but "the world as it is becoming in Christ through the Spirit."⁷⁷ Moreover, what the Spirit declares through the text today does not necessarily coincide with what the prophets and apostles originally said. Hence, "we must never conclude that exegesis alone can exhaust the Spirit's speaking to us through the text."⁷⁸ The Spirit is also active in tradition, leading the church into all truth; we therefore do well to read in community.

What is important to discern is that, for Grenz, the Spirit's speaking is a dynamic, non-foundationalist affair. It is not what is "in" Scripture—revealed propositions, for instance—that counts most, but what the Spirit is doing through Scripture in the present (i.e., creating an eschatological world out of the believing community).⁷⁹ Similarly, past creeds and confessions are not binding in and of themselves but must be tested "by Scripture and by their applicability to our cultural situation."⁸⁰ Here we see Grenz's triangulation at work: rightly to hear the Spirit's speaking involves coordinating the biblical message, tradition, and the cultural moment. What is of special interest is the role Grenz assigns to culture.

On one level, there is nothing objectionable about theology making use of cultural thought forms. How else can the church fulfill its missionary mandate to speak the truth of Jesus Christ? It is just here, however, that Grenz's confusion of source and norm comes home to roost. It is one thing to mine culture for raw materials with which to recast the original biblical message, quite another to correlate the message to the needs of a particular culture.⁸¹ I am not suggesting that Grenz cedes authority to culture. Rather, he strives to coordinate gospel and culture in a dynamic conversation. He neither contextualizes nor correlates but *triangulates*. But this means treating tradition and culture not merely as sources but also, in some sense, norms. As creeds must be tested by Scripture and cultural applicability, so the biblical message must be "balanced" by tradition and culture. This is because Grenz refuses to equate the Spirit's speaking with the *fixed (propositional) content* of Scripture exclusively and exhaustively. Instead, he identifies the

---

77. Here we should register the influence of Wolfhart Pannenberg, Grenz's *Doktorvater*, for whom God's revelation and reality alike are from the future, that point where God will not only be seen to be but actually to be "all in all." Grenz does not deny the objectivity of the present, then, but views the future reality in Christ as even more real (think Plato turned on his side, with the Forms not "above" but "ahead").

78. Grenz, *Beyond Foundationalism*, 74.

79. Grenz, "Articulating," 125.

80. Grenz, *Theology for the Community*, 19.

81. Interestingly, Grenz finds both contextualizers and correlationists to be too foundationalist (*Beyond Foundationalism*, 157).

Spirit's speaking with the Spirit's use of Scripture in particular contexts as an instrumentality of community formation.[82] What the text is ultimately about is not the world "behind" the text (i.e., its historical referent) but the world "*way* in front of" the text (i.e., the new eschatological reality that is coming to be "in Christ"). The church must therefore attend to the world "*immediately* in front of" the biblical text (i.e., the present context), and hence "the Spirit's voice in culture" as well as in the biblical text.[83] This need not result in culture trumping Scripture, for the simple reason that the three sources/norms "are ultimately one speaking."[84] Yet Grenz does tend to identify the Spirit's speaking through Scripture not with the message "behind" the text (i.e., authorial intention), or with the message "of" the text (i.e., its immanent sense), but rather with the message as it has been triangulated as it were "in front of" the text (i.e., in a particular cultural context).[85]

Grenz's systematic theology may therefore lay claim to being Trinitarian in two related senses: first, in the material sense of focusing on community, divine and human; second, in the formal sense of triangulating the Spirit's speaking through Scripture, tradition, and culture. Each sense, however, gives rise to a critical question: (1) Does the material emphasis on community illustrate strong or radical-reductionist Trinitarianism? (2) Does the formal emphasis on the Spirit speaking community into being correctly triangulate Bible, tradition, and culture? I believe the answer to both question depends on how we parse triune communicative action, and it is to that task that we now turn.

A Way Forward? Theodramatic Triangulation (Three Aspects of Communicative Agency)

It should be clear by now that not every triad a Trinitarian theology doth make. Nor, as we have seen, is it a matter of simply positing the doctrine of the Trinity. On the contrary, strong Trinitarian systematics must begin with the central subject matter of Christian theology itself, and this means with

---

82. Grenz fails adequately to emphasize the Spirit's use of Scripture as a ministry of the word whose aim is understanding. Grenz wrongly dissociates the perlocutionary act of the Spirit (i.e., world-building) from the text's illocutions, and hence from exegesis (Vanhoozer, "On the Very Idea of a Theological System").

83. Grenz, "Articulating," 128.

84. Ibid.

85. *Beyond Foundationalism*, 74. Grenz makes some serious missteps here with regard to his use of speech act theory, suggesting that the "Spirit speaking through the Scriptures" is a matter of his performing the illocutionary acts of "addressing" and "appropriating." For a fuller development of this critique, see my *First Theology*, 197–98.

the word and act of God that Scripture attests and Jesus Christ embodies. The way forward is to triangulate: I want to take from Frame the theme of covenant Lordship, from Grenz the motif of community, and modify them both with the notion of communicative action—the action of sharing or making something common. The Trinity is the sum of the gospel because the good news concerns how the Father invites us to share in the divine life in the Son through the Spirit. The gospel of the Trinity (or is it the Trinity of the gospel?) ultimately concerns *communicative action oriented to covenantal communion*. The notion of triune communicative action lies at the heart of both the material and formal principles of Trinitarian theology.[86]

The Material Principle

What Trinitarian theology seeks to systematize is the eternal God's triune outreach to the world—in a word, *theodrama*. The gospel is theodramatic: it is all about the deeds and words of the triune God in a story that begins with creation, progresses to redemption, ends in consummation—"in Christ."[87] Paraphrasing Barth, we might say that God (the Father) communicates himself (the Son) through himself (the Spirit). The triune God is Voice, Word, and Breath: the Father utters his Word; the Son is what gets communicated, the content of the Father's speech; the Spirit is the channel ("breath") that carries the word and ensures that it reaches its destination. That is not all: the God who communicates himself in history to us is also eternally self-communicative in himself. For what God consequently communicates to the world—his light, life, and love—corresponds to what God antecedently is in his own triune life.[88] God the Father relates to everything

---

86. How do these principles relate to what Philip Schaff calls the formal and material principles of Protestantism (in Schaff, *Principle of Protestantism*)? In both cases there is overlap. Scripture is the supreme norm for both the Reformation and my Trinitarian theology (see below). The situation with the material principle is more interesting. Where Schaff identifies the material principle of the Reformation with justification by faith, the "sum of the gospel," I am using it to refer to the sum and substance of the Trinity. However, as we have seen, the doctrine of the Trinity is itself a kind of summary statement of the gospel. Inasmuch as the substance of what God graciously communicates is indeed the light, life, and love of Jesus Christ, and insofar as this gracious communication makes possible a communion, it turns out that the connecting link between the material principles of Protestantism and Trinitarian theology is nothing less than what Calvin identified as the source of the double blessing of justification and sanctification, namely, *union with Christ*.

87. For a further elaboration of this, see my *Drama of Doctrine*.

88. For a further treatment of this theme, see my *Remythologizing*, ch. 5: "God in Three Persons: The One Who Lights and Lives in Love."

else through the work of God the Son and God the Spirit. Hence, in a sense, "there is only one Christian doctrine, the doctrine of the Holy Trinity in its inward and outward movements. . . . All other doctrines are simply extensions of teaching about God and God's works."[89]

The material principle of Trinitarian theology is neither an idea (e.g., relationality) or ideal (e.g., community) but an activity, one that moreover defines God's very being: *communicative activity oriented to covenantal communion*. Father, Son, and Spirit are three communicative agents who subsist in one communicative agency. The triune God shares his light, life, and love first within himself (immanent Trinity) and eventually with creation (economic Trinity). However, in making this triune activity the material principle of my theology, am I too falling into a reductionist Trinitarianism, as Grenz seems to be doing by elevating community to the position of first theology? I think not, and this for three main reasons.

In the first place, unlike reductionists, I do not separate the *meaning* of the doctrine of the Trinity (e.g., relationality) from the doctrine itself, in order then to identify that meaning with the *imago Dei*, as Volf does. On the contrary, I want to acknowledge, with Bavinck, the analogical nature of the claim that human beings image the Trinity, and hence the implied *is not*: "in human beings the trinity is not the persons themselves but something in or about the persons, whereas in God the Trinity is God himself."[90] Communion—being-in-community—is for human creatures not an ontological given (sin *alienates*) but a soteriological gift, the supreme covenant blessing: "I will be your God and you shall be my people" (Lev 26:12). The Trinity does not "represent" but rather *is* interpersonal communicative activity oriented to communion. As Khaled Anatolios notes: "One can after all espouse 'relationality' . . . without actually confessing and worshiping the Triune God as Father, Son, and Spirit."[91] What humans therefore image is not some single characteristic (e.g., relationality), but rather everything that constitutes us as created *communicative agents in covenantal relation oriented to communion*.

Second, communicative action is not an abstract principle—the *meaning* of the Trinity that can be dissociated from it—but a way of describing the economies of both revelation and redemption. The missions of the Son and Spirit are communicative acts, acts by which the Father shares his own light, life, and love with the world by sending his Son and Spirit to bring about union and communion with humans created in his image. Unlike

---

89. Webster, "Principles of Systematic Theology," 68.
90. Bavinck, *Reformed Dogmatics* 2:326.
91. Anatolios, *Retrieving Nicaea*, 6–7.

relationality, or any other abstract principle, the concept of communicative action corresponds to the biblical narrative of the Triune-shaped creation, redemption, and consummation. *Opera trinitatis ad extra indivisa sunt*. The Trinity at every stage shares a common communicative agency, yet each person appropriates this agency in a unique way. The Father initiates, the Son executes, and the Spirit perfects each particular communicative act, be it revealing (making common the knowledge of God), sanctifying (making common the holiness of God), or church-gathering (making common the family of God).

Third, communicative action oriented to covenantal communion is not a discrete teaching but a way of interpreting the entirety of Christian faith.[92] If systematic theology treats God and all things in relation to God, then it "is best drawn from the sequence of the divine economy in which God's relation to creatures is enacted."[93] The whole of Christian faith and life concerns our fitting participation in what the Father is doing in Christ through the Spirit to renew creation. It is this entire communicative project—the sharing of God's light, life, and love with humanity; effecting union with Christ—that I am calling *theodrama*. Scripture depicts the life of the Father, Son, and Spirit as a perfect drama: a *doing than which nothing greater can be conceived*, a ceaseless communicative activity that yields consummate communion. The economic Trinity is the theodrama and the theodrama images or represents in time what the immanent Trinity is in eternity. This Trinitarian material principle is therefore what Christianity is all about, which is why it must inform and influence every other doctrine. Trinitarian systematics may thus be seen to be a matter of thinking about all the theological loci—creation, *imago Dei*, sin, justification and sanctification, the church, etc.—in relation to God's triune communicative (theodramatic) action.

The Formal Principle

Where the material principle of Trinitarian theology focuses on triune communicative agency (the ontological principle of systematics), the formal principle focuses on what we might call the economy of God's *cognitive* communicative action, with Scripture its *principium cognoscendi*. By "cognitive" I mean to include not only the intellect but the imagination and all the other faculties of the mind that enable words to communicate not merely information but knowledge and wisdom, and to direct the desires of the heart. Scripture sets forth the triune communicative activity that describes

---

92. A point made most forcefully by Anatolios, *Retrieving Nicaea*, 11.
93. Webster, "Introduction: Systematic Theology," 12.

what the Father has done to adopt us into his family in Christ through the Spirit. What is more, Scripture is a principal ingredient in the divine communicative action: Scripture is triune discourse.[94] Whereas Grenz's formal principle was the trialogue between Scripture, tradition, and culture as the means of the Spirit's speaking to build a new community, my own focus is on the Spirit's speaking in Scripture to provide theodramatic understanding and direction to the church. My theological triangulating therefore works out a bit differently.

While tradition and culture are important sources, they do not play the same normative role in the economy of triune communication as they do in Grenz. While Grenz rightly cautions against pitting the Spirit's speaking through Scripture with the Spirit speaking through culture, he also says that "culture and biblical text do not comprise two different moments of communication; rather, they are but one speaking."[95] In my view, the Spirit's voice does not speak *from* but rather *to* culture. Specifically, the Spirit enables cultures to hear the word of God spoken definitively in Christ and attested authoritatively in Scripture.[96] Culture is not a fourth form of the word of God.[97] Yes, "whatever [the Spirit] hears he will speak" (John 16:13), but in context, this means that the Spirit speaks only what is the Son's, which is also the Father's (John 16:14–15). It is thanks to the Spirit that we are able to participate in the Father-Son conversation, just as it is only through the Spirit that we can participate in Jesus' filial relation to the Father.

The primary vehicle of the word of God, and hence the focal point in the present economy of communication, is Scripture: triune discourse, "the self-communicating accommodation of the divine to human sensibilities."[98] Taken together, the books of the Bible comprise a canonical communicative act, an act that norms subsequent theodramatic triangulation. It is thanks to Scripture that those of us who live after the apostles know where we are in the drama of redemption and how to participate rightly in the ongoing Trinitarian action: the Father's renewing of creation in Christ through the Spirit.[99] It is thanks to Scripture's depiction of the economy that we can

94. For a fuller treatment of this, see my "Triune Discourse," 75–78.

95. Grenz, *Renewing the Center*, 219.

96. It is important that theology speak the language of the day, but this sensitivity to the present context is not quite the same thing as ascribing authority to one's cultural context.

97. Karl Barth held that Scripture and preaching, in addition to the incarnation, were forms of the one Word of God, Jesus Christ.

98. Anatolios, *Retrieving Nicaea*, 282.

99. There is clearly overlap here with Grenz's notion of the Spirit constructing an eschatological world.

move from "weak" to "strong" conceptions of Trinitarian theology, and it is thanks to Scripture's own triangulating—"plotting" the positions of Son and Spirit throughout the drama of redemption—that we prevent Trinitarian theology from becoming reductionist, focused only on the "meaning" of the doctrine rather than the triune God's missionary movements.

In ministering the Word, the Spirit ministers theodramatic understanding—what the church needs to know in order rightly to participate, in its own cultural time and place, in the ongoing triune theodrama. Theological triangulation coordinates (1) what the Father has done, is doing, and will do in Christ (i.e., theodramatic ontology, because God is being-in-communicative-activity), (2) the Scriptures that authoritatively attest what is and will be "in Christ" (i.e., theodramatic epistemology), and (3) the way the Spirit guides the church and the ways it must speak and act in order to correspond to its being in Christ (i.e., theodramatic ethics). Culture is not the norm of this theodrama, but its staging area.[100]

No doubt much more can, and should, be said. It is only a matter of time before someone triangulates the work of the three evangelical triangulators that I have treated here. If so, I will not protest. Indeed, as a good Reformed theologian, I will applaud the effort in the spirit of *semper triangulanda* ("always triangulating").

Conclusion: Verities of Trinitarian Theology

What is Trinitarian theology and how can it be systematic? I have argued for a strong Trinitarian theology that does not treat the doctrine of the Trinity merely as one of the theological *loci* but rather as the singular *lens* through which to view everything else. I have sought to avoid a reductionist Trinitarian theology that separates the putative meaning of the doctrine from the Trinity's being-in-communicative-activity. I have proposed that the reality of the Trinity spans the biblical narrative from creation to consummation and involves at each step the triune God's communicative initiatives, acts, and effects that establish covenantal relations and expand familial communion. I conclude with three summary theses (of course!).

1. The economic Trinity *communicates* the immanent Trinity. The God who is with and for us in Christ is the God who has perfect light, life, and love in himself.

---

100. On the role and authority of tradition, see my *Drama of Doctrine*, ch. 5.

2. Scripture both describes and is caught up in the triune economy of communication, the historical drama in which the triune God makes common his light, life, and love in revelation and redemption.

3. Systematic theology is a ministry of understanding the length, breadth, height, and depth of the gospel. It is the attempt to set forth in speech *what is in Christ*. As such, systematic theology is always, everywhere, and at all times Trinitarian to the extent that *what is in Christ*—true deity, true humanity, the created order, redemption, the new creation—is a joint work of Father, Son, and Spirit, and requires the work of the Spirit for disciples rightly to grasp, participate in, and do the truth: our adoption in Christ into the family of God.[101]

Bibliography

Anatolios, Khaled. *Retrieving Nicaea: The Development and Meaning of Trinitarian Doctrine*. Grand Rapids: Baker, 2011.

Ayres, Lewis. *Nicaea and Its Legacy: An Approach to Fourth-Century Trinitarian Theology*. Oxford: Oxford University Press, 2004.

Barth, Karl. *Church Dogmatics II/2: The Doctrine of God*. Translated by G. W. Bromiley et al. Edinburgh: T. & T. Clark, 1957.

Bavinck, Herman. *Reformed Dogmatics, Volume 2: God and Creation*. Grand Rapids: Baker, 2004.

Bidwell, Kevin J. *The Church as the Image of the Trinity: A Critical Evaluation of Miroslav Volf's Ecclesial Model*. Eugene, OR: Wipf and Stock, 2011.

Bloesch, Donald. *God the Almighty: Power, Wisdom, Holiness, Love*. Downers Grove, IL: InterVarsity, 1995.

———. *A Theology of Word & Spirit: Authority & Method in Theology*. Downers Grove, IL: InterVarsity, 1992.

Colyer, Elmer M., ed. *Evangelical Theology in Transition: Theologians in Dialogue with Donald Bloesch*. Downers Grove, IL: InterVarsity, 1999.

———. *How to Read T. F. Torrance: Understanding his Trinitarian and Scientific Theology*. Downers Grove, IL: InterVarsity, 2001.

Eglinton, James. *Trinity and Organism: Towards a New Reading of Herman Bavinck's Organic Motif*. London: T. & T. Clark, 2012.

Emery, Gilles. "The Doctrine of the Trinity." In *Aquinas on Doctrine: A Critical Introduction*, edited by Thomas Weinandy, Daniel Keating, and John Yocum, 45–66. London: T. & T. Clark, 2004.

———. *The Trinitarian Theology of Thomas Aquinas*. Oxford: Oxford University Press, 2007.

Frame, John. *The Doctrine of God*. Phillipsburg, NJ: Presbyterian and Reformed, 2002.

———. "A Primer on Perspectivalism" (2008). http://www.frame-poythress.org.

———. *Systematic Theology*. Phillipsburg, NJ: Presbyterian and Reformed, 2013.

---

101. My thanks to James Gordon, Ike Miller, Fred Sanders, and Jason Sexton for their comments on an earlier draft.

Frame, John, and P. Andrew Sandlin. "Reflections of a Lifetime Theologian: An Extended Interview with John M. Frame." In *Speaking the Truth in Love: The Theology of John M. Frame*, edited by John J. Hughes, 75–110. Phillipsburg, NJ: Presbyterian and Reformed, 2009.

Gregory of Nyssa. "An Answer to Ablabius: That We Should Not Think of Saying There are Three God." In *Christology of the Later Fathers*, edited by Edward R. Hardy, 256–67. Philadelphia: Westminster, 1954.

Holmes, Stephen R. *The Quest for the Trinity: The Doctrine of God in Scripture, History and Modernity*. Downers Grove, IL: InterVarsity Press, 2012.

Hughes, John J. Editor, *Speaking the Truth in Love: The Theology of John M. Frame*. Phillipsburg, NJ: Presbyterian and Reformed, 2009.

Husbands, Mark. "The Trinity Is *Not* Our Social Program: Volf, Gregory of Nyssa and Barth." In *Trinitarian Theology for the Church: Scripture, Community, Worship*, edited by Daniel Treier and David Lauber, 120–41. Downers Grove, IL: InterVarsity, 2009.

Jenson, Robert. "Karl Barth." In *The Modern Theologians*, 2nd ed., edited by David F. Ford, 21–36. Oxford: Blackwell, 1997.

Johnson, Elizabeth. *She Who Is: The Mystery of God in Feminist Theological Discourse*. New York: Crossroad, 2002.

Levering, Matthew. *Scripture and Metaphysics. Aquinas and the Renewal of Trinitarian Theology*. Oxford. Blackwell, 2004.

McGrath, Alister. *T. F. Torrance: An Intellectual Biography*. Edinburgh: T. & T. Clark, 1999.

Merriell, D. Juvena. *To the Image of the Trinity: A Study in the Development of Aquinas' Teaching*. Toronto: Pontifical Institute of Medieval Studies, 1999.

Metzger, Paul Louis. "Introduction: What Difference Does the Trinity Make?" In *Trinitarian Soundings in Systematic Theology*, edited by Paul Louis Metzger, 5–8. London: T. & T. Clark, 2005.

Molnar, Paul D. *Thomas F. Torrance: Theologian of the Trinity*. Aldershot, UK: Ashgate, 2009.

Moltmann, Jürgen. *The Coming of God*. Minneapolis: Fortress, 1996.

Poythress, Vern. "Multiperspectivalism and the Reformed Faith." In *Speaking the Truth in Love*, edited by John Hughes, 173–200. Phillipsburg, NJ: Presbyterian and Reformed, 2009.

Rahner, Karl. *The Trinity*. New York: Crossroad, 2002.

Sanders, Fred. *The Image of the Immanent Trinity: Rahner's Rule and the Theological Interpretation of Scripture*. New York: Lang, 2005.

———. *The Deep Things of God: How the Trinity Changes Everything*. Wheaton, IL: Crossway, 2010.

Schaff, Philip. *The Principle of Protestantism*. Eugene, OR: Wipf and Stock, 2004.

Schleiermacher, Friedrich. *The Christian Faith*. Edinburgh: T. & T. Clark, 1928.

Schwöbel, Christoph. "Introduction: The Renaissance of Trinitarian Theology: Reasons, Problems and Tasks." In *Trinitarian Theology Today*, edited by Christoph Schwöbel, 1–30. Edinburgh: T. & T. Clark, 1995.

Sexton, Jason S. "The *Imago Dei* Once Again: Stanley Grenz's Journey toward a Theological Interpretation of Genesis 1:26–27." *Journal of Theological Interpretation* 4 (2010) 187–206.

———. "The State of the Evangelical Trinitarian Resurgence." *Journal of the Evangelical Theological Society* 54 (2011) 787–807.

———. *The Trinitarian Theology of Stanley J. Grenz*. London: T. & T. Clark, 2013.

Shults, F. LeRon. *Reforming the Doctrine of God*. Grand Rapids: Eerdmans, 2005.

Torrance, T. F. "Bloesch's Doctrine of God." In *Evangelical Theology in Transition: Theologians in Dialogue with Donald Bloesch*, edited by Elmer M. Colyer, 136–48. Downers Grove, IL: InterVarsity, 1999.

———. *The Christian Doctrine of God: One Being Three Persons*. Edinburgh: T. & T. Clark, 1996.

———. *Christian Theology and Scientific Culture*. Oxford: Oxford University Press, 1981.

———. *The Trinitarian Faith: The Evangelical Theology of the Ancient Catholic Church*. Edinburgh: T. & T. Clark, 1988.

Vanhoozer, Kevin J., ed. *The Cambridge Companion to Postmodern Theology*. Cambridge: Cambridge University Press, 2003.

———. *The Drama of Doctrine: A Canonical-Linguistic Approach to Christian Theology*. Louisville, KY: Westminster John Knox, 2005.

———. *First Theology: God, Scripture, and Hermeneutics*. Downers Grove, IL: InterVarsity, 2002.

———. "On the Very Idea of a Theological System: An Essay in Aid of Triangulating Scripture, Church, and World." In *Always Reforming: Explorations in Systematic Theology*, edited by A. T. B. McGowan, 125–82. Leicester, UK: InterVarsity, 2006.

———. *Remythologizing Theology: Divine Action, Passion, and Authorship*. Cambridge: Cambridge University Press, 2010.

———. "Triune Discourse." In *Trinitarian Theology for the Church: Scripture, Community, Worship*, edited by Daniel J. Treier and David Lauber, 50–102. Downers Grove, IL: InterVarsity, 2009.

Volf, Miroslav. *After Our Likeness: The Church as the Image of the Trinity*. Grand Rapids: Eerdmans, 1997.

———. "'The Trinity is Our Social Program': The Doctrine of the Trinity and the Shape of Social Engagement." *Modern Theology* 14/3 (1998) 403–23.

Warfield, B. B. "Biblical Doctrine of the Trinity." In *Biblical and Theological Studies*, edited by Samuel G. Craig, 22–59. Philadelphia: Presbyterian and Reformed, 1952.

Webster, John. "Introduction: Systematic Theology." In *The Oxford Handbook of Systematic Theology*, edited by John Webster et al., 1–15. Oxford University Press, 2007.

———. "Principles of Systematic Theology." *International Journal of Systematic Theology* 11 (2009) 56–71.

3

Good News for All People

Trinity, Plurality, and Mission

JOHN R. FRANKE

ONE OF THE MOST basic elements of Christian witness is the notion that the gospel of Jesus Christ is good news for all people. This fundamental idea is at the core of the proclamation of the gospel, as exemplified in Luke 2:8–11: "And there were shepherds living out in the fields nearby, keeping watch over their flocks at night. An angel of the Lord appeared to them, and the glory of the Lord shone around them, and they were terrified. But the angel said to them, 'Do not be afraid. I bring you good news that will cause great joy for all the people. Today in the town of David a Savior has been born to you; he is the Messiah, the Lord.'"

It is one of the great tragedies of the Christian tradition that all too often the proclamation and living out of the Christian message has not been good news for many of the people of the world. It has frequently not been the cause of great joy but rather of pain and suffering. Throughout the history of the church, people have been subjugated, enslaved, and exterminated in the name of Christianity. The missionary expansion of the church has often been an exercise in the extension of empire through the process of colonization, using the Bible as a justification for this activity. While all of the texts that would eventually make up the Christian canon were produced at the margins of empire, the complicity that arose between Christianity and Rome in the advent of Christendom meant that the margins moved to the center and were interpreted accordingly. "Locked in the crushing embrace of the Vulgate, the first official Bible of imperial Christianity, the primary function of the biblical texts became that of legitimizing the imperial status quo, a function that, covertly when not overtly, continued into the modern period."[1]

In keeping with this observation, missiologists have shown that much of the mission activity emanating from Europe and North America over the past two hundred years has been an enterprise centered in the intuitions and assumptions of those settings. The Christian message and its implications have been passed on in the social and cultural shape of the Western church. "The subtle assumption of much Western mission was that the church's missionary mandate lay not only in forming the church of Jesus Christ, but in shaping the Christian communities that it birthed in the image of the church of western European culture."[2] This has resulted in the colonization and oppression of numerous communities in the name God, Jesus, and the Bible with massive consequences.

Commenting on the particular encounter between Christianity and the indigenous people of North America, Richard Twiss, a member of the Rosebud Lakota/Sioux Tribe, puts the matter succinctly, "Christian mission among the tribes of North America has not been very good news. What worldview influences allowed the Creator's story of creation and redemption to morph into a hegemonic colonial myth justifying the genocide and exploitation of America's First Nations people?"[3] Speaking of his own experience he explains the pressure imposed by white Christians to regard the music, dance, drumming, and ceremony of his Native culture as "unclean" and inappropriate for followers of Jesus. The implicit message was that the old and familiar rituals and experiences had passed away and all things had "become white." "This meant I needed to leave my Indian ways behind me, because I had a new identity in Christ, and it WAS NOT Indian! The Bible was used to demonize just about everything important to our cultural sense of being one with God and creation."[4]

1. Moore, "Paul after Empire," 22.
2. Guder, *Missional Church*, 4.
3. Twiss, "Living in Transition," 93.
4. Ibid., 94. Editor's note: For one excellent historical study on complex issues involved in these practices, and how one group of natives harnessed imposed practices in opportunistic educational structures, see Gilbert, *Education Beyond the Mesas*, which acknowledges different contributions of religious (Christian) groups (some good, some bad) and also the deeper issues which highlight different perspectives of those who experienced some of the hegemonic structures for what they provided by way of new opportunities, some of which seems to map onto the social interaction spoken about in the "personhood" section of this chapter.

These social and cultural forms and practices of colonization in the name of Christianity have had devastating consequences and has been all too typical of the interaction between Western mission and the indigenous cultures it has encountered. A particular set of social and cultural assumptions and presuppositions have stamped the Bible and theology in its image, in this case that of Western culture, and then this is imposed on another group of people in the name of God and truth. When this occurs, the voices of those who do not participate in the assumptions and presuppositions of the majority are marginalized or eclipsed, often under the guise of claims that they are not being faithful to Scripture or the Christian tradition.

This is one of the great dangers of the assumption that any particular theology is a universal language. Such an approach will inevitably lead to cultural imperialism and the suppression of voices that do not fit the accepted theological norms. It too easily leads to the conclusion that those who do not share in the assumptions of the majority are culturally, morally, and intellectually inferior. This in turn provides a justification for the political, economic, and racial oppression that are part of the process of colonization. "As the religion of western man, western theology has either preceded him, joined him, or followed him in all missions of world colonization or conquest. It has singularly been unable to wean western man from his white tribalism or nationalism. There is a real sense in which Christianity (not Christ) is a white man's religion."[5] While times have changed and there is greater awareness of these issues, challenges still remain. As Richard Twiss concludes, "Sadly, the hegemony of the prevailing worldview assumptions of the European immigrants that typified the efforts of the Jamestown missionaries not only lingers today, but has morphed into a distinct evangelical bias against Native culture and ways."[6] This bias against Native culture and ways can be extended to other people groups who do not share the Eurocentric assumptions of the hegemonic forms of theology.

Suffice it to say, Christian mission cannot continue in this fashion and be a faithful witness to the gospel of Jesus Christ. Repentance and change are necessary. This essay will explore a Trinitarian rationale for the plurality and diversity that should be characteristic of Christian mission.

---

5. Bentley and Bentley, "Scope and Function," 314.
6. Twiss, "Living in Transition," 94.

Trinity

The twentieth century witnessed the emergence of a broad consensus among Christian theologians concerning the fruitfulness of relationality as a central model for understanding the doctrine of the Trinity. This so-called relational turn is viewed as an alternative to the ontology of substance that dominated theological reflection on the Trinity throughout much of church history. Relationality was deemed to belong to the dimension of attributes, not substance. Consequently, substantialist theologians suggested that God is absolute and immutable in God's essential nature, whereas God maintains relationality to creation through the divine attributes. As Ted Peters notes regarding the classical position, "What could not be countenanced is the notion that the divine essence is contingent upon the relational dimensions of its being."[7] The result, however, has been the obscuring of God's internal relationality and of God's loving relationship to creation in much of the classical literature on the nature of God.

Catherine LaCugna asserts that *person* rather than *substance* is the primary ontological category, noting that the ultimate source of reality is not a "by-itself" or an "in-itself" but a person, a "toward-another." She concludes that the triune God is "self-communicating" and exists from all eternity "in relation to another."[8] Likewise, Robert Jenson writes, "The original point of trinitarian dogma and analysis was that God's relations to us are internal to him, and it is in carrying out this insight that the 'relation' concept was introduced to define the distinction of identities."[9] In a similar manner, Elizabeth Johnson claims that the priority of relation in the triune God challenges and critiques the concentration of classical theism on "singleness" in God. Because the persons are "constituted by their relationships to each other, each is unintelligible except as connected with the others."[10] The assertion that each of the persons in the triune life is constituted only in relationship to the others leads Johnson to the conclusion that the "very principal of their being" is to be found in the category of relation.[11]

David Cunningham notes that the breadth of the current consensus about the priority of relationality in Trinitarian discourse is evidenced by the fact that both Jenson and Johnson may be cited in support of it, even though the two thinkers "are not usually noted for being in close

---

7. Peters, *GOD as Trinity*, 31.
8. LaCugna, *God for Us*, 14–15.
9. Jenson, *Triune Identity*, 120.
10. Johnson, *She Who Is*, 216.
11. Ibid.

agreement with one another."[12] This theological consensus has been seen in the writings of a variety of thinkers such as Jürgen Moltmann,[13] Wolfhart Pannenberg,[14] John Zizioulas,[15] Colin Gunton,[16] Alan Torrance,[17] Leonardo Boff,[18] Millard Erickson,[19] and Stanley Grenz.[20] While these theologians may differ from each other on the precise construction of relationality within the life of God, they have all followed the relational turn.[21]

In addition to the consensus among contemporary theologians, Veli-Matti Kärkkäinen states that the "move to relationality is also in keeping with the dynamic understanding of reality and the human being as well as human community in late modernity." He notes that the ideas and conceptions of isolation, individualism, and independence are the products of modernist thought forms. "Over against the typical modernist bias to classify and categorize everything into distinct units [only think of the methods of the natural sciences], postmodernity speaks of relationality, interdependence, becoming, emerging, and so on. In this changing intellectual atmosphere, the value of communion theology is being appreciated in a new way."[22] Stanley Grenz speaks of this relational turn as envisioning a move "from the one subject to the three persons" with respect to our understanding of God.[23] In other words, God is social not solitary.

The Bible pictures God as having a history in which creation is not the beginning point, but a particular event in the continuing story of the divine life that stretches from the eternal past into the eternal future. Hence, while the acts of God in history provide the basis for speaking of the doctrine of the Trinity, they are also indicative of God's ongoing internal life and Scripture invites us to think through the implications of this history with respect to the character of God. God's love for the created order is that of one who is

12. Cunningham, *These Three Are One*, 26.
13. Moltmann, *Trinity and the Kingdom*.
14. Pannenberg, *Systematic Theology*, vol. 1.
15. Zizioulas, *Being as Communion*.
16. Gunton, *The One, the Three and the Many*.
17. Torrance, *Persons in Communion*.
18. Boff, *Trinity and Society*.
19. Erickson, *God in Three Persons*.
20. Grenz, *Social God*.
21. While the consensus mentioned here has been significant, it is by no means uncontested. For a critical review of this literature see Holmes, *Quest for the Trinity*, and the essays in Sexton, *Two Views of the Doctrine of the Trinity*.
22. Kärkkäinen, *The Trinity*, 387.
23. Grenz, *Social God*, 23–57.

actively and passionately involved in the ongoing drama of life in the world. This expression of love for humanity and creation revealed in Jesus Christ points us to the internal life of God as an eternal Trinitarian fellowship of love shared between Father, Son, and Holy Spirit.

In other words, explication of the triune God in God's self-disclosure in and to creation is at the same time the explication of the triune God in the divine reality. When we affirm with Scripture that "God is love" (1 John 4:8) this points to the eternal life of God lived in a set of ongoing and active relationships of love which constitute God's being in and for Godself. These are the active relationships of God's eternal Trinitarian fellowship in which Father, Son, and Holy Spirit participate in the giving, receiving, and sharing of love that includes both difference and unity. This eternal fellowship of divine love is characterized by both unity-in-plurality and plurality-in-unity in which we affirm that the one God exists in three distinct persons, Father, Son, and Holy Spirit, and that the three together, Father, Son, and Holy Spirit, are the one God.

In understanding God as social plurality rather than a solitary being, the question is therefore raised, what does it mean to affirm that God is one? In John's Gospel, Jesus says, "I and the Father are one" (10:30) and explains that his works were done so that those who saw them might "know and understand that the Father is in me, and I in the Father" (10:38). In seeking to explain this, thinkers in the early church turned to an idea known as *perichoresis*. This refers to the mutual interdependence, even mutual interpenetration of Father, Son, and Holy Spirit in their Trinitarian relation with one another. It seeks to explain the nature of the divine life with the assertion that while the three members of the Trinity remain wholly distinct from each other, they are also bound together, wholly interior to each other, in such a way that the Father, Son, and Spirit are dependent on each other for their very identities as Father, Son, and Spirit. This understanding of *perichoresis* leads us to conclude that the persons of the Trinity—Father, Son, and Holy Spirit—are one by virtue of their interdependent relationality. The contemporary consensus concerning the relationality of the life of God brings us back to the affirmation that God is love. In addition to enjoying the support of the biblical witness and the tradition of the church, love is an especially fruitful term for comprehending the life of God since it is an inherently relational concept. Love requires both subject and object. Because God is a triune plurality-in-unity and unity-in-plurality, God comprehends both love's subject and love's object.

The plurality-in-unity and unity-in plurality that characterizes the life of the triune God means that difference is part of the life of God as Father, Son, and Holy Spirit live in the fellowship of love. The Father is not the Son or the Spirit; the Son is not the Father or the Spirit; and the Spirit is not the Father or the Son. This means that in the life of God is the experience of that which is different, other, not the same. It is important to note that the love of God is not an assimilating love. It does not seek to make that which is different the same but rather lives in harmonious fellowship with the other. The Father, Son, and Spirit are one by virtue of their interdependent relationality but this unity does not make them the same. They are one in the very midst of their difference.

Plurality

The plurality-in-unity and unity-in-plurality of God's life is reflected in the revelation of God as Trinity, the social and cultural reception of revelation, and in the Spirit-inspired witness to revelation contained in Scripture. We will first examine the cultural context in which revelation is received before turning our attention to Scripture. The linguistic turn and the corresponding transition from a realist to a constructionist view of the world are reflective of the finitude of the human experience. This way of thinking suggests that we do not view the world from an objective or neutral vantage point, but instead structure our world through the concepts we bring to it, particularly language. Human languages function as social conventions and symbol systems that attempt to engage and describe the world in a variety of ways that are shaped by the social and historical contexts and perceptions of various communities of discourse. No simple, one-to-one relationship exists between language and the world, and thus no single linguistic description can serve to provide an objective conception of the "real" world. Language structures our perceptions of reality and as such constitutes the world in which we live.

In his frequently cited definition of culture as "a system of inherited conceptions expressed in symbolic forms,"[24] Clifford Geertz reminds us of the central importance of symbols to culture. We construct our world and communicate our understanding of it through a variety of symbols that together form elaborate systems. The primary purpose of these socially devised symbol systems is to convey meanings and facilitate the task of world construction. Hence, the value of symbols lies in their connection to meaning, which in turn resides in the mind rather than in the symbols themselves. Despite the tendency to confuse symbols with their meanings, there is no necessary connection between a symbol and what it symbolizes;

---

24. Geertz, *Interpretation of Cultures*, 89.

the assigning of meanings to symbols is arbitrary. At the same time, symbols are generally public, rather than private. It is this public aspect of symbols that leads to their importance as purveyors of cultural meaning. And the public dimension of symbols, in turn, fosters participation in social groups.

Inherent in the function of symbols is their representative character. Through this representation, a symbol comes to be associated with the meaning of what it stands for. Further, a symbol becomes a means to opening up a level of meaning for which non-symbolic communication is inadequate. While numerous types of symbols are involved in the process of world construction, the most paradigmatic symbolic systems are linguistic. Indeed, language ranks as the central cultural form involved in the world-constructing and meaning-creating task.[25] Language provides the conceptual tools through which we construct the world we inhabit. As Paul Hiebert asserts, "We cannot perceive nature or think or communicate about it without language, but language, to a great extent, also molds what we see and how we see it."[26] In addition, linguistic concepts serve as the vehicles through which we communicate and thereby share meaning with others.

The work of Ludwig Wittgenstein is of central importance in the development of the linguistic turn. Wittgenstein came to realize that rather than having only a single purpose, to make assertions or state facts, language has many functions. This conclusion led to Wittgenstein's important concept of "language games." According to Wittgenstein, each use of language occurs within a separate and seemingly self-contained system, complete with its own rules. Similar to playing a game, we require an awareness of the operative rules and significance of the terms within the context of the purpose for which we are using language. Each use of language, therefore, comprises a separate "language game." And each "game" may have little to do with the other "language games."[27] For Wittgenstein meaning is not related, at least not directly or primarily, to an external world of "facts" waiting to be apprehended. Instead, it is an internal function of language. Because the meaning of any statement is dependent on the context or the "language game" in which it appears, any sentence has as many meanings as contexts in which it is used.

Another key figure in the linguistic turn is the Swiss linguist, Ferdinand de Saussure. In contrast to his predecessors, who viewed language as a natural phenomenon that develops according to fixed and discoverable laws, Saussure proposed that a language is a social phenomenon and that

---

25. Quinn and Holland, "Culture and Cognition," 9.
26. Hiebert, *Cultural Anthropology*, 119.
27. Wittgenstein, *Philosophical Investigations*.

a linguistic system is a product of social convention.[28] Following this line of thought proponents of what has come to be known as "the sociology of knowledge," generated an awareness of the connection between language and culture and both personal-identity formation and social cohesion.[29] Viewing language in this fashion presumes that it does not have its genesis in the individual mind grasping a truth or fact about the world and then expressing it in statements. Rather, language is a social phenomenon, and any statement acquires its meaning within the process of social interaction.

From this perspective, language and culture generate a shared context in which a people engage in the construction of meaning and in the task of making sense out of the world. In the words of Raymond Williams, culture functions as a "signifying system through which necessarily (though among other means) a social order is communicated, reproduced, experienced and explored."[30] In this process, language plays a crucial role. The language that we inherit from our social community, together with non-linguistic modalities such as metaphorical images and symbols, provide the conceptual tools through which we construct the world we inhabit, as well as the vehicles through which we communicate and thereby share meaning with others. In the words of Peter Berger and Thomas Luckmann, "Language objectivates the shared experiences and makes them available to all within the linguistic community, thus becoming both the basis and the instrument of the collective stock of knowledge."[31]

In this social process of world construction and identity formation, language provides the structure of our particular and collective experience, perspective, and understanding. Our conceptions of what it means to be human, the formation and development of our moral, ethical, religious, and ideological convictions, and our understanding of our place and responsibilities in the world are shaped by our language and the discourse and practices of the particular communities in which we participate. We learn to use language and make sense of it in the context of our participation in a community of users that are bound together through common social conventions and rules of practice. Hence, the world we experience is mediated in and through our use of language meaning that to some extent the limits of our language constitute the limits of our understanding of the world. Further, since language is a socially construed product of human construction, forged in the context of ongoing interactions, conversations,

---

28. Holdcroft, *Saussure*, 7–10.
29. Berger and Luckmann, *Social Construction of Reality*, 99–104.
30. Williams, *Sociology of Culture*, 13.
31. Berger and Luckmann, *Social Construction of Reality*, 68.

and engagements, our words and linguistic conventions do not have timeless and fixed meanings that are independent from their particular usages in human communities and traditions. In this sense, language does not represent reality so much as it constitutes reality.

The linguistic turn has gone hand-in-hand with a renewed conception of culture that takes more seriously the historical contingencies of human life and society. Accordingly, contemporary anthropologists have discarded the assumption that culture is a preexisting social-ordering force that is transmitted externally to members of a cultural group, who in turn passively internalize it. They maintain that this view is mistaken in that it isolates culture from the ongoing social processes that produce and continually alter it.[32] Culture is not an entity standing above or beyond human products and learned mental structures. In short, culture is not a "thing."[33] Rather than viewing cultures as monolithic entities, anthropologists tend to view cultures as being internally fissured.[34] The elevation of difference that typifies postmodern thinking has triggered a heightened awareness of the role of persons in culture formation.

Rather than exercising determinative power over people, culture is conceived as the outcome and product of social interaction. Consequently, rather than being viewed as passive receivers, human beings are seen as the active creators of culture.[35] Clifford Geertz provided the impetus for this direction through his description of cultures as comprising "webs of significance" that people spin and in which they are then suspended.[36] Culture resides in a set of meaningful forms and symbols that, from the point of view of any particular individual, appear as largely given.[37] Yet these forms are only meaningful because human minds have the ability to interpret them.[38] This has led contemporary anthropologists to look at the interplay of cultural artifacts and human interpretation in the formation of meaning. They suggest that, contrary to the belief that meaning lies in signs or in the relations between them, meanings are bestowed by the users of signs.[39] However, this does not mean that individuals simply discover or make up cultural meanings on their own. Even the mental structures by which they

32. Tanner, *Theories of Culture*, 50.
33. D'Andrade, *Development of Cognitive Anthropology*, 250.
34. Tanner, *Theories of Culture*, 56.
35. Cohen, *Self Consciousness*, 118–19.
36. Geertz, *Interpretation of Cultures*, 5.
37. Ibid., 45.
38. Hannerz, *Cultural Complexity*, 3–4.
39. Strauss and Quinn, *Cognitive Theory of Cultural Meaning*, 253.

interpret the world are developed through explicit teaching and implicit observation of others. Consequently, cultural meanings are both psychological states and social constructions.[40]

The thrust of contemporary cultural anthropology leads to the conclusion that its primary concern lies in understanding the creation of cultural meaning as connected to world construction and identity formation. This approach leads to an understanding of culture as socially constructed. The thesis of social constructionists such as Peter Berger is that, rather than inhabiting a prefabricated, given world, we live in a social-cultural world of our own creation.[41] At the heart of the process whereby we construct our world is the imposition of some semblance of a meaningful order upon our variegated experiences. For the interpretive framework we employ in this task, we are dependent on the society in which we participate.[42] In this manner, society mediates to us the cultural tools necessary for constructing our world. Although this constructed world gives the semblance of being a given, universal, and objective reality, it is actually, in the words of David Morgan, "an unstable edifice that generations constantly labor to build, raze, rebuild, and redesign."[43]

We inhabit socially constructed worlds to which our personal identities are intricately bound. The construction of these worlds, as well as the formation of personal identity, is an ongoing, dynamic, and fluid process, in which the forming and reforming of shared cultural meanings play a crucial role. Culture includes the symbols that provide the shared meanings by which we understand ourselves, pinpoint our deepest aspirations and longings, and construct the worlds we inhabit. And through the symbols of our culture we express and communicate these central aspects of life to each other, while struggling together to determine the meaning of the very symbols we employ in this process.

To be human is to be embedded in culture and to participate in the process of interpretation and the creation of meaning as we reflect on and internalize the cultural symbols that we share with others in numerous conversations that shape our ever-shifting contexts. It is in the midst of the plurality of these ever-changing contexts that the revelation of God is received and given expression in the witness of Scripture. It is to the plurality of Scripture and its implications that we now turn our attention.

40. Ibid., 16.
41. Berger, *Sacred Canopy*, 3–13.
42. Ibid., 20. See also Berger and Luckmann, "Sociology of Religion and Sociology of Knowledge," 417–27.
43. Morgan, *Visual Piety*, 9.

The Bible is a diverse collection of writings that is not so much a single book as it is a collection of authorized texts, written from different settings and perspectives. Each of the voices represented in the canonical collection maintains a distinct point of view that emerges from a particular time and place. In other words, the Bible is polyphonic, made up of many voices. The self-revelatory speech act of God is received among diverse communities over long periods of time and in a plurality of cultural settings. Scripture paradigmatically reflects this plurality and diversity. In this way Scripture is the constitutive and normative witness for the formation and proclamation of Christian community. At the same time, it is also the first in an ever expanding series of presentations of the Christian faith throughout history. In this multifaceted and diverse collection of writings, each offers a distinct perspective that contributes to the whole.

The fourfold witness of the gospel of Matthew, Mark, Luke, and John indicates the irreducibility of the gospel of Jesus Christ to a single account. A true harmony of the Gospels is neither attainable nor desirable. When we attempt to ease the difficulties of the multiple perspectives in Scripture to make matters more compact, clear, and manageable we suffer the loss of plurality and diversity that is woven into the very fabric of Scripture, and by extension, the divine design of God. This means that true "catholic" or "universal" faith is pluralistic. "It is 'according to the whole,' not in the sense that it encompasses the whole in a single, systematic, entirely coherent unit, but rather in the sense that it allows for the openness, for the testimony of plural perspectives and experiences, which is implied in the fourfold canonical witness to the gospel."[44] Attempts to suppress the plurality of the canonical witness by means of an overarching, universalistic account lead to serious distortions of the gospel and the community that is called to bear witness to it.

The plurality of forms and perspectives imbedded in the biblical witness suggests that no single voice or interpretive approach will be able to do justice to this diversity. Scripture itself authorizes multiple perspectives within a set of possibilities that are also appropriately circumscribed by the shape and content of the canon. However, the plurality of Scripture should not be used as a denial of unity in the canon. But this unity is a differentiated unity expressed in plurality. Indeed, the plurality of the church is a faithful expression of the plurality of Scripture, which is in turn a faithful witness to the plurality-in-unity lived out in the eternal life of God and expressed in the act of revelation. Plurality is the intention and will of God as a faithful expression of truth. In the words of Lamin Sanneh: "For most of us it

---

44. González, *Out of Every Tribe and Nation*, 22.

is difficult enough to respect those with whom we might disagree, to say nothing of those who might be different from us in culture, language, and tradition. For all of us pluralism can be a rock of stumbling, but for God it is the cornerstone of the universal design."[45]

As the Word of God and *normative* witness to revelation, Scripture consists of inspired human speech-acts that bear authentic witness to the divine speech-act of the event of revelation. As such, Scripture is truth written and its pages bear manifold witness to the plurality of truth. As the Word of God and *paradigmatic* human and creaturely witness to the event of revelation, Scripture also invites greater plurality than that contained in its pages, in order that, under the guidance of the Holy Spirit, the witness of the church to the truth in the world may be continually expanded to all the nations in keeping with the mission of God.

The plurality lived out in the life of God, expressed in the pages of Scripture, and manifest throughout the Christian tradition leads to the conclusion that the proper expression of biblical and orthodox Christian faith is inherently and irreducibly pluralist. The diversity of the Christian faith is not, as some approaches to church and theology might seem to suggest, a problem that needs to be overcome. Instead, this diversity is part of the divine design and intention for the church as the image of God and the body of Christ in the world. Christian plurality is a good thing, not something that needs to be struggled against and overturned. Christian witness is, and should be characterized by, an irreducible plurality. In light of this, Justo González has concluded that "the opposite of a pluralistic church and a pluralistic theology is not simply an exclusivistic church and a rigid theology, but a heretical church and a heretical theology!"[46]

Mission

The relational plurality-in-unity of the divine life and the witness to plurality contained in Scripture are significant for the practice of Christian mission. The Christian tradition speaks of the mission of God and the idea that God not only has a mission, but also that God's very character as the one who loves from all eternity is missional. God is a missionary by God's very nature and love characterizes the mission of God from all eternity. Creation itself may be viewed as a missional act, a reflection of the expansive love of God, whereby the triune God brings into being another reality, that

---

45. Sanneh, *Translating the Message*, 27.
46. González, *Out of Every Tribe and Nation*, 25–26.

which is not God, and establishes a covenantal relationship of love, grace, and blessing for the purpose of drawing that reality into participation in the divine fellowship of love. Creation forms the context of God's covenant with humanity in that God's act of creation always has in view the institution, preservation, and execution of the covenant of grace in which God has called human beings into participation and partnership. The covenant of grace is the internal basis of the act of creation, in that God's covenant with humanity constitutes the fulfillment of the very intentions of God in the work of creation.

The missional character of God's eternal life is reflected in the relation of God to the world and the biblical witness of God's concern for engagement with the world. Indeed, mission is at the heart of the biblical narratives concerning the work of God in human history. It begins with the call to Israel to be God's covenant people and the recipient of God's covenant blessings for the purpose of blessing the nations. Hence, the mission of God is at the heart of the covenant with Israel and is continuously unfolded over the course of the centuries in the life of God's people recorded in the narratives of canonical Scripture. This missional covenant reaches its revelatory climax in the life, death, and resurrection of Jesus Christ, and continues through the sending of the Spirit as the one who calls, guides, and empowers the community of Christ's followers, the church, as the socially, historically, and culturally embodied witness to the gospel of Jesus Christ and the tangible expression of the mission of God.

This mission is carried out in the global ministry and witness to the gospel of churches in every culture around the world and, guided by the Spirit, moves toward the promised consummation of reconciliation and redemption in the eschaton. This missional pattern is communicated in the words of Jesus recorded in the Gospel of John, "As the Father has sent me, so I send you" (John 20:21). Hence, David Bosch asserts that mission is derived from the very nature of God, and must be articulated in the context of the doctrine of the Trinity rather than ecclesiology or soteriology. From this perspective the logic of the classical doctrine of the *missio Dei* expressed as God the Father sending the Son, and the Father and the Son sending the Spirit may be expanded to include yet another movement: "Father, Son, and Spirit sending the church into the world."[47] In this context, the church is seen as the instrument of God's mission and its various historical, global, and contemporary embodiments may be viewed as a series of local and contextual iterations of God's mission to all of creation.

---

47. Bosch, *Transforming Mission*, 390.

These local communities are incarnational in that they reflect the interaction between the gospel and the social, historical, and cultural circumstances in which they participate. In addition, because cultures are themselves diverse and fragmentary, these interactions are not uniform among various communities, even those participating in similar cultural settings. In reflecting on this, missiologist Andrew Walls suggests that the history of Christianity has always been a struggle between two opposing tendencies that find their basis in the very substance of the gospel itself. He refers to these as the "indigenizing" principle and the "pilgrim" principle.

The indigenization principle is rooted in the core gospel affirmation that God comes to us where we are and accepts us as such through the work of Christ and not on the basis of what we have been, are, or are trying to become. This acceptance of us as we are points to the notion that God does not relate to us as isolated, self-sufficient individuals, but rather as people who are conditioned by the particular times and places in which we live. As people who in the midst of particular times and places are also shaped and formed by the particular families, societies, groups, and cultures in which we participate. In Christ we are accepted by God in the midst of all the relations, experiences, and cultural conditioning that make us who we are. The impossibility of separating ourselves from our social relationships and the societies in which we belong has led, in principle if not always in practice, to the unwavering commitment to indigenization that has characterized Christian mission at its best. That is, to live life as both a Christian and as a member of a particular society, culture, and people group.

The account of the Jerusalem Council in Acts 15 provides an affirmation of this principle of indigenization, with the decision that the Gentiles should be permitted to enter into the faith without being bound to the rituals and practices of the Jewish Christians. The most significant of these decisions was the determination that male Gentile converts would not need to undergo circumcision. The affirmation that God accepts people as they are means that those who have not participated in such customs as circumcision, dietary restrictions, and ritual cleansings need not do so in order to be part of the community of Christ's disciples.

In light of this, Walls asserts that no particular group of Christians "has therefore any right to impose in the name of Christ upon another group of Christians a set of assumptions about life determined by another time and place."[48] The notion of being a new creation in Christ is not intended to suggest that a convert to the way of Jesus starts a new life in a vacuum with a mind that becomes a blank slate. We are all formed by our social, cultural, and historical circumstances. The affirmation that God has accepted us as

48. Walls, *Missionary Movement*, 8.

we are means that our lives and minds will continue to be influenced by ways in which they have been developed along with the assumptions and presuppositions that we have learned. These are not somehow eliminated from our consciousness and they continue to shape the ways in which we view the world. It is also worth noting that this reality is "as true for groups as for persons. All churches are culture churches—including our own."[49]

In tension with the indigenization principle is the pilgrim principle, which is also intimately connected with the gospel. While it is true that God meets people where they are and as they are, it is also true that the intention of the gospel is transformative. God in Christ calls us to be transformed by the power of the gospel and to participate in the mission of God in the world. This call to transformation means that even in light of the indigenizing principle, which affirms culture and experience, the followers of Christ also find that they are not completely in sync with their cultural and historical surroundings. The transformation principle reminds Christians that we will never be completely at home in this world and that we must always be seeking the renewal of our minds and lives and resisting conformity to many of the social and cultural patterns of our societies. In other words, faithfulness to Christ will often put us out of step with our culture.

While the indigenizing principle affirms that Christians remain appropriately related to the relationships and thought forms in which they are raised and seeks their renewal in Christ, the pilgrim principle points to an entirely new set of relations with others who are part of the community of Christ's disciples. These relations call on us to be accepting of others and all of their group relations just as God has accepted them while at the same time seeking the transformation of all things in Christ in accordance with the will and mission of God. All Christians have dual nationalities and loyalties to multiple Christian faith communities in Christ. These loyalties and commitments serve to link us beyond our own affinity groups to individuals and their communities who are naturally opposed, by cultural and historical assumption and presupposition, to the very things to which we are committed. In addition to these relationships, Christians are given an adoptive past that links us to the people of God throughout all of history. In this way "all Christians of whatever nationality, are landed by adoption with several millennia of someone else's history, with a whole set of ideas, concepts, and assumptions which do not necessarily square with the rest of their cultural inheritance; and the Church in every land, of whatever race and type of

---

49. Ibid.

society, has this same adoptive past by which it needs to interpret the fundamentals of the faith."[50]

Plurality, not uniformity, characterizes the story of Christianity, which did not move in one direction from Palestine to Europe to the rest of the world, but rather was a multi-faceted and multi-directional movement: Palestine to Asia, Palestine to Africa; Palestine to Europe. It is a story that must be understood not simply as "the expansion of an institution but as the emergence of a movement, not as simply the propagation of ready-made doctrine but as the constant discovery of the gospel's 'infinite translatability' and missionary intention."[51]

This translatability continually results in fresh adaptations of the faith as the gospel spreads across the world and engages culture after culture, ethnicity after ethnicity, situation after situation. The church continually reinvents itself to meet the challenges of relating the gospel to new peoples and new cultures. In this activity, the experience of what it means to be church arises from the ongoing engagement of the gospel with culture. "There seems to be an inevitable connection, therefore, between the need for Christian mission, on the one hand, and the need for that mission always to be radically contextual. The urgency of mission is linked to the urgency of change, adaptation and translation—in other words, to context."[52]

What is important to note here is that these cultural translations and adaptations must be indigenous. They cannot be imposed from outside of the situatedness by particular languages and cultures in the name of truth and a universal theology. If they are the result will be the very sort of marginalization and oppression described at the outset of this essay. In such circumstances the gospel will not be received as good news but rather as an instrument of colonization. For the sake of our witness to the gospel of Jesus Christ and love of God we must surrender the pretensions of a universal and timeless theology. Where we are unwilling to do this, we propagate forms of cultural, ethnic, and racial imperialism under the guise of theology and the Word of God. The failure to surrender these pretensions will hinder the witness of the gospel in North America because Christian faith will continue to be defined in ways that are governed by the assumptions and outlooks characteristic of the white experience and its cultural dominance. In the face of our history and its complicity with oppression and colonization, we must reimagine Christian mission in postcolonial perspective.[53]

---

50. Ibid., 9.
51. Bevans and Schroeder, *Constants in Context*, 3.
52. Ibid., 31.
53. Grau, *Rethinking Mission*.

That this is a matter of utmost importance for Christian witness stems from the fact that plurality and mutuality are at the very heart of the gospel. They are the intention and blessing of God who invites all people to participate in the liberating and reconciling mission of Jesus Christ. The Christian community is sent into the world by the Triune God with the calling to live out this mission in order that the love of God might be made visible in the world. In order to be faithful witnesses to the way, the truth, and the life revealed in Jesus the presence of the Christian community must be good news for all people, for the sake of the gospel and the sake of the world.

Bibliography

Bentley, William H., and Ruth Lewis Bentley. "Reflections on the Scope and Function of a Black Evangelical Theology." In *Evangelical Affirmations*, edited by Kenneth S. Kantzer and Carl F. H. Henry, 299–325. Grand Rapids: Zondervan, 1990.

Berger, Peter L., and Thomas Luckmann. *The Social Construction of Reality: A Treatise in the Sociology of Knowledge*. New York: Anchor, 1967.

———. "Sociology of Religion and Sociology of Knowledge." *Sociology and Social Research* 47 (1963) 417–27

Berger, Peter L. *The Sacred Canopy: Elements of a Sociological Theory of Religion*. Garden City, NY: Doubleday, 1969.

Bevans, Stephen B., and Roger P. Schroeder. *Constants in Context: A Theology of Mission for Today*. Maryknoll, NY: Orbis, 2004.

Boff, Leonardo. *Trinity and Society*. Translated by Paul Burns. Maryknoll, NY: Orbis, 1988.

Bosch, David J. *Transforming Mission: Paradigm Shifts in Theology of Mission*. Maryknoll, NY: Orbis, 1991.

Cohen, Anthony P. *Self Consciousness: An Alternative Anthropology of Identity*. London: Routledge, 1994.

Cunningham, David S. *These Three Are One: The Practice of Trinitarian Theology*. Malden, MA: Blackwell, 1998.

D'Andrade, Roy G. *The Development of Cognitive Anthropology*. Cambridge: Cambridge University Press, 1995.

Erickson, Millard J. *God in Three Persons: A Contemporary Interpretation of the Trinity*. Grand Rapids: Baker, 1995.

Geertz, Clifford. *The Interpretation of Cultures*. New York: Basic, 1973.

Gilbert, Matthew Sakiestewa. *Education Beyond the Mesas: Hopi Students at Sherman Institute, 1902–1929*. Lincoln, NE: University of Nebraska Press, 2010.

González, Justo L. *Out of Every Tribe and Nation: Christian Theology at the Ethnic Roundtable*. Nashville: Abingdon, 1992.

Grau, Marion. *Rethinking Mission in the Postcolony: Salvation, Society and Subversion*. London: T. & T. Clark, 2011.

Guder, Darrell L., ed. *Missional Church: A Vision for the Sending of the Church in North America*. Grand Rapids: Eerdmans, 1998.

Gunton, Colin E. *The One, the Three and the Many: God, Creation and the Culture of Modernity*. Cambridge: Cambridge University Press, 1993.

Hannerz, Ulf. *Cultural Complexity: Studies in the Social Organization of Meaning.* New York: Columbia University Press, 1992.

Hiebert, Paul. *Cultural Anthropology.* Grand Rapids: Baker, 1983.

Holdcroft, David *Saussure: Signs, System and Arbitrariness.* Cambridge: Cambridge University Press, 1991.

Holmes, Stephen R. *The Quest for the Trinity: The Doctrine of God in Scripture, Tradition and Modernity.* Downers Grove, IL: InterVarsity, 2012.

Jenson, Robert W. *The Triune Identity: God According to the Gospel.* Philadelphia: Fortress, 1982.

Johnson, Elizabeth A. *She Who Is: The Mystery of God in Feminist Theological Discourse.* New York: Crossroad, 1992.

Kärkkäinen, Veli-Matti. *The Trinity: Global Perspectives.* Louisville, KY: Westminster John Knox, 2007.

LaCugna, Catherine Mowry. *God for Us: The Trinity and Christian Life.* San Francisco: Harper/Collins, 1991.

Moltmann, Jürgen. *The Trinity and the Kingdom: The Doctrine of God.* Minneapolis: Fortress, 1993.

Moore, Stephen D. "Paul after Empire." In *The Colonized Apostle: Paul through Postcolonial Eyes*, edited by Christopher D. Stanley, 9–23. Minneapolis: Fortress, 2011.

Morgan, David. *Visual Piety: A History and Theory of Popular Images.* Berkeley: University of California Press, 1998.

Pannenberg, Wolfhart. *Systematic Theology.* 3 vols. Translated by Geoffrey W. Bromiley. Grand Rapids: Eerdmans, 1991–98.

Peters, Ted. *GOD as Trinity: Relationality and Temporality in Divine Life.* Louisville, KY: Westminster John Knox, 1993.

Quinn, Naomi, and Dorothy Holland., "Culture and Cognition." In *Cultural Models in Language and Thought*, edited by Dorothy Holland and Naomi Quinn, 3–40. Cambridge: Cambridge University Press, 1987.

Sanneh, Lamin. *Translating the Message: The Missionary Impact on Culture.* Maryknoll, NY: Orbis, 1989.

Sexton, Jason S., ed. *Two Views of the Doctrine of the Trinity.* Grand Rapids: Zondervan, 2014.

Strauss, Claudia, and Naomi Quinn. *A Cognitive Theory of Cultural Meaning.* Cambridge: Cambridge University Press, 1997.

Tanner, Kathryn. *Theories of Culture: A New Agenda for Theology.* Minneapolis: Fortress, 1997.

Torrance, Alan J. *Persons in Communion: An Essay on Trinitarian Description and Human Participation.* Edinburgh: T. & T. Clark, 1996.

Twiss, Richard. "Living in Transition, Embracing Community, and Envisioning God's Mission as Trinitarian Mutuality: Reflections from a Native-American Follower of Jesus." In *Remembering Jamestown: Hard Questions about Christian Mission*, edited by Amos Yong and Barbara Brown Zikmund, 93–108. Eugene, OR: Pickwick, 2010.

Walls, Andrew F. *The Missionary Movement in Christian History: Studies in the Transmission of Faith.* Maryknoll, NY: Orbis, 1996.

Williams, Raymond. *The Sociology of Culture.* New York: Schocken, 1982.

Wittgenstein, Ludwig. *Philosophical Investigations.* Translated by G. E. M. Anscombe. New York: Macmillan, 1953.

Zizioulas, John D. *Being as Communion: Studies in Personhood and the Church.* Crestwood, NY: St. Vladimir's Seminary Press, 1985.

4

Uncreated and Created Perichoretic Relations[1]

Kurt Anders Richardson

THERE IS A REASON for the title: "John the Theologian." While Paul's theology is as complex as John's, it dwells primarily with divine action in contrast to John's assertions on God's being, on all things that are not God, and on the divine/human "nature(s)" of the Mediator, Jesus Christ. John is concerned with divine action in the "signs" or miracles of Jesus, but he is intent upon illuminating ontological relations. Relationality is portrayed as to God's eternal being. Divine relationality is discerned through the living, personal appearance God acting at the beginning of all things in the first words of Scripture, speaking into being the creation of all things that are not God. God is the origin of all things in the particularity of time and space, and as such, he is own uncreated Being—thus, he does not belong in any sense to the being of created things, and is conditioned by them only because he has determined to be free for them as he gives them their being. There is nothing that has existence by divine donation that belongs to God's existence—since nothing other than God is eternal and self-existent. But this makes created and redeemed participation in the life, and therefore the existence, of God so determinative of all our knowing of God and creation. Creation itself is at once the revelation of God to all creatures: God's sole initiative for all that is not God and the call to all things to participate in God.

---

1. This essay does not defend any particular "analogy," including the social analogy. Instead, it tries to deal with the implications of perichoresis (which can be operative according to any of the favored analogies for the Trinity).

As the scriptural narrative proclaims this divine cosmology, God's creative and redemptive acts are communicated from his own loving being, the eternally communal and interpenetrating relationality that is now commonly referred to as *perichoresis*. From this God, the divine perichoretic being, generates a true beginning in eternity, fostering relations with all created reality that is not God but from God.

The history of doctrine is rife with disputes over the Trinity, Christology, soteriology, and ecclesiology—each and together is profoundly connected by divine/human relationality. One of the burdens of Christian theology is to show, not only the integral unity of doctrine, but also to explicate the overarching relational cosmology of revelation (i.e., the divine "economy" of salvation). Perhaps the most contested note is to be located at the root question of whether the triune multiplicity in God is a warranted assertion based upon the testimony of Scripture. The texts of the New Testament are unambiguously Abrahamic, Jewish, and monotheist in their homological declarations, while also asserting the full inclusion of the Lord Jesus Christ in the divine "identity."[2] If God's being is Trinitarian, this is disclosed through the incarnation of the Word: "the Son" who becomes truly human. Together with God "the Spirit" and with God "the Father" much of the source material is narrated in John 14–17,[3] along with references that extend throughout the Gospel. Jesus himself declares that he and the Father are relationally, inseparably one. Much of the patristic tradition has inferred that Father, Son, and Spirit are ever "containing" and "contained" in the other: one God of perichoretic, mutually indwelling love.[4] At the same time, the relationality eternally within God (the immanent Trinity) is extended temporally through the mediation of the Son with creation (the economic Trinity).[5] Among many texts, the often-selected *loci* of Jesus for the *perichoresis*, of eternal and temporal relationality, include:

> ". . . the Word was God. . . . All things came into being through him. . . . The Word became flesh . . . and we saw his glory, glory as of the only begotten from the Father. . . . [T]he only begotten God who is in the bosom of the Father . . ." (John 1:1–18; cf. Matt 11:26)

---

2. Bauckham. *Jesus and the God of Israel.*

3. John 17 appears to be the most cited Scripture chapter in patristic Trinitarian theology; cf. Anthansius, *St. Athanasius's Four Orations.*

4. Sorč, *Entwürfe einer perichoretischen Theologie*, 55.

5. The immanent and the economic Trinity are one and the same. God's being is not in any way subject to the conditionality of the creation, except by his own will in his freedom from and freedom for the creation.

"I am he, and that I do nothing on my own, but I speak these things as the Father instructed me..." (John 8:28)

"I am in the Father and the Father is in me..." (John 14:11)

"All that the Father has is mine. For this reason I said that he [the Spirit of truth] will take what is mine and declare it to you." (John 16:15)

"... that they [those the Father has given to Jesus] may all be one. As you, Father, are in me and I am in you, may they also be in us, so that the world may believe that you have sent me." (John 17:21)

"God is love." (1 John 4:8, 16)

"Abide in me, and I in you.... I am the vine, you are the branches. He who abides in me, and I in him, he it is that bears much fruit, for apart from me you can do nothing.... If you abide in me, and my words abide in you.... As the Father has loved me, so have I loved you; abide in my love. If you keep my commandments, you will abide in my love, just as I have kept my Father's commandments and abide in his love. These things I have spoken to you, that my joy may be in you, and that your joy may be full. This is my commandment, that you love one another as I have loved you.... I have called you friends, for all that I have heard from my Father I have made known to you. You did not choose me, but I chose you and appointed you that you should go and bear fruit and that your fruit should abide; ... This I command you, to love one another." (John 15:1–17)

The eternal/temporal relationality of the Creator with the creature is perhaps supremely expressed in the Johannine metaphor of the vine which uses the language of mutual indwelling of the human in the divine and vice versa. With the above and other primary texts the theological tradition fastens upon relationality texts conveying, e.g., that we "became participants of the divine nature" (γένησθε θείας κοινωνοὶ φύσεως; 2 Pet 1:4; cf. Rom 1:20); that by this created relationality, the eternal relationality of God is "God with us." This vision of the divine economy is, more or less, the theological outcome of the centuries of work, right up to current debate and discussion of God.

There are three dimensions of perichoresis in the history and contemporary theological formulations: Trinitarian, christological, and eschatological (or soteriological). Understanding, through Christ, something of God's eternal, perichoretic being is the basis for receiving God's revelation in the fullest sense of both intelligible communication and creative action. Indeed, creation is revelatory by its very nature as created by God (Rom 1:18ff.). Through God's communicative act he speaks creation into existence, and by doing so establishes the economy of Creator/creature relations. The central feature of Creator/creature relationality, however, is that the human is formed according to the *imago Dei* (Gen 1:27f.; Col 1:15), who is Christ. From within the eternally reciprocal interiority of Father, Son, and Holy Spirit, there is created a correspondence in all relationality as human beings are invited into its fullness by the representative and reconciling person of Jesus Christ. This is the christological dimension of Trinitarian perichoresis. Within the divine life, these relations were intentioned from eternity, a primal self-conditioning, self-giving, self-emptying, self-offering of God to God and of God ultimately to us. Ultimately, for the human being in Christ, sharing in his resurrection is to participate in the divine glory through inclusion in the divine life, from henceforth and forevermore. The multi-dimensionality of perichoresis emerges in the Trinitarian perichoresis of the eternal being of God, the christological or incarnate perichoresis of the hypostatic union of two natures, and soteriological perichoresis of our inclusion in the divine life: "Christ in you" (Col 1:27).

The incarnation is the fully human appearing of the eternal Word of God in Jesus Christ and confirming of him by the Spirit and power of God in his acts and words, and the continuous apostolic and prophetic testimony of Scripture and the gospel mission in the world. Jesus Christ discloses the knowledge of the Trinity in the Johannine text, which appropriately receives the metaphor of περιχώρησις "perichoresis" for that which is revealed about the inner life of God. One must acknowledge that the term is neither derived from LXX nor NT, nor from second- or third-century sources, but appeared first in the seventh century in the works of Maximus the Confessor. However, in the context of writing on the two natures of Christ, Gregory of Nazianzen did introduce the verbal form of the term (*perichoreo*) in his Epistle 101.[6] Did Nazianzen think of the triune God in terms of the mutual containment of the three persons in one another, along with the dynamic life of their mutual interpenetration? Certainly Orthodox dogmatics in the eighth century, led by John of Damascus, used the term normatively for explicating what is meant by the triune God.[7] Through the advancing

---

6. According to Nazianzen, the two natures have "perichorized" and so will remain into eternity; they co-inhere in the one person of Jesus Christ. Use of the term, co-inhere, however, does not apply Trinitarianly, since there is only one being or "substance" of God, rather than two or three natures inhering in a unity not original to them.

7. *De fide orthodoxa* 1,8; 3,5; 4,18, et al., cited by Sorč, *Entwürfe einer perichoretischen Theologie*, 52.

formulations of the doctrine of the incarnation, it is accurate to say that Trinitarian perichoresis was achieving its full dogmatic expression.

In God's eternally interpenetrating, mutually containing "persons" we are given to know the richness of being in eternal relations of the one God. The normativity of the term "perichoresis"[8] is such because it appropriately conveys the knowledge of God, not only as God's eternal sociality or having a capacity for relationship, but because God, who is love, is ontologically the basis for relationality itself. God is the Creator of all things whose relationality is determinate from their beginning by him and solely "for him" (Col 1:16). The God who declares of himself "I will be who I will be" (Exod 3:14) is from all eternity, in his freedom, free to be free according to his (free) nature. Perichoresis is interpenetration, with a choreographic aspect; a kind of dance motif that suggests a circulation among the three out of the one, to another, and to yet another and from another, but without beginning or end. In this a mutuality of this One—Father, Son, Spirit—ever circulating and entwining; interpenetrating, enveloping, absorbing, emerging in and from the Others. They are infinitely immanent to one another. Their mutually eternal from-ness and to-ness, one of the other and to the other, all convey this inter-relational sense. The one is only the One and yet with this life of eternal communicativity a unitary multiplicity amounts to nothing other than, the relational God who is Love. The aspect of divine love has its ontological reality in the very life of God—a relationality that is at once Lordship and love, with love as the destination of both uncreated and created being in created relation; an eternal futurity from *dominus* to *amicus*.[9]

No metaphor, however apt, transcends the limitations of the human word and its finitude. This is the case even when divine inspiration envelops the human words and makes them divine. In every cataphatic expression affirming something known about God, there is an arising of greater apophatic reduction of what is known.[10] In the incarnation, what is called hypostatic union entails immanent mutuality of the two natures in one person. The perichoresis of the divine and the human in the person of Jesus Christ is the basis and beginning of new cosmology in which the human participates in the eternal divine glory, and therefore also in the Trinitarian being of God, without ever ceasing to be fully human and entirely creaturely.[11] This does not mean that the incarnation, which is utterly unique,

---

8. Durand, "Perichoresis"; cf. Lee, *Celebrating God's Cosmic Perichoresis*.

9. Cf. Bruteau, *Grand Option*.

10. Boesel and Keller, *Apophatic Bodies*; cf. also Kearney, *The God Who May Be*.

11. Two important treatments: Greshake, "Trinity as 'communio'" and Oster, "Becoming a Person and the Trinity."

becomes the nature of even the church—though called "the Body of Christ," it is clearly only metaphorical so in the NT. While the incarnation happens nowhere else than in the person of Christ, the perichoretic reality of the double-*homoousion* of Chalcedon (one nature with God and one nature with humanity), that participation in the life and glory of Christ and the reception of the divine grace that accomplishes atonement, all find expression in the divine/human relationality of salvation. Although perichoresis is not unproblematic at moments of divine sovereignty and love, as well as on the assumption of sinful humanity,[12] classic normativity does not tend in these ways. We are not redeemed by God becoming us, one, several, or all, but because he has become fully human (enhypostatically, and therefore also anhypostatically) as the divine achievement that is the triumph of grace through Christ.

Perichoretic theology is not completely free from obscurity and contradiction in the tradition[13]—although Augustine seems to believe that in his experimental work the correct part was the relationality of the inner life of God grasping to a degree: Father, Son, Spirit, according to their relations. Augustine had little or no success exploring the human *imago* as a created analogy to the Trinity. As well, there are accounts of the being and holiness of God that bear only indirect and no immediate or direct relation with creatures. The Holy Spirit may dwell with us but not concretely "in" us. Even if the Trinitarian God is actually beyond all analogy—which is the case actually, neither individuals nor communities are incarnations of God. The fact that there is a creaturely/redemptive reality of God in the person of Jesus Christ, the "Word made flesh," is a fundamental divine determinant for created reality. "He is the pre-existent Deus *pro nobis* . . . ."[14] Fundamentally, scripturally conveyed, relationality does not fit with classical models of absolute being either, even though Abrahamic monotheism appropriated these models (whether from Plato, Aristotle, or the Stoics). By the classical model of the One perfect Being, one has in view its paradigm of perfection, aseity, and immutability. Because of the cultural prominence of the classical model, it seemed essential to reject the objectivity of divine relationality because of the internal logic of being. Christian theologians have always rejected certain key elements of the classical model, such as the eternity of the world (i.e., all that is not God must still be co-eternal, just inferior, since all relations require this so as to preserve God's immutability). From earliest

---

12. Crisp, *Divinity and Humanity*.

13. One of the best recent treatments: Polkinghorne, *Trinity and an Entangled World*.

14. Barth, *CD*, IV/1, 52.

times in the Christian tradition the necessary argument for the eternity of the world has been rejected, although with difficulty, and corrections based on the biblical texts. Some corrections have been warranted, others not so much, such as has been proposed in the form of "openness theory." Openness theory holds back from the quasi-pantheistic implications of process theology or abandoning of theism (i.e., a single divine principle of the cosmos). Openness theory is a kind of minority report and is has not been widely persuasive. Perichoretic theology, on the other hand, if followed carefully according to an appropriate understanding of analogy, demonstrates the most constructive integration of classical and scriptural perspectives.

Perichoretic theology, as derived from Johannine materials, has roots in the theology of Hellenistic Judaism's translation of Scripture, called the Septuagint (LXX). The classical tradition is powerfully present, but the content of Scripture commandeers the language and concepts to its own cosmology of Creator/creature relationality. One must ask regarding the demands of the monotheism's arguments for the perfections of the one God and the narratives of the One testified to in Scripture, who is relational livingness from all eternity.[15] One of the reasons why the Tanakh (OT) was translated into Greek was that Judaism had developed its own theological tradition with significant differences to the Platonic tradition; e.g., the case of Philo, who interprets the creation story according to the sole eternity and activity of God to bring it into being and to be its source of order. God's being was not a member of the cosmic order, and therefore the world was not co-eternal: the creation really did have an absolute beginning; was wholly distinct from him—created (not as God is, solely uncreated). This is a fundamental distinction in all knowledge of God and of all that is not God. God was also recognized to be truly living being, truly conscious, truly deliberative, truly volitional, and truly relational, since he is not only truly loving but is love (just as he is light) and is life. Scriptural narrative conveys, from beginning to end, the dynamic relationality of God. God, in all his creative particularity and intimacy with the human, is perichoretic.[16] The freedom of God[17] to be who he wills to be is the only determinative feature of perichoretic relations. While utterly sovereign over all things, God is sovereign over his own being. God is eternally living, and therefore time-full, not timeless—God's time is infinite as is his livingness. There are no boundaries to his time, but he is nevertheless living in complete self-consciousness, and therefore moving through the experience and knowingness of all his

---

15. McCall, *Which Trinity? Whose Monotheism?*
16. Moltmann, *Sun of Righteousness, Arise!*
17. Zizioulas, "Trinitarian Freedom."

relations (self-relations, in the eternity of his instances, and relations with all else, in the temporality of his creative acts and creaturely engagements). The unitary witness of Old and New Testaments provide a coherent model of these relations.

The created connections between God and all else are expressions of the *ad extra*, or "economic" Trinity, which is the God whose action outside himself is always creating, sustaining, and achieving on behalf of his creation as a whole and every creature. This is the God whose act is in his being and whose being is in his act; so expansively that there is unlimited room for the created space of divine/human relation. This is his purpose for all that is or will be. Theology must never reason from sin to God, only the other way around, based upon his judgment—not about how we may define offenses against him. Only he holds the mystery of his judgment. Theology must focus on the totalizing reality of grace. The benefits of grace in God's creative activity instantiate all that is not God. Created existence is nothing but grace. This is why, sin and evil have no abiding or real existence; they are always parasitical, always negative, nugatory; they cannot nullify in any absolute sense—only God can bring an end to being by truly withdrawing grace or passing over possible existents by unelecting them. The speculation that human sins have been eternalized, because the finite has offended the infinite, and whose offenses have thereby been infinitized, is nothing more than bad speculation. Arguing for eternal punishment this way is in all likelihood a significant error in view of biblical portrayals of the consequences of human action and being.[18]

The self-electing God-in-three-persons-yet-one-being is the basis of all relational beings, which are then inseparable from perichoretic being in the ever-livingness of God. This is the God whose mode of being is declared to be his own self-determination (in light of the *locus classicus*: אֶהְיֶה אֲשֶׁר אֶהְיֶה / ἐγώ εἰμι ὁ ὤν / "I will be whom I will be" Exod 3:14). As Barth so succinctly asserts: "God Himself in all His ways and works willed wholly and utterly to bear this name, and actually does bear it: the Father of our Lord Jesus Christ, the Son of the Father, the Holy Spirit of the Father and the Son."[19] God's entirely free, elective volition is the eternal basis of his triune identity, rather than the other way around. Divine self-election has become an immense topic, as well it should, and there will be books on this as well as intensive shorter studies.[20] All theologies are dependent

18. Moltmann, "God in the World," 369–79.
19. *CD*, II/2, 99.
20. Dempsey, *Trinity and Election*, in which the debate over how to interpret Barth on the freedom of God, developing over the last decade between Bruce McCormack and Paul Molnar, along with much accompanying commentary by those close to the

upon the adequacy of language to convey revelation and then to explicate its metaphors. This is necessary because of the ontological distance and difference between the Word of God and human speech for God. The freedom to actually become Creator is not dissimilar to God's eternal determination to be who he is as triune. To wonder fearfully if this would mean that God could be otherwise or that God could just as well be evil rather than good is to get caught in ridiculous questions of infinite potential at the expense of God's pre-determination to exist for the sake of the-other-than-himself. God's determination to free-for-us is not symmetrical with his determination to be free from all contingencies, particularly evil ones. This matter had remained rather open over the centuries and probably will remain so (somewhat similarly, the decree of atonement, and what it entails, has never been decided upon, although it is part and parcel of the matter of election in all its dimensions).

The question of God's eternally self-constituted triune nature, is not whether omnipotence or omniscience is the primal attribute in the divine being, but whether unconditional election is determinative not merely of all things but also of the divine being itself. Ever since the great biblical argument of Isaac Dorner redefined the understanding of the "immutability" of God to mean God's unfailing faithfulness, Christian theologians have rejected any notion of a law of being that would somehow transcend the self-determined being of God. Fortunately scriptural reasoning about the inner life of God has been gradually advancing the reconstruction of theology based upon the narratives of Scripture over and above the classic themes of metaphysics.[21] If God has willed to be who he is in the identity of Father, Son, and Holy Spirit, from all eternity, omnipotently, omnipresently, and omnisciently; the priority of uncontingent freedom rather than perfection becomes evident. The livingness of God is an irreducible norm of the scriptural ontology and determinate of his own being for created being through Jesus Christ. God has not willed to be otherwise from all eternity and so grounds Trinitarian, christological, and eschatological perichoresis in his own volitional self-determination. For Barth, it is the link between the christological and the Trinitarian that is crucial: "That Jesus Christ lives means quite simply that He exists in the manner of God, and therefore prior to all else that exists. . . . But it also means quite simply that He exists in the manner of a man . . . ."[22] He goes on even more definitively:

---

issue, make significant contributions.

21. Dorner, *Divine Immutability*.
22. *CD*, IV/3, 39.

> The Creator, God Himself, exists only as He does so together with this One who also exists as man, and each and everything in the created world exists only together with this One who also exists as man.... As God exists only together with this One, and so too the world, His existence as such is the fact in which God and the world, however they may oppose or contradict one another, are not of course one and the same, but do exist together in an inviolable and indissoluble co-existence and conjunction ... so that His life-action is identical with that of God Himself, His history with the divine history.[23]

There is nothing about God's created relationality with the world that he has not willed eternally to define him.

Perhaps the most crucial point at this juncture is the distinction within God of his freedom from unconditionality, and also the fact that he is entirely self-directed in "freedom for"—for himself and for creation. One might declare that God is absolute will in order to get at the age old question of substance. Theology would declare a "priority" in divine self-determination as constitutive of God's being. This would be the constant clarification of Trinitarian simultaneity and eternity of one being in three persons, each of which cannot take precedence in any respect. There is a consistency with revelation that is remarkable in its constructive correction of the tradition. God corresponds to himself and if perichoresis quite adequately correlates with the triune livingness of God, not only its propriety theologically, but its generative quality is also striking. Like the other view of God that struggles to clarify itself scripturally, namely "open theory," classic theological metaphysics struggles in the face of exegesis and the thoroughgoing possibilities of following through with its narrative logics. But Barth extends Dorner's sense of divine immutability as faithfulness:

> If we are to ... think of the Godhead of God in biblical, rather than pagan terms, we shall have to reckon, not with a mutability of God, but with the kind of immutability which does not prevent Him from humbling Himself and therefore doing what He willed to do and actually did in Jesus Christ.... Even in the constancy (or, as we may calmly say, immutability) of his divine essence He does this and can do it ... not only without violation but in supreme exercise and affirmation of His divine essence.[24]

---

23. Ibid., 39–40.
24. *CD*, IV/2, 85.

What God does in humbling himself is to bring creation into relation with him and to bring himself lovingly into relation with the creation.

This relation is established by the prior determination with the Word and image of God. *Imago dei* is God's relational manifestation, the understanding of which comes to us *a posteriori*—on account of the revelation that humanity is created according to this image (Gen 1:26f.). The image of God is relational because the being of God is perichoretically communicative—God knows himself in the eternal communion that is his being. Christ is the image of God; we are created and recreated/regenerated in this image. Jesus Christ is God's eternal determination to enter into creatureliness. This is christological perichoresis. In the form of our existence he became mortal and fallen, "taking the form of a servant," but remaining without sin. In the fulfillment of this uniquely divine mission, which once by incarnation is never abandoned but forever after joined to his being, we come to serve him and serve together with him in the resurrection. His nature was every bit ours; ours every bit his ("except without sin"), both in terms of the redemptive union of natures and the accomplishment of his mission without fail. But this did not mean that he had anything other than human embodiment common to everyone. Resurrection, of course, is the restoration and elevation of the creaturely image according to the uncreated image, who is Christ (Col 1:15), and who is elevated according to the far greater glory of that which is to come over that which originally became.

So one must give pause to what has become one of the fundamental questions of theology—whether God can be otherwise or wills not to be otherwise. If we say "cannot," we are making a judgment about God's constancy rooted in a law of himself that is above himself because of his nature. If we say that God "will not" be otherwise, we are asserting no substantive change of any kind ever, but that the principle of his livingness and his freedom are not bounded by anything above himself. There are reasonings that would assert something other in priority, but this is not really acceptable. God is who he is in his own infinite power according to whom he wills to be; this is the nature of his revelatory self-disclosure, rather than the inferential demands of our human notions of perfection. They simply do not match up.

The incarnation only reveals the Trinity. One basic rule in theology: revelation primarily answers questions of "why" rather than "how." The negative theology of Chalcedon does not offer any truly cataphatic knowledge of the "hypostatic union" of natures in Christ. But Jesus Christ is God become man in order to accomplish the divine purpose. The fully divine, fully human Christ therefore displays a double *homoousion*—he is one being with God and one being with man. Through this incomparable mediation of the Word, the humanity of Christ becomes and is identical to human being itself. On account of the Word taking flesh, theology becomes just as anthropocentric as it is theocentric. Since it is a product of grace and sovereign self-limitation, this only true anthropocentrism is not contingent upon the cosmos but upon the will of the Creator. The great analogy of baptism (Matt 28:18) is that the being of God truly corresponds to the names, and therefore the relations, of Father, Son, and Holy Spirit, into whom one is baptized. Indeed, this analogy can be said to be the only one that works, since the incomparable God has no analogy with creation other than the *imago dei*. The baptismal analogy is then not actually in the ritual action but in the Word of institution.

The Trinitarian material of the NT of the Johannine Upper Room discourse is actually also the perichoretic in establishing relations with human beings. The Holy Spirit's indwelling is simultaneously the indwelling of Father and Son—making "our abode" with them. The great question then, next to the anthropological, is the ecclesiological. There are many ecclesiologies that claim salvation not apart from the church, but of course it is extra Christum not extra ecclesiam. By extension, in the fullness of created perichoretic relations, it is community, and it is therefore truly ecclesia. But the crucial factor in all created relations is co-equal self-communication and self/social constitution through this generative activity of mutual love from all eternity now in time through incarnation and koinonia.

Koinonia is the umbrella term since also in John the fellowship of the Son becomes the fellowship of all the children of God. Because there is eternal fellowship within the one being of God, this is the basis for the creation and redemption of the human. "Fellowship" is the sharing of necessities, of life, of a meal, of shelter, of labor and leisure. Ultimately "fellowship" is the dwelling together in marriage, and thus the aptness of the nuptial metaphor with Jesus' "let no one sunder" hearkens to the Trinity as well. Creation is God's perichoretic self-expression of love in almighty power and goodness, all human beings manifesting, whatever their disability, God's creative action.[25]

One must consider that the uncreated divine perichoresis envelopes all things; they "hold together" through him whose union of natures also hold together because of the loving graciousness of this living manner of relations. Barth wrote, "the covenant is the internal ground of creation and the creation is the external ground of the covenant." This is the case because of the gracious relations that are grounded in God's action of *creatio continua*, and redemptive restoration. Perichoresis is the ground of the gracious

---

25. Reinders, *Receiving the Gift of Friendship*.

exchange. Perichoresis does what the resurrection of Christ does for human nature through creation and resurrection.

The human is generated and regenerated as dialogical being in relation to God and to other human beings. While it is not correct to categorize creation as a "Trinitarian system" that evidences the Trinity through vestiges of "threeness"; the relational God generates a relational universe that corresponds with his relationality and intelligibility. Thus, the original commands included those address to the non-human vital world; and human beings, in turn, address that world as co-inhabitants. The human being converses with creation, not merely with other humans, about the non-human populations. This is the basis for creative and regenerative acts toward the creation as God's co-creators from their own beginning to end.

The glorification of the human in resurrection becomes the consummate participation of the creature in the eternal glory of God. The metaphors of participation are many and are often conveyed in the context of a child to its mother as she nurses and it takes nourishment (cf. Isa 49:15 "Can a woman forget her nursing child, or show no compassion for the child of her womb? Even these may forget, yet I will not forget you").[26] But the metaphorical primacy goes to the nuptial: "I will bring all the people back to you as a bride comes home to her husband" (2 Sam 17:3); Israel is "like a bride" (Isa 49:18); "For as a young man marries a young woman, so shall your builder marry you, and as the bridegroom rejoices over the bride, so shall your God rejoice over you" (Isa 62:5; cp. John 3:29); the marriage of man and wife is the "great mystery" of Christ and the Church (Eph 5:22–32); "Come, I will show you the bride, the wife of the Lamb" (Rev 19:7; 21:9). Of course, all of this will be fed very early in Christian theology through the commentary tradition on the Song of Songs.[27]

The Christian constellation of revealed truths provides an intriguing model of distinctions and relations. The Creator/creature distinction remains in all of its manifold differentiation where createdness and uncreatedness are un-exchangeable, non-transferable. And yet, christologically, the two are united from the side of God, or even more asymmetrically, God unites himself to the human, to the creaturely, to mediate the two simultaneously to one another and to create a new elevated framework of mutual participation. The mutuality is by no means of equals, but of gracious adoption and elevated reunion. This is wholly a created union where the union itself is already reflective of the divine imago.

---

26. Cf. Haskell, *Suckling at My Mother's Breasts*.
27. King, *Origen on the Song of Songs*.

Created perichoretic relations are ultimately sanctifying. They are the dynamic personal connections with God and the human which produce the entire *ordo salutis*, terminating in the progressive regeneration of the believer. The relationship in divine love progressively excludes all rival loves, renews the mind, and sets the body in motion for Christ's mission through discipleship in the world. The co-eternal missions of Son and Spirit, and the commission of the Father, extends in and through the creatures God has redeemed for himself.

Created perichoretic relations are the work of the Holy Spirit as *vinculum amoris*—"conjunction in love," the realization of Jesus' prayer in John 17. What is so crucial about this chapter is that it not only substantiates the claim of relationship between the uncreated and the created, but it is the core text for the doctrine of the Trinity itself in Jesus' terms as delineated by John's Gospel. "God is love" is the web of perichoretic relations, as Augustine so well perceives. Pauline anthropology, ultimately based upon his understanding of the union of the two natures, makes possible and real the enfolding of that which is created, particularly according to the image of God, in that which is uncreated, the triune life that constitutes the love that is the eternal constitution of the deity. Of course, this is not a love, but the love of God that the God of love declares himself to be—who is irreversibly self-identified as love.

The faith in Christ that participates in his life is a precondition for participation in the church and its liturgies.[28] This goes for ethics as well; while religion has ceased to be an institutional force for politics, religious faith has not. While the nationalist heritage of religion and state have been deconstructed in favor of a proper theology of the human, where the other is recognized and protected, the recovery of theology on a whole new basis has been decisive for this trend.[29]

But participation in divine glory is realized, terminates, and extends dynamically into the age to come through resurrection; this is what Eastern theology has meant by *theosis*[30] ("deification"—by which is meant "clothed with immortality," 1 Cor 15). Although not a universally accepted term, neither is perichoresis. They are neither prohibited terms, and so the rule: "what God permits us to say of him" holds in these cases as well. When either of them is carefully nuanced, always maintaining the Creator/creature distinction, then what God uncontingently, unilaterally, and irreversibly

---

28. Clark, "Presumption, Preparation."
29. Simmons, *God and the Other*.
30. Kharlamov, *Theosis*.

elects to share with the creation in no way undercuts what Scripture discloses revelationally.

Finally, the relationality that is the perichoresis of the triune God is exemplaristic to human beings in relation to God. The interpersonal life of God is the presupposition of interpersonal human life. While human beings are individual persons, they achieve their person-ness, their personability and sociability, through relationships that indwell them, that contribute through address and memory to wholesome formation of the self. This is the delicate balance of subjectivity, where the self must dwell both intrinsically and extrinsically to itself and others. We are generated and regenerated in Christ for others—this is Bonhoeffer's great christological ethic.[31] What we are as human beings is indispensably shaped by the relationality that we perceive in the world around us and in the transcendent coordinates of our consciousness. This is the consciousness that receives revelation and that being-in-relation that is mediated by the Holy Spirit who "spirits" (or incorporates) us into the Trinitarian life according to its own original and originating *oikonomia*.

Bibliography

Anthansius. *St. Athanasius's Four Orations Against the Arians, and His Oration Against the Gentiles*. Translated by Samuel Parker. N.p.: BiblioLife, 2010.

Bauckham, Richard. *Jesus and the God of Israel: God Crucified and Other Studies on the New Testament's Christology of Divine Identity*. Milton Keynes, UK: Paternoster, 2008.

Boesel, Chris, and Catherine Keller, eds. *Apophatic Bodies: Negative Theology, Incarnation, and Relationality*. New York: Fordham University Press, 2010.

Bonhoeffer, Dietrich. *Letters and Papers from Prison*. Edited by Eberhard Bethge. New York: Macmillan, 1972.

Bruteau, Beatrice. *The Grand Option: Personal Transformation and a New Creation*. Notre Dame: University of Notre Dame Press, 2001.

Clark, Tony. "Presumption, Preparation, Parresia, Perichoresis, and Worship." In *The Great Tradition, a Great Labor: Studies in Ancient-future Faith*, edited by Philip Harrold and D. H. Williams, 25–37. Eugene, OR: Cascade Books, 2011.

Crisp, Oliver D. *Divinity and Humanity: The Incarnation Reconsidered*. Cambridge: Cambridge University Press, 2007.

Dempsey, Michael T., ed. *Trinity and Election in Contemporary Theology*. Grand Rapids: Eerdmans, 2011.

---

31. "Our relation to God is not a "religious" relationship to the highest, most powerful, and best Being imaginable—that is not authentic transcendence—but our relation to God in a new life in 'existence for others,' through participation in the being of Jesus" (Bonhoeffer, *Letters and Papers from Prison*, 381).

Dorner, Isaak. *Divine Immutability: A Critical Reconsideration*. Minneapolis: Fortress, 1994.
Durand, Emmanuel. "Perichoresis: A Key Concept for Balancing Trinitarian Theology." In *Rethinking Trinitarian Theology: Disputed Questions and Contemporary Issues in Trinitarian Theology*, edited by Giulio Maspero and Robert J. Woźniak, 177–92. London: T. & T. Clark, 2012.
Greshake, Gisbert. "Trinity as 'Communio.'" In *Rethinking Trinitarian Theology: Disputed Questions and Contemporary Issues in Trinitarian Theology*, edited by Giulio Maspero and Robert J. Woźniak, 331–45. London: T. & T. Clark, 2012.
Haskell, Ellen Davina. *Suckling at My Mother's Breasts: The Image of a Nursing God in Jewish Mysticism*. New York: State University of New York Press, 2012.
Kearney, Richard. *The God Who May Be: A Hermeneutics of Religion*. Bloomington, IN: Indiana University Press, 2001.
Kharlamov, Vladimir, ed. *Theosis: Deification in Christian Theology*. Vol. 2. Eugene, OR: Pickwick, 2011.
King, Christopher J. *Origen on the Song of Songs as the Spirit of Scripture: The Bridegroom's Perfect Marriage-Song*. Oxford: Oxford University Press, 2005.
Lee, Bryan Jeongguk. *Celebrating God's Cosmic Perichoresis: The Eschatological Panentheism of Jürgen Moltmann as a Resource for an Ecological Christian Worship*. Eugene, OR: Pickwick, 2011.
McCall, Thomas H. *Which Trinity? Whose Monotheism? Philosophical and Systematic Theologians on the Metaphysics of Trinitarian Theology*. Grand Rapids: Eerdmans, 2010.
Moltmann, Jürgen "God in the World—the World in God: Perichoresis in Trinity and Eschatology." In *The Gospel of John and Christian Theology*, edited by Richard Bauckham and Carl Mosser, 369–79. Grand Rapids: Eerdmans, 2008.
———. *Sun of Righteousness, Arise! God's Future for Humanity and the Earth*. Translated by Margaret Kohl. Minneapolis: Fortress, 2010.
Oster, Stefan. "Becoming a Person and the Trinity." In *Rethinking Trinitarian Theology: Disputed Questions and Contemporary Issues in Trinitarian Theology*, edited by Giulio Maspero and Robert J. Woźniak, 346–67. London: T. & T. Clark, 2012.
Polkinghorne, John, ed. *The Trinity and an Entangled World: Relationality in Physical Science and Theology*. Grand Rapids: Eerdmans, 2010.
Reinders, Hans S. *Receiving the Gift of Friendship: Profound Disability, Theological Anthropology, and Ethics*. Grand Rapids: Eerdmans, 2008.
Simmons, J. Aaron. *God and the Other: Ethics and Politics After the Theological Turn*. Bloomington, IN: Indiana University Press, 2011.
Sorč, Ciril. *Entwürfe einer perichoretischen Theologie*. Münster: Lit, 2004.
Zizioulas, John. "Trinitarian Freedom: Is God free in Trinitarian Life?" In *Rethinking Trinitarian Theology: Disputed Questions and Contemporary Issues in Trinitarian Theology*, edited by Giulio Maspero and Robert J. Woźniak, 193–207. London: T. & T. Clark, 2012.

Part Two

COMMUNITY

5

The Church Local and Universal

Catholic and Baptist Perspectives on Koinonia *Ecclesiology*

Paul S. Fiddes

Communion Ecclesiology Today

AMONG THE SEVERAL IMAGES for the church to be found in the New Testament, *koinonia* has become the term of choice in ecclesiology of recent years, especially on the ecumenical scene. Variously translated as "communion," "fellowship," "communio," or "community," *koinonia* has, over the last thirty years or so, supplanted the previously preferred terms "body of Christ" and "people of God."[1] The language of "communion" has soaked into the documents that mark bilateral conversations between Anglicans, Roman Catholics, the Orthodox, Lutherans, Reformed, Methodists, and Baptists.[2] To take just one example, the conversations between the Roman Catholic Church and the Lutheran World Federation (1993) explain:

> Participation in the communion of the three divine persons is constitutive for the being and life of the church as expressed in the three New Testament descriptions of it as "people of God,"

---

1. For this shift in thought, see Hahnenberg, "Mystical Body of Christ," 3–30.
2. Fuchs, *Koinonia*, 251–368; Kasper, *Harvesting The Fruits*, 72–77.

"body of Christ" and "temple of the Holy Spirit." Thus the church also shares in the communion of the Father with the Son and of both with the Holy Spirit. The unity of the church as communion of the faithful has its roots in the trinitarian communion itself . . . .[3]

The usefulness of the term "communion" is both its capacity for expressing a diversity of relationships, and its rooting in a vision of God as Trinity. Ecclesially, it can describe the relation of an individual believer to a local congregation, the relating of churches together on various levels of human society, the relation between churches and their leaders (pastors and bishops), and leaders with each other, the communal life created by sharing in the Eucharist, the relation of the local to the universal church, and the participation of all these relations (including the partnership of woman and man in creation) in the loving fellowship of Father, Son, and Holy Spirit. In short, it makes clear that the church is a manifestation in time and space of the eternal relational life of God. The report of recent conversations between the Baptist World Alliance and the Roman Catholic Church states near the beginning:

> The church is thus to be understood as a *koinonia* ("communion," "participation" or "fellowship"), which is grounded in the *koinonia* of the triune God. Believers are joined in *koinonia* through participation in the communion of Father, Son and Holy Spirit. At the same time they are in *koinonia* through their participation in the community of believers gathered by Christ in his church: "that you may have fellowship with us. And truly our fellowship is with the Father and with his Son Jesus Christ" (1 John 1:3). The principle of *koinonia* applies both to the church gathered in a local congregation and to congregations gathered together, whether in a regional association of churches (in the Baptist model) or in a local church (in the Catholic sense), or in still wider expressions of the church universal.[4]

Koinonia has become the "sacred thread"[5] weaving together an ecumenical convergence on the nature of the church, partly because it allows the flexibility of "degrees of communion" or "a certain though imperfect communion,"[6] and so is able to express "the various forms and extent of

---

3. *Church and Justification*, §63.
4. *Word of God in the Life of the Church*, §§11–12.
5. Fuchs, *Koinonia*, 252.
6. *Unitatis redintegratio*, §3, in Flannery, *Vatican Council II*, 455–56; *Ut Unum Sint*, §11.

communion already enjoyed by the Churches"[7] as well as hopes for a fuller visible unity. Further, the Roman Catholic Extraordinary Synod of Bishops in 1985 declared that the ecclesiology of communion was "the central and fundamental idea" of the documents of the Second Vatican Council,[8] a claim backed up by both Joseph Cardinal Ratzinger (later Pope Benedict XVI)[9] and Walter Kasper,[10] who were nevertheless to be the conversation-partners in a dispute about the nature of *koinonia* from 1999–2001, which I will be exploring in this essay. While in fact the theme of Vatican II was more obviously the church as the "people of God," Ratzinger later reflected that it was right in retrospect to regard *koinonia* as a synthesis of all the ideas of the Council about the church and God.[11]

In this focus on *koinonia* we can find an immediate resonance with the thought of the distinguished Baptist theologian we are honoring with this volume, Stanley Grenz. Writing that our fellowship with each other in the church is "nothing less than our common participation in the divine communion" he immediately goes on to quote from the Roman Catholic advocate of *koinonia* ecclesiology, Jean-Marie Tillard, that "the ecclesial koinonia can be defined as the passing of the Trinitarian Communion into the fraternal relations of the disciples of Christ."[12] Later he agrees with the Orthodox theologian John Zizioulas that "The Church is primarily communion, i.e. a set of relationships making up a mode of being."[13] Grenz's particular contribution to this ecumenical convergence is to align the idea of communion with the traditional Baptist idea of covenant, which he expounds as having both a vertical dimension (relating believers to God) and a horizontal one (uniting believers to each other).[14] Further, he stresses that both covenant and communion are eschatological in their orientation; as a sign of the kingdom, while not confusing the two, the church models "in the present the glorious human *fellowship* that will come at the consummation of history."[15] The final experience of a covenant community "comes only at

---

7. *Nature and Mission of the Church*, 22.
8. "Extraordinary Synod," 448.
9. See n. 11.
10. Kasper, *Theology and Church*, 150.
11. Ratzinger, "Ecclesiology of the Constitution on the Church," section headed "Ecclesiology of Communion."
12. Grenz, *Theology for the Community*, 630, citing Tillard, "What is the Church of God?" 372–73; see also n. 58 below.
13. Grenz, *Social God*, 334, citing Zizioulas, "Doctrine of God," 27–28.
14. Grenz, *Theology for the Community* (2000), 626–27.
15. Ibid., 624 (emphasis added).

the consummation of history."[16] It is, he stresses, the nature of every human person to have an eschatological destiny, to be open towards a future of perfect community with others and the whole of creation.

While the debate among Roman Catholic theologians at this time centered on the relation between local and universal church in their *koinonia* with each other, Grenz's interest is elsewhere: it is in communion as the ontology of the human person, uniting individuals to God and other persons both here and now, and in hope, made as they are in a divine image, which is "a shared corporate reality . . . fully present only in community."[17] With this interest in the nature of the "relational self," it is perhaps not surprising that Grenz's treatment of covenant is confined to the local congregation in which he sees persons as coming together in a voluntary agreement.[18] However, we shall see that there is a more expansive sense of covenant in Baptist tradition than the single local church, and that Grenz's own ontology of persons fits well into a network of relations embracing the local and the universal, throwing light in turn on the Roman Catholic debate.

This debate over the place of the church local and universal in *communio* was intensified in an exchange I have already alluded to between Cardinals Ratzinger and Kasper, conducted against the background of Vatican opposition to the understanding of communion promulgated by the liberation theologian Leonardo Boff. During the process of their conversation in print, always friendly but also sometimes sharp, Ratzinger and Kasper engage in a fascinating hermeneutical discussion of some New Testament texts, particularly Acts 2 and Gal 4. But first we must begin with a point of consensus. As well as agreeing on the importance of the concept of *koinonia*, they agree that the communion of the universal church cannot mean a mere collection or aggregation of local churches.

Communion No Mere Federation

In a "Letter to the Bishops of the Catholic Church on some aspects of the Church understood as Communion" issued in 1992 by the Congregation for the Doctrine of the Faith (henceforth CDF), it is made clear that it is a misuse of the idea of communion to understand the universal church as a mere extension of the communion at a local level. The church universal is not simply the sum total or federation of individual local churches. There

---

16. Ibid., 627.

17. Ibid., 231; *Social God*, 305, 321–22.

18. He does not contradict the view that "the covenant is by its very nature local": *Theology for the Community*, 612.

is no question of a kind of spiritual arithmetic through which many small bodies add up to make one large body. Rather, local churches are formed "out of and in the Church universal" (*ecclesiae ex et in Ecclesia universali*); this neat expression matches the phrase *Ecclesia in et ex ecclesiis* (the church in and formed out of the churches) in *Lumen Gentium* §23, and had already appeared in an address of Pope John Paul II to the Roman Curia.[19] Thus, in every "particular" church "the one, holy, Catholic and apostolic Church of Christ is truly present and active."[20]

There is a question of terminology at this point, since some Roman Catholic writers mean by "local church" the diocese, the group of churches centered upon the celebration of the Eucharist by a single bishop, while others refer to the diocese as a "particular" church, regarding the "local" church as the church gathered in one geographical, cultural space (such as the United States of America), composed of a number of "particular" churches. The documents of Vatican II use "local" and "particular" indifferently, and so it seems do Ratzinger and Kasper in their debate, being concerned with the basic relation between the "one church" and the "many churches," as I am in my own argument here. We should recognize that for Baptists "local church" and "particular church" mean neither diocese nor region but a single congregation. However, the difference is not as great as it seems, since in historic Baptist thinking the local minister of word and sacrament may be called "bishop" (*episkopos*),[21] no distinction being drawn between bishop and presbyter (elder) in a basically two-fold order of ministry, *episkope* and *diakonia*. Baptists have, moreover, usually understood that the local pastor *represents* the wider church on the local scene, opening up the vision of a single congregation to the wider mission of God.[22] Baptists do have an office of inter-church *episkope* ("oversight") in an area like a diocese, a pastor who may go by the name of "regional minister," "executive minister," "superintendent," or even "bishop," but this ministry is generally[23] seen as an extension of congregational *episkope* rather than a third office, and he or she has pastoral influence but no executive authority in a local congregation. Reducing the gap between Roman Catholic and Baptist even further, in Roman Catholic ecclesiology the local presbyter *represents* the bishop

---

19. John Paul II, Address to the Roman Curia (1990), 746.

20. "Letter to the Bishops," §9.

21. E.g., The Particular Baptist *Second London Confession* (1677), ch. 26.9, in Lumpkin, *Baptist Confessions*, 287.

22. See Fiddes, *Tracks and Traces*, 88–95.

23. Exceptions include a three-fold order among some General Baptists in seventeenth-century England, and in the Evangelical Baptist Church of Georgia today. See *An Orthodox Creed* (1679) §31, in Lumpkin, *Baptist Confessions*, 319–20.

and shares in the bishop's *episkope* so that the eucharistic assembly at the parish level itself participates in the "local" church (as well, of course, in the church universal). For all these reasons, I suggest that it is illuminating to make some comparison between Baptist and Roman Catholic understanding of the relation between "local" and "universal" church.

The CDF in its letter was opposed to a misunderstanding of "communion" in what it identified as an "ecclesiological unilateralism":

> Sometimes, however, the idea of a "communion of particular Churches" is presented in such a way as to weaken the concept of the unity of the Church at the visible and institutional level. Thus it is asserted that every particular Church is a subject complete in itself, and that the universal Church is the result of a *reciprocal recognition* on the part of the particular Churches. This ecclesiological unilateralism, which impoverishes not only the concept of the universal Church but also that of the particular Church, betrays an insufficient understanding of the concept of communion. As history shows, when a particular Church has sought to become self-sufficient ... it finds itself in danger of losing its own freedom in the face of the various forces of slavery and exploitation.[24]

The letter deals with this danger by proposing that the universal church is "prior" to the local church in both being and time: it is "a reality ontologically and temporally prior to every individual particular church."[25] This is a thesis that Cardinal Ratzinger is going to defend stoutly. Though he writes later that "it all began, not with anything I wrote, but with a 'Letter to the Bishops...,'"[26] the key formulation that the universal Church has "temporal and ontological priority" over local churches appears in Ratzinger's earlier writings about communion,[27] and Kilian McDonnell judges that "obviously this is Ratzinger's personal formulation."[28] While Walter Kasper is opposed to this thesis, he expresses frustration on several occasions that he has in consequence been associated by Cardinal Ratzinger with the "ecclesiological unilateralism" that the CDF is opposing. The chief opponent is in fact Leonardo Boff, as Ratzinger makes clear in a later lecture.[29]

---

24. "Letter to the Bishops," §8.
25. Ibid., §9.
26. Ratzinger, "Local Church and the Universal Church," 8.
27. Ratzinger, *Called to Communion*, 44.
28. McDonnell, "The Ratzinger/Kasper Debate," 228.
29. Ratzinger, "Ecclesiology," section "Subsistit in."

Boff asserts that the "historical Jesus" would not have conceived the idea of a church, nor have founded one. The church as a historical reality is rooted in the whole life and work of Jesus,[30] but it could have only come into existence after the resurrection, on account both of the loss of a sense of eschatological urgency about an immediate coming of the kingdom, and of the inevitable sociological needs of institutionalization.[31] In the beginning, a universal *catholic* church would certainly not have existed, but only different local churches with different theologies, different kinds of ministers, and different kinds of structures. No institutional church could, therefore, say that she was that one church of Jesus Christ desired by God; all institutional forms stem from sociological needs and are human constructions, which can and even must be radically changed again in new situations. The new situation Boff has in mind is of course that of the oppression of the poor by government and the wealthy classes in Latin America. For Ratzinger, this kind of scenario exemplifies not only ecclesiological "unilateralism" but "relativism."

Perhaps the reaction against Boff by the CDF was so severe because Boff had claimed the support of the early Ratzinger, alongside Hans Küng, for his views.[32] In fact, Boff asserts that "the church universal—the mystery of salvation, the *ecclesia deorsum*, the church-from-above—enjoys a primacy over the particular churches because it is this church-from-above that exists in them all."[33] The universal church is not, he emphasizes, a "sum" of its particular parts:[34] instead "the universal church is always the *prima novissima*, the structuring, originating principle of all." The difference between Boff and the later Ratzinger seems to be that Boff makes a distinction between the "universal church" in the mind of God and its manifestation in time, place, and history as the "catholic" church. All actualizations are subject to the shaping of social and political influences, and the historic communion of the church (its catholicity) will therefore be formed by the coming together of local churches. Thus Boff writes that is it the exercise of faith[35] by believers and local churches that "establishes communion with the particular churches that live Jesus' message in the fidelity of the apostolic succession,"[36] and that "this sacramental expression, this visible expression,

30. Boff, *Ecclesiogenesis*, 58.
31. Boff, *Church, Charism and Power*, 146.
32. Boff, *Ecclesiogenesis*, 53; Boff, *Church, Charism and Power*, 74.
33. Boff, *Ecclesiogenesis*, 19.
34. Ibid., 17.
35. Also the exercise of charisms: Boff, *Church, Charism and Power*, 160–63.
36. Boff, *Ecclesiogenesis*, 19.

can grow greater and greater in larger communities, since these have the capacity to render explicit the whole abundance of riches contained in the mystery of salvation...."[37] Ratzinger, by contrast, envisages the church universal as being the same reality both in eternity and in its "catholic" form in history, though he does claim that he is not identifying the universal church in either case with a particular institution such as the Roman Curia.[38] Kasper too wants to distance himself from any notion that the church universal, either in eternity or history, results from the voluntary decisions of local churches.

Commenting on the founding of the church on the Day of Pentecost in Acts 2, Boff finds the origin of the church to be the result of a blending of the work of the Spirit and the apostles' own decisions. The church-as-institution, he emphasizes "was not based as one so often hears on the incarnation of the Word, but on faith in the power of the apostles, inspired by the Spirit, who enabled them to transfer eschatology into time[;] . . . the church was born of a decision of the apostles under the impulse of the Spirit," and so "the power of community decision in the areas of discipline and dogma pertain to the essence of the church."[39] The church will continue to live, he urges, if men and women of faith in the risen Christ and his Spirit permanently renew this decision and incarnate the church in new situations with which they are confronted.

Some Baptists might judge that Boff stands close to Baptist ecclesiology, with his stress on communion as a voluntary decision of churches to gather together. However, it has been a historic Baptist insight that the visible church universal is not merely constructed out of local churches, or by a voluntary association of congregations into a larger unit. For example, a report of the Council of the Baptist Union of Great Britain (1948) speaks of the local as being a "manifestation" of the universal.[40] That this refers to the church universal in human history as well as in eternity is clear from the way that seventeenth-century confessions treat the theme of covenant. Local churches covenant with others, agreeing to "walk together" because they are already members of "one body," that is of the Christ who has gathered them together as the covenant-maker. Local churches have freedom because they exist directly "under the rule of Christ," but associations of churches together also stand under the same rule, setting up a tension between local assembly and association that can only be resolved by mutual

37. Ibid., 20.
38. Ratzinger, "Local Church and Universal Church," 8–9.
39. Boff, *Ecclesiogenesis*, 58; Boff, *Church, Charism and Power*, 147.
40. *Baptist Doctrine of the Church*, 8.

trust, not hierarchical authority. According to the First London Confession of 1644:

> And although the particular Congregations be distinct and severall Bodies, every one a compact and knit Citie in it selfe; yet are they all to walk by one and the same Rule, and by all meanes convenient to have the counsell and help of one another in all needfull affaires of the Church, as members of one body in the common faith under Christ their onely head.[41]

The principle of "one body" must apply to the church universal as well as regional associations, a point I want to return to later, and indeed the confession here in a marginal note includes the reference to the cosmic body of Christ in Col 2. If the church beyond its local manifestation is the body of Christ, then it cannot be merely the *result* of fellowship between many bodies. A theology of covenant has a place for the "decision in faith" helpfully highlighted by Boff, but it also replaces mere voluntarism by the belief that Christ has gathered his church together, so that members of his body are bound to enter into communion together. The Second London *Confession* of 1677 echoes the wording of covenant promises when it states that members of the church "do willingly consent to walk together according to the *appointment* of Christ, giving up themselves, to the Lord & one to another."[42] Here willing consent and Christ's requirement are brought together.

Stanley Grenz observes that some Baptists have made the distinction between a universal church, which is "invisible," a purely spiritual unity, and a local church, which is visible. He himself prefers, however, a three-part delineation into "mystical, universal, and local":

> The broadest manifestation is the "mystical church," the one body composed of all believers of all ages (Heb 12:22–3), the one cosmic fellowship that transcends time. The "universal church" is composed of all believers on earth at any given time, the one world-wide fellowship that transcends spatial boundaries. If frequency of use is the chief indication, however, the New Testament places greatest emphasis on the local manifestation of the church . . . .[43]

---

41. *Confession of Faith* (1644), §47, in Lumpkin, *Baptist Confessions*, 1689; this is virtually identical to article 38 of *A True Confession* (1596), in Lumpkin, *Baptist Confessions*, 94.

42. *Confession of Faith* (1677), ch. 26.6, in Lumpkin, *Baptist Confessions*, 286.

43. Grenz, *Theology for the Community*, 608–9.

Whether he is right to identify the local manifestation as the place where "greatest emphasis" has been, and should be, placed is a matter we shall come to in due time. Nor is it clear here whether he regards the universal church as invisible, that is (ideally) without any kind of organizational structure or social forms. He goes on to write, "As the visible fellowship of believers gathered in a specific location, the local church is the most concrete expression of the covenanting people."[44] If this implies that it is the *only* visible manifestation, then this is not in accord with seventeenth-century Baptist confessions, which make a similar three-fold distinction to Grenz's, but which regard the universal church as having visible form. In both Particular and General Baptist Confessions, we find a threefold form of an "invisible church universal," consisting of all the elect and redeemed, on earth or in heaven, a "visible church universal" consisting of all those who explicitly confess Christ in the world, and a "visible particular church," or the local assembly.[45] This must entail, in covenantal relationship, in searching for some social structures in which the visible unity of the universal church can be expressed. This classification is not unlike Ratzinger's description of an eternal universal church, a universal church in history, and a particular church, or indeed Boff's distinction between the eternal universal church, the *koinonia* of the catholic church in history, and the local church. The question is how these three dimensions of church are related in communion; here Boff's stress on human decision does not seem entirely adequate, as the Baptist understanding of covenant indicates. The solution to which Ratzinger and Kasper come we shall be reviewing shortly.

Grenz argues that evangelicalism has stressed the reality of the "invisible church" (understanding this to be all converted believers) over the visible church, or any institutional forms or empirical social organization of the church. The traditional "marks of the church" have been applied only to a "spiritual fellowship." This has allowed for practical cooperation between evangelical churches in evangelism and social reform, without worrying about unity of structures, as well as generating the "parachurch" movement. Grenz's own solution is to restore church "visibility" through making his focus the triune God, developing what he calls a "theological ecclesiology," affirming that the marks of the church are first the notes of the divine life, active in and through the church, and then only by extension marks of the church as the people through whom God works.[46] The church invisible, fol-

---

44. Ibid., 609.

45. *Confession of Faith* (1677), ch. 26, in Lumpkin, *Baptist Confessions*, 285–86; *Orthodox Creed* (1679), in Lumpkin, *Baptist Confessions*, §§29–31.

46. Grenz, *Renewing the Center*, 321–22.

lowing Luther, is the church "hidden in the life of God," and the church visible is the manifestation in the world of the relational life of God as Trinity: "The church's identity as a community must emerge out of the identity of the God it serves and in whom its life is hidden."[47] The communal fellowship in which Christians share is "nothing less than a shared participation . . . in the perichoretic community of trinitarian persons."

Grenz does not make clear whether he thinks that the visible community, emerging from the communion of God, includes social structures that are wider than the local church. He swings his interest towards the local when he appeals to the "demise of foundationalism" in a postmodern world as undercutting "any illusion of gaining access to some universal reality called 'community.'"[48] He notes among evangelicals a "new focus on the local nature of the church, from which in turn emerges the universal church as the interconnection of all local congregations,"[49] while not overtly committing himself to this view. I want later to argue that his own reflections on the nature of the human person give us grounds for putting as much weight on the visibility of the church universal as of the local, and to questioning any view of the universal church as a mere agglomeration of local congregations. Grenz is certainly in accord with Catholic and Orthodox writing on the church, including both Kasper and Ratzinger, in affirming that "each congregation is nothing less than the local reality of the one church";[50] local church *is* the universal church in local form. I have no doubt that Grenz would be critical of the mindset that, starting from the belief that the local is primary and the universal is secondary, asserts an independence from others, as if local believers could find what it means to share in the mission of God and to profess the faith in the world of today without asking how this is discerned in the whole church, in the South as well as in the North, in the urban shanty towns and favelas of South America and Africa, as well as in the prosperous and secular cities of the West.

It is a practical imperative to ask how the local church can be "from and in" (*ex et in*) the communion of the church universal, and it is here that the debate between Cardinals Ratzinger (as he was) and Kasper is highly illuminating. The debate began with the "Letter to the Bishops of the Catholic Church" issued by the CDF on 28 May 1992, which we have already been considering. Cardinal Ratzinger at the time was Prefect of the CDF. Walter Kasper, then Bishop of Rottenburg-Stuttgart, in a somewhat delayed

47. Ibid., 322.
48. Ibid., 323.
49. Ibid., 312.
50. Grenz, *Theology for the Community*, 609.

response, wrote a sharp critique of the CDF letter in a paper "On the Theology and Praxis of the Office of Bishop" for a *Festschrift* published in 1999. Ratzinger responded in defense of the earlier letter in a lecture given at a symposium in Rome in November 2000, on the theme "The Ecclesiology of the Constitution on the Church, Vatican II, *Lumen Gentium*," published in *L'Osservatore Romane* (2001).[51] Kasper immediately made his response to this lecture in an article appearing in *Stimmen der Zeit*, entitled "The Relation between the Universal Church and the Local Church: A Friendly Conversation"; this appeared in several places in English translation, and first in the American Jesuit review *America* under the title "On the Church" (April 2001).[52] By the time of the appearance of the translation, Kasper had been made a Cardinal and was in Rome as President of the Pontifical Council for Promoting Christian Unity. The editors of *America* then invited Ratzinger to respond to Kasper's article, which he did in the issue of 19 November, 2001, in a piece called "The Local Church and the Universal Church," cautioning that "for a long while I hesitated to accept this invitation because I do not want to foster the impression that there is a longstanding theological dispute between Cardinal Kasper and myself."[53] The editors of *America* finally invited Kasper to respond briefly to Ratzinger's comments, and a letter doing so appeared the following week.

Priority versus Perichoresis

In his "Theology and Praxis" article (1999), Kasper took issue with the position of the CDF letter of 1992, and particularly its assertion that "the universal Church is ontologically and temporally prior to the local church." Kasper wrote that the position criticized by the CDF letter, namely, the local church as a self-sufficient subject, and the universal church as a federation of local churches, is rightly to be rebuked.[54] But, in his view, the response of the CDF is excessive. In asserting the ontological and temporal priority of the universal church over the local church, the CDF goes far beyond Vatican II, amounting to a "departure from the council's teaching," and "more or less

---

51. A summary of the lecture was published in the *Frankfurter Allgemeine Zeitung*, 22 Dec. 2000, 46. In his account of "The Ratzinger/Kasper Debate," Kilian McDonnell seems to have had access only to this summary rather than to the whole lecture.

52. The article also appeared in a different translation as "On the Church" in *The Tablet* 255 (23 June 2001), 927–30. My account uses the translation in *America* (by Ladislas Orsy).

53. Ratzinger, "Local Church and the Universal Church," 7.

54. Kasper, "Zur Theologie und Praxis," 43.

a subversion *(Umkehrung)*" of Vatican II's position. The position taken by CDF is to be understood as "a theological attempt to restore Roman centralism . . . a process which appears to have already begun." In a word, "the relationship of the local church and the universal Church has been thrown out of balance."[55] Kasper suspects that the concern of CDF to assert the priority of the church universal is a hidden program to identify the universal church with the Pope and the Roman Curia, so giving them undue primacy over the College of Bishops.[56] Later he explains that his criticism came from the practical problem about how to guide his flock in a situation where bishops no longer had freedom to implement universal church laws as they thought right, but had to follow detailed regulations coming from Rome; examples he cites are the refusal of communion to all divorced and "the highly restrictive rules for eucharistic hospitality."[57]

Kasper's own alternative to the "priority" of the church universal is to affirm that the universal and the local church should be understood as always being held together in *perichoresis*; one cannot be prior to the other but they must always exist simultaneously.[58] This alternative is set in the context of interpretation of Scripture. The CDF in its letter had argued (implicitly in opposition to Boff's exegesis) that the church founded at Pentecost in Acts 2 was the church universal, the eternal church manifested in time and history, not the church local. The twelve apostles and the one hundred and twenty gathered round Mary had a missionary task, and were "representatives of the one unique Church and the founders-to-be of the local Churches," which were thus to arise "within and out of the universal Church."[59] This exegesis is supported by appeal to Gal 4:26, where the church universal is described as "mother"; she is thus "one and unique, precedes creation, and gives birth to the particular Churches as her daughters." She is the mother and "not the product of the particular churches," and only in this way is she the "communion of churches." In his article Kasper now responds to the CDF's exegesis of Acts 2; he has no objection to identifying the Pentecostal church as the church universal, but because it was the church in Jerusalem it was at the same time "universal *and* local in its single

---

55. Kasper, "Zur Theologie und Praxis," 43; translation by Kilian McDonnell in "Walter Kasper on the Theology and Praxis of the Bishop's Office," 712.

56. Kasper, "Zur Theologie und Praxis," 46.

57. Kasper, "On the Church," section "A Pressing Pastoral Problem."

58. Kasper, "Zur Theologie und Praxis," 43. This coinherence had already been anticipated by Jean-Marie Tillard's concept of mutual 'immanence' of local and universal, in, e.g., *Church of Churches*, 26, cf. 284.

59. "Letter to the Bishops," §9. This corresponds to Ratzinger's exegesis of Acts 2 in *Called to Communion*, 43–45.

reality."⁶⁰ In fact, there must have been already a number of Christian communities in Galilee "alongside the Jerusalem community" so that from the very beginning the church is constituted "from and in" local churches.

In his lecture in Rome on *Lumen Gentium* (2000) in which he responds to Kasper, Ratzinger goes back to the brief affirmations of the CDF letter, and appears to be simply preferring priority to perichoresis, significantly casting priority now in terms of an ecclesiology of story. He argues that the expression of Gal 4:26, "this Jerusalem is our mother" shows that the universal church has a story which precedes any local church. It is a story that begins before creation, as the CDF had affirmed. The mystery of the church is not something that comes into being "at the last moment," but expresses "an inner teleology in creation." The story continues through Israel as the bride of God, as a "love-history" of God with his people. The church pre-exists in the old Israel, and the story comes to fulfilment in the church as the bride of the Son; the image of bride is fused with that of body in the Eucharist, since the creation story tells us that man and wife will be "one body" and here Christ and church will become one. There can only be one bride as there can only be one mother, and so the one universal church must have priority.⁶¹ In line with Gal 4, Acts 2 similarly gives us a story. Reiterating the exegesis of Acts 2 in the CDF letter, Ratzinger adds that this is not the story of a local church, but the story of old Israel made new in the church, the twelve tribes renewed in the twelve apostles—together with a group of 120 who are also to be apostles and church-founders. Thus, "it does not do justice to the Lucan account to say that the original community of Jerusalem was simultaneously both the universal church and the local church."⁶² Returning to the phrase "temporal and ontological priority" in the light of Kasper's point about other communities alongside the Jerusalem community, he concedes that "perhaps it is not necessary to over-emphasize the question of the *temporal* priority of the universal Church," although (in his view) Luke clearly presents it in his account. The point is that the church has an "inner beginning" in time at Pentecost, that is the generation of the universal church in the twelve by the one Spirit for the sake of all peoples.

Ratzinger's exposition of Acts 2 is also intended to address the suspicion of Kasper that the formula of the priority of the universal church would be "completely problematic . . . if the universal church were identified with the local Roman church, *de facto* the Pope and the curia." He insists that this

---

60. Kasper, "Zur Theologie und Praxis," 44.
61. Ratzinger, "Ecclesiology," section "CDF Letter on Communion."
62. Ratzinger, "Ecclesiology," section "Lucan Vision of the Church."

is just not the case, and that this is a merely hypothetical "if."[63] His whole concern, he stresses, is to affirm the church as a creation of the Holy Spirit and as a realization of a Trinitarian dynamic, and not to reduce the church to a sociological, human entity, which would be exactly the case if one empirical church—the Roman church—were to be identified with the church universal. Indeed, this reduction is what is apparent in the "ecclesiological relativism" of those who see the church universal as having its origin in the local church (here he names Boff for the first time),[64] so that communion is simply the result of sociological imperatives. If the Pentecost church *were* to be reduced to the empirical community of Jerusalem, this would leave all the "theological depth" out of one's perspective on the church.

In Ratzinger's lecture he gives a central place to the sacraments in thinking about the way that the church universal both is, and creates, *koinonia*. Eucharistic communion must be universal, he affirms, as there is only one body of Christ. Baptism, Eucharist and episcopacy are all gifts that come from *outside* the local church, making clear that the universal church has priority as the source. Responding to the accusation that he is interested only in an abstract concept of the church as universal, he identifies the concrete and empirical manifestation of the church not in its sociological conditions, but in the "concreteness of the incarnation." The empirical church is founded in the body of Christ, which is known through eucharistic communion.[65]

Pre-Existence, Priority, and Perichoresis

Replying to Ratzinger in his article, "On the Church" (2001), Kasper rejects any attribution to him of a sociological reduction of the church to the empirical, local church. He repeats that his emphasis is upon the *perichoresis* of local and universal church: the local churches and the universal church mutually include each other; they share the same existence and they live within each other, in a mysterious unity which is "constituted after the image of the Trinity."[66] Whenever there is mutual presence and inclusion, there is a perfect relationship and communion. He repeats that in his view the Congregation for the Doctrine of the Faith exceeded these essentials when it used the doctrine of communion as mutual inclusion to assert the "ontological and temporal" priority of the universal church.

63. Ibid.
64. Ratzinger, "Ecclesiology," section "Subsistit in."
65. Ratzinger, "Ecclesiology," section "Ecclesiology of Communion."
66. Kasper, "On the Church," section "Common Foundations in Ecclesiology."

Kasper's argument is based quite largely on exegesis of the same two texts to which Ratzinger appeals. First, he returns to the exegesis of Acts 2 offered by Ratzinger, dissenting from his identification of the Pentecostal church in Jerusalem solely with the universal church, picking up the same theme of "story" but using it in a different way. In Luke's presentation, the Pentecostal community is not only the gathering of the apostles on the day itself; it unfolds in historical actuality "to become the Church of all nations and peoples." He judges that "the correct history of the beginnings of the church is found comprehensively in the *narrations of its initial expansion* and not in Luke's isolated passage about Pentecost."[67] There is a story, but it belongs to many churches. Beginnings are as much about the church in its concrete, empirical forms as about the church universal. As for the exegesis of Gal 4:26, "Jerusalem above who is our mother," Kasper agrees that this is a reference to the church as a pre-existent reality, and strengthens the notion by adding "the city of the living God, the heavenly Jerusalem" from Heb 12:22–23. But he refuses to associate pre-existence with *ontological* priority, as Ratzinger does, since he argues that Paul appeals to pre-existence as a way of expressing the grounding of the church in God's eternal will to save humanity through a community of salvation, the church. Since that church exists in empirical actuality, what "pre-exists" must be the actual church in history, and so the church that exists "in and from" the many particular churches as well as the universal church "in and from which" they themselves exist.[68] It pre-exists, that is, in the sense of being included in God's eternal intentions.

More generally, Kasper asserts that the New Testament portrays an ecclesiology that starts from the local church, led by a single bishop, in which local community the one, universal church of God is represented and is present. For Paul, the focus is on the local community in which the one church of God comes alive; *ekklesia* primarily means the individual church or the individual congregation, and communion arises from the presence of the universal church of God in all of them. There can be no communion that is characteristic first of the universal church, and is then imparted locally: "Because the one church was present in each and all, they were in communion."[69] Kasper supports his reading of the text by reference to the Protestant New Testament scholar Joachim Gnilka, who suggests that it is only later, in the post-Pauline literature that the focus moves to the church

---

67. Kasper, "On the Church," section "Controversy."
68. Ibid.
69. Kasper, "On the Church," section "Historical Dimensions."

universal, for example in the theme of the "cosmic Christ" in Colossians and Ephesians.

In responding to Kasper's article in his own piece in *America* ("The Local Church and the Universal Church," 2001), Ratzinger returns to what he considers to be Kasper's leap from hypothesis to fact, repeating the accusation that Kasper has a hidden agenda of suspicion against Roman centralism. He repeats that the church of Rome is a local church and not the universal church; even though the Roman church has a peculiar, universal responsibility, he claims that the CDF never thought to identify the Pope and Curia with the universal church.[70] Taking up his earlier expression of an "inner beginning," he proposes that the "ontological priority" of the universal church means the "inner precedence" of the one bride over all her empirical realizations in particular churches, or the "inner priority" of unity demonstrated in salvation history,[71] and this has nothing to do with the problem of centralism.

Ratzinger now significantly grants the principle that has been at the center of Kasper's ecclesiology—the simultaneity and *perichoresis* of the universal church and local churches as the church "lives in history." But this, he argues, is not the point of the *pre-existence* of the church, which he sees as equivalent to *ontological priority*. Ratzinger again associates both ideas with the "love story between God and humanity," where God finds and prepares the bride of his Son, citing Gal 4:26 once more—"Jerusalem above, our mother" (quoting from his Rome lecture). There is *only one bride*, he stresses, and hence there is an "inner priority of unity," although he does raise just a slight query about whether we should here speak of a "teleological" rather than an "ontological" precedence.[72] Nevertheless, Ratzinger thinks that Kasper has modified his objection to the ontological and temporal priority of the universal church by accepting the pre-existence of the church, apparently not noticing Kasper's careful distinction between pre-existence and ontological priority. Thus, Ratzinger grants *perichoresis* in history, while still affirming priority; Kasper grants pre-existence, while still denying priority. While there is some convergence, they also still seem to be talking past each other, and not least in the exegesis of Gal 4:26. I shall come to my own proposal about a possible baptistic approach to these issues later.

Ratzinger returns to what he had affirmed about baptism with regard to the universal church; baptism, he had declared in his Rome lecture, was a "trinitarian event . . . far more than a socialization bound up with the local

70. Ratzinger, "The Local Church," 8.
71. Ibid., 10.
72. Ibid. 10.

church." Baptism, as with Eucharist and the ministry, comes from "outside" the local scene, from a Christ who walks through "closed doors." Through baptism the "door of the one church is opened to us," and so the waters of baptism can only flow from the one church, from "the Jerusalem that is above, our new mother," again citing Gal 4:26. He is surprised that Kasper has not responded to this point, and cites an occasion when Kasper had spoken movingly of his own baptism, recalling that he had, early in life, left the parish where he was baptized, and so in baptism had not been socialized into this particular community but born into the one church. For Ratzinger, "this statement clears up the controversy—for that is the issue here."[73] In his final response, Kasper agrees that baptism is of course into the one church, but one is still baptized in a specific (episcopally structured) local church, so the sacraments (and the ministry) must be simultaneous events at both the local and universal level.[74] Anything other, Kasper argues, makes the universal church an abstraction.

In this article Ratzinger declines to comment directly on Acts 2, but takes up Kasper's assertion, following Gnilka, that in the Pauline letters the local church is the focus. Against this opinion of one Protestant scholar, Ratzinger sets the view of another, Rudolph Bultmann, that "the priority of the Church as a whole over the local community" is pervasive in the New Testament; significantly, Bultmann sees this notion worked out in "the equation of the *ekklesia* with the *soma Christou* (body of Christ), which embraces all believers."[75] Bultmann, concludes Ratzinger mischievously, could never be accused of wanting to bring back Roman centralism! Just as mischievously, Kasper notes in his response that Bultmann no doubt has some presuppositions that Ratzinger does not share.[76]

In this final response, an invited letter in *America*, Kasper notes thankfully that Ratzinger has accepted in his last article that he, Kasper, does not hold a doctrine of the church that dissolves it into a "purely sociological entity" through focus on the empirical church. This accusation, he recalls, has caused him some embarrassment in ecumenical circles. Further, he observes that Ratzinger now accepts the principle that the local churches and the universal church interpenetrate one another, "so that one can speak of their being simultaneous," at least as the church has existed throughout history. In the light of this concession, for his part Kasper now declares that "I no longer care to attribute too much importance to the really rather

---

73. Ibid., 11.
74. Kasper, "From the President," 29.
75. Bultmann, *Theology of the New Testament*, 1:94.
76. Kasper, "From the President," 29.

speculative question of whether the situation is precisely the same or perhaps different with regard to the pre-existence of the church." That is, Kasper is not going to insist on the perichoresis of the local and universal church in some pre-existent reality (understanding pre-existence, of course, in his own sense of existing in God's intentions).

Ratzinger is right, Kasper affirms, to insist on "only one bride" and "only one body." But he has now, Kasper is pleased to see, appealed to these images in order to "make over" the thesis of the priority of the universal church into something else—"the priority of inner unity," which Kasper can certainly accept. But in reporting Ratzinger, Kasper uses the term "priority" in an open-ended way; for Ratzinger, by contrast, "inner unity" (as already flagged up in the Rome lecture) is only a way of re-formulating *temporal* priority, and is not at all a modification of "ontological priority." Here again, we must say, there is not an entire meeting of minds.

Personhood and Versions of *Koinonia* Ecclesiology

In this debate we have seen three Roman Catholic versions of *koinonia* ecclesiology. It might mean, first, that the universal church is prior to the local, and so creates *koinonia* (Ratzinger); second, that local church is prior to universal or catholic *koinonia*, and so creates it with others (Boff); and third, that local and universal church exist simultaneously in a *koinonia*, which is their mutual interpenetration (Kasper). A baptistic perspective will, in the end, tend to side with the third version, a *perichoresis* between the church local and universal, because of a baptistic concern for the freedom of the local church and suspicion of hierarchy. Indeed, the joint report of the Baptist World Alliance-Roman Catholic Commission (with the approved status of a "Study Document") takes this approach, stating:

> We agree that the local fellowship does not derive from the universal church, nor is the universal a mere sum of various local forms, but that there is mutual existence and coinherence between the local and universal church of Christ.[77]

However, I want to argue that a baptistic perspective should also learn from Ratzinger's stress on *koinonia* as being the local church "from and in" the universal church. Admittedly, Kasper has a point that an assertion of the "ontological and temporal priority" of the universal church in the present Roman Catholic climate tends to support the magisterium and papal authority over collegiality. Ratzinger's firm denial that this is in mind, on

77. *Word of God in the Life of the Church* §12.

the grounds that the communion is mystical and not institutional, may be a means (as the Catholic theologian Edward Hahnenberg argues)[78] of ignoring the criticism of establishment. Kasper in his final letter rejects Ratzinger's own dismissal of the issue of centralism as mere "politics," or a political reductionism. He urges that the church is a historically-existing divine-human reality, not "some kind of Platonic republic,"[79] and so it is essential to ask about concrete actions in pastoral life. Kasper's original reaction to the CDF letter had arisen from pastoral concerns about the way a bishop could advise and guide his flock over disputed matters, though he later records that he had come to see it as a central ecumenical issue as well.[80]

But within baptistic ecclesiology, where there is no central magisterium, there is a stronger case for combining the first and third approaches, as Ratzinger himself finally attempts to do. *Perichoresis*, it may be argued, can only be possible if the universal is prevenient and originates it. We are led in this direction by a grounding of *koinonia* in a theology of the body of Christ, as Bultmann indicates in the passage cited by Ratzinger.[81] In a baptistic view, the local congregation and an assembly of churches are both "body of Christ," as both make Christ visible in the world; yet Christ in his glorious resurrection body, continuous with his earthly body, must pre-exist both. There was a historic shift in Roman Catholic theology, as Henri de Lubac maintains,[82] from regarding the church as "true body" to "mystic body," so that the empirical reality of "true body" was transferred to the "true body" of the eucharistic bread, previously regarded as the "mystic body." There is a good case to be made, as Hahnenberg does, that ever since this the notion of the universal church as the body of Christ tends to ignore its concrete, historical and social aspects, turning it into a "mystical," non-empirical ideal.[83] But this is not true of a baptistic context, where the sense of a *local* body is prominent (though not exclusive), and where "body" is inseparable from a covenant which includes the willing commitment of members to each other in their everyday life, akin to Boff's concern for the making of *koinonia* through faith at a local level. In this context, it becomes less abstract and hierarchical to affirm the church universal as having a priority which enables *perichoresis*.

78. Hahnenberg, "The Mystical Body of Christ," 25–27.

79. Kasper, "From the President," 29.

80. Kasper, "On One Church," section "Consequences for the Ecumenical Movement."

81. See above, n. 75.

82. De Lubac, *Corpus Mysticum*, 25–130; cf. de Certeau, *Mystic Fable*, 79–90.

83. Hahnenberg, "The Mystical Body of Christ," 7–9, 11–13, 15–16.

In debate with Kasper, Ratzinger comes to accept a simultaneity of the local and universal church in history, but continues to affirm the ontological priority of the universal church as a mystery from eternity. This is the way that he himself holds together the first and third versions of *koinonia*. Kasper at first insists on simultaneity in both history and eternity, though finally he is prepared to leave eternity and pre-existence as mystery, while still not accepting ontological priority. Another way of integrating the first and third approaches to *koinonia* is to affirm *both* priority and simultaneity in *both* history and eternity. Simultaneity does justice to the empirical, concrete aspects of the church, while priority is an inner movement of Christ in the church, where his rule always comes first. This has some affinity to the "inner beginning" identified by Ratzinger and finally accepted by Kasper, but is more christological. It also takes us into the heart of the Trinity, where the *perichoresis* of persons does not deny an inner direction of life and love "from the Father."

This Trinitarian reflection takes us back to the thought of Stanley Grenz, although he never seems to have commented himself on the conversation between Cardinals Ratzinger and Kasper. Grenz, as I argued earlier, is most enthused about *koinonia* in its implications for human personhood. While relationality is basic to secular views of the "social self," the Christian view of the person is an "ecclesial" self, a person only in relation to the community of Christ, participating in the divine communion of love and having an eschatological destiny.[84] The believer is constituted as a person by participation through the church and the Eucharist in Christ's own life, sharing in filial relation of Christ to the father.[85] We can now extend Grenz's approach, in light of the Kasper-Ratzinger debate. If a person is an "ecclesial self," then this must be shaped by the universal as well as the local church. Persons in a local community are persons also because of the wider community. In person-making, both local and universal church must have a role. One way of understanding this is through the notion of story, to which Ratzinger and Kasper both allude, and to which Grenz adds another dimension.

In his *Theology for the Community of God*, Grenz's theology of story concerns the relation of the individual to the local church. The believer cannot be an isolated individual but must be in community, because that community has a larger story of covenant to which the individual can belong: "we participate in a fellowship that has already enjoyed a covenantal history."[86] In *The Social God and the Relational Self* this idea is amplified.

---

84. Grenz, *Social God*, 312.
85. Ibid., 324–25.
86. Grenz, *Theology for the Community*, 614.

Taking up the late-modern philosophical idea that persons are constituted through narrative, he identifies the "larger story" as the Jesus-narrative, which makes sense of life by its eschatological perspective. The Holy Spirit incorporates believers into this transcending narrative, which is the shared story of the community.[87] Persons are formed by accepting the story of the Christian community as their own: "The personal identity of all who are 'in Christ' is bound up with participation in a particular community—namely the fellowship of those who live by means of the connection they share to the Jesus story."[88]

Thus we may see Grenz's theology as adding a baptistic covenantal dimension to Ratzinger's story of the love-affair between God and Israel, which for Ratzinger essentially validates the priority of the universal church. But conversely, we must add to Grenz's perspective that the story is not only that of a local community but of the whole church universal. The perceptions that local and universal church are in perichoresis, and that the universal church has priority because it is the whole body of Christ, add an important element to the idea of the ecclesial self. Practically, the development of the self requires a deliberate immersion into the *koinonia* of the wider church, for example through recollection of the communion of saints, and through active engagement (through prayer and cooperative work) with the church beyond the local scene. This, I suggest, is the direction in which Stanley Grenz's thought was implicitly moving, and which is a momentum he has bequeathed to his grateful successors.

Bibliography

The Baptist Doctrine of the Church (1948). In *Baptist Union Documents 1948–1977*, edited by Roger Hayden, 41–11. London: Baptist Historical Society, 1980.
Boff, Leonardo. *Church, Charism and Power*. Translated by J. Diercksmeieer. London: SCM, 1985.
———. *Ecclesiogenesis: The Base Communities Reinvent the Church*. Translated by R. Barr. Maryknoll, NY: Orbis, 1997.
Bultmann, Rudolph. *Theology of the New Testament*. Translated by K. Grobel. 2 vols. London: SCM, 1952.
Church and Justification. International Lutheran-Roman Catholic Commission on Unity, Phase III (1993). In *Growth in Agreement II : Reports and Agreed Statements of Ecumenical Conversations on a World Level, 1982–1998*, edited by Jeffrey Gros, Harding Meyer, William G. Rusch. Faith and Order Paper 187. Geneva: WCC, 2000.

---

87. Grenz, *Social God*, 329.
88. Ibid., 332.

De Certeau, Michel. *The Mystic Fable*. Translated by M. Smith. Chicago: Chicago University Press, 1992.

De Lubac, Henri. *Corpus Mysticum: The Eucharist and the Church in the Middle Ages*. Edited by Laurence Hemming and Susan Parsons. Translated by G. Simmonds, R. Price, C. Stephens. London: SCM, 2005.

Extraordinary Synod of Bishops. "The Final Report." *Origins* 15 (19 December 1985) 444–50.

Fiddes, Paul S. *Tracks and Traces: Baptist Identity in Church and Theology*. Milton Keynes, UK: Paternoster, 2003.

Flannery, Austin, O.P. *Vatican Council II: The Conciliar and Post Conciliar Documents*. Dublin: Dominican, 1977.

Hahnenberg, Edward P. "The Mystical Body of Christ and Communion Ecclesiology: Historical Parallels." *Irish Theological Quarterly* 70 (2005) 3–30.

John Paul II. Address to the Roman Curia, 20 December, 1990. In *Acta Apostolicae Sedis* 83/9 (1991) 740–49. www.vatican.va/archive/atti-ufficiali-santa-sede/index_en.htm.

Kasper, Walter. "From the President of the Council for Promoting Christian Unity" (letter), *America* (26 November 2001) 28–29. Copy supplied by British Library, ref. 0809.66000.

———. *Harvesting The Fruits. Basic Aspects of Christian Faith in Ecumenical Dialogue*. London: Continuum, 2009.

———. "On the Church. A Friendly Reply to Cardinal Ratzinger." *America* 184/14 (23 April 2001). www.americamagazine.org/issue/333/article/church. Originally published as "Das Verhältnis von Universalkirche und Ortskirche. Freundschaftliche Auseinandersetzung mit der Kritik von Joseph Kardinal Ratzinger." *Stimmen der Zeit* 218 (2000) 795–804.

———. *Theology and Church*. Translated by M. Kohl. New York: Crossroad, 1989.

———. "Zur Theologie und Praxis des bischoflichen Amtes." In *Auf neue Art Kirche Sein: Wirklichkeiten-Herausfoderungen-Wandlungen. Festschrift für Bischof Dr Josef Hohmeyer*, edited by Werner Schreer and Georg Steins, 32–48. Munich: Bernward bei Don Bosco, 1999.

"Letter to the Bishops of the Catholic Church on some aspects of the Church Understood as Communion." Published by the Congregation for the Doctrine of the Faith May 28, 1992, republished *Origins* 22 (June 25, 1992) 108–12. www.vatican.va/roman_curia/congregations/cfaith/documents/rc_con_cfaith_doc_28051992_communionis-notio_en.html.

Fuchs, Loreli F., S.A. *Koinonia and the Quest for an Ecumenical Ecclesiology*. Grand Rapids: Eerdmans, 2008.

Lumpkin, W. L., ed. *Baptist Confessions of Faith*. Philadelphia: Judson, 1959.

McDonnell, Kilian, O.S.B. "The Ratzinger/Kasper Debate: The Universal Church and the Local Churches." *Theological Studies* 63 (2002) 227–50.

———. "Walter Kasper on the Theology and Praxis of the Bishop's Office." *Theological Studies* 63 (2002) 711–29.

The Nature and Mission of the Church. Faith and Order Paper 198. Geneva, WCC, 2005.

Ratzinger, Joseph. *Called to Communion. Understanding the Church Today*. Translated by A. Walker. San Francisco: Ignatius, 1991.

———. "The Ecclesiology of the Constitution on the Church, Vatican II, *Lumen Gentium*." Originally published in *L'Osservatore Romane*, 19 September 2001. English translation online: www.catholicculture.org/culture/library.

———. "The Local Church and the Universal Church." *America* 185/16 (19 November 2001) 7–11. Copy supplied by British Library, ref. 0809.66000.

Tillard, Jean-Marie. *Church of Churches: Ecclesiology of Communion*. Translated by R. C. De Peaux. Collegeville, MN: Liturgical, 1992.

———. "What is the Church of God?" *Mid-stream* 23 (1984) 363–80.

Ut Unum Sint. Encyclical Letter of Pope John Paul II. London: Catholic Truth Society, 1995.

The Word of God in the Life of the Church. A Report of International Conversations between The Catholic Church and the Baptist World Alliance 2006–2010. published in *American Baptist Quarterly*, 31/1 (Spring 2012).

Zizioulas, John. "The Doctrine of God in the Trinity Today." In *The Forgotten Trinity*, edited by Alasdair I. C. Heron, 19–32. London: CCBI/Inter-Church House, 1989.

6

Should We "Welcome" and "Affirm"?

Reflecting on Evangelical Responses to Human Sexuality[1]

Stephen R. Holmes

Introduction

I ONLY HAD THE privilege of meeting Stanley Grenz on a couple of occasions, both when I was a beginning graduate student; as far as I can reconstruct in

---

1. The politics of language in this area is enormously complex; Grenz used the term "homosexuality," which today is regarded as offensive by many; however, almost every alternative term is politically loaded in one direction or another. To speak of the general area being reflected upon as "human sexuality" is perhaps fairly safe; I have, where necessary, adopted the term "same-sex erotic attraction" to speak of a specific human experience, whilst acknowledging that many gay and lesbian people—including many Christian gay and lesbian people—would regard this as unhappy because it is reminiscent of a term—"same sex attraction"—that has been used with the intention of invalidating their felt and owned identities. Equally I know several Christian people who would resist the terms "gay" and "lesbian" and would indeed instead speak of experiencing "same sex attraction." I intend "same-sex erotic attraction" to be a phenomenological term, which is as neutral as possible, and which can be paralleled to "opposite-sex erotic attraction": it seems a matter of human experience in contemporary Western societies that some people experience one of these but not the other; whilst others experience both with varying degrees of intensity. Editors' note: thanks to Megan DeFranza for commenting on an early draft of this chapter.

my memory, it must have been about the time his book on human sexuality, *Welcoming But Not Affirming*,[2] was in press. I certainly was not aware that he was writing in the area; I knew him as an evangelical and Baptist theologian who was responding creatively to broad cultural currents with serious dogmatic insights, and so as someone whose practice might serve as a model for the sort of theology I was trying to imagine myself doing.

Re-reading *Welcoming* fifteen years after its publication, I am struck first by how contemporary it seems: Grenz ran ahead of the rest of us, delineating the debate as it is happening now, not as it was happening as the twentieth century closed. This is particularly true in the deep pastoral concern and insight of the book, unusual for a conservative treatment in its day, but is also evidenced in the nuanced treatment of questions of the origin of same-sex erotic attraction, and in the serious attempts to locate gay/lesbian sexuality within a broad narrative of Christian sexual ethics. Grenz concluded that the calling of the church is to welcome all people, regardless of their desires or indeed actions, but never to affirm homosexual sexual activity as licit or appropriate; in surveying the history since he wrote, it is salutary to notice how rare the position he advocated has been in practice, and how wise it seems with the benefit of hindsight.

In this chapter I want to sketch—I can do no more, and I hope to offer a fuller treatment soon—an evangelical theological account of human sexuality that I believe stands in significant continuity with Grenz's program. I will develop my ideas here in dialogue with Grenz, and stress the continuities, but honesty compels the acknowledgement that this was not the genesis of my ideas; I came to them—as far as I can tell—independently of any specific reflection on his work, and was pleased and encouraged to discover a degree of congruity; as I indicate below, where I go beyond him, I see reasons to hope that he might have followed at least some of the same tracks had he lived longer and chosen to engage further with these issues.

On the Origins of Human Sexuality

Grenz begins his book with a chapter entitled "Homosexuality in contemporary perspective," which addresses two questions: why questions of human sexuality have attained the cultural prominence they have in Western cultures in our generation; and the roots of same-sex erotic attraction in individuals who experience it.

---

2. Hereafter, *Welcoming*.

In much contemporary debate, the second of these is regarded as determinative, while the first is ignored or dismissed; this seems to me to be wrongheaded on both counts, and I suspect from what he wrote that Grenz would agree. To deal with the second first, he surveys the scientific evidence concerning the causes of homosexuality, and cautiously concludes that a "social constructivist" account is most plausible.[3] That said, he rightly claims that the crucial question does not concern causality but normativity: is there a right way to be human or not?[4] Accounts of the biological/psychological/sociological origins of human sexuality are only interesting, ethically speaking, if they can address questions of normativity—but, within a Christian dogmatic framework, it seems inevitable that such matters are largely irrelevant to this issue of norms. The reason for this is not hard to state: once we take with full seriousness a doctrine of the fall, and the ruin of humanity, we are forced to accept a (logical, and potentially actual) distinction between what is "normal" and what is "usual" which makes scientific or social-scientific accounts of the origins of sexuality largely uninteresting in ethical discussion.

Most Christian contributions to contemporary Western debates over human sexuality (on both sides of the argument) work with an unstated assumption that a Christian sexual ethic should celebrate, and enshrine, "normal" sexuality. However, we should notice a fundamental ambiguity in the meaning of the word "normal" which is not often recognized. Indeed, it is so elusive that it is even there in the definition offered by the *Oxford English Dictionary*, where 2a (the relevant meaning) reads: "Constituting or conforming to a type or standard; regular, usual, typical; ordinary, conventional."

It seems at least logically possible that something which "conforms to a standard" might be distinctly unusual, and that something which is "usual" might substantially fail to conform to a standard. If this is right, there is a conflation of two different meanings here, which should be distinguished if we want to think clearly. As indicated above, I distinguish between "usual" meaning "(most) commonly occurring" and "normal" meaning

---

3. Grenz, *Welcoming*, 29–31. By "social constructivist" he meant accounts of the origins of same-sex erotic attraction that acknowledged the possibility of latent biological predisposition, and of the effect of upbringing, but which asserted that the cultural context in which these brute facts were negotiated was also crucial. Although slightly anachronistic, I suspect that Grenz would find congenial contemporary accounts of gender as social construction, and also the recent development of queer theory, of which more below.

4. Grenz, *Welcoming*, 33.

"conforming to a standard" (on the basis that the etymology of "normal" seems to imply a connection to a norm, I retain the word for this sense).

Now, we might argue that in a well-ordered ("normal" . . .) world, this distinction would be formal, not real: most or all examples of a given thing would in fact conform to the standard that governs or defines that thing, and so the sets defined by "usual" and "normal" would be coterminous, or at least broadly so, even if differently defined. It happens that the world we live in is not well-ordered: to take an example, it is *normal* for a (British) banker to adhere to a high level of professional ethics; it is not at all clear, given recent news reports, that this has been *usual*, however. (We could make analogous points about politicians, journalists, and—lest I be thought to be sniping at others—academics and church leaders also.)

I further propose that an adequate account of the fall will suggest to us that this situation, where that which is "normal" is far from "usual," and that which is "usual" is far from "normal," is one which we should expect to be, well, usual in ethical debates. Human life, particularly in its ethical dimension, is fundamentally warped and broken; we are unable to discern the good; our physical existence does not indicate the good; and our social practices do not instantiate the good.[5] Given this, claims that "all societies practice male-female monogamy" or "there is a genetic predisposition to exclusive same-sex attraction" or "culture has moved to a common consensus" are largely irrelevant, even if they could be shown to be true. Because of the catastrophe of the fall, human beings have lost sight of what it is to be good—in the area of sexuality, and in every other area—and, also because of the catastrophe of the fall, examination of our own lives, or of the life of creation, will not help us to regain that sight. So the current preoccupation—on every side of the debate, or so it seems—with questions of the origins of human sexualities is a mistake: even if they could be answered exhaustively and satisfactorily (and what question about the origins of a profound human experience has ever been answered like that?), the answer would not advance the ethical discussion very far.

Where, then, do we find an account of the good? The Christian tradition offers us two answers, which are really one: the natural law, or special

---

5. I am acutely conscious that this series of assertions requires significant unpacking. In particular, I would want to explore the difference between Thomist and Calvinist accounts of depravity, and to work at different theological accounts of the construction of public goods in society. I am confident that the position I have adopted and here gestured at is defensible in any (non-Pelagian) theological system, but for the record my own convictions tend to a Calvinist account of depravity and an Augustinian two-cities theology of the state.

revelation. Natural law, we should note, is also a species of revelation,[6] so in either case we discover what is good by attending to the divine revelation of what will be and always should have been both usual and normal for human life, rather than trying to define what is normal through our own psychological or sociological investigations of what is presently usual.

Cultural Constructions of Sexuality

Grenz's other question concerned the cultural prevalence of debates around same-sex erotic attraction in the West currently. The genealogy of contemporary gender politics is fascinating, and too-often ignored in ethical debates. As Grenz points out,[7] "homosexuality" is a very recent coinage, dating from the last decades of the nineteenth century. Academic study of the history of human sexuality since Grenz wrote has emphasized this, and also stressed that "heterosexuality" was invented at about the same time.[8]

We need to be careful here, of course: whilst the assumption that language determines ontology is, or recently has been, fashionable in certain sorts of postmodern philosophy, it cannot be accepted without reflection, and the fact that words were invented at a particular period does not mean that the reality they name was invented at the same time. That said, recent studies on the history of human sexuality, and recent anthropological studies, do both suggest strongly that the idea that most people are erotically attracted to people of one sex only is held only in the late modern West. Historically and globally, reported sexual attraction and behavior offer, essentially, no support at all to the thesis that people may generally be defined as either "heterosexual" or "homosexual."[9]

This evidence is important, but must not be read as invalidating the experience of gay and lesbian—or indeed straight—people in the contemporary West. It is the case that at this point in history across a substantial proportion of the world, most people are erotically attracted to people of one sex only—I include myself in this group. Grenz's recognition of the

---

6. *Dei Verbum* I.6.

7. *Welcoming*, 13–14.

8. Blank, *Straight* is a readable, intelligent, and well-referenced guide to the broader literature on this point.

9. This thesis is accepted without question by virtually all scholars working in the relevant fields—gender studies; anthropology of sexuality; history of sexuality; etc.—as far as I can see from the literature, and is certainly supported by the evidence given in every study I have read; that said, I have not seen it conclusively and compactly demonstrated in a single work; such a work, written to be accessible to scholars outside these specialist fields, would be of great value.

role of our cultural context in the formation of our gender identities is important here, and seems prescient: recent gender studies, and particularly the development of queer theory,[10] have proposed (and also decried) just such an account of the construction of normative genders. The cultural context in which a human being grows up offers certain models of gender performance as acceptable or even praiseworthy; successful enculturation involves, amongst other things, learning to perform gender in one of these culturally-sanctioned ways; in the late-modern West, people are enculturated into—or resist enculturation into—a set of gender identities that include "straight"; "gay"; "lesbian"; and (perhaps) "bisexual."

History and anthropology, however, suggest that this set of gender identities is not universal; famously, ancient Athenian men (of the ruling class) were enculturated into a gender identity that included attraction to both adult women and pubescent boys; early modern European sexual libertinism similarly involved sexual attraction to people of both sexes; many other examples are available in the literature.

The crucial point here, however, is that such enculturation is profoundly powerful. It is not a "choice"; it is not less "hard-wired" into our identity than a genetic predisposition. This might seem a difficult thing to claim from certain philosophical perspectives, in that it suggests that personal identity is, at least in part, determined by enculturation, rather than by some more basic account of the essence of humanity. When we rephrase the question, however—can ontology really be socially constructed?—it is clear that addressed repeatedly, not least by Grenz himself,[11] in contemporary dogmatics: the doctrine of the Trinity, taken as paradigmatic for our accounts of personal identity, has been heard as teaching of three persons who are constituted by their mutual relations; that my identity is in part constituted by my cultural context does not, then, seem difficult to assume.

One of the places where I would want to go beyond Grenz, but where I suspect he might have gone himself had he lived and done further work in this area, is, on this basis, to resist more seriously than he did the standard "conservative" Christian accounts of sexual ethics that try to draw hard lines between identities and acts:[12] if we truly understand the cultural situation in

---

10. The term "queer theory" is recent and remains somewhat contested; I use it to mean a strand of gender studies that begins in Judith Butler's rejection of the theoretical separation of sex and gender, and insistence that gender is performative (see *Gender Trouble*). Gender is thus endlessly malleable; the illusion of stable gender identities ("male"; "female"; "gay"; "straight") is an inherently violent and oppressive mechanism of social control that needs to be resisted—"queered."

11. Grenz, *Social God*.

12. See, e.g., his engagement with Jeffrey Siker, *Welcoming*, 154–56.

which we find ourselves, we have to accept that being gay/lesbian is a matter of human identity, not a matter of performing (or desiring) certain erotic activities. Thomas Aquinas could properly treat (male) homosexual activity as one amongst many species of lust,[13] because culturally, that was how he and his readers experienced it; we experience our sexual desires as identities—gay, lesbian, or straight[14]—and so as something far more profound and basic to our sense of self than merely another experience of desire, whether disordered or not.[15]

Such an analysis, I suggest, helps us to understand various features of the contemporary Christian debate over human sexuality, particularly the differing strengths that traditional arguments seem to have in different cultures. It is rather obvious that the churches of the West are (generally) considerably more hospitable to recognizing same-sex partnerships of some form as a valid option for Christian ethics than the churches of the Global South (generally) are; given, however, that the same arguments are at play, this obvious fact demands explanation. How is it that the same arguments carry different force in different contexts? Logically, of course, this should not happen. We might propose that the Southern churches are more traditionalist than their Western counterparts, and there is probably some truth in this, but it cannot be pressed too far: on ethical questions concerning social and economic justice issues, for instance, the Southern churches are generally far more ready to propose radical solutions than almost anyone in the West.

I suggest that a part of the reason for the culturally-divergent evaluations of the strengths of the same arguments in our current debate is the sort of analysis I have just offered, built on queer theory: traditional Christian ethical arguments concerning human sexuality assume, as Thomas did, that

---

13. ST IIa.IIae Q154, arts. 11–12. In passing, it is worth noting that, although the heading of Art. 12 suggests that Thomas thought homosexual activity to be "the greatest sin among the species of lust," in fact, as he makes clear in resp. obj. 4, "the most grievous is the sin of bestiality, because use of due species is not observed"—that is, copulation with an animal is further from the norm for human sexual activity than any form of human copulation is.

14. Or indeed bi, trans, queer, or asexual. A proper study of gender would no doubt expand this list considerably.

15. If this notion of "identity" is found difficult, one might consider the different reactions to the revelation that a meal in fact contained bacon: from someone who is trying to cut down on his intake of processed meat for health reasons; from a lifelong vegetarian; and from an orthodox Jew. In different ways, in the latter two cases, not eating bacon is an aspect of personal identity. The analogy with sexuality is at best very approximate, but this scenario perhaps offers some illustration of the way the same discrete action—here, eating bacon—can be more or less bound up with experienced and owned identities.

particular experiences of human sexual desire are discrete, and not shaped by a more basic identity; in a cultural context where this is also assumed, the arguments will be found powerful; in one where questions of identity are to the fore, the same traditional arguments will be found difficult or inadequate. The fascinating difference Foucault finds between Greek and Roman adult male erotic attraction to boys might be a helpful analogy here, in that he finds little difference in desire, or its fulfillment, but considerable difference in the moral debate around such desires and activities: in comparing Rome to Greece, he comments "[w]hat seems to have changed is not the taste for boys . . . but the way in which one questioned oneself about it. An obsolescence not of the thing itself, but of the problem; a decline in the interest one took in it; a fading of the importance it was granted in philosophical and moral debate."[16]

For Thomas, and (generally) for the churches of the Global South, because there is no entanglement with personal identity, the question of the moral status of same-sex genital acts is relatively unproblematic; natural law and/or biblical texts define it as a species of lust, and so it is to be dealt with ethically as other species of lust are dealt with.[17] For the churches of the West, whatever formal stance they take concerning the ethics of human sexuality, there is (generally) an awareness, often acute, of the cruelty of imposing ethical norms that conflict with personal identities. If this analysis is approximately correct, it is no surprise that the same logical arguments produce different responses and attitudes in different cultures.[18]

16. Foucault, *Care of the Self*, 189.

17. This is, of course, too simplistic: anthropological study has demonstrated that male same-sex genital activity is in fact culturally inscribed in many (but certainly not all: see Hewlett and Hewlett, "Sex and Searching for Children," 107–25) sub-Saharan African cultures, in a wide variety of different ways. The recently-retired Anglican Archbishop of Uganda, Henry Orombi, has cited one aspect of this as part of his implacable opposition to revisionist theologies of human sexuality. He describes a tradition similar to that Foucault found in the early Roman empire, in which male same-sex intercourse was a mode of imposing and demonstrating control of social inferiors; when in June 1886 a number of page boys of the king of Buganda refused to submit to his sexual advances, because of their new-found Christian faith, they were killed (see Orombi's influential essay, "What is Anglicanism?").

The truth or otherwise of this historical account is not really to the point: Orombi recounts it as a defining narrative of the faith of his people; if it is such, then it becomes a part of the socially-constructed narratives of gender that define them at present, and it is not difficult to understand the Archbishop's point that this makes the imagination of an ecclesial acceptance of same-sex relationships extremely difficult for his people. Of course, exposure to different cultural expressions of same-sex erotic attraction would over time change these attitudes, and lead to different cultural constructions.

18. As I have suggested, modern gender theory would suggest that social constructions of gender must have happened in Thomas's culture also; but if the constructions

Foucault described a gradual decline of interest in the ways in which adult males were sexually attracted to, or at least sexually active with, pubescent males through antiquity, and, as already noted, identified the cause of this decline of interest as, not a decline of the practice, or the desire, but a decline of moral and philosophical interest in the practice and the desire. The reasons for this, as he analyses them,[19] are inevitably complex, and include, for example, deeply political factors (when one's young male partners are slaves and not apprentices of one's own social class, the ethical questions become less pressing); given this, there is certainly no analogy in causal terms between the situation he describes and the reality of the late modern West. That said, we might profitably invert his language to describe our own, acute, problem: we face a massive increase in the interest people take in sexualities in general, and particularly in gay and lesbian sexualities;[20] and so a huge elevation of the importance these questions are granted in philosophical and moral debate.

In the face of such an elevation, it is not a surprise that inherited arguments, which were adequate to carry the weight of responding to a comparatively unimportant issue, are now found inadequate. This does not mean the arguments were wrong—they might have been, but equally, they might have been right but merely underdeveloped. Such an account, I suggest, can make sense of the present strange state of the worldwide Christian ethical argument over human sexuality—and, in making sense, can help indicate ways to improve the conduct of that argument.

Christian Analysis of Human Sexuality

Grenz offered two chapters outlining Christian ethical discussions of human sexuality. The first surveys biblical material, and the ways in which it has been understood; I do not want to spend much of my available space here discussing that question; suffice to say that Grenz's conclusion, "that

---

happened in such a way that there was no entangling of particular experiences of sexual desire with patterns of personal identity, then his ethics had no particular need to pay attention to the social constructions. Equally, it is possible he was unhappily blind to some real problems; I do not know enough about dominant sexualities in medieval Italy and France to decide between these two options.

19. Foucault, *Care*, 189–232.

20. And, to continue to stress the point, notice here that the emphasis is, very deliberately on sexualities—that is, constructed genders—and not on genital activity; our present cultural fascination is with identities, not with narrow erotic practices.

the Biblical writers condemned homosexual conduct, at least as they had come to know it,"[21] seems to me still to stand.

Grenz's second chapter on Christian ethical discussions turns to church teaching. This is a sophisticated theological discussion, exploring how sexuality relates to more central biblical themes—procreation—as well as to "the sex act."[22] He then turns to options for a constructive ethic, first considering "same-sex intercourse," and then "homosexuality"—again making the distinction between act and identity which, as I have indicated, seems both important and difficult.[23] Finally, accepting that there are "homoerotic persons"—something Grenz never questions—he asks what options there are for sexual activity for these people. His answer is uncompromising: chastity.[24]

In common with many writers on human sexuality, Grenz gives little space here[25] to the biblical teaching about marriage. This seems to me unfortunate, for two reasons. First, most of the ethical material concerning human sexuality in the Scriptures in fact deals with marriage (a positive ethic of chastity only really occurs in a couple of texts, most expansively in 1 Cor 7); if we are to find space in a Christian ethic for gay and lesbian relationships, it will probably be by reflecting on this biblical material on marriage.

To develop this point further, contemporary Western legal approaches to the question of lesbian and gay rights seem to be following, broadly, a pattern: same-sex genital activity is first decriminalized; then provision is made for a parallel pattern of relationship to traditional marriage (in the UK, "civil partnership"); then same-sex marriage is proposed and embraced. This middle step, however, is difficult to narrate in terms of Christian ethics: should it be understood as a way of being married, or as a way of being single?[26] Or is it the construction of a third way, a new ethic of human community that was unimagined in biblical times?

21. Grenz, *Welcoming*, 62.
22. Ibid., 102–9.
23. Ibid., 109–25.
24. Ibid., 125–29.
25. He makes many of these points well elsewhere, and indeed asserts that "[A] central concern of this book has been to evaluate same-sex unions by comparison to heterosexual marriage" (*Welcoming*, 150). This is clearly true, and is another instance of Grenz's perceptiveness in dealing with this issue. That said, the claim that the Bible has very little to say about contemporary questions concerning human sexuality is heard so often today that not pausing, at length, in discussing biblical material to point out the focus on marriage seems unfortunate.
26. The question is potentially not as absurd as it might seem. It could very plausibly be argued that, in biblical perspective, marriage is fundamentally oriented to the bearing of children; it is possible then to imagine an argument that suggests that sexual

It is perhaps important to note that, in genealogical perspective, this "third way" argument has been very important in the struggle for LGBTQIA rights. Strikingly, the mainstream pressure group Stonewall UK only began campaigning for equal marriage in late 2010, some time even after mainstream political figures in the UK had declared their support.[27] At the same time Stonewall was careful to reaffirm the "special and unique status" of civil partnerships for gay and lesbian people. The context here is a suspicion, arising out of the historical entanglement of LGBTQIA rights with feminism and the sexual revolution of the 1960s, that—both for women and for gay men and lesbians—marriage was the problem, not the solution; marriage was an inherently patriarchal and homophobic institution that needed to be overcome, not colonized.

That said, these questions about the ethical status of civil partnerships are sufficiently difficult that the most obvious Christian argument in this area must be an attempt to extend our understanding of "marriage" to include same-sex couples; despite its current popularity, the question of whether churches and Christian ministers might "bless" civil partnerships seems to me to be an unhelpful and unhappy one. So I return to the starting point for this brief excursus: in thinking ethically about human sexuality, the biblical material on marriage should be at the forefront of our discussions.

Pastoral Practice and LGBTQIA People

Grenz's final substantive chapter, entitled "Homosexuality and the Church," is another of the sections of the book that I find to be profoundly helpful in its arguments, whatever one may make of specific conclusions. Simply put, Grenz makes the point that there is necessary distance between ethical/theological doctrine and pastoral practice. This is obviously true in every area of life, but curiously often seems to be missed in considering sexuality.

To take the more general point first, the sacramental/liturgical requiring of confession should already say everything necessary: at the core of the life of the church is a sober acceptance that Christian people remain

---

activity that is not open to the bearing of children is licit within certain forms of single life. I do not presently suppose that such an argument would succeed in any Christian ethical discourse of which I am aware, but it cannot be ruled out *a priori*. The student of anthropology could point to many societies where patterns of relationship like this are recognized and accepted. Indeed, Grenz himself discussed in passing the potential to see "same-sex intercourse" as an acceptable activity within "the friendship bond," although he rapidly dismissed it. *Welcoming*, 114–15.

27. See press release http://www.stonewall.org.uk/media/current_releases/4710.asp.

sinners throughout their lives and, although progressively renewed by the Spirit, repeatedly fail to live lives expressive of God's holiness. So Christian pastoral practice is concerned with people—those pastoring, as well as those pastored—whose lives fail to conform to the ethical standards set by the doctrines we confess. There is anger, lust, greed, spiritual apathy, cowardice, and the rest; there are broken promises and imperfect relationships and petty jealousies and rank hypocrisy. None of this is news.

Curiously, however, in the area of human sexuality there seems to be a refusal to accept this fundamental truth—and this seems to me equally observable in more conservative and more liberal churches. Congregations may differ on which sexual practices or arrangements they regard as licit, but there seems to be a pervasive assumption that if one's actions fall within the bounds laid down (formally or informally) within the congregation, then they are beyond ethical critique[28]—and that if one's sexual desires tend towards actions permitted by these bounds, then one desires rightly.

This, bluntly, is Pelagianism, pure and simple.

The horror of Pelagianism, as Augustine saw so clearly, is threefold: it makes Christian holiness a cheap and tawdry thing; it denies God's grace; and, like Donatism, it creates an artificial and inappropriate division in between the righteous and the sinners. A whole and holy human sexuality is not merely about desiring to have sex with only someone you are allowed to have sex with; it is about valuing the magnificent, beautiful, fragile creation of the human body (your own as well as others) and of human emotions in ways that are profoundly expressive of humility and generosity and other Christian virtues. One does not need to have been a Christian pastor for long to know the deep brokenness and distorted desires that exist in perfectly licit relationships. Again, it is very clear that the message heard by many who somehow fall outside the expected norms is that they have failed in some irreparable way—but it is of the essence of the gospel promise that God's gracious forgiveness is never exhausted in this life.

That said, the response to this can never be simply to move the boundaries slightly. If God's grace is not seen to be available to every human person, it cannot be really be seen to be available to any human person. The language of "inclusive church" is currently the rhetoric of choice for those proposing a revisionist sexual ethics in the UK; it works well as rhetoric, but seems to me to miss the point: so-called "inclusive churches" are—visibly— just as excluding of those they regard as sexual sinners; they just define what

---

28. The repeated, and tragic, failure of churches to address questions of domestic abuse adequately is eloquent testimony to this fact: the (heterosexual) marriage is perceived to be a necessarily good relationship, which therefore should be preserved, almost regardless of what is happening in the home.

counts as "sexual sin" in slightly different ways. Inclusion must mean the promise of an unconditional gospel welcome for every sinner, whatever he or she has done—and the expectation that the gospel will transform the life of everyone who comes, and lead them into new understandings and experiences of holiness. While we say "some are welcome and need no change; others need change before they can be welcomed" we have failed very badly.

So a proper Christian pastoral practice in this area, it seems to me, will be profoundly uninterested in the details of owned gender identities, felt orientations, or experienced desires. The offer of baptism is the offer of a new identity—being in Christ—which relativizes, perhaps erases, every other—"straight/heterosexual" just as much[29] as "gay/lesbian/homosexual"; the gift of the Spirit is the promise of a new orientation towards holiness that will eclipse all other orientations—opposite-sex attraction just as much as same-sex attraction; the call to maturity in Christ is a call to discipline every desire, not just some desires, because, east of Eden, every human desire is wayward and warped, and will in some measure remain so until we are made perfect by the resurrection of our bodies.[30]

In Christian pastoral practice, we have developed, in deep reflection on the Scriptures, two very stable vocations which enable people to discipline their desires in the area of human sexuality: marriage and celibacy.[31] Both are deeply ascetic practices,[32] as already indicated, ways we are given to tame and redirect our wayward desiring so that we may, by self-denial and by ordering our actions in ways that do not conform to our desires, learn more and more to desire well, to be conformed by the Holy Spirit to the pattern of Christ.

---

29. I am in fact inclined to argue that, in the contemporary Western church, the various culturally-dominant performances of "heterosexual" genders are more broken, and more in need of redemption, than other culturally recognized gender performances, specifically those named by the components of the LGBTQIA acronym. This argument needs more development than I can give it here, however.

30. Obviously some desires are more wholly inappropriate than others, hence the inclusion of "in some measure" here; it would seem to me a simple, and devastating, failure of theology to conclude that every particular instance of same-sex erotic attraction is necessarily more distorted than every particular instance of opposite-sex erotic attraction, however.

31. I am aware that to describe marriage as "stable" is presently controversial. Culturally, the institution of marriage changes enormously through the centuries, but the meaning given to marriage as a practice of ascesis through the liturgical celebration of the union does not, as far as I can see, vary at all.

32. The deeply ascetic nature of Christian marriage is witnessed to in the Gospels: "His disciples said to him, 'If such is the case of a man with his wife, it is better not to marry'" (Matt 19:10, NRSV).

Of course, in pastoral practice we welcome those who are failing to live according to the best patterns we can offer, and we conform our counsels for better ways to live in some measure to the present felt desires of a particular person, trying to find their best path towards the shared goal of holiness.[33] This will mean that the Christian pastor in the late modern West needs to understand—at a deep, not a facile, level—what it means for a person to say "I am gay/lesbian/straight/transgendered" (and, while that meaning will be somewhat different for each particular person, understanding deeply the cultural categories, the constructed genders, will be a necessary part of coming to particular meanings). None of those categories—including "straight"—are in any way meaningful descriptions of Christian holiness, however.

In this area of human life, as in every other, the church must welcome all; in this area of human life, as in every other, the church can affirm none. This is the straightforward message of the gospel.

Bibliography

Blank, Hanne. *Straight: The Surprisingly Short History of Heterosexuality*. Boston: Beacon, 2012.

Butler, Judith. *Gender Trouble: Feminism and the Subversion of Identity*. New York: Routledge, 1990.

Foucault, Michel. *The Care of the Self: The History of Sexuality, Vol. 3*. Translated Robert Hurley. Harmondsworth, UK: Penguin, 1990.

Hewlett, B. S., and B. L. Hewlett. "Sex and Searching for Children among Aka Foragers and Ngandu Farmers of Central Africa." *African Studies Monographs* 31 (2010) 107–25.

Orombi, Henry. "What is Anglicanism?" *First Things*, August/September 2007. http://www.firstthings.com/article/2007/07/001-what-is-anglicanism-50.

---

33. 1 Cor 7:9.

7

Divine Hospitality and Communion

A Trinitarian Theology of Equality, Justice, and Human Flourishing[1]

VELI-MATTI KÄRKKÄINEN

Introduction: "Trinity Is Our Social Program"—Or Is It?

TESTIMONIES TO THE INDISPENSABILITY and "usefulness" of the doctrine of the Trinity can be easily found in contemporary theology from across the ecumenical spectrum. To the Eastern Orthodox John Zizioulas, "Trinitarian theology has profound existential consequences,"[2] and to the late (United) Reformed Colin Gunton, "much, indeed everything depends on the way that that particular doctrine [of the Trinity] is articulated."[3] The Baptist Millard J. Erickson mentions no less than twelve reasons for the importance of this doctrine, many of them "practical."[4] And so forth. Certainly the late Stanley Grenz believed not only in the indispensability of that doctrine but also everywhere reflected on its implications for communal and personal life. Just consider the title of his widely used textbook *Theology for the Community*

---

1. The present essay is based on my *Trinity and Revelation*, ch. 13.
2. Zizioulas, "Doctrine of God the Trinity," 19.
3. Gunton, *The One, the Three and the Many*, 149.
4. Erickson, *God in Three Persons*, 29.

of God.⁵ Indeed, having used that book of Stan's for years as an integrative introductory text in systematic theology classes, I recall more than one student making a remark like this: "Why is it that with every theological topic we also end up asking what are the implications for the community?"

So it appears that the doctrine of the Trinity "works" in terms of everyday life benefits—at least a good one does. But is it supposed to "work"? Is the doctrine of the Trinity meant to be a tool for liberation and equality? Are we even supposed to inquire into the "practical" implications of the most revered and mysterious article of our faith, the Trinity? Doesn't that kind of inquiry necessarily lead to, so to speak, a *liberation theology "from below"*—a superficial theology of God put in the service of human social needs? No, it does not have to. Indeed, the present essay is not meant to be an exercise in such a "from-below liberationist theology." Let me list some reasons why not.

To begin, the Trinity, in the first place, was never meant to be primarily a model for human relations; it is a statement about God!⁶ Second, as an affluent white European male theologian—living in the entertainment metropolis of the world, the City of Angels in California—I am hardly qualified to speak of liberation of the oppressed! The third reason this essay is not an exercise in a distinctively liberation theology is that I firmly believe that *all* good theology should have a liberationist impulse embedded in its deep structure. Although I applaud the indispensable contributions of *liberation* theologies (from Latin America, Africa, and say, the perspective of women and other marginalized human beings), I also think that only when the motif of liberation at all levels is adopted as an integral theological theme can Christianity be in a place to make a difference in real life.

The final reason this essay is not an exercise in (liberation) theology *"from below"* is that as much as there is correspondence between the divine and human communities, the differences are even more profound. While affirming the turn to communion theology and its implications for inclusivity, relationality, and belonging, contemporary theology also has to exercise healthy self-criticism. The basic concern boils down to this question: how should we imagine the correspondence, or how much can we claim to learn from the "divine society" for the sake of human societies? A basic similarity has to be assumed, if for no other reasons than because humanity exists as *imago Dei*. However, this correspondence, even at its best, is partial and fragmentary for the obvious reasons that whereas the divine life is uncreated

---

5. Grenz, *Social God*.

6. Grenz, *Rediscovering the Triune God*, 130–31; Cunningham, *These Three Are One*, 51–53.

and infinite, the human is not, and whereas the divine life is perfect, the human is not. And so forth. Hence, the saying "The Trinity Is Our Social Program" has to be handled with great care.[7] The Roman Catholic Brazilian Leonardo Boff's approach serves here as a useful model. Unlike most liberationists, he wishes to begin "from above," even when the goal is to develop a socially and politically relevant liberation program: "The Trinity is not something thought out to explain human problems. It is the revelation of God as God is, as Father, Son, and Holy Spirit."[8] Rather than *praxis* being the matrix out of which Trinitarian communion theology emerges and whose well-being it serves, the order must be the reverse.

With these warnings and caveats in mind, let me first review briefly what the talk about God as communion means and how that is related to the notion of hospitality, the source of gifts essential to flourishing human life, whether individual or social. Thereafter, I will attempt three excursions into specific issues—how we could best think of the formation of human communities, questions of justice and equality, and the topic of human flourishing—through the lens of a Trinitarian communion theology of hospitality. Needless to say, this essay is suggestive and exploratory and meant to inspire conversation rather than attempt any last word.

God's Life as Communion and Hospitality

To say that one God exists as Father, Son, and Spirit is to say that there is communion—personal and eternal communion of the three. The turn to a relational understanding of personhood at large has helped rediscover communion theology.[9] The Orthodox John Zizioulas's formative collection of essays with a telling title, *Being as Communion* (1985),[10] has become a clarion call for contemporary theologians. The main thesis of Zizioulas's theology is simple and profound: God is not first "one substance" and only then exists as "trinity"; rather, the "Holy Trinity is a *primordial* ontological concept and not a notion which is added to the divine substance."[11] In other words, "the substance of God, 'God,' has no ontological content, no true

---

7. For an important discussion of the limitations of the correspondence, see Volf, "'The Trinity Is Our Social Program,'" 403–23.

8. Boff, *Trinity and Society*, 3.

9. Grenz, *Social God*, 3–14.

10. Zizioulas, *Being as Communion*; "Human Capacity and Human Incapacity," 401–47.

11. "In the Beginning Is Communion," in Boff, *Trinity and Society*, 9.

being, apart from communion," mutual relationships of love.[12] God's being coincides with God's personhood, which cannot be construed apart from communion.[13] Biblically that is expressed by the idea of God as "love," which is "*constitutive* of His substance, i.e., it is that which makes God what He is, the one God."[14] Hence, God is person as a community of three persons. God's being coincides with God's *communal* personhood. While there are of course varieties of communion theologies on the contemporary scene, the foundational intuition is that, rather than the individual, the ultimate reality is the communion, personhood, belonging, reflecting the life of the triune God.

While communion theology—and the social analogy[15]—has been embraced widely in contemporary theology, not all appropriate it similarly. Whereas Zizioulas as an Orthodox theologian conceives it hierarchically, making the Father the source (*aitia*) of the Trinity,[16] the Reformed Jürgen Moltmann and a number of contemporary female theologians have passionately argued for an equalitarian notion of communion.[17] Several leading women theologians have reminded us that to the notion of communion belong the principles of mutuality and relationality: "God, too, lives from and for another: God the Father gives birth to the Son, breathes forth the Spirit, elects the creature from before all time. . . . God's rule is accomplished by saving and healing love."[18]

Communion theology brings God and world, God and humanity, close to each other. Whether or not you call it panentheism is not the point.[19] The point simply is this: Behind the appreciation of the communion nature of God is the intuition that while distinct, God and world do not represent two totally different realities; they are intertwined. An older static conception of reality is giving way to a more dynamic one in which "categories such as history, process, freedom, and so on, then dynamism, interplay of relationships, and dialectics of mutual inclusiveness make their appearance." In that kind of worldview, the world poses itself as the "receptacle

12. Zizioulas, *Being as Communion*, 17.

13. Zizioulas, "The Teaching of the 2nd Ecumenical Council," 37.

14. Zizioulas, *Being as Communion*, 46 (emphasis in original); "Human Capacity," 410.

15. For a historical look, see Kärkkäinen, *Trinity and Revelation*, ch. 4.

16. Zizioulas, *Being as Communion*, 41; "On Being a Person," 41.

17. Moltmann, *Trinity and the Kingdom of God*, 17–19; 191–92; Johnson, *She Who Is*, 222.

18. LaCugna, *God for Us*, 383; also Baker-Fletcher, *Dancing with God*.

19. Recently I have advocated a new way of conceiving the God-world relationship, namely, in terms of "Classical Panentheism," a combination of Classical Theism and contemporary forms of panentheism. See my *Trinity and Revelation*, ch. 10.

of God's self-communication" and "begins to belong to the history of the triune God."[20] While God remains God and the world remains the world, they are not separate from each other.

Such an intimate communion theology may best capture the infinite hospitality of God. Theology then, following the feminist Letty M. Russell, becomes an exercise in "reframing the idea of hospitality through identifying characteristics of God's gift of welcome."[21] To speak of God is to speak of giving, gift, hospitality. No one else in the history of theology has spoken of this theme as powerfully as Martin Luther. In his profound theology of love, based on the theology of the cross, the Reformer proclaims: "Rather than seeking its own good, the love of God flows forth and bestows good."[22] God's love seeks that which is worthless in itself and donates not only gifts but one's self.[23] At the cross, God's self-giving, the most profound act of hospitality, came to expression.[24] Indeed, according to the Reformer, the divinity of the triune God consists in that "God gives" himself. The essence of God, then, is identical with the essential divine properties in which he gives himself, called the "names" of God: Word, justice, truth, wisdom, love, goodness, eternal life, and so forth. God is, as Luther put it, the "whole beatitude of his saints"; the name of God donates God's goodness, God himself; the spiritual goods are God's gifts in the Christian.[25] The doctrine of the Trinity expresses profoundly this grammar of giving and hospitality: sent by the Father, the Son unites to himself in the power of the Spirit what was separated.

But is this too good to be true? Not without reason is the whole possibility of hospitality and gift questioned by many contemporary thinkers, from the Jewish Emmanuel Levinas to the late French philosopher Jacques Derrida. Well known are the severe reservations of Derrida concerning the gift and hospitality. His *Given Time*[26] is a massive attempt to deconstruct the whole notion of the possibility of gift. The reason is simply this: in our world, there is no way of giving a gift without the expectation of some kind of reciprocity. Derrida demands absolute unconditionality of a true gift and goes so far in his insistence on "unconditional hospitality" that he advises

20. Boff, *Trinity and Society*, 112–13.
21. Russell, *Just Hospitality*, 77; on "reframing," see Lakoff, *Don't Think of the Elephant!*, 15.
22. *Luther's Works* 31:57 (Heidelberg Disputation, thesis #28).
23. Mannermaa, *Kaksi rakkautta*, 9–11.
24. An important discussion of the theme can be found in Newlands and Smith, *Hospitable God*.
25. Martin Luther, *Psalmenvorlesungen* 1513/15 (Ps 1–84), *Weimarer Ausgabe*, 3:454, 4–10; 158, 18–19; 303, 20–26.
26. Derrida, *Given Time*; Dufourmantelle and Derrida, *Of Hospitality*.

us to "say yes to who or what turns up, before any determination, before any anticipation, before any identification,"[27] even if the guest "may be the devil"![28]

Derrida is, of course, right about the fact that in our kind of world—finite and sinful—absolutely unconditional hospitality is impossible for men and women. Derrida's skepticism, however, must be qualified and put in perspective. First, there is a difference between human and divine hospitality and gift-giving. While the former is limited and imperfect, the latter is absolute and possible. Only the divine gift can be a "pure gift."[29] Second, when it comes to human hospitality, only with the coming of the eschatological kingdom it is possible for men and women to participate in hospitality without the limits of the fallen world. Third, granted that in the meantime we have to be content with less than absolute standards for gift and hospitality, it still is far better to give a gift and show hospitality even in an imperfect form than take away from others, be complacent, or just ignore the other. The same "already"–"not-yet" dynamic characterizes all Christian existence.

In an important recent study, *The Hospitable God*, George Newlands and Allen Smith note that "[t]hough we may not find the word 'hospitable' on every page of the doctrinal tradition about God, we suggest that hospitality provides a summative term which may express eloquently affirmations and concerns which lie at the heart of the Christian gospel. Hospitality reflects the understanding of God, and of the shape of service to God and to our fellow human beings, that is central to other major world faiths."[30] Consequently, "Hospitality is not optional for Christians, nor is it limited to those who are specially gifted for it. It is, instead, a necessary practice in the community of faith."[31]

Any talk about hospitality, however, raises the question of whether it "sound[s] dangerously like a particularly comfortable religious title, a coffee table Christianity to soothe away the cares of the actual world in which we live."[32] True, *hospitality* can be easily abused—similarly to *love* and *mercy*—yet in light of biblical revelation, the opposite is the case: "hospitality carries risks," it includes sacrifice, self-giving, discipleship, turning to others.[33] Indeed, in Christian tradition, "it is the hospitality of cross and resurrection.

27. Dufourmantelle and Derrida, *Of Hospitality*, 77.
28. Derrida, "Hospitality, Justice, and Responsibility," 70.
29. See Tanner, *Economy of Grace*, 58, 63.
30. Newlands and Smith, *Hospitable God*, 22.
31. Pohl, *Making Room*, 31.
32. Newlands and Smith, *Hospitable God*, 3–4.
33. Ibid., 4.

It acts often in spite of unpalatable reality. It arises as a protest against rights violations, a hope against hope.... The hospitality of God is dynamic. It invites active human commitment in reciprocal, specific, sensibly executed hospitable action."[34] Letty Russell aptly characterizes some key features of the divine hospitality: "In the Bible, God's welcome—hospitality—has at least four overlapping central components: (1) unexpected divine presence; (2) advocacy for the marginalized; (3) mutual welcome; and (4) creation of community."[35] The radical nature of hospitality is intensified in light of the fact that we live in a world that often is not hospitable.[36]

Hospitality and Community of Equals

Famously, Jürgen Moltmann has juxtaposed what he calls "monotheism," which for him is nothing less than "monarchism,"[37] whether it manifests itself in politics[38] or church life,[39] with Christian Trinitarianism, a theology of communion. In his view, nontrinitarian "monotheism" supports domination and abuse of power, whereas Trinitarian imagination supports equality, fairness, and mutuality.[40] The way to combat the hierarchical and power-laden way of life for Moltmann is to imagine the Trinitarian God as a "community of equals, vulnerable and open to the human suffering, who experiences this suffering in himself."[41] Trinity is not a hierarchical entity, but rather a fellowship of persons: "We understand the scriptures as the testimony to the history of the Trinity's relations of fellowship, which are open to men and women, and open to the world."[42]

Indeed, at the heart of Trinitarian communion theology is the insistence on the Trinity as a dynamic, lively symbol. That approach wishes to replace the derivationist, subordinationist, and hierarchical ways of conceiving the triune God with a relational, equalitarian, and inclusive way, one that is "a relational pattern of mutual giving and receiving."[43] As the mod-

34. Ibid., 9.
35. Russell, *Just Hospitality*, 82.
36. Newlands and Smith, *Hospitable God*, 13. See also Caputo and Scanlon, *God, the Gift and Postmodernism*.
37. Moltmann, *Trinity and the Kingdom*, 191; cp. 130.
38. Ibid., 192–200.
39. Ibid., 200–202.
40. Similarly Boff, *Trinity and Society*, 139–40.
41. Matei, "The Practice of Community in Social Trinitarianism," 217.
42. Moltmann, *Trinity and the Kingdom*, 19; cp. 17–18, 191–92.
43. Johnson, *She Who Is*, 194–97.

erate Roman Catholic Feminist Elizabeth Johnson succinctly puts it, "The symbol of the triune God is the specific Christian shape of monotheism."[44] It speaks of "one God who is not solitary God but a communion of love."[45] For such a discourse, essential values are the following three: First, the symbol of Trinitarian communion speaks of mutual relationality. The triune God can be spoken of with the help of the metaphor of friendship, which is the "most free, the least possessive, the most mutual of relationships, able to cross social barriers in genuine reciprocal regard."[46] Second, the symbol of the triune God speaks of radical equality. The Christian symbol of the Trinity for Johnson bespeaks a community of equals with patterns of differentiation that are nonhierarchical.[47] Third, the symbol of the Trinity speaks of "community in diversity," expressed in classical theology with the term *perichoresis*, a picture of an eternal divine round dance.[48]

An integral communion theology may help overcome the rampant individualism of much of modern theology, particularly in the Global North. The Cuban-born Justo González claims that this is one area in which Euro-American theology needs to be mentored and corrected by the theologies of the Global South, in this case by the Hispanic tradition for which "[t]he best theology is a communal enterprise," as opposed to "Western theology—especially that which takes place in academic circles—[that] has long suffered from an exaggerated individualism. Theologians, like medieval knights, joust with one another, while their peers cheer from the stands where they occupy places of honor and the plebes look at the contest from a distance—if they look at all." Communion theology and theology done by and in the community, in contrast, "will not be a theology of theologians but a theology of the believing and practicing community."[49]

The rampant individualism of much of Western theological tradition is not politically innocent, argues the Uruguayan Jesuit Juan Luis Segundo. According to his analysis, Christian tradition's replacement of the biblical and patristic communion orientation is not only a historical matter, stemming from Greco-Roman and particularly European Enlightenment-based cultures; it is also ideological at its core. The Western cultural emphasis on the "private" underwrites the capitalistic economy with its protection of the individual's rights, particularly economic. In this outlook, God was

---

44. Ibid., 211.
45. Ibid., 222.
46. Ibid., 216–18.
47. Ibid., 219.
48. Ibid., 220.
49. González, *Mañana*, 29–30.

looked to as the "private" *par excellence*. This, in turn, is nothing other than "shift[ing] onto God the features wherewith the individual feels he can find self-fulfillment in a society based on domination."⁵⁰

As mentioned above, the correspondence between the divine communion and human communities is partial and suggestive. But even then, it has to be taken seriously. As Boff succinctly puts it, "Human society is a pointer on the road to the mystery of the Trinity, while the mystery of the Trinity, as we know it from revelation, is a pointer toward social life and its archetype. Human society holds a *vestigium Trinitatis* since the Trinity is 'the divine society.'"⁵¹ This is not to hide the obvious fact that indeed all theological claims—as analogues, metaphors, symbols—derive from human experience and utilize tools available in human cultures. There is no "God's point of view" available to us.⁵² Rather, the methodological caution has everything to do with the danger of making theological doctrine a cheap tool for fixing human problems at the theologian's wish. In this outlook, rather than being a social program, the Trinitarian divine communion serves "as a source of inspiration, as a utopian goal . . . [for] the oppressed in their quest and struggle for integral liberation."⁵³

Systematic theology also has to negotiate carefully and dynamically the complicated question of the hierarchy in the divine life. Christian tradition until recently, and Eastern Orthodox tradition even today, insists on the primacy of the Father and hierarchy.⁵⁴ For Zizioulas, in the Divine Hierarchy, there is reciprocity if not symmetry. Reciprocity means that Spirit and Son are the "presupposition of [the Father's] identity."⁵⁵ On the other side, the Son and Spirit exist only through the Father; the Father is the "ground" of God's being.⁵⁶ Moltmann could not disagree more vehemently. Similarly, most female theologians and other liberationists simply dismiss the whole idea of any kind of hierarchy in the divine communion. Wolfhart Pannenberg steers a middle course that seems most appealing to the current project.

---

50. Slade, "Theological Method of Juan Luis Segundo," 68.

51. Boff, *Trinity and Society*, 119.

52. Ibid., 112.

53. Ibid., 6–7.

54. A main reason for Zizioulas to insist on the primacy of the Father (apart from his desire to align with Christian tradition, particularly that of the Christian East) is his understanding that this is the only way to secure the "personal" basis of the Trinity, as the Father is person. The alternative would be an "ontology of substance," i.e., a nonpersonal basis. Zizioulas, "Teaching of the 2nd Ecumenical Council on the Holy Spirit," 36n18. For commentary see Volf, *After Our Likeness*, 79.

55. Quoted in Volf, *After Our Likeness*, 78.

56. Zizioulas, *Being as Communion*, 89.

On the one hand, he rejects the role of the Father as the "source" of the Trinity, insisting on the mutual—although highly distinct—dependency of each Trinitarian person on others for their deity. On the other hand, in keeping with tradition, he affirms the monarchy, albeit not in a way that would violate the principle of mutuality or subordinate the Son and Spirit.[57] It seems to me this is the most nuanced and theologically most sustainable way of conceiving the dynamic relationality and communion of the Trinitarian life. It also helps systematically negotiate the biblical data, which unabashedly seems to assign to the Father the role of primacy in the godhead. This primacy—monarchy—following Pannenberg, however, does not have to lead to hierarchy nor asymmetrical relations. In this eternal Trinitarian life of love, there is mutual conditioning, respect, and honoring. Diversity is being affirmed in strict unity. Could one imagine anything more appropriate as an inspiration and critique for human relationships and communities?

Hospitality and Advocacy of Justice

In his brilliant and striking manner, the American Robert McAfee Brown notes that in the Bible "justice" appears to be God's middle name![58] Following Russell, we "understand hospitality as the practice of God's welcome, embodied in our actions as we reach across difference to participate with God in bringing justice and healing to our world in crisis."[59] Recall also her note above that among the several features of the divine hospitality is "advocacy for the marginalized."[60] Hospitable constructive theology not only advocates inclusivity and equality, it also makes every effort to actively promote liberation and freedom. While the task of hospitality as advocacy has been, and continues to be, the major focus of liberation theologies of various stripes, it is essential, as mentioned, for the current constructive theology to remind us of the fact that at its core all Christian theology is "liberation theology." As long as liberation is merely an "added thing," an auxiliary element, it can be sought or dismissed—and the theological task continues as it is. However, the gospel means liberation at all levels.[61] The God of the Bible is committed to liberation. "God is God who saves us not

---

57. Pannenberg, *Systematic Theology*, 1:324.
58. Brown, "The 'Preferential Option for the Poor,'" 10. I am indebted to Russell, *Just Hospitality*, 106.
59. Russell, *Just Hospitality*, 2; for an extended discussion of "just hospitality," see ch. 5.
60. Ibid., 82.
61. Boesak, *Farewell to Innocence*, 9.

through his domination but through his suffering. ... And it is thus that the cross acquires its tremendous revelatory potential with respect to God's weakness as an expression of his love for a world come of age."[62]

Although "praxis" *per se* cannot of course be made uncritically the basis for doing theology, neither can it be ignored. Theology does not happen in a vacuum. All theology is contextual in the sense that it is shaped and lived out in a context. From a liberationist perspective, this praxis is not merely the common human experience, but more specifically the human experience and reality of the poor, the despised, the marginalized, those without opportunities. This is the specific "praxis" of theology.[63] The adoption of "praxis" as the point of departure for God-talk does not, of course, mean sidetracking biblical revelation and Christian tradition. Rather, it means an intentional and robust dialectic between critical theological reflection in a specific context and in light of action to address impending needs and challenges.[64]

The African American senior theologian James Cone reminds us that the context of praxis in black theology is the experience of blacks in the United States. Consequently, "Black theology ... [is] the affirmation of black humanity that emancipates black people from white racism, thus providing authentic freedom for both white and black people. It affirms the humanity of white people in that it says NO to the encroachment of white oppression." This is an important affirmation of black praxis as a point of departure into liberative speech about God. However, it has to be qualified and complemented by two critically important points. First, even such a specific point of view as "black experience" is not an unnuanced, generic phenomenon. This black experience may be different for African American *women* than for men. This is what the Womanist theologians argue. Delores S. Williams wishes to replace her male counterparts' focus on Exodus as the paradigmatic narrative of God's liberative work with the Genesis story of Hagar, the dismissed slave woman. Whereas in the Exodus narrative liberation stands in the forefront, in Hagar's story survival is the key; God participates in Hagar's and her child's survival.[65] What is most instructive in the Hagar story—and paradigmatic for black women—is that Hagar is the only person in the Bible attributed with the power of naming God (Gen 16:3). Not that she does not use the designations for God used by Abraham and Sarah, her oppressors, but she also gives God a new name, *El Roi,* "God

---

62. Gutiérrez, *Essential Writings,* 39.
63. Chopp, "Latin American Liberation Theology," 412.
64. On the "hermeneutical circle," Segundo, *Liberation of Theology,* 9.
65. Williams, *Sisters in the Wilderness,* 5.

of seeing."⁶⁶ The main point for this discussion is simply this: The nature and conditions of liberative speech about God vary in different contexts. This is not to pit one discourse of God against others. It is to make room and facilitate diverse, mutually enriching, and specific conversations.

The second qualification for Cone's methodology of beginning from black praxis has to do with the principle of complementary inclusivity, lest the discourse—in this case black speech about God—become exclusive and even violent, as it did with the young Cone.⁶⁷ The limitation of hospitality to only one race, the blacks (or, alternatively, to whites or others), has to be rejected as violence. Hence, the mature Cone's conciliatory and hospitable note of an inclusive nature about paying theological attention to "color" should be affirmed. Utilizing Paul Tillich's concept of the symbolic nature of theological talk, he says, "The focus on blackness does not mean that *only* blacks suffer as victims in a racist society, but that blackness is an ontological symbol and a visible reality which best describes what oppression means in America."⁶⁸ Always conciliatory in his approach, another African American theologian, James H. Evans, maintains that in Black theology God is experienced as impartial, "no respecter of persons" (Acts 10:34). In a world of injustice, African Americans have put their faith in the One who deals justly with them, but not only with them but also with whites.⁶⁹ The expression "inclusive partisanship" of the God of the Bible, utilized by liberationists from various contexts—including female theologians of Hispanic origin⁷⁰ working in the context of emerging *Mujerista* theologies,⁷¹ and theologians from the context of the First Nations of North America⁷²—helps avoid exclusion and foster liberative inclusivity. God's preference for a particular group of people—be it blacks, Hispanics, Asians, or white Europeans—is not meant to exclude others.⁷³

Meaningful and healthy human life requires not only belonging to community but also equality and justice, as well as a sense of self-worth. That kind of life is best described in terms of human flourishing.

---

66. Ibid., 20–27.
67. Cone, *A Black Theology of Liberation*, 111.
68. Ibid., 7.
69. Evans, *We Have Been Believers*, 67–76.
70. Rodríguez, *Racism and God-Talk*.
71. Isasi-Díaz, *En la Lucha [In the Struggle]*.
72. Warrior, "Canaanites, Cowboys and Indians, 261–65.
73. This tendency was evident in Cone's early theology.

Hospitality and Human Flourishing

Cartographing the cultural changes across two millennia, the famed Canadian philosopher Charles Taylor, in *A Secular Age*, makes a sweeping statement: "Every person, and every society, lives with or by some conception(s) of what human flourishing is: what constitutes a fulfilled life? What makes life really worth living? What would we most admire people for?"[74] During the past five hundred years, the overall framework for such reflection has dramatically changed as there are two main options, radically different from each other: religion or what Taylor calls "exclusive humanism." These two frameworks articulate the quest for human flourishing in totally different ways:

> Does the highest, the best life involve our seeking, or acknowledging, or serving a good which is beyond, in the sense of independent of human flourishing? In which case, the highest, most real, authentic or adequate human flourishing could include our aiming (also) in our range of final goals at something other than human flourishing. . . . It's clear that in the Judaeo-Christian religious tradition the answer to this question is affirmative. Loving, worshiping God is the ultimate end. Of course, in this tradition God is seen as willing human flourishing, but devotion to God is not seen as contingent on this. The injunction "Thy will be done" isn't equivalent to "Let humans flourish," even though we know that God wills human flourishing.[75]

The senior American theologian David H. Kelsey rightly notes, "Christian theology has a large stake in making it clear that its affirmations about God and God's ways of relating to human beings underwrite human beings' flourishing." Not only outspoken atheists and critics of religion but also many popular mindsets of the contemporary world share the "widespread and deep suspicion that Christians magnify God and God's power and dominion by systematically minimizing human beings, making them small, weak, and servile—anything but flourishing." Hence, the "challenge to Christian theology has been to develop conceptual and argumentative strategies by which to show that, properly understood, human flourishing is inseparable from God's active relating to human creatures such that their flourishing is always dependent upon God."[76]

---

74. Taylor, *A Secular Age*, 16.
75. Ibid., 16–17.
76. Kelsey, "On Human Flourishing," 1.

Mindfulness of the importance of human flourishing, however, should not lead us to replace the theological concept of "salvation" with mere "flourishing,"[77] as the late British, feminist philosopher-theologian Grace Jantzen wants to do. There are two problems here. First, as argued above, to make religion (or God) a function of serving human needs is a failing enterprise; ultimately, it ends up serving neither humanity nor the cultivation of genuine religiosity. Second, and more importantly for this discussion, it can be argued that salvation and flourishing are rather an integral part of the one pluriform, holistic Christian vision, namely, hope for the life to come and a fulfilling, meaningful life on this earth. Not only "flourishing," as Jantzen one-sidedly claims,[78] but also the Christian holistic vision of salvation includes both physical and spiritual, earthly and mental, this-worldly and otherworldly dimensions.

True, in Christian tradition—as well as in other religious traditions (and perhaps, differently, even in secular utopias)—there are plenty of instances in which the idea of flourishing in this life has been lost because of concentrating merely on hope for the life to come. But how many contemporary theologians are there who would consider that kind of "eschatology" genuine and balanced *Christian* hope? On the other hand, in the final analysis, the power of the classical Christian hope for this life is grounded in the coming eschatological redemption and new creation wrought by the same faithful and loving God who is also the Creator and Provider. If religion were merely a matter of flourishing in this life, even the most flourishing life would not have any lasting significance, particularly when put in the vast cosmic perspective in which human life, as a "last minute" phenomenon in the almost fifteen-billion-year history of the universe's evolution, is an utterly tiny and insignificant thing. Similarly, following the logic of the outdated and rejected Classical Liberal Quest, Jantzen[79] also seems to make Jesus merely a fine example of life lived to its fullest, without any notion of sin and need for salvation, which seems to the systematic theologian an utterly naive and unnuanced claim.

What kind of view of God supports and underwrites the goal of human flourishing? It is *theologically* "Christocentric," Kelsey explains,

> in the sense that it is in large part generated out of, and governed by, reflection on implications concerning God of Christian claims that the God who relates to created human beings also relates to them to draw them to eschatological consummation

---

77. Jantzen, *Becoming Divine*, 160–61.
78. Ibid., 166–67.
79. Jantzen, *Becoming Divine*, 162–63.

and, when they are estranged from God, to reconcile them to God, by giving them Godself in an exceedingly odd way, namely, in the concrete personal life and particular personal identity of Jesus of Nazareth.[80]

Robustly Trinitarian theology adds to that the presence of the ever-present, life-giving, life-supporting, and energizing Spirit of God. What is there in this classical picture of the Christian God that would frustrate human flourishing, one should ask? On the contrary, there is much that bespeaks flourishing; that much can be said without making the doctrine of God a cheap function of human interests. If human beings are creatures of God, then where else could they find the fulfillment of their deepest desires? The divine hospitality alone can deliver the promise.

It is highly significant that it is in his study *The Trinity*, dealing with the doctrine of God, that St. Augustine penned these famous words: "God is the only source to be found of any good things, but especially of those which make a man good and those which will make him happy; only from him do they come into a man and attach themselves to a man."[81]

A Closing Word

A few years before his untimely passing away, Stan Grenz articulated wonderfully the meaning of the doctrine of the Trinity in relation to faith and human life:

> Stating the matter simply, "community" is central to my theological thinking because I am convinced that it is both at the heart of the biblical narrative and speaks clearly to the contemporary context. More specifically, I would add that community is crucial because it arises out of the very essence of God. At the heart of Christian theology is the doctrine of the Trinity, which declares that God is not only the one who enters into relationship with creation, and hence relates to us in time. Rather, God is internally relational within the Godhead, and hence eternally relational. Moreover, the Christian teaching declares that God is a trinity, rather than merely a binity; God is three-in-one. This suggests that mere one-to-one relationality does not exhaust the essence of God. Instead, the one God of the Bible is the fellowship of Father, Son, and Holy Spirit, to cite the traditional

---

80. Kelsey, "On Human Flourishing," 3–4.
81. Augustine, *On the Trinity* 13.10, cited in Volf, "Human Flourishing," 4.

Trinitarian terminology. In short, the God revealed in Jesus is communal, or community.[82]

Ascending "from below," as it were, from the signs of the gracious presence of the triune God in the economy of salvation to glimpses into the nature and "personhood" of the one God—Father, Son, Spirit—yields indeed a beautiful picture of community, relationality, equality. Name it Gift or Love or—as often done nowadays—Hospitality, it all speaks of the infinite fountain of goodness. God the Giver is also the divine gift.

Theology—thinking after God—at its best, therefore, may become an act of hospitality, giving and receiving gifts, reflecting the Christian vision of the triune God as the Giver and Sustainer of Life. The basic Greek verb *didomi* appears over 400 times in the New Testament. It is used of both human and divine giving, and it encompasses all levels from the most concrete to the most abstract.[83] The Finnish ecumenist Risto Saarinen aptly notes, "In religious life, giving can also be portrayed as divine action. God is the supreme giver, whereas human persons remain receivers."[84]

For the constructive theologian in search of such a vision of hospitality, the word of advice from Moltmann is in order: it is a call to "the fellowship of mutual participation and unifying sympathy," looking for a "free community of men and women, without privilege and without discrimination ... the earthly body of truth." According to Moltmann, "Christian theology would wither and die if it did not continually stand in a dialogue like this, and if it were not bound up with a fellowship that seeks this dialogue, needs it and continually pursues it."[85] That kind of hospitable dialogical pursuit of truth reflects—albeit dimly and in a less than perfect way—the nature of the Divine Truth.

Bibliography

Baker-Fletcher, Karen. *Dancing with God: The Trinity from a Womanist Perspective*. St. Louis: Chalice, 2006.

Boesak, Allen. *Farewell to Innocence: A Socio-Ethical Study on Black Theology and Black Power*. Maryknoll, NY: Orbis, 1977.

Boff, Leonardo. *Trinity and Society*. Translated Paul Burns. Maryknoll, NY: Orbis, 1988.

---

82. "Community and Relationships," interview with Grenz.
83. Saarinen, *God and Gift*, 36–45.
84. Ibid., 1.
85. Moltmann, *Trinity and the Kingdom*, xii–xiii (emphasis in original).

Brown, Robert McAfee. "The 'Preferential Option for the Poor' and the Renewal of Faith." In *Churches in Struggle: Liberation Theologies and Social Change in North America*, edited by William K. Tabb, 7–17. New York: Monthly Review, 1986.

Caputo, John, and Michael Scanlon, eds. *God, the Gift and Postmodernism*. Bloomington, IN: Indiana University Press, 1999.

Chopp, Rebecca S. "Latin American Liberation Theology." In *The Modern Theologians*, edited by David F. Ford, 409–25. Oxford: Blackwell, 1997.

Cone, James H. *A Black Theology of Liberation*. 2nd ed. Twentieth Anniversary Edition. Maryknoll, NY: Orbis, 1986.

Cunningham, David S. *These Three Are One: The Practice of Trinitarian Theology*. Oxford: Blackwell, 1998.

Derrida, Jacques. *Given Time: 1. Counterfeit Money*. Translated by Peggy Kamuf. Chicago: University of Chicago Press, 1995.

———. "Hospitality, Justice, and Responsibility: A Dialogue with Jacques Derrida." In *Questioning Ethics: Contemporary Debates in Philosophy*, edited by Richard Kearney and Mark Dooley, 65–83. London: Routledge, 1999.

Dufourmantelle, Anne, and Jacques Derrida. *Of Hospitality*. Translated by Rachel Bowlby. Stanford: Stanford University Press, 2000.

Erickson, Millard J. *God in Three Persons: A Contemporary Interpretation of the Trinity*. Grand Rapids: Baker, 1995.

Evans, James H. *We Have Been Believers: An African-American Systematic Theology*. Minneapolis: Fortress, 1992.

González, Justo L. *Mañana: Christian Theology from a Hispanic Perspective*. Nashville: Abingdon, 1990.

Gunton, Colin E. *The One, the Three and the Many: God, Creation and the Culture of Modernity*. Cambridge: Cambridge University Press, 1993.

Gutiérrez, Gustavo. *Essential Writings*, edited by James B. Nicholoff. Minneapolis: Fortress, 1996.

Isasi-Díaz, Ada María. *En la Lucha [In the Struggle]: A Hispanic Women's Liberation Theology*. Minneapolis: Fortress, 1993.

Jantzen, Grace. *Becoming Divine: Towards a Feminist Philosophy of Religion*. Indianapolis: Indiana University Press, 1999.

Johnson, Elizabeth A. *She Who Is: The Mystery of God in Feminist Theological Discourse*. New York: Crossroad, 1992.

Kärkkäinen, Veli-Matti. *The Trinity: Global Perspectives*. Louisville: Westminster John Knox, 2007.

———. *Trinity and Revelation, Constructive Christian Theology for the Pluralistic World*, Vol. 2. Grand Rapids: Eerdmans, 2014.

Kelsey, David H. "On Human Flourishing: A Theocentric Perspective." Yale Center for Faith and Culture Resources, n.d. http://www.yale.edu/faith/downloads/David%20Kelsey%20%20-%20God%27s%20Power%20and%20Human%20Flourishing%202008.pdf.

LaCugna, Catherine Mowry. *God for Us: The Trinity and Christian Life*. San Francisco: Harper/Collins, 1991.

Lakoff, George. *Don't Think of the Elephant!* White River Junction, VT: Chelsea Green, 2004.

Mannermaa, Tuomo. *Kaksi rakkautta: Johdatus Lutherin uskonmaailmaan*, 2 painos. Helsinki: Suomen Teologisen Kirjallisuusseura, 1995.

Matei, Eugen. "The Practice of Community in Social Trinitarianism: A Theological Evaluation with Reference to Dimitru Staniloae and Jürgen Moltmann." Ph.D. diss., Fuller Theological Seminary, 2004.

Moltmann, Jürgen. *The Trinity and the Kingdom: The Doctrine of God.* Minneapolis: Fortress, 1993.

Newlands, George, and Allen Smith. *Hospitable God: The Transformative Dream.* Surrey, UK: Ashgate, 2010.

Pannenberg, Wolfhart *Systematic Theology,* Vol. 1. Translated by Geoffrey W. Bromiley. Grand Rapids: Eerdmans, 1991.

Pohl, Christine D. *Making Room: Recovering Hospitality as a Christian Tradition.* Grand Rapids: Eerdmans, 1999.

Rodríguez, Rubén Rosario. *Racism and God-Talk: A Latino/a Perspective.* New York: New York University Press, 2008.

Russell, Letty M. *Just Hospitality: God's Welcome in a World of Difference.* Louisville: Westminster John Knox, 2009.

Saarinen, Risto. *God and Gift: An Ecumenical Theology of Giving.* Collegeville, MN: Liturgical, 2005.

Segundo, Juan Luis. *The Liberation of Theology.* Maryknoll, NY: Orbis, 1976.

Slade, Stanley David. "The Theological Method of Juan Luis Segundo." Ph.D. diss., Fuller Theological Seminary, 1979.

Tanner, Kathryn. *Economy of Grace.* Minneapolis: Fortress, 2005.

Taylor, Charles. *A Secular Age.* Cambridge: Harvard University Press, 2007.

Volf, Miroslav. *After Our Likeness: The Church as the Image of the Trinity.* Grand Rapids: Eerdmans, 1998.

———. "Human Flourishing." Presentation at the Institute for Theological Inquiry, n.d. http://www.yale.edu/faith/jewishchristianconference/documents/Miroslav_Volf.pdf (accessed 6 January 2013).

———. "'The Trinity Is Our Social Program': The Doctrine of the Trinity and the Shape of Social Engagement." *Modern Theology* 14/3 (1998) 403–23.

Warrior, Robert Allan. "Canaanites, Cowboys and Indians: Deliverance, Conquest and Liberation Theology Today." *Christianity and Crisis* 49/12 (11 September 1989) 261–65.

Williams, Delores S. *Sisters in the Wilderness: The Challenge of Womanist God-Talk.* Maryknoll, NY: Orbis, 1993.

Zizioulas, John D. *Being as Communion: Studies in the Personhood and Church.* Crestwood, NY: St. Vladimir's Seminary Press, 1985.

———. "The Doctrine of God the Trinity Today: Suggestions for an Ecumenical Study." In *The Forgotten Trinity 3: A Selection of Papers Presented to the British Council of Churches Study Commission on Trinitarian Doctrine Today,* edited by Alasdair I. C. Heron, 19–32. London: British Council of Churches, 1991.

———. "Human Capacity and Human Incapacity: A Theological Exploration of Personhood." *Scottish Journal of Theology* 28/5 (1975) 401–47.

———. "On Being a Person: Towards an Ontology of Personhood." In *Persons, Divine and Human,* edited by Christoph Schwöbel and Colin E. Gunton, 33–46. Edinburgh: T. & T. Clark, 1991.

———. "The Teaching of the 2nd Ecumenical Council on the Holy Spirit in Historical and Ecumenical Perspective." In *Credo in Spiritum Sanctum: Atti del congresso teologico internazionale di pneumatologia*, edited by José Saraiva Martins, 29–54. Vatican: Liberia Editrice Vaticana, 1983.

Part Three

ESCHATOLOGY

8

Aesthetics of the Kingdom

Apocalypsis, Eschatos, and Vision for Christian Mission

JONATHAN R. WILSON

SINCE NOVEMBER 2012, MY Friday evenings have gone something like this. I gather with friends for evening prayer and a quiet meal. Then around 8:30 I board a bus that takes me through Vancouver's downtown eastside (DTES), sometimes labeled the poorest neighborhood in North America. I travel through the DTES to the downtown core of Vancouver, where I walk and pray for two hours or so. My walk encompasses the blocks in proximity to an expensive, exclusive strip club, and weaves through the financial district of Vancouver. The strip club is on the second floor of a five-story building. The financial district is marked by towering (well, by modest towers—we are Canadian) phallic symbols of power and prosperity with names displayed in glowing signs.

As I have walked and prayed on these Friday evenings, I have begun to see this district with very different eyes. Indeed, for the first several weeks that I walked and prayed, I would not have described the district as I did above. I simply committed myself to this practice in response to a call from God. As I have walked and prayed, I have begun to envision the humiliation of the proud towers of financial success and the dissolution of the walls of the strip club, exposing its bondage and liberating the women who are held captive by covert and overt violence. For me, this is an unexpected and unsought vision of God's judgment on the intertwining principalities and powers that dominate our world and destroy the goodness of life.

These prayers and visions coincide with my deeper reading of works on NT apocalyptic and the works of some theologians who are assimilating NT apocalyptic and extending it into the mission of God's people today.[1] The mutual illumination of these two practices—prayer and reading apocalyptic theology—leads me to a stronger and more sure foundation for the ministry and mission of God's people, especially in places where the principalities and powers that would crush and destroy life are so well-established.

In order to bring the resources of apocalyptic to bear on the mission and ministry of God's people, I will first address the problem of the distorted apocalypticism that especially marks so much of American Christianity and affects Christianity everywhere. Then I will "rehabilitate" apocalyptic—but watch for a twist here—and eschatological ways of seeing the world and engaging in mission. After this, I will support my proposal by testing the "apocalyptic vision" that follows from the proposal. Finally, I will bring this proposal and vision back onto the streets of Vancouver to find cracks in the concrete where the gospel can take root and faithful discipleship to Jesus Christ may be nourished and flourish.

The Renewal of Apocalyptic

To propose that "apocalyptic" is a resource for the ministry and mission of the church will strike many people as theological insanity, or, at best, foolishness. Various forms of apocalypticism, especially in American Christianity but also in other parts of the world, have been sources of end-times fever, date-setting, and withdrawal from public life to await the return of Christ and the end of the world. Surely apocalyptic thinking diverts the people of God from our mission in the world and turns discipleship into a passive indolence brought on by an end-times fever.

Alternatively, apocalypticism locates the work of God in "the American empire"—its military power, and its sacred mission to extend democracy

---

1. Recent work in apocalyptic has produced a lot of material. For surveys, see O'Regan, *Theology and the Spaces of Apocalyptic*, and Congdon, "Eschatologizing Apocalyptic," in Davis and Harink, *Apocalyptic and the Future of Theology*, 118–36, and his blog entry http://fireandrose.blogspot.ca/2013/01/two-apocalyptic-families-modest-proposal.html (accessed 23 Mar. 2013). See also his link to Fleming Rutledge's proposal in Davis and Harink, *Apocalyptic*.

around the world through the exercise of empire.[2] When apocalypticism takes this form, the mission of the church is co-opted by or, quite often, surrendered to the nation-state as surrogate for principalities and powers. How, then, could apocalyptic be a resource for the mission and ministry of the church? Is not apocalyptic so captive to these distortions that it is utterly incapable of being a resource for ministry and mission? This judgment of the dangers and emptiness of apocalyptic come readily to those who recognize Christ's call to discipleship in the Sermon on the Mount and locate the mission and ministry of God's people in such passages as Luke 4:16–21.

The first step toward "rehabilitating" apocalyptic Scripture and theology is to realize that the very things that are most co-opted and corrupted may be the very things that are most important to God's people in identifying, understanding, and being faithful to our mission. That is, if this particular place is where the enemy is sowing confusion and corruption, then it may be the very place for us to look more closely.[3] The abuse and misuse of apocalyptic calls us to look more closely at Scripture to see what is being obscured by the apocalypticism of doom-sayers and date-setters.

As developed by scholars such as J. Christian Beker, J. Louis Martyn, Joel Marcus, Christopher Morse, John Howard Yoder, Fleming Rutledge, Douglas Campbell, and Douglas Harink, apocalyptic theology powerfully illuminates of God's mission in the world.[4] In their hands, apocalyptic teaches us the conflict between the kingdom of God and the fallen principalities and powers, between the kingdoms of light and darkness; in short, apocalyptic reveals the conflict between life and death that is taking place every moment in every space of the cosmos. Apocalyptic rips away the cover-up that allows us to go on our way as if nothing of significance is happening. Apocalyptic exposes the true conflict that takes place within, above, under, and around all the conflicts that seem merely to be conflicts between the forces of this age—corporations, nations, ideologies, religions, people. These conflicts are real, but apocalyptic teaches us the deepest reality of these conflicts: a cosmic battle between life and death.

This leads us to the second step—the crucial step in "rehabilitating" apocalyptic: realizing that the one apocalypse, the one revelation of this conflict, the one exposure of the fallen principalities and powers, the final

---

2. Northcott, *An Angel Directs the Storm*.

3. This is not to say that the only places to look more closely are those where we see confusion and corruption. The enemy is also successful when we neglect portions of God's teaching.

4. See essays in Davis and Harink, *Apocalyptic and the Future of Theology*. There is still much work to be done. In particular, this recent work needs to be extended beyond Paul to the OT and to Jesus.

battle between life and death, is *Jesus Christ*. Here is Douglas Harink's brilliant and oft-quoted proclamation:

> all apocalyptic reflection and hope comes to this, that God has acted critically, decisively, and finally for Israel, all the peoples of the earth, and the entire cosmos, in the life, death, resurrection and coming again of Jesus Christ, in such a way that God's purpose for Israel, all humanity, and all creation is critically decisively, and finally disclosed and effected in the history of Jesus Christ.[5]

When confronted with this proclamation of the good news of Jesus Christ, we begin to see that it is not apocalyptic but *we* who need "rehabilitation."

Apocalyptic Vision

Our rehabilitation begins by first confessing that we all too often keep something in reserve even when we proclaim Christ's lordship and declare ourselves to be his disciples. Even as we proclaim and declare these truths, we depend, overtly and covertly, on other powers—economic, political, managerial, ideological—for making our way in the world under the supposed lordship of Christ. Apocalyptic theology is "theology without reserve."[6] A theology without reserve leaves no space for any power in addition to or alongside of God's work in Jesus Christ. This is most stringently and clearly argued by Paul in his letter to the Galatians, where his concern is not the conflict between human faith and works, but between God's apocalyptic action in Jesus Christ and all other claims about God's action. Drawing on the work of Beverly Roberts Gaventa and J. Louis Martyn, Harink writes that

> in Galatians Paul is concerned to affirm "the singularity of the gospel"—that God's relationship to and purpose for the nations and all creation is exclusively determined by and through God's cosmic-eschatological-healing in the cross and resurrection of Jesus Christ and the outpouring of the Holy Spirit. For this reason, and this alone, any other cosmic principle . . . is ruled out as constituting and determining God's relationship with the cosmos and humanity.[7]

---

5. Harink, *Paul among the Postliberals*, 68.

6. Lowe, "Prospects for a Postmodern Christian Theology," in Davis and Harink, *Apocalyptic*.

7. Harink, *Paul among the Postliberals*, 71–72. The internal quote is from Beverly

This and other descriptions of this apocalyptic theology may seem a bit too, well, apocalyptic for readers who are new to this conversation or have not worked through the biblical and theological expositions. But the arguments and expositions are sound.[8]

"The singularity of the gospel" must not be mistaken for christocentrism.[9] Rather, the apocalypse of Jesus Christ is the triumph of God. Thus, rather than a christocentrism, apocalyptic theology advances a theocentrism that must be radically Trinitarian.[10] We may advance this radical Trinitarian theocentrism in three ways. First, the radical Trinitarian theocentric apocalypse of Jesus Christ teaches us that the gospel is the work of God. This may sound commonplace and obvious. But it is not. Paul's letter to the Galatians confronts the very concrete reality of a people who call themselves Christians but who seek to add to what God has done in Christ to assure their participation in the new covenant and consequently their salvation. These additions make "another gospel" (Gal 1:6–9), one that proclaims "Jesus *and* . . . ." In the case of the Galatians, this other gospel is Jesus *and* the works of the law. But the "and" takes many different forms throughout history and in our lives and mission. For apocalyptic theology, the new creation, which is the good news of Jesus Christ, is God's work wholly, from beginning to end.[11] In Jesus Christ, that new creation has apocalypsed the cosmic conflict between life and death. The question for us is simply the question of our participation in that apocalypse and the shape of that participation. (I ask my readers' patience with and submission to my strange use of "apocalypse." Following others who write on this topic, I adopt this unfamiliar usage precisely to drive home the shock, the rupture, the newness, irrupting in the world through Jesus Christ.)

Roberts Gaventa (see ibid., 71 n. 9).

8. It might be helpful for me to note that this particular conversation has simply revitalized attention to this kind of apocalyptic theology. There have been periodic resurgences of this kind of apocalyptic theology throughout the twentieth century and now in the twenty-first. By writing "this kind of apocalyptic theology," I mean to distinguish it from the "apocalypticism" of doom-sayers and date-setters, who are always with us.

9. Beker, *Paul's Apocalyptic Gospel*, 32–34.

10. At this point, there needs to be a continuing confluence of biblical studies and theology on apocalyptic that mutually illuminate and strengthen one another. Biblical studies has been strong on theocentrism but weak on *Trinitarian* theocentrism. Theology seems to have not known what to do with apocalyptic and at times has perhaps over-compensated by being christocentric. The new confluence of biblical studies and theology in apocalyptic is beginning to show us the way to profess the singularity of the gospel in a radical Trinitarian theocentrism. (It is "radical" in being Trinitarian to its roots.)

11. Later we will consider two dangers that arise out of this apocalyptic without reserve: passivity and exclusivity.

PART THREE—ESCHATOLOGY

Second, apocalyptic theology teaches us that the conflict between life and death has been decisively fought in the incarnation, life, death, resurrection, ascension, and coming again of Jesus Christ. In another place we might take the space to open each of these according to the insights of apocalyptic theology. Here I will simply note that, taken as a whole, the actualities of Jesus Christ listed just above are the climactic engagement of God with the final enemy, death, and all of death's servants. Jesus Christ did not come to teach us a few things, show us a better way to live, embarrass the rich and powerful, encourage the poor and needy. *Jesus came to die.* Hans Urs von Balthasar says it this way: "One can meaningfully put the question in a Christian way. Did the Son of God become man in order to act or to die? Many church fathers—for example, Tertullian, Gregory of Nyssa, Leo the Great—have unhesitatingly answered: he was born in order to be able to die."[12] Balthasar endorses this answer as well.

In these teachers of the church and many others, the crucifixion of Jesus apocalypses the cosmic conflict between life and death. Here, in the crucifixion of the one human who is not subject to death, we see the wrongness of death, its misrule of the world, its opposition to God and thus to life. Jesus was not subject to death, but in his free willingness to endure death he exposes the impotence of death. Fear of death is one of the weapons of death by which death rules over us and defeats us. By Jesus' willingness to undergo a death that was "unnecessary," he apocalypses the actuality that death does not have the final word. The actuality of the resurrection of Jesus reveals and confirms the truth of his death as the exposure, the public humiliation of the impotence of death.

In light of Jesus' crucifixion and resurrection, we may now see that what he taught, how he lived, his conflict with the rich and powerful and liberation of the poor and needy, are instances of this cosmic conflict with the power of death and death's servants. He was born not to act but to die. However, his "dying" marked his entire life—what he taught, how he lived, his conflicts and his invitations.

But may we perhaps take one more step? He was born to die—and to live. The coming of Jesus apocalypses the fundamental, cosmic battle between life and death. That battle climaxes with the death of Jesus. And then life goes on. Jesus' resurrection is the shocking irruption of life in the midst of death.[13] However, it is shocking only because death seems to be the

---

12. Balthasar, *Life Out of Death*, 25. I am indebted to Soohwan Park for directing me to this little gem by Balthasar.

13. My use of the language of "irruption" here and throughout this paper is not an indication of any metaphysical dualism. Indeed, apocalyptic, understood as shorthand for Jesus the Messiah, acknowledges no dualism. Yes, there is a cosmic conflict that

inevitable, unavoidable finality. Jesus' resurrection, shocking in the midst of death, is actually and simply the "natural" and inevitable telos of life with God. Life not death is the "final" word. Life not death is the telos of God's creation. John Howard Yoder unleashes this actuality when he announces,

> the point that apocalyptic makes is not only that people who wear crowns and who claim to foster justice by the sword are not as strong as they think. . . . It is that people who bear crosses are working with the grain of the universe. One does not come to that belief by reducing social processes to mechanical and statistical models, nor by winning some of one's battles for the control of one's corner of the fallen world. One comes to it by sharing the life of those who sing about the Resurrection of the slain Lamb.[14]

Thus, apocalyptic is not a rupturing of God's work of creation but a rather an irruption of God's life in the midst of a fallen world ruled by death. This irruption is for the healing of people and the redemption of creation. To follow Jesus in the way of the cross is to follow Jesus to life by participation in the work of the Father, Son, and Spirit. This account of the apocalypse of Jesus the Messiah depends upon an indispensable Trinitarian grammar, because the event to which it witnesses is an act of the one God: Father, Son, and Spirit.[15]

After we ourselves have been "rehabilitated" by apocalyptic, another step may be taken—discovering that apocalyptic and eschatological need not be antipathetic. Indeed, *apocalypsis* and *eschatos* must be sympathetic because both ultimately refer to God's triumph in Jesus Christ. We have already noted that "apocalypse" is really shorthand for "Jesus Christ." Now, receive these words from G. B. Caird:

> The end is not an event but a person. In much that has been written during the last thirty years on the subject of eschatology the debate has turned on the nature of the *eschaton*, the

---

pervades all of life. But the apocalypse of the Messiah enacts and proclaims the actuality of only one Lord, one living God: Father, Son, and Spirit. Thus, the only "irruption" is the irruption of life in the midst of death, and the various images that may be used to proclaim this irruption. I am grateful to Sam Adams, Director of Graduate Studies at the Kiln's College, Bend, OR, for the basic insight into the nature of "irruption" in apocalyptic thought.

14. Yoder, "Armaments and Eschatology," 58.

15. See my further development of this in *God's Good World*, ch. 5, and *God So Loved the World*. I am writing a new Christology book in which this Trinitarian grammar of God's act in Jesus Christ will be prominent, tentatively titled, *Jesus Christ, Life of the World*.

final event, and whether this *eschaton* can be properly said to have entered history in the person of Jesus Christ. But the word *eschaton* (neut.) does not occur in the New Testament. John knows only of the *eschatos* (masc.), a person who is both *the beginning and the end*.[16]

Since *apocalypsis* and *eschatos* proclaim Jesus Christ, we must reconsider how to relate these two terms as witnesses to Jesus. To do so fully is beyond the scope of this essay.[17] However, we may begin the process by recognizing that we have often set them against one another by regarding apocalyptic, on the one hand, as a sudden irruption for which there is no preparation, no continuity with preceding events, and no way of discerning an approaching apocalypse. On the other hand, we have often regarded eschatology as a movement of God in history that has some continuity with preceding events, that may be revealed by signs of progress, and that is foretold by events presaging the approaching "eschaton" (remember Caird). We might say roughly that we often place apocalyptic on a vertical axis while placing eschatology on a horizontal axis.

There is something to this common placing of apocalyptic and eschatology, but we must first identify what is wrong in the way that we so often do this. We go wrong in the way that we place eschatology on a horizontal axis when we teach that God's work *progresses* in history. From our experience of time, it seems to us that history "progressed" to the time of the coming of the Messiah, that gradually God unfolded God's plan and put everything in place for the birth of the Messiah. This is a common reading of history eschatologically.[18] However, what apocalyptic discloses is that up to the coming of the Messiah, the world is in bondage: "Bondage to the powers of Sin, Disobedience, Injustice, and Death. Every character in this history has been "handed over" to these powers *by God* (only here may we speak of God's "plan"), kept in prison under them, until the singular event of God's own invasive and liberating act in the crucifixion and resurrection of Jesus and the coming of the Holy Spirit."[19] Through the coming of the Messiah, there is now a new reality: new creation.

This new creation is the actual breaking of the bondage, the liberation of those under the rule of death. But once again, this rupture is so decisive,

---

16. Caird, *Revelation of St. John the Divine*, 266 (his emphasis, writing in 1966).

17. One good place to read more is Beker, *Paul's Apocalyptic Gospel*, 99–104.

18. For much of what follows I am dependent on Harink, "Partakers of the Divine Apocalypse," in Davis and Harink, *Apocalyptic*, 73–95, esp. sec. on history, 82–90.

19. Harink, "Partakers," in Davis and Harink, *Apocalyptic*, 85–86; Harink has especially in view here Paul's letter to the Romans.

so radical, that there is no "progress" toward it in history or in the lives of those under bondage. One is either living in the freedom of new creation or bound to the rule of death. Likewise, God is not gradually and progressively redeeming the world so that we can chart the growing percentage of the world that has been redeemed. Nor can we track the redemption of the world on a rising thermometer.

The error in placing eschatology on a horizontal axis is thinking that we can then track a progressive work of God's redemption of the world. But there is an appropriate way to think about and live eschatology on a horizontal axis. We do this when we recognize that Scripture calls us to mature as the body of Christ and as members of that body (Eph 4). Since Jesus himself is the eschatos, then once we are made partakers of the divine life by the Holy Spirit through the work of the Messiah, we grow in Christ (2 Pet 1). As we grow in Christ, we become "little apocalypses," who in our corporate and individual life display the conflict between life and death. We take up our crosses in order to live "with the grain of the universe" (Yoder). We live in the right-side-up kingdom of God, the new creation, in a world that is upside down. We do so as signs of the final apocalypse in which the Messiah will return and the entire cosmos will be turned right-side-up to live eternally with God.

Misappropriating Apocalyptic

I have already set aside the obvious and persistent misappropriation of apocalyptic by doom-sayers and date-setters. But even after setting those aside and developing a mature, biblically shaped apocalyptic theology such as we find in the authors I have been referencing, there are still potential misappropriations of this apocalyptic theology. One misappropriation is to think that since this is all God's action in Christ, we can leave the saving to God and simply relax in a comfortable seat on the bus of redemption. Those who misappropriate apocalyptic in this way have not really been grasped by the apocalypse of Jesus. This apocalypse is a present irruption in the rule of death that looks toward a future, climactic irruption that will destroy the last enemy (1 Cor 15). The present actuality of this apocalypse as new creation in Christ is the form of life that follows the crucified Messiah. This form of life is "the Christian ethic" that does not seek to "change the world"—because God is doing something infinitely greater: God is redeeming the world as God's creation. Thus, to be grasped truly by the apocalypse of Jesus Christ is to be drawn into a new life that takes shape and bears witness in this world, where the apocalypse of Jesus began and where it continues.

Another misappropriation of apocalyptic cultivates an "ethic of excess" that sees "partakers of the divine apocalypse" as living on a different plane from non-partakers. Beker notes that for apocalyptic theology "all forms of Christian elitism or of Christian self-fulfillment *over against* the world of the other creatures of God are rejected. . . . Christians must know that as long as any section of God's creation suffers, they cannot and should not as yet participate in the eschatological glory of God."[20] This knowledge should help keep us from regarding our participation in the apocalypse of Jesus as conveying superior status on us. And when we do fall into that sin, this knowledge calls us to repentance.

The final potential misappropriation that we will consider is similar to the first. As the first misappropriation led to retirement from the world while God takes us to our destination, this misappropriation withdraws from the world in a misguided quest to maintain the "purity" of the new creation. This misappropriation is once again a failure to be grasped by the apocalypse of the Messiah. This apocalypse does not allow Christians to withdraw from the world into the new creation because the new creation in Christ occurs precisely within the world ruled by death. Thus, as we will see in more detail below, "the Christian ethic" is the way of being in the world apocalypsed by the life, death, resurrection, ascension, and coming again of Jesus Christ. At the same time, this apocalyptic theology—theology without reserve—also disallows recourse to any other power than God for the work of new creation. Thus, it has a "purity" of devotion and of action that may appear to other eyes to be a withdrawal from the world. But the purity of the apocalypse of the Messiah is the purity of heart that sees God (Matt 5:8). Those who receive this gift become our guides to the mission of God's people.

With the preceding in mind, we may now take one more step in our "appropriation" of apocalyptic theology by acknowledging the offense of apocalyptic theology and various strategies for removing the offense.[21] One response is to acknowledge that Paul indeed taught an apocalyptic gospel rooted in Jesus, but that both were wrong. In Albert Schweitzer, this judgment resulted in a "reverence for life" that saw no future overcoming of death. In others, the apocalyptic events of history are transferred to an existential stance toward life or a symbolic way of interpreting our situation apart from any expectation of God's triumph over death in any concrete way. Still others reduce apocalyptic to immanent historical processes. Beker

---

20. Beker, *Paul's Apocalyptic Gospel*, 37–38.

21. Beker devotes much of *Paul's Apocalyptic Gospel*, chs. 5 and 6, to this topic, and *passim*.

reaffirms Paul's apocalyptic gospel against these interpreters, observing that they "fail to discern that the apocalyptic emphasis on the triumph of God celebrates not only God's initiative in Christ but also God's coming victory in Christ that will be a victory over those powers of evil and death that human initiative and responsibility alone cannot conquer."[22]

Apocalyptic Vision for Mission

We may think that what is required of us is to take the apocalypse of the Messiah seriously and appropriate it—but that is not quite right. It is not that we appropriate the apocalypse of the Messiah but rather that the Messiah "appropriates" us in his apocalypse. So, when we are appropriated by apocalyptic without reserve, we begin to be made pure in heart. We become intentional and aware participants in the cosmic conflict that runs through each of us as well and as we grow in purity of heart in and as new creation, we see God. And when we see God, we see what God is doing in the world and become "partakers of the divine apocalypse" (Harink).

This vision of the divine apocalypse is vision for mission. Theology without reserve—that is, apocalyptic theology—is always also mission.[23] The resources that we receive for mission from apocalyptic are manifold and quite nourishing. I will not do them full justice here, but will point toward some of the ways that being appropriated by the apocalypse of the Messiah nourishes and guides Christian mission. Some of this nourishment and guidance may seem commonplace, but grounded in the divine apocalypse they take on cosmic depth and breadth and height.

(1) Apocalyptic keeps always before us the priority of God's work. This apocalyptic priority is not a priority followed by something that is secondary, such as our own work. Rather it is a priority that always goes before us; we participate in it. It is not that God has started something and we now must complete it. Rather, God's kingdom has broken into the world and continues this irruption even today. Our mission is to participate in

---

22. Beker, *Paul's Apocalyptic Gospel*, 102. This paragraph is merely a sampling of the mistaken responses to apocalyptic theology and Beker's critique of them.

23. This is the central thesis of Kerr, *Christ, Apocalyptic, History*. Kerr's book is concerned with parsing some distinctions among various theologians for the purpose of advancing a particular "politics" of mission. While there are things to be learned from Kerr's analyses and arguments, I find that his powers of analysis lead to over interpretation and the ferreting out of minutiae from which he infers too much too confidently. These obscure his important aim and undercut his contribution to an apocalyptic vision for mission.

that irruption and bring others into that same participation: make disciples, baptizing and teaching them (Matt 28:18–20).[24] Jesus' opening and final statements in this great commission point to apocalyptic: "all authority in heaven and on earth has been given to me. . . . And remember, I am with you always, to the end of the age."

(2) This is once again the apocalyptic reminder that God's apocalypse in Jesus Christ triumphs over the cosmic powers that are also manifest concretely in our systems and our bodies. We must always then remember that the conflict in which we fight as partakers of the divine apocalypse is cosmic in scope, even when it is manifest quite concretely in our bodies and systems. It is the conflict with death and death's surrogates. This power, these rulers cannot be defeated by rearranging the system by which they rule nor can death be defeated by feeding the hungry, clothing the naked, sheltering the homeless, liberating the captive, caring for the poor. Rather, these things become signs of and participation in the kingdom of God *because* death has been defeated by the apocalypse of the Messiah.

(3) In this apocalyptic actuality, there is no tension between the social and the personal, no problem of "social gospel or personal salvation." Beker describes how this bifurcation arises as a recoil away from apocalyptic hope in the future resurrection of the dead to view the

> history of the world . . . as the permanent stage upon which Christian activity takes place, that is, the stage for ethics and missions, whereas the natural and historical world as such was no longer considered to be the object of God's saving and judging intervention. And so Christian hope was no longer directed to the cosmic theophany of the glory of God but became restricted either to hope in a God who "is always One who comes" and is "permanent futurity" (Bultmann), or hope in the Spirit-endowed ethical activity of Christians in the world (C. H. Dodd and Walter Rauschenbusch).[25]

Beker then describes the consequence: "One did not notice that the reduction of Paul's hope in the public manifestation of God's glory actually caused a crippling of the ethical imagination. Ethical activity focused now either on the private sphere of the individual or on the social power of Christian witness in the world."[26] Because we did not recognize the root of this

---

24. Mangina, "Baptism at the Turn of the Ages," in Davis and Harink, *Apocalyptic*, 315–33.

25. Beker, *Paul's Apocalyptic Gospel*, 86.

26. Ibid.

bifurcation in the transposition of the divine apocalypse into something different, these problems have bewitched us for some time. The recovery of apocalyptic dispels this bewitchment and enables a mature, theologically deep practice of integral mission that does more than simply tie together the social and the personal.[27] Apocalyptic enables us to see the deep, inescapable, undeniable actuality of the kingdom that is God's cosmic triumph. This goes deeper than the connection between the social and the personal for human salvation. This cosmic triumph requires a cosmic anthropology that reflects the wholeness of redemption proclaimed by Paul.[28]

(4) As apocalyptic dissipates our bewitchment with the problem of the personal and the social, it also deconstructs the alternatives of Christian being in the world as historically progressive or spiritually private. Of course, very few movements, institutions, or people live purely in one of these two alternatives, but they are articulated as two programs or ideals toward which we strive. Apocalyptic puts an end to these. The apocalypse of the Messiah that declares and enacts the coming triumph of God is the life, death, and resurrection of Jesus. This dying and rising is the actuality of our participation in the irruption of God's kingdom.

Since this apocalypse took place with the world that is ruled by death, we who have been appropriated by this apocalypse cannot escape into a supposed realm of private spirituality. The apocalypse of the Messiah continues to take place in this same world in which it began. To participate in this apocalypse is to be engaged in God's mission, and it is to be inescapably in the world. At the same time, because the divine apocalypse reveals the coming triumph of God, the work of God and the mission of God's people cannot be found in the progress of history. We do not progressively get rid of death. We do not see a reduction in the percentage of creatures who die. Yes, we make a kind of "progress" by eliminating some causes of death and by ameliorating the process of death. We also make a kind of "progress" in ameliorating the conditions under which creatures live toward their deaths. But the apocalypse of the Messiah proclaims and enacts the only triumph over death and its surrogates through the work of God.

This apocalyptic reality gives us the shape of the mission of God's people in the world. As Yoder reminds us, "people who bear crosses are

---

27. "Integral mission" has its roots in the *Fraternidad Teologica de Latino America* (Latin America Theological Fellowship) as misión integral. http://www.micahnetwork.org/.

28. Beker, *Paul's Apocalyptic Gospel*, 36–37, where he references Rom 7:7–25 and 8:18–30. See also my exposition of Rom 8 in *God's Good World*, 142–46.

working with the grain of the universe."²⁹ These are people whose lives have been appropriated by the apocalypse of the Messiah. From the vantage point of the coming triumph of God, we have been set free from sin and have been raised from the dead. From the vantage point of our continuing life in the world, we are dying and rising daily. This is because our life is lived in the apocalypse of the Messiah, the one whose life irrupted in this world and participated in its full reality to make it possible for this world to be made once more God's creation. In Rom 8, Paul describes this as the groaning of creation in which we also groan. As Beker notes, this groaning is not the groaning of those who have transcended this world and now groan in sympathy. Rather, our groaning is the groaning of solidarity: "as long as any section of God's creation suffers, [Christians] cannot and should not as yet participate in the eschatological glory of God."³⁰

(5) This knowledge that our mission in the world is shaped by dying and rising teaches us how to be in the world as God's apocalypsed people without seeking to escape the world or remake it. We have a "this-world" gospel of the future world. Once again Beker is perceptive.

> The demand for a social gospel, however authentic its impulse, nevertheless contained a tragic aspect which was not given due recognition. For it should be clear that unless that demand is viewed against the horizon of *God's initiative* in bringing about his kingdom, it threatens to become a romantic exaggeration of the ethical capability of the Christian. For although Christians must do battle against the power of death and against the unjust power structures of this world, they should not overrate their own capabilities. Otherwise God's will and power become too easily identified with the will and power of Christians.... In other words, unless Christians know that their ethical activity is essentially an anticipation of that greater reality of God's coming kingdom, they cannot but wonder about the futility of their efforts in view of the overwhelming structures of evil and suffering in our world.... [N]ot only the sheer magnitude of the ethical task will suffocate them, but also their frequent inability to measure ethical progress will stifle them.³¹

Beker's observations about the social gospel in this long and illuminating passage apply just as forcefully and perceptively to much Christian mission

---

29. See above, n. 14.
30. Beker, *Paul's Apocalyptic Gospel*, 37.
31. Ibid., 86–87.

today, particularly when it is engaged with death and its surrogates in their most destructive work.

When we see that the gospel calls us out of a privatized spirituality, often the only alternative that we can identify is "the social gospel." But then we are led into the apparent futility, discouragement, and stifling that Baker identifies. When we locate our call to mission in the apocalypse of the Messiah we are given a vision for mission that can sustain us in the midst of the overwhelming structures and sheer magnitude of the task.

At the same time the vision for mission given by this apocalypse also calls us to the individual and their "conversion" to this apocalyptic vision and way, which is life in the midst of death. Under the guidance of apocalyptic the salvation of the individual is understood in a new way. Here's Philip Ziegler's description:

> The victory God wins when Christ takes power over us is won *for us* even as it is won *against us* insofar as we are exponents and instruments of that false lord, i.e., insofar as we are ourselves "a piece" with the world vanquished and overturned. To speak of our redemption out from under the power of Sin is to speak therefore of a liberation whose form is precisely that of judgment and forgiveness, for it involves the overcoming of enmity and the reconciliation of renewed creatures with the God who is in fact God. As liberation, salvation includes rather than bypasses personal sin: the gospel promises that God wills to wrest the earth out from "our deep-seated indolence and hypocrisy," and that he does so by freeing us from the tyrannical powers that enslave us. These are two aspects of the one rectifying movement of God's sovereign grace.[32]

(6) This apocalyptic vision for mission gives us our place in history without history determining the scope, limits, and success of mission. As we have seen above, the apocalypse of the Messiah takes place in this world of death and calls us to mission here. But we are taking one step beyond that now in seeing that although our mission takes place in this world and is fully immersed in this world, it is not determined by this world. The powers and authorities of this age, of the history of the world, have no power or authority over us. Of course, it appeared that they did have power when they judged, condemned, and crucified the Messiah. In this vision, Jesus is a "historical failure." But that is how it had to be. Apocalyptic exposes the powers that rule the history of the world as the servants of death. For Jesus to have been

---

32. Ziegler, "Christ Must Reign," in Davis and Harink, *Apocalyptic*, 208–9.

a "historical success," he would have had to accept death as the final and determining authority, the last word. Then, perhaps, he could have played by the rules of death, engaging death on its own ground with its own powers. Then, perhaps, he could have been a historical success. Of course, this never could have been. Jesus is the Messiah, and as the Messiah he could not have subjected himself to the authority of death. Moreover, anyone who accepts the final authority of death and plays by death's rules, using the surrogate weapons of death, has already lost the war with death.

Instead, Jesus the Messiah apocalypses the way to be in history in the midst of the rule of death without succumbing to death's rule. Again, the two alternatives that we see in the church's mission are an escape from history into a privatized spirituality or an immersion in history that seeks to "make progress" in the history of the world. Apocalyptic calls us into a fully "this world" mission, but it does so in light of the future apocalypse that will destroy death, and new creation will be all in all in God. Those who are guided by the apocalyptic vision of mission will know that although their mission may make the world a "better" place in which to die, the divine apocalypse actualizes the redemption of creation for new creation, in which there will be no death. We do not progress toward that. The Christian mission, then, is to participate in and bear witness to the Messiah in whom and through whom God actualizes new creation. None of our labors in this apocalyptic reality are in vain. We know this not because we can trace success and progress in the history of the world, but because we know that the cosmic conflict has an end. The end is the triumph of God in new creation.

(7) This leads to one final point that comes as a proposal for further thought. If we take seriously the irruptive character of the divine apocalypse, what happens to the cherished and wide-spread affirmation that we live in the already but not yet of the kingdom of God? Does not that already-not yet scheme draw us back into the kind of historical captivity that opens the door to "theology-with-reserve"? That is, doesn't "already here but not yet fully here" place Christian mission in a space where authorities and powers other than the Messiah circumscribe the sphere, range, and possibilities for Christian mission?

In place of this familiar scheme, I propose that we consider submitting to an "irruptive" view of the kingdom of God. That is, let us imagine that the divine apocalypse—the kingdom of God, which is the new creation actualized by the redemption of creation—continually irrupts into this world. It is irrupting wherever we find "righteousness, peace, and joy in the Holy Spirit" (Rom 14:17). If our imagining this leads us to seeing and believing the actuality of this apocalypse, then we will be more deeply grounded for mission in the life, crucifixion, resurrection, ascension, and coming again of Jesus the Messiah.[33]

Conclusion

The most appropriate conclusion to this excursion into the possibilities of apocalyptic for the "aesthetics of the kingdom" as vision for mission will be "written" by those who work at the frontiers of the conflict between the powers of light and of darkness, where the contest between life and death is clear and ever present. If such workers are grasped by this apocalyptic theology, then they may work with thankfulness that they are called to places where the ultimate reality apocalypsed by the Messiah is so evident and so wonderfully redemptive. They will know that the kingdom is always irrupting not progressing, that moments of goodness and light are signs of the kingdom's actuality in their midst, even if structures do not change and people succumb to the powers of death. Rather than "success," they will celebrate the joy of being faithful to the way of the cross as the way of everlasting life and love, even in the midst of this age. They will delight in the times when the systems of death are subverted. And they will live in the hope of new creation enacted by the apocalypse of the Messiah, the coming triumph of God, in which death will be destroyed.[34]

In addition to this fairly obvious—if unconventional—conclusion, I hope for another very appropriate and just as significant conclusion: when a new and apocalyptic vision for mission is written by those who live and work in places where the conflict between the powers of light and darkness, where the contest between life and death, is opaque and hidden. This too is a frontier. Indeed, although the contest between life and death daily is waged out in the open on the downtown eastside of Vancouver, the contest is no less fierce in the proud towers and slick clubs of downtown Vancouver or on the tidy westside, the hipster eastside, or the sprawling suburb of Surrey. The apocalypse of the Messiah reveals to us the one reality that encompasses us all: the cosmic conflict between light and dark, good and evil, life and

---

33. Although I cannot develop it here, I am intrigued by the possibilities in Julian Hartt's argument that we are not confined to a cyclical or linear view of time. He proposes periodicity as the proper view of time rooted in the gospel. I would call this "apocalyptic time." Hartt, *Christian Critique*, 142–44.

34. This entire essay has been an extension of Stanley Grenz's exploration of eschatology and his focus on the guidance for Christian life and mission. The new developments in apocalyptic theology have opened up new ways of pursuing Grenz's vision, especially in relation to Christian mission. For Grenz's teaching, see *Theology for the Community*, 603–6, 644–49, 650–59.

death, in which the one God—Father, Son, and Spirit—acts in Jesus for the redemption of the world. This actuality, this redemption, takes place in the world in which we live and follow Christ today. This Messiah Jesus is the apocalypsis and eschatos of God who commissions us and is our vision for mission.

Bibliography

Balthasar, Hans Urs von. *Life Out of Death: Meditations on the Paschal Mystery*. Translated by Martina Stöckl. San Francisco: Ignatius, 2012.

Beker, J. Christiaan. *Paul's Apocalyptic Gospel: The Coming Triumph of God*. Philadelphia: Fortress, 1982.

Caird, G. B. *The Revelation of St. John the Divine*. Harper's New Testament Commentaries. New York: Harper and Row, 1966.

Davis, Joshua B., and Douglas Harink, eds. *Apocalyptic and the Future of Theology: With and Beyond J. Louis Martyn*. Eugene, OR: Cascade, 2012.

Harink, Douglas. *Paul among the Postliberals: Pauline Theology beyond Christendom and Modernity*. Grand Rapids: Brazos, 2003.

Hartt, Julian N. *A Christian Critique of American Culture: An Essay in Practical Theology*. New York: Harper and Row, 1967.

Kerr, Nathan K. *Christ, History, and Apocalyptic: The Politics of Christian Mission*. Theopolitical Visions. Eugene, OR: 2009.

Lowe, Walter. "Prospects for a Postmodern Christian Theology: Apocalyptic without Reserve." *Modern Theology* 15/1 (1999) 17–24.

Northcott, Michael. *An Angel Directs the Storm: Apocalyptic Religion and American Empire*. London: I. B. Tauris, 2004.

O'Regan, Cyril. *Theology and the Spaces of Apocalyptic*. Milwaukee: Marquette University Press, 2009.

Wilson, Jonathan R. *God So Loved the World: A Christology for Disciples*. Grand Rapids: Baker, 2001.

———. *God's Good World: Reclaiming the Doctrine of Creation*. Grand Rapids: Baker, 2013.

Yoder, John Howard. "Armaments and Eschatology." *Studies in Christian Ethics* 1 (1998) 43–61.

9

Kerygmatic Hope

Another Look at Karl Barth's Resistance to Universalism

DAVID GURETZKI

> The one who is awakened and gathered to being in the Church has every cause for the full assurance of faith, but none at all for certainty or over-confidence.[1]

AT THE END OF his 1924 lecture on Schleiermacher, Karl Barth concluded by saying: "Schleiermacher is a force with which one cannot expect to come to terms at a first or second or third attempt. I should like to have this summary of his thought accepted not as my 'settlement' with him; but in expectation of further attempts at understanding him."[2] Little could Barth, the young lecturer in dogmatics, have known that he himself would also a theologian with which those to follow could not expect to come to complete terms at first, second, or even third attempt. This is illustrated perhaps nowhere better than in the ongoing debate about Barth's view of the final destiny of humanity.

Many have argued that Barth's novel doctrine of election appears to lead him down the path to a particular form of the doctrine of universalism.

---

1. Barth, *Church Dogmatics*, I/1, 49. Hereafter, *CD*.
2. Barth, *Theology and Church*, 199.

Nevertheless, it is also well known that Barth consistently resisted all attempts to characterize him as a universalist. Thus, Stanley Grenz rightly noted when it came to the question of universalism, Barth "remained somewhat ambivalent so as not to place limits on God's grace."[3] Indeed, it may be Barth's ambivalence that has kept scholars attempting to come to terms with Barth on this question, particularly the puzzle of how Barth can, on the one hand, appear to lead in a universalist direction, and on the other hand, explicitly deny that he was a universalist. In this regard, this essay will be less an attempt to provide a definitive solution to the puzzle as much as a modest attempt to lay one more piece of the puzzle on the table—a piece of the puzzle that has not yet been acknowledged in the debate and which, it is hoped, may add some clarity.

In what follows, I will provide an overview Barth's doctrine of election and its commonly understood universalist trajectory alongside his vocal resistance to the concept of universalism. A survey of major scholarly critiques of Barth will follow after which I will point out a couple of perspectives on the problem not yet considered in the literature. I will argue that both Barth's resistance to historical metaphysics and his understanding of the nature and interrelationship of both proclamation and dogmatics (as outlined in *Church Dogmatics* I/1) serve as two additional factors to consider in better understanding Barth's position without having to conclude that his position suffers under theological or logical inconsistency. In the end, I will suggest that Barth's position, though still significantly different from traditional evangelical perspectives, may also be more compatible than may have been previously acknowledged.

I. Election and the Problem of "Universalism"

Barth's novel reconstruction of the doctrine of election has loomed large in virtually every discussion about Barth's supposed universalist tendencies.[4] (Universalism is defined here as the doctrinal affirmation that the redemptive purposes of God in Christ and the Spirit will result in an eschatological restoration of all creation into fellowship with God, or at the very least, all of humanity. Such a position has been classically called *apokatastasis*.[5]) Central to Barth's doctrine of election is his affirmation that Jesus Christ is both

---

3. Grenz, *Theology for the Community* (1994), 827.
4. For Barth's outworking of the doctrine of election, see *CD*, II/2, 3–506.
5. George Hunsinger notes that the doctrine of *apokatastasis* (first associated with the writings of Origen) was the church's "minority report." Hunsinger, *Disruptive Grace*, 234.

subject and object of election. Or as he put it, "Jesus Christ is the electing God, and . . . He is also elected man."[6] Barth thus argues that Jesus Christ, in the unity of his divinity and humanity, is both the acting subject of election (i.e., the one who elects), and the receiving object of election (i.e., the one who is elected). Without at all downplaying the longstanding debate about the significance of Barth's reworking of the traditional Reformed doctrine of election on both sides of his equation,[7] it is the second half of Barth's equation that is typically of primary concern when it comes to the question of whether Barth is ultimately to be reckoned a universalist.

According to Barth, Jesus Christ is to be understood to be the object of election, the elected man. In one sense, this is in accord with traditional Reformed theology, and indeed, with much evangelical theology. Theologians of varying stripes have long pointed out that Jesus Christ is the object of election, in so far as Jesus Christ is the one whom God elected to be the mediator between God and humanity (Eph 1:3–4).[8] Put another way, in the traditional Augustinian/Calvinist construction of the doctrine of election, God determined in eternity past to elect Jesus to be the agent of salvation and judgment for the elect and the reprobate, respectively. Those individuals whom God had foreordained in eternity to be the recipients of salvation would receive the gift of faith by which the atoning merits of Christ would be applied to them, while those who were not elect (the reprobate) would be passed over to face Christ's judgment of their sin as deserving of eternal damnation.

It is here that Barth digressed from the Augustininian/Calvinist framework of the doctrine of election, not by denying the two-sidedness of the doctrine (i.e., that there are elect and reprobate), but by insisting that Jesus Christ in his person is the proper and primary recipient both of God's election and rejection.[9] It is not, Barth argued, that certain individuals are elect

---

6. *CD*, II/2, 103.

7. McCormack, perhaps more than anyone, has emphasized the impact on the doctrine of God and theological anthropology consequent to Barth's insistence that Jesus Christ is the electing God. For a recounting of the influence of Pierre Maury upon Barth's novel reformulation of election, see McCormack, *Critically Realistic Dialectic Theology*, 457ff.

8. McCormack, "Grace and Being," 94. Cf. Article VII of the Canons of Dort which declares: "The elect God hath decreed to give to Christ to be saved by him, and effectually to call and draw them to his communion by his word and Spirit; to bestow upon them true faith, justification, and sanctification." Schaff, *Creeds of Christendom*, 582.

9. The priority given to the place of Christ in election did not mean there was no room for either the individual or the people of God. To be sure, Barth goes on to develop the doctrine of election as applied to the community or *Gemeinde* (§34 "The Election of the Community [*Gemeinde*]") and to individuals (§35 "The Election of the

and others are rejected and that Christ is thus the Savior only of the elect. Rather, God has acted definitively by electing Jesus Christ to be the one who is both elected and rejected on behalf of every individual human. As Barth puts it, "In Jesus Christ God . . . takes upon Himself the rejection of man with all its consequences, and elects man to participation in His own glory."[10] And to make it even clearer, he insists, "[Jesus Christ] is *the* Rejected, as and because He is *the* Elect. In view of his election, there is no other rejected but Himself."[11] Given these statements, McCormack observes that "it is hard to imagine a more solid basis for a final reconciliation of all things than the one Barth has laid in his doctrine of election and reprobation. And if what is accomplished in Jesus Christ is the reality of redemption and not merely its possibility, then surely all *must* be saved!"[12]

Despite what appears to be the unavoidable conclusion that Barth's doctrine of election drives him logically to a universalist position, he repeatedly denied the charge. Though several passages could be adduced, the following sufficiently highlights Barth's resistance to the charge:

> We should be denying or disarming that evil attempt and our own participation in it if, in relation to ourselves or others or all men, we were to permit ourselves to postulate a withdrawal of that threat and in this sense to expect or maintain an *apokatastasis* or universal reconciliation as the goal and end of all things. *No such postulate can be made even though we appeal to the cross and resurrection of Jesus Christ*. Even though theological consistency might seem to lead our thoughts and utterances most clearly in this direction, we must not arrogate to ourselves that which can be given and received only as a free gift.[13]

Barth's denial of universalism may be full of conviction, yet there is a reason why he continues to be suspected of being, at the very least, a closet universalist. As Eberhard Jüngel pointed out, Barth was once quoted as saying, "I do not teach it, but I also do not not [sic] teach it."[14] In other words,

---

Individual [*Einzelnen*]")—in that order. However, Barth is clear that Jesus Christ is the primary recipient of election *through* whom the community and the individuals receive their election. In this regard, Barth declares that his own reworking of the doctrine of election is an attempt to correct the axiomatic starting point receive in the Augustinian tradition that "predestination has to do exclusively with the eternal establishment of the relationship between God and the 'individual'" (*CD*, II/2, 307).

10. *CD*, II/2, 94.
11. *CD*, II/2, 353.
12. McCormack, "Merciful to All," 246.
13. *CD*, IV/3.1, 477 (emphasis added).
14. "*Ich lehre sie nicht, aber auch nicht nicht.*" Jüngel, *Barth-Studien*, 51; ET: Jüngel,

as Jüngel explains, "Barth thought that it was safer to risk the danger of implicitly teaching the *apokatastasis pantōn* (Acts 3:21) . . . than to risk the greater peril of restricting the power of the Gospel and the sovereign will for salvation."[15] Clearly, then, it is the tension between Barth's denial of and his affinity to universalism that has continued to fuel the debate.

II. Surveying the Critical Responses to Barth

The apparent logical direction toward universalism in Barth's doctrine of election and his own denial of the doctrine has stirred up no small amount of debate about how to understand this dynamic in Barth. Barth's interpreters, friend and foe, not surprisingly, have come to conflicting conclusions. An historical analysis of the literature reveals that attempts to deal with this tension in Barth occurred in three phases of interpretation and under four basic categories.

A. Phase 1: Contemporary Responses to Barth

The first category of response also corresponds to some of the earliest commentary on Barth's eschatology, responses penned even while Barth himself was still churning out volumes of the *Church Dogmatics*. Three representatives stand out here: Emil Brunner, G. C. Berkouwer, and Hans Urs von Balthasar. Each of these three examined *Church Dogmatics* as they rolled off the press, and all three come to a similar conclusion: the trajectory of Barth's argument leads him unavoidably to a doctrine of universalism.

Though Brunner characteristically saw himself standing with Barth in "the desire to state the doctrine of Election . . . in harmony with revelation and the thought of the Bible as a whole,"[16] in the end he remained unconvinced that Barth had sufficiently demonstrated the biblical basis for Jesus, the God-man, being the eternal ground of all election. Furthermore, Brunner was also concerned that Barth's christologically-intensive doctrine of election logically led to the loss of freedom and responsibility for humans because he felt that everything had been decided in advance in the sphere of the pre-existent election of Christ.[17] Consequently, Brunner could only

---

Karl Barth, 44.

15. Ibid., 44–45.
16. Brunner, *Christian Doctrine of God*, 346.
17. Ibid., 347, 351.

surmise that Barth's election logically led to the conclusion that it was impossible for anyone ever to be finally lost.[18]

Berkouwer, in consonance with Brunner, agreed that the net outcome of Barth's doctrine of election led him, at the very least, "to the verge of the apokatastasis."[19] However, unlike Brunner who emphasized the loss of human freedom, Berkouwer perceived exactly the opposite theological effect! "When Barth's vision has been pursued to the end, it is no longer possible to appeal to God's freedom in election."[20] This is because, Berkouwer argued, in his all-encompassing pre-temporal election of Christ, God's decision in regard to individuals has been closed off from the very start. God, as it were, had locked himself into non-freedom as soon as he elected all in Christ.

Hans Urs von Balthasar, a Swiss Catholic contemporary of Barth's, discerned also in Barth an unstoppable movement toward universalism. Even though Barth had already given advance warning that a positive doctrine of *apokatastasis* is eschatologically irresponsible, von Balthasar insisted that Barth's doctrine of election makes universalism an "inevitable and necessary" conclusion.[21] (Not that von Balthasar necessarily disagrees with this conclusion. In fact, he asks, "Shouldn't this certainty of victory be the real Christian pathos?"[22])

These three respondents to Barth are placed in a phase and category of their own because all three provided critiques which they acknowledged were anticipatory and tentative in their conclusions. They understood well that Barth was still actively writing and that he had not yet reached the starting point of developing his formal eschatology in the much anticipated (though never started) fifth volume of *Church Dogmatics*.[23] Though all concluded that Barth was on a universalist trajectory, Brunner probably spoke for them all when he said, "we cannot see, either, how [Barth] could accept [this conclusion]. It is therefore definitely to be expected that . . . he has not yet said his last word."[24]

---

18. Ibid., 352.
19. Berkouwer, *Triumph of Grace*, 295.
20. Ibid.
21. Balthasar, *Theology of Karl Barth*, 186.
22. Ibid., 187.
23. The last projected volume of *CD* was supposed to be entitled, "The Doctrine of Redemption."
24. Brunner, *Christian Doctrine of God*, 352.

B. Phase 2: Assessing or Resolving the Tension in Barth

Brunner's prediction that Barth would have more to say was fulfilled when Barth took pains to incorporate a generous response to Berkouwer's book in *Church Dogmatics* IV/3,[25] in addition to providing a few more explicit paragraphs in which he ponders the possibility of a doctrine of *apokatastasis*. And what was Barth's "final word" to *apokatastasis*? *Nein*! "Even though theological consistency might seem to lead our thoughts and utterances most clearly in [the direction of *apokatastasis*], we must not arrogate to ourselves that which can be given and received only as a free gift." But having closed off the option of holding to the *doctrine* of universal salvation, Barth nevertheless went on to opine, "there is no good reason why we should forbid ourselves, or be forbidden, openness to the possibility that in the reality of God and man in Jesus Christ there is contained much more than we might expect and therefore the supremely unexpected withdrawal of that final threat, i.e., that in the truth of this reality there might be contained the super-abundant promise of the final deliverance of all men."[26]

These oft-quoted words led into a distinct second phase of interpretation whereby, unlike Brunner, Berkouwer, and von Balthasar preceding, interpreters now had the added responsibility of making sense of a heightened tension in Barth which, if previously implicit, was now explicit and very much out in the open. Thus, in this second phase of inquiry, readers of Barth attempted to resolve the tension in one of two (or three, depending how the second way is understood) basic ways.

1. Barth has to be understood as an incoherent universalist

Some took Barth's statements to mean nothing less than that Barth had fallen into a logically incoherent position. Cornelius Van Til's critique was perhaps the most forceful, and he approached Barth consistent with his distinctive form of apologetics: by seeking to uncover Barth's underlying presuppositions. Van Til was convinced that Barth made uncritical use of neo-Kantian philosophical assumptions and generally argued that though Barth was speaking in the language of orthodoxy, his meanings were far from orthodox.[27] Beyond this, Van Til was himself committed to "inter-

---

25. Berkouwer's original book, *De Triomf der Genade in de Theologie van Karl Barth* (ET: *The Triumph of Grace in the Theology of Karl Barth*), was published in Dutch, 1954. Barth's response was published in 1959 (*CD,* IV/3.1, 173–80).

26. Ibid., 477–78.

27. It should, of course, be noted that Van Til was right about Barth's underlying

nal coherence"[28] as a significant test of theological veracity. In this regard, Van Til was of the opinion that Barth couldn't have his cake and eat it, too. That is to say, Barth couldn't insist that "no one can finally deny his election in Jesus Christ,"[29] while continuing to deny that it led to a universalist conclusion. Thus, Van Til sees no option but to assert, unavoidably, that Barth is to be counted in the company of universalists, his own protestations notwithstanding.

More recently, Oliver Crisp has offered an analytico-logical approach to the problem of Barth's denial of universalism. Crisp is convinced that when broken down into propositional form, Barth's theology logically leads to a universalist conclusion, but that Barth "retreats from its consequences" and is therefore "happy to withhold [the] requirement of theological consistency, because he deems that such a move would compromise divine freedom."[30] Crisp's conclusion, therefore, is that Barth is simply and unavoidably logically inconsistent: "One cannot consistently hold both that all humanity have been (derivatively) elected, so that all their sin has been efficaciously atoned for by Christ, *and* that the soteriological status of all humanity is uncertain."[31]

There is something to be said about the charge of logical inconsistency in Barth. But there are two fundamental problems with this charge. First, a reading that charges Barth with a glaring inconsistency that he apparently could not discern is unlikely at best and uncharitable at worst. As Colwell aptly puts it, "Either Barth remained blissfully oblivious to the most obvious implication of a fundamental tenet of his theology; or there must be some factor in his doctrine of election that has been overlooked by his critics."[32] Colwell and I am drawn to the latter as more probable than the former.

Second, the assumption that internal logical consistency is the fundamental or even axiomatic test of theological veracity is an assumption that Barth himself would not hold. As McMaken rightly complains in his review of Crisp, such logical analyses of Barth are attempts "to force Barth's thought into traditional dualities"—dualities which Barth *consistently* sought to resist.[33]

---

neo-Kantianism, even if one does not finally agree that Barth's use of it was uncritical. See McCormack, *Critically Realistic Dialectical Theology*, 43–49.

28. Frame, *Van Til the Theologian*, 9.
29. Van Til, *Christianity and Barthianism*, 28–29.
30. Crisp, *Retrieving Doctrine*, 128–29.
31. Ibid., 129.
32. Colwell, "Contemporaneity of Divine Decision," 139.
33. McMacken, "'Review of Crisp," 125. Furthermore, it must be remembered that Barth's primary theological concern in his work (and certainly in *CD*) was not to strive

2. Barth has to be understood as a coherent (non-)universalist

Some scholars have, understandably, lined themselves up on either side of the debate and attempted to show either that Barth is a coherent, *qualified* universalist, or that Barth is a coherent non-universalist, given his own stated reservations. To be sure, most scholars who take one side or the other have sought to absorb Barth's warning that a doctrine of *apokatastasis* cannot be appealed to as a matter of principle, lest one rob God of his freedom to do what he deems it just to do in the eschaton, whether to save all, or only some. Consequently, few (if any) interpreters would actually categorize Barth as holding to *apokatastasis* in the classical sense of the term, and thus no one justifiably calls Barth a universalist pure and simple. Nevertheless, some scholars such as Greggs readily affirm that "Barth's theology clearly points in a universalist direction," even while qualifying that Barth remains committed to the particularity of salvation being found in Christ alone.[34] Greggs, in other words, sees the trajectory of Barth's doctrine of election as a means of breaking down what he calls "the endless and dreadful dividing of humanity into categories" of saved and damned.[35]

On the other hand, and more commonly, some scholars have sought to defend Barth against charges of universalism. In this category, Bettis stands as perhaps the most well known and most quoted early apologist on behalf of Barth as a coherent non-universalist.[36] Bettis is not only concerned to remind readers of Barth's principled rejection of universalism as a matter of retaining God's freedom, he also suggests that attention to Barth on this question is important because his theology resists being squeezed into either a double-predestinarian (i.e., Augustinian/Calvinist) or Arminian doctrine of election.[37]

---

after a tight internal logical coherence, but to attempt to reiterate as a witness, even if falteringly, to the Word of God attested to in Holy Scripture. It is more important, as Barth once put it, to "seek expressions that resemble the ratio and relations of the Word of God in a proportionate and, as far as feasible, approximate and appropriate way." Or earlier, "theology is modest because its entire logic can only be human ana-logy to that Word" (*Evangelical Theology*, 17).

34. Greggs, "Jesus is Victor," 210.

35. Ibid., 212. For a full scale comparison between the doctrine of *apokatastasis* in Origen compared to Karl Barth, see Greggs, *Barth, Origen, and Universal Salvation*.

36. Bettis, "Is Karl Barth a Universalist?" 423–36.

37. Ibid., 423. Donald Bloesch says something structurally similar, even while using different categories: "It can be perhaps be argued that Barth transcends the polarity between universalism and particularism in that he denies both of these as rational principles or even as necessary conclusions of faith." Bloesch, *Jesus is Victor*, 70. Despite Timothy Scheuers' observation that there is inconsistency in Barth, he nevertheless is in agreement that Barth is not to be regarded as a universalist, not only because of

C. Phase 3: A Third Way through the Impasse?

The third phase of response to the so-called "impasse" on Barth and universalism isn't designated as "third" only because it is chronologically latest. Rather, I designate it as a "third" phase because I believe this group of interpreters are trying to find a new direction—a third way, as it were—of navigating through the impasse. If there was a common weakness I discern in the first two phases of response to Barth, it was each appealed to external theological or philosophical criteria foreign to, or even antithetical to, Barth's own theology. In contrast, von Balthasar rightly discerned, even in the 1950s, that Barth's theology displays

> a quite define *form of thought* [*Denkform*], a structure that determines his whole world view. This framework is quite different from other Protestant forms of thought as it is also from the Catholic framework.... Intending, therefore, to understand Barth's theology more fully and to contrast it all the better against other thought forms, we shall raise this question of the perspective from which Barth has gained his vast panoramic view. *Whoever wants to understand him will above all have to make the effort to stand on the same promontory. Only in this way can we even approach seeing what he has claimed to have seen.*[38]

In other words, to understand Barth on the question at hand, we will need to search for some clues *internal* to his thought—clues arising from his own thought-forms—which might be used to solve the puzzle. In this way, we can resist, as much as possible, imposing a foreign framework upon his thought. Ultimately, one may or may not agree with Barth, but at least we will have better grounds for assessing his position.

1. Barth's Rejection of Historical Metaphysics

Bruce McCormack has pinpointed a major factor that has been largely overlooked in the debates about Barth's resistance to universalism. It is true, he says, Barth resisted a doctrine of *apokatastasis pantōn* because he felt that to do so would make grace out to be a principled outworking of a logical cause. But that is simply a formal, negative reason for rejecting universalism, not a substantial theological reason in itself. Thus, McCormack argues

---

Barth's rejection of *apokatastasis* as a principle, but also because he sees in Barth the markers of demarcation expected in a non-universalist theology. Scheuers, "Evaluation of Barth's Election," 161–73.

38. Balthasar, *Theology of Karl Barth*, 187–88.

that the ultimate reason Barth rejects universalism is because Barth is wary of imposing an understanding of historical causation that is contrary to that which he sees developed in Scripture. He is, McCormack declares, resistant to any and all "historical metaphysics."[39]

In the very midst of his discussion of on the "Determination [*Bestimmung*[40]] of the Elect" Barth argues that God's freedom must be protected when it comes to a doctrine of universalism. He says:

> If we are to respect the freedom of divine grace, we cannot venture the statement that it must and will finally be coincident with the world of man as such (as in the doctrine of the so-called *apokatastasis*). No such right or necessity can legitimately be deduced. Just as the gracious God does not need to elect or call any single man, so He *does not need* to elect or call all mankind. *His election and calling do not give rise to any historical metaphysics, but only to the necessity of attesting them* on the ground that they have taken place in Jesus Christ and His community.[41]

Here some important qualifications need to be made about Barth's form of thought.

Barth insists that God does not *need* to elect anyone. There is no necessity in God, he says, that makes it a foregone conclusion about what God will or will not do. Though God is faithful, he is also free to do as he wills.

Furthermore, Barth insists that we resist the temptation to produce a historical metaphysics. What does he mean by this?

For Barth, the notion of historical metaphysics could be defined as the belief that the future can be predicted and explained by going back to a first cause in history. It is the notion that everything in history (and even perhaps beyond history) can be explained by going back to the first domino pushed in a long chain of dominos. In this regard, Barth was unwilling to play dominos!

In direct contradiction to historical metaphysics, particularly when it comes to the outworking of the doctrine of election, Barth says that all can only be "explained" through attestation to Jesus Christ. Christians, he argues, do not believe that the eschaton will be the last effect of the sum total of historical causation, but will be what it is (including the destiny of those

---

39. McCormack, "Merciful to All," 247.

40. It is unfortunate that the English translation of *Bestimmung* has been rendered "determination," especially given the philosophical overtones of materialistic causation it has in English. A better phrase might be something along the lines of "The Defining Relation of the Elect." I am indebted to Bruce McCormack for a better suggested word here.

41. *CD*, II/2, 417 (emphasis added).

there) on the basis of Christ's perpetual free reality in history. Jesus Christ is, Christians confess, Immanuel, God with us, not just a man trapped in history "back then." On the contrary, Jesus is the living Lord who is free to come to us in every moment of our own history. "Jesus Christ is not only the One who has come (in the incarnation); He is also the One who comes (in the power of the eschatological Spirit) and the One who will come (in his visible return)."[42] Consequently, an understanding of anything which happened, is happening, or will happen from the perspective of a theological interpretation of the God revealed in Jesus and attested in Holy Scripture must resist an appeal to the notion of historical causation. Rather, we must instead perpetually attend to the active and living presence of the Lord Jesus Christ. Elsewhere Barth explains,

> Our present [time] is not like the millions of identical oscillations of the clock with which we measure it. It would be like this if we had to live it without God. . . . The fact that the living God is present makes our present not only real but weighty and therefore important. It encloses the mystery of what God has for us now, of what He has to say to us, to allow, to command us, to give us. It encloses the opportunity which He wills to be realised in and through us now.[43]

In an important article, T. F. Torrance has sought to explore the theology of the atonement in a way similar to Barth's rejection of historical metaphysics (a lesson which Torrance undoubtedly learned from Barth). Torrance, in fact, calls the reliance upon what he calls "logico-causal explanation" (="historical metaphysics") as applied to theological reality a "heresy" (together with what he provocatively calls the twin heresies of universalism and limited atonement).[44]

Torrance explains that the widespread and deep belief in logico-causal explanation in Christian theology has resulted in a mistaken assumption that the atonement is the efficient cause of salvation, some*thing* which is applied to humans in such a way as to result in their salvation. (Notice the commonly used words "sufficient and efficacious" when applied to the atonement both reflect an Aristotelian notion of causation). On the contrary, Torrance says, salvation is to be attributed to the historical agency of the *person* of Jesus Christ. That is to say, a logico-causal perspective would understand that Christ's death for the sins of the world set in motion a chain of events such that the ultimate salvation of believers is assumed to be the

---

42. McCormack, "Merciful to All," 247–48.
43. *CD*, III/2, 531.
44. Torrance, "The Atonement," 248.

end result of the application of that atonement. Such a way of looking at it, Torrance explains, is why the concept of limited atonement arose in the post-Calvinist traditions.[45] Once the atonement was understood to be applied to people as an abstract causal outworking of the death of Christ, rather than as a personal act of Jesus Christ himself, then there is need *either* to say that the atonement is sufficient for all but only efficacious (i.e., efficiently caused) for some, or to limit the atonement strictly only to the elect such that both the sufficiency and efficaciousness of the atonement is only for a few. But in both cases, Torrance argues, atonement is misunderstood as being applied as a logical or historical cause of the effect of salvation.

In all of this, I believe Torrance and McCormack to be essentially right about Barth's rejection of logico-causal explanation (or historical metaphysics), and thus to offer a vital clue as to why Barth outright rejects universalism. Barth doesn't simply resist *principalization* (which he does), but he resists the notion that something abstract can be attributed to be the cause of salvation rather than the personal, concrete action of the Lord Jesus Christ. By cutting out historical metaphysics from the equation, the statement "Jesus is the atoning sacrifice for our sins, and not only for ours, but for the sins of the whole world" (1 John 2:2) does not need to be (1) understood as a soteriological statement of universalism (in which atonement for all becomes the salvation of all), or (2) further qualified through the use of sufficient and efficacious as traditionally done in non-universalist theologies, or (3) limited only to the elect.

The same then also applies to the question of election. Does Barth believe that Jesus Christ, as elect man, takes both election of all and the rejection of all up in himself? Without a shadow of a doubt! But what has not been so clearly understood is how a declaration that in Christ Jesus the election of all of humanity is to be understood as another instance of logico-historical causation of salvation. To miss this point is to be in danger of misunderstanding Barth's doctrine of election entirely. To be clear: For Barth, election is not the pre-temporal logico-historical cause of salvation. On the contrary, all humans, for Barth, are elect in Christ *to be his witnesses* and to bear fruit in accordance with discipleship. But most importantly, according to Barth, when humans do this, they are living in the here and now in light of their election; when they don't, they are, in an impossible possibility, living against their election, even while not negating or undoing their election in Christ.

---

45. Interestingly, Torrance insists that Calvin "explicitly rejected the proposition that Christ suffered sufficiently for all, but efficaciously only for the elect." Citing *De aet. Pred.* XI.5. See ibid.

So the question that is begged, then, is: What is the "cause" of salvation? According to Barth, Jesus Christ, the personal agent of salvation. Not the atonement or election *per se*. As the Barmen Declaration put it, "*Jesus Christ, as he is attested for us in Holy Scripture, is the one Word of God which we have to hear and which we have to trust and obey in life and in death.*"[46]

2. Distinguishing between Kerygmatic and Dogmatic Statements

A second important aspect of Barth's distinctive thought form which has, to my knowledge, never been considered in the question of Barth's resistance to universalism is his understanding of the relationship between the church's tasks of proclamation and dogmatics. I posit that the supposed tension in Barth between election and his resistance to universalism may be diminished once it is understood how these two species of theological statements are understood and illustrated in Barth's own writing. I offer, therefore, a theo-linguistic analysis of Barth on the question at hand through the dual lens of proclamation and dogmatics, two tasks that Barth argues are proper to the church's witness to the gospel.

In the first volume of the *Church Dogmatics*, Barth seeks to define and delineate a relationship between proclamation (*Verkündigung*) and dogmatics (*Dogmatik*). Proclamation and dogmatics share several characteristics: both are subject to God and his living Word, Jesus Christ, attested to in Holy Scripture;[47] both are functions of the church as she fulfills her calling to be witness to God and his Word;[48] both are the work of fallen, faltering human tongues;[49] and both are continuously practiced in history and in ever changing circumstances.[50]

Despite the similarities between proclamation and dogmatics, however, there are pointed differences, differences that help to define them as such, but also that point to their relation to one another.

On the one hand, proclamation (which, for Barth, broadly includes both preaching and sacrament, Word and deed)[51] is not simply an important task of the church but is *essential* to its very character.[52] That is, a non-

46. Leith, *Creeds of the Churches*, 520.
47. *CD*, I/1, 60–61; Cf. *CD*, I/1, 16.
48. *CD*, I/1, 17.
49. *CD*, I/1, 72, 82; Cf. *CD*, I/1, 76.
50. *CD*, I/1, 56; Cf. *CD*, I/1, 77.
51. *CD*, I/1, 56.
52. "The essence of the Church is proclamation." Barth, *Homiletics*, 40.

proclamational church, according to Barth, is an oxymoron, for the church is the church only as it proclaims the gospel of Jesus Christ. In this regard, statements of proclamation (or kerygma) are viewed by Barth as a kind of "first order language" that arises immediately in the church's encounter with the living God as mediated in Jesus in the communion of the Spirit. Thus, Barth says, "Church proclamation and not dogmatics is immediate to God in the Church."[53]

Furthermore, one of the most common ways Barth speaks about proclamation is that it is the reiteration or repetition of God's promise, his gospel, in human words as attested to us in Scripture.[54] Such a human reiteration of God's promise by the church is something that takes place continually in history and is directed by the church to every tongue, tribe, and generation, even as it continually falters to do so with full veracity. Finally, as a reiteration of God's *promise*, proclamation is always an eschatologically oriented *announcement* or *kerygma*. "Proclamation must mean announcement— announcement as distinct from the real 'I am with you' as future fulfilment. . . . i.e., announce the future revelation, reconciliation and calling."[55] Thus, *the proclamation or kerygma of the church is a declaration, arising from an analysis of God's triune self-revelation, discerned in advance by faith, and in hope of its fulfillment in the coming kingdom of God.*

Dogmatics, on the other hand, is a distinct ecclesial practice from proclamation, even while remaining intricately related to it. Most importantly, dogmatics, Barth insists, is subservient to proclamation: "Dogmatics serves Church proclamation."[56] In this regard, Barth is clear that proclamation is required of the church as an "execution of God's command to the Church." But as the church executes its command to announce the good news, dogmatics is necessary, precisely because even proclamation is a human, fallible work.[57] Dogmatics, like proclamation, as a form of human speech is fallible, but is nevertheless demanded precisely because the church ceases to be church if it were to cease to carry out its task of proclamation. Thus, dogmatics constantly inquires[58] whether the church's proclamation is faithful to, and corresponds to, the self-revealed God of the gospel. Dogmatics, thus, serves a critical function for the church. It unendingly asks, "Did the Church's proclamation measure up to its responsibility yesterday? Will it do

---

53. *CD*, I/1, 87.
54. *CD*, I/1, 58, 59, 60, 67, 70.
55. *CD*, I/1, 59, 60.
56. *CD*, I/1, 83.
57. *CD*, I/1, 82.
58. "Dogmatics as Enquiry" (*CD*, I/1, 11ff.).

so tomorrow?"[59] And in whatever manner dogmatics seeks to answer that evaluative question, Barth insists, it must always do so in fear and trembling before God himself, who alone can render the verdict of the suitability and truthfulness of the dogmatic statements.

When speaking of the relation of proclamation and dogmatics, Barth makes the connection clear: "Church proclamation," he says, "is the raw material of dogmatics. But it would be a fatal conclusion to try to reverse this and say that dogmatics is the raw material of proclamation."[60]

Given this relationship, Barth warns,

> It is a familiar and perhaps unavoidable beginner's mistake of students and assistants to think that they can and should confidently take the content of their preaching from their treasured college notebooks and textbooks of dogmatics. On the other hand, older preachers are usually far too confident in removing themselves from the jurisdiction of this critical authority.[61]

The distinction drawn by Barth between these two species of linguistic statements could be very helpful in negotiating the apparent tensions between Barth's emphasis in election—that all humans are elect in Christ—and his explicit resistance to universalism.

For Barth, the very core of the good news is the confession "Jesus is Lord!" Or to use another phrase, which is central to his discussions on election, "Jesus is Victor!" These statements are of the sort that Barth would designate as a form of proclamation, as kerygma, or, as I am suggesting, a confession of kerygmatic hope. It is here that Barth declares, "there can be no qualifying or calling in question the statement that Jesus is Victor. At this point there is no room for counterpoint. The statement does not contain any paradox. It is incontrovertible. It gives no ground for suspicion. Where does the Bible teach the contrary?"[62]

To be clear, Barth is not saying that the statement, Jesus is Victor, in itself, is beyond critical scrutiny, because as a proclamation of the gospel, it is still human and subject to critical inquiry and clarification. Indeed, upon proclaiming that Jesus is Victor, the preacher and theologian are thrown back to the Bible to test the truth and the meaning of that very statement. If this statement is indeed understood as an instance of Christian kerygma, an announcement in advance of the church's ultimate witnessing of its historical

---

59. *CD*, I/1, 75.
60. *CD*, I/1, 79.
61. *CD*, I/1, 79.
62. *CD*, IV/3.1, 176.

culmination and fulfillment, dogmatics goes back to the Bible critically to analyze whether in fact this proclamation is faithful to God's self-revelation of himself in Jesus. This is where Barth's dogmatic inquiry leads him in the doctrine of election, a manifestation of which Barth believes to be a faithful expansion of the kerygmatic declaration that Jesus is Lord. For Jesus to be Lord, for Jesus to be Victor, Barth suggests, means that there are none beyond his saving influence, none left without hope of salvation, none outside of his election. How can, Barth asks, Jesus be Victor if some are not in fact saved, or if some are not elect? Herein lies Barth's universalist optimism.

Yet in the midst of the discussion on proclamation and dogmatics, Barth declares, "The one who is awakened and gathered to being in the church has every cause for the full assurance of faith, but none at all for certainty or over-confidence."[63] If we understand him correctly here, Barth views the church's role in proclamation as a declaration of what God *will do* in the future based on the full assurance of faith of what God has already and is continuing to enact in the risen Lord Jesus Christ in the power of the Spirit. However, Barth's view of dogmatics is such that such an announcement, given in full assurance of faith, cannot be confused with a certainty or overconfidence born of dogmatic, logical, intellectual, or exegetical skill. This would be a kind of dogmatic certainty evident in a doctrine of universalism that is constructed along the lines of logical or historical necessity; it is for this reason that Barth rejects such universalism. This is why "universalism" can never be a dogmatic conclusion for Barth, for such certainty or assurance can only reside in God himself, not in our human dogmatic statements.

For Barth, proclamation accomplishes two things: (1) It announces with full confidence of faith and hope of what God will do in Jesus Christ (i.e., Jesus is the atoning sacrifice for our sins, and not only for our sins, but for the sins of the whole world, cf. 1 John 2:2); and (2) It turns that same proclamation back upon the human as a "summons" to obedience. Barth describes the doctrine of election as the "sum of the Gospel."[64] When did it turn into something else, he asks? When did the election of God turn into good news for some and bad news for others? If election is gospel, then the announcement is indeed good news to the one who hears. As Barth explains,

> the hearer or reader can fully realise what we are talking about only when he observes that in this final connexion the whole definitive investigation and exposition of the object of

63. *CD*, I/1, 49.
64. *CD*, II/2, 3.

predestination transcends all definition and is transformed into a direct summons to himself: Thou art the man! Thou art the object of predestination in this its final connexion! We are talking about thee, nay—we are actually talking *to* thee when we talk about the individual human person in relationship to the election of Jesus Christ and the community![65]

It is in this light that I suggest that the tension between Barth's statements that in Christ all humans are elect (i.e., a statement of proclamation) and his *Nein!* to universalism (i.e., a statement of dogmatic criticism), if not falling away, is at the very least mitigated. That is to say, the former statement summarizes not only what the church has always proclaimed, but what the church *must* proclaim: that in Christ, you too, whoever it is that hears these words in faith, are chosen to be holy and blameless in his sight (Eph 1:4). However, the latter statement is a dogmatic conclusion to which Barth comes as a result of his resistance of historical metaphysics and his affirmation that salvation comes about only in and through the agency of the man Jesus Christ, the mediator between God and man—not through the logico-mechanical-historical application of atonement of election, by the grace and mercy of the Living Savior, Jesus Christ.

Conclusion

Understanding Barth's own distinction between proclamation and dogmatics helps us, hopefully, to see how Barth's openness to universalism could be characterized as a spirit of kerygmatic hope, borne on arrival of the good news in Jesus Christ. Such proclaimed hope is evident in Barth when he says, "There is no good reason why we should forbid ourselves, or be forbidden, openness to the possibility that in the reality of God and man in Jesus Christ there is contained much more than we might expect and therefore the supremely unexpected withdrawal of that final threat."[66] Thus, as an utterance of the kerygma, Jesus is Victor! not only *can* be, but *must* be announced by the church. This is what the church, and indeed, all individuals, are elected to do.

And such an announcement is good news, indeed! In fact, I would argue that this has been the hopeful message that evangelicals have always sought to sound (even if sometimes it sounds like we are more convinced of the inevitability of hell than the surety of the Savior!). Even for those who

---

65. *CD*, II/2, 323.
66. *CD*, IV/3.1, 478.

might hold to a double-predestinarian form of election in the Augustinian/Calvinist heritage, evangelicals can properly be characterized as "good news'ers": We announce the good news of Jesus *in full expectation* that it is a message open to each and every human being. It is precisely in light of its universal applicability that it is so good! But regardless of where one lands in regard to the doctrine of election, surely it can be agreed that the church's task is to announce and proclaim that Jesus is the Savior of the whole world, regardless of the success or failure of human response. This is, I believe, close to the spirit of what Barth was trying to affirm, and is at the heart of the Reformation cry *sola gratia*! By grace alone!

But as a critical dogmatician, whose job it is to put fallible human proclamation into critical scrutiny, Barth also goes on to insist that in declaring the hopeful kerygma, we cannot tell God what he *must* or *must not* do. We cannot, therefore say that *because* Jesus is Victor, God *must* save all. Nor can we say that because Jesus is Victor that he must *not* save even the most vile, wicked, and rebellious of all humans. In either case, a dogmatic deduction arising from critical inquiry into the Christian kerygma has been illegitimately allowed to become the content of our preaching. The function of dogmatics, thus, is meant not as an exercise in shoring up human epistemological certainty through logical reasoning, but to ensure that proper dogmatic limits are set on what we can know.

Or to put it one more way, it would be difficult to conceive of any Christian proclamation that would be unable to declare Jesus is Victor! But it *is* conceivable that such a proclamation in the end *may* mean that God, the Just and Merciful Judge, saves all, even while being conceivable that the declaration Jesus is Victor! could equally mean that some are saved and others are damned to eternal separation and judgment from that same Just and Merciful Judge. It is simply not up to us to decide. Proclamation tells us what we must preach, to every soul, tribe, nation and tongue, but dogmatics serves to remind us continually that it is not the logic of an argument or the application of an abstract principle that saves or damns, but only the personal action of the free, loving, just Judge whose judgment is still yet to come.

Bibliography

Balthasar, Hans Urs von. *The Theology of Karl Barth: Exposition and Interpretation*. San Francisco: Ignatius, 1992.
Barth, Karl. *Church Dogmatics*. Edited and translated by G. W. Bromiley et al. 4 vols. Edinburgh: T. & T. Clark, 1975–61.

―――. *Evangelical Theology: An Introduction*. New York: Holt, Rinehart and Winston, 1963.

―――. *Theology and Church: Shorter Writings 1920-1928*. Translated by Louise Pettibone Smith. New York: Harper and Row, 1962.

Berkouwer, G. C. *The Triumph of Grace in the Theology of Karl Barth*. Grand Rapids: Eerdmans, 1956.

Bettis, Joseph D. "Is Karl Barth a Universalist?" *Scottish Journal of Theology* 20 (1967) 423–36.

Bloesch, Donald G. *Jesus is Victor!: Karl Barth's Doctrine of Salvation*. Nashville: Abingdon, 1976.

Boring, M. Eugene. "The Language of Universal Salvation in Paul." *Journal of Biblical Literature* 105/2 (1986) 269–92.

Brunner, Emil. *The Christian Doctrine of God*. Philadelphia: Westminster, 1950.

Colwell, John. "The Contemporaneity of the Divine Decision: Reflections on Barth's Denial of 'Universalism.'" In *Universalism and the Doctrine of Hell*, edited by Cameron, Nigel M. de S., 139–60. Grand Rapids: Baker, 1992.

Crisp, Oliver. *Retrieving Doctrine: Essays in Reformed Theology*. Downers Grove, IL: InterVarsity, 2010.

Frame, John. *Van Til the Theologian*. Phillipsburg, NJ: Pilgrim, n.d. http://www.reformed.org/apologetics/index.html?mainframe=/apologetics/frame_vtt.html.

Greggs, Tom. *Barth, Origen, and Universal Salvation: Restoring Particularity*. Oxford: Oxford University Press, 2009.

―――. "'Jesus is Victor': Passing the Impasse of Barth on Universalism." *Scottish Journal of Theology* 60 (2007) 196–212.

Hunsinger, George. *Disruptive Grace: Studies in the Theology of Karl Barth*. Grand Rapids: Eerdmans, 2000.

Jüngel, Eberhard. *Karl Barth, a Theological Legacy*. Philadelphia: Westminster, 1986.

McCormack, Bruce. "Grace and Being: The Role of God's Gracious Election in Karl Barth's Theological Ontology." In *The Cambridge Companion to Karl Barth*, edited by John Webster, 92–110. Cambridge: Cambridge University Press, 2000.

―――. *Karl Barth's Critically Realistic Dialectic Theology: Its Genesis and Development, 1909–1936*. Oxford: Clarendon, 1995.

―――. "So that He May be Merciful to All: Karl Barth and the Problem of Universalism." In *Karl Barth and American Evangelicalism*, edited by Bruce L. McCormack and Clifford B. Anderson, 227–49. Grand Rapids: Eerdmans, 2011.

McMaken, W. Travis. "Review of Oliver D. Crisp, Retrieving Doctrine: Essays in Reformed Theology." *Koinonia: The Princeton Theological Seminary Graduate Forum* 23 (2011) 123–26.

Schaff, Philip, ed. *Creeds of Christendom: The Evangelical Protestant Creeds*. 3 Vols. Rev. ed. Grand Rapids: Baker, 1984.

Scheuers, Timothy. "An Evaluation of Some Aspects of Karl Barth's Doctrine of Election." *Mid-America Journal of Theology* 22 (2011) 161–73.

Van Til, Cornelius. *Christianity and Barthianism*. Philadelphia: Presbyterian and Reformed, 1962.

Torrance, Thomas F. "The Atonement, the Singularity of Christ and the Finality of the Cross: The Atonement and the Moral Order." In *Universalism and the Doctrine of Hell*, 225–56. Grand Rapids: Baker, 1992.

10

"Living as Jesus Did"

Practicing an Embodied Future in the Present

CHERITH FEE NORDLING

The *imago Dei* is the divinely intended vocation of all humankind and the shared goal of our existence. This vocation, in turn, defines our very being. God's intention is that we might experience eschatological transformation after the pattern of the resurrected Christ, who is the Second Adam. Or, viewing our destiny from another perspective, God desires that we find our being as we are caught up in the narrative of the Son. In this manner, the *imago Dei* emerges as the christologically focused and eschatologically oriented, universal human vocation.[1]

THE JOYFUL CONFIDENCE THAT permeates Stan Grenz's theology for the community of God, specifically his understanding of what it means to be truly human, is due in no small part to his eschatological orientation of our communal life as *with* God, *from* God, and *by* God. When Stan tells the Christian story we hear repeated themes of creation, exodus, and new creation, of God's lavish, relational love and covenantal compassion, justice, and hope, of faithfulness and unwavering commitment to his good creation. We hear the stunning grandeur of the good news in all its life-giving,

---

1. Grenz, *Named God*, 360–61.

death-defying, indescribably costly beauty and hope, as the first creation is redemptively recapitulated in the full career of Jesus Christ, whose resurrection by the Holy Spirit and gift of the same Spirit guarantee its complete restoration.

Stan's strength is to frame theological anthropology from this grand scope and from the eschatological perspective opened up in Jesus Christ. As God's human children, we are the creaturely ministers of the divine life and love on the earth. We are vice-regents in God's image and likeness, whose human being, identity, and calling are made manifest as we manifest God's presence, character, power, and *shalom*. In its context as an ancient Near Eastern creation narrative, Genesis places human beings as the communal image of God in creation's temple-palace-garden to function as God's royal suzerain, mediating within creation the immanence of the transcendent Creator.[2] As humanity's embodied existence testifies to Yahweh's kingship, God's creative act of making human beings "'*in our image, according to our likeness*' . . . *male and female*" (Gen 1:26–27), asserts the destiny and vocation of humanity to be God's representatives on the earth. The biblical language indicates that all human beings, in our embodied maleness and femaleness, individually and communally, are intended to be living pictograms of Yahweh, our Creator, enlivened by his breath and his indwelling Spirit.[3]

Because the original creation narrative gives no specifics as to what this vocation actually looks like, argues Grenz, the biblical quest leads to Jesus Christ.[4] Our anthropological center is Jesus whose life, death, and resurrected glory enfold our relation to God, our lives in the image of God, our redeemed brokenness and sin, and our human restoration in eternal life. As God's true image and ours, Jesus Christ is the divine agent and redeeming Lord of all creation, who has been moving all things to their final destiny with the Father and the Spirit.[5] As Athanasius saw so clearly: "*[T]he renewal of creation has been wrought by the Self-same Word Who made it in the beginning. There is thus no inconsistency between creation and salvation*[;] . . . *it was He alone, the Image of the Father, Who could recreate man made after*

---

2. Ibid., 361.

3. Watts, "The New Exodus," 15–41.

4. "Genesis 1:26–27 does not, however, define the *imago dei* in detail but rather opens the door to the possibility of the answer emerging from the broader biblical narrative. . . . At the heart of this wider narrative is the life, death, resurrection and exaltation of Jesus of Nazareth" (*Social God*, 223).

5. Grenz, *Theology for Community* (1994), 849–50; Grenz, *Named God*, 364.

the Image."[6] In the Word made flesh, Jesus Christ, the reality and meaning of the *imago Dei* have been reordered forever.

Although Jesus is the center of the biblical narrative, he is not its end *per se*: Rather, Jesus' story opens to include all those born into his family by the resurrecting, eschatological Spirit, who receive his life and story as their own and come to be conformed ultimately to his likeness.[7] The divine intention is for those who are in Christ to participate in his destiny and thereby replicate his glorious image: "*For those God foreknew he also predestined to be conformed to the image of his Son, that he might be the firstborn among many brothers and sisters*" (Rom 8:29).[8] This "final exegesis" of Gen 1:26–27 indicates that this new creation community of men and women conformed to the image of Christ has been the object of God's foreknowledge and foreordaining mercy from the beginning. If the triune God's purpose from the beginning was to have a "new humanity conformed to the *imago Christi*," then the *telos* toward which the original creation narrative points "is the eschatological community of glorified saints who have joined their head in resurrection life by the power of the Spirit."[9]

Grenz regularly asserts that the New Testament "imperative is always bound up with the indicative": Those who are destined to be the new humanity and reflect the divine image carry the ethical responsibility to live out that reality in the present.[10] We are the communal *imago Dei*, already grounded but not yet fully realized in the resurrected Lord and the life-giving Spirit. Precisely as those who see "our present life in the light of God's future," we are oriented by "the question as to how we as the church of Jesus Christ ought to understand ourselves and our mission in the present age."[11]

From the New Testament perspective, the answer is thoroughly eschatological and pneumatological in the already/not yet space of the kingdom of God. It is not abstractly or generally ethical, but precisely reordered to Christ and his life lived by the Spirit in daily obedience to the Father—"in this world *we are like Jesus*" (1 John 4:17). It assumes that our conformity to

---

6. *On the Incarnation*, 26, 44 (original emphasis). F. F. Bruce reiterates: "It is because human beings in the creative order bear the image of their Creator that the Son of God could become incarnate as a human being and in his humanity display the glory of the invisible God." Moreover, "[t]he old creation in itself is insufficient for the realization of this goal: it requires the redemptive work of Christ and His consequent status as Head of the new creation" (*Colossians*, 58; *Romans*, quoted in *Social God*, 225–26).

7. Grenz, *Social God*, 224.

8. Ibid., 225.

9. Ibid., 231–32.

10. Ibid., 251.

11. Grenz, *Theology for the Community*, 854.

the image of Jesus Christ has begun, that we are already empowered by the Spirit poured out from the Father and the Son, and thus that we are to enact our vocation and final destiny as women and men together in the power, authority, and character of God. As we pray and live into our vocational identity every day, we practice the life to come, previewing our destiny as "children of the resurrection" (Luke 20:36) in the midst of God's beloved world. We ask, as Jesus instructed us, for the Holy Spirit (Luke 11:13) so that we might authentically participate in the life of the kingdom of God.

We join in the work of new creation, the eruption of life and cruciform love in the midst of a presently broken creation. We are to speak and enact the evidence of the life to come, of a future hope that actually looks like Jesus. We are to participate in signs and wonders and in the fellowship of Jesus' suffering until he speaks the final "it is finished" over our suffering. In short, if we are becoming who we already are and will be, then we should be doing what we were destined for in the manner and likeness of our Lord. It could not be more explicit: "*This is how we know we are in him: Whoever claims to live in him must live as Jesus did. . . . This is how love is made complete among us . . . in this world we are like Jesus*" (1 John 2:6; 4:17).

The Indicative as the Source of the Imperative

> The eschatological destiny of bearing the divine image is present in the here and now as the Spirit is at work transforming those who are in Christ into the image that Christ bears. In this process humans are becoming the new humanity in accordance with God's intent from the beginning. New Testament writers, however, repeatedly declare that an imperative is always bound up with the indicative. Those who are destined to be the new humanity and as such to reflect the divine image, and therefore are already in the process of being transformed into that image, carry the ethical responsibility to live out that reality in the present.[12]

"An imperative is always bound up with the indicative." The Spirit is transforming God's people "into the image that Christ bears." We are the communal *imago Dei* whose ground is the resurrected Lord and the life-giving Spirit. As such, we are eschatologically oriented in every way. We live out our call in a kingdom that has begun but is not yet consummated, whose Lord is *busy*, reigning and bringing all things under his feet in heaven and

---

12. Grenz, *Social God*, 251.

on earth, extending the influence of his kingdom through his image-bearing brothers and sisters. Our life in the Spirit is to reflect Jesus' life in the Spirit. Our destiny is be like Jesus; to look and act like Jesus. We are to see and do by the Spirit what we see the Father doing, to speak for God and for the world as Jesus did and does as God's anointed Son and messianic High Priest. In this world we are to be like him. Such is the witness of the New Testament. Period.

And yet, the fundamental imperative of our life "in Christ" by which we enact the ethics of the kingdom through the radicalizing person and power of the Spirit, is often taken less seriously as we get closer to the indicative, Jesus Christ, who enacted the ethics of the kingdom in the same way. We seem to skirt around Jesus himself—our new Adam *through his whole life*—as our true indicative. Instead, the source of the imperative is some version of the church's early experience in the New Testament (however idealized or watered down), or perhaps a version of the great command to love one's neighbor. When the indicatives are social justice, outreach/activism, or even Spirit-gifting for its own sake, the ensuing imperatives quickly lead us to an over-realized eschatology (with or without the Spirit) in this world. Alternatively, if the indicative becomes equivalent to "being saved" out of this world, then the imperative may manifest as an under-realized eschatology of quietism. Here *agape* is unrecognized as God's cruciform character *in and for* the world, and is easily replaced by "niceness" toward our neighbor while we await a disembodied life in heaven. Mission is understood as saving souls out of creation rather than saving a people for participation in God's renewed creation through the redemption of their bodies (Rom 8:23).

The New Testament, however, points us to only one indicative—Jesus of Nazareth and the whole of his life, death, and resurrected exaltation. He is the source and norm against which all other indicatives and imperatives are tested and weighed. He is the manifestation of God's true image on the earth in obedience to the Father, even unto death—precisely for the sake of salvation as new creation and restored communion. If we miss the true indicative, the Word made flesh, then we miss the meaning of our lives and the clarity of our destiny made evident in his resurrected life, where he reigns with the Father as "the faithful witness, the firstborn from among the dead, and the ruler of the kings of the earth" (Rev 1:3). We also miss our participation in his eschatological, Spirit-filled kingdom on earth already in which we practice our future vocation in the present.

In a word, we fail to take our Spirit-empowered, resurrection-oriented humanity seriously. Why? It is because we fail to take Jesus' Spirit-empowered, truly human life seriously. We disparage his daily obedience to the Father, doing only what the Father was doing and *not* doing what the Father was not doing, tempted as he might be to do otherwise. As we shift away from Jesus, this lack of eschatological focus makes us aimless, purposeless, caught up in other narratives that compete with the truth of our life in the kingdom and our call to manifest the kingdom on the earth.

The reasons for this failure are many, but among them are some predominating views of salvation, on one hand, and some interrelated views of the life of Jesus, the Spirit, and the kingdom of God, on the other hand. Evangelical descriptions of salvation, and their corresponding atonement theories, often have to do with something we "get" (heaven) or "get saved *from*" (hell). "Salvation is reduced to what Christian believers experience as forgiveness of sins, personal justification before God, and virtuous living, with spiritual immortality in heaven after death."[13] If salvation is giving mental assent to propositions about Christ's Lordship, about forgiveness through the past event of his death, and about freedom from this mortal body when our *souls* go to heaven, then we attempt to love God and our neighbor *in spite of* being human. We look back to who Jesus *was* and to his crucifixion with little account for his whole career as the image of God. From this perspective Jesus seems wholly unrelated to our present humanity; it is difficult to see who Jesus *is* and what he is *presently doing*, let alone to see that all he did in the past was accomplished precisely "because God was with him," having "anointed Jesus of Nazareth with the Holy Spirit and power" (Acts 10:38).

We seldom recognize the deeply inbred gnosticism and docetism that consistently frame our articulated and lived witness of the gospel. These heresies, both of which make Jesus only seem to be human, or certainly less human than we are, significantly change the content of the good news. Without the truth that Jesus presently embodies and mediates the hope of an embodied, broken world, we are left wondering what salvation really means, namely,

> that the promise of God made in the bodily resurrection of Christ is holistic and all-encompassing: for whole persons, body and soul, for all the networks of relationship in human society that are integral to being human, and for the rest of creation also, from which humans in their bodiliness are not to be detached. In other words, it is God's creative renewal of his whole creation.[14]

Our lack of eschatological focus and orientation around the grand reality of salvation for the whole person and the whole of creation, forever,

---

13. Bauckham, "The Future," 268.
14. Ibid.

can be tied to a lack of attention to the integrity of the *homoousion*—not only is the Son "of one being with the Father" but he is of one being with us as well—forever. The Word not only took on flesh, but he stayed that way. In other words, Jesus' incarnate life is a permanent reality. He is *still* like us, though glorified. Thus, we really will be like him as glorified human beings. This lack of attention to the incarnation as a permanent act within, and on behalf of, creation, in the loving purposes of God, leads to a lack of eschatological purpose in terms of our own human, embodied destiny, now and in the future.

This inattention to the vitality and the vital importance of Jesus' authentic, and ongoing, human life as the key to our embodied, eschatological life in the present is linked to a dire neglect of the person and work of God the Spirit in Jesus' life and ours. We tacitly perpetuate the christological heresies that over-emphasize Jesus' divinity (giving him a pass to do all that he did because he was God). Concomitantly, we perpetuate pneumatological heresies that undermine the person and work of God the Holy Spirit, who from creation has been Immanuel, God with us. "With the Father and the Son he is worshipped and glorified," states the Creed, precisely as "the Lord, the Giver of Life," from Genesis 1 to Revelation 22. We domesticate the Holy Spirit either by directly claiming or merely assuming from experience that he is not present and active as Yahweh's presence upon the earth in the same ways that he was throughout the Old Testament, and in the life of Jesus, and in the church throughout history.

Just as christological heresies run to the "mostly divine" or "mostly human" so that we do not expect the Spirit to manifest the power of the kingdom of God among us, so do our interpretations of the kingdom. Over-realized eschatologies expect everything now, often in "spiritual" terms along the lines of the church in 1 Corinthians and versions of the "name it/claim it" *anti-christos* in our time. Or the kingdom is so under-realized and future-oriented (not of this world or its restoration) that expectations and manifestations of the kingdom present are viewed with suspicion, particularly if the signs of new creation look greater than what we can ask or imagine.

As Jesus ushered in, and continues to extend, the kingdom of God, however, he manifested the life of God on the earth precisely as God's divinely human image-bearer. The kingdom was described and made evident by Jesus as both a present but not yet fully realized reality, and his obedience manifested both aspects of that reality. Furthermore, as the divine Son, Jesus nevertheless did not consider his divine prerogatives to be used to his advantage in his union with us (Phil 2:6–11). Uniquely born of the Spirit and of a young woman from Galilee, Jesus lived a life of openness to God the Father as his truly human image-bearing Son. Becoming like us in every way so that we could become like him, he exercised the power of God in the same way that every other image-bearer does, and must do—by the Spirit. The Scriptures are adamant that we recognize this for what it was—*obedience* to God his Father (Isa 52–53; Heb 2:17–18; 4:15; Phil 2:6–11). His anointing for the fulfillment of his vocation and ministry was the calling of true humanity to do the work of God on the earth *by the power of the Holy Spirit*, joined in love to the purposes of God, making evident the future kingdom in this present evil age, and guaranteeing its destiny under God's judgment in favor of eternal life over death.

Jesus' Life in the Kingdom—and Ours

Jesus' Spirit-empowered life is what the *imago Dei* has always been intended to be—the human, embodied presence of God on the earth. Jesus' life in the Spirit is not to be misunderstood as unique *to* Jesus, however uniquely the Spirit ministered in and *through* Jesus.[15] Rather, from Genesis forward, the biblical assumption is that where God's image and likeness is, so is God in all divine power and authority. This reality is recapitulated in Jesus and remains the eschatological destiny of God's children even now; "the Spirit is at work transforming those who are in Christ into the image that Christ bears . . . in accordance with God's intent from the beginning."[16] The Spirit, the image-bearer and creation/new creation are inextricably linked.

At first creation, as God's male and female image-bearers are set in the temple-palace-garden, God breathes his presence upon and vivifies these living images (vs. idols of stone and wood). As the Spirit hovers over the water of first creation, Noah sees the sign of the Spirit—a dove—hovering over the floodwaters with the promise of new creation. Multiple signs of God's presence (Spirit) are with Abraham as the father of a new nation of people for God's Name on the earth. They multiply as God had promised under the protection, and then oppression, of Egypt. The new creation story is recapitulated in the exodus through the waters of the Red Sea. God anoints Moses, his chosen image-bearer, promising to fill his mouth and make him like a god to Pharaoh. Moses is given authority to exercise life and death in order to bring redemption and freedom to God's people, so that they might walk with God once again in a new "garden" land.

---

15. Hawthorne, *The Power*, 227–43.
16. Grenz, *Social God*, 251.

When Israel rejects the power and authority of God on Sinai, Moses knows that it is only God's presence that marks them as God's people on the earth (Exod 33:12–16). God's faithful promise not to abandon them, but to lead them, is seen in the glory-cloud that guides them through the wilderness. God the Spirit rests among his people so that they manifest his presence in their life together among the nations. Israel is a people set apart for precisely this vocation.[17] The divine presence comes to rest uniquely in power and glory upon the tabernacle (itself a microcosm of God's temple-palace-garden) as he does again in Solomon's dedication of the temple (Exod 40:34–35; 1 Kgs 8:10–11).

Israel is established and called God's "firstborn son," fathered (like Adam) in the likeness of God's image—corporately and individually. In submitting to the law (Torah), Israel accepts its subordination to God, repudiating the autonomy sought by Adam and Eve in the Garden by eating from the tree of "knowledge" and "wisdom." In contrast, wisdom is to follow the law, which is "perfect, reviving the soul; the decrees of Yahweh are sure, making the wise simple; the precepts of the LORD are right, rejoicing the heart; the commandment of the LORD is clear, enlightening the eyes" (Ps 19:7–8). Israel, God's new "son," is to look collectively like a holy nation-kingdom of priests (Exod 19:6), who keep God's commands and so enjoy God's personal presence. Through Israel's anointed judges, prophets, and kings, God speaks to a people with ears to hear, who listen, obey, and thus act for God, with eyes that see from God's perspective and mouths that speak his truth. As God dwells among them, his people serve as God's "living image" to the surrounding nations. Elected to be a source of blessing, Israel is to demonstrate the divine justice, mercy, righteousness, compassion, and long-suffering in the world that God showed to her. They are to walk and live this way because they *know* God; knowledge expresses itself through obedience.[18]

Israel, however, rejects her identity, calling, and empowerment as God's true image on earth. As the "idolater's curse" in several Old Testament moments so powerfully expresses (Pss 115, 135, and Isa 6:9–10), Israel instead reflects the image of the blind and deaf gods she worships. She has eyes but will not see; ears, but will not hear; she staggers naked. "Who is blind but my servant, and deaf like the messenger I send? Who is blind like the one in covenant with me, blind like the servant of the LORD?" (Isa

---

17. I am indebted to Watts, "The New Exodus," for this section.

18. "The lack of knowledge of God does not imply intellectual inadequacy in comprehending God. Rather it points to a moral failure, to a lack of faithfulness and obedience. Those who know God live according to the way God prescribes" (Thompson, *1–3 John*, 55).

42:19). The result is not only exile; most tragically the Spirit's manifest presence departs from them (Ezek 10:4–5, 18–19).[19]

Resounding in hope throughout the prophets is the promised return of the eschatological Spirit and Israel's salvation as the final restoration of God's kingdom. Isaiah's starting point and main theme is that God will initiate a great reversal of all things by the sending of the Spirit so that the blind see, the lame walk, the deaf hear, the dead are raised, stone hearts become flesh, the poor are lifted up, and the exalted made low in the presence of the Lord's anointed (Isa 32:15; 35:1–7; 41:16–17; 43:19–20; 44:1–5; 61:1–3). "'My Spirit, who is on you, and my words that I have put in your mouth will not depart from your mouth, or from the mouths of your children, or from the mouths of their descendants from this time on and forever,' says the LORD" (Isa 59:21). This same promise is beautifully rendered in Ezekiel (36:26–7; 37:14, 26–7), Jeremiah (31:33) and Joel (2:28–9). With the coming of the promised messianic king (Isa 9:2–7; 52:13—53:12), God's "salvation" is for the whole of God's good creation; with the restoration of the image-bearer comes the restoration of the land (Ezek 36, 37) ultimately as "new heavens and new earth" (Isa 66:17–19). The expectation of the Spirit-filled Messiah is the climax of Israel's eschatological expectation based on her long history of God's manifest presence and power resting upon his human image-bearers throughout the Old Testament.

This grand narrative, and eschatological expectation, is always in the background and foreground of the Gospels and the whole of the New Testament. Looking specifically at Luke's account of Jesus' career by the Spirit and that of the first decades of the church, both are characterized by a robust, Spirit-led and gifted life *allelon* (for one another) that manifests the character and power of God.[20] Reverberating with Old Testament eschatological hope, Luke begins his gospel by demanding his readers to pay attention: God has ushered in his eschatological kingdom through Jesus of Nazareth, his anointed one. Pay attention! The Spirit of God is once again present in power. The stories of Zechariah's angelic visitation, Elizabeth's miraculous pregnancy, Mary's angelic visitation and the ensuing immaculate conception, the (pre-natal) recognition and affirmation of God's presence and work by these sets of cousins, the angelic proclamation to shepherds that God's *shalom* has come, the testimony of Simeon and of Anna the prophet, all make abundantly clear that God's long-expected, Spirit-anointed king is present on the earth in prophetic fulfillment.

---

19. Fee, *Paul, the Spirit*, 13.
20. Ibid., 66.

Jesus' story is that of the true, Spirit-enlivened image bearer who reflects God's image in the world and is understood only in light of the older story of Israel's genesis and eschatological hope. Jesus ushers in Israel's new exodus/new creation return from final exile. John the Baptist proclaims Isaiah's promised messianic deliverer and baptizer in the Holy Spirit (Luke 3:16, 21–22). Jesus' baptism and temptation recapitulate Israel's passing through the waters. He is declared God's "beloved Son" and receives the anointing of God the Spirit (a dove over the waters of new creation) to enact his divine-human calling.

Led by the Spirit into the wilderness to face the testing of his firstborn sonship, God's Son remains faithful to his image-bearing identity and calling, reorienting the meaning of image and likeness to him. Jesus submits to the word and will of the Father in the power of the Spirit, claiming the prophetic fulfillment of Israel's messianic hope and new creation in his own person (Luke 4:1–21). He preaches the coming of this long-awaited restoration and through "signs and wonders" and "mighty deeds" (deliberate echoes of the language of exodus and new creation—Deut 3:24; 4:34; Pss 65:6; 107:24). He exercises power over the waters, gives daily provisions of bread, fish, and wine (Ezek 47:9–10; Joel 3:18; Amos 9:13), and re-establishes the reign of God on earth. This new Davidic king, the "branch of the Lord," is prophet, priest, and king. In his prophetic role, God makes his mouth "like a sharpened sword" to tell of the kingdom that has come and is still coming. As priest he mediates between God and world, offering his life of love and service to God for humanity, and receiving atonement and blessing from God on their behalf. As king, the Son of Man executes justice for the oppressed and judgment against evil and sin. He comes with justice and righteousness for all nations in the new covenant inaugurated through his death (Isa 11:4–5). He is vindicated by God through his resurrection and exalted as Lord precisely because of what he suffered (Acts 2:22–36; 4:8–12; Heb 2:3–18; Phil 2:6–11).

Just as Jesus' anointing for ministry is utterly dependent upon the anointing of the Spirit, his expectation is that those who follow him will receive that same anointing to enact the loving power and character of God through their lives. His twelve disciples reconstitute a new community of Israel. He demonstrates the "new law" of love (Matt 22:37–39) among them and through his self-giving obedience summons them also to become a cruciform community of love in word and action. In a kind of Spirit-baptism, as is his privilege (Luke 3:16), Jesus further conforms the twelve and the seventy-two to his image by partially conferring upon them the anointing he eventually opens up for all humanity through his death, resurrection, and exaltation: "he gave them power and authority to drive out all demons and to cure diseases, and he sent them out to proclaim the kingdom of God and to heal the sick" (Luke 9:1; cf. Acts 2:32-33). Both groups return to testify that this is precisely what happened (Luke 9:1-10; 10:1,10). Jesus, who sees the eschatological picture in full, reminds them that their true cause for rejoicing is in their identity as children of God—their names are already "written in heaven" (Luke 10:20)—rather than in the accompanying evidence of that fact. The parallels to the synoptic descriptions of Jesus' Spirit-filled life are unmistakable.

> Jesus went throughout Galilee, teaching in their synagogues, proclaiming the good news of the kingdom, and healing every disease and sickness among the people. News about him spread all over Syria, and people brought to him all who were ill with various diseases, those suffering severe pain, the demon-possessed, those having seizures, and the paralyzed; and he healed them (Matt 4:23-24; cf. Mark 1:32-34; Luke 4:40-43).

The New Testament declaration (and experiential assumption) is that Jesus' followers will do what Jesus does, acting out of love and power in his name and character, as children of their Father in heaven. *They will be like Jesus.* John's Gospel reiterates that as they are united to him and the Father in love (John 15:17), they will be led by the Spirit to live out their eternal life in the present in Jesus' name, and will thus see "greater things than these!" In Acts, Luke presents this as the "new normal" for those who follow Jesus and bear witness to the resurrected Lord. Those who bear Jesus' name will manifest the evidence of the Spirit's presence among them in both "signs and wonders" and in the power to participate in the fellowship of his suffering. Throughout the remainder of the New Testament, God's new community of image-bearing children are called to imitate, both in suffering and glory, the life of their embodied resurrected Lord. They are imperatively joined to their indicative—Jesus Christ.

"This is how we know we are in him: whoever claims to live in him must live as Jesus did." (1 John 2:6)

If Jesus was never really like us, then it seems futile to take seriously a mandate to be like him. He, however, was and is like us. Therefore, we must take his entire life—past, present, and future—with the utmost seriousness. Here alone can we recognize truly human life and remember what we are waiting for—for him and for our final glorious humanity completed in him. Because our life is already a participation "in Christ," our waiting is active, attentive, oriented to Jesus' life and kingdom. We practice eternal life already through the power of the Spirit, in divine humility and authority, power and perseverance, all given in the context of divine and human community. We are the living "testimony of God" (1 John 5:10b): "And this is the testimony: God has given us eternal life, and this life is in his Son. . . . Those who keep his commands live in him, and he in them. And this is how we know that he lives in us: we know it by the Spirit he gave us" (1 John 5:11; 3:24).

John's first epistle is full of eschatological imperatives that stem from the one indicative (the crucified, resurrected Lord Jesus Christ) traced back to the apostolic eyewitness,[21] "which we have looked at and our hands have touched—this we proclaim concerning the Word of life. The life appeared; we have seen it and testify to it, and we proclaim to you the eternal life, which was with the Father and has appeared to us[;] . . . our fellowship is with the Father and with his Son, Jesus Christ" (1:1–3). The community's fellowship is given through the life-giving Spirit, whose most dramatic sign of anointing upon them is God's *agape* among them which gives them eschatological confidence in Jesus who guarantees their eternal life: "This is how love is made complete among us so that we will have confidence on the day of judgment: In this world we are like Jesus" (4:17).

Despite this, and other imperatives tied directly to Jesus' life found in 1 John, this affirmation (along with John's Gospel) has been historically relegated to a "high Christology" that docetically undermines the call to be like Jesus. Indeed, Ernst Käsemann famously declared (in opposition to Bultmann) over half a century ago, John's view of Jesus is "naively docetic."[22] Thankfully, this docetic declaration has not gone uncontested. Marianne Meye Thompson is among the biblical scholars whose work challenges Käsemann as she argues for the humanity of Jesus in John.[23] She contends that failure to see God's Self-revelation precisely in Jesus' humanity is to misunderstand John and the revelation of the Spirit. Jesus walks in truthful correspondence to his identity with the Father and with us, as the authentically human divine Son. His humanity is assumed not least in the objection by some of his own opponents that *as a man* Jesus makes himself equal to God (John 10:33). If divinity threatens to overwhelm the humanity of Käsemann's docetic Jesus, the objection raised by Jesus' opponents assumes that "*anthropos* and *theos* can be construed in contradistinction to one an-

---

21. Just how direct that tracing might be is a matter of extensive Johannine scholarship not taken up here. See, e.g., Brown, *Epistles of John*, 3–45.

22. Käsemann, *The Testament of Jesus*, cited in Thompson, *The Humanity*, 1–2. Käsemann was refuting Bultmann's claim in *The Gospel of John* that "the revealer is nothing but a man."

23. Thompson, *The Humanity*, 117.

other—[that] they represent different realities or realms."²⁴ However, John's testimony does not make this kind of quasi-Nestorian distinction, nor is it docetic. Were either the case, it would be impossible to draw our imperative from Jesus.²⁵ We would be left without hope, and certainly without the true image of God.

In John, the "Word became flesh," which means we must say "the signs are deeds done by a human being."²⁶ John's Gospel emphasizes that in the flesh of Jesus *God* is revealed (John 1:14), while the emphasis of 1 John is that God is revealed *in the flesh* of Jesus (4:2), states Thompson.²⁷ In both texts Jesus' truly human life is taken for granted, even as he displays divine power and identifies with the Father.

> Jesus repeatedly asserts that he works not by his own power and authority, but by God's, and not by his own will, but in submission to that of the Father. . . . On the one hand, the signs do not efface Jesus' humanity. . . . On the other hand, the signs underscore the claim that the works of this human being reveal God's own activity.²⁸

Precisely because this is so we are called to be like him (2:6; 4:17). As he was anointed by the Father and received the empowerment of God the Spirit to live out his identity and vocation "in this world," so it is with us. In *this world* "we are like 'that one'" (3:3, 5, 7, 16; 4:17). Those who are "in God" are shaped by the character and behavior of God's righteousness, truth and love. More specifically, "Whoever claims to live in him must live as Jesus did" (2:6). This is not merely imitation by example or adopting ethical behavior. "The concept is more profound than merely mimicking externals or even obeying Christ's expressed will in a formal way"—rather it "has to

---

24. Ibid.

25. "In Jesus' life the course of God's action towards man is identical with his own existence in the flesh. There is no gap between a realm of truth and a realm of event here. He is the truth; he does the truth; he speaks the truth; he enacts the truth in physical flesh, and what he does in the flesh he is in himself, in his own person" (Torrance, *The Incarnation*, 107).

26. Thompson, *The Humanity*, 121.

27. Ibid., 122. While Thompson's study analyzes Jesus' humanity primarily in John's Gospel, she makes important parallels to the Johannine epistles within the warrants of her study.

28. Ibid., 121. D. Moody Smith argues that the Johannine epistles are specifically written against docetic teaching (probably taught by the schismatics): "Seemingly, the non-Jewish Jesus has become a nonhuman Jesus. The epistle writer insists upon Jesus' humanity, but not his Jewishness." This failure, says Moody, contributes to the problem it seeks to correct ("The Historical Figure," 323).

do with living the whole of life *coram deo,*" in God's presence, as Jesus did.[29] It is to bear the image of Christ, the *eikon* of the invisible God, in obedience to and fellowship with the Father by the power of the Spirit.

John's epistle speaks powerfully and pragmatically about our reality as eschatological image-bearers, using familial language rather than *eikon.* God's "children" are loved by God, who gave his Son for them, and whom God loves as he does his Son. They have been given the Spirit and thus *look like* the Son in their lives together, thereby testifying to the truth of God in their love for one another in word and deed. They bear the family likeness in contrast to the idolaters or false image-bearers who have sought to influence them by bearing false witness through the claim that there is life apart from God and his Son, Jesus of Nazareth. In the face of the deceptive message of these "false teachers" and their "anti-*Christos*" message, this Johannine community of Spirit-anointed people perceives the truth: Their eternal, eschatological life is through Jesus and his fellowship with the Father, having been "born of God" and thus having received their "anointing from the Holy One" (2:20; 3:9).

In a marvelous wordplay, their identity and character as "anointed ones" (*chrisma*) (2:20), who know the truth given by the anointing Spirit, is set in contrast to those who are *anti-Christos*, who point away from Jesus of Nazareth.[30] The Spirit alone makes it possible to see Jesus as the Son of God, just as the Spirit alone can reveal Jesus' crucifixion as a sign of God's glory (love, light, truth, and obedience) rather than "of this world" (darkness, falsehood, hatred, and disobedience).[31] As this community lives their anointed life "in God" in imitation of or participation with Jesus Christ, they live *en Christo*, vs. the *anti-christos*, whose message and manifestation look away from Jesus as God's love in the flesh.[32]

They are Spirit-breathed, empowered children who walk in the light, who do not sin, who keep God's commands as Jesus did and who love one another as an expression of their love for God and his love for them. As image-bearers of God, there is no deceit in them. They can discern truth from falsehood, test the spirits, and recognize idolatry that sets itself up as truth but defames the name and character of God. As Spirit-anointed

---

29. Yarbrough, *1–3 John*, 88. In reflection on this same text, Howard Marshall states: "The test of our religious experience is whether it produces a reflection of the life of Jesus in our daily life; if it fails this elementary test, it is false" (*I John,* 128.)

30. Fee, *How to Read*, 412–13.

31. "True understanding of Jesus' death, resurrection, and exaltation occur only after these events and in light of the teaching of the Spirit . . . the later perspective is the Spirit-inspired one" (Thompson, *The Humanity,* 111–12, 114).

32. Fee, *How to Read*, 411–12.

brothers and sisters who resemble their older brother and Lord, they manifest their participation in his life by caring for one another's basic needs. They know God. They know and rely on the love God has for them, and they know that they live in him and he in them because God has given them "of his Spirit" (4:13, 16).

If that is *what* the community knows, this is *how* they know it: The truth is known at least in part through the enacted imperative of their lives. "This is how we know that we love the children of God: by loving God and carrying out his commands" (5:2). "This is how we know what love is: Jesus Christ laid down his life for us. And we ought to lay down our lives for one another" (3:16); "This is how we know that we live in him and he in us: He has given us of his Spirit" (4:13); "This is how we know who the children of God are . . ." (3:10), and so on. This repeated idiom in 1 John assumes no disconnect between what the community *knows* as eternal life in Christ and how they *enact* it together.[33] Ultimately, they are being transformed as a new creation in this divine-human fellowship of *agape*: "We know that we have passed from death to life, because we love each other"; "This is how we know what love is: Jesus Christ laid down his life for us. And we ought to lay down our lives for one another"; "Dear children, let us not love with words or tongue but with actions and in truth" (3:14–18).

Toward the end of his letter, John sums it up beautifully and somewhat surprisingly: "God is love. Whoever lives in love lives in God and God in them. This is how love is made complete among us so that we will have confidence on the day of judgment: In this world we are like Jesus.[34] There is no fear in love. But perfect love drives out fear, because fear has to do with punishment. The one who fears is not made perfect in love. We love because he first loved us" (4:16b–19). In summary, because we already live in him, look like him, participate in his communion with the Father, share his life through the Spirit, have the apostolic testimony that God sent his Son to save us; because we confess Jesus as God's Son in word and deed and, above all, because of God's love for us, we can rest assured that God's day of eschatological judgment, like the coming of Christ, will find us "confident and unashamed" (4:12–16; 2:28).[35]

---

33. The idiom "*en touto*" or "in this . . ." is rendered "this is how . . ." in most modern translations. It occurs twelve times in 1 John (2:3, 5c; 3:10, 16, 19, 24; 4:2, 9, 10, 13, 17; 5:2). Brown makes specific distinctions between its usage as it refers to something preceding or following. *The Epistles of John*, 248–51.

34. As with 1 John 2:6, to *live* like Jesus is to *be in* and to *know* God (Marshall, *1 John*, 126–27).

35. Johnson, *1, 2, and 3 John*, 112–13.

In this context, love and fear are completely incompatible, since fear has to do with punishment. As Johnson reminds us, "although we will be judged, we will not be punished or condemned (John 3:18; Rom 8:1) . . . the believer in Jesus has already passed from death (spiritual death and its concomitant punishment) to life (John 5:24; 1 John 3:14)."[36] Or, as Marshall states, "This experience of mutual love is fully realized in the fact that we can have confidence on the day of judgment[;] . . . we stand in the same relationship to God as that of Jesus to his Father and we live as Jesus lived (2:6)."[37] Thus in freedom and joy, and in the power of the Holy Spirit, we live out our eternal life and destiny already, like Jesus, as children who bear his Name.

"See what great love the Father has lavished on us, that we should be called children of God! And that is what we are! Dear friends, now we are children of God, and what we will be has not yet been made known. But we know that when Christ appears, we shall be like him, for we shall see him as he is" (1 John 3:1–2). Although we haven't yet seen what we will look like in our final glory in "the redemption of our bodies" when "completeness comes" (Rom 8:18–23; 1 Cor 13:10), we have seen the prototype, the image of the invisible God and the firstborn from among the dead (1 Cor 15: 5–7, 12–49; Col 1:15). We do not yet see all things in heaven and on earth brought to unity under Christ (Eph 1:10), nor do we see all enemies put under his feet (1 Cor 15:25–28). We do not yet see everything put under our feet as God's image bearers (Heb 2:5–10), but "we do see Jesus, who was made lower than the angels for a little while, now crowned with glory and honor because he suffered death" (Heb 2: 9).

The one who makes us holy and we who are made holy are of the same family. Since we have the same Father, Jesus unashamedly calls us his brothers and sisters (Heb 2:11). And he will complete what he started with the Father before the creation of the world (Eph 1:4–5). He will perfect us in his image by the Spirit so that we too will embody love in our relational, eternal life together with him. Just as *agape* will never perish but remains, eternally encompassing faith and hope,[38] we will remain in God and image God's *agape* forever, joined to eternal life in him through the *agape* of the Father, Son, and Spirit.

Eschatology is the end *from the beginning*. In a word, it is about things finally getting to *be* what they were destined for, in relation to God and everything else. The New Testament speaks of Jesus' coming again as God's final judgment over sin and brokenness, speaking his first and last word

---

36. Ibid., 113.
37. Marshall, *I John*, 223–24.
38. N. T. Wright, "Faith, Virtue," 472–97; Fee, *Corinthians*, 369, 641–51.

of life through his Son, and thereby finishing everything through the life-giving Spirit. This triune act of consummation is creation's *telos*. We finally get to be who we are—in unbroken, glorious correspondence to the character, beauty, and love of God. We will become like Jesus in every way that he has become like us.

This anticipation casts out any possibility of fear of judgment. We have already heard God's last word spoken over all things and that word is Jesus Christ. We live and proclaim Jesus—God's eternal life given to us. When Jesus returns with judgment and justice, he will speak his own final word of new creation once more, completely destroying evil and swallowing up the last vestiges of death through unstoppable life. We have no fear because we are *already* participating with Jesus in what he is doing; no fear, because we are joined to the resurrected one and his shared love with the Father; no fear because the one who will come to judge the living and the dead has received the judgment that is ours and given us what is his; no fear, because nothing can separate us from the love of God in Christ (Rom 8:38–39). As we actively wait for Jesus' return, living and loving with heart, soul, mind, and strength, we, as partial glimpses of new creation, join him against all that is evil, broken, anti-*christos* and anti-*agape* in his beloved world. In the process, we become more conformed to his image as we live our lives in correspondence to the self-giving *agape* of our resurrected Lord, the alpha and omega, who mediates the promise that "as it was in the beginning, is now, and ever shall be—world without end." Amen.

Conclusion

Dear Stan,

What a gift to be writing in your honor, to pick up the conversation with you again about being the *imago Dei* and our life in communion with the triune God—including our life to come. If a story is only as good as its ending, the end of a great story brings everything together from the very beginning, and then makes us long for it to go on into "ever after." You told the great story well, because you were and remain deeply embedded in it. Led by the Holy Spirit, bringing great delight to your Father in heaven, you walked with, lived for, hoped in, and spoke lovingly of God's first and last Word—Jesus Christ, Son of Mary, Son of the Father, and firstborn Son over heaven and earth from before the creation of the world to its consummation. You faithfully narrated our hope from a place of joyful communion with God, experienced and anticipated. You also left us in anticipation of what is coming while reminding us of our place in that future *now*. All the while you knew, and now know differently, that it is a far, far better story than we can imagine. We are better for being in community with you.

While writing I have been aware of your presence with me, as the Holy Spirit has enabled our fellowship with the Father and the Son and the communion of the saints. I have frequently had to stop, arrested by holy wonder, as I reflect on what you knew and said so well while simultaneously realizing that now you *know* in a whole new way. I write this in dialogue with what you wrote, knowing that my words echo yours as truth. Nevertheless, at this intersection of new creation, we each bear witness to the truth in different ways. You know what I only know in part. And yet even as you see already what I cannot yet see, *we both still see in part* the consummation of the kingdom from our distinct vantage points. When all is finished, when we know as we are known, we will both tell the story again in a new way.

Stan, my friend, you are already present to the hope that awaits us all. From your place in the divine drama, you testify to the final defeat of our last enemy. You have passed through its jaws, permanently ripped open by the firstborn from among the dead and left gaping until he closes them forever. Moreover, as you presently inhabit a new space or dimension in our eschatological life together, you can hear the Word in ways our ears cannot, echoed by languages of heaven that we rarely speak, hear, or interpret, and even then, only in part. From "further in and further up" you see what we have not yet seen, heard, looked at, or touched with our hands. Though we all have yet to see things finished, you can uniquely say with the Elder in 1 John 1:2: "The life appeared; we have seen it and testify to it, and we proclaim to you the eternal life, which was with the Father and has appeared to us."

Bibliography

St. Athanasius. *On the Incarnation: The Treatise* De Incarnatione Verbi Dei. Crestwood, NY: St. Vladimir's Seminary Press, 1996.

Bauckham, Richard. "The Future of Jesus." In *The Cambridge Companion to Jesus*, edited by Markus Bockmuehl, 265–80. Cambridge: Cambridge University Press, 2001.

Brown, Raymond E. *The Epistles of John*. The Anchor Bible, Vol. 30. Garden City, NY: Doubleday, 1982.

Bruce, F. F. *The Epistle to the Romans*. Tyndale New Testament Commentaries. Grand Rapids: Eerdmans, 1963.

Fee, Gordon. *The First Epistle to the Corinthians*. The New International Commentary on the New Testament. Grand Rapids: Eerdmans, 1987.

———. *Paul, the Spirit and the People of God*. Peabody, MA: Hendrickson, 1996.

Hawthorne, Gerald F. *The Presence & the Power: The Significance of the Holy Spirit in the Life and Ministry of Jesus*. Dallas: Word, 1991.

Johnson, Thomas F. *1, 2, and 3 John*. New International Biblical Commentary, Vol. 17. Peabody, MA: Hendrickson, 1993.

Marshall, I. Howard. *The Epistles of John*. New International Commentary on the New Testament. Grand Rapids: Eerdmans, 1978.

———. *New Testament Theology*. Downers Grove, IL: InterVarsity, 2004.

Thompson, Marianne Meye. *1–3 John*. The IVP New Testament Commentary Series. Downers Grove, IL: InterVarsity, 1992.

———. *The Humanity of Jesus in the Fourth Gospel*. Philadelphia: Fortress, 1988.

Torrance, T. F. *Incarnation: The Person and Life of Christ*. Milton Keynes, UK: Paternoster, 2008.

Watts, Rikk E. "The New Exodus/New Creational Restoration of the Image of God." In *What Does it Mean to be Saved?*, edited by John Stackhouse, 15–41. Grand Rapids: Baker, 2002.

Wright, N. T. "Faith, Virtue, Justification and the Journey to Freedom." In *The Word Leaps the Gaps: Essays on Scripture and Theology in Honor of Richard B. Hays*, edited by J. Ross Wagner, C. Kavin Rowe, and A. Katherine Grieb, 472–97. Grand Rapids: Eerdmans, 2008.

Yarbrough, Robert W. *1–3 John*. Baker Exegetical Commentary on the New Testament. Grand Rapids: Baker, 2008.

Part Four

SCRIPTURE

11

Triangulation in the Psalms of Lament

ELLEN T. CHARRY

Poems that Complain

WITH WHAT STANLEY GRENZ called the "world-creating function of the text" he gave us a supple tool for discerning theological meanings of Scripture.[1] It is a limber application of the Protestant Scripture principle, *sola scriptura*, that argues that the world that the poets intend to create for us to dwell in is the work of the Spirit to form us into a community of believers clustered under a sacred canopy that links us both back to the events that constitute the handholds of Christian identity and forward to God's glorious future onto which we can happily latch. Speaking through the text's authors, the Spirit creates a socially and morally engaged world that shapes our spiritual and moral identity, our longings and our hopes.

This hermeneutic embeds Scripture interpretation within the larger theological task of interpreting the doctrines of the Creed so that they provide a historico-spiritual framework of meaning on which the Christian community stands and from which it lives. Theological interpretation is in the service of the Spirit. Scripture interpretation and doctrinal exegesis undertake the same project. Not only that, but through Scripture and doctrinal interpretation the Christian community offers its framework of meaning to the general community as a Christian suggestion for grounding a wholesome society.

---

1. Grenz, "The Spirit and the Word," 357–74.

This essay is a specific application of Grenz's interpretation of the Protestant Scripture principle. While he, like many hermeneuts, may have been thinking primarily of the scriptural narratives as he wrote, this essay applies his approach to biblical poetry, specifically, the psalms of lament. Prayers of supplication offered to the entire community by individuals in distress, by and for the sick, and those bent under the weight of their own chagrin dominate the Psalter.

Laments are complaints addressed directly to God that cry for help. They often include cries of "how long, O Lord" can this continue (Pss 6:3; 13:1–2; 35:17; 74:9; 79:5; 80:4; 89:46; 90:13; 94:3). They depict the speaker's difficult straits in general terms. The speaker is surrounded by unnamed enemies (17:9, 11; 22:12; 43; 49:5; 88:17; 118:11–12; 140:9), marginalized by family and friends (22:7; 31:11; 38:11; 44:13; 55; 69:8), misunderstood or ostracized, sometimes for due cause (38; 40; 51; 79; 90), but also for no reasons that the speaker understands or accepts (25; 31; 43; 55). Most terrifying of all, the speakers feel inexplicably forgotten or abandoned by God (10; 22; 42; 44; 74; 79; 88; 115). There is a Kafkaesque quality to those lament psalms where the speaker presents himself as an upright and faithful Israelite who is suffering needlessly, while friends and acquaintances scoff gleefully at the complainant's pleading for divine aid that may never come (70:1; 74:10; 79:5; 80:4; 89:46). In these psalms the speaker is triangulated between his faith in God's powerful compassion and empirical evidence.

The Psalter's opening words proclaims God's way of life for Israel: "Blessed are those who do not follow the advice of the wicked, or take the path that sinners tread, or sit in the seat of scoffers" (1:1). And the last verse of this psalm sums up what the complainants believe or strive to hold onto believing in the face of their anguish: "the LORD watches over the way of the righteous, but the way of the wicked will perish." The first poem, not itself a lament but an admonition to Israel to hold fast to God's teaching, points toward the dilemma of the laments without naming the problem. Israel is divided between the righteous who keep to God's teaching and the wicked who scoff at those who do. This stark confrontation between the pious (who will in the long-term be vindicated) and the impious (who will in the long-term perish) pulses throughout the lament psalms. It will be a desperate verse by verse struggle to bring the skeptics back to God by imploring him to act graciously as the history recited in Psalm 106 reminds readers.

In the laments, the circumstances behind the speaker's current plight are rarely if ever specified. What led to the situation is not as important as the fact that the faithful speaker is being scorned by those who neglect God because they fail to see God rescuing the faithful! It seems to be a catch-22.

On one hand, the faithful are scoffed at for their faithfulness. On the other hand, God seems to be on vacation when he should be rescuing those who trust and take refuge in him. Doubters scorn the speaker's faithfulness because they doubt that God is "there" (3:2; 10:4; 14:1/53:1; 42:3, 10; 59:7; 69:9; 70:3; 71:11; 137:3). God is again being forgotten in Israel, as Psalm 78's summary of Israelite history makes clear! Here we have the sloughing off of obedient living in response to the silence of God.

Triangulation saturates the lament psalms. On one level there is of course the immediate confrontation of the believers by scoffers. The issue here is not simply that some are disobedient when they should be delighting in the teaching of God and meditating on it constantly (1:2) but that the speaker(s) cannot meaningfully exhort other Israelites to faithfulness when his own life suggests the absence of God. On another level, the Israelite scoffers are undermining the speaker's call to make God known among all nations (2; 9; 18; 22; 46; 47; 57; 67; 72; 79; 82; 86; 96; 98; 102; 108; 117; 126). The speaker is triangulated among God, other Israelites, and his suffering is not only immediately humiliating and painful but it is undermining his strength to proclaim the goodness and power of God and that righteous way of life to which God lays claim. The complainant understands how much is at stake here for God and Israel while others simply seem not to notice or care.

One theme underlying several of the lament psalms is that by not rescuing the faithful, the impious are not called back to faith based on evidence. Further, by not rescuing corporate Israel from military defeat, exile, and other humiliating international incidents the nations do not see the power of God and so remain in idolatry, taking some Israelites with them. Similarly, by not punishing the nations mounted against Israel God allows them to persist in false faith. Laments whose purview extends beyond the speaker's personal suffering imply that God's failure to vindicate the righteous or to rescue Israel from corporate defeat and suffering in the short-term is self-defeating, if his goal and that for which he has deputized Israel is to bring the whole world under his authority and the way of life he commends to all through the torah of Israel. The complainant is caught between his theological convictions and his personal circumstance.

While on one hand the suppliant confronts God directly, believing that he certainly can attend to the needs of the righteous faithful, on the other, doubt about God's reality or perhaps his power or interest in us, or yet again, perhaps about his faithfulness to his covenantal promises, lurks only slightly beyond the words reported of the complainant's enemies. Now the suppliant, stretched to the limit by God's silence, is exhausted. The only poem to appear twice in the Psalter (14; 53) begins, "Fools say in their hearts, 'There is no God.'" Numerous other psalms reinforce this doubt about God's very existence. "Many are saying to me, 'There is no help for you in God'" (3:2), and "In the pride of their countenance the wicked say, 'God will not seek it out'; all their thoughts are, 'There is no God'" (10:4). Psalm 35:21 identifies the scoffers again: "They open wide their mouths against me; they say, 'Aha, Aha, our eyes have seen it,'" when the suppliant's enemies rejoice. Similarly, Psalm 70:3 has the scoffers saying, "Let those who say, 'Aha, Aha!' turn back because of their shame." "My tears have been my food day and night, while people say to me continually, 'Where is your God?'" and yet again, "As with a deadly wound in my body, my adversaries taunt me, while they say to me continually, 'Where is your God?'" (42:3, 10).

The deepest terror here, however, is not of the immediate enemy or even of God's possible failure to win the nations, whether through gracious love or a coarse display of power, but that the scoffers may be right! It may not be that the true enemy is the scoffers who deny God but that God simply may not be there, or at least is resisting the cries of the faithful, or perhaps is powerless to help, although such embarrassing thoughts are only obliquely hinted at. Worst of all, the terrifying thought arises in the sensitive soul that God may stand behind the scoffers; indeed, God might be the real enemy![2] Job is often pointed to as the biblical book focused on theodicy (the question of the justice and power of God), but the lament psalms explore the same issue far more pointedly since there is no opening scene that depicts God as intentionally testing the suppliant.[3] How is the faithful Israelite to advance the cause of Israel's God among the nations when God's power and goodness are not evident? Our speaker looks silly indeed.

A still further arena of tension, of course, is between the complainant and himself. The weight of Israel's international responsibilities rests on his shoulders. But unless and until God shows his face instead of hiding it, the scoffers may not only get the upper hand with other Israelites and gentiles who exploit every military and political setback that Israel experiences, but with the faithful complainant as he is himself tempted to abandon hope in God and fall over into the camp against which he rails (141).

When Complaint Is Warranted

The Psalter may be the most commented upon text in all of written history and it is presumptuous to think that I might contribute something to

---

2. Fløysvik, *When God Becomes My Enemy*.
3. Moore, *Psalms of Lamentation*, 4–6.

that venerable conversation. Yet the reason no generation can neglect these poems, even if one can no more than rehearse and at best refresh what earlier commentators have said, is perhaps seen most clearly in the prayers of supplication. While recent theologians who long to reclaim the Bible for the more liberal wings of the church admit that there is an intellectual and ontological gap between the world of the Bible and our own, there is no such problem with the psalms, and especially with the psalms of lament. The biblical supplications are irresistible because there is no emotional gap at all between the speakers of pain and suffering and the experience of believers today. Today's believers have little problem understanding the psalms, for the experience of being triangulated between belief in what God ought to be doing and what is actually happening is widespread.[4] Despite intervening millennia, some things simply have not changed. We share the lurking doubt with these poets: maybe God is not! Even staunch believers who can quote Scripture fluently, attend public worship regularly, and cultivate wholesome Christian friendships can be knocked over by suffering and find themselves gasping for spiritual breath. We are emotionally at home with lamentation because we too experience the frustration, anger, sense of abandonment, betrayal, fear, and humiliation (in spite of doing our best at living virtuously) that drove the psalmist(s) to pen these verses. The comfort of the Psalter then lies not only, perhaps not even primarily, in patting us on the hand and saying "God will provide," but in permitting us to doubt even as the psalmist doubts, and to scream against the silence of God even as the poet screams.

At the same time, Christian theology is not quite at home with the lament psalms for it is not comfortable confronting God. From a Christian theological perspective, the lament psalms are somewhat of an embarrassment. Feeling called to protect divine benevolence and power, some Western Christian theologians have insisted that all that happens to us is good and that whatever our circumstance God is to be thanked and gratefully praised. As understandable as the motivation here may be in order to defend the perfection of God, defending divine perfection challenges our readily complaining to God about our plight. Seeking divine intervention to make the problem go away, thereby restoring us to a place of honor in our community and punishing those who have wronged us is to argue with God. The lament psalms are ingenuous or human, even all too human, to steal a phrase from Nietzsche.[5] The tension here is not only between the believer's faith and empirical evidence but also between tending to the philosophical

---

4. Ibid., 115. Quoting Viktor Frankl, *Man's Search for Meaning*.
5. Nietzsche, *Human, All Too Human*, I.

desire to defend the absoluteness of God and the pastoral desire to support the genuine psychological needs of suffering people.

The theological perspective just identified would not see the tension quite this way however, for the pedagogy behind mainstream Christian theology is that people should not take their own suffering all that seriously. Trust in divine absoluteness should suffice to mute one's psychological desire to be vindicated and rescued from suffering. Christian theology absorbed strong doses of Stoicism, Platonism, and Neo-Platonism, as well as Aristotelian philosophy. Christianity's exceptionally high doctrine of sin that makes it difficult to confront God is in part the result of the philosophical insistence on divine absoluteness, of which the psalms know little, although the plea for rescue implies that God is perfectly capable of doing so. Such a staunch belief in one's sinfulness combined with belief in divine absoluteness suggests that whatever one's suffering, it is deserved, and complaining about it is an affront to God's perfect knowledge, goodness, or power. On this view, moving beyond personal pain and the need for succor into acceptance of divine benevolence and power as meting out what is best for us is considered to be spiritual growth. Humility, gratitude, and temperance are the chief virtues and the complainant's reliance on his personal faithfulness as grounds for calling God to account seem Christianly untoward because they challenge belief in the divine perfections inherited from classical Hellenistic philosophical-moral thought.

Despite the clear value of the high-minded Stoic insistence on self-control that squirms at the imprecatory psalms for example, the gap between the comfort that the lament psalms afford and the rather stern emotional restraint required by the desire to defend the absoluteness of God may not be biblically defensible, at least from the perspective of the Psalter. Indeed, reflection on the nature of God, in this case, on the attribution of absoluteness is part of Christianity's philosophical rather than its biblical heritage. Saying that does not impugn the legitimacy of the philosophical inheritance of Christian thought—Christianity would be impossible without it—but awareness of the distinction, with us for about a century now since Adolf Harnack, does free us to read Scripture on its own theological terms, indeed in the terms that Grenz encourages us to read, believing that the Spirit is creating a world for us to dwell in through the scriptural author's gift.

Since Christianity's earliest days, theologians have constructed Christian doctrine using Hellenistic philosophy.[6] The absoluteness of God is one such set of interrelated concepts. The absolute knowledge, goodness, and power of God are not central to the biblical writers as they were by

---

6. Harnack, *History of Dogma*. See vol. 3, ch. 4 on the doctrine of God.

later Christian theologians, although they may reside silently behind the text. Pious Christians insisting on divine absoluteness are now likely to be embarrassed or perhaps confused by the emotional candor of the lament psalms in which the speaker challenges God. The confusion is unbecoming on three levels. At one level, it encourages scorning the candor as sub-Christian or more derisively, "Jewish," that is impious. It is also unbecoming because it suppresses the message of the text. Avoiding the theodicy question may silence the pastoral cry of the speakers with whom we can identify. If we are psychologically honest with ourselves we must own the feelings that some classic Christian interpretation wants to suppress, for they are our own, even if, with Christian training, we hope to be discomfited by them. Finally, it is unbecoming at the theological level because Christians claim that the Holy Spirit inspired the biblical authors, so that their thought is only set aside at the cost of challenging the claim that Scripture has on the church.

Grenz's suggestion that we read Scripture as the work of the Spirit creating a godly world for us liberates us from automatically subordinating our reading of the lament psalms to post-biblical theological principles. There is certainly a time and place for that but trusting that the Spirit is guiding the poesy of the psalmist(s) invites us to heed the independent voice of the text boldly so that Scripture is freed to speak not only to us personally when we seek succor in times of trouble but to the theological tradition itself. Another level of confrontation at work then in our reading of the lament psalms is that between the psalmists and classical Christian theology.

Complaints that Challenge

Several psalms commentators have observed that the psalms seem to traverse the entire gamut of human emotion, and indeed they do span a vast emotional array. Athanasius of Alexandria, for example, identified an appropriate personal circumstance for reciting every psalm.[7] Yet, as suggested above, there is a strong cluster of psalms that depict a faithful Israelite abjured by his community experiencing isolation, censure, and humiliation with concomitant feelings of anger, bewilderment, confusion, and consternation caused by God, or at least by God's inaction. The hope here is to probe that experience, so central to the spirit of the Psalter, as the Holy Spirit's way of creating a world for us to dwell in.

---

7. Athanasius, "Letter to Marcellinus."

Among the lament psalms, several challenge God because the suffering of the suppliant has simply gone on too long (6; 13; 35; 74; 80; 90; 94). There is a natural assumption in these poems that the suffering is caused by God's anger at Israel. Yet, prolonged anger clashes with the suppliant's belief that God is compassionate, restrains his anger, and is able to act compassionately (30:5; 78:38; 85:3, 5; 86:15; 103:8–9; 145:8; cf. Jonah 4:2b). On this basis, the psalmist feels quite comfortable calling on God to explain himself. "Where are you when I need you?" is the basic cry. It is an unspeakably bold question from the perspective of Augustinian-Calvinist piety, which seeks to humble the believer at all costs, but the sheer number of lament psalms cast as Scripture and used in public worship set the complaint's call in larger perspective than personal supplication. Several of these poems promise to proclaim God's goodness and faithfulness publicly once the speaker is rescued (22; 35; 43; 69; 71; 109). Ultimately, the call for God to act functions evangelistically for the sake of God's lordship over all creation. To achieve his own goal of universal sovereignty, as we see it nailed down in Isa 2–4, for example, God must begin by vindicating his most faithful adherents.

While we see the speaker of the lament psalms triangulated between his belief in the compassion and power of God and his suffering at the hands of cynical opponents, we also see God triangulated between the plight of his faithful followers, suffering either unjustly or beyond the term of reasonable chastisement, and his own identity construed as compassionate, slow to anger, and faithful to his followers. In a word, both the speaker of the psalms and God are on the spot, alienated from one another, not because the speaker is overcome by sin before God but because God's very identity calls him to rescue those who are faithful to him when they experience serious setbacks. Indeed, the complainants who call for God to attend to their plight seek to embarrass or flatter God into being faithful to his best and most compassionate self. God may be angry but there are limits to pedagogically helpful punishment. The complaint is for God to be God lest he be lost to all people on earth, beginning with those who should be most faithful to God's torah.

There is a genuine give and take here between God and his followers, suggesting mutual need. We need God to show us the way of righteousness, to discipline us when we fall away and become wicked, and to restore us when discipline succeeds in its pedagogical task, when God's anger abates, and it is time for God to rehabilitate us. In Pss 6, 13, 35, 74, 80, 90, and 94 there is no suggestion that God's anger is implacable. On the contrary, rehabilitation is assumed throughout the laments, with the single exception of Ps 88, which has the speaker completely enclosed in darkness. It may be worth noting, however, that the very next verse of the Psalter jumps to the very opposite view: "I will sing of your steadfast love, O Lord, forever; with my mouth I will proclaim your faithfulness to all generations" (89:1). Although this poem devolves into yet another lament, the long initial upbeat section reminds the speaker's audience of God's longstanding love for and covenant with Israel to which God promises to be faithful and on which even sinful Israel may rely. The other side of the conversation is that God wants or perhaps needs us to remind him of his past graciousness to Israel and to recall him to his covenantal obligations not only to those who take refuge in him, but to all of Israel, despite its failings, and to the nations well beyond, that God may be universally recognized.

Based on the preceding discussion, it is not difficult to see why many Christian commentators on the psalms, perhaps especially on the psalms of lament, sought to Christianize them by christologizing them as part of the larger project of Christianizing Jewish Scripture in light of Jesus Christ. Yet if we are to take the Protestant Scripture principle seriously, fitting the psalms into an external theological framework that derives from events that occurred centuries after they were written obstructs listening to the theology of the text itself. Grenz's premise, that the world-creating power of the Holy Spirit is expressed through the author rather than through later interpreters who were pressured to christologize the psalms, moves us ahead. Rather than explaining the text, christologization may actually be bypassing the work of the Spirit in the life of the original authors of these poems, thereby suppressing their world-creating power.

If the Protestant Scripture principle calls us to attend to the texts themselves, as Grenz seems to intend, as a body of sacred Scripture, the lament psalms challenge the urge of some Christian commentators to domesticate the text in order to render it compatible with later intellectual and theological assumptions. To Christianize the lament psalms anachronizes them and mutes their ability to speak to the Christian tradition on their own terms. Allowing the lament psalms to speak freely, as Grenz's version of the Protestant Scripture principle commends, reveals a society thrashing out its theological identity publicly in pressured situations where suffering unsettles presuppositions and expectations of who God is and how the world is expected to function. Psalm 22 is an especially dear lament for Christian piety, and it has often been christologized. To exemplify the ability of the lament psalms to speak their very own word to us, and to explore how the movement of the psalm illuminates the story of Jesus for Christian devotion and nurture, I examine it here. The examination proceeds in three parts: the canonical context and theme of the psalm, its structure and dynamic, and finally its theological pedagogy.

Psalm 22

Canonical Context and Theme

It is often noted that both Abraham and Moses pressured God to save the people. It is rarely noted that the psalmists are doing the same, but Ps 22 does just that through the complaint of an individual. Like Pss 7 and 13, this poem laments God's absence, and then celebrates rescue to reassure the community that God's love and power are active. There is no need to ask whether the laments are finally for or about the individual, or finally for or about the larger community, for just as Augustine's *Confessions* are deeply personal and published for the sake of the church, Psalms like 9 and 22, by proposing to celebrate or by celebrating personal rescue, offer hope to other sufferers that they too may be vindicated by God's power. After pleading for help for twenty-one verses, Ps 22 suddenly bursts into exultant praise of God, without explaining anything except that the petition was answered. At this good news, the community will celebrate, and that will broadcast knowledge of who God is and what he has done for the supplicant across the world so that both the nations currently and posterity will know that the God of Israel lives, and they will "turn to the Lord" (v. 27). The lament is instrumental to the spread of the good news of God and the establishment of his universal recognition.

Despite being a Davidic psalm, Ps 22 has inspired some commentators to associate it with other biblical figures. While Theodore of Mopsuestia, Abraham Ibn Ezra, and Calvin associate it with David, Midrash Tehillim associates its most poignant phrases with Esther in her days of fasting before the king, and many Christian commentators associate it in part or whole with Jesus (Theodoret of Cyrus, Augustine, and recently John Goldingay, who uses the association to better understand Jesus, not the psalm[8]). Although Theodore and Calvin demur from the identification, wholesale association of the complainant with Jesus was encouraged by the fact that Matthew and Mark have Jesus speaking the first verse of this psalm on the cross, that Mark incorporates verses 7 and 8, and Mark, Luke, and John cite verse 18 at the crucifixion.[9]

---

8. Goldingay, *Psalms 1:1–41*, 342–43.

9. Augustine is the most brilliant of the christological interpreters. He comments twice on this psalm, once with a running commentary and once in a long and exhaustive sermon. He is persuaded both that the speaker is Christ and that the poem is written to the catholic church against the Donatist church that Augustine was fighting at the time. A vivid reading of the psalm will enable us to read our own suffering through Christ's suffering on the cross to realize that God is a doctor, and that our troubles are a medicine bringing us to salvation, not a punishment leading to damnation. Under

Structure and Dynamic

Our bedraggled suppliant is desperate (vv. 1–21a), and in typical fashion addresses God directly, adducing all sorts of reasons why God should hurry to rescue him. Verse 21 is itself both a plea for rescue and a dramatic and sudden announcement of rescue in unexplained succession.[10] With the abrupt shift from imploring God in the imperative to proclaiming being answered in the perfect tense, the poem segues into public worship and praise (vv. 21b–26), and further outward from there to "the ends of the earth" and into the future (vv. 27–31).

The dynamic is typically expansive beginning with personal distress that is likely to arouse the hearer's sympathy, then turning outward in communal praise of God, and then, in this case, to global conversion of those who learn of God's wonderful work on behalf of the suppliant from the laudatory congregation. The rescue of one is for the expansion of God's reign beyond Israel. The dynamic of this psalm resonates deeply with the evangelistic commitment of the Christian gospel, based on personal testimony. Now we shall take a closer look at the dynamic movement within the psalm's segments.

I am a mess! (1–21a)

In this long lament, the speaker complains of feeling abandoned by both God (vv. 1–5) and other people (vv. 6–8). Despite being in extremis, he cannot bring himself to abandon God and turns back to him pleading for rescue from the enemies, depicted as multiple wild beasts, on account of both the longstanding enemies, the relationship he has with God (vv. 9–11) and the dire straits he is in (vv. 12–21). He thinks that this will surely rouse God to action.

---

medical treatment you undergo cautery, or the knife, and you scream with pain. The doctor does not listen when you beg him to stop, but he does listen to your need for healing" Augustine, *Expositions of the Psalms: 1–32*, 230.

10. Both Amos Haham and Goldingay hold the two cola of verse 21 together by interpreting the second verb, עֲנִיתָ֫נִי, to be in the precative mood, indicating a request rather than in the past tense as NRS and Alter do because, as Goldingay says, the shift within one verse from the imperative to the past tense "seems artificial" (Hakham, *The Bible: Psalms with the Jerusalem Commentary*, 164; Goldingay, *Psalms 1:1–41*, 335). Alter points to this verse as the turning point of the psalm precisely because it accounts for the next and concluding segment that bursts into praise by stating that God has indeed answered, rescuing him from the horns of wild oxen (*The Book of Psalms*, 75). Reading as a precative, however, is even more jarring than reading it as a past tense because that leaves no point at which the complainant receives an answer.

Where are you, God? (vv. 1–5)

Our sufferer finds no warrant for God not acting given his (the sufferer's) constant imploring.[11] He is exhausted by the intensity of his own prayers (v. 2), and appeals to the faithfulness of Israel's patriarchs, who trusted and were released from their suffering without reproach, as a reason for God to heed his cries. Appealing to the ancestors suggests that the current generation is not as worthy, perhaps not as faithful as those in ancient times, and God must be relied upon to act mercifully on account of the past praises of Israel, not the faithfulness of the present generation within which the speaker is so distastefully embroiled. By the end of the poem, however, the author is inviting the congregation back into those very praises based on the dramatic reversal of the speaker's circumstance. Rhetorically, the poet is reminding his congregation of the standard of piety they are called to as much as he is reminding God of the piety of Israel's ancestors who set the standard for Israel's faithfulness. An effect of this rhetoric is to call Israel to faithfulness indirectly, not haranguing or scolding them, but encouraging them to honor their heritage and live into the best of their identity.

I am mocked (vv. 6–8)

From attention to Israel's noble past, the complainant turns to his personal circumstance, offering a second reason God should act decisively. Our speaker feels like a worm from the shame he is suffering, and mentions both non-verbal and verbal forms of contempt that he is experiencing (v. 6). He reads contempt in people's facial gestures (v. 7), and is taunted verbally as well (v. 8). While the Rule of Benedict appreciated the power of the analogy to a worm to cultivate monastic humility, other commentators were arrested

---

11. Verse 1 gained special notoriety because Jesus speaks the first colon after the superscription from the cross, according to Matt 27:46. This causes some consternation in Christian circles since, being God, Jesus could not abandon himself! Relying on orthodox two-natures Christology worked out by the mid-fifth century, the remark was often attributed to Christ's human nature to protect involvement of the divine nature. E.g., Theodoret says that the abandonment does not suggest separation from his divine nature but "the permission given for the Passion: the divinity was present to the form of a slave in his suffering and permitted him to suffer so as to procure salvation for the whole of nature. Of course, it was not affected by suffering from that source: how could the impassible nature suffer? It is Christ the Lord as man, on the contrary, who speaks these words, and since he was the first fruits of human nature, it is on behalf of all nature that he utters the words in what follows: *The words of my failings are far from saving me*" (Theodoret of Cyrus, *Commentary on the Psalms*, 146).

by such a negative metaphor and sought to turn it to good effect.[12] Midrash Tehillim used it to comfort: "Like a worm whose only resource is its mouth, so the children of Israel have no resource other than the prayers of their mouths. Like a worm which roots out a tree with its mouth, so the children of Israel with the prayers of their mouths root out the evil decrees which [hostile] nations of the earth devise against them."[13] Even Calvin, who does not usually shy away from reminding his readers of their failings using discouraging imagery, finds the worm image off-putting. "This, it is true, seems at first sight to have a tendency to discourage the mind, or rather to destroy faith; but it will appear more clearly from the sequel, that so far from this being the case, David declares how miserable his condition is, that by this means he may encourage himself in the hope of obtaining relief."[14]

The verbal taunt of verse 8 takes us back to the struggle played out in Pss 10:4 and 14:1, where the suppliant finds his faith challenged by disbelief, and ahead to Jesus on the cross, where his messianic pretensions are ridiculed with this verse (Matt 27:43). Sarcasm is the voice of cynicism and it is easily arrayed against anyone who suffers willingly, and even dies in the integrity of earnest conviction. When the stakes are high, the cynic hides from becoming embroiled in the struggle for the common good, feeling prudent for having avoided risk. The thwarted risk-taker looks foolish by comparison, at least in the short run.

Come to me! (vv. 9–11)

This strophe offers God another reason to help our afflicted one; it is God's job. God has been taking care of our sufferer since the womb; why should he stay far away now when no one else can help? God assumed responsibility for people's well-being by creating them, and until now has stayed faithfully at his post. Our pleader knows himself to have been cared for by God all his life. The complaint is that God is now shirking the responsibility that he took on at the dawn of human life itself. The suppliant is not pointing to any virtue or merit of his own, but only to God's role as giver and sustainer of life. The assumption is that God has no right to "slumber or sleep," as Ps 121:4 would put it. His watch does not end at midnight, or at dawn. The poet is reminding God that care for people is a full-time job. God does not get vacations.

---

12. Benedict, *Rb 1980*, 199.
13. Braude, *Midrash on Psalms*, 315–16.
14. Calvin, *The Book of Psalms: 1–35*, 1:365.

The theology here is the precise opposite of the thought that suffering is punishment for sin or that God is angry and justly punishes in order to break rebellious spirits. On the contrary, God is accountable for failing to alleviate the suffering. His love for the sufferer is so obvious to both the speaker and the local audience that it does not need to be stated but can be called upon almost to embarrass God into acting. The supplicant is not passive; his deep trust in God's providential care attests palpably to his tenacious clinging to his belief that God has not, nor even could, abandon him. The opening verse is an attention-getting device set against this deeper revelation that the speaker cannot abandon God or fully and finally believe that God has abandoned him. Neither can he, our speaker, abandon God. He just can't.

In contrast to pieties that teach that suffering should stimulate introspection on one's sinfulness to generate humility and a turn to God in self-despair, our poet here teaches that celebrating God's powerful deeds of rescue will arouse confident devotion. The psalmist's interest is not in fostering humility, but in eliciting devotion. Surely there is need for both; one need not be forced to choose since both will speak their own voice in due season.

I am perishing! (vv. 12–21a)

That God has been faithful throughout the speaker's life sets the stage for the next reason he offers to God in his argument for immediate rescue; his suffering is acute. The urgency is heightened by the analogies between the vicious oppressors and wild beasts: bulls, stallions, lions, wild dogs, and wild oxen. The images aggregate to paint a picture of the supplicant surrounded by feral forces that are not subject to reason and will not be assuaged until the victim is no more. Verse 18, famously quoted by all four evangelists at the crucifixion of Jesus, depicts both enemies and cynical bystanders unable to restrain their crude urge to seize the victim's clothes, even before he is dead! The beastly analogies attest to the subhuman character of the victim's pursuers, portrayed by the analogies to the brutes.

One of the most arresting features of this psalm is its graphic portrayal of the psychosomatic effects of the experience of rejection and persecution by these "animals". He tells us what it feels like. He is poured out like water; his bones are falling apart; his insides are melting like wax (v. 14). His whole body is dried out so that his tongue sticks with aphasia (v. 15), and his limbs falter from constriction (v. 16).

No conversation passes between victim and persecutors. There is nothing to say. It is too late for words. Each side has dug in its heels. His pursuers look at and stare right through him as he struggles to "count his bones" and stand up straight, pulling himself up to whatever dignity he can muster (v. 17) as he feels his life tottering at sword point (v. 20). With one last "save me from the lion's mouth," verse 21b continues with either "and from the horns of wild oxen," or shockingly catapults to "you have saved me from the horns of wild oxen."

The community celebrates (vv. 21b–26)

Regardless of whether verse 21b requests deliverance or announces it, the following strophe finds the speaker publicly celebrating what has happened to him, for this is not news one can keep to oneself (v. 22). One is reminded of the inability of observers of Jesus' healing miracles not to tell everyone what they had seen, despite Jesus imploring them not to do so (Mark 1:44–45 [Luke 5:14–5]; 7:36), as well as of the speed with which the proclamation of Jesus' resurrection spread abroad. In all cases, word of mouth is the way the good news of God spreads. Our former victim calls those who revere the Lord—indeed, every single Israelite—to praise, honor, and admire God for his personal rescue, which tells out the truth of who God really is. Whether that happened "on-stage" in verse 21b or "off-stage" in some other unmentioned moment is not clear, but by verse 24 it is accomplished. God is not preoccupied with the rich and famous but with the weak and lowly. God listens.

The next verse of this strophe begins with an odd phrase. It reads literally "my praise is from you (מֵאִתְּךָ)" and is usually translated that way.[15] Perhaps the fuller thought of the verse, in keeping with the preceding verses, is that the transformation of pleading into public praise is "from God" in the sense that praise results from what God has done. The public testimony has cash value too; the celebrant offers to keep his vows with total disclosure. While here the fulfillment of vows—perhaps a sacrifice of thanksgiving—is spontaneous, Jesus commends the same practice when, after healing a leper, he prods the man to go to the priest and offer sacrifice "as a testimony to them" (Mark 1:44).[16] In this psalm, the experience of release from suffering is not a private exchange between God and an individual but an opportunity

---

15. To avoid the awkwardness, Alter translates it "for you" (*Book of Psalms*, 75).

16. Jesus' instructions to the healed man both not to tell anyone what had happened and yet to go right to the priest to offer sacrifice as a public testimony seems a bit odd if not disingenuous since telling the priest is a sure way to publicize the healing.

to strengthen the community spiritually and materially through various expressions of gratitude.

At this point, the celebrant's personal victory gives way to the larger point the poet says God is making though him. His rescue makes way for others to hope as well. The poor will eat their fill and, like our speaker, praise the Lord. Now our singer sings with double joy. Not only is he experiencing his own rescue but is able to bring the good news of God to the poor everywhere so that those who seek God may join his thanksgiving. The strophe ends with a rousing cheer: "May you be enlivened forever!"

Everyone will worship God (vv. 27–31)

We have traveled from anguished despair to public celebration and far-ranging hope. Now our psalmist carries that hope in yet another outward streaming direction. The last five verses of this psalm reach to the ends of the earth to gather all the families of the gentiles to God in worship. The phrase "all the families" immediately calls to mind Gen 12:3, of which Paul made much ado. The single rescue operation—although it occurred in Israel—constitutes evidence that extends far beyond this locale. Our psalmist concurs with the conviction of Isa 2:2–4 that God's scope includes the gentiles. With the dynamic rescue of this one Israelite we have a model for that later Jew who did succeed in bringing masses of gentiles to the God of Israel, that perhaps our psalmist envisioned but did not witness. I will say more on this in our conclusion. This vision of the universal scope of God's reign is no prediction of the events so long after, although the Christian imagination may have difficulty resisting connecting them. Indeed, this poem authenticates the theological contiguity of the latter events not only with Scripture but with the sensibility of the community shaped by many experiences of deliverance, this being but one of them.

While verse 30 transposes this eschatological vision of God's worldwide reign into temporal terms—God's reign is not only geographically but also temporally extended—verse 29 offers a perspective that is out of keeping with other expressions of psalmic theology. Taken at face value, the verse suggests that God will be worshipped not only around what we now call the globe (vv. 27–28) and on into posterity (v. 30), but that the dead will also bend the knee. That the dead are in some sense able to worship God may resonate with medieval Christian eschatology, which has souls distributed in various locales awaiting reunion with their bodies, but other psalms are quite clear that the dead are dead and do not praise God (6:5;

88:10; 115:17).[17] If these dramatic closing verses are the psalmist's distinctive theology, he employs it to give us a grand vision of the triumph of the reign of God. It emerges from one Israelite's plaintive cry for recompense and spreads outward in dramatic concentric circles first to all Israel (the congregation, especially the poor), then to the ends of the earth to embrace the gentiles, and finally includes those who have passed on and those yet to be born (vv. 30–31).

Theological Pedagogy

Our psalmist is a deft pastor and evangelist. He has been very busy gently leading Israel indirectly to rely unflinchingly on God, even as they are tempted to cynicism observing God's seeming absence from one who clings to him. While he depicts the enemies as vicious animals, he surely allies his audience with his own situation, calling forth their sympathy, compassion, and support, even as they realize that someday they could be in his place. He works two fronts simultaneously, teaching compassion for the suffering and the poor, and binding together in mutual support those who revere God and nourish community morale and well-being. Finally, he lays a third responsibility on the shoulders of his hearers. By their compassion, mutual support, celebratory worship, and devotion to God they extend the reign of God in both space and time.

While this psalm covers many bases, finally it is about God's responsibility for Israel's well-being, for the ingathering of the gentiles under the dominion of God, and gloriously for those who have gone before and those who are yet to come. Yet all of this is without a harsh word, without threat, and without embarrassing his audience. The writer trusts his hearers to take up the challenges he lays before them because he and they are fundamentally of one accord—or so he treats them. That is, his theology and his call dignify his auditors as the Israel of God, elected for the great and noble purpose of the glory of the Lord to which he lifts them.

---

17. Ibn Ezra was understandably uncomfortable with the idea that the dead worship God; it is not a Jewish idea. He interprets דִּשְׁנֵי־אֶרֶץ (those who sleep in the ground) as "fat ones of the earth," "who enjoy themselves in this world. They eat all kinds of fat food. *The fat ones* are the opposite of *the humble* [of verse 27].... If the fat ones enjoy themselves in this world, they will ultimately bow to God who gathers their spirit at the end of their lives."

Conclusion

If indeed, we do believe the Holy Spirit to be at work in the original contexts of the writing of Scripture—however limited our understanding of it may be—we need to come to terms with the theology of the texts, even when it upends later theology that is comfortable and comforting. The lamenting poets strive with God, not only because they suffer, but because they refuse to accept God's silence in the face of covenant promises that identify God's willingness to stand by them. God simply cannot be permitted to abandon those who love and revere him and seek to have his name honored among all nations everywhere. Those who truly honor God call him to account just as we must call one another to account.

Unlike later Christian theology, these poems are not afraid to grapple with the terrible possibility both they and we face that God is not, all the while knowing that we cannot long survive with such bare atheism that can easily lead to despair in the face not only of life's unavoidable contingencies but also in light of sin, both our own and that directed against us. Those who simply cannot not believe are burdened with facing the theodicy question head on, and for the Psalter the answer to the question is offered even before we see the extent of the problem that the lament psalms lay before us. Psalm 1 gives us the answer to the despair the theodicy dilemma shadows. The righteous who live by the torah of God, even when spurned for doing so, are privileged, honored, blessed, in the same way that those who practice the way of life depicted in the Matthean "beatitudes" are.

Taken together, the message of the lament psalms and the beatitudes is that personal integrity is foundational for well-being. Remaining faithful to high principles and standing tall against the temptations that would corrupt the soul is the source of satisfaction with one's life, even when the going is morally tough. Psalm 1, in its terse six verses, only hints that it has the answer to the problem the collection will raise. When it concludes "the LORD watches over the way of the righteous, but the way of the wicked will perish" it may not be only saying that if we can just hold out long enough our circumstances will improve. It may also be hinting that *even if* our circumstances do not improve, God is still watching over us because our integrity as faithful followers of God is not impugned, even in difficult straits.

Yet this tough encouragement is not easy to glean from the laments themselves. They leave the impression rather that the poems have failed to bring Israel back to God's teaching, and so have failed to bring the nations to God. Indeed, Christianity's eventual legalization and subsequent disenabling of Judaism to pursue the evangelization of the nations on its own terms forced the Jewish tradition to turn inward, guarding its own flame of devotion to God as best it could, frequently under trying circumstances. Yet the Isaian hope that the nations would stream to the mountain of the Lord God of Israel was realized through the tortured death and proclaimed resurrection of one Jew. Paul, the first to grasp this change in the fortunes of Israel by which the resurrection overturned the despairing psalmist(s)' cry, put the astounding reversal of understanding success and failure this way: "God's foolishness is wiser than human wisdom, and God's weakness is stronger than human strength" (1 Cor 1:25). Together then, Jews and Christians continue to sustain knowledge and love of God among the discouraged, the mocked, and the despised by clinging to the poems they share.

Bibliography

Alter, Robert. *The Book of Psalms: A Translation with Commentary*. New York: Norton, 2007.
Athanasius. "Letter to Marcellinus." In *The Classics of Western Spirituality*, edited by Robert C. Gregg, 101–47. New York: Paulist, 1980.
Augustine. *Expositions of the Psalms: 1–32*, edited by John E. Rotelle. Translated by Maria Boulding. Vol. 1, Works of Saint Augustine: A Translation for the 21st Century. Hyde Park, NY: New City, 2000.
Benedict. *Rb 1980: The Rule of St. Benedict in Latin and English with Notes*. Translated by Timothy Fry. Collegeville, MN: Liturgical, 1981.
Braude, William Gordon, ed. *Midrash on Psalms*. 2 vols. Yale Judaica Series. New Haven: Yale University Press, 1959.
Calvin, John. *The Book of Psalms: 1–35*. Translated by James Anderson. Vol. 1, Calvin's Commentaries. 1854. Reprint. Grand Rapids: Baker, 1998.
Fløysvik, Ingvar. *When God Becomes My Enemy: The Theology of the Complaint Psalms*. St. Louis: Concordia, 1997.
Goldingay, John. *Psalms 1:1–41*. 3 vols. Baker Commentary on the Old Testament Wisdom and Psalms. Grand Rapids: Baker, 2006.
Hakham, Amos. *The Bible: Psalms with the Jerusalem Commentary*. Translated by Rabbie Israel V. Berman. The Koschitzky Edition. The Jerusalem Commentary, 3 vols. Jerusalem: Mosad Harav Kook, 2003.
Harnack, Adolf. *History of Dogma*. Translated by Neil Buchanan. English from the 3rd German edition. 7 vols. New York: Dover, 1961.
Harries, Richard. *After the Evil: Christianity and Judaism in the Shadow of the Holocaust*. Oxford: Oxford University Press, 2003.
Moore, R. Kelvin. *Psalms of Lamentation and the Enigma of Suffering*. Vol. 50, Mellen Biblical Press Series. Lewiston, NY: Mellen, 1996.
Nietzsche, Friedrich Wilhelm. *Human, All Too Human, I*. Translated by Gary J. Handwerk. Stanford: Stanford University Press, 1997.
Theodoret. *Theodoret of Cyrus: Commentary on the Psalms*. Translated by Robert C. Hill. The Fathers of the Church. Washington, DC: Catholic University of America Press, 2000.

12

Renewing a Doctrine of Scripture

A. T. B. McGowan

Introduction

THE PURPOSE OF THIS chapter, in dialogue with the writings of Stan Grenz, is to explore the relationship between the Word of God and the Spirit of God, and to highlight the dangers that can occur when a careful biblical and theological balance between the two is not maintained.

When I was first asked to write a chapter for this *Festschrift*, one of the editors suggested I might use it to respond to some of the criticisms of my book, *The Divine Spiration of Scripture*.[1] In making this suggestion he pointed out that, when arguing for a pneumatological view of Scripture, I had noted the influence of Stan Grenz on my thinking. This is what I said:

> This pneumatological approach to the doctrine of Scripture was advocated by Stanley Grenz in his *Revisioning Evangelical Theology*.[2] He said that, "our bibliology must revision the link between the Holy Spirit and Scripture" on the grounds that "the purpose of Scripture is instrumental to the work of the Spirit."[3] He argued that, although Reformed theology in its confessional documents advocated a pneumatological approach to Scripture, this had often been neglected or forgotten, sometimes due to the

---

1. Also, in U.S., *Divine Authenticity of Scripture*.
2. Grenz, *Revisioning*.
3. Ibid., 113.

adoption of a particular theological method. "Consequently, the reestablishment of the integral link between Spirit and Scripture must begin methodologically through the reorientation of the doctrine of Scripture under the doctrine of the Holy Spirit."[4]

As I developed this theme, it led me to two conclusions, one concerning the *location* of our doctrine of Scripture and one concerning the *content* of our doctrine of Scripture. First, I argued that we should speak about God before we speak about his Word, hence in our system of doctrine (the structure of our systematic theology) Scripture should be placed under the doctrine of God, as an aspect of the work of the Holy Spirit, rather than at the beginning, to provide grounds for an epistemology. Second, I argued that our whole doctrine of Scripture must be viewed pneumatologically, and I sought to spell out the Holy Spirit's work in relation to Scripture, from the time it was written through to the use he makes of it today.

Unfortunately, because I argued that "infallibility" was a better term to use than "inerrancy," in describing our doctrine of Scripture, this pneumatological emphasis was overlooked by most of the articles and reviews that appeared in response to the book, almost all of which focused on the issue of inerrancy.

The separation of my arguments for a pneumatological view of Scripture from my discussion regarding inerrancy, actually leads to serious misinterpretation. My suggestion that "infallibility" was a better word than "inerrancy" was not intended to weaken the argument for a high view of Scripture but was a natural consequence of a pneumatological view of Scripture. As we shall see below, both Calvin and the *Westminster Confession of Faith* make it clear that the authority of Scripture is not to be located in the existence of inerrant *autographa* but rather in the fact that Scripture is the vehicle used by God the Holy Spirit to make God and his will known to us. It was my contention that Herman Bavinck and the Dutch tradition more accurately maintained the import of what Calvin and the *Westminster Confession* say on Word and Spirit, than the tradition emanating from Princeton.

In this chapter, I would like to do three things. First, to restate my convictions regarding the relationship between Scripture (the Word of God written) and the Holy Spirit; second, to offer some evidence of what can happen when this relationship is undermined by neglecting the person and work of the Holy Spirit; and third, to offer some evidence of what can happen when this relationship is undermined by neglecting the authority of God's Word. I have entitled these sections as follows: Word and Spirit; Theological Method; and Theological Balance.

4. Ibid., 114.

Word and Spirit

In seeking to develop a pneumatological doctrine of Scripture, I made four affirmations regarding the relationship between the Holy Spirit and Scripture. First, the Holy Spirit brought the Scriptures into existence; second, the Holy Spirit enabled the church to recognize what was Scripture and what was not; third, the Holy Spirit helps us to understand the meaning and interpretation of Scripture; and fourth, the Holy Spirit empowers the preaching of Scripture. It is perhaps useful to spell these out in a little more detail.

The Holy Spirit Brought the Scriptures into Existence

This first affirmation regarding the relationship between the Holy Spirit and Scripture refers to the origins of Scripture. After the disciples had witnessed the ascension of Jesus, they returned to Jerusalem and spent time in prayer in an upper room in the city. During this time, Peter said something about Judas Iscariot that has a bearing on our subject. As we read in Acts 1:15–17: "In those days Peter stood up among the believers (a group numbering about a hundred and twenty) and said, 'Brothers, the Scripture had to be fulfilled which the Holy Spirit spoke long ago through the mouth of David concerning Judas, who served as guide for those who arrested Jesus—he was one of our number and shared in this ministry.'"[5] Peter was probably referring to Ps 109:8, but the key point is his statement that it was the Holy Spirit who spoke "through the mouth of David." This is part of the evidence for the argument that the Holy Spirit is the ultimate author of the Scriptures. David himself recognized that he had been an agent of the Holy Spirit, as we see from 2 Sam 23:1–2: "These are the last words of David: 'The oracle of David son of Jesse, the oracle of the man exalted by the Most High, the man anointed by the God of Jacob, Israel's singer of songs: The Spirit of the LORD spoke through me; his word was on my tongue.'"

In the New Testament, both Paul and Peter attest to the action of the Holy Spirit in bringing the Scriptures into existence. Paul reminds young Timothy that he had known the Holy Scriptures from childhood and then says, in 2 Tim 3:16–17, "All Scripture is God-breathed and is useful for teaching, rebuking, correcting and training in righteousness, so that the man of God may be thoroughly equipped for every good work." This statement that all Scripture is breathed out by God is an affirmation that God is the ultimate author of Scripture. Taken together with what we have seen above, there can be little doubt that it is God the Holy Spirit who was the

---

5. Scripture references in this chapter are from the NIV.

agent of this divine spiration. Peter supports this interpretation when he writes in 2 Pet 1:20–21: "Above all, you must understand that no prophecy of Scripture came about by the prophet's own interpretation. For prophecy never had its origin in the will of man, but men spoke from God as they were carried along by the Holy Spirit." The writers of Scripture were not putting down their thoughts for posterity, they were under the compulsion of the Holy Spirit and could do no other.

Having emphasized that it was the Holy Spirit who brought the Scriptures into existence, we must also be careful to emphasize the active involvement of the human authors. In other words, what we have said about the Holy Spirit in relation to the writing of Scripture should not be taken to imply a "dictation theory" of the origins of Scripture, as if the minds of the human authors simply went blank and then God started speaking words which they hurriedly wrote down. God the Holy Spirit is certainly the one who "breathed out" the Scriptures, but he did not overrule or undermine the humanity and creative ability of the authors. For example, at the beginning of his gospel, Luke tells us that he had "carefully investigated everything from the beginning," and so had written "an orderly account." There was hard work involved in the research and writing of his gospel, and this is not in any way undermined by also affirming that what he wrote came about because of the work of the Holy Spirit "carrying" him along. Certain expressions of the inerrantist position, while formally rejecting the concept of a "dictation theory," nevertheless do not say enough about the human authors. As Peter said, it was "men" who spoke, yet they spoke "from God" as they were "carried along" by the Holy Spirit. Any doctrine of Scripture must affirm that these documents had their origins in the sovereign action of God the Holy Spirit, while also taking account of the fact that it was "men" who spoke from God.

The Holy Spirit Enabled the Church to Recognize What Was Scripture and What Was Not

This second affirmation regarding the relationship between the Holy Spirit and Scripture refers to issues of canonicity. I did not deal with this subject in my book on Scripture because it is such a huge area, with a significant literature. I simply wanted to make the point that in determining the canon of Scripture I believed that the church was guided by the Holy Spirit. In terms of the Old Testament, the church received these books as canonical because they were the books used by Christ and the apostles. For example, when writing his account of the crucifixion and its aftermath, the apostle

John sets the whole account in the context of the fulfilment of Scripture (John 19:24, 28, 36–37). Jesus himself frequently spoke of Old Testament Scriptures being "fulfilled" through his own life and ministry (Mark 12:10; Luke 4:21; John 13:18; 17:12). The most significant statement regarding this fulfilment came after his resurrection, when he met with two of his followers on the road to Emmaus. As we read in Luke 24:27: "And beginning with Moses and all the Prophets, he explained to them what was said in all the Scriptures concerning himself."

The church had a more difficult task in relation to the canonical formation of the New Testament. Some decisions were perhaps easier than others. For example, it seems clear that the apostle Peter regarded Paul's writings as Scripture. This is what he says in 2 Pet 3:15–16: "Bear in mind that our Lord's patience means salvation, just as our dear brother Paul also wrote to you with the wisdom that God gave him. He writes the same way in all his letters, speaking in them of these matters. His letters contain some things that are hard to understand, which ignorant and unstable people distort, as they do the other Scriptures, to their own destruction." Notice, there were people who distorted Paul's teaching "as they do the other Scriptures." He does not say, "as they do the Scriptures" but "as they do the *other* Scriptures," thus placing Paul's writings on a par with Old Testament Scripture.

Other decisions must have been more difficult. There were many "gospels" and other books being written, but which of them should be included? The Roman Catholic Church has always argued that, the church having "discerned" which books were to be recognized as Scripture, the authority of these books cannot be separated from the authority of the church itself.[6] Other theologians argue that it was simply a case of durability: some books quickly fell into disuse, others were regularly copied and used and establishing the canon amounted to the "survival of the fittest." Over against these views, evangelical theologians largely support the view articulated very

---

6 See the following from the Catechism of the Catholic Church. 85. "The task of giving an authentic interpretation of the Word of God, whether in its written form or in the form of Tradition, has been entrusted to the living teaching office of the Church alone. Its authority in this matter is exercised in the name of Jesus Christ." This means that the task of interpretation has been entrusted to the bishops in communion with the successor of Peter, the Bishop of Rome." 95. "It is clear therefore that, in the supremely wise arrangement of God, sacred Tradition, Sacred Scripture and the Magisterium of the Church are so connected and associated that one of them cannot stand without the others. Working together, each in its own way, under the action of the one Holy Spirit, they all contribute effectively to the salvation of souls."

persuasively by F. F. Bruce,[7] namely, that the church was enabled by the Holy Spirit to recognize those books which were truly "God breathed" Scripture.

This is not to ignore the fact that, in determining the canon, the church followed a process in which it was guided by some basic principles, for example, that a book could only be included if had been written by an apostle or endorsed by an apostle. Nevertheless, there was great debate over the canon in the early centuries of the Christian church. Even at the end of the second century there were still arguments over 2 Peter, 2 John and 3 John, Jude, Hebrews, and Revelation. It was the challenge of the heretic Marcion that forced the church to give consideration to finalizing the canon of Scripture during the third and fourth centuries. In AD 367, Bishop Athanasius, in his Easter letter, gave a list of the New Testament books. Later, at the Synod of Carthage in AD 397, this was confirmed to be the position of the church as a whole, hence the New Testament canon as used today was agreed.

The question of which Old Testament books were canonical was compounded by discussion of the "Deutero-canonical" or "Apocryphal" books. Later versions of the Septuagint (Greek Old Testament) contained books that were written between 300 BC and AD 70. These books are called the "apocryphal" books, from a Greek word meaning "hidden things." They are also sometimes called "deutero-canonical," which means "belonging to the second canon." The Roman Catholic Church and the Eastern Orthodox Churches include some of these books (different ones) in their Bibles. This argument re-surfaced at the Reformation. The Roman Catholic Church has included these books in the Bible but the Protestant churches have not, preferring to remain with the definitive list given by Athanasius in the fourth century in his Easter letter.

The Jews held a council at Jamnia in c. AD 100 when they agreed the canon of the Hebrew Bible, not including any of the apocryphal books. At the Reformation, the Protestant churches said that the Bible should contain the Hebrew Bible as approved at the Council of Jamnia and the New Testament as finalized in the fourth century. Martin Luther, however, did include in his German Bible the apocryphal books, but in a separate section and with a clear statement that, although they were helpful and valuable, they were not Scripture. Even the *Westminster Confession*, while excluding the apocryphal books from the canon, agrees that they may be read with profit, as with other human writings.

Despite these disagreements over the apocryphal books, theologians from all of the major traditions, whether Orthodox, Catholic, or Protestant,

---

7. Bruce, *Canon of Scripture*.

would agree that the Holy Spirit oversaw the whole process of canon formation and guided the church.

The Holy Spirit Helps Us to Understand the Meaning and Interpretation of Scripture

This third affirmation regarding the relationship between the Holy Spirit and Scripture refers to meaning and interpretation. Immediately prior to Luke's description of the ascension, Jesus speaks some words to his disciples, as recorded in Luke 24:44–45: "He said to them, 'This is what I told you while I was still with you: Everything must be fulfilled that is written about me in the Law of Moses, the Prophets, and the Psalms.' Then he opened their minds so they could understand the Scriptures." Despite the fact that they had been with Jesus for some time and despite the fact that they had heard him teach on numerous occasions, it was necessary for Jesus to "open their minds" before they could understand the Scriptures. The noetic effects of sin are such that the human mind is damaged and only functions properly when enabled by divine action.

We find similar teaching in 1 Cor 2:11–14:

> For who among men knows the thoughts of a man except the man's spirit within him? In the same way no-one knows the thoughts of God except the Spirit of God. We have not received the spirit of the world but the Spirit who is from God, that we may understand what God has freely given us. This is what we speak, not in words taught us by human wisdom but in words taught by the Spirit, expressing spiritual truths in spiritual words. The man without the Spirit does not accept the things that come from the Spirit of God, for they are foolishness to him, and he cannot understand them, because they are spiritually discerned.

The "things that come from the Spirit of God" (which surely includes Scripture) cannot be understood by "the man without the Spirit," because spiritual discernment is needed in order to understand the things of God. There is, of course, a sense in which any human being can read a portion of Scripture and understand what it is saying. There are many biblical scholars who would freely admit that they are not Christians, yet this in itself does not prevent them from being skilful exegetes. The point that is being made here is that true understanding of the meaning of Scripture only comes to those in whom the Spirit of God lives. To that extent, the most gifted biblical scholar who is an unbeliever has less "real" knowledge than the young person who only recently became a Christian.

This third affirmation covers what are normally called "illumination" and "perspicuity." In my book on Scripture, I proposed that we supplement the word "illumination" with the word "recognition," so as to avoid any misunderstanding. My intention was to make the point that it is not the Scriptures that need to be "illumined," but rather it is the human mind, damaged by the noetic effects of sin, that needs to be acted upon by the Holy Spirit so that we can "recognize" Scripture as the revealed truth of God. It is not Scripture that needs to be acted upon but *us*. In the book, I also recommended supplementing the word "perspicuity" with the word "comprehension." My point here was that, although the Reformers were right to insist that the Scriptures should be translated into the common languages and that they could be read without the interpretation of a priest, one might then think that there was no locus for the Holy Spirit. The word "comprehension" was intended to convey the idea that only through the work of the Holy Spirit can we properly understand the Scriptures.[8]

The Holy Spirit Empowers the Preaching of Scripture

This fourth affirmation regarding the relationship between the Holy Spirit and Scripture refers to empowerment. In Isa 61:1, the prophet describes his calling to a preaching ministry in the power of the Holy Spirit: "The Spirit of the Sovereign LORD is on me, because the LORD has anointed me to preach good news to the poor." These words were later read by Jesus in the synagogue and declared to be a description of his own ministry, as we read in Luke 4:18–19: "The Spirit of the Lord is on me, because he has anointed me to preach good news to the poor. He has sent me to proclaim freedom for the prisoners and recovery of sight for the blind, to release the oppressed, to proclaim the year of the Lord's favor."

In the Acts of the Apostles, we find that several times the followers of Jesus were filled with the Spirit. On one such occasion, there is a sequence of events which helps to underline this fourth affirmation regarding the work of the Holy Spirit. It is found in Acts 4:31: "After they prayed, the place where they were meeting was shaken. And they were all filled with the Holy Spirit and spoke the word of God boldly." Now it might be argued that being

---

8. Incidentally, the first review of my book on Scripture, published in the *Banner of Truth* magazine, said that I wanted to "replace" the words illumination and perspicuity with the words recognition and comprehension, whereas I clearly said "supplement." Two or three later reviewers repeated this error.

"filled with the Spirit" and "speaking the Word of God boldly" are simply consequential events rather than the one being "caused" by the other but I would argue that the natural reading of the text is that they spoke the Word of God boldly precisely because they had been filled with the Spirit.

It can also be seen from Scripture that the Holy Spirit not only empowered the preaching of God's Word but also directed where the Word was to be preached. We see that in Acts 16:6–8: "Paul and his companions travelled throughout the region of Phrygia and Galatia, having been kept by the Holy Spirit from preaching the word in the province of Asia. When they came to the border of Mysia, they tried to enter Bithynia, but the Spirit of Jesus would not allow them to. So they passed by Mysia and went down to Troas."

There are other scriptures that support this interpretation. For example, in Rom 15:19 Paul makes it clear that everything he did for God was done in the "power of the Spirit," including his bold proclamation of the gospel. The disciples were also told not to worry about what to say when brought before the authorities, as we read in Mark 13:11: "Whenever you are arrested and brought to trial, do not worry beforehand about what to say. Just say whatever is given you at the time, for it is not you speaking, but the Holy Spirit."

Christians are those who have been "baptized in the Spirit" and who have then been sent out to "make disciples" of all nations. In carrying out this dominical mission, the Holy Spirit enables believers to speak the Word of God. As the *First Helvetic Confession* says, "The Preaching of the Word of God is the Word of God." No wonder, then, that Paul could say this to the Thessalonians, in 1 Thess 2:13: "And we also thank God continually because, when you received the word of God, which you heard from us, you accepted it not as the word of men, but as it actually is, the word of God, which is at work in you who believe."

Theological Method

Having stated these four aspects of the relationship between Scripture and the Holy Spirit, it can perhaps more clearly be seen why the criticisms of my book in respect of my decision not to use the word "inerrancy" did not take seriously enough the pneumatological context in which I made that decision. In other words, I wanted to argue that the authority of Scripture does not depend on the inerrancy of the original *autographa* but rather on the relationship between Scripture and the Holy Spirit.

As a Minister of the Church of Scotland and a Reformed theologian, my tradition includes John Calvin and the *Westminster Confession of Faith*.

Both Calvin and the *Westminster Confession* grounded their view of the authority of Scripture on the work of the Holy Spirit. Calvin wrote,

> Since for unbelieving men religion seems to stand by opinion alone, they, in order not to believe anything foolishly or lightly, both wish and demand rational proof that Moses and the prophets spoke divinely. But I reply: the testimony of the Spirit is more excellent than all reason. For as God alone is a fit witness of himself in his Word, so also the Word will not find acceptance in men's hearts before it is sealed by the inward testimony of the Holy Spirit. The same Spirit, therefore, who has spoken through the mouths of the prophets must penetrate into our hearts to persuade us that they faithfully proclaimed what had been divinely commanded.[9]

Calvin is saying clearly that the truth and infallibility of Scripture is not established on the basis of some rational proof but by the internal persuasion by the Holy Spirit. He says that we only become convinced of the authority of Scripture when "it is sealed upon our hearts through the Spirit."[10] This is the view I have sought to advocate.[11]

The *Westminster Confession of Faith* in chapter 1, sections IV and V, follows Calvin in grounding the authority of Scripture on the "inward work of the Holy Spirit':

> IV. The authority of the Holy Scripture, for which it ought to be believed, and obeyed, depends not upon the testimony of any man, or Church; but wholly upon God (who is truth itself) the author thereof: and therefore it is to be received, because it is the Word of God.
>
> V. We may be moved and induced by the testimony of the Church to an high and reverent esteem of the Holy Scripture. And the heavenliness of the matter, the efficacy of the doctrine, the majesty of the style, the consent of all the parts, the scope of the whole (which is, to give all glory to God), the full discovery it makes of the only way of man's salvation, the many other incomparable excellencies, and the entire perfection thereof, are

---

9. Calvin, *Institutes*, 1.7.4.

10. Ibid., 1.7.5.

11. In a paper given at a conference in Geneva to mark the quincentenary of Calvin's birth, I spelled out Calvin's view in more detail and sought to demonstrate that my understanding of the relationship between Word and Spirit and my advocacy of the "infallibility" of Scripture, are both in line with Calvin's own position: "John Calvin's Doctrine of Scripture," 356–80.

arguments whereby it does abundantly evidence itself to be the Word of God: yet notwithstanding, our full persuasion and assurance of the infallible truth and divine authority thereof, is from the inward work of the Holy Spirit bearing witness by and with the Word in our hearts.

The authority of Scripture is not founded upon inerrant autographic texts but upon the voice of God speaking by his Spirit through Scripture, which is, in its entirety, the Word of God. In making this statement, one is not required to say that such inerrant autographic texts did not exist, merely that this is not the basis upon which we affirm the authority of Scripture. It is also important to remind ourselves that even those who hold to the doctrine of inerrancy are only arguing that the original autographic texts are "inerrant." Given that we do not possess those original *autographa*, but only a collection of manuscripts, texts, and translations, which betray signs of copying errors and apparent contradictions, it is sometimes difficult to see why this argument has become so polarized, at least in North America.[12]

Reformed Theology is a broad enough vehicle to permit various ways of defending a high view of Scripture, since it is a "school of thought" and not a "strand of thought," as I have argued elsewhere.[13] There has been an unfortunate tendency in recent years to act as if there was only one single strand of Reformed thought that is "truly Reformed," and to reject all others. From its inception, Reformed theology has been a school of thought with many strands, and if we lose this we shall be impoverished.

The recognition that different Reformed theologians expressed their doctrine of Scripture in different ways enriches rather than diminishes our movement. For many of us, Herman Bavinck was the most distinguished Reformed theologian since John Calvin. In my book, I set his view of Scripture over against that of the standard Reformed account of the doctrine as represented by B. B. Warfield. In my view, Bavinck's account of the doctrine of Scripture took much more cognizance of the human authorship and maintained a better balance between the work of the Holy Spirit and the actions of these authors. The response to this contrast between Warfield and Bavinck was most surprising. It was asserted categorically that Warfield and Bavinck had precisely the same view of Scripture. There was no account taken of Bavinck's critique of the Hodge/Warfield theological method, nor

---

12. Apart from the numerous publications on this theme, the debate still maintains its energy. An example of this is the fact that the theme of the Evangelical Theological Society meeting in 2013 in Baltimore was, "Evangelicalism, Inerrancy, and the Evangelical Theological Society: Retrospect and Prospect."

13. "Crafting an Evangelical, Reformed and Missional Theology." Published in association with the World Reformed Fellowship.

any serious recognition of the differences between Bavinck's "organic" view and Warfield's more "mechanical" view.

Several of the reviewers suggested that I had not taken sufficient account of Richard Gaffin's two articles in the *Westminster Theological Journal* on the doctrine of Scripture in Kuyper and Bavinck, especially as it was written in response to Rogers and McKim's argument for the use of the term "infallibility" rather than the term "inerrancy." Since my book was published, these articles have been published in book form as *God's Word in Servant Form*.[14] I said very little about these articles because I was in agreement with the substance of the argument. This is what I said:

> Rogers and McKim claimed that Kuyper and Bavinck supported their view of Scripture. This was ably and comprehensively challenged by Richard Gaffin.[15] As Gaffin demonstrated, Rogers and McKim held to a form-content distinction between the humanity of Scripture and the divine Word which is spoken through it. Neither Kuyper nor Bavinck held to this distinction. Unfortunately, many people assumed (because of the closed, two-option dichotomy in the American discussion of the topic) that, since Kuyper and Bavinck could not be cited in support of Rogers and McKim, therefore they must have been inerrantists! In fact, this is not the case.[16]

Gaffin was quite right to critique the interpretation of Kuyper and Bavinck found in Rogers and McKim, and I agreed with his criticism. Nevertheless, it does not follow from the claim that Rogers and McKim failed convincingly to demonstrate that Bavinck was on their side that Bavinck was an inerrantist. This is a false dichotomy, as demonstrated by the doctoral dissertation of Professor Henk van den Belt.[17] This comprehensive study of Bavinck's doctrine of Scripture confirms that his organic view was indeed different to that of Warfield.

In all of this there is a deeper problem and it is the one with which Grenz was particularly concerned, namely, the question of theological method. Grenz, as a member of the Evangelical Theological Society until his death, affirmed inerrancy, but he believed that some expressions of this view led to a deeply flawed theological method. It is clear that many of those

---

14. Gaffin, *God's Word in Servant Form*.

15. In a two part article in the *Westminster Theological Journal*, one dealing with Kuyper, the other dealing with Bavinck, both by Gaffin and titled, "Old Amsterdam and Inerrancy."

16. McGowan, *Divine Authenticity*, 138.

17. Van den Belt, *Autopistia*.

who hold to a doctrine of inerrancy believe that this is the only way to defend a high view of Scripture.[18] Grenz believed this to be mistaken, and argued that many who took this view were wedded to a theological method that stemmed from Enlightenment modernism. In seeking to expose the philosophical underpinning of their method, Grenz traces the position to Charles Hodge of Princeton who was influenced both by Thomas Reid's Scottish Common Sense Realism and by a Baconian scientific method. Hodge argued that theology is a science and that, like the scientist, the task of the theologian is to identify, arrange and exhibit the truth found in Scripture, this truth being revelation in the form of "propositions."[19] Grenz argued that this foundationalist approach had to be abandoned, in order to be able to speak the gospel appropriately to a postmodern age.

The theologians who take a foundationalist approach either discuss the doctrine of Scripture in a section on *prolegomena* at the beginning of their systematic theologies, or they place the doctrine of Scripture as the first locus in their theology. The doctrine of Scripture thus becomes a basis for epistemology and is separated from the doctrine of God the Holy Spirit, where it more properly ought to be situated. Grenz put it like this:

> One of the least obvious means of dividing the Spirit from the Scriptures is latent in the theological methodology of Protestant systematic theology which separates bibliology from pneumatology. Consequently, the reestablishment of the integral link between Spirit and Scripture must begin methodologically through the reorientation of the doctrine of Scripture under the doctrine of the Holy Spirit.[20]

Grenz argued that a complete revisioning of the doctrine of Scripture was needed, in order to escape the static categories of a foundationalist approach, rooted in modernism, and instead to seek a postmodern expression of the doctrine by re-establishing a pneumatological understanding of Scripture.

Theological Balance

There is much to commend itself in Grenz's analysis, but we must now turn our attention to what he wanted to put in place of the Princetonian, foundationalist theological method.

---

18. E.g., Geisler and Roach, *Defending Inerrancy*.
19. Grenz, *Renewing the Center*, 70–77.
20. Grenz, *Revisioning*, 114.

Grenz notes that the Princetonian, foundationalist account of theological method is only one of several approaches that evangelicals have used in order to provide a philosophical underpinning for their theology. Another approach is the "Wesleyan Quadrilateral," where theology is not constructed simply on the basis of the text of Scripture but on a four-source theory: Scripture, tradition, experience, and reason.[21] Grenz had long argued that there was merit in the Wesleyan Quadrilateral, which says that the four sources or norms for theology are Scripture, tradition, reason, and experience. Indeed, in his *Revisioning Evangelical Theology* he seems to prefer it to a more biblicist approach.

Although Grenz can see the strength of the Wesleyan approach, he argues that it also has significant weaknesses, not least that most Wesleyans tend to lay more emphasis on one of the four sources than on the others, and hence the method is open to widely differing results, ranging from liberalism to evangelicalism. His deeper concern is about using "experience" as one of the sources for theology. He wrote, "The Wesleyan quadrilateral is not without its problems. Perhaps its gravest difficulty lies in its appeal to experience as constituting a theological norm separate from the others." Following Tillich he argues that experience is "not the source of theology but the medium through which theology's sources are received." This led him to conclude:

> Carrying this consideration a step further, experience cannot form a separate source simply because we never receive experience uninterpreted. It is always filtered by an interpretive framework or worldview grid. In fact, the framework facilitates the reception of experience, for there is no "pure experience." This being the case, experience cannot serve as a source for theology separate from the worldview that makes its reception possible.[22]

Grenz argues that, instead of the Princetonian "propositionalist" method or the Wesleyan quadrilateral method, theology should be constructed on "three pillars."[23] The three pillars are Scripture, church tradition, and historical-cultural context. To avoid the problems of the Wesleyan approach, where no one source is privileged more highly than the others, he argues that Scripture is the "primary norm" or the "norming norm."

In his 1993 book *Revisioning Evangelical Theology*, Grenz laid out his pneumatological view of Scripture. Although disagreeing with the older evangelical propositionalism, he insisted that it had "captured a central

21. Ibid., 90–93.
22. Ibid., 92.
23. Ibid., 93–101.

truth" in its insistence that "God has disclosed himself to humankind" and that "the Bible is the deposit of the divine revelation in history."[24] There are two principles that together enable access to the knowledge of this divine revelation, the "internal principle" being inspired Scripture and the "external principle" being the witness of the Holy Spirit. Thus he concludes, "The Scriptures are the vehicle or instrumentality of the Holy Spirit through which he chooses to speak to the people of God."[25] He goes on to note that within evangelicalism this nuanced account of the relationship between the Holy Spirit and Scripture has not always been maintained: "rather than maintaining the proper relation between Spirit and Scripture, we have sometimes been guilty of rending the two asunder or collapsing the two together."[26] Grenz argued that in the "classical Reformed approach" a separation had taken place between bibliology and pneumatology because of its theological method and the place given to Scripture as a foundation for epistemology. His conclusion was, as we noted earlier: "Consequently, the reestablishment of the integral link between Spirit and Scripture must begin methodologically through the reorientation of the doctrine of Scripture under the doctrine of the Holy Spirit."[27]

Grenz went on to argue that the classical view underplayed the significance of the human character of Scripture, noting that "it tends to deemphasize the Spirit's ongoing activity in speaking through Scripture in favor of a focus on the Spirit's completed work in inspiration. . . . [M]any evangelicals view illumination as only a secondary work, subservient to the primary matter of inspiration."[28] In a striking statement he says, "In this manner, we often collapse the Spirit into the Bible. We exchange the dynamic of the ongoing movement of the Spirit speaking to the community of God's people through the pages of the Bible for the book we hold in our hands."[29]

Much of what Grenz outlined in that 1993 book later found its way into his one volume systematic theology.[30] Speaking of the authority and trustworthiness of Scripture he writes,

> Whatever authority the Bible carries as a trustworthy book, it derives from the trustworthiness of the divine revelation it

24. Ibid., 109.
25. Ibid., 114.
26. Ibid.
27. Ibid.
28. Ibid., 117.
29. Ibid.
30. Grenz, *Theology for the Community* (1994), 494–527.

discloses and ultimately from the Spirit who infallibly speaks through it.

In declaring the trustworthiness of the Bible, therefore, we must keep in mind that it is ultimately not the book itself which we are affirming. Rather we are confessing our faith in the Spirit who speaks his revelatory message to us through the pages of Scripture. In declaring its infallibility and inerrancy, we are actually affirming the trustworthiness of the Spirit whose vehicle the Bible is.[31]

Having spelled out this high view of the relationship between the Holy Spirit and Scripture, Grenz began increasingly to consider the sources and norms for theological reflection. In 1998 he wrote an article entitled "An Agenda for Evangelical Theology in the Postmodern context."[32] In that article, he had a section on "The sources or tools of the theological enterprise" in which he described scholars like Wayne Grudem, who insist that Scripture alone is the source for theology, as "evangelical modernists."[33] By contrast, he argued that theologians have always had several tools or sources for theological construction: "These tools consist of the biblical message, the theological heritage of the church, and the thought forms of contemporary culture. Only by consciously bringing these three tools into insightful conversation can we construct a truly helpful evangelical theology."[34]

In one reading of this discussion, Grenz was simply affirming what many theologians would take to be a normal theological method. The Bible, to use Grenz's expression is the "norming norm"[35] but we also learn from tradition. This is evidenced by the importance most theologians place on the decisions of the Councils of Nicaea and Chalcedon in respect of our doctrine of the person of Christ. The difficult issue has always been the place given to "culture" in theological reflection. Grenz recognized that this was more problematic and stated his argument clearly,

> I am not elevating culture above either the biblical message or our theological heritage. I am not proposing that contemporary thinking about religion and morals sit in judgment over Christian teaching on these matters. Rather I am advocating that theologians not attempt the impossible task of withdrawing

31. Ibid., 524.
32. Grenz, "An Agenda for Evangelical Theology," 1–16.
33. Ibid., 8.
34. Ibid., 9.
35. *Beyond Foundationalism*, 57–92.

from their social and historical context into some supposedly culture-free realm in which only the "language of Zion" is spoken.[36]

The problem with having four (Wesleyan Quadrilateral) or three (Grenz) sources for theology, raises the important question regarding which has most authority. This was expressed well by Brian Harris: "In moving from a single source for theological construction to a trio of sources filtered through three focal motifs, a fundamental methodological problem appears. Grenz uses the image of the three sources acting as conversation partners, but how does one decide if a conversation partner is speaking too loudly?"[37] Harris himself went on to argue that the introduction of Wolterstorff's concept of "control beliefs" might be helpful in regulating the "volume" of each source.[38]

To affirm the importance of a pneumatological view of Scripture, with a strong emphasis on the close relationship between Word and Spirit, based on these three "pillars," requires some qualification and much careful theological work because there are dangers here. In recent years, some evangelicals who agreed with Grenz that a purely propositional and foundationalist account of the doctrine of Scripture was no longer possible, have moved in an even more revisionist direction. The problem has been the way in which the relationship between Word and Spirit is conceived, in the context of establishing the sources for theological decision-making. More particularly, the problem has come through the way in which "culture" is used as a source informing the content of theology.

The problem lies not so much in the careful and nuanced way that Grenz explains his three sources but the way in which some have used sources other than Scripture to determine their views on certain matters. The question ultimately becomes: How does the Holy Spirit lead the church?

When the General Synod of the Church of England recently decided not to approve of women bishops, a bishop who was very much in favor of women bishops and who was very annoyed at the decision, was heard to say, "If we'd won, we'd have said it was the leading of the Holy Spirit . . . ." Clearly he did not believe that the actual decision taken was the leading of the Holy Spirit.

How is one to adjudicate in such situations? Are we free to state any theological position, and then argue that we were "led" to it by the Holy Spirit? One contemporary issue which illustrates the problem is that of same-sex

36. Ibid., 13.
37. Harris, "Can Evangelical Theology Move Beyond Foundationalism?" 10.
38. Ibid., 11–12.

relations. In the current debates in various denominations regarding the legitimacy or otherwise of homosexual acts, the Holy Spirit is often quoted in support of a revisionist position. Those who advocate that the church should accept homosexual acts as a legitimate expression of sexuality for Christians will often admit that the Bible is completely against homosexual acts but then argue that the Holy Spirit is now leading us in a new direction.

I served as a member of the Church of Scotland's Theological Commission on Same-Sex Relations and the Ministry, which reported to the General Assembly of May 2013. The Commission had three members who were evangelical (called "traditionalist" in the report) and three members who were liberal (called "revisionist" in the report). It was often argued (both in the Commission and in the debate in the wider church) that, despite the apparently clear teaching of Scripture on the subject of homosexual acts, the Holy Spirit is speaking a new word for today, which allows us to affirm homosexual practice. Alternatively, it was argued that the passages of Scripture are not clear and the traditionalist interpretation has come, not from good exegesis, but from importing into the argument human prejudices which the Holy Spirit is now breaking down.

This might be expected from those of a more revisionist persuasion, but recently prominent evangelicals have begun to argue the case for recognizing a homosexual lifestyle as being just as legitimate as a heterosexual lifestyle. The problem with this approach is that the teaching of Scripture on this matter is clear, consistent, and unanimous. It is not a question of "interpretation"; it is a concern to avoid the plain meaning of the text in order to accommodate the politically correct views of modern Western society. That is to say, this is not a matter of a striking new exegetical alternative, but a departure from the clear teaching of the Holy Spirit in Scripture. Surely he cannot contradict himself? Some of the most prominent of these revisionists, on both sides of the Atlantic, have come from the "emerging church" movement, over which Grenz and his co-author John Franke have had so much influence. This is not to say that Grenz or Franke would support these views coming out of the emerging church, as Grenz's *Welcoming But Not Affirming* demonstrates, but it might be argued that their theological method may have opened the way for this.

Brian McLaren, one of the leaders of the emerging church movement in the United States has come to the place where he accepts homosexual acts as a legitimate Christian expression of sexuality. He insists that this was not due to the decision of his son to marry his same-sex partner but he did admit that the "stories" of homosexuals had a defining influence on his change of mind.[39] In the UK, Steve Chalke, the leader of Oasis, an evangelical youth movement, has recently come to similar conclusions.[40]

There seems little doubt that "culture" has been allowed to become the determining factor in the discussion, rather than Scripture, and here lies the danger of the third of Grenz's "three pillars." It might well be argued that Grenz's critique of "experience" as a source for theology in the Wesleyan quadrilateral, could equally well be applied to his own use of "culture" as a source for theology.

McLaren and Chalke would argue that the Holy Spirit has shone new light for them on the Scriptures, and that it is a matter of interpretation, but that is hard to substantiate. It seems much more likely that the prevailing culture has so influenced them that they have sought ways of avoiding the clear teaching of Scripture on this issue. It is worth recognizing the fact that Christian arguments in favor of legitimizing same-sex relations are largely to be heard in the decadent, sex-obsessed culture of the northern hemisphere, whereas Christians in the southern hemisphere are, by and large, appalled by what they regard as a departure from biblical teaching.

Now, the same-sex debate is simply one example of the problem being highlighted here. We might express it like this: What is the proper relationship between Word and Spirit, and is there ever a time when we can ignore the plain teaching of Scripture on the grounds that the Holy Spirit is leading us into new truth? Surely it is one thing to argue that the Holy Spirit can lead us into a deeper or more accurate understanding of Scripture, as we study the Word in a prayerful attitude, seeking the guidance of the Holy Spirit, but quite another thing to say that the Holy Spirit can lead us to theological positions or perspectives which are clearly contrary to Scripture?

Grenz himself believed that we ought to listen to the voice of God speaking to us through culture but clearly states that the Spirit speaking through culture cannot be set against the Spirit speaking through the Scriptures. He wrote,

> To pit the Spirit's voice in culture against the Spirit speaking through Scripture would be to fall prey to the foundationalist trap. It would require that we elevate some dimension of contemporary thought or experience as a human universal that forms the criterion for determining what in the Bible is or is not acceptable. Hence, while being ready to acknowledge the Spirit's

---

39. http://www.patheos.com/blogs/exploringourmatrix/2013/02/genesis-3-how-it-should-have-ended.html (accessed 14 Feb. 2013).

40. http://www.oasisuk.org/inclusionresources/Articles/MOIabridged (accessed 14 Feb. 2013).

voice wherever it may be found, Evangelical theology must always give primacy to the Spirit's speaking through the biblical text. Even though we cannot hear the Spirit speaking through Scripture except by listening within a particular historical-cultural context, hearing the Spirit in the biblical text provides the only sure canon for hearing the Spirit in culture, because the Spirit's speaking everywhere and anywhere is always in concert with this primary speaking through the Bible.[41]

Having noted this disclaimer, it must be said that, in our view Grenz moved from an early position where he emphasized the importance of understanding the culture so as to appropriately communicate the gospel, to a later phase where he saw culture as making a material contribution to the content of theology.

Conclusion

As a Presbyterian minister and theologian in the European Reformed tradition, my primary standard of authority is Scripture, which I hold to be, in its entirety, the Word of God written. My "Principal Subordinate Standard" (to use the language of my ordination vows) is the *Westminster Confession of Faith*. The *Westminster Confession* speaks of the infallibility of Scripture (as did Calvin, Knox, Rutherford, Boston, and all of the leading scholars in my tradition) and I believe that using the word "infallibility" rather than the word "inerrancy" fits better with a balanced view of the relationship between Word and Spirit and also helps to avoid both rationalism and fundamentalism.

One can understand why many in the American Reformed theological community have chosen to use the word "inerrancy," not least because of the way in which the word "infallibility" was used by Rogers and McKim to describe a doctrine of Scripture that, in the view of many, significantly weakened the authority of God's Word. That having been said, it is perfectly possible to use the language of "infallibility" in precisely the way that Calvin and the *Westminster Confession* did, thus maintaining a high view of the authority of God speaking by his Spirit through his Word.

One can also understand the desire for an epistemology that enables answers to be read off the page of an inerrant text, but the importance of listening to the voice of the Holy Spirit speaking in and through Scripture is also vital. If we emphasize the fact that the Holy Spirit brought the Bible into existence but downplay the fact that he is its interpreter and the final

---

41. Grenz, *Renewing the Center*, 210–11.

judge in any controversies, then we run the risk of imagining that we do not require the Holy Spirit in our biblical and theological discussions. We might be tempted to think (or to act as if) he has done his work historically, in giving us the inerrant text, and now we are left alone to interpret and apply it.

It is also clear that nothing must compete with Scripture as an alternative "pillar" or "source" for theology. Yes, we must highly value the theological heritage of the church through the ages, not least in its creeds and councils. Yes, we must recognize the importance of reason, while seeking to avoid rationalism. Yes, we must value Christian experience as the gateway to a true understanding of the mind of God. Yes, we must seek to understand the culture into which we must speak the gospel. At the same time, we must not allow any of this to undermine the fundamental authority of the voice of God speaking by his Holy Spirit in and through the Scriptures.

If we emphasize the Word and neglect the Spirit, then we end up in a fundamentalist biblicism, which is cold and dead. If we emphasize the Spirit and neglect the Word, then we can persuade ourselves that the Holy Spirit is leading us in whichever direction we have already decided we wish to travel. Only when Word and Spirit are held together in a close and unbreakable bond, as Calvin did, can we be sure that we are travelling not on our own chosen path but on God's.

Bibliography

Bruce, F. F. *The Canon of Scripture*. Downers Grove, IL: InterVarsity, 1988.
Calvin, John. *Institutes of the Christian Religion*. Edited by Ford Lewis Battles. The Library of Christian Classics. Philadelphia: Westminster, 1977.
Gaffin, Richard B. *God's Word in Servant Form*. Jackson, MS: Reformed Academic Press, 2008.
———. "Old Amsterdam and Inerrancy." *Westminster Theological Journal* 44 (1982) 250–89.
———. "Old Amsterdam and Inerrancy." *Westminster Theological Journal* 45 (1983) 219–72.
Geisler, Norman L., and William C. Roach. *Defending Inerrancy: Affirming the Accuracy of Scripture for a New Generation*. Grand Rapids: Baker, 2011.
Harris, Brian S. "Can Evangelical Theology Move beyond Foundationalism? Some Insights from the Theological Method of Stanley J. Grenz." *Crucible* 1/1 (May 2008) 1–17.
McGowan, A. T. B. "Crafting an Evangelical, Reformed and Missional Theology for the Twenty-first Century." In *Reformed Means Missional: Following Jesus into the World*, edited by Samuel T. Logan, 237–52. Greensboro, NC: New Growth, 2013.
———. *The Divine Spiration of Scripture*. Leicester, UK: InterVarsity, 2007. (US: *The Divine Authenticity of Scripture*. Downers Grove, IL: InterVarsity, 2007.)

———. "John Calvin's Doctrine of Scripture." In *Tributes to John Calvin: A Celebration of his Quincentenary*, edited by David W. Hall, 356–80. Phillipsburg, NJ: Presbyterian and Reformed, 2010.

Van den Belt, Henk. *Autopistia: The Self-Convincing Authority of Scripture in Reformed Theology*. Leiden: Brill, 2008.

13

On (Still) Taking St. Paul Seriously

The Hermeneutical Function of Sin and Vice in Scriptural Interpretation

MARK ALAN BOWALD

> What all this has to do with taking Paul seriously is simply this. As long as we operate in some foundationalist framework sin does not need to be an epistemological category.... In that project method becomes the means, not of grace, but of our own self-purification. (Merold Westphal)

IN 1990 MEROLD WESTPHAL argued forcefully that Christian philosophers were not taking St. Paul's teachings on sin seriously in their epistemological proposals.[1] His questions are directed toward philosophical approaches to the question of how human beings acquire and validate knowledge, especially those working in the Reformed Epistemology tradition (represented by Alvin Plantinga, Nicholas Wolterstorff, and their compatriots). Westphal's concerns are that these represent a general trend in philosophy in which the models that philosophers use to explain the mechanisms and processes by

---

1. Westphal, "Taking St. Paul Seriously," 200–26. This paper's title recalls Westphal's. Although written to different audiences and with different interlocutors, my concerns here are consistent with his. Quote above is on page 211. Westphal's paper inaugurated a subsequent debate about the role and place of sin in accounts of knowledge. This history is detailed in Moroney, *Noetic Effects*.

which human beings acquire knowledge are models in which the senses and capacities of human beings are both functioning properly and functioning well. Westphal's simple but penetrating argument is that sin presents challenges and problems for acquiring knowledge which these proposals, and any which share this feature, fail to properly take into account.[2] What are those ways that sin and vice complicate, misdirect, undermine, and even prevent human beings from acquiring and giving warrant to knowledge? The more that any epistemology claims to comprehensively account for knowledge without addressing these issues is the degree to which that account is likely to be incompatible with a Christian biblical anthropology.

Westphal issued a charge to theologians to join in this project of "taking St. Paul seriously."[3] The challenge is taken up here with respect to recent proposals for using virtue as a foundation for thinking about a hermeneutics of Scripture. These proposals build upon developments in philosophy called "virtue epistemology."[4] The argument pursued here parallels Westphal's. Virtue hermeneutics, insofar as they rest upon an anthropology that focuses with (near) exclusion on human persons acting and interpreting Scripture well and faithfully, virtuously, they (also) fail to take adequate account of the place and role of sin and vice in biblical hermeneutics. We will see that, in the case of virtue hermeneutics, the stakes and pitfalls are, in practice, more potentially distortive of their subject matter than in Westphal's case.[5] We begin by turning our attention to how Scripture depicts the character of its anticipated reader(s)/interpreter(s).

Introduction: The Divine Author and the (Mis)Interpreter

The task of a hermeneutics of the holy canon of Scripture is to depict the character of the participants and practices ingredient in its reading and interpretation. Its goal is to describe these in ways that carefully and transparently display that character. The holy canon stands uniquely at the crossroads of the communicative practices of its divine author, human authors, editors, and interpreters; its character reflects, reveals, and refracts their character; it displays the love, majesty, and grace of the triune author, and

---

2. Wolterstorff recently published an article that begins to address this problem (among others), setting up a new corrective tangent from within the Reformed epistemological tradition. See his "Historicizing the Belief-forming Self," 118–43.

3. Westphal, "Taking St. Paul Seriously," 219.

4. We will introduce and discuss this movement below.

5. It cannot be pursued here, but there is a deep need for a similar criticism to be pursued with Virtue Epistemology.

the mixed character of the practices of human creatures, which stand in both harmony and dissonance both with God and the good creation. This exclusive mediate relationship that Scripture possessed and enjoys, and the priority and authority that this mediation implies, means that a hermeneutics of Scripture must give priority to how Scripture itself witnesses to the character of the divine triune author and creature interpreters.[6]

Scripture is the written witness and record of the announcement of the creative, redemptive, and perfecting drama of the triune God in the narrative of the keystone events in the shared history and relations with human creatures. Scripture's purpose is not simply to report this narrative[7] but to enact the transformation of the creature's character and practices by way of re-presenting and re-calling the histories, poetry, wisdom, and other literary forms that comprise the Word of God in the holy canon. Thus, the character of the reader of Scripture is presumed by Scripture to be one that requires salvation, redemption, and transformation, and can be by this re-calling. The Bible addresses human creatures as practiced sinners; it announces the reality of judgment on sin and the hope of redemption from its violence and enslavement. The holy canon is the gospel, the collective announcement that the blessings of the kingdom are fulfilled in Christ (Luke 4:21), and that repentance is therefore available for the forgiveness of sins (Luke 24:47).

The focus of our attention turns here toward the complexity of the character of the reader/interpreter of Scripture to which the gospel is addressed. Our subject matter is, then, a matter of theological anthropology in the phenomena and practices of the encounter and transformation by the Word of God. The inherent limits of writing theology dictate that greater attention will be given here to the person in the reading: There is, then, an assumed imbalance in this exposition; the priority and foundational disposition of triune God who creates the human creature in their image will be treated with pragmatic, but necessary, brevity.

The character of the self-revealing and self-announcing divine author of Scripture is not *de novo* defined by the act of the creation and redemption of the creature and the *cosmos*, but is *revealed* in these economies. The eternal life of the triune godhead is one of perfect unity in balanced and

---

6. The architecture of Stanley Grenz's *Theology for the Community* locates the doctrine of Scripture in a mediate relationship, being positioned at the conclusion of his pneumatology, anticipating the next section, which is on ecclesiology proper. Scripture stands, positioned to be the instrument of the Holy Spirit to create the community (Grenz was a Baptist, after all, through and through) *by* presenting the necessity and possibility of conversion through repentance and faith, which are the two subsections which follow the section on Scripture and introduce the church.

7. Although it does so, faithfully and truthfully.

harmonious reciprocity and differentiation: love. The creation of the *cosmos* is the natural extension and expression of this love; it is an undetermined, spontaneous, and self-caused practice of the love of God the Father, with and through the Word of the Son, in the binding and effecting power of the Holy Spirit.

Both the character of the triune God and that of the creatures—who are created by the Word of God, and to whom the Word of God is directed— are intrinsically and reciprocally related. Creaturely being is framed and inaugurated by the gracious and free initiative of God; this loving unmerited grace marks the order of creation and the ordered place for human creatures within it. In turn, the character of the human creature is, by design, intended to image and mirror the love of God in care for other creatures and the created order in virtue. The narration of the fall into sin in Gen 3 describes the loss of humanity's inherent, created virtue: the defiance of the creature against the rule of God's love and the vacation of the stewardly vocation of love. Scripture's *raisin d'être* is God's Word in the work of redressing this fallen, sinful, and vicious character, which humankind then and now possesses in rejecting its Maker and Namer, in seeking its own self-making and self-naming (Gen 11:4). This story, of the creation, fall, and redemption of humanity, is that metanarrative of Scripture and is the ennarrated and enacted summary of the rule of faith, which is the fitting and harmonious disposition with which readers come to read and interpret the canon.

However, the reader who comes *perfectly* or *simply* to Scripture with the disposition, rule, or *kanon*, of faith, in virtue, is an ideal; it is never accomplished or performed in this present dispensation.[8] Scripture narrates the fall of the creaturely disposition into sin and vice; a state of affairs with which human beings struggle until their death or the arrival of the future eschatological rule of Christ. A theological hermeneutics of Scripture that focuses primarily or only on the function of virtue in the phenomena of reading Scripture, *as if* this were the complete picture, would be ironic; it would turn Scripture into an archive of some completed task from a past era looking back from that future eschaton. To the utter and complete contrary: Scripture itself assumes throughout that its reader(s) is (are) sinful, and prone to vice. This is not simply a rhetorical stance; it is the divine pronouncement and verdict of the character of human creatures in their fallenness. A fuller account of this subject of Scripture's address and reading requires the account of the hermeneutical function of sin and vice as an intrinsic, and fundamental, feature of scriptural hermeneutics. The

---

8. With only a few exceptions, the deep and broad consensus of the Christian tradition is that sin is a perennial struggle for every person and community.

hermeneutical function of faith and virtue are not set aside in this fuller accounting, but qualified, necessarily, and put into better and more fitting balance and proportion. We will pursue a sketch of that fuller account here, beginning with a review of recent related work.

The Corrective of Virtue Hermeneutics

There is a significant and growing body of writing that has recently argued for the positive role for faith and virtue as tangible and necessary dimensions to the practices of scriptural interpretation. These can be organized under the rubric "virtue hermeneutics." They have inaugurated a necessary and timely corrective to the theological anthropology of the subject/reader of Scripture. That corrective relates to the picture of the ideal reader that is portrayed in those all too familiar portraits of scientific objectivity arising in the Enlightenment, and which came to become the default setting for many and most forms of modern critical biblical scholarship. Just as Scripture is determined to be, famously, read "like any book," so the ideal reader purportedly reads like a generic and objective reader. In both cases the text and the reader are stripped of their specific character; in their places stand generic, hollow shells and mannequins: artificial, plastic, barren, and mundane reductions. The ideal text of modernity is filled with blank pages; the ideal reader is nameless, faceless, without history or place.

One of the main streams that has fed virtue hermeneutics and the recovery of the character of the reader of Scripture originates with virtue ethics. Alistair Macintyre stands in the background[9] as an inspiration for the application of virtue ethics in the theological work of Stanley Hauerwas, L. Gregory Jones, Steve Fowl, and others.[10] Virtue ethics has now evolved and been applied in the recent works on virtue epistemology,[11] and with specific application with regard to our topic: how virtue operates and informs hermeneutics.

Reading in Communion: Scripture and Ethics in Christian Life (1991) by Stephen Fowl and L. Gregory Jones[12] stands as an important and sig-

9. MacIntyre, *After Virtue*; *Whose Justice? Which Rationality?*

10. Modified proposals for thinking about theology in terms of the pursuit and practices of virtue in an explicitly evangelical mode have been pursued by Vanhoozer, *Is There a Meaning in This Text?* and by one of his students: Treier, *Virtue and the Voice of God.*

11. See Zagzebski, *Virtues of the Mind*; Roberts and Wood, *Intellectual Virtues.*

12. Fowl and Jones, *Reading in Communion*. See also Jones, "Formed and Transformed by Scripture," among a set of recent articles that stand in clear continuity with this stream in Brown, *Character and Scripture*, 18–33.

BOWALD—*On (Still) Taking St. Paul Seriously* 263

nificantly influential early seminal work in this vein. There are two clear corrective points to that quintessential modern reader/subject named above that Fowl and Jones pursue with rigor. The first is to insist that the proper way to frame the reading of Scripture is as a collective practice of Christian communities, over against the solitary independent reading tendencies of modernity. The second is to begin to recover the place for virtues within the practices of reading as a way of framing the communal relationship of Scripture and ethics. The value of these two points is significant, and the influence of this approach on subsequent reflection on scriptural hermeneutics continues to be felt.

What emerges from their account is a reader of Scripture that is more familiar and recognizable; it is a person who possesses and embodies their character, who is properly embedded in a community of readers; a community that seeks to engender the characters and virtues for which humanity was created, and for which this community was specifically called in the covenant with Abraham to engender as a witness to the character of the triune God: to be a people who will be a blessing to all the nations.

Insofar as it goes, the hermeneutic sketched by Fowl and Jones is timely and sets off in directions that are more fitting both to the nature of Scripture and to the reader. The picture is incomplete, however, insofar as it tends to focus attention with some narrowness on the production of virtue in the reading community as the sole effect of the practices of scriptural interpretation. This tendency has continued to characterize works that pursue different versions of virtue hermeneutics. We will complete the picture by taking the logic of virtue hermeneutics to its fuller conclusion, recognizing how vice and sin, as the shadow of virtue, are *both* effected in the practices of those addressed by the Word of God in Scripture, and also how virtue *and vice* not only are the byproduct of scriptural hermeneutics but also comprise the character of the assumed reader of Scripture, and are therefore substantive for the entirety of the hermeneutical spiral and practices of biblical interpretation.

Scripture itself anticipates readers who, at best, of a mixed character, possessing both sinful propensities and (sometimes) evidence of covenant faithfulness. Scripture also describes and expects that those who are confronted by the Word of God will depart that encounter producing both faith and sin. A full hermeneutics of Scripture should account for all of these facets. The result is a clearer picture both of the nature of the subject reader as well as of the character of Scripture as the written witnessing Word of God.

Why is it, though, that only the production of virtue in readers is the focus of present discussions around scriptural hermeneutics? In one regard, it is both understandable and even, in a qualified respect, appropriate. We long for the full effects of God's redemptive work to be felt in our lives and in the world. Waiting for the joy and relief of salvation is painful; it is the agony of childbearing, the "groaning" of which Scripture itself speaks. Indeed Scripture constantly directs our attention to that future when we may experience the fullness of this redeemed life. It is fitting that we fix our attention on these redemptive hopes. However, the captivation of that future can cause us to overlook and misplace the difficulties of our present dispensation, to ignore the very real judgment that is its alternative, and ultimately to misperceive the place, and function, of Scripture in both. The compellingness of the beauty and joy of the eschatological hope only receives its proper proportion and scale *over against* the negative relief of the destructive power of sin, from the perennial reminder in Scripture of the very real judgment that is both deserved and applied. The grandeur and gravity of Scripture is tied to its singular role in serving as the witness to that hope in this present age. The shock and miracle of the gospel message, as the unifying point for the *skopos* of the canon, is that repentance is available for the forgiveness of sins. The terrifying side of this news, which Scripture itself bears witness, is that many will not take the opportunity to repent and thereby refuse forgiveness.

In this sense, then, it is understandable that much of the work in virtue hermeneutics has tended to continue to focus with some exclusion on virtue as the hermeneutical *byproduct* of reading practices: reading *for* virtue. The judgment of which Scripture speaks is distasteful, unfashionable, and repellent to modern sensibilities. The preoccupation with virtue does serve a rhetorical function; our descriptions of what occurs in the interpretation of the holy canon should hope for, and compel others toward, the virtues that contribute to our participation in the divine life, in the expression of love of God and neighbor. It is easily explainable how the *production* of virtue, as the present sign of that eschatological hope, would occupy the attention of hermeneutics utilizing virtue theory.

More recently, work has also appeared that considers also how virtue might profitably guide us *into* the reading of Scripture: So not just reading *for* virtue but reading *with* virtue.[13] Recently, Richard Briggs has produced a powerful contribution to this in his recent work *The Virtuous Reader: Old Testament Narrative and Interpretive Virtue.*[14] This work is all the more noteworthy in that Briggs is a professional biblical scholar and his book signals how deeply this interdisciplinary link between virtue and scriptural

---

13. The seminal article is Rogers, "Virtues of an Interpreter," 64–81
14. Briggs, *Virtuous Reader.*

hermeneutics has penetrated (rightfully!) into the self-reflection on methodology in the biblical studies guild.[15]

The focus of Briggs's work is to focus attention on the "moral character of the implied reader" of the Old Testament.[16] In other words, from the OT texts themselves Briggs wishes to draw out pictures that anticipate the moral character of biblical readers.[17] Briggs compellingly demonstrates how, in turn, specific texts in the Old Testament hopefully anticipate humility, wisdom, trust, charity, and "receptivity" in the reader. His argument establishes an important beachhead in both supplementing the earlier work of Fowl, Jones, Vanhoozer, and others in raising the broader question of the role of virtue in biblical interpretation from a theological standpoint. Like these others, Briggs focuses attention on the virtuous characteristics of the reader. Tellingly, in the last six pages of the book, he enters a line of discussion in which the role of sin and vice begins to also emerge.

The title of this section of his book is "What is Normative about This Picture? Real Readers of the Old Testament."[18] Here he draws out a contrast between the implied reader and the "real" reader, and touches, ever so briefly and lightly, on the line of the argument pursued here. He quickly poses the very pregnant question: Is the implied reader "incapable of attaining to perfect reading" and "'sinful' in some sense and this assumed to be equipped to read the text only by the various graces of [God ?]"[19] Briggs signals sensitivities and leanings similar to virtue ethics by not pursuing this line of questioning to its substantive conclusions, but continuing to hold the strained former line. He does this by insisting that the implied reader of Scripture is one who comes with virtue, while the "real" reader is one who cannot attain to the perfection of the virtues that the text anticipates. This hermeneutical tension is unsustainable in light of the text of Scripture itself. The moral character of the implied reader that Scripture itself anticipates is mixed (at best!). The interpretive virtues that the reader is called to possess are the ideal *to which* Scripture rhetorically directs our attention and practices. The implied reader is one for whom sin and vice is still a real and

---

15. Briggs teaches at Durham University, and is presently joined there by colleagues Walter Moberly and Francis Watson, two other biblical scholars whose works stand at the forefront of their respective fields in the reconsideration of the ethical, theological, and confessional character of scriptural hermeneutics.

16. Briggs, *Virtuous Reader*, 38.

17. See the perceptive article by Pardue, "Athens and Jerusalem Once More," 295–308, for a discussion of this work by Briggs as a way into a broader assessment of the value and deficiencies of virtue hermeneutics.

18. Briggs, *Virtuous Reader*, 206–12.

19. Ibid., 206.

present danger; one who has not yet fully attained the virtues but, hopefully, is by grace on the way to them. And, if not, then the specter of judgment is the only other, very real, alternative. Briggs rightly remarks that between these options "[r]eal readers, then, still have a choice."[20] That choice is not between virtue and ignorance: it is virtue or vice, repentance or refusal, forgiveness or judgment.

The preoccupation with virtues and the positive dimensions of the anthropology of the interpretation of Scripture reflect a preoccupation with the *desired* outcome of the reading. Certainly we all hope to be virtuous readers. There is a substantial difference, however, between the ideal of reading with and for virtue and the fuller account of the phenomenon of scriptural interpretation. None of us interpret Scripture perfectly in practice. We all have knowingly and unknowingly used Scripture to underwrite our sin; this is why our perennial prayer, which in many of our traditions we overtly give before we hear the word in preaching, is that we might be forgiven both for what we have done and what we have left undone. Hoping, praying, and working for virtuous interpretation is one thing; the full account of the conditions, practices, and effects of the interpretation of Scripture according to its character as the Word which pierces through to the division of soul and spirit, judging the thoughts and intentions of the heart, is another (Heb 4:12).

The Hermeneutics of Vice

The limited picture of the character of the reader in virtue hermeneutics is seen in that it remains primarily, even exclusively, interested in the role of *virtue* in the reading subject as a dimension of the practices of either coming *to* Scripture and/or as the byproduct *of* interpreting Scripture. What is missing is the hermeneutical role of sin and vice as both the anticipated penchant of the hearer/interpreter who comes to Scripture and that results as the byproduct of the encounter of the reader with the Word of God in Scripture. Why is this important?

First, as already alluded to above, the proper proportion and magnitude of the problem of sin and vice is necessary to keep in view in order to properly understand the nature of redemption and virtue to which the reader is called. Scripture itself, as we will briefly survey below, is perennially reminding its hearers/interpreters of the ever-present problem of sinful practices, and their deep propensity toward such. Canonical readings of

20. Ibid., 207.

Scripture reveal the miraculous scale and proportion of the accomplishment of salvation and redemption in Christ: the announcement of the gospel as the center of gravity of the canon; the heights and depths of the love of the triune God, as seen in the narrative of redemption—all these are properly set before us together in their presentation in the holy canon. The singling out of faith and virtue, as positive features of a theological anthropology, apart from the shadows of sin and vice from which they emerge and are reborn, constricts and reduces the scale of the effects of redemption and portrays an imbalanced, and even misshapen, biblical anthropology.

Second, one of the primary correctives that virtue hermeneutics has brought to bear on scriptural hermeneutics is to interrogate and deconstruct the modernist account of the subject reader, which sees some sort of neutrality as being the ideal. The ideal modern reader is "objective" in their reading,[21] supposedly setting aside any and all personal bias. Virtue hermeneutics, like virtue ethics and virtue epistemology, properly and effectively recovers the way that *character* formation is both central to, and saturates all human practices, including those of ethicists, philosophers, and theologians. The focus on virtue *alone*, however, leaves that corrective of the mythical faceless and characterless subject of modernity incomplete.

If we only focus our attention on the human subject in their practices of *virtue*, we run the very real risk of permitting a residue of the modern neutral person in neglecting to see and thoroughly articulate what is their character when they are not practicing virtuously. We can put this question another way, with specific reference to biblical interpretation: In virtue hermeneutics of Scripture, what is the alternative to virtue in the interpreter? What is the character, the constitution, of the person who engages Scripture *in addition to*, or *apart from*, whatever virtue they might possess? Virtue hermeneutics are largely silent on this point. In the vacuum of this silence there are two possibilities: either that non-virtuous character is sin and vice, or it is some sort of ethically and morally neutral characteristic.

Some might describe this as a state of "ignorance." But what is the character of that ignorance? Is it some sort of suspended neutrality? A reflective moment of escape? Does it lack moral character or bearing? What fills the void in the fuller phenomenological picture of the subject/reader apart from virtue? There is a subtle but familiar lacuna formed here with respect to the character of the reading subject. In virtue theory the possibility is sometimes permitted, or even encouraged, of envisioning or assuming an *unformed* subject, a close kin to the mythical neutral and purely "objective"

---

21. For a broader discussion of this particular issue see my "Objectivity" in *Dictionary of the Theological Interpretation of the Bible*.

agent that is often posited in modern accounts of agency and epistemology. There is here a lingering temptation to suppose the kind of neutral observer or neutral character. This would not have been a temptation in pre-modern hermeneutics of Scripture. Pre-modern readers of Augustine's *De Doctrina Christiana*, for example, would have properly understood the gravity of the alternative to his call to read with the Rule of Faith and Rule of Love. The alternative to faithful reading is not a benign naiveté, it is to remain under the curses of Gen 3.

The degree to which neutral or unformed dimensions are permitted in anthropology under the guise of some form of hermeneutical neutrality is the degree to which the scale, proportion, and character of the gospel is, likewise, distorted and undermined. We need to more intentionally and thoroughly remove and resist any notion of a neutral reader. We will see below, that Scripture itself anticipates both the reader who comes to the text without understanding and also the reader who departs without understanding. The character of this ignorance is not of a person innocently seeking, or simply naïve; it is the hard and difficult lesson of the universal complicity in sin.

Third, as mentioned at the outset, we are bound by Scripture's own character in preserving the balance of virtue and vice in our prescriptions of scriptural hermeneutics. To represent only one side of the anthropology of the reader as if it is the complete picture not only distorts the character of the person, it also, in turn, creates imbalances and distortions in the character of Scripture itself, and ultimately projects and maps that imbalance and distortion onto the very character of the triune God. In the next section we will offer one key example of how this distortion occurs as a way of extending our appreciation for the role of sin and vice in the picture of scriptural hermeneutics.

Virtue Hermeneutics and the (Mis)Character of Scripture

As we noted at the outset, the character of Scripture itself hangs in a perennial and porous, mediate relationship between the divine Trinitarian authorship and the human recipient readers. As it hangs, it is influenced easily by the perceived character of the authors and readers on both sides. Scripture is highly sensitive and vulnerable to these misconceptions; these misconceptions are often difficult to discern but operate with great influence in particular ways of reading.[22] Thus, to misperceive the nature of the reader (in this particular case, to focus on the role of virtue in an unbal-

---

22. It was one of the chief goals of my *Rendering the Word* to uncover some of these hidden dimensions and tensions.

anced manner) will result in a corresponding imbalance in the perception of the character of Scripture and to restrict and narrow the effectiveness of Scripture as God's written Word.

A striking example of this type of restriction comes from Fowl and Jones. At the end of a section where they effectively outline how the goal of Christian hermeneutics should be the embodiment of virtuous practices and character, they draw the following conclusion about Scripture: that, "[u]nless Christian communities are committed to embodying their Scriptural interpretation, the Bible loses its character as Scripture."[23] This way of unilaterally connecting the character of Scripture with the production of virtuous character in the community of readers is a tendency we commonly find in actualist[24] accounts of the theology of Scripture and its hermeneutics.

This is a problem that many see as tainting the theological wells from which virtue hermeneuticians have drawn water. It is argued to be found in Karl Barth's theology of Scripture and the work of Postliberal theology, particularly Hans Frei and George Lindbeck.[25] Barth's theology of Scripture was, and is, controversial insofar as he decides to honor Scripture's perennial relationship to God as God's Word written by describing its ontology in actualist terms: Scripture "becomes" the Word of God.[26] The rationale for why Barth does this, and the question of whether he is guilty of theological sins, is complex and beyond our concerns here.[27] What is telling for our purpose is how, in the *Church Dogmatics*, as he describes this "becoming," Barth does so focusing, like virtue hermeneutics, primarily on the positive and successful reactions that readers may have to Scripture.[28] This, inten-

23. Fowl and Jones, *Reading in Communion*, 20.

24. Broadly put, there are two ways that theologians have talked about Scripture's character as the Word of God. Some approach it by way of some essence that Scripture tangibly possesses; these may be named "essentialist" accounts. "Actualist" accounts define Scripture's character as God's Word not in terms of what Scripture is, but in terms of what Scripture *does*. Scripture expresses God's Word because God speaks through it is an actualist way of describing it; Scripture is God's Word because it is inerrant, holy, perfect, or possesses some intrinsic character is an essentialist mode of description.

25. It should be noted that Barth's influence on Frei is well known. Barth's influence on Lindbeck is less so.

26. *CD*, I/2, 110.

27. I don't think he is, but it would take some space to work out; space which we do not have here. My own solution to the problem of how to responsibly describe Scripture's character *vis-a-vis* actualist or essentialist accounts is sketched briefly below. It should also be noted that Barth himself was aware of the problem and indicated some flexibility on the historical and contextual appropriateness for both actualist and essentialist ways of framing a doctrine of Scripture. Barth, *Table Talk*, 1963.

28. It is important to note that Barth, as far as I am aware, only puts the argument in the positive form, that Scripture "becomes" the Word of God, but does not put the

tionally or otherwise, creates the impression that Scripture *only* becomes the Word of God on the occasion of those positive reactions. This, many argue, makes (literally) the Word of God contingent upon human subjectivity in the event of the successful and faithful response.

Similar accusations have been made against Hans Frei and George Lindbeck. In Lindbeck's famous case, from *The Nature of Doctrine*, he argues that when the crusader cries out "Jesus is Lord" just prior to cleaving the head of his enemy, this statement is false. "Jesus is Lord" is only true as a truth claim for those who engender that lordship in ways that are faithful to Scripture. In both cases, the ontological character of Scripture, and of the truth of confessions, is descriptively tied to the *positive* manifestation of its effects in or through the hearer/confessor. This is the same unilateral tie we saw in Fowl and Jones above, and is a general tendency in virtue hermeneutics. We can beneficially describe, interrogate, and correct this problem, supplementing and completing the helpful corrective of virtue hermeneutics, if we treat it as a form of "occasionalism."

The basic argument of seventeenth-century developments of the idea of occasionalism is that the direct cause of all events in the world is God, and that all of the events that happen in time and space are simply "occasions" of that direct causality. In this view, the role for any mediate or secondary cause is minimized or even disappears. This results, arguably, in a loss of things like secondary causality and free will in human actions. The cause and effect relationship we see operating in the world is, then, only an apparent relationship; the "real" cause for all things and actions being God.[29] The concern with the views of the relationship of Scripture and human agency raised with respect to actualistic accounts such as those of Barth, Frei, Fowl, and others can be viewed as a kind of occasionalism insofar as the Bible only becomes Scripture on the occasion of the positive response of the human creature.[30] If the lack of faith in the response of the interpreter of Scripture causes it to lose its status as Scripture then it is difficult to see how the opposite is not also the case, that the faith of the interpreter also causes Scripture to gain its status as such. Scripture's character is unilaterally produced by the occasion of the faith of the interpreter.

---

assertion in the negative form, that Scripture is something less than or other than the Word of God if the church or readers fail to respond in faith, such as in the quote from Fowl and Jones above. Insofar as this is true, Barth has greater space to avoid the problems of occasionalism that we describe here.

29. For an overview of the history and basic lines of the argument for occasionalism see: "Occasionalism," *Stanford Encyclopedia of Philosophy*: http://plato.stanford.edu/entries/occasionalism/.

30. For a recent forceful articulation of this argument see Legaspi, *Death of Scripture*.

Framing this tendency as a form of occasionalism helpfully exposes a simple path by which the problem might be corrected. Simply put, we might ask: why is the character of the truthfulness of the speech of Lindbeck's crusader, or the character of Scripture as God's written word, only effective in the *faith* of the speaker or interpreter? The occasionalist problem is averted if we see how the proclamation "Jesus is Lord" is effectively true and Scripture is effectively the Word of God in the effect and practices of those who respond *unfaithfully* as well.

Let's assume, for the sake of argument, that the crusader in Lindbeck's account is, in fact, acting unfaithfully, sinfully, and viciously in his violent crusading activities. We need not be distracted by debates about violence and just war to make this point. We can assert that the confession "Jesus is Lord" is still true in that it hangs, ironically, in truthful judgment on the lips of the murdering crusader. Lindbeck requires something like this in order to make his famous point. He sees the truth of the confession in a pattern of practices that are irreconcilable with what the crusader is doing. Those practices of grace and peacemaking, and their necessary inclusion in the character of those for whom Jesus is Lord, is the truth of the confession which is required if the murder of the crusader is to be named as such.

Likewise, we will explore below how Scripture is effective as the Word of God in, with, and under the response of the interpreter, whether that response be faithful or sinful. Scripture itself expects this, as its effect in the world and in the practices of human creatures. The language "in, with, and under" is chosen intentionally here. Scripture bears an analogous relationship to the Eucharist in its perennial effectiveness: just as the Eucharist is effective both in communicating grace to those who receive it in faith as well as in bringing judgment to those who eat of it unworthily (1 Cor 11:27), so Scripture affects those who interpret it with faith, as well as with resistance or indifference. The Bible's effectiveness in its speech action is absolute and total. It is always effective in the fullness of its power and intention, as the Word of God. That effectiveness is revealed in the production of virtue in the reading community, it is also produced in the uncovering and confirmation of sin as vice.

We may still usefully employ actualist ways of talking about Scripture and its effects with this correction in place. Indeed actualist accounts are of great benefit for other theological reasons we cannot explore here. They still offer a framework for a more thorough and consistent theology of Scripture. They preserve the perennial relationship of the canon with the actions of the Trinity in the economy of grace and reconciliation. They also offer a more comprehensive and robust anthropology of practicing reader(s). By way of the virtue hermeneutics corrective actualist accounts contribute to resist any neutral moment or permit the neutered character of modern views of personhood to reassert themselves. We also preserve and affirm the perennial and pervasive power and presence of God's Word in the holy canon of Scripture; an effectiveness that is always "becoming," always speaking, always calling humanity to return to its faithful imaging of God, and revealing the ways in which we do not.

The Witness of Scripture to the Character of Its Interpreter/Hearer

Above we indicated the importance of allowing Scripture itself to inform how we understand the character of the divine author and human interpreters. We now turn our attention to that point. What is the character of the reader and reading community that Scripture itself anticipates?

First of all, it is important to recall that Scripture does not address, either initially or primarily, a virtuous reader or reading community. From the beginning in Gen 1 and 2 the Word of God anticipates hearers who will be confused about who or what is worthy of worship; it seeks to fend off from the beginning the strong human propensity to idolatry, violence, and injustice. Genesis 3 sets the stage for the rest of Scripture, outlining the problem of human sinfulness and violence that will ebb and flow all the way through, until the final resolution in the eschaton of John's Revelation. Scripture's hermeneutical metanarrative arc assumes the presence, practices, and problems of sin and vice. Stanley Grenz puts it well: "The central purpose of this story is to be the Spirit's instrumentality in bringing sinful humans to change direction."[31] Even if we take the valuable insights of virtue hermeneutics and of Briggs and others into account, Scripture, painted with the most generous of brushes, anticipates readers with mixed (at best) characters. This complicated character is fundamental to the ethos of scriptural hermeneutics.

Further, and more exactingly to the point, Scripture does not anticipate addressing readers who are simply ignorant or neutral in the bearings of their moral and ethical character. Virtue hermeneutics helpfully reminds us that *all* practices of human interpretation are saturated with character: with moral, ethical, political, and religious dynamics and texture: "The ways in which people read and write texts are decisively shaped by material circumstances and by the kinds of people they are and hope to become."[32]

---

31. Grenz, *Theology for the Community* (2000), 390.
32. Fowl and Jones, *Reading in Communion*, 21. Works of Fowl and Jones remain

BOWALD—*On (Still) Taking St. Paul Seriously* 273

The logical extension of that all important insight is to exhaustively interrogate all human practices and the character that they implicitly possess: to name all that is not virtue as vice, all that is not faith as sin and idolatry. Virtue hermeneutics has a tendency to ignore this point, to be hesitant in naming the character of those practices that are not virtuous. But to allow any hint of a dimension of neutrality in the character of human practices is to allow a possibility that unravels and undoes the foundation of the argument that gives virtue hermeneutics its value and importance in the first place.

So, to complete the line of argument of virtue hermeneutics, not only do we never come to Scripture neutrally, we also never depart Scripture neutrally. Not only does Scripture anticipate readers who are both vicious and virtuous; it also anticipates, expects, and even can be seen as *producing* mixed character as the "successful" by-product of its reading. Both the ethos and the pathos of reading Scripture are anticipated to be of a mixed character.

One way that we might explore this is in the theme within the Bible of those who, in the presence of God's Word and the gospel, are said to have "closed" eyes and ears, who do not hear or understand. This is a strong thematic thread throughout Scripture, describing this response as an apathetic or vicious reaction to the Word of God. Isaiah 6:9–10 is the focal point of this theme in the Old Testament. The passage that perhaps gives it its greatest hermeneutical gravity in the New Testament is found in the last, culminating passage in the book of Acts, where Isaiah is quoted.

Paul is under house arrest in Rome, but is free to preach the gospel. Chapter 28:23–25 describes how a Jewish contingent who heard him responded to hearing Paul's preaching. Some were persuaded, others "would not believe." Paul then issues one last closing comment explaining to them why there was this mixed reaction. He begins:

> The Holy Spirit rightly spoke through Isaiah the prophet to your fathers, saying "go to this people and say: you will keep on hearing, but will not understand; and you will keep on seeing but will not perceive."

And why do they not understand? Paul continues:

> For the heart of this people has become dull, and with their ears they scarcely hear, and they have closed their eyes; lest they should see with their eyes and hear with their ears, and

---

the clearest and most persuasive publications on the topic.

understand with their heart and return, and I should heal them. (NASB)

Why don't they see, hear, or understand? Is it, in the popular idiom, "through no fault of their own"? Is it simply a byproduct of a lack of skill or ability to comprehend the words that Paul was speaking? A lack of language facility to grasp what Paul was saying is not the problem. They are, to continue using Paul's metaphor, sick and injured, in need of healing, but unwilling or unable to acknowledge their injury and accept the work of the healer. Paul elaborates on this condition in Rom 1:18-24.[33]

> For the wrath of God is revealed from heaven against all ungodliness and wickedness of men who by their wickedness suppress the truth . . . for although they knew God they did not honor him as God . . . but they became futile in their thinking and their senseless minds were darkened . . . (RSV)

The "darkening" of human minds, of which Paul writes here, ties into a longstanding biblical theme that describes the darkening in terms of a spiritual blindness and deafness. To gain a greater perspective let's look briefly at the extensiveness of this theme of not hearing or seeing in response to the Word.

There are anticipations of it in Deut 29:4 and 29:10. It appears explicitly in Isa 43:8, Jer 5:21ff., Eze 12:2, and Zech 7:11-12. Each of the Gospels records Jesus as referencing it in order to describe the reaction of those who rejected or resisted his teaching: in Matt 13:14-15, Mark 4:12 (for the purpose of parable teaching), 8:18, Luke 8:10 (cp. Mark 4:12), 19:42, John 8:43-44, 9:39-41, and 12:40. It also appears in Rom 10:16, 11:8, 2 Tim 4:4, and perhaps allusively in Heb 5:1. The prevalence of this theme in Scripture, especially in the New Testament writings, gives it substantial hermeneutical gravity; we must allow this gravity to inform our thinking about the character of the Word of God and the nature of the reader to which the Word is addressed.

For example, with regard to the anthropology of the reader, there is an ambiguity in these texts as to who does the blinding of the eyes which prevents understanding. John's Gospel and Romans variously attribute the blinding either to God or leave the cause ambiguous. Paul in Acts, and others, attribute the closing of the eyes to the willfulness of the person who is not seeing. Regardless of the range of report here, Paul leaves no doubt that

---

33. This is a pivotal passage for the epistemological framework for the Augustinian-Reformed tradition, which extends through Karl Barth, and is also a pivot point for Westphal: "Taking St. Paul Seriously," 201-2.

it is the human creature who is ultimately responsible for their blind and deaf condition; that this is the direct result of their sin.

Scripture itself does not envision the lack of understanding in the response to hearing and seeing the Word of God as a morally or ethically neutral characteristic. Taking the biblical witness about the character of the persons it addresses results in "not so much a spiritual vacuum as idolatry."[34] Not understanding is a sign of sinfulness and judgment, it is a sign that people remain in the darkness through their own volition and through their covenant participation in the curses of the fall. There is no ambiguity on this point in 2 Cor 3:12—4:6, where Paul expressly explains how those who read fail to see the face of Jesus when they read "Moses"[35] are reading from behind a veil of idolatry. That,

> [I]f our gospel is veiled, it is veiled only to those who are perishing. In their case the god of this world has blinded the minds of the unbelievers, to keep them from seeing the light of the gospel of the glory of Christ, who is the likeness of God. (2 Cor 4:3, 4)

With respect to God's Word, ignorance is not bliss; ignorance is grief; ignorance is sloth and pride; ignorance is idolatry and vice.

Here we only briefly surveyed the theme of blindness to understanding the Word of God. The "hardening of heart" is another theme that helpfully illustrates and supplements our understanding of Scripture's anthropology of those who are confronted by God's Word. The famous example of this is found in the Exodus passages related to the confrontation of the pharaoh by Moses and Aaron.

Throughout the familiar narrative in Exod 7–14, upon hearing the demands of Moses, Scripture describes the so-called "hardening" process that the pharaoh's heart undergoes as he resists and rejects their requests. Again, we do not need to sort out the problem of the cause of his hardening, which, in the narrative is attributed at different points to God and to Pharaoh, but rather, to understand how this narrative illustrates the effectiveness of this encounter with God's directive word through Moses on the pharaoh.

As the narrative progresses the plagues and the sign becomes increasingly more dramatic, inflicting greater and greater harm and difficulty on

---

34. Westphal, "Taking St. Paul Seriously," 201.

35. On how Moses is transformed into a text in this passage, and the highly relevant discussion, see Behr, *Formation of Christian Theology*, 26ff. Grenz also affirms the necessary role of prevenient divine agency in enabling the church to read Scripture properly (*Theology for the Community*, 382–83). Grenz's emphasis here, and the way he positions Scripture deeply in pneumatology, is unique amongst American evangelicals of his time.

the Egyptian people. Reading the story we inevitably ask how it is that the pharaoh can continue to refuse. This is the process of "hardening" that is taking place as an effect of his rejection and resistance to God's message through Moses. Anthropologies of "practice" are of some assistance in helping us picture the hermeneutical function of vice as a productive effect of reading Scripture in this example.

Practices that are repeated produce tendencies in their practitioners; practices produce character. Training for sports is an apt example. In basketball, there is an ideal way of shooting the ball, with one's elbow set perpendicular to the ground, with one's arm at something of a 90 degree angle, allowing the ball to be balanced on one's hand as the shot is taken. The goal is to train the body to produce the same shot every time. The only way to achieve this goal is to repeatedly practice well-formed jump shots. The best shooters literally take thousands of shots in practice every week. The only way to possess the character of a good jump shot is to engage in this high level of practical repetition. It is often the case that basketball players will, unknowingly, practice with poor form in their shot. It is well known that the more one has practiced with poor form, the more difficult it is to correct that form.

This example holds true for other sports, for football, for musical performance, for acting, for all kinds of practices. Practice makes perfect. Practice also makes one more fundamentally flawed. The lesson is that, incrementally, as one repeats a practice, the character of that way of practicing becomes more and more ingrained; it feels more and more "natural" to the practitioner, despite the fact that it is demonstrably a poor and unproductive, even a "false," practice. The practiced lives of human creatures are a liturgy of struggle; the wrestle between practices of harmony and dissonance in relation to the melody of the love of the Trinity resonant in the good order of creation.

Each time the pharaoh says "no" to the word of God he becomes just a bit more practiced and inclined to say "no" again. It becomes more and more natural to see and respond *this* way. This also explains how it is that people come to read Scripture in odd or eccentric ways that bear little to no resemblance to more orthodox and traditional readings. The more a person persists in reading in one particular way the more that way feels normal, and a trajectory is established that takes that person's (or community's) practices in a direction that, over time, bear little resemblance to the mainstream of Christianity. This is the "hardening" of practice and the heart against the grain of God's Word. This is an example of how we might think of Scripture being effective as God's written Word in the unfaithful practices of response.

There are numerous other biblical themes that also would illuminate the effectiveness of the practices of reading Scripture in both faith and unfaith. Time will not permit any further exploration here, and we move to the conclusion.

Conclusion: Toward a Fuller Accounting of the Subject of Scriptural Interpretation

Here we have pressed the point of the complex character of readers, as manifest in both the ethos and the pathos of reading, and as attested to by both Scripture and the Christian theological tradition. Character formation perennially and effectively occurs in the interpretive encounter with the Word of God. That formation may be toward faithfulness and virtue, in harmony with the character of the divine image and the *cosmos*; that character may also be formed in sin and rebellion, in dissonance with the created order and against the grain of the practices for which human being were created. The character formation may be a mix of these, indeed this is the most likely outcome.

It reinforces and expands the fundamental and valuable insight that Fowl, Jones, Briggs, and others have initiated in exploring how virtue leads the reader into Scripture more deeply by setting the production of readerly virtues within the accompanying effects and practices of vice, as these pertain to Scripture's ethos and pathos.

This corrective also assists with a complaint that has been lodged against various contemporary forms of virtue ethics, epistemology, and hermeneutics. That is, that the call for virtue lacks any concrete description of virtues. Briggs' book *The Virtuous Reader* redresses this with great success. Even greater clarity on the character of virtues is achieved with the relief that is achieved in setting virtue over against the perennial presence and pressures of vice.

In the end, if we keep the broader picture of the phenomenon of scriptural hermeneutics in view, as a horizon against which we articulate a hermeneutics of virtue, it would not undermine the latter but, rather, frame and underscore the gravity and importance of investing in ways of promoting biblical literacy and faithful and virtuous church practices. If the very real possibility of vice, sin, and judgment is an ever-present and real presence in our practices, the care and attention we will give to confession, repentance, and the practices of faith and virtue, will receive all the greater contrast, relief, and importance as a result.

Here we have endeavored to lay out more broadly and thoroughly what is the character of readers and interpreters of Scripture. We have listened to what Scripture itself speaks to that character as it anticipates the address of human creatures who battle and succumb to the power of the proclivities of their sinful practices and natures. We have supplemented the picture offered by virtue hermeneutics, adding the hermeneutical role of sin and vice. Once this larger picture is clarified, we are in a better position to articulate and write treatises that intend to teach others how best to read Scripture.

We have waxed on these points so as to also see how Scripture itself resists and deconstructs any of that doggedly persistent modern myth of what Thomas Nagel called "the view from nowhere."[36] We cannot fall back into a modern temptation to allow our scriptural hermeneutics to posit or permit either a reader of Scripture who is reading from nowhere, or more to the point, a reader who is reading as no one.[37] Westphal, in a warning that resounds just as strongly today as it did a quarter of a century ago, wrote that,

> [I]t is entirely possible to find in the ashes of foundationalism only finitude and not sinfulness, to discover preunderstandings that are perspectival but not perverse. This is just what has happened for many, if not most, of those who have played major roles in the undermining of foundationalism.[38]

In contrast to the one-sided and incomplete picture painted by virtue hermeneutics, Scripture anticipates, perennially, readers who, despite whatever virtues they may possess, continue to struggle with their sinful character and pictures the encounter with the Word as always addressing and affecting that character. The reader is transformed, encouraged in the direction of virtue, and confirmed, if they so choose, in their vice. The reader reads with either sympathy or antipathy; there is no "third" category or character of reading practices.[39]

Once this fuller larger picture is set in place, we may quite effectively rejoin in the efforts of virtue hermeneutics and the deeper traditions of theological reflection on the practices of reading Scripture as found in places like Augustine's *De Doctrina Christiana* and the *Didascalicon* of Hugh

---

36. Nagel, *View from Nowhere*.

37. This is one of the main concerns raised by Westphal in complaint against contemporary Christian philosophers, primarily exemplified (ironically) in the work of Reformed epistemologists Alvin Plantinga and Nicholas Wolterstorff. See Westphal, "Taking St. Paul Seriously," 212–18.

38. Westphal, "Taking St. Paul Seriously," 211.

39. Apathy is really a form of the latter.

of St. Victor, and direct our efforts toward developing more deeply faithful ways of reading and interpreting Scripture.

The holy canon of Scripture is like a sacrament, giving grace and life to those who read in faith, and judgment to those who do not (1 Cor 11:27). The faithful reading practices of virtue are attractive to those seeking repentance and faith, and a repulsive stench to those who reject repentance. The practices of interpretation should be undertaken with repentance and prayer, in the spirit of 2 Cor 2:14-17:

> But thanks be to God, who always leads us in His triumph in Christ, and manifests through us the sweet aroma of the knowledge of Him in every place. For we are a fragrance of Christ to God among those who are being saved and among those who are perishing; to the one an aroma from death to death, to the other an aroma from life to life. And who is adequate for these things? For we are not like the many, peddling the word of God, but as from sincerity, but as from God, we speak in Christ, in the sight of God.

Bibliography

Barth, Karl. *Church Dogmatics*. Edited and translated by G. W. Bromiley. 4 vols. Edinburgh: T. & T. Clark, 1975.

———. *Table Talk*. Nashville: John Knox, 1963.

Behr, John. *Formation of Christian Theology. Volume 1: The Way to Nicaea*. Crestwood NY, St. Vladimer's Seminary Press, 2001.

Bowald, Mark Alan. "Objectivity." In *Dictionary of the Theological Interpretation of the Bible*, edited by Kevin J. Vanhoozer et al., 544-46. Grand Rapids: Baker, 2005.

———. *Rendering the Word in Theological Hermeneutics: Mapping Divine and Human Agency*. Aldershot, UK: Ashgate, 2007.

Briggs, Richard. *The Virtuous Reader: Old Testament Narrative and Interpretive Virtue*. Grand Rapids: Baker, 2010.

Fowl, Stephen E., and L. Gregory Jones. *Reading in Communion: Scripture and Ethics in Christian Life*. Grand Rapids: Eerdmans, 1991.

Jones, L. Gregory. "Formed and Transformed by Scripture: Character, Community, and Authority in Biblical Interpretation." In *Character and Scripture: Moral Formation, Community and Biblical Interpretation*, edited by William P. Brown, 18-33. Grand Rapids: Eerdmans, 2002.

Legaspi, Michael C. *The Death of Scripture and the Rise of Biblical Studies*. Oxford: Oxford University Press, 2010.

MacIntyre, Alasdair. *After Virtue: A Study in Moral Theology*. Notre Dame, IN: University of Notre Dame Press, 1981.

———. *Whose Justice? Which Rationality?* Notre Dame, IN: University of Notre Dame Press, 1989.

Moroney, Stephen K. *The Noetic Effects of Sin: A Historical and Contemporary Exploration of How Sin Affects Our Thinking*. Oxford: Lexington, 2000.

Nagel, Thomas. *The View from Nowhere*. Oxford: Oxford University Press, 1986.

Pardue, Stephen T. "Athens and Jerusalem Once More: What the Turn to Virtue Means for Theological Exegesis." *Journal of Theological Interpretation* 4/2 (2010) 295–308.

Roberts, Robert C., and W. Jay Wood, *Intellectual Virtues: An Essay on Regulative Epistemology*. Oxford: Oxford University Press, 2007.

Rogers, Eugene F. Jr. "How the Virtues of an Interpreter Presuppose and Perfect Hermeneutics: The Case of Thomas Aquinas." *The Journal of Religion* 76/1 (1996) 64–81.

Treier, Daniel J. *Virtue and the Voice of God: Toward Theology as Wisdom*. Grand Rapids: Eerdmans, 2006.

Vanhoozer, Kevin J. *Is There a Meaning in This Text? The Bible, the Reader, and the Morality of Literary Knowledge*. Grand Rapids: Zondervan: 1998.

Westphal, Merold. "Taking St. Paul Seriously: Sin as an Epistemological Category." In *Christian Philosophy*, edited by T. P. Flint, 200–226. Notre Dame, IN: University of Notre Dame Press, 1990.

Wolterstorff, Nicholas. "Historicizing the Belief-forming Self." In *Practices of Belief: Selected Essays, Volume 2*, edited by Terence Cuneo, 118–43. Cambridge: Cambridge University Press, 2010.

Zagzebski, Linda. *Virtues of the Mind: An Inquiry into the Nature of Virtue and the Ethical Foundation of Knowledge*. Cambridge: Cambridge University Press, 1996.

Part Five

TRADITION

14

A Tale of Two Pietist Theologians

Friedrich Schleiermacher and Stanley Grenz

GLEN G. SCORGIE *and* PHIL C. ZYLLA

SYSTEMATIC THEOLOGY AND HEART religion sound odd together. The intellect and experience can indeed make for an awkward marriage, but theirs is a union that has to work if the Christian faith is to flourish. Humans are holistic beings, and no option that saws off the head or eviscerates the soul will work very well. This is a study of two theologians who tried to bring heart and mind together in fresh ways they hoped would revitalize Christian faith. It compares and contrasts two theologians indebted to the Pietist impulse in Christian history.

Friedrich Schleiermacher (1768–1834)[1] and Stanley Grenz (1950–2005) were divided by almost two centuries and a certain asymmetry in stature and influence. After all, Schleiermacher is regarded as "the father of modern (liberal) theology," and the most influential Protestant systematic theologian since John Calvin. Yet both were gifted theologians nurtured in the German Pietist tradition, and both bore the marks of its shaping influence in their subsequent lives and thought.

It is a fair assessment that most theology is autobiographical.[2] Personal experience may not singlehandedly determine everything a theologian af-

---

1. See Redeker, *Schleiermacher*.

2. "There is an important relation, not always clearly recognized, between personal life and theological interest and methodology" (Baum, *Journeys*, 1); cf. Nelson,

firms, but it will influence a lot of it. Personal narrative and experience become lenses through which a theologian sees life, decides what is most important, and comes to understand the things of God. Like a lot of other intellectual historians, Stanley Grenz observed that "Schleiermacher's theology is inseparable from his biography."[3] He was right, and he might just as easily have made the same observation about his own work.

Many influences converge in the formation of a theologian, but the early ones are often the most profound and enduring. Most theologians are deeply sensitized and shaped by the religious traditions in which they are nurtured. Even if they come later in life to reject their religious heritage, or at least differentiate themselves from it, they seldom shake free of it altogether.

Friedrich Schleiermacher's father was a minister of the Reformed Church and a chaplain in the Prussian army. At mid-life, while his children were still young, he was deeply influenced by local Moravian Brethren (*Herrnhuters*, followers of the Pietist Ludwig Nicholas von Zinzendorf) and entered into the close relational web of their religious community. The senior Schleiermacher treasured his own spiritual transformation so much that when the time came he insisted that his son Friedrich should be educated at Pietist institutions—first at a boarding school the Moravian Brethren operated, then at their nearby "seminary," and eventually at the University of Halle, founded by Pietist Auguste Francke and others of a kindred disposition a century or so earlier.

However, a couple of major problems emerged early on. The first was that he had trouble genuinely identifying with the Moravian community's claims to personal experiences of "companionship with Jesus."[4] They seemed to elude him. The second problem was that he also developed reservations about some of the central doctrines of the orthodox Christian faith espoused by the Moravians—Christology in particular. In anguish he confessed to his father: "I cannot believe that He who called Himself the Son of Man, was the true Eternal God: I cannot believe that His death was a vicarious atonement."[5] He was distraught because he knew this was a significant departure from both his father's expectations of him and the doctrinal core of the Moravian belief system and devotional experience.

Nevertheless it is also clear from what has survived of his tortured correspondence with his disappointed father that Friedrich still considered himself a Christian, and one who continued to regard Jesus Christ with profound and affectionate esteem. He never renounced this spiritual heritage.

Theologians in their Own Words.
3. Grenz and Olson, *Twentieth Century*, 40.
4. Gerrish, *Prince of the Church*, 25.
5. Schleiermacher, *Life of Schleiermacher*, 46.

For the remainder of his life he retained a dispositional regard for Pietism's emphases on communal fellowship, Christian affections, and devotional feelings. In a famous statement, penned in 1802 after a visit back to the geographic site of his early Moravian education, he declared that he was still a Pietist (lit., *Herrnhuter*), but "of a higher order."[6]

In his famous *Speeches on Religion* (1799) Schleiermacher attests to both his doctrinal struggles and the enduring impress of his Pietist heritage in the face of them:

> Piety was the mother's womb, in whose sacred darkness my young life was nourished and was prepared for a world still sealed for it. In it my spirit breathed ere it had yet found its own place in knowledge and experience. It helped me as I began to sift the faith of my fathers and to cleanse thought and feeling from the rubbish of antiquity. When the God and immortality of my childhood vanished from my doubting eyes it remained to me.[7]

It is surprising, in light of such statements by Schleiermacher himself, and the obvious affinities between the Pietists' emphases on feeling, experience, and community, and his own theological paradigm-shifts in these same directions, that so few of Schleiermacher's intellectual biographers have paid much attention to this. For example, the otherwise erudite *Cambridge Companion to Friedrich Schleiermacher* (2005) makes only a single, passing reference to the influence of Pietism.[8] The same is true of Richard Crouter's otherwise brilliant study *Friedrich Schleiermacher: Between Enlightenment and Romanticism* (2005). However, things are starting to change. Some recent scholarship on Schleiermacher is rediscovering this influence on his creative theological work.[9]

Our second theologian was the son of Richard and Clara Grenz, a German-speaking Protestant minister and his wife. Their home was in the United States, in the mid-twentieth century, and they were Baptists, not Reformed. Stanley Grenz's father pastored in what had been a tightly-knit regional community of German-speaking pietistic Baptist immigrants seeking to build new lives on the windswept prairies of the American upper Midwest and the Canadian prairies. Many of these European immigrant

---

6. The quotation is ubiquitous in studies of Schleiermacher; e.g., Gerrish, *Continuing the Reformation*, 149. It is from a collection of Schleiermacher's correspondence (*Briefen*) still not translated into English.
7. Schleiermacher, *On Religion*, 9.
8. Marina, *Cambridge Companion to Schleiermacher*, 231.
9. Eaghll, "Pietism to Romanticism."

families were affiliated with the North American [German] Baptist Conference, although as English language proficiency developed some were integrating into existing English-speaking denominations. It was natural, therefore, that Grenz should take his seminary training at the Conservative Baptist seminary in Denver, and even more understandable that he was ordained into the North American [German] Baptist clergy, and later taught at their seminary in Sioux Falls, South Dakota.

One of the most significant differences between these two theologians is that Grenz, unlike Schleiermacher, never rejected any significant elements of his doctrinal heritage as he matured intellectually. He owned it and honored it in its entirety, and for the rest of his life readily identified himself as a Pietist. At the height of his tragically abbreviated career he acknowledged "how deeply steeped I am in the warm-hearted, relational, Pietistic conception of the Christian faith that I saw as a child in my father's ministry and imbued in the churches he served."[10] The only significant way in which he differentiated himself from this spiritual tradition was by acknowledging that he was "a Pietist with a Ph.D."[11] This made him different from most of his co-religionists, and, as he came to believe, also helped define his unique vocation.

As we shall see, Schleiermacher and Grenz moved along divergent theological trajectories. They did this by selectively appropriating elements and dispositions from their shared heritage. The first made feeling (or sensibility) his epistemological foundation, while the latter promoted a "tethered" Pietism—one characterized by robust evangelical experience and abiding allegiance to Scripture and the contours of a scriptural worldview. Schleiermacher became the father of modern liberal theology, while Grenz became an important spokesperson for orthodox evangelical renewal at the beginning of this millennium.

In what follows we will review the origins of Pietism, profile its character, and trace the diffusion of its influence. After this we will explore how the Pietist impulse informed the distinctly different visions of these two theologians. We will conclude with some constructive reflections on a Christianity of the heart and mind.

---

10. Grenz, "Concerns of a Pietist," 58–59.
11. Ibid.

The Origins and Character of Pietism

Pietism signifies a Continental European movement launched in the seventeenth century to reclaim the experiential and transforming dimensions of the Christian faith.[12] It is difficult to encompass all the interconnected themes comprising Pietism into a single, succinct definition.[13] Perhaps we come closest to doing so when we think of Pietism as "a religion of the heart, where the heart is understood as the controlling and affective center of the self."[14]

The movement originated in Germany, where many Protestant Christians were expending their energies arguing—and in some instances literally fighting—amongst themselves over details of doctrine. Lutheran mystic and church superintendent Johann Arndt (1555–1621) called such Christians back to the importance of a vibrant relationship to the living Christ, and "brought to light again the spontaneity of Christian service as the true fruit of a living faith."[15] The title to his multi-volume admonition, *True Christianity* (1605ff.), conveyed his conviction that this, not complacent confessionalism, is original and genuine Christian faith. "True Christianity," he wrote, consists "in the exhibition of a true, living faith, active in genuine godliness and the fruits of righteousness." Christians bear the name of Christ "not only because we ought to believe in Christ, but also because we are to live in Christ and he in us."[16]

Arndt's work was frequently contested by confessional Lutherans because it reclaimed elements of the pre-Reformation medieval mystical tradition. Nonetheless, it enjoyed enormous popularity among Protestant laypersons, and became ubiquitous in Christian homes. Many early German immigrants to America brought treasured copies with them. Demand for the work prompted Benjamin Franklin to publish a new edition in 1751. It was the first German-language book printed in the New World.[17]

The Pietist movement per se emerged in the late seventeenth century when another Lutheran pastor, Philip Spener, building on Arndt's work, escalated the reaction against a coldly intellectual Lutheran orthodoxy. His little classic *Pia Desideria* (1675), originally intended as a preface to a

---

12. Lotz, "Continental Pietism," 448–52; Stoeffler, *Rise of Evangelical Pietism*; Weborg, "Pietism."

13. Olson has helpfully collated a number of credible definitions of Pietism in "Reclaiming Pietism."

14. Carlson, "Pietism," 673.

15. Oberman, "Preface" to *True Christianity*, xv.

16. Arndt, *True Christianity*, 21.

17. Wallmann, "Johann Arndt," 21–22.

reprinting of Arndt's work, took on a life of its own. As a stand-alone publication, it became a highly-influential call for a return to a faith characterized by sincerity, devotion, and heartfelt experiential love for Christ.

We are hard-pressed to find a better summary of the contours of Pietism than the constructive proposals found in *Pia Desideria*. In this Pietist manifesto, Spener commended such innovations as: devout Bible study in small groups (*collegia pietatis*), significant layperson participation and empowerment, showing practical love toward others, maintaining a charitable spirit under fire, providing pastoral training with a spiritual formation component, and preaching that nourished spiritually, rather than merely informed, congregants.[18]

In short strokes Spener had sketched a vision of devout Christianity liberated from large, formal institutional structures, and known for its warmly genuine, egalitarian relationships. He offered a vision of the Christian life characterized by affective dispositions toward God and others, and overflowing responsiveness to human need—responses prompted by compassion rather than mere duty. Such dispositions were not acquired naturally; they demanded a supernatural work of grace in the human heart.

This is genuine Pietism. The original Pietists did not disparage the mind or doctrine, but they did insist that a Christian faith commitment sequestered in the intellect falls well short of the biblical ideal. When Pietism launched as "a religion of the heart," the term *heart* did not imply a dimension of human existence divorced from reason or thought. Rather, *heart* conveyed a sincere and holistic commitment to God in Christ that also encompassed moral responsibility and the life of the mind.

The Diffusion of the Pietist Heritage

The Pietist vision and disposition stayed alive after Philip Spener and his contemporaries passed on, even after the Enlightenment had molded the secular European consciousness. At first this was mainly through the emergent Moravians and their charismatic leader Nicholas Ludwig von Zinzendorf (1700–1760). The international Moravian communities served as tiny fire-pots for the Pietist impulse, keeping it alight until it was fanned into a large flame in the broader contexts of the First and Second Evangelical Awakenings in the mid-eighteenth and early nineteenth centuries.

Through the Moravians, as we have noted, Schleiermacher was exposed to the Pietist impulse. It remains an open question how much the

---

18. Spener, *Pia Desideria*, 88–122.

original Pietism had already mutated in the hands of Zinzendorf. Much of his writing was aimed at fostering an experiential intimacy with Christ—a heart-felt personal relationship described by more recent critics as a kind of sublimated eroticism or sanctified sexuality.[19]

Perhaps we can also discern in Zinzendorf the beginnings of a disparagement of reason that has come to infect many subsequent aberrations of original Pietism. Zinzendorf was convinced that the essence of religion was "something quite different from holding an opinion."[20] It was, he maintained, something that everyone, regardless of relative mental ability, is able to grasp "through experience alone, without any concepts."[21] In at least one instance Zinzendorf went so far as to suggest to his students that "reason weakens experience."[22] Peter Vogt sums up Zinzendorf's view as follows: While doctrine may have some usefulness, "it is not the conceptual knowledge of particular points of doctrine but the personal, experiential, and preconceptual grasp of the spiritual realities to which these doctrines refer that matters in the life of a believer."[23]

Most intriguing of all is Zinzendorf's suggestion that human beings have an awareness, as created beings, of their "dependence on something superior."[24] Even though this limited consciousness of God was insufficient for eternal salvation, and needed to be supplemented by an encounter with the living Christ, it was a baseline consciousness upon which Christ-centered religion might build. Peter Vogt plausibly concludes that Zinzendorf "paved the way for Friedrich Schleiermacher's concept of religious intuition. Reared in the Moravian Church, Schleiermacher largely rejected the doctrinal content of Moravian piety but held on to its experiential and communal orientation."[25]

On the European continent and elsewhere, small Moravian communities continued to practice their Pietistic faith until the Second Evangelical Awakening broke out in the early nineteenth century. For example, Emile Guers, one of the Swiss leaders of *Le Réveil*, the francophone manifestation of this international awakening, later reflected: "The Moravian church was our spiritual cradle."[26]

19. Vogt, "Zinzendorf," 219, 222.
20. Ibid., 213.
21. Erb, *Pietists*, 291.
22. Ibid., 292.
23. Vogt, "Zinzendorf," 213.
24. Ibid., 231.
25. Ibid., 220.
26. Quoted by Stunt, *From Awakening*, 27.

The Second Evangelical Awakening[27] was pietistic, but this influence was now supplemented by a strong infusion of Romantic tenor and tone. Throughout Europe people were reacting against the rationalistic spirit of the Enlightenment, and this was true of many people associated with established Protestant churches. The Awakening's affirmation of heart-felt religion offered an appealing alternative. It resonated with the concurrent counter-cultural shift toward Romanticism, which found intellectualism deficient, and gloried instead in feeling and human emotion. More often than not awakened evangelicals expressed themselves in the newer florid, highly affective speech, prose and hymnody of those Romantic times. This awakened sensibility has been described as a matter of heart-felt piety "that flows from the love of the Redeemer as a personal affair."[28]

Leaders of the established Protestant churches of northern Europe frequently resisted this emergent religious enthusiasm. This led to the formation of (often illegal) small conventicles for fellowship and Bible study. Convinced that the established ecclesiastical structures were spiritually moribund, such ardent evangelicals hived off into new "free church" groups that were sometimes harassed by the religious establishment and civil authorities. For these small groups, the adversarial stance of religious authorities seemed to reinforce the earlier Pietist valuation of the inner life and intimate fellowship. Social marginalization also meant that these small fellowships of believers had to fall back on an elemental brand of religion, devoid of aesthetic, ritual and sophistication, and centered instead on simple Bible study, hymn-singing, and prayer.

The Moravians were responsible for connecting John Wesley (1703–91), the preeminent leader of the Great Awakening, to Continental Pietism. It was, after all, in a small Moravian chapel in London, in 1738, that Wesley's heart was strangely (and famously) warmed. Thereafter the Methodists and the Wesleyan tradition, alongside the spiritual descendants of the Puritans, helped carry the flag for experiential conversion and heart-felt religion in the English-speaking world.

Pietism and Evangelicalism

Pietism contributed in a substantive and formative way to the evangelical tradition that has flourished on the North American scene since colonial

27. We are designating the Great Awakening of the mid-eighteenth century as the First Evangelical Awakening, and therefore describing as the Second Evangelical Awakening the subsequent renewal movement circa 1790–1830.

28. Cramp, *Memoir*, 15.

times. Its contributions are now widely recognized as seminal to the evangelical emphases on conversion, on real change of heart, and on a personal relationship with Jesus Christ.[29] Much of this, as we have noted, was mediated to evangelicalism through John and Charles Wesley, and the Wesleyan movement generally.

According to historian David Bebbington, the evangelical tradition is *both* Bible-centered *and* conversion-focused—both biblically orthodox and experiential in character.[30] However, there has been a long-simmering tug-of-war within evangelicalism over whether evangelical identity should be determined *primarily* by adherence to a set of orthodox doctrines, or by sharing in a transforming experience of the grace of God in Christ.[31] John Wesley appears to have tilted toward prioritizing the experiential. He recognized the impossibility of complete Christian agreement in matters of opinion. But he was also convinced that it was nevertheless right and good to work together in a spirit of brotherhood. "Is your heart right with mine?" he wrote. "If so, I give you my hand."[32]

The Pietism impulse also entered North American Christianity by a smaller, quieter second route. This route was more directly from Europe, and less colored by intervening American influences and events like the Fundamentalist-Modernist controversies of the early twentieth century. I refer to the waves of mid- and later-nineteenth century European immigrations to the United States that included Pietistic Lutherans and adherents of the "free church" tradition in Germany, Scandinavia, and other parts of northern and Eastern Europe.

Some of these pietistic immigrants to North America were German Baptists. This little community revered Johann Oncken (1800–1884) as their pioneering leader, often rehearsing the stories of his courageous and iconic baptism by immersion in 1833 in the wintry waters of the river Elbe, downriver from Hamburg, "under the friendly light of the stars." Despite persecution and imprisonment, Oncken's prodigious evangelistic efforts, extending internationally to German communities in Poland and Russia, led in 1849 to the organization of the Union of Baptist Churches of Germany.[33]

Some of these immigrants found land in the American upper Midwest, and in Western Canada, where, due to geographic and especially language

---

29. Lovelace, *Dynamics of Spiritual Life*, 35–38; also, *American Pietism of Cotton Mather*.
30. Bebbington, *Evangelicalism*, 5–14.
31. Rawlyk and Noll, *Amazing Grace*.
32. John Wesley, "Catholic Spirit," 299–310.
33. Effa, "Diaspora Strategist."

barriers, they remained somewhat isolated. Their isolation was exacerbated by mainstream American and Canadian suspicion of ethnic Germans during the two World Wars. Such enforced separateness, combined with economic stringency, compelled them to perpetuate the very simple, heart-felt and Bible-centered spirituality with which they had come to North America.

A Pietist disposition survived among these German immigrants for at least two reasons: sustained memory of their Pietist heritage, and the new circumstances in which they found themselves. Without easy access to educational opportunities, or the time and energy to devote themselves to a rigorous life of the mind, they drew nourishment from what remained accessible to them—a religion of the heart. It provided an orientation of quiet transcendence amid the earthy demands of agrarian life. Farmers hummed memorized hymns as they plowed long, pungent furrows across their fields. Isolated homemakers prayed in tiny wind-battered houses. Weekly assemblies for worship satisfied deep longings for community, while the simply-expounded Bible grew into an object of reverent delight.

These far-flung congregations first united in 1865 as the General Conference of German Baptist Churches in North America. Later, to clarify their patriotism, the word *German*, was discarded and they became the North American Baptist Conference. Among their leaders was German-born Pietist August Rauschenbusch (1816–99), a highly-successful itinerant evangelist and church-planter who later chaired the German-speaking department of the (Baptist) Rochester Theological Seminary in upstate New York.[34]

August Rauschenbusch had an even-more-famous son Walter (1861–1918), known for his evangelistic endeavors, social ministries in the inner-city, and seminal contributions to the twentieth-century Social Gospel movement. Walter Rauschenbusch famously declared that the only convincing evidence of a genuine conversion lay in the inward transformation of the heart toward unselfishness. Otherwise, "accepting" an offered gift of free and eternal salvation, and thereby avoiding hell, was simply a manifestation of unconverted self-interest "on a higher level."[35] Such a provocative challenge to complacent Protestants was precisely what might be expected from a *bona fide* Pietist. Despite his controversial social views, Rauschenbusch remained in the eyes of his German Baptist peers "a man of deep piety. Religion to him meant more than mere intellectual assent. God and Jesus were very real to him."[36]

34. Cindy Wesley, "Pietist and Baptist," 257–68.
35. Rauschenbusch, *Theology for the Social Gospel*, 108.
36. Von Berge, *Glorious Years*, 93–94.

This is the Pietist heritage in which Stanley Grenz was nurtured, and which he wholeheartedly embraced. For a while, apparently, other intellectual influences muted the force of this tradition in shaping his outlook. But during a study sojourn in Germany, he later reflected, he renewed his commitment to Pietism in a deep and decisive way.

He was profoundly aware of the "twin bloodlines" of evangelicalism, as he called them—experiential piety and Bible-based doctrine. He vigorously validated both. But he left no question about which of the two he was convinced must be privileged. "The commitment to the gospel of heartfelt transformation and the accompanying suspicion of any reduction of saving faith to simple *assensus* has been the lifeblood of evangelicalism throughout its history. It may well remain the movement's central contribution to the renewal of the church of Jesus Christ." Then he added: "The *sine qua non* of evangelicalism is not primarily doctrinal uniformity, but a vibrant spirituality."[37]

Pietist Theologians

Richard Crouter refers to questions of theological method and the appropriate starting point for theological reflection as "the standard divinity school problems."[38] It is precisely these "standard problems," we wish to investigate. More specifically, in what ways does the Pietism impulse shape theological content or method? To put it another way, do Pietist theologians understand their craft any differently than their theological peers view it?

This question led us to *The Pietist Theologians* (2005), a collection of sixteen illuminating profiles edited by Carter Lindberg. The locus of the volume is the seventeenth and eighteenth century, beginning with Arndt and culminating with Wesley. It does not examine subsequent theologians whose work bears the impress of the Pietist impulse. The book reveals that these Pietism theologians tend to give proportionately greater attention to the dynamics of the Christian life, and to cultivating the dispositions of the heart from which life and service issue. To use the contemporary term, they incline toward spiritual theology.

Generally speaking, they do not seem overly exercised by epistemological issues, preferring to rest their case for the truthfulness of the Christian faith on the self-authenticating quality of their experience of the living Christ and, for those who need more objective evidence, the human

---

37. Grenz, "Concerns of a Pietist," 69–70.
38. Crouter, *Schleiermacher*, 170.

transformations that follow from such experience. Finally, the uniting power of divine love, which Pietists celebrate, is often assumed by these theologians to override the relational divisions created by colliding opinions and belief systems. In some instances, then, the Pietist disposition may actually undermine commitment to the rigorous construction and defense of carefully-parsed theological systems. For this reason it is especially intriguing to study Schleiermacher and Grenz. Both were theologians informed by Pietism yet with an unusual capacity and commitment to building summative theological systems.[39]

Similarities between Schleiermacher and Grenz

Schleiermacher and Grenz had much in common beyond their shared Pietist heritage and systematizing gifts. At a personal level both were ordained clergy and professors. They studied attentively the spirit of their respective times, and the hearts and minds of their contemporaries. And both sensed a vocational imperative to contextualize the Christian faith for their generation.

Modern people tend to think of history as a positive linear progression. Nevertheless, a case can be made that it often advances in something more like a spiral pattern, or in a curiously oscillating manner. As it turns out, the cultural and intellectual contexts to which Schleiermacher and Grenz tried to speak were not entirely dissimilar. Romanticism rose in reaction to Enlightenment rationalism, and later on postmodernism emerged as a cry of protest against the pretensions and dehumanizing excesses of scientific modernity. Schleiermacher framed his work in a way that appealed to Romantic sensibilities, while Grenz framed his in a manner designed to draw in postmodern persons.

It may seem merely coincidental that both men's funerals—the one in Berlin in 1834 and the other in Vancouver in 2005—were exceptionally well-attended public events. On the other hand, the unusually larger number of mourners, and the countless and often moving testimonials of regard for their theological contributions, at both, may suggest something about the extent to which their persons and their proposals resonated at a deep level with many of their contemporaries.

---

39. Scorgie, "Systematics," 1:156–60.

Differences between Schleiermacher and Grenz

There were also some differences between these two Pietist theologians. First of all, they differed in the extent to which they were able to embrace the Pietist heritage. It was no small matter that Schleiermacher could not accept orthodox Christology, and so had to think of himself as *a different kind* of Pietist. This led him eventually to redefine the sense in which he could affirm all the classic Christian doctrines.

For his part, Grenz modestly rearranged the familiar sequence of Christian doctrines, and gave some neglected doctrines relatively more emphasis (like the illumination of Scripture) and some prominent ones relatively less (like the wrath of God). At the same time he continued to believe that all the doctrines derived from divine revelation are true in the old-fashioned sense that they reliably witness to what is real.

In a sense Grenz flipped Schleiermacher's theological system upside down. The doctrine of the Trinity, which was a stumbling-block for Schleiermacher, became a chief cornerstone for Grenz. Schleiermacher treated the doctrine dismissively in his *The Christian Faith*, where he consigned it to a brief appendix.[40] In his opinion, it did not contain anything essential to his overarching system of theology. By contrast, and following the lead of Karl Barth, Grenz took the same doctrine and utilized it as an important organizing principle for his mature theology.[41]

Third, Grenz did a much better job than Schleiermacher in linking Christian experience to ethical behavior. Schleiermacher's ethical reflections were essentially philosophical in nature, divorced almost entirely from his theological work.[42] Perhaps he was reticent to embrace anything that might be confused with the moralism of Immanuel Kant. In any event, he was insufficiently engaged in the subject of theological ethics to publish on it. For Grenz, the pursuit of the kingdom of God and the cultivation of authentic community combined to create a compelling vision that moved the Christian out beyond self-centeredness, to be caught up into something much larger, more animating and infinitely more fulfilling.[43]

This is the vision that informs the earnest spirituality of Grenz's *Prayer: The Cry for the Kingdom*, the sensitivity of his *Welcoming But Not Affirming* response to homosexuality, and the love-grounded substance of his ethics textbook *The Moral Quest*. If Schleiermacher had focused more

---

40. Schleiermacher, *Christian Faith*, sec. 170–72.

41. Esp. Grenz, *Social God*.

42. Beiser, "Schleiermacher's Ethics," 53.

43. The ultimate goal of the kingdom is "nothing less than the establishment of community on the highest plane" (*Moral Quest*, 271).

on theological ethics, as Grenz did, perhaps Albrecht Ritschl (1822-91) would not have been so eager categorically to denounce Pietism for its other-worldly narcissism and false claims to genuine personal relationship with Christ, as he did in his multi-volume *History of Pietism*.[44]

Religious relativism is implicit in Schleiermacher's work. It prompted him to welcome a future in which Christianity would become a thing of the past. He rhapsodized that "Christianity, exalted above [all the other religions], more historical and more humble in its glory, has expressly acknowledged this transitoriness of its temporal existence. A time will come, it says, when there shall no more be any mediator, but the Father shall be all in all . . . I would gladly stand on the ruins of the religion I honor."[45]

To be fair, Schleiermacher was not celebrating the death of Christianity but its fulfillment. Still, his vision of the end of all memory of the Mediator is dissonant with the eternal gratitude toward, and endless adoration of, the Son of God that Grenz and other orthodox Christians anticipate. "On that great day," wrote Grenz, "the Spirit will mold us into one great chorus of praise to the eternal Creator and Savior. . . . Through our union with Christ, the Father's lavish glorification of the Son overflows to us (John 17:24)."[46]

Fourth, Schleiermacher claimed that the religious experience he espoused was universally accessible to everyone (reflecting, many think, a Romantic quest for universals), but Grenz commended a distinctly Christian experience that was particularized and restricted to those who have encountered Jesus Christ clothed in the same gospel the apostles taught and the historic Christian confessions have always affirmed.

A Parting of the Ways

As constructive theologians both Schleiermacher and Grenz gave priority to the experiential element of religion, to the lived experience of the Christian. Schleiermacher began his *Brief Outline* with this definition: "Theology is a positive science, whose parts join into a cohesive whole only through their common relation to a particular mode of faith, i.e., a particular way of being conscious of God." And Grenz *seems* to have said something quite similar when he described the Christian faith as "a piety cradled in a theology," and

---

44. The *History of Pietism* has not yet been translated into English; the prolegomena, however, has been, in Ritschl, *Three Essays*, 51-147.
45. Schleiermacher, *On Religion*, 251; compare *On Religion*, 122.
46. Grenz, *Theology for the Community* (1994), 844-45.

defined theology as "reflection on the faith commitment of the believing community."[47]

Both boldly organized their theological systems around the Christian life (the sphere of what is often identified now as Christian spirituality). Both treated everything else, including doctrine, as auxiliary to this dimension of Christian existence, which they regarded as of ultimate importance and concern. And both gave considerable attention to the formational power of community, and the church's role in nurturing and sustaining faith.

Nevertheless, these affinities must not be allowed to mask a *seminal difference* between these two theologians' understandings of the Christian faith and the theological enterprise supporting it.

Schleiermacher's creative theological efforts were motivated by his inability any longer to accept traditional Protestant authority and doctrines, and by his missional concern for contemporaries in the same boat. He no longer had confidence in the Bible as an infallible revelation, viewing it instead as a fallible record of human reflections on religious experience.

He believed, however, that Christianity could be salvaged if a new path were followed. And so, against a backdrop of tired biblicism, rationalism and moralism, and with nostalgic memories of Pietism, he drew from the resources of emergent Romanticism to rebuild Christian faith on a foundation of inward sensibility, feeling, and intuition of beauty. It was precisely in such a universally-shared experience (or awareness) that he believed the ground and essence of all religion lay.[48]

Schleiermacher described this seed of religion as "an immediate feeling of the infinite and eternal,"[49] and with that "a sense of absolute dependence" upon this infinite and eternal Other. It is a direct, existential perception that one is not self-sufficient, but belongs to, and is grounded in, an infinitely larger reality. He then took up the task of reformulating conventional theology, modifying it wherever necessary to conform to his bottom-line test of validity, the absolute-dependence feeling. Theological statements were not truth statements in the conventional sense (that is, statements that faithfully reflect an objective reality), but provisional intellectual attempts to express religious feeling and talk about experience through the unavoidable medium of ideas.[50] University of Chicago historian B. A. Gerrish notes that Schleiermacher's theological reconstruction was "so brilliant and subtle that one does not know which to marvel at more: the startling creativeness

---

47. Grenz, *Revisioning*, 62, 87.
48. Mackintosh, *Types of Modern Theology*, 31–100.
49. Schleiermacher, *On Religion*, 16.
50. Schleiermacher, *Brief Outline*, sec. 2.

of his innovations or the ingenuity of his carefully forged links with the past."[51] Depending on the reader's interpretation, this may or may not be a compliment.

Schleiermacher's proposal was prompted by a crisis of faith. Stanley Grenz's revisioning of evangelical theology was motivated by a desire to foster more effectively real experience of inward renewal through the presence and work of Jesus Christ, with all the transformational and vocational effects of God's loving nature "shed abroad" in the regenerate soul.

His great fear was that "creeping creedalism" might gain ascendency in the evangelical community and gradually squeeze out the experiential vitality that lay at the heart of the evangelical movement, the very thing that had prompted Philip Spener's seventeenth-century Pietist protest in the first place.[52] He feared the prospect of theology operating callously in a silo entirely sealed off from the signature saving and transforming experience granted by the Holy Spirit.

An imminent danger, as he saw it, was that doctrinaire theologians could latch on to an epistemological ground independent of the actual experience of faith, and on that basis feel empowered to go their own way. He was convinced there were theologians, even within the evangelical tradition, who were inclined to treat the Bible as precisely such a basis for their autonomous intellectual enterprise. His counter-proposal was simply to begin with, and stay tethered to, the work of grace that the Spirit of God has done, and continues to do, in believers' hearts in the context of Christian community.

Grenz did not "bury" the doctrine of Scripture under pneumatology in his *Theology for the Community of God* because he had somehow lost faith in it or was embarrassed by it.[53] He located it there to preempt the temptation to re-establish Scripture as a kind of "secular" intellectual foundation, a source of doctrine independent of the divine work of Christ-centered redeeming grace in the hearts of believers.[54] It was strategic to his agenda "to preserve the priority of the new birth and reiterate that doctrine is the servant—a crucial servant to be sure, but a servant nonetheless—of the transforming work of the Spirit."[55] The most important thing Christians need to know

---

51. Gerrish, *Continuing the Reformation*, 148.
52. Grenz, "Concerns of a Pietist," 74.
53. Grenz, *Theology for the Community*, ch. 14.
54. He avoided such an approach to Scripture because of its deleterious effects on the spiritual life and because he concurred with aspects of the postmodern and postfoundational critique of modern-style epistemology. See Grenz, *Primer on Postmodernism*, 161–74.
55. Grenz, "Concerns of a Pietist," 75.

about Scripture is that it is the chief means by which the Spirit speaks to, and enlivens, those with ears to hear.[56]

Unlike Schleiermacher, Grenz never experienced a crisis of faith about the trustworthiness of Scripture, or the truthfulness of Christian doctrine. He embraced Anselm's classic dictum "faith seeks understanding," taking it to signify that the experience of assured believing is first granted through God's grace, and is then to be reflectively unpacked (together) as believers mature.

Grenz had a much higher regard for doctrine than Schleiermacher ever did. Grenz wrote: "Every experience is necessarily tied to an understanding of reality, an interpretive framework that both facilitates it and emerges from it. So also the saving encounter with God in Christ through the Spirit . . . must be cradled by the constellation of beliefs, arising from the Bible, that comprise the Christian interpretive framework."[57] His ownership of this interpretive framework was not tongue-in-cheek, nor was he playing (as some do) a clever language game. When he described the Christian faith as an experience "couched" in a doctrinal framework, he never intended to suggest that doctrine was arbitrary or whimsically concocted. He might just as easily have said that the Christian experience is both *shaped by* and becomes *embodied* in doctrine. He believed in the truths proclaimed in the Bible and the wisdom of the church's historic interpretations of it. But—and this was his main point—these doctrines remain means to a greater end. They are penultimate. Even in their grandeur they serve a purpose higher than themselves.

Conclusion

The Pietist impulse has been strong and influential in Christianity through the years. Within evangelicalism it has been a defining force. The Pietist invitation to a vital, holistic, and communal experience of the Christian faith appears to have perennial appeal. Perhaps this is because it touches a felt-need in the human spirit that cannot be satisfied by reason or doctrine alone; and because it resonates, according to the Gospels, with so many themes (like the blessedness of purity of *heart*) that Jesus himself prioritized.

Admittedly, history shows that the Pietist impulse is also prone to volatility. It can mutate rather easily, and explode outward along myriad trajectories. On numerous occasions it has morphed into such alien

---

56. Grenz, *Theology for the Community* (1994), 495–507.
57. Grenz, "Concerns of a Pietist," 74–75.

manifestations as unorthodox subjectivity, anti-intellectualism, quietism, and legalism. Many Christians, theologians included, are understandably guarded against it, or dismissive of it, precisely because of these incipient dangers. Such reactions might seem safe and prudent, but they are actually short-sighted.

As Michelle Clifton-Soderstrom sagely observes, "Pietism has caused trouble. Nevertheless, its trouble is worth redeeming."[58]

Pietism is a perennial witness to something essential to the Christian faith—the lived experience of the believer as a transforming encounter with God revealed in Christ. Whenever this dimension of lived experience is allowed to atrophy in the church, there has been and there will be a reaction against it in favor of genuine, holistic experience. Neither rationalism nor moralism satisfied the human longing for spiritual reality in the early nineteenth century. And neither confessionalism nor biblicism will be able to do so in this century.

Pietism offers an enduring witness to an essential dimension of a sustainable Christianity. The Pietist prioritization of experience rocks the boats of those invested in more rationalistic approaches to Christian faith. Yet thoughtful, earnest evangelicals should appreciate the sometimes-provocative proposals of doctrinally-orthodox Pietists like Stanley Grenz, who recognized that living faith is evoked, nourished, and sustained in the framework of orthodox belief and within the reinforcing locus of the community of faith.

We have noted how misleading it is to paint all theologians influenced by Pietism with the same brush. There are profound differences among them. So much depends on what they choose to appropriate, and how they choose to apply elements of it. The legacy of Stanley Grenz is particularly heuristic because he assigned priority to believers' lived, shared, and transforming experience of God through Christ. And he did so all the while as a "tethered" Pietist, with steady loyalty to orthodox beliefs and the uniqueness of Christ as the one and only Savior of the world.[59]

Bibliography

Arndt, Johann. *True Christianity*. Translated by Peter Erb. New York: Paulist, 1979.
Atwood, Craig. "Sleeping in the Arms of Christ: Sanctifying Sexuality in the Eighteenth-Century Moravian Church." *Journal of the History of Sexuality* 8 (1997) 25–51.

---

58. Clifton-Soderstrom, *Angels*, 10.
59. Grenz, *Renewing the Center*, 2nd ed., 293–94.

Baum, Gregory, ed. *Journeys: The Impact of Personal Experience on Religious Thought*. New York: Paulist, 1975.
Bebbington, David. *Evangelicalism in Modern Britain: A History from the 1730s to the 1980s*. London: Unwin Hyman, 1989.
Beiser, Frederick. "Schleiermacher's Ethics." In *The Cambridge Companion to Friedrich Schleiermacher*, edited by Jacqueline Marina, 53–71. Cambridge: Cambridge University Press, 2005.
Carlson, G. William. "Pietism." In *Dictionary of Christian Spirituality*, edited by Glen G. Scorgie, 673–74. Grand Rapids: Zondervan, 2011.
Clifton-Soderstrom, Michelle. *Angels, Worms, and Bogeys*. Eugene, OR: Cascade, 2010.
Cramp, J. M. *A Memoir of Madame Feller*. London: Evangelical Society of the Grande Ligne, [1876].
Crouter, Richard. *Friedrich Schleiermacher: Between Enlightenment and Romanticism*. Cambridge: Cambridge University Press, 2005.
Eaghll, Tenzan. "From Pietism to Romanticism: The Early Life and Work of Friedrich Schleiermacher." In *The Pietism Impulse*, edited by Christian Collins Winn et al., 107–19. Eugene, OR: Pickwick, 2011.
Effa, Alan. "Diaspora Strategist: The Missionary Work of Johann Oncken." *Global Missiology English* 4/4 (2007). http://ojs.globalmissiology.org/index.php/english/article/view/305.
Erb, Peter, ed. *Pietists: Selected Writings*, 291–330. New York: Paulist, 1983.
Gerrish, B. A. *Continuing the Reformation: Essays on Modern Religious Thought*. Chicago: University of Chicago Press, 1993.
Gerrish, B. A. *A Prince of the Church: Schleiermacher and the Beginnings of Modern Theology*. Philadelphia: Fortress, 1984.
Lotz, David. "Continental Pietism." In *The Study of Spirituality*, edited by Cheslyn Jones et al., 448–52. Oxford: Oxford University Press, 1986.
Lovelace, Richard F. *The American Pietism of Cotton Mather: Origins of American Evangelicalism*. Grand Rapids: Christian University Press, 1979.
Lovelace, Richard. *Dynamics of Spiritual Life*. Downers Grove, IL: InterVarsity, 1979.
Mackintosh, H. R. *Types of Modern Theology*. London: Nisbet, 1937.
Marina, Jacqueline, ed. *Cambridge Companion to Friedrich Schleiermacher*. Cambridge: Cambridge University Press, 2005.
Nelson, Derek, Joshua Moritz, and Ted Peters, eds. *Theologians in Their Own Words*. Minneapolis: Fortress, 2013.
Oberman, Heiko. "Preface." In *True Christianity*, by Johann Arndt, xi–xvii. Translated by Peter Erb. New York: Paulist, 1979.
Olson, Roger. "Reclaiming Pietism." 16 March 2011. http://www.patheos.com/blogs/rogereolson/2011/03/reclaiming-pietism/#_ftn1.
Rauschenbusch, Walter. *A Theology for the Social Gospel*. New York: Macmillan, 1917.
Rawlyk, George, and Mark Noll, eds. *Amazing Grace: Evangelicalism in Australia, Britain, Canada, and the United States*. Grand Rapids: Baker, 1993.
Redeker, Martin. *Schleiermacher: Life and Thought*. Translated by John Wallhausser. Philadelphia: Fortress, 1973.
Ritschl, Albrecht. "Prolegomena to the *History of Pietism*." In *Three Essays*, 51–147. Translated by Philip Hefner. Philadelphia: Fortress, 1972.
Schleiermacher, Friedrich. *Brief Outline on the Study of Theology*. Translated by Terrence Tice. Atlanta: John Knox, 1966.

———. *The Christian Faith*. Edinburgh: T. & T. Clark, 1928.

———. *The Life of Schleiermacher as Unfolded in His Autobiography and Letters, Volume 1*. Edited by Frederica Rowan. London: Smith, Elder and Co., 1860.

———. *On Religion*. Translated by John Oman. New York: Harper and Row, 1958.

Scorgie, Glen. "Systematics." In *Encyclopedia of Christian Literature*, 2 vols., edited by George Thomas Kurian and James D. Smith III, 1:156–60. Lanham, MD: Scarecrow, 2010.

Spener, Philip. *Pia Desideria*. Translated by Theodore Tappert. Eugene, OR: Wipf & Stock, 2002.

Stoeffler, F. Ernest. *The Rise of Evangelical Pietism*. Leiden: Brill, 1965.

Stunt, Timothy. *From Awakening to Secession: Radical Evangelicals in Switzerland and Britain, 1815–35*. Edinburgh: T. & T. Clark, 2000.

Vogt, Peter. "Nicholas Ludwig von Zinzendorf." In *The Pietist Theologians*, edited by Carter Lindberg, 207–23. Malden, MA: Blackwell, 2005.

Von Berge, Herman, et al. *These Glorious Years: The Centenary History of German Baptists of North America 1843–1943*. Cleveland, OH: Roger Williams Press, 1943.

Wallmann, Johannes. "Johann Arndt." In *The Pietist Theologians*, edited by Carter Lindberg, 21–37. Malden, MA: Blackwell, 2005.

Weborg, C. J. "Pietism." *Christian History* 5/2 (April 1986) 17–18, 34–35.

Wesley, Cindy. "Pietist and Baptist: Examining the Influence of August Rauschenbusch." In *The Pietism Impulse*, edited by Christian Collins Winn et al., 257–68. Eugene, OR: Pickwick, 2011.

Wesley, John. "A Catholic Spirit" (1750). In *John Wesley's Sermons: An Anthology*, edited by A. Outler, 299–310. Nashville: Abingdon, 1991.

15

Lost in an Epistemological Maze

WILLIAM J. ABRAHAM

> Don't get involved in partial problems, but always take flight
> to where there is a free view over the whole single great problem,
> even if this view is still not a clear one.[1]

ONE CRUCIAL ELEMENT IN Stanley Grenz's work represents an elegant and sustained attempt to provide a fresh epistemology of theology.[2] As such, it is a substantial effort to contribute to the health of evangelicalism, to render the Christian gospel intelligible within postmodernity, and to engage the standard questions taken up within epistemology more generally. As such it is also represents a longstanding feature of Christian theology that stretches across space and time; there is a tacit assumption that there can be no serious Christian theology without first sorting out the epistemological challenges that have to be faced. I find myself with a dilemma as I respond. On the one hand, I genuinely and sincerely appreciate what Grenz has achieved. His work is wonderfully clear, theologically informed, historically dense, acutely penetrating at times, and full of wisdom. On the other hand, I think

---

1. Wittgenstein, entry for 1 Nov. 1914, *Notebooks 1914-1916*.
2. My focus in this essay will be various elements in the work that Grenz co-authored with John R. Franke, *Beyond Foundationalism*. Given that Franke and Grenz are in substantial agreement and make that abundantly clear in that volume's preface, I shall henceforth refer to this work as indicative of Grenz's position. This in no way involves a marginalization of Franke and his contribution to the ideas in the book.

his work represents the end of the line; it makes visible the emergence of a sophisticated scholasticism that takes one into an interminable maze which has unfortunate consequences for the health of the church. Scholasticisms have their own marvelous virtues; I have no interest in demonizing them. Yet I speak of scholasticism here as a stage within contemporary theology when its adherents keep going round in circles. As will appear towards the end, the challenge this observation evokes is twofold. First, what do we do with the questions that Grenz seeks to answer in *Beyond Foundationalism: Shaping Theology in a Postmodern Context*? And, second, what alternative am I canvassing in facing the arrival of postmodernity?

The Role of Tradition in Epistemology

A useful point of entry into the debate about epistemology is the topic of tradition. The crucial move developed by Grenz can be stated succinctly at the outset: the role of tradition is to "provide a hermeneutical context and trajectory of faithfully Christian theology."[3] We see immediately that Grenz has already down-graded the epistemological role of tradition; in fact, we might say that in fact it has no really deep epistemological role at all in theology; that coveted position goes to Scripture, theology's norming norm. The task of tradition is to provide indispensable but not exclusive help in securing what Scripture means; it does not function as a norm that can call into question the truth of Scripture. To put it in other words, tradition functions as a hermeneutical norm not as an epistemological norm; the truthfulness of Christian theology is to be secured by Scripture alone; the correctness of our interpretation of Scripture is to be partially secured by appeal to tradition.

Historically speaking, Grenz sees this as the retrieval and extension of an earlier vision of the relation between Scripture and tradition. Drawing on the seminal work of Hieko Oberman, he opts for what Oberman labels "Tradition I" over "Tradition II." In Grenz's words, "Tradition I represents the single-source understanding in which the emphasis is on the sufficiency of Scripture as the exclusive and final authority in the church."[4] From this perspective one is not permitted to extra-scriptural or ecclesiastical tradition; one relies on the faith handed down by God in Holy Scripture. "Tradition II maintains a two-source conception of authority in which both the written *and* the unwritten, oral components of the apostolic message, as

---

3. *Beyond Foundationalism*, 129.
4. Ibid., 97.

approved by the church, are deemed to be equally authoritative. Here the emphasis shifts away from the interpreters, or doctors, of Scripture and towards the bishops who determine the content of the authentic tradition."[5] From this perspective one is permitted to appeal to oral tradition, to material not recorded in the canonical books of Scripture, and even to canon law.

For Oberman and Grenz both these traditions were held within the church prior to the fourteenth century. Their theoretical origins, as they read the evidence, go back to Basil the Great and of Augustine, but the full consequences of the relevant distinction between tradition and Scripture were not really observed until the debates between canon lawyers and theologians in the Middle Ages. Thereafter much energy was spent sorting out which of these options should be deployed within theology proper. By the time of the Reformation a third element was introduced, namely the illumination granted to the teaching of popes and councils. The Reformers, generally speaking, rejected Tradition II, while the Council of Trent, even as it insisted that both Scripture and tradition were dictated by the Holy Spirit, left open how best to construe the relation between the two. Even so, Trent was often read both within and without Western Catholic circles as an endorsement of Tradition II, which in turn led to a hardening of a negative attitude towards tradition on the part of Protestantism. Anabaptists went so far as to eliminate tradition. In the Enlightenment, tradition was dramatically undercut, paving the way for the overthrowing of tradition in Protestant Liberalism. Materially this meant a search for the naturalistic origins of tradition in political, social, and economic factors, and a turn to religious experience as the only proper foundation for theology. While conservative Protestants represented by most evangelicals rejected the turn to religious experience, they sustained the modern prejudice against tradition and became preoccupied with a two-party dispute with liberals. Within this dispute they tacitly relied on tradition hermeneutically in their appeal to their distinctive confessional identities.

Grenz's strategy at this point is to make a virtue out of this reality.

> It is simply not possible to step back from the influence of tradition in the act of interpretation or the ascription of meaning. Interpretive communities that deny the reality of this situation and seek an interpretation unencumbered by the "distorting" influence of "fallible" traditions are in fact enslaved in patterns that are allowed to function uncritically precisely because they are unacknowledged.[6]

5. Ibid. (emphasis in original).
6. Ibid., 113.

This argument amounts to nothing less than a nuclear strike in favor of the place of tradition in Christian theology. Its initial premise is taken as self-evident in a broad, non-technical sense; opponents are taken to be subject to self-denial or self-deception. It constitutes a decisive rejection of modern versions of evangelicalism that at the very least have approached tradition with suspicion, if not outright hostility. It also represents an olive branch to the more recent treatments of tradition as seen in the work of Vatican II. Most of all, it represents what Grenz sees as pivotal in our current situation, namely, a move from an explicit foundationalist to a non-foundationalist understanding of Scripture and tradition.

What one expects at this point is the application of Grenz's earlier treatment of foundationalism.[7] What one actually gets is an interesting pneumatological diversion. What matters in the appeal to Scripture, understood as the norming norm of Tradition I, is not some quality that inheres in the scriptural text but the work of the Holy Spirit that works in and through the text and which is also at work in the formation of the Christian community, the church. It is the work of the Spirit that constitutes the authoritative element in the appeal to Scripture. How this is supposed to relate to the debate about foundationalism and non-foundationalism is at this point, to say the least, opaque. Conceptually we have moved away from the domain of foundationalism and its conceptual alternatives and begun developing a material, first-order theological thesis on the work of the Holy Spirit. Broadly speaking, we have shifted from epistemology to pneumatology.

Yet this is not quite fair to Grenz, for he is committed to a narrative that inscribes his favored epistemological vision of Scripture within the work of the Holy Spirit in the history of the church. To put the issue succinctly, the Holy Spirit works within the Christian community, first to produce various texts, then to the selection of these texts as canonical, and finally to the judgment that these texts of Scripture constitute a "distinctive collection of documents to which it makes itself accountable".[8] The further payoff of this narrative, it is thought, is that it mandates the role that tradition must now play in the economy of theology. Given that the Spirit works to produce the church's norming norm, the appropriate context in which to interpret Scripture is the tradition of the church. The same Spirit that governs the church's judgment on the normative character of Scripture works to illuminate the meaning of Scripture both in the past (as available in tradition) and in the present (as the church applies Scripture afresh to deal with contemporary challenges). It is this work of the Spirit that somehow signals that we have

7. Ibid., ch. 2.
8. Ibid., 116.

moved to a non-foundationalist epistemology as mandated by the collapse of foundationalism in the turn from modernity to postmodernity.

> A nonfoundational understanding of scripture and tradition locates ultimate authority only in the action of the triune God. If we must speak of a "foundation" of the Christian faith at all, then, we must speak of neither scripture nor tradition in and of themselves, but only of the triune God who is disclosed in polyphonic fashion through scripture, the church, and even the world, albeit always normatively through scripture.[9]

Clearly we have now moved to a position that is within shouting distance of the position developed in Vatican II in *Dei Verbum*. How does Grenz's position differ?

The difference surfaces in Grenz's account of the role of tradition in the construction of Christian theology. Here it is not difficult to glimpse the solidly Protestant character of his position. Following a clue of Alasdair MacIntrye, he proposes that we think of tradition as the history of the interpretation and application of canonical Scripture by the church as it listens to the voice of the Spirit speaking in the text across the ages up to present.

> *The Christian tradition is comprised of the historical attempts by the Christian community to explicate and translate faithfully the first order language, symbols, and practices of the Christian faith, arising from the interaction among community, text, and culture, into the various social and cultural contexts in which community has been situated.*[10]

So far so good, we say. The crucial giveaway shows up in the ambivalence on the significance of the "classical" theological formulations and symbols of the tradition. Crucial within these, of course, are the great canonical doctrines enshrined in, say, the Nicene Creed and the Chalcedonian Definition. We have already seen that some vision of the work of the triune God is crucial for Grenz. Moreover, he goes to great lengths to hammer home the importance of continuity of tradition across the history of the church. However, the ultimate assessment is in the end substantially Protestant. The classical theological formulations are logically dispensable: "they must always and continually be tested by the norm of canonical scripture";[11] and "it is the *intent* of the creeds, confessions, and formulations, and not the specific construction and order of their wording, that is significant for

9. Ibid., 117–18.
10. Ibid., 118 (emphasis in original).
11. Ibid., 124.

contemporary theology."[12] What is on offer here is somehow a living and dynamic, as opposed to static, conception of tradition; what is on sale, as befits a "truly" evangelical vision, is an open, as opposed to closed, confessionalism. And the best way to honor these observations, Grenz thinks, is to construe tradition as a hermeneutical context or trajectory for the Christian theological enterprise.

My aim to this juncture has not been to give a comprehensive account of Grenz's vision of tradition, nor of the wider epistemological or cultural context in which his work is self-consciously embedded. My goal has been the modest one of identifying crucial elements in his position as a whole. Grenz, in fact, provides a very intricate account of the resources and interlocutors that inform his work; every page is studded with apt references to a host of insights and historical figures that he has read and pondered. *Beyond Foundationalism* is effectively a fully worked out prolegomenon to systematic theology. This is in part its value and initial attraction. We are taken on a whirlwind tour that is intricate, measured, self-confident, and full of vigorous enthusiasm. One comes away from the text grateful for the historical sensitivity, the felicitous internal organization, and the wide range of judgment on display. Yet, as I indicated at the outset, I find myself deeply dissatisfied; so much so that I have been bold to identify Grenz's effort here as an exercise in sophisticated scholasticism. What we have in the end is one more foray into the epistemology of theology that seeks to break new ground but that leaves us trapped inside a maze without the prospects of an exit. I need now to unpack what lies behind this prima facie unfriendly, and indeed for me, unwelcome response.

Difficulties of Grenz's Understanding of Tradition

I want to begin by noting some of the difficulties that lie at the heart of this treatment of tradition. Consider initially what I earlier described as a nuclear strike type argument Grenz took to be virtually self-evident in a broad sense. "It is simply not possible to step back from the influence of tradition in the act of interpretation or the ascription of meaning." If we think of this with respect to the normative interpretation of Scripture it is either patently false or hopelessly vague. Suppose we have been taught to read John 6 as contextualized within a eucharistic reading of the references to the eating of the bread of life. We are reading the text influenced, say, by the tradition of the Western Catholic tradition. However, it is surely obvious

12. Ibid. (emphasis in original).

that we can stand back from the text and read it without being influenced by the relevant eucharistic reading. In fact, we might argue, as I would, that being influenced by the eucharistic reading may hinder a proper reading of the text. So Grenz's hermeneutical platitude is false. We can easily fix this, of course, by claiming in response that in developing any alternative interpretation we will be influenced by some alternative tradition. However, now the claim about the role of tradition is so vague that virtually anything we bring to the text by way of presupposition will count as being "influenced by tradition"; tradition will cease to do any interesting work in the interpretation of the text.

There is a further but important logical difficulty in the neighborhood. Grenz is confusing the psychology (or sociology) of what may influence a reader or a community in the interpretation of a scriptural text with the epistemology of justification of any particular reading of a scriptural text. It is a platitude that when we read the books of the Bible we do not do read them naked, as if we did not come to them with minds already clothed in a host of prior assumptions, presuppositions, prejudices, and the like. In that broad sense we rely on a host of traditions that we already inhabit. However, if we are to justify our particular reading, we cannot always fall back on those traditions to secure any particular interpretation we may offer. Thus suppose someone reads the book of Exodus influenced by the interpretation of these texts provided by his initiation into the Orange Order in Ireland. He takes the text to be a charter for political liberation as represented by the British Imperial order. Even if the Orange Order is broadly right in its interpretation of the book of Exodus, and even if one comes to this reading because of the influence of the Orange Order, appeal to the influence of this tradition will not secure the justification of the text as a charter for liberation as understood by the Order. The psychology of discovery should not be confused with the logic of justification. I am not offering in this instance even the beginnings of a hermeneutics; that is way beyond the scope of this essay. I am simply making a crucial epistemological point that is easily overlooked in the appeal to the influence of tradition as somehow constitutive in the interpretation of scriptural texts. Moreover, I think that ignoring this distinction not only tends to sideline the justification of this or that interpretation; it can readily become the source of self-deception, a clever way to insulate one's favored interpretation from criticism, and a cheap way of dismissing alternative readings that may well be more accurate and illuminating.

A very different worry about Grenz's vision of tradition arises when one presses the question of how to identify tradition. Consider at this point another distinction, the distinction between custom and tradition. The concept of tradition in theology must carry much more weight than custom. Customs are habitual practices that are repeated again and again. Traditions, if they are to be taken seriously, should be understood as "manifestations of judgments; customs are manifestations of preferences for predictability and continuity."[13] I borrow this distinction from the field of jurisprudence, but it has salience within theology. In the early days of the Anglican tradition this insight was captured in the claim that tradition, represented by the patristic tradition, carried weight because it embodied the sanctified reasoning of those who were closest to the original texts of Scripture. In fact, tradition can readily be construed as reason in the sense that it is the articulation of good judgments. A version of this sense of tradition is also at work in the appeal to the work of Alasdair MacIntyre that shows up in Grenz in various places. A tradition, for MacIntyre, is the embodiment of an argument within a social space where participation in the practices of the tradition is constitutive of internal appropriation and their successful operation. By initiation into traditions the human agent acquires the very capacity to see the intrinsic telos and validity of the tradition; moreover, there is no tradition without embodiment in a social space and agenda. The recurring challenge this poses for MacIntyre and those who follow him is that of relativism, a challenge that also haunts the turn to postmodernity.[14] My initial difficulty with Grenz is that the idea of tradition is underdeveloped and may readily be confused with custom. Hence it is not always clear when we are appealing to tradition rather than a neighboring phenomenon like custom or general usage.

My recourse to jurisprudence in unpacking a substantive conception of tradition was a deliberate one in the present context.[15] It opens up another avenue of inquiry. Can Grenz's appeal to tradition really work in practice? In the legal case we can already identify the mechanisms and practices without which the whole domain becomes a morass of abstractions that really get us nowhere in the search for resolution of contested issues. Thus, even though there are rival traditions of interpretation with respect to the American Constitution, at the end of the day, when contemporary issues have to be resolved, there is a Supreme Court, which settles the issue one way or another. As we have seen in the recent case of Justice Roberts in his

13. Brown, "Tradition and Insight," 177–78.
14. For a defense of MacIntyre against this charge see Lott, "Reasonably Traditional," 315–19.
15. Brown's essay, cited earlier, brings out the salience in a most pleasing manner. The relevance of her work is enhanced by the fact that she belongs self-consciously to the Reformed tradition and readily perceives the significance of the debate on Scripture and tradition for her work as a legal scholar.

judgment on the Affordable Care Act, there is even a tradition of interpreting the text of the law in terms of what is permitted rather than what is strictly required. It is no accident that scholars have seen an analogue with the interpretation of Scripture. Given the privileged status of Scripture, any interpretation in the tradition or the academy that permits a reading that is compatible with what we know to be the case on other grounds (or that we think is essential on other grounds) is acceptable if not mandated. This practice shows up in both Aquinas and in modern evangelicals committed to the authority of Scripture; thus, if a literal meaning does not make sense, given what we know, say, from empirical observation, then they shift to a figurative meaning to save the text from nonsense.

The problem with Grenz's progressive evangelicalism (as with contemporary evangelicalism more generally) is that while there is endless theorizing about how to read the text understood as the norming norm of theology, there are no functional equivalents such as we find in jurisprudence or in Vatican Catholicism that get us beyond the endless gesturing to this or that proposal in theology. The text has morphed into an account of the Holy Spirit speaking through the text or using the text instrumentally; it is not clear what we should pick out as tradition as opposed to custom; it is not clear whether the evidentiary appeal to tradition as a hermeneutical context and resource is positive, or negative, or merely permissible; it is not clear what role it plays relative to other sources like current context, reason, or experience; and there is no institutional procedure or mechanism for resolving contested issues. Hence there is no way of really finding out what the norming norm actually mandates in the constructing of a contemporary theology. It should surprise no one that those who begin to take Grenz seriously will either retreat into a more classical Protestant tradition (and adopt a hardline, simpler version of *sola scriptura*), or they will move forward towards the household of the Bishop of Rome (who will, with the teaching magisterium, provide the epistemic practices and mechanisms to end the chaos).[16] The other option is to move forward into some version of liberal or revisionist Christianity. Grenz will not take such an option; but others who take up his proposals on tradition will be sorely tempted to do so.[17]

16. The latter option, in fact, provides a much more realistic and practical rendering of the claim that Scripture is the norming norm of theology than the option laid out by Grenz.

17. Basil Mitchell in a splendid paper on tradition captures the issues very nicely in what follows. "Conservative theologians who attach importance to tradition, who are not, that is, Biblical Fundamentalists, look for certainty in religious truth and argue that it can be secured only if the Church as *the* repository of tradition is guaranteed against error. The tradition must be safeguarded by a continuing institution whose role is, indeed, supported by reason, but whose deliverances are open to criticism only within

Beyond Foundationalism?

Some will no doubt worry that my objection here betrays a hidden if not overt commitment to foundationalism. I am looking, it will be thought, for a secure foundation that will transcend the range of interpretations that now flourish in the shift to postmodernity. I want some definitive, final word that will settle matters once and for all and operate as the foundation for truth in theology. I do indeed think that there is a sure Word from God that we can rely on; and in general terms I am indeed committed to a version of moderate foundationalism in epistemology. This is not the place to defend either of these. However, the more pertinent response to this objection is that those who take up the defense of Grenz are in no position to press this point. Grenz in fact is fully aware that foundationalism is by no means a dead-end epistemology. He recognizes that Alvin Plantinga, for example, the most trenchant critic of classical foundationalism, is in fact a moderate foundationalist.[18] Plantinga allows, as I do, that we are entitled to all sorts of beliefs as basic beliefs without necessarily having to secure their truth by appeal to some other beliefs. If this is the case, it is out of order to play the anti-foundationalist cards at this point. That said, I think that Grenz is simply confused here. There are clear signs that he is sympathetic to a coherentist position in epistemology, which is the real alternative to foundationalism in epistemology.[19] If he is, then we need a really serious defense of this highly contested option. More generally, as already noted, he somehow thinks that a shift to pneumatology can be a serious alternative to strong evangelical foundationalism. The deep worry here is that the theologian knows enough epistemology to make him dangerous when it comes to dealing with the salient problems of epistemology. It runs the risk of being an erudite scissors-and-paste epistemology.

I want to register one other fascinating and astonishing observation before I turn to the last section of this essay. Grenz is, in the end, a traditional Protestant. This is made clear in his commitment to Scripture as the norming norm of theology. It is also made clear when he insists that all claims in the tradition, including the classical faith of the church, must

---

narrow limits. Liberal theologians maintain that the Christian tradition has always been subject to controversy, which is a condition of growth and by risking error allows fuller understanding. The Church should look not for an unattainable certainty but a reasonable faith of the sort that is characteristic of the human situation. The guidance of the Holy Spirit is itself the postulate of such a faith." See Mitchell, "Tradition," 596.

18. *Beyond Foundationalism*, 47.

19. Ibid., 38–39. It is not clear to me how far coherentism is simply a stick with which to beat up foundationalists or a bridge beyond foundationalism or both.

be tested again and again against Scripture. It is, in the end, the intent of the early creeds—not the content—that is to be honored in theology. The intent presumably here is to capture faithfully what the Holy Spirit teaches through Scripture. Yet when it comes to the interpretation of Scripture and to its norms and resources, ultimate authority is to be found in the action of the triune God. Moreover, it is clear that when we actually do theology the doctrine of the Trinity is its structural motif. The puzzle now is a simple one. We are initially told that everything has to be tested by Scripture; but now somehow the doctrine of Trinity will be built into our very interpretation of Scripture; there is no way (outside torturous epistemological footwork) that Scripture can challenge the doctrine of the Trinity. So now tradition is governing Scripture rather than vice versa. Moreover, in actually doing theology we will rely on the doctrine of the Trinity rather than any other reading of Scripture as a whole to provide its structural motif. Again, Scripture is drifting off into the margins. Of course, generally speaking, this is more or less what we find in the Reformers. They develop varied visions of *sola scriptura* but they vigorously retain the great Trinitarian faith of the church and read Scripture in the light of it. However, sooner or later the tension becomes explicit and folk begin to worry about whether the Trinity can really be derived from Scripture. Initially this can be halted by the use of state power; however, this has had its day. So the development of liberal Protestantism is simply an accident waiting to happen. The journey will begin by adopting Scripture as the norming norm and find fault with a host of traditional Christian teaching; it will then worry about the norming norm itself and turn to grand abstractions like reason and experience to save the day.[20] Grenz is caught up in this modern struggle and cannot avoid it. His postmodernity is effectively modernity transposed into another key; he is looking for one more way to resolve the epistemological challenges precipitated by the failure of Scripture as the norming norm of theology. He is providing one more effort, exploiting a rhetoric and sociology of postmodernity, to shore up his Protestant epistemology of theology. This is not new; the game is an old one and shows no signs of a final whistle.

---

20. It cannot be repeated too often that classical foundationalism was first developed by theologians at the Reformation before it was secularized in various versions of the Enlightenment. It is ironic in the extreme to watch sophisticated Reformed theologians lament the vices of foundationalism when in their own way they still cling to the intellectual impulses in their own tradition that led to classical foundationalism in the first place.

Grenz and Contemporary Evangelical Theology

My assessment of Grenz's vision of tradition will appear to be harsh to many readers. Truth be told, I could have extended the catalogue of woe. I have focused merely on the problems that emerge when we try to distinguish tradition from custom; when we search out the evidentiary value of tradition as a norm in the task of the hermeneutics of Scripture; when, allowing the appeal to tradition, we seek to reach some kind of resolution to contested theological proposals; when we explore the meaning of, and alternatives to, foundationalism; and when we look carefully at the relation between the doctrine of the Trinity and Scripture. I have left to the reader to ponder other crucial questions that are in the neighborhood and that are salient to Grenz's project. How can we develop a vision of Scripture and tradition without a robust vision of divine revelation? How can we secure a robust vision of divine revelation without tackling the thorny problem not just of its interpretation but of its proper identity given the arrival of Islam and other competing understandings of revelation in our contemporary world? Why should we assume the basic legitimacy of Heiko Oberman's account of Tradition I and Tradition II? Does this not already cook the books by developing an oversimplified account of the complex range of arguments actually deployed, say, in the patristic period? Can we really speak of the Enlightenment when we now know that there were a variety of Enlightenments in Europe and North America in the modern period? How do we get beyond railing at the correspondence theory of truth and respond to the full range of theories of truth available in contemporary philosophy? If we are not metaphysical realists on Christian doctrine, how do sustain serious commitment to the great teachings of the faith? It looks now as if I am adding insult to injury by piling up a whole new round of queries.

Yet I want also to insist that Grenz's work is as good as it comes in contemporary theology when considered as a prolegomenon in systematic theology. Indeed, within the canons of theology it deserves high praise. So why display so brazenly my intellectual schizophrenia at this point? Why am I such a curmudgeon? The answer is simple: Grenz's work shows that something has gone wrong at a very deep level. It takes us into a maze where there appears to be no exit. To change metaphors, it goes round and round in circles with no end in sight. It draws us into an epistemological underworld where we become disoriented but fail to see straight any longer. It offers to cure the patient but only adds to the deeper disease that has been either ignored or misdiagnosed.

Toward an Epistemology of Theology

We have now arrived at the two challenges that this last observation presents. What do we do with the questions that Grenz so eagerly seeks to answer? And, second, what alternative am I canvassing in facing the arrival of postmodernity? Here is my response.

In dealing with the central questions raised by Grenz in *Beyond Foundationalism* we should lodge it in a proper and systematic treatment of the epistemology of theology. At this point we need extended work in epistemology. If the object of inquiry is profoundly relevant to the means adopted to seek the truth about the object of that inquiry then theology, as much as history or natural science, will be subject to its own object-relative evidentiary paraphernalia. To be sure, there will be general considerations that will be deployed. Hence debates about generic stances in epistemology will be worth considering; we will need to look at not just at foundationalism and coherentism but at all the other "isms" and theories that have been invented: internalism, externalism, contextualism, methodism, particularism, virtue theory, social epistemology, and the like. However, the heavy-lifting in the epistemology of theology will entail a discussion of matters that are unique to theology. I have in mind such themes as the spiritual senses, testimony, religious experience, tradition, divine revelation, spiritual discernment, Scripture, and papal infallibility. The time is long past when we can tackle the desiderata on an ad hoc basis. We need extended collaborative work that will involve philosophers and theologians. We need a new sub-discipline that operates in the boundaries between philosophy and theology that can felicitously be identified as the epistemology of theology. Grenz's forays into philosophy and theology in search of a way forward for a renewed commitment to Scripture as the norming norm in theology and to tradition as a crucial hermeneutical resource in the interpretation of Scripture belong in the arena. As already indicated I am skeptical of the cogency of his position as it stood here; but they absolutely belong at the table and deserve a careful hearing.

Depending on how we chart the terrain, work in the epistemology of theology will be inescapable in dealing with the current debates about a proper response to postmodernity. At one level postmodernity is a normative doctrine about the collapse of one vision (or family of visions) in epistemology and how to proceed epistemologically in the future. At another level postmodernity is a generic term used to capture certain crucial features of Western culture. We need to keep this distinction in mind as we proceed.

Taken in the first sense, postmodernity is in reality a rhetoric of disillusionment and a rhetoric of hope. As such, like modernity, it is also a family of visions that calls for critical assessment from an epistemic point of view. Grenz is right in thinking that Christian theologians should take advantage of the shifts in sensibilities that make the rounds in the academy and in culture more generally. He is also partly right in deploying the narrative of postmodernity to unmask the hidden judgments that have been absorbed in modern expressions of Christian theology, both liberal and conservative. Moreover, we certainly need to deal head on and systematically with the epistemic challenges posed within and without theology. However, if we remain at this level of response then we are still enmeshed in the world of epistemology; we are contributing to a scholastic enterprise that has captured the energy and imagination of Western Christians and become something of an obsession. There are important problems to be addressed in their own right but they are partial problems and, as Wittgenstein advised, "Don't get involved in partial problems, but always take flight to where there is a free view over the whole single great problem, even if this view is still not a clear one."[21]

The whole single great problem here is the failure to step back and evaluate the place of the epistemology of theology in the intellectual economy of the church. Grenz, in keeping with both modernity and postmodernity, gives it a place of privilege if not primacy. Getting the right epistemology comes across as the first order of business; once we get this done, it is thought, we can then get on with the work of theology. Consequently theology exists as an ever-changing enterprise that is subject to the wider developments in epistemology.

I reject this whole way of thinking. Putting the matter pastorally, this whole enterprise deprives the church of pivotal resources, creates endless disunity, destabilizes the faith of ordinary believers, and, in most of its biblicist forms, readily distorts the faith at its deepest levels. Putting the matter historically, the early church was well able to develop and adopt its canonical doctrines without agreeing to any particular epistemology. In fact, a variety of epistemological insights, proposals, and theories were allowed to flourish. Putting the matter theologically, the Holy Spirit, contrary to what Oberman and Grenz claim, did not in leading the church to canonize Scripture also lead it to adopt Scripture as its norming norm. The latter option was one option some theologians adopted in their initial efforts to resolve epistemological queries about the proper norm for theology as an academic enterprise, but there was no agreement on this option and it was never canonized. What was at stake in terms of the working of the Holy Spirit was the provision of a network of canonical persons, materials, and practices

21. Wittgenstein, entry for 1 Nov. 1914, *Notebooks 1914–1916*.

that initiated disciples of Jesus Christ into the life of God. Scripture takes its place within this arena as an indispensable means of grace.

Turning to a very different and second sense of "postmodernity," suppose we take postmodernity in a more deflationary fashion. Suppose we think of it as a term of art that captures certain features of contemporary culture as a whole. It matters marginally how we spell this out either negatively or positively. We may wax eloquent and learned on the importance of narrative, images, social location, tradition, restless innovation, power relations, particularity, the Other, the Internet, and whatever else we may prefer. The really massive challenge facing the church in this version of postmodernity is not finding a new epistemology to fit a new age but the much more mundane one of preaching the gospel and initiating folk inside and outside the church into the kingdom of God. The critical challenge is not first and foremost in epistemology but in basic proclamation and catechesis. The general assumption at stake in the imagination of postmodernists is that we must reverse these priorities; we will not be able to engage in relevant proclamation and catechesis unless we get clear on the host culture and learn how to translate the faith into the categories it deploys. I reject this assumption. It makes the faith hostage to the prevailing epistemic regimes and, without realizing what is happening, reconceives the faith in epistemic terms. Once again there is a failure to step back and evaluate the place of epistemology in the intellectual economy of the church. At this level, epistemology in any shape or form must take a back-seat to the actual practice of proclamation and catechesis. It is the demands of the latter that should be foremost in our thinking and practice. This is one of the deepest and most pressing challenges facing the church in the West.

To be sure, this radical reversal also calls for a whole reconceptualizing of the very nature of theology itself. We need a whole new era of theology proper, that is, of theology conceived along the lines of university level catechesis that equips the church as a whole to teach and live the faith with flair and confidence. It is only after we have really grounded converts, nominal believers, and confused believers in the gospel and the kingdom that we should introduce them to the challenges of theology proper. Moreover, when we get that far we need to be clear how such work is to be distinguished from rigorous work in epistemology. One reason for inventing the epistemology as a new sub-discipline in the academy is precisely to free up theology to get on with its proper work in the life of the church. Perhaps Grenz was stumbling into this insight when he inadvertently offered his material proposals in pneumatology as an alternative to foundationalism. He has naturally switched from epistemology to theology proper, that is, a material account of the activity of the Holy Spirit. I think other important elements in his legacy would bear out my sense that he would welcome the change in perspective I am advocating. It remains to those of us who admire him to develop the radical consequences this change of perspective involves for both the future of theology and the life of the church as whole. Insofar as we succeed we will be offering nourishing bread as opposed to one more round in the maze of epistemology.

Bibliography

Brown, Rebecca L. "Tradition and Insight." *The Yale Law Journal* 103 (1993) 177–222.
Lott, Micah. "Reasonably Traditional: Self-Contradiction and Self-Reference in Alasdair MacIntyre's Account of Tradition-Based Rationality." *Journal of Religious Ethics* 30 (2002) 315–39.
Mitchell, Basil. "Tradition." In *The Blackwell Companion to Philosophy of Religion*, edited by Philip L. Quinn and Charles Taliaferro, 591–99. Oxford: Blackwell, 1997.
Wittgenstein, Ludwig. *Notebooks, 1914–1916*. 2d ed. Edited by G. H. von Wright and G. E. M. Anscombe. Oxford: Blackwell, 1979.

16

The *Corpus Theologicum* of the Church and Presumptive Authority

GREGG R. ALLISON

STAN GRENZ WAS A good friend of mine. When I became the director of the Th.M. program at Western Seminary in the late 1990s, Stan would come down to Portland twice a year to do lectures for my students. We were always eager for Stan's insightful content and engaging style of presenting theology, and he was similarly keen to try out new material—e.g., the Trinitarian shape of theological method, the history of theology, worship, the non-genderedness of God—on budding theologians. Our friendship extended beyond these two yearly events, as we regularly met at the annual meetings of the Evangelical Theological Society to renew our relationship. In terms of his greatest impact on me, the vision of full conformity to the image of Jesus Christ that he communicated in *The Social God and the Relational Self* forever changed my eschatological hope.

Because of Stan's impact on my life, I count it a great privilege to contribute a chapter to this *Festschrift* in his honor. Because I have written a work on historical theology,[1] I will address the theological legacy of the church that played such an important role in Stan's theology.

As is widely known, Stan's methodology featured "three sources or norms for theology," with the second being "the theological heritage of the church."[2] Scripture holds the place of primacy, and the contemporary culture

1. Allison, *Historical Theology*.
2. Grenz, *Theology for the Community* (1994), 21.

of the church is theology's tertiary source.³ To be clear about what Stan affirmed, I will first review his notion of theological tradition,⁴ for which he referenced Jude 3 in terms of biblical support: "the faith that was once for all delivered to the saints."⁵ Next, I will offer one critique of Stan's notion of theological heritage—its vagueness—and seek to bring some concreteness to the discussion by means of the concept of presumptive authority, followed by three case studies showing how the presumptive authority of the *Corpus Theologicum* could guide the church in its contemporary theological task. Finally, I will anticipate some concerns with and criticisms of my proposal, and seek to address them.

Grenz's Notion of Theological Heritage and the Issue of Vagueness

In terms of definition, the theological heritage as conceived by Stan "is the flow of church history as it describes the conclusions of past theological discussions"⁶ or "the history of the interpretation and application of canonical scripture by the Christian community, the church, as it listens to the voice of the Spirit speaking through the text."⁷ Such valid biblical interpretations and sound theological formulations from the past are "instructive in our quest for a relevant theology" and are indeed a necessary component of the theological task because "they alert us to some of the pitfalls to avoid, and they point out some of the directions that might hold promise for our attempts to engage in the theological calling in the present."⁸ In

---

3. In my essay, I will assume, and occasionally comment on, the role of Scripture, but will not address the role of contemporary culture, as that is material for other essays in this volume.

4. Stan was careful to distinguish his notion of tradition from the "medieval Roman Catholic idea of a twofold source of truth" (*Renewing the Center*, 2nd ed., 216). I would want to modify Stan's understanding of Catholic tradition by bringing it in line with Vatican Council II's notion of it, as expressed in *Dei Verbum* (Dogmatic Constitution on Divine Revelation; 18 Nov. 1965), but that is another matter for another time. The important point is that he did not view the historical legacy of the church, or tradition, as a source of divine revelation. Indeed, he insisted that "tradition plays an important albeit *secondary role* in theology" (ibid., emphasis added).

5. The Holy Bible, English Standard Version. The appeal to this passage is made in Grenz and Franke, *Beyond Foundationalism*, 119.

6. Grenz, *Theology for the Community* (1994), 23.

7. Grenz and Franke, *Beyond Foundationalism*, 118.

8. Grenz, *Theology for the Community* (1994), 24; *Renewing the Center*, 2nd ed., 217; *Revisioning*, 95–96; Grenz and Franke, *Beyond Foundationalism*, 121–23.

particular, Stan underscored "classic" theological statements or "symbols of the faith"[9]—what he also called "the 'universal doctrine' of the church"[10] and what others might call "the great tradition"[11] (the specific examples he offered are the Apostles' Creed and the Nicene Creed).[12] He especially appreciated the potential they offer for uniting Christians and churches of different stripes:

> Certain past formulations carry special significance, in that they have withstood the test of time. As "classic" statements of theological truths—milestones in the history of the theology of the church—these expressions have a special relevance for every age.... Because we desire to participate in the one church of Jesus Christ—that is, to retain continuity with the entire body of the people of God—we must take seriously what has become the doctrine of the church throughout the ages. This doctrine is expressed in those formulations that have gained broad acknowledgement among Christians of many generations.[13]

This affirmation was accompanied by two caveats. First, Stan would not permit the historical consensus of the church to be considered apart from theology's other two sources: "Of course, past creeds and confessions of faith are not binding in and of themselves. They must be tested by the Scriptures and by their applicability to our cultural situation."[14] Second, Stan emphasized that all well-established doctrines were forged in particular situations and thus must be understood "within their historical and philosophical contexts."[15] When all is said and done, this properly understood, re-appropriated[16] theological tradition "serves as a source or a resource for theology,

9. Grenz and Franke, *Beyond Foundationalism*, 123.
10. Grenz, *Revisioning*, 97.
11. Cutsinger, *Reclaiming the Great Tradition*.
12. Grenz and Franke, *Beyond Foundationalism*, 123.
13. Grenz, *Theology for the Community* (1994), 24; Grenz, *Renewing the Center*, 2nd ed., 217; Grenz, *Revisioning*, 96; Grenz and Franke, *Beyond Foundationalism*, 123–24.
14. Grenz, *Theology for the Community* (1994), 24.
15. Ibid. Cf. Grenz, *Renewing the Center*, 2nd ed., 216–17; Grenz, *Revisioning*, 95, 97, 124. This caveat is in keeping with Stan's definition of tradition: "The Christian tradition is comprised of the historical attempts by the Christian community to explicate and translate faithfully . . . the Christian faith . . . into the various social and cultural contexts in which that community has been situated" (Grenz and Franke, *Beyond Foundationalism*, 118).
16. As suggested by Rodney Clapp: "There can, there must, be a re-appropriation of Christian tradition (and not just of its first three centuries), but it is necessarily a *re*-appropriation, not simply a rote imitation or repetition of the tradition as it was embodied centuries earlier" (*Border Crossings*, 98).

not as a final arbiter of theological issues or concerns but a hermeneutical context or trajectory for the Christian theological enterprise."[17] The church has inherited a legacy from the past and, following along the trajectory of this tradition, it engages in the task of formulating theology in its contemporary context.[18] As Stan concluded, "In confessing faith today, therefore, we are but the contemporary embodiment of a legacy of faith that extends through time and encompasses believers of all ages. Hence our expression of faith is to be not only contemporary but also the confessing of the faith of the one people of God."[19]

Without subscribing to all the details of Stan's proposal for the theological tradition of the church as a resource for the theological task today, I do agree with its broad contours and many of its particulars. One mild critique that I have, and which stimulates this essay, is some of the proposal's vagueness.[20] I offer three examples. The first concerns Stan's view of the nature of this inherited body of theological wisdom, specifically, whether it is unchanging or not: "The assumption that tradition comprises an unchanged body of Christian doctrines articulated by the ancient church for all time, *while in one sense true*, can also be indicative of an understanding that fails to comprehend properly the dynamic character of tradition, viewing it instead in static terms."[21] In what sense is it true that this legacy is constant, such that modifications to it cannot be made without imperiling the contemporary theological endeavor by overly separating from the Christian faith? Indeed, when Stan affirms that the church's contemporary theology "must also place us *in continuity with the faith* of the one people of God,"[22]

17. Grenz and Franke, *Beyond Foundationalism*, 120.

18. In one sense, then, this approach is the antithesis of Kant's agenda of shirking off "the symbol [i.e., creed] of the church" (Kant, *What is Enlightenment?*, 464).

19. Grenz, *Revisioning*, 96; *Beyond Foundationalism*, 124. In one sense, this proposal overlaps with Oden's call for "tradition-maintenance" (Oden, *Beyond Modernity . . . What?*, 151).

20. Stan addressed this problem of ambiguity in his brief article "Virtue of Ambiguity," 361–65. Though his response was directed at Archie Spencer's criticism of ambiguity in relationship to Stan's proposal for the role of culture and community in theological construction, Stan's reply may be broadened to encompass the role of the theological heritage of the church in such theological work. If this move is permitted, then I concur with Stan's assessment that one possible reason for this ambiguity was the fact that he was "a *relatively* young theologian" (364, original emphasis) who was still working through understanding the proper role for the church's tradition in his theological project. Importantly, I hope that my critique of Stan's ambiguity is not due to my misunderstanding of his project, as was often the case with many critiques of it.

21. Grenz and Franke, *Beyond Foundationalism*, 119 (emphasis added). Cf. Grenz, *Revisioning*, 95.

22. Grenz and Franke, *Beyond Foundationalism*, 123–24 (emphasis added).

does he place parameters on theological development or erect boundaries for the extent of the trajectory on which the church in its theological elaboration is permitted to travel? The second example involves the degree of importance that is/should be attached to this theological heritage. When Stan quotes approvingly Gabriel Fackre, who calls tradition "a *weighty resource* in Christian theology,"[23] and when Stan himself proposes that "the theological tradition of the church must be *a crucial component* in the construction of our contemporary theological statements,"[24] the question is raised as to how much weight it should be accorded and how crucial a role it is expected to play. The third example, which is related to the preceding one, treats the nature of the authority of this theological legacy. As Stan offers, "Insofar as the tradition of the Christian church is the product of the ongoing reflection of the Christian community on the biblical message, it is in many respects *an extension of the authority of scripture*."[25] Given Stan's high view of the authority of Scripture, this affirmation prompts reflection on the nature of this transferred authority of the church's theological tradition. Specifically, what authority is/should be accorded the unchanged/constant, classic doctrinal consensus that is a weighty/crucial component of the contemporary church's theological enterprise?

The Presumptive Authority of the *Corpus Theologicum*

Before answering my own question, I want to sketch what this *corpus theologicum* of the church might include in terms of broad doctrines (one's understanding of this consensus may include more or less features, it may be more or less detailed, but I believe that widespread agreement approaching this sketch does exist), the notion of which I developed by summarizing the elements of the early creeds and adding beliefs that were assumed by the church from its outset (and thus no council of the church felt compelled to articulate them) and were regularly and extensively promulgated in its writings, sermons, and liturgies:[26]

---

23. Fackre, *The Christian Story*, 18 (emphasis added), cited in Grenz and Franke, *Beyond Foundationalism*, 123.
24. Grenz and Franke, *Beyond Foundationalism*, 124 (emphasis added).
25. Ibid., 119 (emphasis added).
26. As Stan emphasized, I also affirm that this consensus is not just doctrinal; liturgical, spiritual, and ecclesial elements also find common agreement. But following Stan's focus on doctrinal matters as key to the church's theological heritage, I confine my discussion to these creedal or dogmatic matters.

- the inspiration, authority, truthfulness (inerrancy), power, and centrality of divine revelation, Scripture
- the existence, knowability, and nature/attributes of God
- the Trinity (God as Father, Son, and Holy Spirit)
- creation and providence as the works of God
- the reality and work of spiritual beings (angels, demons, Satan)
- human dignity as image bearers of God
- human depravity as fallen into sin (including original sin and actual sin)
- the deity and humanity of Jesus Christ (including his virgin birth)
- Christ's work of salvation (e.g., incarnation, death, burial, resurrection, ascension) on behalf of fallen human beings
- the person and work of the Holy Spirit
- the application of salvation (e.g., the forgiveness of sins, regeneration, conversion, transformation) as a gracious work of God appropriated by faith
- the church as the people of God, the body of Christ, the temple of the Holy Spirit
- the church as characterized by unity, holiness, catholicity/universality, and apostolicity
- means of grace (e.g., baptism, the Lord's Supper) through the church
- personal eschatology in terms of death and the intermediate state
- cosmic eschatology in terms of the return of Jesus Christ, the resurrection, the last judgment, and eternal punishment
- the new heaven and new earth as the ultimate hope

If this doctrinal consensus, or something approximating it, will be granted, then what authority is/should be accorded it as a vital component of the contemporary church's theological enterprise?

Following Stan's theological method, Scripture is the first source for the contemporary theological task; as such, Scripture enjoys *primary* authority. It is not the only authority—and the Protestant formal principle of *sola scriptura* is not a rejection of other authorities—but in all theological matters, Scripture is the ultimate authority.[27] But the theological corpus is

---

27. As the relevant section of the Westminster Confession of Faith, which Stan was

the second source for the task; in terms of my proposal, this theological tradition enjoys *presumptive* authority. This notion is derived from the field of law. Presumption is commonly defined as "a rule of law which permits a court to assume a fact is true until such time as there is a preponderance (greater weight) of evidence which disproves or outweighs (rebuts) the presumption."[28] A presumption is not absolute, being instead derived from other facts that are certain and conclusive. Moreover, a presumption is rebuttable; it is possible to marshal other facts or evidence that would overturn the presumption. At the same time, in court proceedings, the burden of proof rests with the one who challenges the case that is undergirded by the presumption. To take several examples from the legal field: an accused person is presumed to be innocent until proven guilty; the child of a couple living together is presumed to be the biological offspring of the man until evidence is presented to the contrary; a woman who has been missing for seven years or more is presumed to be dead, but the presumption could be refuted by evidence that she is indeed alive. Applied to the discussion at hand, the ascription of presumptive authority to the *corpus theologicum* means that it provides probable contours and grounds for the contemporary church's doctrinal developments, and it gives this shape and warrant in a subsidiary or auxiliary way (with Scripture, from which the consensus is derived, being the direct source). Conceptually, specific elements of this corpus—indeed, the entire body—could be overturned by Scriptural evidence to the contrary. That is, it stands as the church's theological consensus—and each element in turns stands as a component of the whole—until contrary evidence is produced in rebuttal to dismiss it/each element. At the same time, the burden of proof rests with theologians who challenge the *corpus theologicum* with its presumptive authority and who neglect or depart from the contours of this consensus in their theological endeavors.

Because of its presumptive authority, the church's theological tradition plays a secondary role in the contemporary theological enterprise. The primary role belongs to Scripture, which possesses supreme authority.

Let me contrast the presumptive authority of the theological consensus of the church with several other possible views. For the sake of his people and their progress in doctrinal maturity, God would intend that the church

---

so fond of quoting, states: "The Supreme Judge, by which all controversies of religion are to be determined, and all decrees of councils, opinions of ancient writers, doctrines of men, and private spirits, are to be examined, and in whose sentence we are to rest, can be no other but the Holy Spirit speaking in the Scripture" (Westminster Confession of Faith, "On the Holy Scripture," 10).

28. Legal Dictionary, public domain. http://legal-dictionary.thefreedictionary.com/presumption.

would develop a body of beliefs to be embraced by the whole church, and the church would need to become aware of this consensus. If this is the case, we may rightly expect that God would provide guidance for discerning this corpus. He could provide such guidance in several ways: raising up an authoritative church magisterium (teaching office) and maintaining an authoritative church tradition; producing individual believer conviction; fostering particular church/denominational affirmation; or providing ecclesial-wide wisdom. Catholics affirm the first way, but the church's magisterium and tradition go beyond presumptive authority, possessing instead primary authority as the divinely-appointed discerner and interpreter of divine revelation, which is composed of both Scripture and tradition. Protestants are caricatured as affirming the second way, but such an understanding, while a portrait of some Protestants, does not ring true with respect to all Protestants (e.g., the high regard for the early creeds within Lutheranism).[29] Protestants often settle for the third way. The fourth way is what I propose: God has provided wisdom to his church throughout the centuries, enabling it to acknowledge and embrace the cardinal doctrines of the faith, and this wisdom is located in the historical consensus of the church. Such wisdom is not divinely inspired; hence, no category of tradition exists in my proposal as it does within Catholicism. Such wisdom goes beyond individual acknowledgement, though individual conviction on such doctrines is certainly the privilege of all Christians. Such wisdom goes beyond particular church/denominational affirmation, though such acknowledgement is certainly the privilege of all churches. Rather, such wisdom has as its source God's guidance, in accordance with his promise to direct his people through the ages, that is manifested in a consensus that has demonstrated itself across the centuries to be true. It is this *corpus theologicum*, possessing presumptive authority, which serves as the secondary resource in the church's theological task today.

An alternative is to imagine that the theological task appeals to Scripture, which possesses supreme authority, but to nothing more;[30] or else, such an enterprise would look to both Scripture with its main authority and

---

29. In addition to affirming the supreme authority of Scripture, Lutheran theology insists on the importance of certain church traditions "(such as are the *Apostles'*, the *Nicene*, and the *Athanasian Creeds*). We publicly profess that we embrace them, and reject all heresies and all dogmas that have ever been brought into the church of God contrary to their decision" (Formula of Concord, Epitome 1: "Of the Compendious Rule and Norm," in Schaff, *Creeds of Christendom*, 3:95).

30. Of course, the claim to appeal "to nothing more" can be demonstrated to be a false claim, as some species of hermeneutic, a denominational distinctive or distinctives, a particularly dynamic leader, and the like exercise strong influence in the theological process.

the church's theological consensus with its presumptive authority. The latter proposal better accounts for the broad doctrinal unity in terms the Trinity, the deity and humanity of Jesus Christ, a gracious salvation, human dignity and depravity, and the like, as presented earlier, doctrines that are held not just by individual Christians on the grounds of their individual convictions based on Scripture, nor just by particular churches/denominations on the grounds of their particular church/denominational affirmation grounded on Scripture, but by both individual Christians and particular churches/denominations on the grounds of the presumptive authority of the historical consensus of the church in addition to the supreme authority of Scripture.

Presented in this way, my proposal clarifies why the *corpus theologicum* serves as a weighty resource for, or crucial component of, the contemporary theological task. Though not possessing primary authority (which belongs to Scripture), it possesses presumptive authority. The *corpus theologicum* does possess a subsidiary authority to the main authority of Scripture. As theologians today present and argue their constructive theological proposals, appeals that they make to the historical consensus of the church are/should be accorded great significance. Berkouwer provides a fine illustration of this posture toward the church's heritage regarding the doctrine of sin, specifically what he calls "the biblical *a priori*," which is "the message that confronts us, inescapably, in the whole of the biblical witness. What concerns us at this point is *the truth that the Church has confessed* on the basis of this witness: that God is not the Source, or the Cause, or the Author of man's sin."[31] He emphasizes the normative status of this historical position: "There is every reason for us to give full attention to the *a priori* character of this cautioning witness. For this apriority can be seen in the fact that, in the light of God's revelation and faith oriented to that revelation, *a decision has already been made of far-reaching and even normative significance*. This is not a theoretical or a speculative decision but a thoroughly religious one. With it the purity of our doctrine of sin must stand or fall."[32] From Berkouwer's perspective, contemporary theological formulation of the doctrine of sin must pay heed to the church's consensus on this point, for "[i]f anything is clear, it is certainly that the Church has addressed herself to this issue in unequivocal terms."[33]

Presented in this way, my proposal also addresses in what sense it is true that this "tradition comprises an unchanged body of Christian

---

31. Berkouwer, *Studies in Dogmatics: Sin*, 27 (emphasis added).
32. Ibid. (emphasis added).
33. Ibid., 28.

doctrines articulated by the ancient church for all time,"[34] such that modifications to or abandonment of it would imperil contemporary theological projects. This corpus properly summarizes biblical affirmations, narratives, psalms, prophecies, etc., that give rise to its cardinal doctrines. As Stan expressed it, the consensus "is in many respects *an extension of the authority of scripture*."[35] Arising from Scripture and possessing presumptive authority that is an extension of biblical authority, the *corpus theologicum* has for its incubation period the early church, but it is not limited to that epoch for its full development.[36] Moreover, the constancy of this theological tradition is particularly seen against the backdrop of deviations from it, aberrations that have consistently been exposed and denounced as heretical departures from the Christian faith (e.g., Arianism, modalism). Furthermore, the Christian church expresses and fosters its unity through theologians embracing this heritage.

The issue is thus raised: What could possibly overturn/defeat this historical tradition of the church, in whole or in part? To use an analogy from (American) football, what might constitute "indisputable . . . evidence"[37] to the extent that a call by the referee on the field is to be overturned—that is, that the corpus is wrong, in whole or in part, and stands in need of correction/revision? Because presumptive authority can and must yield to primary authority, such unassailable evidence would come from a reinterpretation of Scripture that up to the point of revision supported the consensus or any element therein. Moreover, this reinterpretation would have to establish

---

34. Grenz and Franke, *Beyond Foundationalism*, 119.

35. Ibid., 119 (emphasis added). This affirmation echoes that of Article 8 of the Thirty-Nine Articles: "The Three Creeds, Nicene Creed, Athanasius's Creed, and that which is commonly called the Apostles' Creed, ought thoroughly to be received and believed: *for they may be proved by most certain warrant of holy Scripture*" (emphasis added).

36. For Stan, as the Holy Spirit guides the church, "to focus on his work in the Fathers is to emphasize the beginning point to the neglect of the current and future points." Grenz, Th.M. lecture on the Trinitarian shape of Christian Theology, Western Seminary. He underscored the development of doctrine throughout the centuries, but also emphasized that such development be closely tied to Scripture and the historical consensus. Indeed, he quoted approvingly Fackre: "The circle of tradition is not closed, for the Spirit's ecclesial Work is not done. Traditional doctrine develops as Christ and the Gospel are viewed in ever fresh perspective. Old formulations are corrected, and what is passed on is enriched. The open-endedness, however, does not overthrow the ancient landmarks. As tradition is a gift of the Spirit, its trajectory moves in the right direction, although it has not arrived at its destination" (*The Christian Story*, 18–19, cited in Grenz and Franke, *Beyond Foundationalism*, 127).

37. *2012 Official Playing Rules and Casebook of the National Football League*, Rule 15, Sec. 9.

itself as being more valid than the historical interpretation. Alternatively, such incontrovertible evidence would come from a demonstration that the manner in which the Scriptural support was put together in constructing the consensus or any element thereof was incorrect. Alternately, it could be demonstrated that some relevant biblical affirmations, narratives, psalms, prophecies, and the like were overlooked in constructing the consensus such that, when those biblical matters are brought into consideration, the consensus or any element therein demands revision. The notion of presumptive authority includes corrigibility, and the historical tradition of the church or any component of it could be defeated in these (and probably other) ways.[38]

If such a scenario would play itself out, other issues would need to be raised: Does the corrected corpus/element mean that for the last two thousand years the church has been in error with regard to the consensus/ that element? How could the church today, developing its theological task in a corrected direction, claim unity with the historic church, from which it breaks over the historical consensus or a particular element thereof? Could this unity still be preserved in some sense if the contemporary church distances itself from the historic church on only one of the elements of the corpus? A few of its elements? Half of its elements? At what point should/ must the contemporary church, because of its thoroughgoing revisioning of the consensus or because of its correction of particular elements therein, abandon hope of claiming continuity with the church of the past and admit that it has become a new entity?

These questions raise important issues that would be the entailment of the contemporary church's abandonment or significant modification of the corpus/elements thereof in its theological task. Perhaps this specter will prompt the church take to heart Stan's perspective: the bulk of the church's theologizing is restatement, being not so much an advancement as a retrieval of old truth.[39]

Three Case Studies

I introduce three case studies to illustrate several key points of my proposal and show how it could guide the contemporary church in its theological

---

38. An example of such corrective activity is the "ransom to Satan" theory of the atonement, a model that held sway in the church for nearly a millennium, from the time of Origen to that of Anselm and Abelard.

39. Grenz, Th.M. lecture on theological method, Western Seminary. Cf. Oden's discussion of the impulse toward conservation of earlier theology that typified the later ecumenical councils. Oden, *Beyond Modernity . . . What?*, 161.

task: first, the virgin birth of Jesus Christ; second, the reality and work of angels, Satan, and demons; and third, the eternal conscious punishment of the intractably wicked in hell.

The primary authority for the virgin birth of Christ rests almost exclusively on one biblical prophecy (Isa 7:14) and two biblical narratives (Matt 1:18–25; Luke 1:26–38).[40] The presumptive authority for this belief is the church's doctrinal consensus affirmed very early on: Ignatius,[41] Tertullian,[42] and the early creeds—Nicene, Apostles', Athanasian, Chalcedonian—make reference to the virgin Mary. Criticisms abound: biblical support is minimal; conception by a virgin is biologically impossible; the virgin birth has numerous parallels with ancient Near Eastern and Greek mythology; and others. The contemporary church, engaged in the task of articulating its Christology, should continue to affirm the virgin birth because of both the main authority of Scripture and the subsidiary authority of the classic tradition; indeed, Stan provides a fine example for the church on this doctrine.[43] To deny that the Son of God became incarnate through normal sexual relationships between Mary and Joseph (or some other man) or in some other way than the virginal conception would entail establishing a more valid interpretation of the biblical prophecy and narratives and a dismissal of the historic tradition, reckoning it as wrong and breaking with the church throughout the centuries. For those who might respond by questioning the importance of such a "peripheral" doctrine, this belief does not stand in isolation from other doctrines. Indeed, historically, rejection of the virgin birth was an entailment of the rejection of divinely wrought miracles, a reason why its affirmation became one of the five fundamentals of the faith during the fundamentalist-modernist conflict.[44]

Second, the reality and work of angels, Satan, and demons is established on the primary authority of numerous biblical writings and enjoys the presumptive authority of the historical consensus of the church from its earliest writings. It would be hard to overstate the traditional case for this matter: St. Antony regularly wrestled with demons;[45] St. Augustine's *City of God* envisioned angels and demons as the foundations of the two cities;[46]

---

40. Other possible "hints" at the virgin birth include Mark 6:3 in contrast with Matt 13:55; Luke 4:22; and Gal 4:4.
41. Ignatius, *Letter to the Ephesians*, 18–19 (ANF 1:57).
42. Tertullian, *The Five Books against Marcion*, book 4, ch. 10 (ANF 3:358–59).
43. Grenz, *Theology for the Community* (1994), 409–23.
44. E.g., Orr, "The Virgin Birth of Christ," 2:247–60.
45. Athanasius, *Life of Antony* (NPNF 2 4:195–221).
46. Augustine, *The City of God*, 14.28 (NPNF 1 2:282–83).

Thomas Aquinas is not without reason referred to as the "Angelic Doctor" of the Catholic Church.[47] Since the advent of modernism, the existence and role of angels, Satan, and demons has been challenged, mocked, and roundly dismissed, and the church (at least in the rationalistic West) has struggled to maintain its traditional belief. Criticisms include the demonstrably non-authoritative, speculative traditional material (e.g., Dionysius the Pseudo-Areopagite's *Celestial Hierarchy*) on which later theologians (e.g., John of Damascus, Thomas Aquinas) rested their doctrine; the mythological worldview of Scripture that would affirm the existence of these disembodied creatures; their superfluity; and others. The contemporary church's enterprise of describing the creation of the universe and its many creatures, and its task of constructing its angelology and demonology, should continue to affirm the reality and work of angels, Satan, and demons because of both the main authority of Scripture and the subsidiary authority of the classic tradition. To capitulate to the view that these beings are nothing more than mythological creatures would be a serious departure from the theological consensus of the church, and would entail tossing both biblical contributions and the historical position of the church onto the ash heap of an outmoded supernaturalistic worldview that is out of step with contemporary society. It would also distance the contemporary Western church—in which this departure could be envisioned as occurring—from the rest of the global church, which continues to embrace and live in light of the reality of angelic and demonic activity.

This second example serves another purpose, and that is to illustrate how corrections to the *corpus theologicum* may and should be made. One of the chief criticisms of the heritage concerning angelic beings is the church's reliance on fanciful extra-biblical writings in its development of the tradition. Speculation on the part of this tradition—for example, basing its nine-tiered angelic hierarchy[48] on Dionysius's *Celestial Hierarchy* rather than Scripture—opens it up to—indeed, even demands—correction. In the hands of Karl Barth, the criticism (based on Heb 1:14) was leveled at the church's overemphasis on angels as "ministering *spirits* sent out to serve"—leading to a fascination with the *nature* of angels—instead of a proper focus on them as "*ministering* spirits *sent out* to serve"—encouraging a proper attention on the *function* of angels in playing a mediating role between God and human beings.[49] But correction in this case did not translate into a denial of the reality and work of these created beings. Whatever one may

---

47. Thomas Aquinas, *Summa Theologica*, pt. 1, q. 50–64.
48. Dionysius, *The Celestial Hierarchy*, 7–8. In *Pseudo-Dionysius*, 162–68.
49. Barth, *CD*, III/3, 453, 478.

think of Stan's proposal, which linked the doctrine of angels and demons to "the structures of existence," it stands as an example of constructing a contemporary angelology and demonology with the resources of Scripture and a chastened tradition.[50]

As for the third case study, the eternal conscious punishment of the intractably wicked in hell is grounded on the main authority of Scripture and the presumptive authority of the church's tradition[51] that included defenses of the traditional view (e.g., how material bodies could suffer fiery torment without being all consumed;[52] why eternal conscious punishment is not cruel and unjust punishment;[53]) and denouncements of alternative positions (e.g., universalism,[54] annihilationism[55]). Other criticisms raised against the traditional doctrine—critiques that were occasionally voiced prior to the nineteenth century but that have increased in intensity since then[56]—include a dismissal of the retributive justice of God that would demand such punishment; biblical and theological support for universalism, conditional immortality, or annihilationism; a hoped for post-mortem opportunity to hear the gospel and embrace it; the irreconcilability of the envisioned eternal, tortured existence of the impenitent in hell with biblical affirmations of God's love for the world and his ultimate triumph over evil such that all things will be summed up in Christ; the emotional cost of believing the traditional view; and others. The contemporary church's theological engagement in formulating its eschatology should continue to affirm—with sadness and an impassioned evangelistic concern—the eternal conscious punishment of the intractably wicked in hell because of both the supreme authority of Scripture and the presumptive authority of the *corpus theologicum*. Disavowal of the tradition would not only put the

---

50. Grenz, *Theology for the Community* (1994), 276-314.

51. Frederick Farrar distanced himself from the traditional view because "none of the first four general councils lay down any doctrine whatever concerning the eternal misery of the wicked, or directly or indirectly give any interpretation of the Scriptural expressions that describe their condition" (Farrar, *Eternal Hope*, 167). His position was challenged by Edward Pusey, who explained that the silence of the councils was due to the fact that the doctrine of the eternal punishment of the wicked in hell was not an issue needing conciliar articulation, as the overwhelming majority of the early church held to a consensus view. Pusey, *What is of Faith, as to Everlasting Punishment?*, 136-37.

52. E.g., Augustine, *City of God*, 21.3-9 (NPNF 1, 2:453-61).

53. E.g., ibid., 21.11-12 (NPNF 1, 2:462-63).

54. E.g., the Synod of Constantinople in 543 condemned the universalism of Origen with its ninth anathema; this denunciation was reiterated in canon 1 of the Second Council of Constantinople in 553.

55. E.g., Augustine, *City of God*, 21.17; in NPNF 1, 2:466.

56. Bauckham, "Universalism," 48.

contemporary church at odds with the traditional interpretation of scores of biblical affirmations, narratives, psalms, prophecies, etc., but it would also align itself with positions explicitly condemned by the church of the past. Moreover, the rejection of this doctrine could entail the rejection of numerous other biblically and traditionally warranted beliefs such as retributive divine justice, the uniqueness of Christ's death and resurrection appropriated by faith, the dishonoring of human choice against God, the sealing of human destinies at death with no possibility of post-mortem repentance,[57] and so forth. Whether one agrees or disagrees with Stan's proposal, which linked the eternal dark destiny of the wicked with the experience of "God's love in a terrifying manner"[58] as "protective jealousy or wrath,"[59] it stands as an example of constructing a contemporary doctrine of the future eternal fate of the wicked with the resources of Scripture and the *corpus theologicum*, including its rejection of universalism and conditional immortality/annihilationism.[60]

By means of these three case studies, I have illustrated several key points of my proposal for the presumptive authority of the theological heritage of the church and shown how it could guide the contemporary church in its theological task.

Addressing Anticipated Concerns with and Criticisms of the Proposal

A first objection to my proposal: such a *corpus theologicum* does not exist, either in whole or in part. This criticism could come from several camps. For example, it could derive from an ignorance of historical theology. Contemporary scholars who offer such a criticism often assert, when constructing their own theology, that their proposal is superior to those of other theologians with whom they disagree; yet, these contemporary scholars are unaware of the fact that the other theologians actually stand in the tradition of the church and have that consensus on their side. To illustrate, I turn to liberal scholar Kirsopp Lake, whose vivid and opinionated comments about

---

57. Even the doctrine of purgatory does not affirm the possibility of purification for the intractably wicked—i.e., those who have died in mortal sin—because their doom is sealed in hell.

58. Grenz, *Theology for the Community* (1994), 839.

59. Ibid., 836.

60. Ibid., 826–39. Stan used the terms "conditional immortality" and "annihilationism" interchangeably.

both fundamentalism and liberalism underscore a fine point about the presumptive authority of the church's theological consensus:

> It is a mistake, often made by educated men who happen to have but little knowledge of historical theology, to suppose that Fundamentalism is a new and strange form of thought. It is nothing of the kind: it is the partial and uneducated survival of a theology which was once universally held by all Christians. How many were there, for instance, who doubted the infallible inspiration of all Scripture? A few, perhaps, but very few. No, the Fundamentalist may be wrong; I think he is. But it is we who have departed from *the tradition*, not he, and I am sorry for the fate of anyone who tries to argue with a Fundamentalist on *the basis of authority*. The Bible and the *corpus theologicum* of the church is on the Fundamentalist side.[61]

This example seems to be a case of ignorance of historical theology, and such a lack of awareness could lead to the mistaken objection that the *corpus theologicum* does not exist.

Alternatively, the objection might be offered from the standpoint that the historic consensus is a figment of the church's imagination. This objection usually is articulated by those whose attention is riveted on the immense diversity that divides (often with great hostility) the churches of Christendom, making it difficult if not impossible for these objectors to acknowledge any unity on doctrinal matters. With such widely divergent views on so many issues—e.g., justification, baptism, the Lord's Supper, church polity—the church is hopelessly divided, and any claim that a *corpus theologicum* exists so as to unite it is wishful thinking.

In response, I reiterate that the consensus that I advocate and defend is a broad one that must be grasped at a general level; placed under a microscope and assessed at a detailed level, diversity and disagreement rather than unity and agreement come into focus.[62] For example, the theological consensus has always embraced two future destinies for all human beings: heaven and hell. The addition of a third temporary destiny—purgatory—upon which Catholic, Orthodox, and Protestant churches have disagreed,

---

61. Lake, *Religion of Yesterday*, 61–62 (emphasis added).

62. According to Williams, our interpretation and incorporation of the theological tradition faces some key obstacles, one of which is the diversity of biblical exegesis and theological formulation throughout the church's history. He insists that we move beyond the mere recitation of the idealistic dictum of Vincent of Lerins—"that which has been believed everywhere, always and by everyone"—and realistically confront this diversity by finding "a central axis of faithful self-awareness that functioned within the historical process." Williams, *Retrieving the Tradition*, 30.

does not negate the broad agreement on the ultimate fate of the righteous in eternal conscious blessing and of the unrighteous in eternal conscious punishment. Certainly, the entailments of belief in purgatory—e.g., an insufficient view of justification, an improper notion of the communion of saints and the correlative treasury of merits—enter into the discussion, but these entailments are circumscribed. For example, belief in purgatory does not entail a false belief about the deity and humanity of Jesus Christ and heretical notions about the Trinity. Broad consensus still exists despite these disagreements and what they entail.[63]

A second criticism to my proposal: The notion of presumptive authority is unnecessary because we have the primary authority of Scripture—and that is all we need. This objection will be especially voiced by those who think my proposal attacks or dismisses *sola scriptura*. However, as noted above, the formal principle of Protestantism, in its classical expression, did not entail the rejection of the historic consensus of the church,[64] so my proposal is actually more in keeping with *sola scriptura* than are those that divorce the primary authority of Scripture from the presumptive authority of the theological heritage.

Besides this point, those who champion the motto "no creed but the Bible" are naïve; no such immaculate reading of Scripture is actually possible—nor desirable (assuming a sound theological framework is brought to the interpretive and theological tasks to illumine them properly).[65] An illustration of this troubling naiveté is Alexander Campbell: "I have endeavored to read the Scriptures as though no one had read them before me, and I am as much on my guard against reading them today, through the medium of my own views yesterday, or a week ago, as I am against being influenced by any foreign name, authority, or system whatever."[66] Campbell was denying that his biblical understanding and theology was influenced by Scottish sectarians, but even if this particular point were true, his contention that his interpretation of Scripture was removed from all influences was surely mis-

---

63. My proposal further acknowledges the prolonged and often contested nature of the historical progression of this consensus. The development of doctrines such as the deity of Christ, the hypostatic union, and the Trinity featured heretical proposals, orthodox counterpoints, attempts at compromise, intense wrangling, ongoing disagreement, and excommunication. From a theological standpoint of a high view of divine providence, I embrace these contrasting developments as coming from the hand of God and occurring by his design for the purpose of forging the consensus.

64. As Timothy George phrases it, "*Sola scriptura* was not *nuda scriptura*" (*Theology of the Reformers*, 81, cf. 315; cf. also McGrath, *Reformation Thought*, 144–47).

65. The very point that prompted John Calvin to write his *Institutes*. Calvin, "John Calvin to the Reader," 4.

66. Campbell, "Reply," 204.

taken. All interpreters and theologians bring their preunderstanding—their worldview, religious experience, ecclesial involvement, theological formulation, and the like—to their enterprise.[67] My proposal calls for an awareness of the theological heritage that interpreters of Scripture and theologians should bring to their undertakings, together with an embrace of the presumptive authority of this theological consensus to drive their tasks along the proper trajectory. This authority is not binding; to Scripture belongs that authority. But for the theological tradition, the alternative is not between absolute, binding authority and no authority whatsoever. My proposal calls for an acknowledgment of the church's *corpus theologicum* to help Christian scholars "to commit themselves firmly to formulations from the past"[68] that enjoy presumptive authority for their contemporary theological formulations. I agree with Alister McGrath, that though "there is no privileged vantage point *independent of tradition*" for theological formulation, there is a privileged vantage point *within tradition* for engaging in the theological enterprise: the *corpus theologicum* of the church.[69]

A third concern with my proposal: The idea of a secondary source of theology seems to embrace the Catholic notion of tradition and flies in the face of free church rejection of an infallible resource outside of Scripture. In response, I reiterate what was underscored earlier: my proposal is far removed from the Catholic idea of tradition, which consists of teachings that Christ passed down orally to his apostles (alternatively, they learned these matters from the Holy Spirit), who in turn passed them down to their successors, the bishop. This tradition is maintained in the Catholic Church, and occasionally promulgated as official church dogma, specifically, the immaculate conception of Mary and her bodily assumption.[70] My proposal bears no resemblance whatsoever to this orally transmitted body of divinely inspired and authoritative revelation. Furthermore, as I argue for the presumptive authority of the church's theological heritage, I do indeed underscore its truthfulness, to the degree that it conforms to and properly summarizes and amplifies biblical affirmations, narratives, psalms, prophecies, and the like. But I also account for its corrigibility when such conformity and fittingness are shown to have failed. Accordingly, I embrace the truthfulness of the *corpus theologicum* but not its infallibility, and these two matters, while related, are different.

67. For an evangelical discussion of preunderstanding, see Osborne, *The Hermeneutical Spiral*, 376–84; Thiselton, *Two Horizons*, 103–14 ; Carson, "A Sketch of the Factors," 12–15.
68. Sweeney, "Mercerburg Doctrine," 106.
69. McGrath, "Engaging the Great Tradition," 148 (emphasis added).
70. *Catechism of the Catholic Church*, sec. 74–83; *Dei Verbum*, sec. 1–2.

In summary, the *corpus theologicum* does exist in broad doctrinal agreements at a general level; its presumptive authority does not detract from the primary authority of Scripture; having the latter does not mean that the church can and should dispense with the former (we are not faced with the alternative of either-or, but we can and need to embrace both primary and auxiliary authority); and my proposal is not an invitation to journey down the road leading to Catholicism.

Conclusion

I offer this essay in tribute to Stan Grenz, for whose friendship I am thankful. I have taken his notion of the theological tradition of the church as constituting a second resource for the contemporary church's theological task and developed it in several areas: Stan's understanding of the nature of this heritage; a mild critique of its vagueness, countered by means of a proposal that the *corpus theologicum* possesses presumptive authority in theological construction today; three case studies illustrating how this theological heritage can serve the theological enterprise; and responses to a few anticipated concerns with and criticism of my proposal.

Stan's emphasis on this theological heritage was important for various reasons: its recognition that tradition does indeed affect theological formulation today; its offer of hope for uniting divided churches around their common doctrinal beliefs; its promise of wisdom from the past to guide the church of today and tomorrow; and others. D. H. Williams underscored another benefit, one that particularly addresses the free church tradition to which Stan belonged, and to which I belong. The benefit has to do with confronting "the problem of how far we should accommodate the Christian message to the surrounding culture without losing Christian identity."[71] According to Williams (and surely confirmed by Grenz),

> Without the church's Tradition, I will contend that Free church communions, especially independent and "community"-type churches, (1) will increasingly proliferate a sectarian approach to Christian faith, characterized by an ahistorical and spiritual subjectivism which Philip Schaff aptly called "the great disease which has fastened itself upon the heart of Protestantism," and (2) will be more susceptible to the influences of accommodating the church to a pseudo-Christian culture such that the

---

71. Williams, *Retrieving the Tradition*, 12.

uniqueness of the Christian identity is quietly and unintentionally traded way in the name of effective ministry.[72]

May Stan's focus on the church's *corpus theologicum*, hopefully taken another step by means of my proposal, help the contemporary church engage in its theological task in a wiser manner, thereby staving off the impetus toward accommodation and compromise.

Bibliography

Allison, Gregg R. *Historical Theology: An Introduction to Christian Doctrine*. Grand Rapids: Zondervan, 2011.
Barth, Karl. *Church Dogmatics*, III/3. Translated and edited by G. W. Bromiley. Edinburgh: T. & T. Clark, 1960.
Bauckham, Richard. "Universalism: A Historical Survey." *Themelios* 4/2 (1979) 48–54.
Berkouwer, G. C. *Studies in Dogmatics: Sin*. Grand Rapids: Eerdmans, 1971.
Calvin, John. "John Calvin to the Reader." In *Institutes of the Christian Religion* (1559). Translated by Ford Lewis Battles. Library of Christian Classics, Vol. 20. Philadelphia: Westminster, 1960.
Campbell, Alexander. "Reply" to a letter from Robert B. Semple of Virginia. In *The Christian Baptist*, Volume 3 (3 April 1826).
Carson, D. A. "A Sketch of the Factors Determining Current Hermeneutical Debate in Cross-Cultural Contexts." In *Biblical Interpretation and the Church: The Problem of Contextualization*, edited by D. A. Carson, 11–29. Nashville: Nelson, 1984.
Catechism of the Catholic Church. New York: Doubleday, 1995.
Clapp, Rodney. *Border Crossings*. Grand Rapids: Brazos, 2000.
Cutsinger, James S. *Reclaiming the Great Tradition: Evangelicals, Catholics and Orthodox Dialogue*. Downers Grove, IL: InterVarsity, 1997.
Dei Verbum (Dogmatic Constitution on Divine Revelation). In *Vatican Council II, Volume 1: The Conciliar and Post Conciliar Documents*, rev. ed., edited by Austin Flannery. Northport, New York: Costello, 1975.
Dionysius the Pseudo-Areopagite. *The Celestial Hierarchy*. In *Pseudo-Dionysius: The Complete Works*, translated by Colm Luibheid and Paul Rorem. New York: Paulist, 1987.
Dunzl, Frank. *A Brief History of the Doctrine of the Trinity in the Early Church*. London: T. & T. Clark, 2007.
Fackre, Gabriel. *The Christian Story: A Narrative Interpretation of Basic Christian Doctrine*. 3rd ed. Grand Rapids: Eerdmans, 1996.
Farrar, Frederick W. *Eternal Hope*. London: Macmillan, 1897.
George, Timothy. *Theology of the Reformers*. Nashville: Broadman and Holman, 1988.
Kant, Immanuel. *What is Enlightenment?* In *Kant: Selections*, edited by Lewis White Beck. New York: Macmillan, 1988.
Lake, Kirsopp. *The Religion of Yesterday and Tomorrow*. Boston: Houghton, 1926.

---

72. Ibid., 14.

McGrath, Alister E. "Engaging the Great Tradition." In *Evangelical Futures: A Conversation in Theological Method*, edited by John Stackhouse, 139–58. Grand Rapids: Baker, 2000.

———. *Reformation Thought: An Introduction*, 2nd ed. Oxford: Blackwell, 1993.

Oden, Thomas C. *Beyond Modernity . . . What? Agenda for Theology*. Grand Rapids: Zondervan, 1990.

Orr, James. "The Virgin Birth of Christ." In *The Fundamentals: A Testimony to the Truth*, edited by R. A. Torrey, 2:247–60. 4 vols. Los Angeles: The Bible Institute of Los Angeles, 1917.

Osborne, Grant. *The Hermeneutical Spiral: A Comprehensive Introduction to Biblical Interpretation*. Revised and expanded ed. Downers Grove, IL: InterVarsity, 2006.

Pusey, Edward Bouverie. *What is of Faith, as to Everlasting Punishment? In Reply to Dr. Farrar's Challenge in His "Eternal Hope," 1897*. Oxford: Parker, 1880.

Schaff, Philip. *Creeds of Christendom*. 3 vols. New York: Harper, 1877–1905.

Sweeney, Douglas A. "Mercersburg Doctrine as a Double-Edged Sword: A Response to Darryl G. Hart." In *Evangelicals and the Early Church: Recovery, Reform, Renewal*, edited by George Kalantzis and Andrew Tooley, 104–7. Eugene, OR: Cascade, 2011.

Thiselton, Anthony C. *The Two Horizons: New Testament Hermeneutics and Philosophical Description*. Grand Rapids: Eerdmans, 1980.

Williams, D. H. *Retrieving the Tradition and Renewing Evangelicalism: A Primer for Suspicious Protestants*. Grand Rapids: Eerdmans, 1999.

Part Six

CULTURE

17

Church Matters[1]

STANLEY HAUERWAS

1. The Theological Politics of the "And"

I AM A CHRISTIAN. I am even a Christian theologian. I observe in my memoir, *Hannah's Child*, that you do not need to be a theologian to be a Christian, but I probably did. Being a Christian has not and does not come naturally or easily for me. I take that to be a good thing because I am sure that to be a Christian requires training that lasts a lifetime. I am more than ready to acknowledge that some may find that being a Christian comes more "naturally," but that can present its own difficulties. Just as an athlete with natural gifts may fail to develop the fundamental skills necessary to play their sport after their talent fades, so people naturally disposed to faith may fail to develop the skills necessary to sustain them for a lifetime.

By training I mean something very basic, such as acquiring habits of speech necessary for prayer. The acquisition of such habits is crucial for the formation of our bodies if we are to acquire the virtues necessary to live life as a Christian. For I take it to be crucial that Christians must live in a manner that their lives are unintelligible if the God we worship in Jesus Christ does not exist. The training entailed in being a Christian can be called, if you are so disposed, culture. That is particularly the case if, as Raymond Williams reminds us in *Keywords*, culture is a term first used as a process

---

1. In honor of Stan Grenz, who from an evangelical perspective helped us to see why the church matters.

noun to describe the tending or cultivation of a crop or animal.[2] One of the challenges Christians confront is how the politics we helped create has made it difficult to sustain the material practices constitutive of an ecclesial culture to produce Christians.

The character of much of modern theology exemplifies this development. In the attempt to make Christianity intelligible within the epistemological conceits of modernity, theologians have been intent on showing that what we believe as Christians is not that different than what those who are not Christians believe. Thus MacIntyre's wry observation that the project of modern theology to distinguish the kernel of the Christian faith from the outmoded husk has resulted in offering atheists less and less in which to disbelieve.[3]

It should not be surprising, as David Yeago argues, that many secular people now assume that descriptions of reality that Christians employ are a sort of varnish that can be scraped away to reveal a more basic account of what has always been the case. From a secular point of view it is assumed that we agree, or should agree, on fundamental naturalistic and secular descriptions of reality, whatever religious elaborations may lay over them. What I find so interesting is that many Christians accept these naturalistic assumptions about the way things are because they believe by doing so it is possible to transcend our diverse particularities that otherwise result in unwelcome conflict. From such a perspective it is only a short step to the key socio-political move crucial to the formation of modern societies, that is, the relegation of religion to the sphere of private inwardness and individual motivation.[4]

Societies that have relegated strong convictions to the private, a development I think appropriately identified as "secularization," may assume a tolerant or intolerant attitude toward the church, but the crucial characteristic of such societies is that the church is understood to be no more than a "voluntary association" of like-minded individuals.[5] Even those who identify as "religious" assume their religious convictions should be submitted to a public order governed by a secular rationality. I hope to challenge

2. Williams, *Keywords*, 77–78.
3. MacIntyre, *Religious Significance of Atheism*, 24.
4. Yeago, "Messiah's People," 147–48.
5. I have no intention to enter into the never ending debates about secularization and the corresponding discussions concerning the demise of "religion." Suffice it to say, I am in general sympathetic with David Martin's contention that secularization is best understood in terms of social differentiation correlative of the division of labor, with the result that discrete sectors of social life are assumed autonomous. Martin, *The Future of Christianity*, 124.

that assumption by calling into question the conceptual resources that now seem to be givens for how the church is understood. In particular, I hope to convince Christians that the church is a material reality that must resist the domestication of our faith in the interest of societal peace.

There is a great deal going against such a project. For example, in his book, *Civil Religion: A Dialogue in the History of Political Philosophy*, Ronald Beiner argues that in modernity the attempt to domesticate strong religious convictions in the interest of state control has assumed two primary and antithetical alternatives: civil religion or liberalism. Civil religion is the attempt to empower religion not for the good of religion but for the creation of the citizen. Indeed the very creation of "religion" as a concept more fundamental than a determinative tradition is a manifestation that, at least in Western societies, Christianity has become "civil."[6] Rousseau, according to Beiner, is the decisive figure that gave expression for this transformation because Rousseau saw clearly that the modern state could not risk having a church capable of challenging its political authority.[7] In the process the political concepts used to legitimize the modern state, at least if Carl Schmitt is right, are secularized theological concepts.[8]

In contrast to civil religion the liberal alternative rejects all attempts to use religion to produce citizens in service to the state. Liberalism, in its many versions, according to Beiner, seeks to domesticate or neutralize the impact of religious commitment on political life.[9] Liberalism may well result in the production of a banal and flattened account of human existence, but such a form of life seems necessary if we are to be at peace with one another. In other words, liberalism as a way of life depends on the creation of people who think there is nothing for which it is worth dying. Such a way of life was exemplified by President Bush, who suggested that the duty of Americans after September 11, 2001 was to go shopping. Such a view of the world evoked Nietzsche's bitter condemnation, ironically making Nietzsche an ally of a Christianity determined by martyrdom.[10]

An extraordinary claim to be sure, but as Paul Kahn has observed, the Western state exists "under the very real threat of Christian martyrdom; a threat to expose the state and its claim to power as nothing at all."[11] The

---

6. Bill Cavanaugh provides an invaluable account of how the creation of "religion" was a correlative of the modern state: *Myth of Religious Violence*, 60–71.
7. Beiner, *Civil Religion*, 1–7.
8. Schmitt, *Political Theology*, 5, 35.
9. Beiner, *Civil Religion*, 301–5.
10. Ibid., 374–94.
11. Kahn, *Putting Liberalism In Its Place*, 82.

martyr does so, according to Kahn, because when everything is said and done sacrifice is always stronger than murder. The martyr wields a power that defeats the murderer because the martyr can be remembered by a community more enduring than the state. That is why the liberal state has such a stake in the domestication of Christianity by making it but another lifestyle choice.

In contrast, the modern nation-state, Kahn argues, has been an extremely effective sacrificial agent, able to mobilize its populations to make sacrifices to sustain its existence as an end in itself. The nation-state, therefore, has stepped into the place of religious belief, offering individuals the possibility of transcending their finitude. War becomes the act of sacrifice by which the state sustains the assumption that, though we die, it can and will continue to exist without end.[12]

I have earned the description of being a "fideistic, sectarian, tribalist" because of my attempt to imagine an ecclesial alternative capable of resisting the politics Beiner (and Kahn) describe.[13] For as Yeago observes, most churches in the West, with the possible exception of the Roman Catholics, have acquiesced in this understanding of their social character, and have therefore collaborated in the eclipse of their ecclesial reality.[14] As a result the church seems caught in a "ceaseless crisis of legitimation" in which the church must find a justification for its existence in terms of the projects and aspirations of that larger order.[15]

In his extraordinary book, *Atheist Delusions: The Christian Revolution and Its Fashionable Enemies*, David Bentley Hart observes that the relegation of Christian beliefs to the private sphere is legitimated by a story of human freedom in which human kind is liberated from the crushing weight

---

12. Ibid., 276–77. I am indebted to Sean Larson for suggesting the importance of Kahn's understanding of liberalism for the argument I am making in this paper.

13. Kahn argues that there is a liberalism of the will that can and does demand sacrifice. Liberalism of interest and reason, however, cannot acknowledge the sacrifices required by the state. The result is what Kahn calls the "paradox of democratic self-government," that is, "the more the nation believes itself to be a product of the will of the popular sovereign, the less democratic it becomes—if by democratic, we mean subject to control through broadly participatory electoral mechanisms." Kahn suggests this is the modern form of Rousseau's distinction between the general will and the will of all (*Putting Liberalism In Its Place*, 161).

14. For an extremely informative comparison of the Catholic and Protestant responses to secularization see Martin, *The Future of Christianity*, 25–44. Perreau-Saussine's *Catholicism and Democracy* is a fascinating account of the rise of the political importance of the papacy after the French Revolution was at once the manifestation as well as the result of the Catholic agreement with the liberal presumption that there is "something irreducibly secular about the modern state" (p. 2).

15. Yeago, "Messiah's People," 148–49.

of tradition and doctrine. Hart, whose prose begs for extensive quotation, says the story goes like this:

> Once upon a time Western humanity was the cosseted and incurious ward of Mother Church; during this, the age of faith, culture stagnated, science languished, wars of religion were routinely waged, witches were burned by inquisitors, and Western humanity labored in brutish subjugation to dogma, superstition, and the unholy alliance of church and state. Withering blasts of fanaticism and fideism had long since scorched away the last remnants of classical learning; inquiry was stifled; the literary remains of classical antiquity had long ago been consigned to the fires of faith, and even the great achievements of "Greek science" were forgotten until Islamic civilization restored them to the West. All was darkness. Then, in the wake of the "wars of religion" that had torn Christendom apart, came the full flowering of the Enlightenment and with it the reign of reason and progress, the riches of scientific achievement and political liberty, and a new and revolutionary sense of human dignity. The secular nation-state arose, reduced religion to an establishment of the state, and thereby rescued Western humanity from the blood-steeped intolerance of religion. Now, at last, Western humanity has left its nonage and attained its majority, in science, politics, and ethics. The story of the travails of Galileo almost invariably occupies an honored place in this narrative, as exemplary of the natural relation between "faith" and "reason" and as an exquisite epitome of scientific reason's mighty struggle during the early modern period to free itself from the tyranny of religion.[16]

This "simple and enchanting tale" is, Hart observes, captivating in its explanatory power. According to Hart, however, there is just one problem with this story. The problem is that every detail of the story, as well as the overarching plot, just happens to be false.[17] Hart's book provides the arguments and evidence to sustain that judgment. What I find so interesting, however, is even if the narrative may be false in every detail, it is nonetheless true that believer and unbeliever alike assume, though they may disagree about some of the details, that the main plot of the story is true.

That this story now has canonical status has deep significance for how Christians should understand the relation between faith and politics. Put even more strongly, in the interest of being good citizens, of being civil,

16. Hart, *Atheist Delusions*, 33–34.
17. Ibid., 34.

Christians have lost the ability to say why what they believe is true. That loss is, I want to suggest, a correlative of the depolitization of the church as a community capable of challenging the imperial pretensions of the modern state. That the church matters is why I resist using the language of "belief" to indicate what allegedly makes Christians Christian.[18] Of course Christians "believe in God," but far more important for determining the character of Christian existence is that it is constituted by a politics that cannot avoid challenging what is normally identified as "the political." For what is normally identified as "the political" produces dualisms that invite questions such as, "What is the relation between faith and politics?" If I am right, that "and" prematurely ends any serious theological reflection from a Christian perspective.

As I have already indicated, to make this argument necessarily puts me at odds with the attempt to make Christian convictions compatible with the epistemological and moral presumptions of liberal social orders. That project presumed a story very much along the lines suggest by Hart. Theologians trimmed the sails of Christian convictions to show that even if the metaphysical commitments that seem intrinsic to Christian practice cannot be intellectually sustained it remains the case that Christianity can claim some credit for the creation of the culture and politics of modernity.

In particular, Christian theologians sought to justify Christian participation in the politics of democratic societies. The field of Christian ethics, the discipline with which I am identified, had as one of its primary agendas to convince Christians that their "beliefs" had political implications. The determinative representative who exemplified this mode of Christian ethical reflection was Reinhold Niebuhr. Thus his claim that "the real problem of a Christian social ethic is to derive from the gospel a clear view of the realities with which we must deal in our common or social life, and also to preserve a sense of responsibility for achieving the highest measure of order, freedom and justice despite the hazards of man's collective life."[19] Niebuhr reminded Christians that we do not live in a world in which sin can be eliminated, but we nonetheless must seek to establish the tentative harmonies and provisional equities possible in any historical situation.

18. In his magisterial book, *The Unintended Reformation*, Brad Gregory observes that the Reformation placed an unprecedented emphasis on doctrine for identifying what made Christians Christians. Such an emphasis led Protestant and Catholic alike to emphasize the importance of an "interior assent to the propositional content of doctrinal truth claims, whatever they were." Gregory observes this development "risked making Christianity seem more a matter of what one believed than how one lived—of making the faith a crypto-Cartesian matter of one's soul and mind, *rather than* a matter of what one does with one's body" (p. 155).

19. Niebuhr, *Reinhold Niebuhr on Politics*, 153.

Niebuhr, who prided himself for being a sober realist challenging what he took to be the unfounded optimism of liberal thinkers such as John Dewey, would have in a like manner called into question the optimism of the story Hart associates with the celebration, if not the legitimization, of modernity. But Niebuhr's support of liberal democratic political arrangements drew on a narrative very much like the one Hart identifies as the story of modernity.[20] The result is ironic, a category Niebuhr loved, because Niebuhr's arguments for the political engagement by Christians presupposed a narrative that legitimates political arrangement that requires the privatization of Christian convictions. One of the consequences being the loss of any attempt to say what it might mean for the gospel of Jesus Christ to be true.

For instance, one of the curiosities associated with what has been popularly called "the new atheists" is their assumption that the most decisive challenges to the truthfulness of Christian convictions come from developments in the sciences, or perhaps more accurately put, the "method" of science. Such a view fails to appreciate that the most decisive challenge to the truthfulness of Christian convictions is political.[21] The politics of modernity has so successfully made Christianity but another life-style option that it is a mystery why the new atheists think it is important to show what Christians believe to be false. Such a project hardly seems necessary given that Christians, in the name of being good democratic citizens, live lives of unacknowledged but desperate unbelief just to the extent they believe that what they believe as a Christian cannot be a matter of truth. As a result Christians no longer believe that the church is an alternative politics to the politics of the world, which means they have lost any way to account for why Christians in the past thought they had a faith worth dying for.

2. The Witness of Karl Barth

I need an example of what the connection between the truthfulness of Christian speech and politics might look like. An example is necessary because I am not sure we know what Christianity so understood would look

---

20. For a fuller defense of this account of Niebuhr see my *Wilderness Wanderings*, 32–62, and *With the Grain of the Universe*, 87–140.

21. David Martin nicely shows the assumption that science makes theological claims unintelligible is simply not sustainable. See his *The Future of Christianity*, 119–31. Brad Gregory observes that "empirical investigation of the natural world has not falsified any theological claims." Much more troubling for the status of the truthfulness of Christian convictions, according to Gregory, was the unresolved disputes between Protestant and Catholic concerning the meaning of God's actions (*The Unintended Reformation*, 47).

like. I think, however, we have the beginnings in the work of Karl Barth. Barth, more than any theologian in modernity, recognized that the recovery of the language of the faith entailed a politics at odds with the world as we know it. For Barth there is no kernel of the Christian faith, because it begins and ends with the extraordinary claim that what we mean when we say "God" is to be determined by Mary's willingness to be impregnated by the Holy Spirit.

That is not where Barth began. Barth began presuming the work of Protestant liberal theologians was a given. It was, however, a political event that called into question Barth's liberalism. On a day in early August of 1914, Barth read a proclamation in support of the war policy of Wilhelm II, signed by ninety-three German intellectuals. To Barth's horror almost all his venerated theological teachers were among the names of those who had signed in support of the war. Barth confesses he suddenly realized that he could no longer follow their theology or ethics. At that moment the theology of the nineteenth century, the theology of Protestant liberalism, came to an end for Barth.[22]

Barth characterized the theology he thought must be left behind, a theology identified by figures such as Schleiermacher and Troeltsch, as the attempt to respond to the modern age by underwriting the assumption that Christianity is but an expression of the alleged innate human capacity for the infinite. From such a perspective Christianity is understood to be but one particular expression of religion. Such a view of the Christian faith presumed that the primary task of Christian theology is to assure the general acceptance of the Christian faith for the sustaining of the achievements of Western civilization. Barth observed theology so conceived was more interested in man's relationship with God than God's dealings with man.[23]

For Barth, however, a theology understood as the realization, in one form or another, of human self-awareness could have no ground or content other than ourselves. "Faith as the Christian commerce with God could first and last be only the Christian commerce with himself."[24] The figure haunting such an account of Christianity is Feuerbach, whom Barth thought had powerfully reconfigured the Christian faith as a statement of profound human needs and desires.

---

22. Barth, *The Humanity of God*, 14.

23. Ibid., 24. Barth noted, however, that theology so understood could be in continuity with Melanchthon's emphasis on the benefits of Christ. So there is no reason that an attempt should not be made to develop a Christian anthropocentrism in which theology is done, so to speak, from the bottom up.

24. Ibid., 26.

Drawing on Kierkegaard, Dostoevsky, and Overbeck, as well as his discovery of what he characterized as "the strange new world of the Bible," against the theology of his teachers, Barth proclaimed: "God is God."[25] Barth did not think such a claim to be redundant, but rather to be the best expression of who God is; it is a response to the particularity of a God who has initiated an encounter with humankind. Barth says, "the stone wall we first ran up against was that the theme of the Bible is the deity of *God*, more exactly God's *deity*—God's independence and particular character, not only in relation to the natural but also to the spiritual cosmos; God's absolutely unique existence, might, and initiative, above all, in His relation to man."[26]

So Barth challenged what he characterized as the accommodated theology of Protestant liberalism using expressions such as God is "wholly other," breaking in upon us "perpendicularly from above." There is an "infinite qualitative distinction" between God and us, rendering any presumption that we can know God on our terms to be just that, namely, a presumption based on sinful pride. Thus, Barth's sobering claim that God is God and we are not means that it can never be the case that we have the means to know God unless God first makes himself known to us.

Barth later acknowledged that his initial reaction against Protestant liberal theology was exaggerated, but any theology committed to clearing the ground for a fresh expression of the Christian faith could not help but sound extreme. Barth acknowledged that his first salvos against Protestant liberalism seemed to be saying that God is everything and man nothing. Such a God, the God that is wholly other, isolated and set over against man, threatens to become the God of the philosophers rather than the God who called Abraham. The majesty of the God of the philosophers might have the contradictory results of confirming the hopelessness of all human activity while offering a new justification of the autonomy of man. Barth wanted neither of these results.

In retrospect Barth, however, confesses he was wrong exactly where he was right, but at the time he did not know how to carry through with sufficient care the discovery of God's deity.[27] For Barth the decisive breakthrough came with the recognition that "who God is and what He is in His deity He proves and reveals not in a vacuum as a divine being-for-Himself, but precisely and authentically in the fact that he exists, speaks, and acts as

---

25. Timothy Gorringe suggests that Barth may well have seen *A Midsummer Night's Dream*, whose "Well roared Lion!" he liked to use to characterize his reaction against Protestant liberalism (*Karl Barth*, 25).
26. Barth, *The Humanity of God*, 41.
27. Ibid., 44.

the *partner* of man, though of course as the absolute superior partner."[28] In short, Barth discovered that it is precisely God's deity which includes and constitutes God's humanity.

We are not dealing with an abstract God, that is, a God whose deity exists separated from man, because in Jesus Christ there can be no isolation of man from God or God from man. In Barth's language:

> God's deity in Jesus Christ consists in the fact that God Himself in Him is the *subject* who speaks and acts with sovereignty. . . . In Jesus Christ man's freedom is wholly enclosed in the freedom of God. Without the condescension of God there would be no exaltation of man. . . . We have no universal deity capable of being reached conceptually, but this concrete deity—real and recognizable in the *descent* grounded in that sequence and peculiar to the existence of Jesus Christ.[29]

I am aware that this all too brief account of Barth's decisive theological turn may seem but a report on esoteric methodological issues in Christian theology. But I ask you to remember that Barth's discovery of the otherness of God, an otherness intrinsic to God's humanity, was occasioned by his recognition of the failure of the politics and ethics of modern theology in the face of the First World War. I think it not accidental, moreover, that Barth was among the first to recognize the character of the politics represented by Hitler. Barth was a person of unusual insight, or as Timothy Gorringe describes him, he was a person of extraordinary vitality who was a profoundly political animal.[30] But his perception of the threat the Nazis represented cannot be separated from his theological turn, occasioned by his reaction against his teachers who supported the war.

Tim Gorringe rightly argues in his book, *Karl Barth: Against Hegemony*, that Barth never assumed his theology might have political implications because his theology *was* a politics. That way of putting the matter, that is, "his theology was a politics" is crucial. The very structure of Barth's *Dogmatics*, Gorringe suggests, with its integration of theology and ethics displayed in his refusal to separate law from gospel, was Barth's way of refusing any distinction between theory and practice. Barth's Christocentrism meant that his "theology was never a predicate of his politics, but also true that politics is never simply a predicate of his theology."[31]

---

28. Ibid., 46.
29. Ibid., 48.
30. Gorringe, *Karl Barth*, 11.
31. Ibid., 9.

Gorringe's argument that Barth was a political theologian was confirmed in 1934, the same year Barth wrote the Barmen Declaration,[32] by Barth's response to a challenge by some Americans and English critics that his theology was too abstract and unrelated to actual lives. Barth begins his defense by observing that he is, after all, "a modern man" who stands in the midst of this age. Like his questioners he too must live a life, not merely in theory but in practice, in what he characterizes as the "stormy present." Accordingly he tells his antagonists that "exactly because I was called to live in a modern world, did I reach the path of which you have heard me speak."[33]

In particular, Barth calls attention to his years as a pastor in which he faced the task of preaching the gospel in the face of secularism. During this time he was confronted with the modern world, but he was also confronted with the modern church. It was a church, a church of great sincerity and zeal with fervid devotion to deeds of charity, too closely related to the modern world. It was a church that no longer knew God's choice to love the world by what Christians have been given to do in the light of that love, that is, to be witnesses to the treasure that is the gospel. The problem, according to Barth, is that the church of the pious man, this church of the good man, this church of the moral man, became the church of man.[34] The result was the fusion of Christianity and nationalism.[35]

Consequently the modern church is a near relative to the Godless modern world. That error, Barth suggests, began two hundred years before the present with Pietism's objections to orthodoxy. In the Reformation the church heard of God and of Christ, but love was not active.[36] The fatal error

---

32. The Barmen Declaration was the statement of protest by the Confessing Church, that is, the church in opposition to Hitler's formation of the German Christian Church. The synod met in Barmen on 4 Jan. 1934. Though the Barmen Declaration was a joint effort of several theologians, Barth was the primary author.

33. Barth, *God In Action*, 133. This little gem of a book contains lectures Barth gave in response to the Nazis in 1934.

34. The role of Pietism for the development of Protestant liberal theology as well as the legitimating discourse for the subordination of the church to the state is a story in itself. It is not accidental that Barth was the great enemy of pietism. David Martin suggests that pietism was the ultimate working out of the implications of the Protestant Reformation for the development of the centralized sovereignty necessary to legitimate the formation of the nation state. He observes, "German Pietism inculcated disciplines that helped ensure the smooth running of the state" (*The Future of Christianity*, 199).

35. Barth, *God in Action*, 134–35.

36. In his book, *The Unintended Reformation*, Brad Gregory convincingly argues "that the Western world today is an extraordinarily complex, tangled project of rejections, retentions, and transformations of medieval Western Christianity, in which the Reformation era constitutes the critical watershed." The secularization that was the result of the Reformation was, according to Gregory, unintended but no less a reality (p. 2).

was the Christian response: they did not say, let God be even more God, and Christ be even more the Christ, but instead they said let us improve matters ourselves. Reverence for the pious man became reverence for the moral man, and finally, when it was found that man is of so large an importance, it became less important to speak of God, of Christ, of the Holy Spirit. Instead men began to speak of human reason.[37]

Barth then directly addresses his questioners, whom he identifies as "friends," to tell them he is well aware of what is happening, and that is exactly why he insists that he must speak of God. He must speak of God because he must begin with the confession, "I am from Germany." Because he is from Germany he knows that he stands in a place that has reached the end of a road, a road that he acknowledges may be just beginning in social orders like America and England. Yet Barth claims he is sure that what has been experienced in Germany, that is, the remarkable apostasy of the church to nationalism, will also be the fate of those who think Barth's theology to be a retreat from political engagement. Thus, Barth's challenge to his critics: "if you make a start with 'God *and* . . .' you are opening the doors to every demon."[38]

Barth early recognized such a demon had been let loose in the person of Hitler. He was able to do so because Hitler's attempt to make Christianity a state religion by creating the German Church meant the free preaching of the gospel was prohibited. Theological speech and politics were inseparable. It is, therefore, no accident that Barth in the Barmen Declaration challenged the "German Christians" on Christological grounds. He does so because Barth assumes that Jesus' claim, "I am the way, and the truth, and life; no one comes to the Father, but by me" (John 14:6), is the defining politics of Christianity. Barth writes:

> Jesus Christ, as he is attested for us in Holy Scripture, is the one word of God which we have to hear and which we have to trust and obey in life and in death. We reject the false doctrine, as though the Church could and would have to acknowledge as a source of its proclamation, apart from and beside this one word of God, still other events and powers, figures and truths, as God's revelation.[39]

The witness that is Karl Barth, that is, how such a life fits into the ongoing story we must tell as Christians of our faithful and unfaithful living out

---

37. Barth, *God in Action*, 137.
38. Ibid., 138.
39. I am quoting from Cochrane, *The Church's Confession Under Hitler*, 172–78.

the gospel, means there is no way we can avoid making clear to ourselves and the world that we believe a new world began in the belly of Mary.

3. Where Are We Now? Where Do We Need To Go?

You may be rightly wondering, if not worried, where all this has gotten us. I should like to be able to say more about where we are now and where we need to go but I am unsure who the "we" or the "us" may be. I have assumed I should, or perhaps more truthfully, I can only speak from a first person perspective, but hopefully it is one shaped by my Christian identity. Yet just as Barth confessed that he was German, so I must acknowledge I am American. Indeed, it may be I am more American than Christian, and thus tempted to confuse the Christian "we" and the American "we." That confusion tempts Americans to assume we represent what any right-thinking person should say because our "we" is the universal "we."

American presumption is always a problem, but the problem is deeper than my American identity. For I think none of us can assume an agreed upon "we" or "us" to be a manifestation of the cultural and political challenges that befall us at any time. Given the difficulty of locating the "we," some may worry that directing attention to Barth in order to show the political character of Christian convictions is morally and politically the exemplification of a profoundly reactionary position. In Nazi Germany a Barmen Declaration may have seemed "prophetic," but "after Hitler" a Barmen-like account of the politics of Christian convictions suggests theocracy.[40]

I confess I often enjoy making liberal friends, particularly American liberal friends, nervous by acknowledging I am, of course, a theocrat. "Jesus is Lord" is not my personal opinion; I take it to be a determinative political claim. So I am ready to rule. The difficulty is that following a crucified Lord entails embodying a politic that cannot resort to coercion and violence; it is a politic of persuasion all the way down. A tiring business that is slow and time consuming, but then we, that is, Christians, believe that by redeeming time Christ has given us all the time we need to pursue peace. Christ, through the Holy Spirit, bestows upon his disciples the longsuffering patience necessary to resist any politic whose impatience makes coercion and violence the only and inevitable response to conflict.

---

40. During a visit to the Holocaust Museum in Washington, DC, my wife and I encountered school children wearing shirts emblazoned with the slogan, "Celebrate Diversity." There is much good no doubt in training the young to enjoy difference, but I worry for those who think the celebration of diversity an adequate response to a movement like National Socialism.

For fifteen hundred years Christians thought Jesus' lordship meant they should rule the world. That rule assumed diverse forms, some beneficial and some quite destructive. "Constantinianism" or Christendom are descriptions of the various ways that Christians sought to determine the cultural and political life of the worlds in which they found themselves. Some Christians look with nostalgia on that past, seeking ways to recapture Christian dominance of the world. That is obviously not my perspective.

For as David Hart observes, Christianity's greatest historical triumph was also its most calamitous defeat. The conversion of the Roman Empire in which it was thought the faith overthrew the powers of "this age" found that the faith itself had become subordinate to those very powers. Like Hart I have no reason to deny the many achievements of Christendom. I think he is right to suggest that the church was a revolution, a slow and persistent revolution, a cosmic sedition, in which the human person was "invested with an intrinsic and inviolable dignity" by being recognized as God's own.[41] But this revolution, exactly because it was so radical, was absorbed and subdued by society in which nominal baptism became the expression of a church that was reduced to an instrument of temporal power and the gospel was made a captive to the mechanism of the state.[42]

In *The Stillborn God*, Mark Lilla has written in defense of what he calls "the great separation" of politics and religion represented by Hobbes. He observes that though Christianity is inescapably political it has proved incapable of integrating this fact into Christian theology.[43] The problem, according to Lilla, is that to be a Christian means being in the world, including the political world, but somehow not being of it. Such a way of being, Lilla argues, cannot help but produce a false consciousness. Christendom is the institutionalization of this consciousness just to the extent the church thought reconciliation could be expressed politically.[44] Politics so constituted cannot help but suffer from permanent instability.

---

41. Hart, *Atheist Delusions*, 167.

42. Ibid., 194. It is true, nonetheless, as Brad Gregory argues in *The Unintended Reformation*, that the church was never coextensive with or absorbed by any secular political entity. A thousand years after Constantine, from the papacy to the parishes into which Christendom was parceled, the church remained distinct from secular political entities, such as medieval kingdoms, principalities, duchies, and cities and city states (pp. 136–37). One of the great virtues of Gregory's book is his treatment of the often ignored Anabaptist. He rightly understands the Anabaptist alternative to represent a political alternative to the magisterial Reformers just to the extent the latter led to the increasing control of the church by the state.

43. Lilla, *The Stillborn God*, 85.

44. Ibid., 169

Lilla, I think, is right that the eschatological character of the Christian faith will challenge the politics of the worlds in which it finds itself. But that is why, even at times when the church fails to be true to its calling to be a political alternative, God raises up a Karl Barth. For as Barth insisted, this really is all about God, the particular God of Jesus Christ. The humanity of that God Christians believe has made it possible for a people to exist who do in fact, as Nietzsche suggested, exemplify a slave morality. It is a morality Hart describes as a "strange, impractical, altogether unworldly tenderness" expressed in the ability to see as our sisters and brothers the autistic or Down syndrome or disabled child, a child who is a perpetual perplexity for the world, a child who can cause pain and only fleetingly charm or delight; or in the derelict or broken man or woman who has wasted their life; or the homeless, the diseased, the mentally ill, criminals and reprobates.[45]

Such a morality is the matter that is the church. It is the matter that made even a church in Christendom uneasy. From the church's standpoint today, Christendom may be a lamentable world now lost, but it is not clear what will replace or shape the resulting culture or politics. Hart observes that when Christianity passes from a culture the resulting remainder may be worse than if Christianity had never existed. Christians took the gods away and no one will ever believe them again. Christians demystified the world, robbing good pagans of their reverence and hard won wisdom derived from the study of human and nonhuman nature. So once again Nietzsche was right that the Christians shaped a world that meant that those who would come after Christianity could not avoid nihilism.[46]

Why this is the case is perhaps best exemplified by how time is understood. Christians, drawing as they must on God's calling of Israel to be the promised people, cannot help but believe that time has a plot, that is to say, Christians believe in history. A strange phrase to be sure, but one to remind us of how extraordinary it is for Christians to believe we come from a past that will find its fulfillment in the future. Accordingly, we believe that time has a narrative logic, which means time is not just one damn thing after another. The story of creation is meant to remind us that all that exists lends witness to the glory of God, giving history a significance otherwise unavailable. Creation, redemption, reconciliation are names for Christians that we believe constitute the basic plotline that makes history more than a tale told by an idiot.[47]

---

45. Hart, *Atheist Delusions*, 213–14.
46. Ibid., 229–30.
47. Ibid., 201–2.

Yet the very assumption that history has a direction is the necessary condition that underwrites the story of modernity earlier characterized by Hart. The story that has underwritten the new atheist's presumption that if history is finally rid of Christianity we will discover that through unconstrained reason how our politics can be made more just and humane. Thus Hart speculates that the violence done in the name of humanity, a violence that is now unconstrained, might never have been unleashed if Christianity had not introduced its "peculiar variant of apocalyptic yearning into Western culture."[48] Hart rightly observes that such a judgment is purely speculative given the reality that past great empires prior to Christianity claimed divine warrants for murder. Yet Hart thinks that the secularization of Christian eschatological grammar is the "chief cause of the modern state's curious talent for mass murder."[49] An exaggerated claim, perhaps, but it is at least a reminder that it is by no means clear why the killing called war is distinguishable from mass murder.[50]

This last observation, I hope, draws us back to Karl Barth's theological work. I suggested Barth exemplifies the politics of speech that is at the heart of Christian convictions. At the heart of Christian convictions is the belief in "the humanity of God," a humanity made unavoidable by our faith in Jesus Christ as the second person of the Trinity. Christ's humanity means no account of the church is possible that does not require material expression that is rightly understood as a politic. Church matters matter not only for the church, but we believe what is a necessity for the church is a possibility for all that is not the church.

48. Ibid., 222–23.
49. Ibid., 223–24.
50. In a recent blog post entitled "Bend Your Knee," *The Hooded Utilitarian*, Noah Berlatsky, defends my arguments for pacifism against Eric Cohen's critique of my book, *War and the American Difference*, that appeared in the conservative magazine, *First Things* (April 2012), http://www.firstthings.com/article/2012/03/the-sacrifices-of-war (accessed 24 June 2013). Cohen described my views as "a form of eschatological madness"—a description that Berlatsky quite rightly suggests I would happily accept. Berlatsky suggests that Cohen missed my argument that war produces its own logic and morality. In fact, according to Berlatsky, Cohen's defense of war as a heroic story exemplifies the view of war I was criticizing; when war becomes a "heroic story" it becomes idolatry. He observes that though I would like to get rid of war, what I really want to get rid of is a church of war. What Cohen missed is that my argument is aimed at Christians. Berlatsky then makes what was for me the surprising claim that he finds this to be a relief for someone like him because he is an atheist, so he can cheerfully continue to support Caesar. Yet he observes there is a bit of discomfort because if Christians began to take up non-violence, and he hates to have to say it, "it would be hard to escape the suspicion that that might actually be the work of God." http://hoodedutilitarian.com/2012/04/bend-your-knee/ (accessed 24 June 2013).

I suspect humans always live in times of transition; what is time if not transition? But I believe we are living in a time when Christendom is actually coming to an end. That is an extraordinary transition whose significance for Christian and non-Christian has yet to be understood. But in the very least it means the church is finally free to be a politic. If I may summarize what I take to be one appropriate response to this observation it is quite simply this: let Christians make the most of it.

Bibliography

Barth, Karl. *God In Action*. Reprint. Eugene, OR: Wipf & Stock, 2005.
———. *The Humanity of God*. Richmond, VA: John Knox, 1963.
Beiner, Ronald. *Civil Religion: A Dialogue in the History of Political Philosophy*. Cambridge: Cambridge University Press, 2011.
Berlatsky, Noah. "Bend Your Knee." *The Hooded Utilitarian* (18 April 2012). http://hoodedutilitarian.com/2012/04/bend-your-knee/ (accessed 16 March 2014).
Cavanaugh, William T. *The Myth of Religious Violence*. Oxford: Oxford University Press, 2009.
Cochrane, Arthur. *The Church's Confession Under Hitler*. Philadelphia: Westminster, 1962.
Cohen, Eric. "The Sacrifices of War." *First Things* (April 2012). http://www.firstthings.com/article/2012/03/the-sacrifices-of-war (accessed 16 March 2014).
Gorringe, Timothy. *Karl Barth: Against Hegemony*. Oxford: Oxford University Press, 1999.
Gregory, Brad. *The Unintended Reformation: How a Religious Revolution Secularized Society*. Cambridge: Harvard University Press, 2012.
Hart, David Bentley. *Atheist Delusions: The Christian Revolution and Its Fashionable Enemies*. New Haven: Yale University Press, 2009.
Hauerwas, Stanley. *War and the American Difference*. Grand Rapids: Baker, 2011.
———. *Wilderness Wanderings: Probing Twentieth-Century Theology and Philosophy*. Boulder, CO: Westview, 1997
———. *With the Grain of the Universe: The Church's Witness and Natural Theology*. Grand Rapids: Brazos, 2001.
Kahn, Paul. *Putting Liberalism in Its Place*. Princeton: Princeton University Press, 2005.
Lilla, Mark. *The Stillborn God: Religion, Politics, and the Modern West*. New York: Knopf, 2007.
MacIntyre, Alasdair. *The Religious Significance of Atheism*. New York: Columbia University Press, 1966.
Martin, David. *The Future of Christianity: Reflections on Violence and Democracy, Religion and Secularization*. Farnham, UK: Ashgate, 2011.
Niebuhr, Reinhold. *Reinhold Niebuhr on Politics*. Edited by Harry Davis and Robert Good. New York: Scribner's, 1960.
Perreau-Saussine, Emile. *Catholicism and Democracy: An Essay in the History of Political Thought*. Princeton: Princeton University Press, 2011.
Schmitt, Carl. *Political Theology: Four Chapters on the Concept of Sovereignty*. Chicago: University of Chicago Press, 2005.

Williams, Raymond. *Keywords: A Vocabulary of Culture and Society.* Oxford: Oxford University Press, 1976.

Yeago, David. "Messiah's People: The Culture of the Church in the Midst of the Nations." *Pro Ecclesia* 6/2 (1997) 146–71.

18

Theology After Pandora

The Real Scandal of the Evangelical Mind (and Culture)

F. LeRon Shults

Introduction

STAN GRENZ LOVED TO make connections between theology and popular culture, and he had a special predilection for science fiction—especially *Star Trek* (Next Generation, of course) and *X-Files* (like agent Mulder, he believed the truth was "out there"). He also knew that our fascination with extra-terrestrials is more about our own alienation, our own strangely anxious and hopeful sentience, than it is about imagined alien creatures. More than most evangelical theologians, Stan focused on what was happening here and now on planet Earth. Nevertheless, like every other evangelical I know, he also anticipated an eschatological renewal of this world, a new earth (and a new heaven), re-created in some sense by the supernatural agency of Christ. In this essay I borrow one of Stan's well known methodological strategies, reflecting on theological themes in the context of engaging a popular science fiction film. Although he almost certainly would not have agreed with my material proposal, I know he would have welcomed the conversation.[1]

---

1. I want to thank the editors of this *Festschrift* for their generosity in allowing me to contribute such a scandalous essay. As they wisely suggested, I have done my best to

One might think that the reference to "Pandora" in the main title of this chapter was to the Greek myth in which the first woman, modeled of clay by Hephaestus as part of Zeus's punishment of mankind for Prometheus' theft of fire, released evils into the world by opening a box (or jar) given to her by the gods. In the conclusion I will return to poor Pandora, but the reference here is actually to the planet Pandora in the 2009 film *Avatar*.[2] The film portrays the conflict between the Na'vi, the (mostly) friendly natives of Pandora, and the invading human forces of the RDA mining corporation, the (mostly) nasty humans bent on acquiring the aptly named "unobtainium" buried beneath the surface of the planet. I use this fictional account of a conflict of ideas and societies on Pandora as material for reflecting on the possibilities for theology to respond in new ways to the intellectual and political challenges we face here and now on planet Earth.

My sub-title plays on the title of the influential book by Mark Noll, *The Scandal of the Evangelical Mind*, which he begins by asserting that "the scandal of the evangelical mind is that there is not much of an evangelical mind. . . . American evangelicals have failed notably in sustaining serious intellectual life."[3] In his more recent *Jesus Christ and the Life of the Mind*, Noll finds some signs for modest optimism but remains "largely unrepentant" of his negative evaluation.[4] Stan Grenz was an obvious exception. His scholarship set a standard of excellence among those who self-identified as part of the North American evangelical subculture. Fundamentalists were often scandalized by his writings, not for Nollian reasons, but because he challenged the *status quo* they were so concerned to protect. Nevertheless, the existence of a few such scholars does not diminish the larger point: Noll is right to decry the lack of intellectual rigor among evangelicals. The problem, however, is much deeper and more serious than Noll acknowledges.

The real scandal of the evangelical mind cannot be separated from the scandal of the evangelical *culture*, and vice versa. Balancing piety with more appreciation of the Christian intellectual tradition will not solve the problem. Balancing social concern with better scholarship will not solve the problem. Such efforts merely reorganize the chairs on the deck of the sinking Titanic (to allude to another film by James Cameron). The deeper problem facing evangelicalism is one that is shared by other religious coalitions. Although the material details of evangelical belief in and hope for eschatological renewal have their own particularities, they are formally structured

---

maintain an irenic tone.

2. Directed by James Cameron, 2009 (20th Century Fox).
3. Noll, *Scandal*, 3.
4. Noll, *Jesus Christ*, 151.

by the same evolved tendencies that have contributed to the emergence of religion in every known human society: widely shared imaginative engagement with person-like supernatural agents who are interested in the moral activity of specific groups.[5]

Evangelicals will continue to stumble as long as they cannot see the hidden cognitive and coalitional mechanisms that shape their mental and social life. This essay is an attempt to unveil these mechanisms by engaging recent scientific discoveries about (and philosophical reflection on) the emergence, evolution, and transmission of human religiosity. Once we can see what we are doing, it will be easier to explore new possibilities for the discipline of theology. In the concluding section of this chapter, I propose a way of doing theology that does not appeal to extra-terrestrials (or supernatural agents) who favor a particular human coalition. For reasons I will try to make clear, I call this the *iconoclastic* trajectory of theology.

The first three sub-sections set out the basic argument of the chapter. First, I outline a conceptual framework that describes a convergence of findings and theories in the bio-cultural sciences of religion, which help to explain why "religion" is so prevalent in human cultures. Second, I use this framework to analyze the "theological" options portrayed in the movie *Avatar*, as the (increasingly) evil capitalists fight the (initially) naïve tree-huggers for control of the planet Pandora. This then sets the stage for a description of evangelical groups as examples of a particular kind of supernatural agent coalition, typical of those religions that trace their roots to the axial age, which normally follow what I call the *sacerdotal* trajectory of theology. The *real* scandal of the evangelical mind (and culture) is that evolved mechanisms are surreptitiously shaping its theological practices, reinforcing the psychological repression and political oppression that everyone sees but no one is sure what to do about. The last two sub-sections explore the possibility of a quite different approach to doing theology.

Bearing Gods in Mind and Culture

Why are we religious? Empirical findings and theoretical reflections across a variety of fields, including archaeology, cognitive science, evolutionary neurobiology, moral psychology, social anthropology, and political theory suggest that the contemporary human beliefs, activities, and emotions normally associated with "religion" are shaped by naturally evolved

5. I will explain my use of some of these contentious terms below. Some of the themes in this essay are treated in more detail in Shults, "Bearing Gods," "Problem of Good," "Science and Religious Supremacy," and *Iconoclastic Theology*.

mechanisms that are part of our shared phylogenetic heritage. There is no space here to analyze, or even list, all of the important developments in these disciplines that bear on the bio-cultural study of religion. For my purposes here, however, it will suffice to provide a broad sketch of some of the significant trends within these fields, which coalesce in support of the general claim that shared imaginative engagement with gods naturally emerges in contemporary human minds and cultures as a result of cognitive and coalitional tendencies that helped our early hominid ancestors survive in small-scale groups, granting them a competitive advantage in the late Pleistocene environment. The question that faces us today is whether these tendencies are still adaptive in our rapidly changing, pluralistic, global environment. First, let me clarify my use of some key terms.

The term *bearing* has a double meaning, indicating the naturally evolved processes by which gods are *born* in human cognition (by the hyper-active detection of agency in the *natural* environment) and *borne* in human culture (by the hyper-active protection of coalitions in the *social* environment). By referring to these as *theogonic* (god-bearing) mechanisms, I mean to emphasize not their expression in literary accounts of the genesis of the gods, such as Hesiod's *Theogony*, but the way in which they engender any narrative imaginative engagement that reinforces the detection and protection of a specific supernatural agent coalition.

Scholars in the disciplines that contribute to the bio-cultural study of religion often use the term *god* as shorthand for any culturally-postulated, discarnate intentional force—as synonymous with "supernatural agent" or "superhuman entity."[6] In other words, not only Yahweh, Zeus, or Vishnu, but also ghosts, genies, and ghouls would be referred to as *gods*. The differences between these kinds of gods are obviously significant, but for the sake of participating in this interdisciplinary dialogue I will follow this usage in this essay. At this point, it is important to note that they all share at least two key features: intentionality and contingent embodiment.

I am using the term *supernatural* in this context to mean not necessarily embodied in the causal nexus of space-time-matter-energy as generally understood by contemporary physical cosmology. The qualifier "not necessarily" allows for the possibility that an imagined agent could be called supernatural if it is temporarily embodied but has not always been, or is potentially embodied although it might not ever be. By *agent* I mean any entity or force that is attributed intentionality or related human-like features, such as consciousness or the capacity for symbolic communication. In this

---

6. E.g., Tremlin, *Minds and Gods*; Atran, *Talking to the Enemy*; Boyer, *Future of an Illusion*; Pyysiainen, *Supernatural Agents*; and Guthrie, *Faces in the Clouds*.

sense, gods are agents postulated to have some interest in and causal power over the members of the coalition that imaginatively engages them.

A supernatural agent *coalition* is a social nexus that is held together, at least in part, by appeal to the power or authority of gods allegedly watching the group and concerned about its members' evaluative judgments and moral actions.[7] That is to say, the way in which members of the group evaluate one another's (and their own) beliefs, behaviors, and attitudes is in some way constituted or regulated by supernatural agents, who are taken to be strategic players in the survival of the group. All of this leads to my use of the term *religiosity* in this context to refer to "shared imaginative engagement with axiologically relevant supernatural agents."

With these definitions in place, I now turn to a conceptual grid (figure 1) that can help clarify the relation between some of the cognitive and coalitional tendencies studied by the bio-cultural sciences of religion. The relevant theories are more complex than I can convey here, but this framework is sufficient for its purpose, namely, as a heuristic device for showing the possible interactions between two basic sorts of proclivity found among all *Homo sapiens* (including evangelicals).

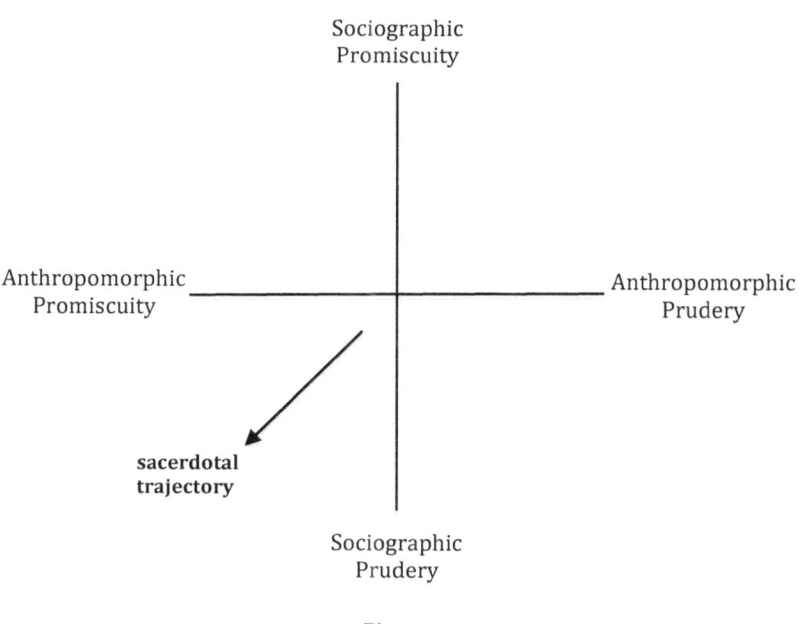

Figure 1

---

7. For theories that contribute to such claims, see Bulbulia, "Nature's Medicine"; Sosis, "Religious Behaviors"; Boyer, *Religion Explained*; Teehan, *In God's Name*.

Along the spectrum represented by the horizontal line one can mark the extent to which a person will tend to guess "human-like intentional form" when confronted with ambiguous phenomena in the natural environment. Those who are *promiscuous* in their anthropomorphic detection are always on the lookout for supernatural agents, and leap rather quickly at opportunities to attribute causality to the gods of their group. An anthropomorphic *prude*, on the other hand, resists the temptation to appeal to disembodied intentional forces when interpreting an event. He or she will reflect more carefully before giving in to the intuitive desire to grab at supernatural explanations for strange occurrences.

The vertical line represents a spectrum that registers the way in which a person holds on to conventional modes of inscribing the social field, i.e., to the proscriptions and prescriptions that regulate the evaluative practices and boundaries of the coalition(s) with which he or she primarily identifies. The sociographically *prudish* are strongly committed to the authorized social norms of their in-group, following and protecting them, even at great cost to themselves. They are more likely to be suspicious of out-groups and to accept claims or demands that appeal to authorities within their own coalition. The sociographic *promiscuity* of those at the other end of the spectrum, on the other hand, leads them to be more open to interaction with out-groups about alternate normativities and to the pursuit of new modes of creative social inscription. Such persons are also less likely to accept restrictions or assertions that are based only or primarily on appeals to convention.

The integration of anthropomorphic promiscuity and sociographic prudery was an evolutionary winner. In the early ancestral environment the selective advantage went to hominids whose cognitive capacities enabled them to quickly *detect* relevant agents (such as predators, prey, protectors, and partners) in the natural environment, and whose groups were adequately *protected* from the dissolution that could result from too many defectors and cheaters in the social environment. Hyper-sensitive detection often led to false positives, e.g., identifying a noise in the forest as a predator (or prey) when it was really the wind. However, occasionally it really was a predator (or prey), and those whose detective capacities were weak or lazy—it's probably just the wind—got eaten (or failed to eat), and so their genes were not passed on. Hyper-sensitive protection often led to serious punishment of cheaters, the demand for costly signals of commitment from those suspected of considering defection, and willingness to attack and kill members of out-groups. The good news (for the in-group) is that these strategies did in fact lead to stronger (longer-lasting) coalitions.

In fact *over*-sensitive detection and protection increased the chance of survival during a critical period of time in human history. A growing body of evidence in archaeology, anthropology, and other fields suggests that by 90,000 years before the present some *Homo sapiens* groups had developed more complex beliefs and rituals in which they imaginatively engaged supernatural agents (such as animal-spirits) they detected in the environment.[8] These contingently embodied intentional forces were believed to have the power to punish cheaters or defectors (or their family members); moreover, they might be watching at any time. Such beliefs would have increased the motivation to follow social norms. By around 60,000 years ago it appears that some of these "god-bearing" groups left Africa, out-competing all other hominid species and spreading out across the Levant and into Europe and Asia, eventually incorporating other kinds of supernatural agents such as ancestor-ghosts into their rituals and belief systems.

All living humans are the genetic offspring of these groups, and so share a suite of inherited traits that support the tendency to detect supernatural agents and protect supernatural coalitions. In other words, human beings today are intuitively and "naturally" drawn into the bio-cultural gravitational force of the integrated theogonic (god-bearing) mechanisms in the lower left quadrant of figure 1. These evolved traits were tweaked differently in various contexts, which led to the diversity of manifestations of religious life we see across cultures. That is to say, supernatural agent conceptions are never immaculate; the particular features of our gods betray our religious family of origin.

During the axial age (800–200 BCE), the challenges of pluralism and organizational hierarchy in complex literate states across west, south, and east Asia required more complicated and stronger forms of coalition. In other words, bigger cultures needed bigger gods. In the monotheistic religions that trace their roots to Abraham (Judaism, Christianity, and Islam), this takes the form of belief in an infinite person-like supernatural agent who has power over all coalitions whatsoever. These religions are *sacerdotal* insofar as they require their members to signal commitment to the group by costly participation in "priestly" rituals that are intended to mediate the power of the "sacred." When *theology* follows this sacerdotal trajectory, it reinforces detection of the particular supernatural agent concerned about the well-being (and obedience) of a particular coalition. Such an organizational strategy has worked relatively well for centuries, at least from the perspective of those coalitions whose crusades against and colonization of religious others has enhanced their own prosperity.

---

8. E.g., Rossano, *Supernatural Selection*; Lewis-Williams, *Conceiving God*.

Avatar Theology

What does any of this have to do with the imaginary planet of Pandora? Like most science fiction, the movie *Avatar* portrays a mixture of dystopian anxieties and utopian idealizations projected from the writers' own concerns or hopes about contemporary human society. As far as we can tell, nothing like an axial age had occurred on Pandora; the writers depict the Na'vi (and other indigenous tribes) as an odd combination of shamanic small-scale clans and proto-barbarian despotic states. The RDA corporation is a stereotypical organizational cog within an industrial-military complex, driven by nothing more than a lust for more profit. Some of the scientists hired by RDA, however, want to study (and perhaps even learn from) the Na'vi.

As we saw above, the evolutionary default for human beings on planet Earth is toward the integration of theogonic mechanisms, falling into the lower left quadrant of the grid introduced above. The two main groups combating in the movie *Avatar*, the Na'vi and RDA, can be taken to represent the upper left and lower right quadrants of the grid (figure 2) respectively. The way in which they integrate cognitive and coalitional tendencies lead to what I call the prodigal and penurious trajectories of theology.

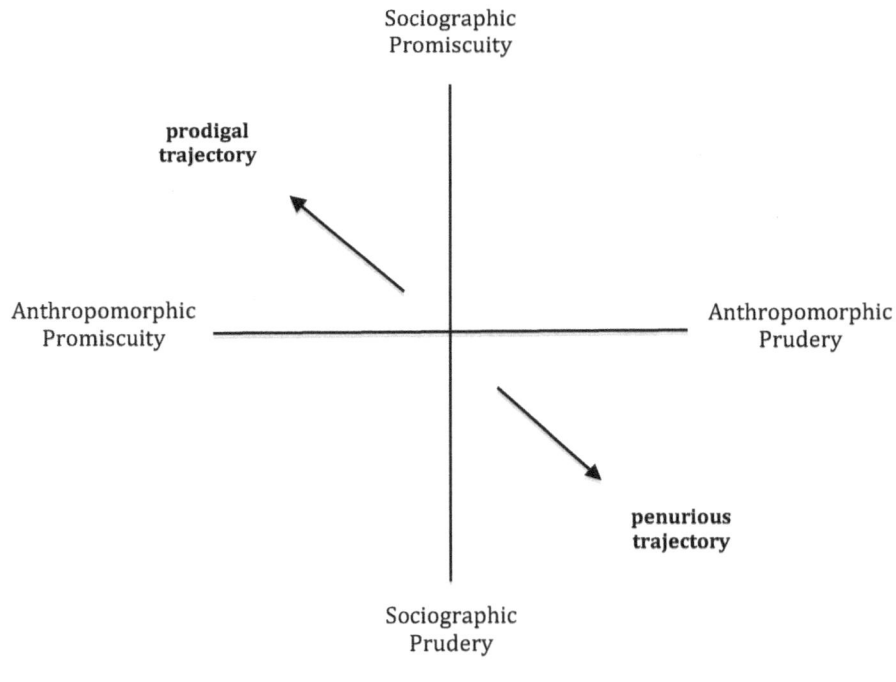

Figure 2

The Na'vi are anthropomorphically promiscuous: supernatural agency is detected at work in moss, trees, animals, and mountains. They are quite open (at least initially) to other modes of inscribing the socius, enthusiastically sending their children to the school run by the RDA scientists. The corporate leaders of RDA, on the other hand, are anthropomorphic prudes, refusing to acknowledge even the human-like agency of the Na'vi, whom they refer to as "blue monkeys." Members of the RDA coalition are also prudish in their sociography, forcing their own norms upon others, with little patience for anything that challenges their capitalist inscriptions.

I call the trajectory in the upper left corner *prodigal* because it is promiscuous in relation to *both* the cognitive and coalitional tendencies; i.e., it can lead to an extravagant expenditure of energy on imaginative engagement with supernatural agents (ubiquitous detection of intentionality) and on profligate pursuit of ever new experiences with other groups (inadequate protection of sociality). The lower right trajectory is *penurious* in the sense that it is stingy in relation to *both* types of evolved mechanisms; i.e., it can lead to a tightfisted refusal to acknowledge members of out-groups (failure to "see" actual, natural intentional agents), and miserly resistance to sharing with and learning from other cultures (stubborn maintenance and expansion of in-group norms).

What does any of this have to do with *theology*? For the sake of this essay, I want to suggest a broad description of this field of inquiry: theology is the critique and construction of hypotheses about the conditions for finite axiological engagement. In this sense, both the Na'vi and RDA had their own theologies. Each group had its own (more or less explicit) hypotheses about that which makes possible the experience of valuing and being valued. Here we are not talking about this or that particular value, but that which generates the conditions for all valuation whatsoever. Now the *sacerdotal* trajectory in theology, by far the most common on Earth since the axial age, develops hypotheses that appeal to particular supernatural agents and their coalitions; "*our* God" is the basis of and judge over all values and actions. I will return below to the upper right quadrant, which I call the *iconoclastic* trajectory of theology.

My point here, however, is that the trajectories represented by the Na'vi and the RDA are indeed *theological*. What is it that makes possible (perhaps even originates, orders, and orients) value-laden engagements? The hypothesizing that guides the prodigal trajectory of the Na'vi is characterized by a relatively loose and open interaction with a pervasive field of supernatural agency that (early in the story) is not specifically concerned with protecting a particular coalition. The penurious hypothesizing of the RDA is guided by a strict allegiance to the invisible (yet quite "natural") hand that guides the flow of capital-money, and whose alleged neutrality justifies the behavior of those who learn to control it.

In the movie, of course, the planet of Pandora is portrayed as actually infused with the supernatural energy of a mother tree-goddess who (spoiler alert) eventually makes the animals of the planet fight against RDA. Jake Sully (the hero) becomes a kind of warrior-priest who is able to convince her of the evil of RDA. Because of her intervention, the RDA is thwarted and forced to leave the planet; the Na'vi coalition is saved.

But let's come back to Earth. Clearly there are some groups on our planet too who resemble the RDA and others who live somewhat like the Na'vi. However, neither of these theological strategies will be adequate for saving *our* planet; in our late modern, pluralistic, globalizing context, we will not be able to *live together* under these conditions. As several cinematic observers pointed out, the movie Avatar is rather obviously intended as a negative commentary on U.S. interventions in the Middle East. The Colonel with a southern accent (George W. Bush?) and the RDA Administrator in charge of doling out contracts (Dick Cheney?) are blind to everything but the "unobtainium" (oil) hidden under the land of indigenous peoples (Iraqis, Afghans, etc.).

My point here is that although we may well celebrate the movie's denigration of the trajectory represented by RDA, we humans do not actually live on Pandora and so the trajectory represented by the Na'vi is also doomed to fail. If in fact there were tree-goddesses to whom the colonized worldwide could appeal, things would be different; invading forces (military or economic) could be defeated by petitioning such supernatural agents who could harness the powers of nature. But there are not. And they cannot. Earth is not Pandora. I believe that the upper right quadrant is our best theological option, and can open up new ways to think about *God*. Before exploring this possibility, however, let me back up and demonstrate the way in which contemporary evangelicalism illustrates the *sacerdotal* trajectory, which has been the most popular mode of theological hypothesis construction for the last two millennia here on Earth.

Evangelical Supernatural Agent Coalitions

First, what is an "evangelical"? The question is not merely academic, as Stan Grenz, and those who tried to exclude him from this category, knew quite well.[9] For my purposes, it suffices to use a broad definition of the term,

---

9. See D. A. Carson, "Domesticating the Gospel."

referring generally to those who participate in religious coalitions shaped by various attempts in the mid-twentith century (by the likes of Billy Graham) to find a middle way between fundamentalism and liberalism in Christianity. Such groups have achieved dominance in many areas in the United States and Britain, and continue to expand in many parts of the world, including my new homeland of Norway. Although this was my own religious "family of origin," I did not know how important this appellation was until I was informed of my "evangelical" identity at college.

Now many (but certainly not all) evangelicals would laugh at the idea of a tree-goddess who controls animals and cares about a small-scale coalition. However, most evangelicals do imaginatively detect a whole host of ambiguously discarnate or contingently embodied intentional forces who are interested in *their* coalition: angels, demons, disembodied ancestors (saints), etc. They also believe in a powerful and wise supernatural agent, God, who will punish cheaters and defectors and protect those who remain faithful to an in-group, rewarding them a place in an everlasting heavenly coalition. The fact that members of out-groups (other religions, or even other sorts of evangelicals who disagree on some point of polity or biblical interpretation) believe that *their* coalitions will be protected by the gods (or God) that *they* have detected is explained away as the result of demonic delusion or even sin. In my view, this appeal to the noetic effects of sin is one of the most appalling of noetic sins. But I digress.

While most evangelicals find themselves comfortably in the sacerdotal trajectory (the God we detect protects our coalition), it is interesting to observe how differently their right and left wings typically respond to the other two trajectories so far explored. In my experience, those on the evangelical "right" are usually more worried about New Agers (the prodigals) than they are about capitalist corporations that ravage the poor and the environment (the penurious). On the other hand, those on the evangelical "left" tend to react more harshly to RDA types and are less anxious about the touchy-feely spiritualism that characterizes some recent forms of the ecclesial socius. Which is more important—rejecting the (interpretation of) gods detected by others or expanding our own coalition by loosening social norms?

Wherever evangelicals fall in their answers to such questions, they remain within the sacerdotal trajectory. Here they are in good (or at least plentiful) company. Like the other Abrahamic religions, evangelical coalitions are held together by shared imaginative engagement with particular kinds of contingently embodied intentional forces. These may be explicitly divine figures detected at rituals (the presence of Jesus at the Eucharist, the Holy Spirit at a baptism) or lesser supernatural agents detected in everyday life (an angel when in need of protection, a demon when feeling temptation, a former saintly coalition member when in need of inspiration). Evangelicals may be well trained in theological doctrine, and give orthodox answers to questions about divine infinity, immutability, aseity, and omniscience, but (like everyone else) they easily fall back into "theologically incorrect" models of God as a human-like intentional entity who is emotionally concerned with the struggles of their coalition in real space and time. This is because the default to evolved theogonic mechanisms naturally leads to images of finite gods who are watching over small-scale groups.[10]

Most professional theologians (at least in North America) are paid by institutions that support a particular religious coalition or set of coalitions that follow the sacerdotal trajectory. A great number of these institutions require faculty to sign "statements of faith," signaling their commitment to the in-group. As one example, let us take the institution with which Mark Noll has been associated for much of his career. Wheaton College demands that the scholars it employs—the "evangelical minds" it hires—assert and re-assert every year that they believe *inter alia* in supernatural agents like Satan, that out-group members will be punished eternally, that a text revealed by a supernatural agent is the final authority on all matters it discusses, and that physical death entered the world when Adam and Eve, the historical parents of the entire human race, disobeyed God.[11]

Similar claims could be culled from other statements of faith imposed by hundreds of similar institutions. But let us set aside for a moment the plausibility of particular assertions within such statements. The very fact that intellectual exploration is policed and restricted by forcing scholars to limit their claims (in any field) to assertions that are consistent with a particular coalition's appeal to supernatural agents (which only they can appropriately detect and properly interpret) is a symptom of the *real* scandal of the evangelical mind (and culture).

Stan Grenz was a leader in reforming, renewing, and revisioning evangelical theology.[12] He was often attacked by other scholars who seemed to perceive his intellectually rigorous engagement with contemporary culture and science as a threat to their own coalitions. I always admired Stan's courage and integrity in setting out his positions. He was the epitome of irenicism and never insisted that someone agree with him before (or after) engaging in serious theological conversation. I'm quite sure he would have

10. Slone, *Theological Incorrectness*.

11. http://www.wheaton.edu/About-Wheaton/Statement-of-Faith-and-Educational-Purpose (accessed 6 Jan. 2013).

12. His massive corpus is engaged in a variety of ways in other chapters in this *Festschrift*. Excellent examples of his efforts at reformation include *Renewing the Center*, and *Revisioning*.

resisted the radical proposals that I set out in the next section, but equally sure he would have encouraged me to tell it like I see it.

Iconoclastic Theology for Terrestrials

We do not live on Pandora. There are no tree-goddesses to save us. Those of us who agree that unbridled capitalism requires an infinite expansion of resources, and is rapidly depleting our finite ecological limits, have little faith in the RDAs of planet Earth. Given our evolved tendencies to detect supernatural agents, and our social entrainment within west Asian religious traditions, it is easy to believe that our only and best option is the sacerdotal trajectory. This adaptive strategy may have worked well (in terms of holding together complex social groups) during the axial age; it still feels natural to us, but the integration of these cognitive and coalitional mechanisms lead us to misinterpret ambiguous natural events (like tsunamis) or to ignore clear natural events (like global warming), appealing instead to supernatural causes or promises. The same evolved tendencies that aid in the coalescence and maintenance of relatively large religious coalitions, like evangelicalism, also fuel antagonism toward perceived in-group defectors (like Stan Grenz) and a willingness to sanctify violence against out-groups. The sacerdotal trajectory helped the species hold together during a difficult period, but the exponential growth and rapidly increasing global connectedness of the human population require new ways of constructing and criticizing hypotheses about the conditions for axiological engagement.

How could theologians possibly participate in the iconoclastic trajectory, which is diametrically opposed to the theogonic forces that have nurtured their traditions? In fact, most Christian theologians have indeed followed this trajectory—at least sometimes, at least partially. The real question is whether they can follow it consistently.

When theologians resist their evolved tendencies to over-detect agency and over-protect groups, they are pressing toward the upper right corner of Figure 3. In this case they construct and criticize hypotheses about the conditions for axiological engagement without immediately appealing to a particular supernatural agent revelation or to the rituals and social norms of their in-group. In other words, they become more sociographically promiscuous and anthropomorphically prudish. I call this trajectory *iconoclastic* because the integration of these tendencies has a jarring, and potentially destructive, effect on the religious images (icons) shared by the coalition, weakening their explanatory and cohesive power.

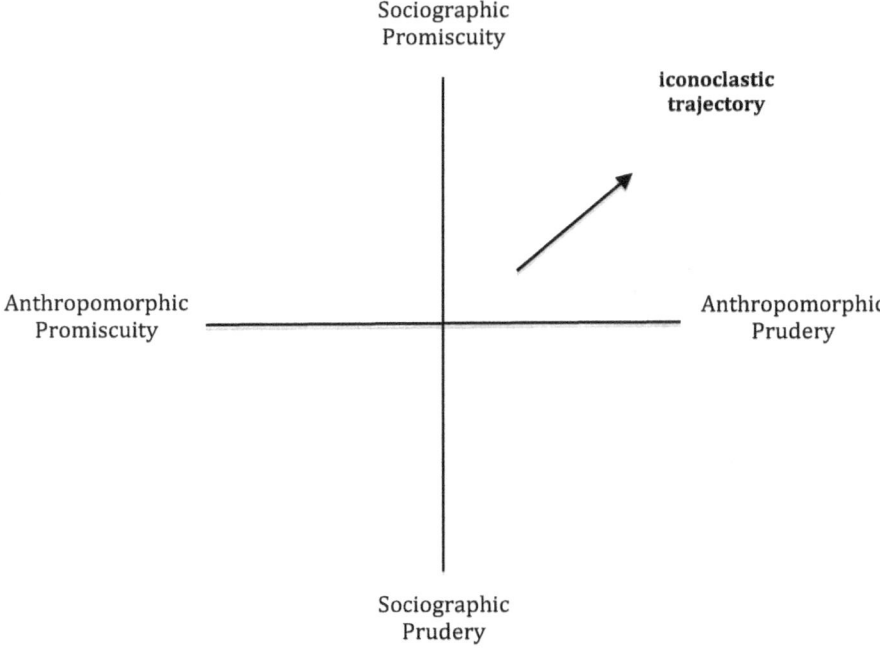

Figure 3

Before offering examples of sacerdotal *theology*, let me illustrate the integration of these mechanisms in non-theological scholarship. In sciences such as physics and chemistry, for example, scholars resist (or at least try to resist) the tendency to appeal to discarnate intentional forces or to the beliefs of politicized organizations with some investment in the research. If something strange happens in a test tube, the chemist's first guess is not "ghost." If a laboratory heavily funded by a pharmaceutical company announces that the drug produced by that company is more effective than previously thought, other scientists will remain skeptical until the research is repeated by another group. Even in sciences like sociology and political theory, which do indeed need to detect human agents and whose subject matter includes the dynamics of group cohesion, their *scientific* explanations of these phenomena do not appeal to supernatural agents or insights available only through revelation to a particular coalition. If they did, they would not be taken seriously as scholars. Anthropomorphic prudery and sociographic promiscuity are the (preferred, ideal) defaults of the academic community.

What about *theologians*? Can someone who is anthropomorphically prudish and sociographically promiscuous still talk about *God*? Could an *evangelical* theologian? Yes. In fact, many—perhaps even most—evangelical theologians sometimes do resist (or at least strongly qualify) the idea of God as a coalition-favoring, person-like being. The problem is that their movement in this direction is pulled back by the bio-cultural gravitational force of the theogonic mechanisms. The sacerdotal trajectory easily and "naturally" overrides the iconoclastic because such theologians are operating within coalitions whose cohesion depends on shared imaginative engagement with supernatural agents. A first step for theologians interested in pursuing the iconoclastic trajectory—if they dare—is to trace and liberate lines of flight already present within the axial age religions, in which they are expert; for evangelicals, this usually means Christianity.

We can identify at least three different pathways or *modes of intensification*, already present (albeit suppressed) in the Christian tradition, which lead in this direction. The first is what I call the *intellectual* mode, in which the intensification of *conceptual analysis* leads to a recognition of the logical incoherence of the idea of *an* infinite supernatural agent. If "the infinite" cannot be thought as one object distinct from "the finite," else it would be limited by the finite and so itself finite, then *a fortiori* it cannot be thought of as one supernatural *person* distinct from other persons, who favors one *polity* distinct from other polities. This is the pathway (partially) taken by most of the leading theologians of the axial age religious traditions. Stan Grenz's robustly Trinitarian theology is an excellent example; he clearly saw the logical problems with the idea of a single infinite subject.

A second mode is *pragmatic*; here, the intensification of *compassionate action* leads to liberating efforts on behalf of those oppressed or excluded by the dominating policies of the elite within a supernatural agent coalition. Many evangelicals, especially those interested in challenging the racism, sexism, and classism within their coalitions have proactively developed new ways of inscribing the socius and questioned the extent to which particular interpretations of supernatural agents (and their role in personal and social transformation) are necessary conditions for fellowship. It is easy to see why such "emergent" movements are so vigorously and violently vilified by the (white, male, upper middle class) evangelical power elite. In fact, reaching out with authentic openness to members of out-groups (and defectors, like ex-evangelicals) is indeed dangerous for such religious in-groups, whose cohesion depends on clear statements about the boundaries of faith.

Third, there is a *mystical* mode in which the intensification of *contemplative awareness* leads to experiences that alleviate anxiety about being-limited by an infinite person-like supernatural agent and the need to protect the power of a particular group. One can find examples of this mode within all of the religious traditions that trace their roots to the axial age, and often evangelicals who begin to follow this trajectory explore meditative practices that evolved within other traditions (e.g., Buddhism, Daoism, Sufism, etc.). In Christianity, this mode is often linked to the apophatic way, in which the power of human language to comprehend the divine is rigorously denied. Evangelicals are permitted to express their ignorance about the essence of a transcendent supernatural agent, as long as they *also* express their confidence in cataphatic statements about the anthropomorphic attributes of that agent. In other words, the risky adventure of the iconoclastic trajectory must be domesticated within and subordinated to the sacerdotal trajectory.

For obvious reasons, most theologians have preferred the intellectual pathway. Not uncommonly, however, concerns about the plausibility of the idea of God as an infinite supernatural agent who favors a human coalition are driven by moral and aesthetic sensitivity as well as by conceptual reflection. It is important to ask why it is usually systematic theologians, rather than biblical scholars or historians (like Noll), who get drawn into evangelical heresy trials. Scholars of Scripture or Christian history are not required, and indeed sometimes actively discourage one another, from trying to provide a coherent, explanatory account of the discrepancies within the texts or disparities across the eras they study. Systematic theologians, on the other hand, are pressured to follow out the logical implications of the assertions of their religious coalitions as far as possible—before appealing to mystery. If a theologian follows the intellectual mode too far, she gets in trouble. This is the real scandal of evangelical culture and its oppression of evangelical minds.

Noll decries the lack of integration between intellectual rigor and *piety* in evangelicalism. This is only a symptom, not the root of the problem. Insofar as pious devotion imaginatively engages ritually-mediated, discarnate intentional forces concerned about "my" in-group, it *is* the hyper-active detection of coalitional gods—postulated as causal explanations for ambiguous natural phenomena. Insofar as pious activism is driven by an attempt to participate in and expand the kingdom of "our" God, it *is* the hyper-active protection of a supernatural coalition—interpreted as the best way to inscribe the global socius. In this sense, piety directly compromises inter-subjective discourse about natural phenomena and inter-communal discourse about social phenomena. It cannot be integrated with the intellectual rigor that is characteristic of the other sciences, which attempt to follow the trajectory in the upper right corner of Figure 3.

Sacerdotal appeals to "mystery" use the in-conceivability of infinity as a veil of ignorance—a learned ignorance that veils the hyperactivity of the religious family's shared imaginative engagement with God. The inability of finite creatures to conceive the infinite (or even all finite things), suggests an (infinite) vacuum in human knowledge. Abhorred, the theogonic mechanisms quickly and easily fill it by detecting and protecting manifestations of a particular coalition's supernatural agent.

In contrast to the domesticating effect of the sacerdotal forces, the *iconoclastic* trajectory of theology de-personifies, de-politicizes, and, in a certain sense, de-objectifies the existential conditions for axiological engagement. It is true that the "object" of theology is not like the objects of other disciplines; the relation between infinity and intentionality cannot be objectified like finite relations. That which conditions the existence of all finite valuations cannot itself be finite or even evaluated in the same sense. Rather than using this as an excuse for appealing to the mystery of a particular coalition's interpretation of a supernatural agent, however, the iconoclastic theologian can explore other ways of making sense of this being-limited of thought (or being-thought of limitation) which can indeed be "objectified" (as the reader is currently doing).

The integration of anthropomorphic prudery and sociographic promiscuity are not merely *destructive* of certain religious images; as we can see from the other sciences, it also has a *creative* power. In the case of theology, it can facilitate the construction of new hypotheses about the conditions for axiological engagement that avoid personifying or politicizing "infinity." For example, one might think of the conditions for finite human intentionality as in some sense "infinitely" enfolded within and unfolding among the energetic relational fields of space-matter-time (*intra*-natural, rather than *super*-natural). I do not have the space to set out such a proposal here, so I devote the remainder of the chapter to a discussion of the possibility and promise of the iconoclastic trajectory.

Theology After Pandora (and Eve)

Back to Pandora—but not the planet this time. The ancient Greeks were not the only ones to develop a myth in which the actions of the first woman are blamed for the evils in the world. Like Pandora, Eve's curiosity killed the race—or at least its chance for immortality. Both in early Greek and in Abrahamic religions, new and other gods were invented; (mostly) male heroes whose supernatural powers could provide remedies for humanity. The stories of Pandora and Eve teach us that it is dangerous (especially for women) to question divine things, to look into the forbidden black boxes of divine intentionality. Inquiring too persistently into the mechanisms by which discarnate intentional forces punish and reward us threatens the shared imaginative engagement that holds the coalition together, and so it is taboo. As long as evangelicals, or members of any other religious in-group, protect the cohesion of their communities and institutions by encouraging detections of hidden supernatural powers only "we" know how to interpret by, for example, insisting that theologians sign coalitional statements of faith, they will not ever be able to engage in serious constructive scholarship in dialogue with other sciences.

I was an evangelical theologian long enough to know how my friends and former colleagues might respond to such claims. St. Paul acknowledges that God uses the "folly of what we preach to save those who believe," and that Christ crucified is "a stumbling block to Jews and folly to Gentiles" (1 Cor 1:21–22). Blessed are those who are not scandalized, but signal their commitment to the coalition by faithfully adhering to apparent foolishness. Similar texts and similar strategies are present in other religions. But why accept the Bible as the revelation of a contingently embodied intentional force in the first place? Or why not accept the Qur'an, the Book of Mormon, or the Dhammapada? Human beings have evolved cognitive and coalitional mechanisms that short-circuit such questions. We know that our (interpretation of) shared imaginative engagement with *our* supernatural agents is true. Every other religious group (or denomination) says the same thing. At best, the leaders of such groups come to abstract agreements that have little effect on everyday religious practice; at worst, they start "holy" (or "just") wars against one another. Is it any wonder that intellectuals in other fields hesitate to take (sacerdotal) theology seriously?

Several other objections will certainly arise from my religious family of origin. Wouldn't my proposal for taking more seriously the discoveries of the bio-cultural study of religion mean the dissolution of evangelicalism, indeed the destruction of Christianity itself? Doesn't the fact that Shults has clearly gone off the deep end prove that, in fact, engaging modern science and culture really is dangerous—too dangerous? Perhaps the conservative Christian political "right" is right; sectarianism may be the only hope for protecting the purity of particular Christian coalitions.

I have several responses to these kinds of questions and concerns. First, we should begin by admitting that the dissolution of *other* supernatural coalitions is exactly the goal of most Christian evangelism and missions. If evangelicals want believers in other supernatural agents (whom they take to be "false" gods) to consider with all seriousness that they may be wrong, they should be willing to take their own medicine.

Second, do evangelicals want to believe what is true or do they want what they already believe to be true? Is being a Christian, or an evangelical, more important than being right—or even making sense? We have evolved to think that fitting into our coalition is indeed the most important thing in the world. We have learned to stifle our questions about the contents of the divine "black box" hidden in plain sight in the religious imagination and rituals of our in-groups. We are cognitively and coalitionally wired to ignore the psychological repression and political oppression caused by our own religious tribes.

Scholars, activists, and contemplatives are trained *not* to ignore them. My challenge to evangelicals who are also *iconoclasts* (in any of the three modes of intensification) is to take seriously the importance of the following questions: is contemporary shared imaginative engagement with supernatural agents the result of evolved hyper-active perceptive and cooperative strategies that helped our ancestors survive in small-scale societies? Are these strategies now obsolete in a complex, pluralistic social environment? If so, what can we do about it? What new ways can we find of talking about "God" in this context?

Third, iconoclastic theology does not necessarily lead to the destruction of social groups; the complete dissolution of evangelical coalitions is not the only option here. Like many other such religious in-groups, evangelicals have played an important role in developing strategies for caring for human persons and coalitions, including out-groups. The hard work ahead for the iconoclastic theologian (or activist, or contemplative) is to imagine and enact new and creative ways to live in community that do not rely on the mechanisms of the sacerdotal trajectory. This may very well, indeed we should expect that it would, include forms of axiological engagement that are inspired by exemplars like Jesus of Nazareth (among others).[13]

The best hope for theologians to join other scholars of religion in serious inter-disciplinary conversation, and to participate with other groups in serious inter-cultural conversation, is to liberate the iconoclastic trajectory from the sacerdotal. Like their colleagues in other disciplines, theologians must learn to resist the evolutionary defaults that reinforce cognitive and coalitional biases. This does not at all mean giving up on the real *intensity* of the human experience of being-limited, the intense *reality* of being-conditioned in all of our axiological engagements. Reflecting on these really intense experiences of encountering infinite intensities remains an important task in human life.

Even if we could reconstruct this discipline into a critique of axial age religious conceptions and new hypothesis-construction, would it be appropriate to call it "theology"? In fact this term has been used historically,

---

13. Cf. Shults, "Ethics, Exemplarity and Atonement."

from Aristotle to Žižek,[14] to refer to arguments about the existential conditions for human axiological engagement that do *not* appeal to human-like, coalition-favoring gods. In the long run, whether or not we keep the term "theology" is less important (I vote "yes" for now) than undertaking the task of reconstructing this mode of inquiry so that it can fully enter into the significant dialogue among academic disciplines on these issues. This can only happen if we honestly discuss how God is born(e) among us, however embarrassing the "facts of (religious) life" may be to evangelical (and other sacerdotal) theologians.

Bibliography

Atran, Scott. *In Gods We Trust: The Evolutionary Landscape of Religion*. Oxford: Oxford University Press, 2002.
Barrett, Justin. "Dumb Gods, Petitionary Prayer and the Cognitive Science of Religion." In *Current Approaches in the Cognitive Science of Religion*, edited by I. Pyysiainen and V. Anttonen, 93–109. New York: Continuum, 2002.
Boyer, Pascal. *Religion Explained: The Human Instincts that Fashion Gods, Spirits and Ancestors*. London: Random House, 2001.
———. *The Fracture of an Illusion: Science and the Dissolution of Religion*. Göttingen: Vandenhoeck and Ruprecht, 2010.
Bulbulia, Joseph. "Nature's Medicine: Religiosity as an Adaptation for Health and Cooperation." In *Where God and Science Meet, Volume I: Evolution, Genes and the Religious Brain*, edited by Patrick McNamara, 87–122. London: Praeger, 2006.
Carson, D. A. "Domesticating the Gospel: A Review of Grenz's *Renewing the Center*." In *Reclaiming the Center: Confronting Evangelical Accommodation in Postmodern Times*, edited by Millard Erickson et al., 33–58. Wheaton, IL: Crossway, 2004.
Guthrie, Stewart. *Faces in the Clouds: A New Theory of Religion*. Oxford: Oxford University Press, 1993.
Lewis-Williams, David. *Conceiving God: The Cognitive Origin and Evolution of Religion*. New York: Thames and Hudson, 2010.
Noll, Mark. *Jesus Christ and the Life of the Mind*. Grand Rapids: Eerdmans, 2011.
———. *The Scandal of the Evangelical Mind*. Grand Rapids: Eerdmans, 1995.
Pyysiainen, Iikka. *Supernatural Agents: Why We Believe in Souls, Gods and Buddhas*. Oxford: Oxford University Press, 2009.
Rossano, Matt. *Supernatural Selection: How Religion Evolved*. Oxford: Oxford University Press, 2010.
Shults, F. LeRon. "Bearing Gods in Mind and Culture." *Religion, Brain & Behavior* 1/2 (2011) 154–67.
———. "Ethics, Exemplarity and Atonement." In *Theology and the Science of Moral Action: Virtue Ethics, Exemplarity and Cognitive Neuroscience*, edited by James A. van Slyke et al., 164–78. London: Routledge, 2012.
———. *Iconoclastic Theology: Gilles Deleuze and the Secretion of Atheism*. Edinburgh: Edinburgh University Press, 2014.

14. *Metaphysics* 1025a.19, 1064b.3; Žižek, *Parallax*, 68.

———. "The Problem of Good (and Evil) Arguing about Axiological Conditions in Science and Religion." In *Science and the World's Religions, Volume I: Origins and Destinies*, edited by Wesley Wildman and Patrick McNamara, 39–68. New York: Praeger, 2012.

———. "Science and Religious Supremacy: Toward a Naturalist Theology of Religions." In *Science and the World's Religions, Volume III: Religions and Controversies*, 73–100. New York: Praeger, 2012.

Slone, Jason D. *Theological Incorrectness: Why Religious People Believe What They Shouldn't*. Oxford: Oxford University Press, 2007.

Sosis, Richard. "Religious Behaviors, Badges and Bands: Signaling Theory and the Evolution of Religion." In *Where God and Science Meet, Volume I: Evolution, Genes and the Religious Brain*, edited by Patrick McNamara, 61–86. London: Praeger, 2006.

Teehan, John. *In God's Name: The Evolution of Religious Violence and Ethics*. Oxford: Wiley-Blackwell, 2010.

Tremlin, Todd. *Minds and Gods: The Cognitive Foundations of Religion*. Oxford: Oxford University Press, 2006.

Žižek, Slavoj. *The Parallax View*. Cambridge: MIT, 2006.

19

Revelation, Community, and Culture

A Dramatic Inquiry

DAVID S. CUNNINGHAM

PROTESTANT THEOLOGIES OF ALL stripes face a perennial problem: how to draw upon the insights of the traditions of the church and the insights of secular culture, while still maintaining the centrality of the Bible as the sole source of Christian revelation. Every reference to a post-biblical ecclesial development, every gesture in the direction of a cultural phenomenon from which something can be learned, seems to demand some form of *apologia* to clarify that such references should not be taken as evidence that the biblical text is somehow insufficient to answer every question that one might raise. All forms of Protestantism are haunted by the ghost of *sola scriptura*—accompanied by a nagging sense that there remains, in fact, something more to be said than what the Bible has to say.

By describing this as a "Protestant" problem, I do not mean to suggest that Catholic theologians (whether Roman, Orthodox, or Anglican) have somehow managed to develop an ideal account of the respective roles of Scripture, tradition, and reason as sources of divine revelation. I only mean to observe that many forms of Protestantism have pointed to one particular source—the Bible—as the sole source of divine revelation. In some cases the Bible is not described as the only source, but it is always at least *primus inter pares*. Protestant theologians have thereby created for themselves the very real challenge of finding an appropriate place for the church and the world as *loci*, or at least as mediators, of divine revelation. This is, however, a task which some forms of Protestantism have sometimes studiously avoided, hoping that a well-placed biblical proof-text or a lengthy round of exegesis will somehow put all questions to rest. This has been a particular hazard for those forms that describe themselves as "evangelical"—a term which, by its very etymology denotes a high degree of attention to the Gospels and, by extension, to the whole of Holy Scripture.

There have been exceptions, of course. Karl Barth, a theologian deeply *evangelisch* if not downright evangelical, famously called for preaching that held the Bible in one hand and the newspaper in the other.[1] Recent evangelical writers in a more popular vein, including Brian McLaren and Rob Bell, have sought to draw more heavily on church tradition (i.e., McLaren's advocacy of Hans Frei's "generous orthodoxy"[2]) or on personal experience of the lives of non-Christians (Bell's suggestion that salvation might ultimately be universal[3]). Others have sought to evade the ghost of *sola scriptura* by describing their work as simultaneously catholic *and* evangelical theology.[4] All of these approaches could be read as attempts to maintain the centrality of the biblical witness while calling for greater attention to community and culture; and in this endeavor, one of the leading American voices during the second half of the twentieth century was that of Stanley Grenz.

Professor Grenz was able to persuade many of his fellow evangelicals to take community and culture more seriously by demonstrating that the Bible demanded that they do so. Biblically-grounded doctrinal claims, ranging from the Trinity as the "social God"[5] to human beings as "created

---

1. This frequently-cited trope doesn't seem to exist in exactly this form in any of Barth's published materials, but both the Eberhard Busch biography and several interviews point to the sentiment. Perhaps the clearest version occurs in an interview for *Time*: "[Barth] recalls that 40 years ago he advised young theologians 'to take your Bible and take your newspaper, and read both. But interpret newspapers from your Bible.'"

2. McLaren, *A Generous Orthodoxy*; the title refers to a phrase of Hans Frei's, though not a published one. The spirit is well conveyed in the essays in Hans Frei, *Theology and Narrative*. Interestingly, McLaren's link to Frei is via Stanley Grenz, who credits Frei with the phrase in *Renewing the Center* (2000), 325, 331.

3. Bell, *Love Wins*.

4. Most notably, theologians associated with the Center for Catholic and Evangelical Theology, and its journal, *Pro Ecclesia*. (Full disclosure: I once counted myself among this tribe, but eventually felt the need to distance myself from the reactionary politics espoused with increasing frequency by some of its members.) Truth be told, however, the word *evangelical* in this group's title was largely a gesture toward the German *evangelisch* as a descriptor of Protestantism, and had very little in common with contemporary American evangelicalism.

5. Grenz, *Social God*.

for community"[6] to the church as the "community of God,"[7] all demand a fairly high degree of attention to the world—and even to those parts of the world that seem to lie outside or beyond the range of direct biblical reference. In a 1999 interview, responding to the criticism that his approach to Scripture was not sufficiently "evangelical," Grenz described the heart of the evangelical ethos as "understanding oneself and telling one's story in accordance with the biblical categories of 'having once been lost' but 'now being found.'"[8] In other words, it was this key biblical insight, and not the Bible itself, that Grenz took to be the bedrock of the evangelical witness. In doing so, he probably came a great deal closer to grasping the depth of *sola scriptura*, at least as Luther understood it, than have many who have cited it as their mantra. And it was this insight, I think, that allowed him to explore such a wide swath of modern and postmodern culture while remaining firmly committed to the Bible as the primary locus of Christian revelation.

In that same spirit, I offer this exploration of the relationship among revelation, community, and culture. My primary vehicle is that of the theater: I am interested in the ways that dramatic literature, in its performance, helps us better understand the Christian doctrine of revelation.[9] I believe that such an exploration, if not exactly following in Professor Grenz's footsteps, does honor his memory and his theological perspective in a number of different ways. First, like Professor Grenz, I do not want to abandon the claim that the Bible is the genuine source and primary locus of revelation; therefore, I have argued elsewhere that the ultimacy of Holy Scripture can be better understood by comparing it to the dramatic script as the "source" of the production of drama in the theatre.[10] Similarly, I would emphasize the person and work of Christ as key to any doctrine of revelation; in other words, I would agree with Professor Grenz's claim, here summarizing the argument of the Epistle to the Hebrews, that "God's self-disclosure through Jesus supersedes all previous revelation and bestows on him a superior status."[11] Hence I have written about Christ as the "lead actor" whose willingness to fully inhabit his role helps us to understand his person and work as revelatory.[12] In this essay, I want to suggest that *the acting company* can

---

6. Grenz, *Created for Community*.
7. Grenz, *Theology for the Community*.
8. Bos, "Next-Wave Interview."
9. This is part of a larger project I am completing on drama and revelation, *Theater to the World*.
10. Cunningham, "Is Scripture a Script?"
11. Grenz, *Social God*, 218.
12. Cunningham, "Christ the Actor."

help us understand the role of the church—the community of God—in the process of divine revelation. I would like to think that Professor Grenz would approve of this analogy, because it is ultimately Christocentric: revelation is always in Christ, and indeed takes place through the body of Christ, which presents itself to us in a variety of forms: textual (Holy Scripture), physical (the Incarnate Word), and ecclesial (the church). If this last form seems less "evangelical" than the other two, it would be good to remember Professor Grenz's emphasis on the communal character of the ecclesial self and on the *imago dei* as a social reality. "Those who are 'in Christ' form a 'corporate personality.' They share a common identity, a solidarity, that fosters the new sense of personhood enjoyed by each participant in the ecclesial community."[13]

But how, precisely, can that "corporate personality" become a locus of divine revelation? Here, I believe, the analogy to drama and the theatre is particularly useful to us, because of the way that the acting company—working with the script and aware of the ultimate significance of the lead actor—contributes to the revelatory nature of drama in performance. I will frame this exploration with accounts of two plays; I begin with a brief account designed to make the *prima facie* case for drawing an analogy between the acting company and the church, and I conclude the essay with a more extended illustration of some of my claims by examining a play in performance. Within the space that is framed by these two accounts, I will construct my analogy—first by taking note of certain features of the church that ally it with the acting company, and then by outlining the means by which revelation takes place, both in the church and on the stage.

I. God's Spies[14]

In one of the most poignant moments in any of Shakespeare's plays, an aged father, beset with grief for having cast out the daughter who loved him best, now promises her that they will share a happy life—even if they must experience it in prison.

> So we'll live,
> And pray, and sing, and tell old tales, and laugh

13. Grenz, *Social God*, 332.

14. Sec. I, III, and IV of this paper were presented in an abbreviated form as "God's Spies," in the Christian Systematic Theology Group at the American Academy of Religion, Atlanta, Oct. 2010. My thanks to the Louisville Institute and the Alexander von Humboldt Stiftung, which provided funding for a sabbatical year in Freiburg (2009–10) during which much of the research of this paper was carried out.

> At gilded butterflies, and hear poor rogues
> Talk of court news; and we'll talk with them too—
> Who loses and who wins; who's in, who's out—
> And take upon's the mystery of things,
> As if we were God's spies. (*King Lear* V.iii.12–18)

In fact, imprisonment will make the whole process easier: no longer the object of every courtier's attention and every commoner's speculation, the fallen king and the formerly favored princess get to be the observers instead of the observed. Ironically enough, only the enclosure of the prison walls provide an adequate vantage-point for making sense of the mystery of things; here, says Lear, we will be able to see things as they really are. We will see them as God might, in their proper perspective, from just the right distance.

Of course, this much-desired vision never comes to pass. And yet, it is somehow made present when the actor playing Lear speaks these lines; if things go as they should, the vision of Cordelia and her father whiling away the hours in each others' presence will be conjured up in the imagination of those who are watching the play. The members of the audience may even be able to get a glimpse of why the prisoners might indeed gain a clearer perspective on things, why they might come to have broader knowledge and deeper wisdom as a result of the limitations imposed upon them by circumstances. Just as the audience has witnessed how the Earl of Gloucester develops better vision after losing his eyes, they may also come to understand the freedom that Lear expects to gain from his and his daughter's confinement.

Shakespeare was fond of writing theatrical meta-commentary into his plays, and although this passage is not one of the more obvious examples of that genre, one wonders whether he might not have considered the stage to have some affinities with the comfortable jailer's cell that Lear imagines. As the play unfolds, the players and the company seem to be imprisoned within its confines, unable to escape; and yet, from within this cockpit, one can see not only the vasty fields of France, but indeed, the whole world. The acting company, like Lear and Cordelia in prison (or indeed, like "God in His heaven"), view the world from a realm apart—which is part of why they are able to take upon themselves the mystery of things.

Of course, this represents an ironic inversion: we have been taught to assume that prisoners are the *objects* of this gaze, not its agents. They are the victims of the Benthamite panopticon, the powerless laboratory rats who scurry about while the people in white coats undertake their mission of *surveiller et punir*.[15] By this analogy, the theatre company—and particularly

---

15. Foucault, *Discipline and Punish*.

the actors on the stage—are the prisoners: those whom the audience has come to observe. And yet, only these imprisoned, bounded characters have a fully-rounded perspective on things; their apparent confinement actually gives them the power of sight and insight. Think of the moment when the play begins: only the acting company really knows what is in store for the audience over the next few hours; only they can see the whole world, insofar as the performance of this play will define it. It is the outside observer, whose gaze is not rooted in any true understanding of the object gazed upon, who cannot truly see and therefore cannot know. In the theatre, it is not the cast and crew, but rather those who sit in the *audience* who cannot see, and therefore cannot know how all the pieces fit together.

To put the matter differently: the theatre is a place where the apparent freedom of the audience, which can come and go as it pleases, actually puts it at a disadvantage with respect to the acquisition of knowledge and wisdom—whereas the acting company, having committed itself to work within the severely confined quarters of the theatre, achieves the most expansive insight into the unexplored niches of the world's mysteries. This inversion, I believe, provides a *prima facie* case for thinking about the acting company, alongside the script and the lead actors, as one of the primary *loci* of revelation in the theatre; by producing the play, this group of people brings about new knowledge. And this in turn provides us with a point of entry for thinking through the role of the church, the ecclesial body of Christ, in the Christian doctrine of revelation.

II. The Theatrical Company and the Church

At first glance, the church's role in God's self-revelation may seem primarily receptive; the members of the body of Christ can be seen as those *for whose sake* revelation takes place. But such an account fails to recognize the "event" character of revelation and wrongly characterizes it as a mere "deposit of faith"—an account that I have argued against in various venues, and that is increasingly out of favor among Christian theologians of all persuasions. If we are to make the transition from thinking about revelation primarily as a noun (an object that is handed on) to thinking about it as a verb (a manifestation that is perpetually re-enacted), we will need to break the habit of describing it within a "sender-receiver" model of communication.[16] Thus, revelation does not simply describe nuggets of knowledge being passed along from the one who knows (God) to those who do not

---

16. Such a model has already been discredited in any case, and not only with respect to revelation. See, Ong, *Presence of the Word*; Ong, *Orality and Literacy*.

(the church). The church's role is not merely to receive revelation, but to embody it and to be transformed by it, thereby bearing it bodily into the world. In fact, the church must actually *enact* revelation in some way—to put its knowledge of God into words and movement, to allow the invisible mystery of God to become visible through human signs and actions.

This explains why, in the analogy that I want to construct here, the church should not be understood in parallel to the audience that watches a play; it is, rather, the analogue to the theatrical *company*. Audiences may come and go, may pay attention or find themselves distracted, may care or not care about what is enacted on the stage. Needless to say, this rather lax attitude may well characterize a number of those who actually sit in the pews in any given church on any given Sunday morning. But my task here is not to offer a sociological account of those who attend church; it is, rather, to offer a theological account of what the church is meant to be—what it properly must be, if it is to live into its true role as the body of Christ. And this theological conviction makes the acting company the appropriate analogue to the church as the community of God.

This is not to say that the theatrical company is the only "active" entity in this process, while the audience remains passive; on the contrary, the theatrical audience must be active and engaged for the entire enterprise to have its proper effect. In my view, however, the audience is more analogous to "the world" for whom the play is performed, for whom the self-revelation of God has serious implications, and for whose sake the whole drama of salvation is enacted (John 3:16). Of course, as Augustine taught us long ago, there can be no neat and tidy dividing line between church and world; the church is a *corpus permixtum* in which only God knows where each person's allegiances truly lie. Still, given the kind of dedication and attention to God's revelatory action that should be operative within the church, its theatrical analogue must operate with a similar degree of dedication and attention to the revelation that occurs in drama; and here, only the theatrical company can serve the purpose.

By "the theatrical company," I mean everyone who is involved in the production of a play: supporting actors, designers, directors, and technicians, as well as front office staff, producers, financial backers, bartenders, and the people who keep the toilets clean. This is, obviously, an extraordinarily diverse group of people: different levels of interest in the particulars of any given production, different educational backgrounds and preparatory work, all of which have differing effects on various elements of an audience's experience. Of course, it is precisely this diversity, this chaos-inducing range of roles, that makes the theatrical company such an exceptional analogue for the church. Just as the theatre's motley crew works to make drama present to the contemporary audience, so does the church, in all its diversity, provide the means by which divine revelation is mediated to the entire world in every age.

The viability of this analogy depends, first and foremost, on the fact that the church is communal. This seemingly obvious point nevertheless requires exposition, since the contemporary Western church is so deeply affected by the hyper-individualism of the various cultures in which its members live. In an age of individual freedom and choice, the accent falls heavily on one's "personal relationship with God," and on freedom of conscience as the ultimate criteria in determining one's status as a Christian. Churches underwrite the individualist convictions of the wider culture even through the means they use to compete for members—offering an appealing range of social and personal services, rather than making ecclesiological claims about the alignment of a particular community with Christ.

Neither the biblical witness nor the history of Christian belief makes it particularly easy to justify such wide-ranging capitulation to individualism. From Jesus' call of his disciples to the structure of the early Christian communities as described in Acts, the conception of Christian belief has always been staunchly communal. Indeed, the very idea of a lone believer in a "personal relationship" with God seems, in light of the gospel, to be something of a category error. If the point were not already obvious, Paul makes it so with his analogy of the body in 1 Cor 12–14; only in the diversity of its members are believers rightly accounted as attached to the Head, which is Christ. The theme continues through the history of Christianity: from Cyprian's *extra ecclesia nulla salus* to Augustine's *civitatis Dei*, from the collegial ecclesiology of the Eastern church to the conciliar traditions of the post-schism West, and even in the more attenuated ecclesiology of the magisterial reformers, the believer's relationship to God was always corporate in character. When Luther promoted a doctrine of universal priesthood, he clearly meant that no one stands between the believer and God; he did not mean that each believer stands in splendid isolation from everyone else. Fortunately, a number of contemporary theologians have reasserted the communal nature of the church; and in fact, Stanley Grenz is an important example of this trend.

By taking seriously the history of the church, including a re-appropriation of the Eastern fathers, and by entering into conversation with a wide range of postmodern thinkers, Professor Grenz sought to nudge his audience away from a too-easy reliance on their "personal walk with God" and toward a fully-articulated communal account of the Christian faith.

I believe that the theatrical analogy can help press this point further by reminding us of the illusory nature of dyadic relationships. In the realm of drama and the theatre, we find it almost impossible, and certainly unfulfilling, to experience the work of art in isolation from others. Reading a play is important and necessary work, but to anyone who has seen even one production, it will always rank far behind the experience of the play's enactment. (This is unsurprising, since plays are, necessarily, written not merely to be read but to be performed. And, for the matter, so is the Bible.) And while it might be possible to experience a play as an audience of one, most of us would find it a less than complete experience (even if it mercifully prevented the play's most poignant moment from being interrupted by a coughing fit in the back row). One-person shows have their place, but even this is a misnomer and an illusion; William Luce's play *Barrymore*[17] starred Christopher Plummer, but my program contains credits for over a hundred people, from designers to stagehands to directors and assistants—and even that fails to account for all the people who kept the theatre open and operating.

All of this seems obvious enough. We would tend to feel either derision or pity for anyone who might say something like "I really love Shakespeare, but I never go to plays, because that would just get in the way of my personal relationship with the playwright." First of all, we'd probably think that the "personal relationship" was largely imaginary, constructed by means of textual fragments and the commentary of other lovers of the Bard. Second, we'd worry about the supposed claim to "love" someone who wrote work that was meant to be enacted in community, while disdaining the community in which it is enacted. And finally, we'd recognize the illusory nature of the claim to have unmediated access to Shakespeare—as though one's reading of the text didn't depend on thousands of editors, annotators, and an entire history of production that has kept these texts in circulation for centuries.

Yet as foolish and pitiable as this claim may be, many contemporary Christians are apt to give a great deal of credence to the structurally similar claim that "I love God, but I avoid the church, because that would get in the way of my personal relationship with Christ." While some might claim a degree of "spiritual" access to God (through prayer and contemplation) that might not be possible with a historical human figure, any careful observer will have to admit that this access is heavily mediated through textual and historical traditions that allow the believer to shape and re-shape the "personal relationship with God" to fit whatever needs and desires might stand out in the given moment. Even more analogous are the other two details

---

17. Technically a two-person play, though only one of them appears on stage—the other interacts with him over a loudspeaker. Luce, *Barrymore*.

mentioned in the previous paragraph: the facts that, first, God's intention in the creation of the world and the inspiration of the Scripture is clearly for the prospering of the human community; and second, that one's understanding of God depends on evangelists and theologians and pastors and ordinary believers through the ages, who have kept the Christian tradition alive by enacting it in a communal setting.

In both the theatre and the church, a focus on community is necessary, but it is not sufficient. Both entities are *ordered* communities, in which particular roles are played (some on the stage, some in the wings) and in which there is a balance of mutuality and subordination. The church has sometimes suffered from a certain lack of clarity about its own internal order; it has, at various times and places, imitated political structures, ranging from pure democracy to absolute dictatorship, and organized itself into every form of order, ranging from a military-like structure of ranks to an anti-hierarchical circle of friends. A good theological argument can be made for both order and equality, but it seems that the church may have lacked good models for such simultaneity of mutuality and subordination.

The theatre company may be one such model. Each member has a role to play (even if many of these roles, like those of the technical crew, are not seen directly by the audience). If one or more members fail to fulfill their roles, the entire production suffers. An excessively firm directorial hand may hold a production together, but sometimes only at the cost of snuffing out its creative energy. The best companies develop a good sense of when to make suggestions and to assert an individual perspective, and when to allow other members of the company to go their own way. All of this seems like it would transfer easily from the theatre to the church (or to the inner workings of any other group). But there is a difference: the theatre company knows that its ability to strike the right balance will be tested when the audience arrives to see the play being performed. Too often, the church operates without the sense that its organizational mechanisms are on public display—that an audience is watching its performance. Its tendency is to dismiss criticism with the claim that it comes from "outsiders" who don't share the church's common assumptions and divinely-given mission. In doing so, it fails to recognize that it thereby damages the credibility of its own witness to God's self-revelation. By contrast, the members of the theatre company know that while they may be disappointed, annoyed, or simply flummoxed by an audience's reaction to its performance, they cannot simply ignore it. Like it or not, the audience has the final say: it is for the sake of the audience that the play is being performed.

A complete discussion of the analogy between the church and the theatrical company would eventually require a much deeper and broader foray into ecclesiology, rather than the surface-skimming that I have done here. And in turn, an adequate account of the role of the church in the doctrine of revelation can only be justified in light of a fully-developed pneumatology. Such an account would need to affirm that God is the initiating agent of all divine revelation, which means that the church can never be seen as displacing God or taking over this agency for itself. Nevertheless, because of the work of the Holy Spirit in the practices of the church,[18] that account would also need to explain how, in the church, God can still go about the business of revealing Godself to the world.

Does this perspective allow too much freedom to the church in illuminating the revelation of God to the world? Some theologians have certainly thought so. For example, in Hans Urs von Balthasar's Trinitarian analogy, God is the author, actor, and director of the play; but he is unwilling to grant these three equal agency. Balthasar is very nervous about the tendency of directors to go their own way, failing to submit themselves with sufficient obedience to the will of the author. As a result, his intra-trinitiarian hierarchy tends to drift well beyond mere *taxis* or ordering; for him, the author of the play determines its meaning, and the job of the director (and anyone else who is involved in the performance) is to get into line.

My account contrasts with Balthasar's here, in two important ways. First, my emphasis on the entire theatrical company, rather than only the director, helps move the focus away from a potential contest of individual wills (in which authors and directors argue over who's really in charge), and toward the notion of *communal discernment* as the means by which the author's spirit comes to inhabit the actual production of the play. Second, I have specifically avoided Balthasar's allocation of the roles of author, actor, and director to Father, Son, and Spirit. Although I once found his approach to be fruitful, I have become increasingly convinced that it cannot help but push the entire account in the direction of a modalist monarchianism— Balthasar's caveats to the contrary notwithstanding. Rather, with greater attention to the dictum that the external works of the Trinity are undivided, I prefer to think of all three theatrical moments—authorship, enactment, and production—as the unified work of the Three, in which each moment is initiated by the Source carried out through the Wellspring, and perfected in the Living Water.[19] If there is a special emphasis on the Spirit's role among the acting company, this can be justified by the doctrine of appropriation; it

---

18. See essays in Buckley and Yeago, *Knowing the Triune God*. The authors of the essays in this vol. are representative of the "catholic and evangelical theology" mentioned above.

19. This alternative naming of the divine Three is described and defended in Cunningham, *These Three are One*, 71–74.

does not deny that the Spirit is also at work in the authorship of the script and in the actor's craft.

In sum: I believe that the proper role of the church in God's revelatory work can be usefully compared to the role of the theatrical company in performing the play. While attention must be paid to the script, and while a lead actor may often carry the show, the performance cannot take place without a diverse, active, and well-ordered company that brings it to life and allows the audience to participate in the play's revelatory character.

III. Revelation by Means of the Ecclesial Body: Three Elements

Having identified some key features that ally the church with the theatrical company in a more general sense, I now turn to the doctrine of revelation in particular. What elements characterize the revelatory role of the ecclesial body of Christ, and how are these elements related to the analogue of the theatrical company? Here, I will identify three such elements: repetition, diversity, and embodiment.

Non-identical repetition

Acting companies are aware that they are not the first people to enact drama in general; indeed, in almost all most cases, they are not the first to enact any particular play. Their own production of a work of theatre takes its place in the ongoing history of that play's productions. Moreover, over the past two centuries, companies have become more and more aware of the place of their own work within the context of a play's production history. During this period of time, theatres have seen the rise of the *dramaturg* as playing an important role in this process. It was not always thus; the discipline of dramaturgy is widely seen as an invention of Gotthold Lessing, whose *Hamburger Dramaturgie* is the archetype of the genre.[20] But well before that point in history, acting companies were aware that, most of the time, they were doing something that had been done before—by other companies, in other places, at other times.

Or, in fact, by the same company, in the same place, at roughly the same time. After all, theatres typically offer more than one performance of any given play; indeed, the kind of work that goes into staging a work of

---

20. Lessing, *Hamburg Dramaturgy*; an excellent introduction to the text, and further developments in dramaturgy, can be found in Luckhurst, *Dramaturgy*.

drama—from memorizing lines to building sets to organizing movement—would hardly be worth the while if the production could only be seen once. Multiple performances also mean that more people can see the play, thereby overcoming some of the obvious physical limitations to the number of people who can simultaneously witness the same work of live theatre without resorting to artificial forms of aural and visual magnification. So the members of the acting company are typically doing something that has been done many times before—not only by others, but also by themselves. And yet, at the end of the performance, most of the people involved will not focus on how tonight's version was the same as last night's, but rather, how it was different.

The performance of a play is therefore an act of *non-identical repetition*. This phrase, at least in its specifically theological usage, is usually attributed to the work of Catherine Pickstock and of John Milbank.[21] The worship liturgy of the church, for example, is often characterized as an act of non-identical repetition. Here, I want to make a broader point: that the church engages in something analogous to the theatrical company's work of non-identical repetition not only in its worship life, but simply in being the church. At its core, the church is properly seen as the non-identical repetition of God's work in the world, doing so in ways that continue to be revelatory in every new moment.

The theatrical company engages in an act of non-identical repetition in ways that it expects to be revelatory for its audiences. And even if the members of those audiences are very familiar with the play as written, they do indeed often find each new production, and even successive performances of the same production, to be revelatory in their own ways. As such, the theatrical event is as noteworthy for its *lack* of identity with the "original" performance as it is for its supposedly "repetitive" quality. Audiences are presented with a kind of embodiment of the drama that is analogous to (though distinct from) its original incarnation (the details of which, at least for classical drama, are largely lost to us in any case).

The enactment of a play in the theatre shows forth its "both/and" character in a very transparent way. It is, quite obviously, both a repetition of a previous event and also something new. This has important implications for the question of whether revelation is "continuing" or "closed"; indeed, it reframes the question, suggesting that these two accounts are not really opposed, but that they derive their meaning from one another. Only a work of drama that is relatively fixed can be meaningfully repeated; yet this very

---

21. Pickstock, *After Writing*; Milbank, *Word Made Strange*.

act of repetition, new in its every instance, testifies to the "ongoing" nature of the revelatory event.

Diversity and Divergence

I noted in the previous section that both the theatre and the church are highly communal in character: neither is the work of one person, but requires a company of people who bring their particular talents to the task at hand. Here, however, I want to take this claim one step further, and argue that both of these enterprises require not simply *multiple* people, but *a diverse array of* people. Moreover, and perhaps more controversially, I want to argue that both enterprises are at their best when a certain degree of divergence marks their respective communal lives.

The matter of diversity is the more obvious point. The actors cannot say to the lighting designers, "I have no need of you," nor could the costumers ply their trade if they had no actors to clothe. But the example of the theatre may actually take us beyond Paul's metaphor of the body in 1 Cor 12, which may have become all too familiar to us through its regular invocation as a reminder of the virtues of diversity. The body metaphor is a bit too easy, because for most of us, our experience of our own bodies is that our heads keeps them under pretty good control; my brain says to my arm, "Hold up your hand," and I do it. But for all our talk of the headship of Christ, the ecclesial body seems to be little less docile; its members have wills of their own in the way that, in a healthy physical body, the hand and the foot do not. The diverse and sometimes divergent wills of the members of the acting company provide us with a more adequate analogy for the church's tendency to propagate a thousand mutually exclusive interpretations.

The theatre may also give us a clue as to what keeps this multifarious system from splintering into ruins. Those without much experience of the production of plays tend to assume that unity is maintained through one of two means—either "the script," that is, whatever the author wrote; or "one designated person" in the performance of the script, usually the director or producer, or perhaps a "star" actor. As I will shortly observe, however, neither of these options is actually the case. Interestingly enough, however, these two attempted answers do reflect the inadequate ecclesiologies that dominate, respectively, Protestantism and Roman Catholicism, which wrongly assume that potential disagreements about divine revelation can be thwarted by appeals to a mutually-agreed-upon text or to definitive pronouncements by a single human being. But no one who has worked in theatre is under the illusion that either the script or the director will resolve the tensions. On the contrary, the tensions and divergences are precisely what makes the whole thing work. On this point, the reflections of director and drama theorist Peter Brook are especially *a propos*, particularly in his accounts of the degree of control that scripts and directors have (or, more frequently, do not have) over the production.[22]

The theatre company can live with its internal disagreements because these radically divergent wills have to pull things together for long enough to put on a play—and they have to do it nearly every day (and twice on Saturday). So long as they give each other credit for being deeply familiar with the script and dedicated to the specific features of their various crafts, they can live with a great deal of divergence in their interpretive perspectives. They do not need to assume that everyone will recognize the same obvious features of the text, nor that they must all bow to the director as the great final arbiter of all difference. They just need to perform the play.

With regard to revelation in particular, this suggests that church could stand to become a great deal more comfortable with incongruity and difference from within, but that, at the same time, it needs to become more aware of its audience. I will not here repeat the argument I offered above, to the effect that the audience casts the final vote by receiving, or refusing to receive, the revelation that the theatrical company offers. If the play is nothing more than a scattered assortment of divergent performances, the audience may well fail to see the point. But they are unlikely to return to the theatre very often if it becomes nothing more than a didactic vehicle through which only one authoritative voice is allowed to speak.

Flesh and Blood

What takes place in the theatre is physical and bodily, not merely cerebral, oral, aural, or conceptual. In order for theatrical enactment to take place, it requires the physical presence of people in the same physical space, able to experience one another as embodied persons. In certain instances, voices may be electronically amplified or entire performances recorded for posterity; but everyone is aware that something significant is lost in the process. The theatre is a physical, corporeal reality—a "work of the flesh," though not in the pejorative sense that St. Paul employs when contrasting this to the fruit of the spirit. In fact, one can probably attribute a great deal of Christianity's historical animosity to the theatre to a too-simplistic dualism of flesh

---

22. See, as one example among many, his reflections on the very different experiences of performing the same production of King Lear for very different audiences, in *The Empty Space*.

and spirit, along with a failure to recognize the thoroughly material, bodily, and indeed *flesh-and-blood* nature of the Christian witness.

The church's ability to be a true means of revelation depends, in part, on its willingness to be a genuinely material reality, a presence in the flesh. Too often, theology has assumed that revelation can be ecclesially-mediated primarily through the intellect without this kind of physical presence. Examples include not only theological texts and official pronouncements (which are often communicated only, or at least primarily, in written form), but also conceptual claims about Christian belief and practice that are largely abstracted from their concrete instantiation in the life of the church. These tendencies toward non-corporeal forms of communication about God are only exacerbated by contemporary trends in virtual media.

In contrast, the *ekklesia* was, from the beginning, a group of people who met face to face. Even after its transformation into a diasporic setting, the need to gather the community again, in the flesh, continued through the office of the bishop and its collegial relationships and occasional councils. We have tended to assume that the physical presence of church members toward one another is primarily an accident of history; we also assume that if new technologies allow us to communicate in non-corporeal ways, we should take advantage of them. But no one imagines that an audience has the same experience of theatre by watching it over a live video stream. We should consider whether ecclesial mediations of divine revelation might not require the same kind of physical presence and face-to-face encounter that transpires in the theater.

In practice, this means that "revelation by means of the church" has less to do with what theologians write or what church officials announce, and more to do with the actual performances of Christians as they participate in ecclesial gatherings for worship, fellowship, and action. These are the "performance spaces" in which God acts in a revelatory way, and in which believers and non-believers alike actually learn something about this God in whose name Christians gather. If these performances are carried out well, with close attention to the various attributes that make for good theatre, then this too can facilitate, and even contribute to, God's revelatory work.

The last few decades have seen a number of interesting discussions of "performance" as a key theological category, but the focus has tended to be on the meaning and significance of this for the performer. Nicholas Lash's seminal essay "Performing the Scriptures"[23] focuses on performance as a better way of thinking about how we interpret the Bible; Stephen Barton

---

23. Lash, "Performing the Scriptures."

has offered similar reflections.[24] Sam Wells has demonstrated how Christian ethics is mostly a matter of performance,[25] but again his focus is primarily on Christians as the actors (or in his case, the improvisers), rather than on how such acting might ultimately serve as a means of God's revelatory act. Still, these accounts point us in the right direction; the next logical step, I think, is to reconsider our understanding of revelation along these kinds of "performative" lines.

In an effort to illustrate this point, as well as the other claims in this paper, I now turn to a concrete case: an actual performance of a play in the theatre. It may help that, in this case, the play happens to about the performance of a play.

IV. Corporeal, Combative, Non-Identical Repetition (on the South Bank)

Alan Bennett's new play *The Habit of Art* is, ostensibly, an account of a hypothetical meeting between W. H. Auden and Benjamin Britten, together with the events leading up to it. Their relationship to one another, and to the other people in their respective lives, provides the audience with a profound meditation on the creation and reception of art (specifically poetry and music) in twentieth-century Britain. But what makes this play unusually interesting, and particularly useful for my purposes here, is that it is set as a play within a play. We watch, not the play itself, but rather, the people who are involved in its performance—a group of actors, the technical crew, and even the author—as this often combative community works its way through the rehearsal process. As such, Bennett's play also allows for a great deal of meta-reflection on the art of the theater and the business of stagecraft. The work forces us to shift our attention back and forth between the interior play's own dramatic content concerning the complex lives of these two brilliant artists, and the people who make the play happen: the stage manager, the technicians, and the actors, both in and out of role. I now want to show how this play underscores the three points I have just made.

First: non-identical repetition. This notion is, of course, part and parcel of the art of theatre, but audiences rarely get to experience it; they typically see a play once. The theatre company experiences it again and again, first in the rehearsal process, and then throughout its run. Bennett's play gives audiences some insight into this experience by complicating the sequencing of

24. Barton, "New Testament Interpretation as Performance."
25. Wells, *Improvisation*.

the interior play: actors stop in the middle of a line, stage managers back up the action and start it again, designers rework scenes on the fly. The play also inserts a number of tricks to help the audience imagine the other aspects of this process; for example, the interval/intermission takes place during a tea break that is called for by one of the technicians. Fifteen minutes later, as the audience drifts back into the theatre, they find the theatre company still on stage, enjoying their tea, and wonder briefly at the actor incongruously dressed in animal skins and a furry hat—until they remember the reference, earlier in the play, to a particular actor who's not there for rehearsal because he's in the Chekhov matinee over in the theatre next door. The play thereby brings the audience into the company's experience of the play as repeated and yet not repetitive.

This leads, in turn, to the question of whether the church thinks seriously about its own rehearsal process, and its own repeating productions, when it thinks about its various activities—and here I am thinking of everything from the liturgy to the soup kitchen to the summer camp. Do Christians take these activities seriously as moments in which divine revelation might well occur? Do they give these moments the kinds of careful consideration that the theatre company gives them, pausing every fifteen seconds to think about what the words mean, why it matters where one stands, what kind of impression is being generated? Shannon Craigo-Snell has written thoughtfully of the way that more attention to the *process* through which drama is produced might help us to extend and deepen our understanding of the Christian life as performance;[26] Bennett's play offers a great deal of support for her argument.

Second point: the diverse and divergent community of interpretation. Here, Bennett's play is especially valuable to us, because it demonstrates the value of this *frisson* in practically every line. Actors stop and wonder about the meaning of a line or an action; the author complains about some section that has been cut or a new emphasis that has been added; technicians point out problems, remind the actors of their lines, and occasionally make mistakes themselves. But the result of all this divergence is not chaos; on the contrary, what the audience can see happening is an incredibly generative process, in which art comes to be understood on a deeper, broader sense— in a way that relates it to everything else in life, and strongly discourages us from either idolizing it or marginalizing it. This notion is nicely encapsulated in the performance when Richard Griffiths, playing an actor named Fitz, who is in turn playing Auden, offers the memorable line, "In the end, *art* is small beer. The really serious things in life are earning one's living and

26. Craigo-Snell, "Command Performance."

loving one's neighbour."²⁷ Of course, this is an Alan Bennett play, so things can't stay too serious for too long; this delicate sentiment is followed by the stage direction, "*He farts*," which is in turn followed by Fitz saying to everyone in the room, "That's Auden farting, not me."

One may point out, of course, that such comic moments—as well as all the instances of interaction, divergence, and combat—that take place in this particular play are themselves carefully rehearsed. These elements are, in fact, part of the play that the audience has come to see; as such, the play is prevented from disintegrating into chaos by the fact that these actors (by which I mean the actors of the actors—Richard Griffiths, Alex Jennings, and Frances de la Tour) are, in fact, performing a script. In other words, there is a meta-script (and a meta-production-company) that controls the action of the whole play (i.e., the one written by Bennett), as well as the interior play (i.e., the one described as having been written by the man who appears on stage as the author).

All of this is true, of course, but I would still argue that the illustration is a good one, because it mirrors the actual rehearsal process of the theatre. There, of course, there is no meta-script and meta-tech-staff to keep the author and director from killing one another; but everyone in the room is working toward a common goal (namely, putting on the play), and usually doing so under a fairly tight deadline. As anyone who has worked in the theatre will testify, this tends to concentrate the mind wonderfully.

All that I wish to take from this illustration is a caution that we not assume that the ecclesial mediation of revelation occurs through neat and tidy categories, systematic theologies and carefully-wrought encyclicals. It seems to me that it might occur just as much in the midst of divergence and argument, in the generative combat among people who are all motivated by a common goal and who work within a common framework. As I noted at the outset, only the theatrical company really gets a whole view of the world of the play; and I want to suggest that the church is a vehicle of revelation only because it operates within this confined space and is therefore able, in spite of the quarrels and occasional cabin fever, to speak the truth about God to the world.

Third, and finally, a few words about corporeality, about physical presence. Of course, live theatre in general is all about being in the same room with other people: the actors, the audience, and—even though they may be just off stage or tucked away behind glass somewhere—the stage managers and technicians who make it all happen. But plays often create all kinds of artificial separations; audience members don't talk with one another,

---

27. Bennett, *Habit of Art*, 28.

technicians can't shout out changes to the actors, and the notorious "fourth wall" sometimes separates audiences from actors in a way that may feel every bit as palpable as the glass screen of a television.

Of course, certain productions of certain plays sometimes toy with these conventions; but the masterstroke of Bennett's *The Habit of Art* is to put these often-separated groups of people into one another's physical presence, and thereby to remind us of how much the theatre depends on that reality. Here we watch actors and technicians interacting with each other, as well with their temporary audiences: actors not currently on stage, chaperones of child actors, and the play's author are all occasionally sitting to the side, watching the play, and sometimes intervening. The end result is a clear demonstration of how much difference it makes when people are physically present to one another.

Having mentioned briefly the significance of this example for the three points I offered in the previous section, I want to conclude by harking back to my comment that preceded them. There, I demurred from Balthasar's association of the Holy Spirit with the director of the play, arguing that this both over-emphasizes the director's role (to the exclusion of the rest of the theatrical company) and that it isolates the Spirit's inspiration to one person, when the more adequate theological claim would be to recognize the way that *the entire church* is the vehicle of the Holy Spirit. One of the things that I like best about Bennett's *The Habit of Art* is that, of all the people involved in the production of the play, the one who never shows up is, in fact, the director. Early in the play, the stage manager receives a phone call and announces, "Bad news, people. The director cannot be with us. Even as we speak Stephen is on his way to Leeds, having forgotten that he was due to speak at a conference on the relevance of the theatre in the provinces."[28] Through this device, the theatrical company (and the audience) is prevented from expecting any disagreement to be resolved, or any final and definitive interpretation imposed, by a single individual. All that we are offered is the effort of various people, primarily the stage manager, to communicate a few of the director's thoughts and choices to the group. It strikes me that this approach might allow us to redeem Balthasar's description of the Holy Spirit as the director of the play; it works best if the director is not physically present only in the body of one human individual (as, after all, the Spirit is not), but has to be interpreted and discerned by the entire company.

---

28. Ibid., 6.

V. Conclusion

In the end, I'm not sure whether Professor Grenz would have approved of my project, with its willingness to draw so heavily on a contemporary cultural phenomenon—the realities of the theatre—to illuminate the doctrine of revelation and, in particular, the role of the church within it. But I am relatively certain that he would have asked the right questions about it; and these are exactly the questions that I would want to be asked: does it align with the overall arc of the biblical story? Does it assert that God is the ultimate agent of revelation? Does it make use of culture in support of a theological claim, rather than the other way around? As I continue my work on this project, I hope that these questions will retain their force in my mind, and that—even if only in that same conjured world of the audience's imagination which Lear invokes—I will continue to hear them being asked by Stan Grenz. For he was, and I suspect that he still remains, one of God's best spies.

Bibliography

Balthasar, Hans Urs von. *Theo-Drama: Theological Dramatic Theory*. 5 vols. San Francisco: Ignatius, 1990–95.
Barth, Karl. Interview in *Time Magazine*, Friday, 31 May 1963.
Barton, Stephen C. "New Testament Interpretation as Performance." *Scottish Journal of Theology* 52/2 (1999) 179–208.
Bell, Rob. *Love Wins: A Book about Heaven, Hell, and the Fate of Every Person Who Ever Lived*. New York: HarperOne, 2011.
Bennett, Alan. *The Habit of Art*. New York: Faber and Faber, 2010.
Bos, Rogier. "Next-Wave Interview with Stanley J. Grenz." Carey/Regent College, Vancouver BC, 20 April 1999. http://www.next-wave.org/may99/SG.htm.
Brook, Peter. *The Empty Space*. New York: Simon and Schuster, 1968.
Buckley, James J., and David Yeago, eds. *Knowing the Triune God: The Work of the Spirit in the Practices of the Church*. Grand Rapids: Eerdmans, 2001.
Craigo-Snell, Shannon. "Command Performance: Rethinking Performance Interpretation in the Context of *Divine Discourse*." *Modern Theology* 16/4 (2000) 475–94.
Cunningham, David S. "Christ the Actor: The Revelatory Power of the Enfleshed Word." Presented at the Society for the Study of Theology, Manchester, England, April 2010.
———. "God's Spies: The Acting Company (and the Church) in a Dramatic Doctrine of Revelation." Presented at the American Academy of Religion Annual Meeting, Atlanta, October 2010.
———. "Is Scripture a Script? Reading and Performing the Revelatory Text." Presented at the University of Exeter, England, February 2010.
———. *Theater to the World: Toward a Dramatic Doctrine of Revelation*. Grand Rapids: Eerdmans (forthcoming).

———. *These Three are One: The Practice of Trinitarian Theology*. Challenges in Contemporary Theology. Oxford: Blackwell, 1998.
Foucault, Michel. *Discipline and Punish: The Birth of the Prison*. New York: Pantheon, 1977.
Frei, Hans. *Theology and Narrative: Selected Essays*. Edited by George Hunsinger and William C. Placher. Oxford: Oxford University Press, 1993.
Lash, Nicholas. "Performing the Scriptures." In *Theology on the Way to Emmaus*, 37–46. London: SCM, 1986.
Lessing, Gotthold Ephraim. *Hamburg Dramaturgy*. New York: Dover, 1962.
Luce, William. *Barrymore*. New York: Samuel French, 1998.
Luckhurst, Mary. *Dramaturgy: A Revolution in Theatre*. Cambridge: Cambridge University Press, 2006.
McLaren, Brian. *A Generous Orthodoxy*. Grand Rapids: Zondervan, 2006.
Milbank, John. *The Word Made Strange: Theology, Language, Culture*. Oxford: Blackwell, 1997.
Ong, Walter J., S.J. *Orality and Literacy: The Technologizing of the Word*. London: Methuen, 1982.
———. *The Presence of the Word: Some Prolegomena for Cultural and Religious History*. 1967. Reprint. Minneapolis: University of Minnesota Press, 1981.
Pickstock, Catherine. *After Writing: On the Liturgical Consummation of Philosophy*. Challenges in Contemporary Theology. Oxford: Blackwell, 1997.
Shakespeare, William. *The Tragedy of King Lear*. The New Folger Shakespeare. New York: Simon and Schuster, Washington Square, 1993.
Wells, Samuel. *Improvisation: The Drama of Christian Ethics*. Grand Rapids: Brazos, 2004.

Part Seven

CONCLUSION

20

Evangelical Theology After Grenz

Evangelical Theology and Global Evangelicalism

DEREK J. TIDBALL

STANLEY GRENZ'S CONTRIBUTION TO evangelical theology came at the end of a century that had been one of immense change and progress for evangelicals. Although there were significant differences between evangelicalism in the United Sates and the United Kingdom, it is a fair generalization that evangelicalism emerged from its fundamentalist cocoon in the middle of the century and, in its renewed form, grew in vitality and impact.[1] Growth and developments within the evangelical movement as a whole resulted in concomitant developments in evangelical theology. During the century evangelical theology was marked by expansion, moving into the mainstream of both the church and the academy, diversification, and adaptation to its changing cultural context of postmodernism, secularism, and globalization.[2] Each of these aspects presented its own challenges and frequently resulted in evangelical theology being highly contested. By the end of the century one commentator claimed of Christian theology as a whole that it "has simply become too large, too divided, too abstract, and too worldly to

---

1. Bebbington, *Evangelicalism*; Hutchinson and Wolffe, *Short History*; Marsden, *Understanding Fundamentalism and Evangelicalism*; Marsden, *Evangelicalism and Modern America*; Marsden, *Reforming Fundamentalism*; Warner, *Reinventing English Evangelicalism*.

2. Noll, *Faith and Criticism*; Larsen and Treier, *Evangelical Theology*; and Grenz, *Renewing the Center*.

407

connect God and a pluralistic reality."[3] The same claim might be made even more of evangelical theology, which is split today not just by its historical division between Arminians and Reformed, but between what Gerald McDermott has called Meliorists and Traditionalists, and what Roger Olson has called Conservatives and Postconservatives.[4] Even that, however, oversimplifies the complex mosaic of evangelical theology.

Stanley Grenz was a key participant in the field of evangelical theology and, given the state of the art, inevitably a contested one since he adopted, in the view of McDermott and others, a meliorist stance. He had an influence that reached far beyond the academy. He had a rare ability, among theologians, to engage issues of contemporary culture and use popular analogies that belonged to the world of "ordinary" Christians. His well-known (and repeated!) use of the changes that occurred in the starship *Enterprise* between the first and second series of *Star Trek* to explain the differences between modernity and postmodernity is a case in point.[5] This went hand in hand with his ability to write in a clear and accessible style, again, not a gift that all academic theologians possess, as his writings in the areas of sexuality, millennial views, and women in ministry, together with his more popular books on theology and doctrine demonstrate. He was active in the church and its mission, both locally and globally. That kept his feet on the ground even if he was able to engage more than competently with the more rarefied atmosphere of contemporary theological and philosophical debate. In these respects, and others, Grenz modelled what evangelical theology should be like—not perfectly, and sometimes controversially—but even so, essentially, as the last part of this essay will explain.

Evangelical Theology and the Evangelical Movement

Evangelical theology may be defined both by what characteristics make it evangelical[6] and also by its relationship to the evangelical movement. By definition it has a symbiotic, if uneasy, relationship with this wider movement.[7] Evangelicalism is essentially a popular religious movement that has

3. Vondey, *Beyond Pentecostalism*, 2.

4. McDermott, "Evangelicals Divided"; Olson, *Reformed*, 7–35. The terms "right" and "left" to describe the differences, as Erickson does in *The Evangelical Left*, is unhelpfully misleading.

5. Grenz, *Primer*, 5–9; "Christian Integrity in a Postmodern World," 7, 10.

6. E.g., Henry and Kantzer *Evangelical Affirmations*; Packer and Oden, *One Faith*.

7. I have deliberately chosen to sidestep debates about the identity of evangelicalism and the evangelical movement for the sake of space. I take it to be a diverse coalition

as much to do with experience as theology, and does not always sit comfortably with academic theology.[8] It has consistently harbored an anti-intellectual stream that is suspicious of theology, not least because of the historical fear that theology leads to liberalism and unbelief.[9] As a movement, at least until very recently,[10] it has been more comfortable with action than with thinking, as Mark Noll concluded, "The tendency of American evangelicals, when confronted with a problem is to act." Adding, "for the sake of Christian thinking, that tendency must be suppressed."[11] He had earlier cited N. K. Clifford as "aptly" stating the problem: "The Evangelical Protestant mind has never relished complexity. Indeed its crusading genius, whether in religion or politics, has always tended toward an over-simplification of issues and the substitution of inspiration and zeal for critical analysis and serious reflection."[12] Furthermore, its primary theological statespersons have been "organic intellectuals," that is, those who emerged from within a community and remain closely in touch with it, rather than being imposed by a community, such as an academic community, from without. John Stott served as the classic evangelical organic intellectual during the second half of the twentieth century, while never holding an academic post.[13] There has always been respect for Bible teachers and commentators within evangelicalism. In fact, when evangelicals emerged from the fundamentalist ghetto in the mid-century their major entrée into the academic world took place through biblical scholars, like F. F. Bruce, who were not trained in theology and often employed classical or historical skills rather than theological tools. Serious engagement with what might be termed theology proper was a later twentieth-century development.[14]

---

of groups and churches that gather around a particular combination of emphases in doctrine and spiritual practice. Thus I am supportive of Bebbington's approach in *Evangelicalism*, 1–19. See Naselli and Hansen, *Four Views on The Spectrum*; and Bebbington's review, "About the Definition of Evangelicalism . . ." Bebbington's approach is more satisfactory than Grenz's definition of evangelicalism in terms of "convertive piety" (*Revisioning*, 22–24; *Renewing*, 46–47) simply because it is fuller.

8. Grenz recognized this and argued that in seeking to understand the movement "we must move beyond the 'fixation with theology' . . . ." (*Revisioning*, 30).

9. McGrath, *Passion for Truth*; Noll, *Scandal*.

10. See assessment in Noll, *Scandal*, 211–39.

11. Ibid., 243.

12. Cited in ibid., 12.

13. McGrath, *Passion for Truth*, 18–20; McGrath, "Evangelical Theological Method," 19.

14. A typical mid-twentieth-century evangelical publication was Manley, *New Bible Handbook*, whereas a collection of articles such as those found in *The Cambridge Companion of Evangelical Theology* would have been unthinkable. These volumes

The relationship between evangelical theologians and the evangelical community is reciprocal.[15] From one perspective evangelical theology derives its life and identity from the wider movement. At its simplest, if evangelical churches were not nurturing people in an evangelical faith, if evangelical parachurch agencies were not engaging in and resourcing mission,[16] if evangelical colleges and seminaries were not training them to build from an evangelical foundation, and evangelical conferences and publishing houses were not disseminating their ideas, evangelical theology would struggle for existence. The fluctuating fortunes, moods, contexts, and agendas of the wider evangelical movement significantly influence the work undertaken by evangelical theologians. This is amply demonstrated by tracing, for example, the work done about mission at the time of Lausanne 74, in pneumatology during the period of charismatic renewal, in recent shifting views concerning the atonement, questions about the openness of God, an emphasis upon communitarian theology, with the recent emphasis on the Trinity and the nature of the church. Each of these mirrors the developing agenda of the parent movement and issues in the wider social context. The future of evangelical theology is, then, in some measure significantly shaped by the future shape of evangelicalism as a movement.

The influence, however, does not flow exclusively, or even primarily, in one direction. Evangelical theologians do more than react. They are not imprisoned by the evangelical movement, and their training teaches them to think independently and creatively. While some evangelical theologians are in ecclesiastical positions, and therefore subject to some interference from those who pay them, many are independent of such pressures. They are often at the frontier of the evangelical movement, shaping its thinking for the future, with ideas that gradually filter down to pew level. When, a decade ago, a popular evangelical leader provoked a furious storm in the UK because he appeared to be jettisoning penal substitution, the central evangelical interpretation of the cross, that leader legitimately protested that evangelical scholars had been raising the same questions and writing in a similar vein for several years.[17] For much of the time there seems a discon-

---

demonstrate the distance travelled in the second half of the twentieth century.

15. McGrath, "Theology and the Futures of Evangelicalism," 15–39, is a rare attempt to address this relationship which deserves much more thought and research than it currently receives.

16. Stackhouse persuasively argues that the interdenominational and parachurch nature of evangelicalism should be a fifth characteristic added to the Bebbington quadrilateral (*Evangelical Landscapes*, 165–83).

17. Chalke and Mann, *Lost Message*; cf. Green and Baker, *Recovering the Scandal*; Wright, *Radical Evangelical*. Other debates, such as, those that cluster around

nection between evangelical theologians and evangelical Christians sitting in the pews, or who are active supporters of its multiplicity of agencies. Yet the views of the theologians have their effect, at least eventually, and, after initially creating fierce counter-reaction, often gradually become adopted as mainstream.

Nonetheless, evangelical theology has no independence apart from the evangelical movement, and it will, therefore, necessarily change as the wider movement itself undergoes transformation. A recent assessment of the evangelical movement[18] points out that in the late twentieth century it enjoyed great global success with a Western brand of evangelicalism being exported and enculturated in many diverse regions of the world. The evidence suggests it has bucked the trend of religious decline that is widespread in the West with the advance of secularism. Yet under the surface, this produces complex challenges, and may well mean evangelicalism does not survive in its present form. The evangelical movement (buttressed by evangelical theology) was a suitable religious expression of Western democracy, individualism, and voluntarism in nation-states where there was a moral and spiritual consensus, but is having to adapt to the immense shifts in transnational agendas. To use an economic metaphor, the export arm of evangelicalism's business is currently more successful than the market at home, but its success has come at a price. Evangelicalism has become "irretrievably"[19] diverse, as well as widespread, calling into question the integrity and identity of evangelicalism as it used to be understood.

The average evangelical today is not from the West, but young, poor, and from the southern hemisphere. As Chris Wright has observed, "Today it is estimated that at least 75% of the world's Christians live in Africa, Asia and Latin America—that is, outside the West, which is becoming increasingly peripheral to the heartlands of Christianity."[20] The activism of evangelical missions has proved successful and as a consequence evangelical theologians will have to adapt if they are to serve the cause of the gospel. So far this change has had much more impact on evangelical missions than on evangelical theology, leading John Mbiti to comment, "It is utterly scandal-

---

postmodernism (cp. Grenz with Tomlinson, *Post-Evangelical*) or universalism (see MacDonald, *The Evangelical Universalist*; Bell, *Love Wins*) have followed the same course.

18. This paragraph is based on the insightful and complex argument of Hutchison and Wolffe, *Short History*, 209–74.

19. Ibid., 270. See Lewis, *Christianity Reborn*. Similarly McLeod wonders if future developments in the church will not depend on China rather than the West ("Being a Christian," 646–47).

20. Wright, "Future Trends in Mission," 153.

ous for so many Christian scholars in [the] old Christendom to know so much about heretical movements in the second and third centuries, when so few of them know anything about Christian movements in areas of the younger churches."[21] Engagement with these churches will change the agenda, making it resonate simultaneously both with the contemporary global agendas and more exactly with the concerns of the Bible, which contemporary Western evangelicals sometimes find embarrassing. As Philip Jenkins observed,

> For the growing churches of the global South, the Bible speaks to everyday, real-world issues of poverty and debt, famine and urban crisis, racial and gender oppression, state brutality and persecution. The omnipresence of poverty promotes an awareness of the transience of life, the dependence of individuals and nations on God, and the distrust of the secular order.[22]

These evangelicals do not engage in precise debates about authority and inerrancy, since they know the Bible speaks authoritatively to their situation. They do not replay historic debates from the Reformation era, since they know the Bible is about their ability to endure and persevere as disciples of Jesus Christ today. They do not endlessly discuss postmodernity, which Pauline Rosenau once described as, in part, the luxury of a bored generation for whom scarcity is remote and who are preoccupied with liberty rather than necessity,[23] since they are in search of survival. It is not that these issues are unimportant. It is vital we connect with the on-going story of the Western world as well, or else we lose our identity. But the focus will inevitably shift towards the agendas set by the most significant areas of evangelical vitality; and Western evangelical theology, reflecting the mission impulse of evangelicalism itself, should be at the forefront of encouraging that shift.

This change will have a major impact on the future course of evangelical theology, whether willingly embraced or reluctantly imposed. Like pastors leading their church through transition, seeking to minister to their committed insiders (often old-timers!) while seeking simultaneously to win those from a younger generation who are strangers to the church and its ways (if not total aliens to it), theologians need to be looking several ways at once and to learn the skills of addressing very different audiences and questions simultaneously. The tensions that already exist between traditionalist

---

21. Cited by Jenkins, *Next Christendom*, 4.
22. Jenkins, *New Faces*, 5.
23. Rosenau, *Post-Modernism and the Social Sciences*, 11.

and "postconservative"[24] evangelical theologians, and those that are inherent in theologians needing at present to address both the academy and the church, will be eclipsed by those spawned by the voices of global evangelicalism. Before returning to the global dimension, though, we need to say something of the present state of Western evangelical theology.

Grenz and the Future of Evangelical Theology

Grenz, although repudiating the label, was perceived by many as a postconservative theologian, because of his method and approach.[25] Yet his conclusions were often distinctly conservative, as is very evident in his writings on ethics. Perhaps Roger Olson puts his finger on the crucial issue when he explains, the difference between traditional and postconservative evangelical theologians is not that one group value the authority of Scripture more highly than the other, but that they engage in theology differently.[26] The traditional emphasis on the Bible as containing information and doctrinal propositions is subsumed under a wider encounter with Scripture that sees it as narrative as well and as primarily transformational.[27] Postconservatives are more exploratory and view their calling as more provisional rather than being a confident assertion of "received doctrinal paradigms."[28] They also emphasize spiritual experience alongside doctrinal correctness rather than allowing the latter to eclipse the former. They reach back to evangelicalism's Pietist roots, not just its Enlightenment beginnings, and are prepared to question the received evangelical tradition. However, some elements of postconservatism do not apply easily to Grenz. Olson claims postconservatives are more critical of the impact of the Enlightenment on evangelical theology than traditionalists, and less concerned with boundaries, viewing evangelicalism more as a centered-set than a boundaried movement. But Grenz reserved an important place for "the theological heritage of the church" as one of the three sources of theology, alongside Scripture

---

24. The choice of any word to describe evangelical theologians who are not traditionalist is fraught with difficulty, but "postconservative" is as good as any. Olson, *Reformed*, 7–65.

25. Olson claims Grenz was "the epitome of postconservative theologians," although rejected the label (*Reformed*, 15).

26. Ibid., *passim*.

27. On Grenz's view of evangelical propositionalism see *Revisioning*, 65–72.

28. Pinnock, cited by Olson, *Reformed*, 55.

(primarily) and the contemporary cultural context.[29] And he viewed evangelicals as "a boundaried community," albeit not in any simply way.[30]

Grenz set out his agenda for the development of evangelical theology in his *Revisioning Evangelical Theology: A Fresh Agenda for the 21st Century*, a work that was complemented and expanded by his *Renewing the Center* and by *Beyond Foundationalism* (with John Franke),[31] and he had begun to work it out in depth in the early volumes of the series he proposed.[32]

After a necessary chapter exploring evangelical identity, *Revisioning Evangelical Theology* gives its attention to evangelical spirituality, rather than to doctrine. This is no accident. It both follows from the nature of evangelicalism, which was essentially, in Grenz's view, one of "convertive piety," and also from the quest among contemporary evangelicals for a renewed spirituality. Far from being a new development, this was, he argued, a return to the earlier evangelical heritage in Puritanism and Pietism, and even the patristic era.[33] It was not that doctrine was unimportant to him. Far from it. But "the evangelical ethos is more than mere theology," and has profound implications for the way we do our theology.[34] While it "ought never to lose as its central goal the intellectual pursuit of truth," "speculative theology" was "best served" by its integration with piety and led naturally to theology being rooted in the life of the community and the Trinity, which were to become Grenz's twin foci.[35] In seeking in his early methodological work, with others, to correct the balance between doctrine and experience Grenz was performing a vital service to the movement, but one that, for the reasons he explores in the following chapter, caused concern to more traditional and propositionally oriented evangelical theologians.[36]

Turning to theology itself, Grenz traced the increasingly rational path it had taken, and the way in which in evangelicalism it came to stress the rationality of God's revelation, and saw systematic theology as "a crystallization

---

29. Grenz, *Revisioning*, 93–101

30. Grenz, "Die Begrenzte Gemeinschaft," 301–16.

31. Note also, Franke, *Character of Theology*, maps out a similar approach to Grenz.

32. The first two volumes of his proposed series on "The Matrix of Christian Theology" were *Social God* and *Named God*.

33. Grenz, *Revisioning*, 39, 57.

34. Ibid., 34.

35. Ibid., 57–58.

36. Olson claims "Stan was absolutely bewildered by some of the reactions to his *Revisioning* proposal, especially the one that equated it with Schleiermacher's project" ("Stanley J. Grenz's Contribution," 27–28). My own conversations with Grenz confirm this.

of biblical truth into a set of universally true and applicable propositions."[37] However, if the task of theology, "is to assist the contemporary believing community to fulfil its responsibility of proclaiming and living out the message that God has appeared in Christ for the sake of the salvation of humankind" then it is necessarily contextual.[38] Since the contemporary context was perceived to have changed from a modern to a postmodern one, inevitably one's approach to theology and the language used must change as well. While all evangelical theologians would agree in theory, the outworking of this principle becomes highly controversial in practice, and explains some of the current divisions. It throws up questions about many things: novelty *versus* tradition; the importance of words, and so of the Word, that is, the text of sacred Scripture, and of propositions; the place of evidentialism; and the clarity of narrative. Grenz's approach was to accept a modified form of Lindbeck's understanding of theology as a "second-order discipline" that functions in the "regulative" way that grammar functions to make sense of language.[39] Thus it is essentially concerned to help the community explore its symbols, beliefs, and experiences, and to create order and make sense out of them. Theology, then, does not describe the ontological reality of God himself directly, but provides a model of how that reality is experienced in a particular historical context. The question of truth, however, cannot be sidestepped since faith communities make truth claims that need to be publicly defensible. Nonetheless, the vocation of theology becomes a chastened and humbled one in comparison with the confidence of previous generations of evangelical theologians, who believed they were dealing directly and as a first order discipline with the revelation of God.[40]

This approach logically raises the question of what sources contribute to the undertaking of contemporary theology. Acknowledging the Reformation emphasis on *sola scriptura*, he takes issue with Wesley's quadrilateral since he sees experience as the medium though which theology is received rather than a source in itself. For Grenz, theology's three primary pillars or "norms" are the biblical message, the theological heritage of the church, and "the thought-forms of the historical-cultural context in which the contemporary people of God seek to speak, live and act."[41] Among this triad, Grenz asserts the Bible is "the primary norm for theology" and that its authority may be "assumed," because it is "universally acknowledged" by evangelical

37. Grenz, *Revisioning*, 65.
38. Ibid., 77.
39. Lindbeck, *Nature of Doctrine*.
40. Grenz, *Revisioning*, 72–85.
41. Ibid., 93.

theologians and is part of our Reformation heritage.[42] However, he rejects attempts to justify the Bible's role by reference to external and internal evidence, as evangelical theologians have traditionally done. He rejects the approach both because he believes it to be unnecessary and also because such justification is required by a modern rather than postmodern culture.[43] While Scripture is primary, the other sources of theology need to be integrated and balanced with it rather than being approached as separate and distinctive disciplines. Whether one is able to produce a genuinely evangelical theology depends precisely on the balance and integration of these three elements, and this becomes another battlefield with, perhaps inevitably, the book *Revisioning Evangelical Theology* being somewhat too simple to assist us in the task.

Grenz's more detailed exploration of Scripture illustrates the problem. There is much in it that all evangelical theologians would wish to affirm. The Bible exists to give a true knowledge of God and nourishment to the spiritual life. The Scriptures are the result of the Holy Spirit's revelation and inspiration. They can only be properly understood if approached from within the believing community, in which they have a "constitutional role."[44] Yet Grenz also offers a challenge to common evangelical approaches to the Bible, believing that although evangelicals acknowledge it to be both a divine and human book, they tend only to pay lip service to the latter and present it in a somewhat distorted fashion as if it only comes "from above." This leads to the errors of bibliolatry, and to equating the "Word of God" with a book rather than to the actual words God spoke.[45] In separating Scripture from the doctrine of the Spirit, Grenz believes the Reformers made a mistake and robbed Scripture of its dynamic character, playing down the continuing role of the Spirit in interpreting Scripture through the believing community for the contemporary context. Inspiration and illumination need to be kept close together.[46] Rather than debating the Bible's reliability, as understood through the lens of historical evidence, linguistic critical method, or a doctrine of inerrancy, the debate is rather about how it is to be interpreted as canonically received, that is, how old truths can be interpreted to meet new

---

42. Ibid. Personally, I am always anxious when the place of the Bible is "assumed" because what is "assumed" by one well-taught generation is often relegated by the next and entirely forgotten by the one that follows.

43. Ibid., 94.

44. Ibid., 111–13.

45. Ibid., 116–18.

46. Ibid., 115, 117.

challenges.[47] In a somewhat similar vein to Spurgeon's oft quoted, "Defend the Bible, I would as soon defend a Lion. Unchain it and it will defend itself,"[48] Grenz sees some value in the functional justification of Scripture: "The Church ... came to confess the inspiration of Scripture because they experienced through these writings the power and truth of the Spirit of God. These documents were, they knew, 'animated with the Spirit of Christ.'"[49]

Grenz's assertions concerning Scripture are the crux of the matter. In seeking to rescue the Bible as a living book and replacing a deductive approach to its authority with an inductive one, in seeking to stress the need for illumination alongside inspiration, and in stressing the human as well as the divine nature of the Bible, has he conceded too much? In saying "our Bible is the product of the community of faith that cradled it.... And the writings contained in the Bible represent the self-understanding of the community in which it developed" does he not make the opposite error to the one he criticizes among more traditional evangelicals?[50] Fears are not allayed when he writes of the Bible as "the enduring trajectory of that community," because such statements raise questions, which I know he did not intend, about the sufficiency and finality of Scripture.[51] To some evangelicals, it is not a matter of whether Grenz concedes too much but whether he has a fundamentally wrong starting point.[52] The issue is whether the Bible is the product of the church or the church the product of the word of God, in other words, the Bible. Perhaps it is a chicken and egg question. But it is one which divides an evangelical community in transition.

Grenz then examines the integrative motif of theology. In contrast to previous integrative motifs, Grenz initially proposes the eschatological kingdom of God as the key point of integration.[53] This seems to recapture the emphasis on New Testament eschatology about which recent evangelicalism has been largely silent. Our recent eloquent silence about eschatol-

47. Ibid. 118, 130–31.

48. This would seem to be a paraphrase of a longer quotation from an address Spurgeon gave to the Bible Society in 1875, Variations occur in at least two of his Metropolitan Tabernacle Sermons (Nos. 2004 and 2467).

49. Ibid., 121.

50. Ibid.

51. Ibid.

52. See the helpful critique of Grenz as a representative of postconservative evangelical theology in Erickson, *Evangelical Left, passim,* and the harsher critique of Carson in *Reclaiming the Center,* 33–55.

53. Grenz, *Revisioning,* 137–48. There is some ambiguity in Grenz's view as, having proposed the eschatological kingdom as an integrative motif, he then appears to have second thoughts about it, and downgrades it to being an orienting motif in favor of community.

ogy may have been the result of two counter movements: a reaction to the embarrassment caused by so much crass premillennialism which has proved false time and again, and an over-dosing on the present and material world which evangelicals rightly rediscovered when their social conscience were reawakened in the mid and late twentieth century.[54] He avoids treating eschatology as about "pie in the sky when you die," and connects the current church and its mission, as "a laboratory of the kingdom"[55] to its future destination.[56] Yet he admits that the concept of the kingdom is somewhat limited as it is "undefined."[57] Sadly, rather than pursuing this theme in more depth and explaining on what basis God's eschatological kingdom can be discerned and how it can be distinguished from merely human experiments for improvements, he turns his attention to the more defined theme of community.

Grenz developed the significance of community in a number of directions, especially in *Theology for the Community of God*. It draws its life from, and models itself on, the relational God who, as a Trinitarian God, is God in community. Community becomes the locus of interpretation of Scripture, as well as being the body that proclaims the kingdom and anticipates it in its own arrangements and lifestyle.

Grenz's agenda is courageous and illustrates the complexity and difficulty of proposing the future path of evangelical theology. It attempts to contextualize the evangelical theological tradition and enable it to make sense to contemporary postmodern culture. It focuses on the hallmarks of evangelicalism, the experience of God, the primacy of Scripture, and the mission of the church, although it does not give as much attention to sin and redemption as found in classic evangelicalism. Some feel that it is insufficiently critical of postmodernity[58] while, although a number of younger critics charge them of being guilty in this respect, conservative evangelicals refuse to plead guilty to the counter claim of being insufficiently critical of modernity. Indeed, postmodernity's understanding of truth does raise fundamental questions for a more conservative evangelical epistemology. Yet, in the ferment of seeking to express old truths for a new context, it is

---

54. An early sign of the reawakening is seen in Henry, *Uneasy Conscience*.

55. Grenz, *Revisioning*, 162.

56. In arguing this he is not unique but a representative of a growing trend in evangelical scholarship, as seen in such diverse works as Beale, *New Testament Biblical Theology* and Wright, *Surprised by Hope*.

57. Grenz, *Revisioning*, 148; cf. Sexton, *Trinitarian Theology*, 145–49.

58. E.g., Carson, "Domesticating the Gospel," 43; Wells, *Above All Earthly Pow'rs*, 73.

surely often true that pioneers get the balance wrong. Wiser perspectives develop with time.

Some of those who are confident of their definitions and have a very defined view of what evangelicalism is[59] see Grenz's approach as hardly evangelical.[60] Others, however, who perhaps have a less restricted definition of evangelicalism, perceive his method as a genuine attempt to translate an evangelical gospel for the contemporary context. The former, perhaps, have something of a limited view of the evangelical tradition, and fail to take account of the breadth of perspective and beliefs that have characterized the evangelical coalition. The pietistic stream of evangelicalism emphasized experience long before Schleiermacher, and definitions of the Bible's authority have not always taken the form they currently do among inerrantists. The former also tend to assume, in McGrath's words, "the inerrancy of the evangelical tradition." May it not be that evangelicals in the past have got some things wrong and that they sometimes fail to distinguish between the inerrancy of Scripture and the inerrancy of their own interpretations of it?[61] The charge of cultural captivity cuts both ways.[62]

Given this, it is hard to see how evangelical theology as an enterprise can do anything but continue to fragment.[63] Grenz represents one stream of those influenced by postmodernity,[64] but among them other currents flow. Vanhoozer's approach to Scripture is another example of a way of handling the same issues of post-propositionalism and post-foundationalism.[65] In the eyes of many, he is more successful in integrating doctrine and experience rather than leaving them somewhat bifurcated, as many wearing Grenz's spectacles do.[66] But the continuous coming on-stream of those who agonize how to give the evangelical tradition currency today does not remove existing streams and often gives them new vigor as they reassert positions

---

59. This is a major issue in the debate: Naselli and Hansen, *Four Views*; Olson, *Reformed*; and n.7 above.

60. Carson, *Gagging*, 481.

61. McGrath, "Evangelical Theological Method," 31.

62. This would be my critique of the various writings of David Wells, whose provocative challenge to the contemporary church I have always greatly valued and believe to have some substance.

63. McDermott, "Evangelicalism Divided."

64. McDermott astutely argues, however, that "what finally divides Evangelical theologians is not their view of foundationalism but their attitude to tradition and Scripture"(Ibid.).

65. Vanhoozer, *Is there a Meaning in this Text?*; "The Voice and the Actor," 61–107; and *The Drama of Doctrine*.

66. McDermott, "Evangelicalism Divided."

worked out in previous contexts. The river, then, is bound to get fuller and fuller, and at times, when crosscurrents flow, become turbulent.

What of the global dimension of evangelical theology mentioned above? Stanley Grenz's career shows that he was personally well aware of it, as he gave some of his time to teaching in Africa and East Asia and to the world Baptist family. Yet the deeper dimensions of globalization had yet to occur and his writings, although putting the right topics on the agenda, inevitably reflects the preoccupations and questions of the Western world and church.

Characteristics of Evangelical Theology

The reality is that while I believe Grenz identified the right topics— Trinitarian God, nature of humanity, Bible, kingdom, eschatology, church, and community—and bravely grappled with an attempt to recontextualize a genuinely *evangelical* theology, his approach to the debates, together with those of his conversation partners, may soon be overtaken by the growth of evangelicalism in the Global South.[67] The symbiotic relationship between evangelical theology and the evangelical movement will mean that the younger evangelicals from the Global South—African, Asian, and South American—will be setting the agenda more in the future, and producing their own contextualized evangelical theology.[68] It is, I believe, a mistake of the arrogant West to assume that globalization means that Western culture, with its preoccupation with postmodernity, will conquer everywhere. The resurgence of Islam and of what Westerners often feel is a more "primitive" form of Christianity shows that the triumph of Western liberal democracy, its cultural concomitants, and a spiritually "sophisticated" worldview cannot be assumed.[69]

---

67. I have chosen to use "Global South" to identify new churches, although I recognize its problematic nature. Rebecca Catto, in her work on reverse mission, discusses the term and, at one point, concludes that "non-Western" would be a more appropriate term because of the significance of Korea, which is in the northern hemisphere. But "Global South" remains the most common shorthand in the literature. Catto, "Reverse Mission," 99–100.

68. To this point much theology undertaken by younger theologians in the Global South has had a Western world complexion, but this is increasingly changing. See Nkansah-Obrempong, "Evangelical Theology in Africa"; Tiénou, "Evangelical Theology in African Contexts," 213–24. This volume contains similar essays on Asia and South America.

69. Micklethwait and Wooldridge, *God is Back*, records the implications from an American perspective.

Having no expertise in what the question of the future will be,[70] all one can do is affirm the contours of what evangelical theology will look like, since "Evangelical theology must be Evangelical."[71]

It Must Be Biblical in Focus

The first hallmark of evangelical theology, as almost everyone would agree, is the centrality and authority of the Bible. This commitment, however, cannot and should not be taken for granted, especially in the contemporary context. Scripture, not culture, must always be primary, but, having said this, that still leaves plenty of questions unanswered.

Evangelicalism's recent approach to Scripture has been anything but static.[72] When evangelicalism initially emerged from its fundamentalist captivity, many scholars sought to authenticate the Bible and its text (and so its message) by reference to archaeology and history.[73] Moving beyond that proved more problematic, and approaches to historical criticism of the text and to formulations of the exact nature of its authenticity led to debates swirling around questions of inerrancy and infallibility.[74] These debates remain fierce in some evangelical circles, but were overtaken elsewhere by the introduction of different forms of biblical criticism, such as rhetorical or canonical criticism, and the introduction of hermeneutics. British evangelicals were first introduced to hermeneutics through Anthony Thiselton's contribution to the National Evangelical Anglican Assembly in 1977.[75] While evangelicals had always proposed some wise principles of how Scripture should be interpreted,[76] not least, so that any apparent tensions within could be reconciled, this propelled evangelical theology into a new orbit by the introduction of hitherto unknown philosophical categories to the debate. The contributions of Grenz and Vanhoozer, and many others, including their critics, to the discussion about the Bible's nature and authority

---

70. Predicting the future, other than the second coming, is a precarious enterprise as so many have found in the past as unpredictable "events" threw their projections off course.

71. Stackhouse, "Evangelical Theology Should be Evangelical," 39–58.

72. See chs. 11–13 of the present vol.

73. As seen in the work of E. M. Blakelock, F. F. Bruce, Donald Guthrie, R. K. Harrison, Ken Kitchen, Donald Wiseman, E. J. Young, and others.

74. See Marsden, *Reforming Fundamentalism*; Lindsell, *Battle*.

75. Thiselton's fuller exposition of the theme came in *The Two Horizons* and in many subsequent books.

76. E.g., Berkhof, *Principles*; Ramm, *Protestant Biblical Interpretation*; Stibbs, *Understanding God's Word*.

is but the latest phase of an on-going and ever-developing discussion among evangelical theologians about their primary source.

The sea changes occurring on the global scene reverberate much more in practice with an approach to Scripture as outlined by Grenz or Vanhoozer, than more traditional views. Expressing frustration at an American who was stressing the need for the Bible to be interpreted using the apparatus of modern critical scholarship, an African bishop asked, "If you don't *believe* the scripture, why did you bring it to us in the first place?"[77] In many Western evangelical seminaries, while the formal defense of an evangelical view of Scripture has been resolute, the use of critical approaches to Scripture as taught has often been confusing, and left many knowing how *not* to preach the Bible rather than how to do so, and undermined their confidence. In the newer churches of Africa, however, the whole Bible is credited with an authenticity and an immediacy often lacking in the West.[78] The reality of the spirit world, God communicating through dreams, the working of miracles, the sense of oppression by corrupt political powers, grinding poverty, and the experience of warfare bring the Bible alive to them in ways long muted in the West, and spawn entirely different hermeneutical approaches than are customary in our seminaries. It is a book that is credited with authority chiefly because of experience; it is a book to be experienced, and one that recapitulates the drama of life and redemption. The Bible and its message should be released.

It Should Be Preoccupied with the Gospel

Evangelical theology will be gospel-centered theology. All manner of implications flow from this deceptively simple statement.

First, it leads us to the content of the gospel that we have to communicate, which will be about what God did in Christ to overcome sin through his cross and resurrection. We will, therefore, dig deep into Scripture to understand God's revelation about salvation, and how it was first experienced and communicated by the apostles. This is normative for what we say today. Yet we should also strive to communicate that same gospel, as they did, with fresh metaphors, expressions, and applications so that the message hits its target. Doing this is to practice Jesus' admonition to his disciples to

---

77. Jenkins, *New Faces*, 1.

78. I recognize that what follows is a grossly black and white picture that needs careful qualifications. Not all Western theology is guilty as charged, and not all Global South church life is as ideal as presented. But the concern is with the major shift in currents rather than precise details.

imitate house owners who bring out "new treasures as well as old" from the storeroom.[79] We are, in Vanhoozer's words, to be engaged in "faithful performance and creative improvisation," which need not be at odds with each other.[80] This will involve the unmasking of the idols of our age, whether they are materialism, pop psychology, violence, mystical experiences, or whatever. It will involve the diagnosis of our ills in terms of our alienation from God and sin, identifying sin in all its varied forms as described in the Bible. But in a world where the evidence of failure and breakdown is all too evident, it is the good news to which we should pay most attention.

Evangelical theologians will keep the big picture of what God is doing to rescue his fallen creation in mind. This concerns both the salvation of individuals and the recreation of the cosmos—the "reconciliation of all things."[81] To concentrate on the one at the expense of the other is a distortion of the gospel. As a child of the Enlightenment, evangelicalism has often emphasized the personal and individual nature of salvation, and understandably so. But to do so exclusively when the Bible speaks, for example, of the resurrection as the first fruits of a new creation[82] and when its eschatological trajectory leads us to the creation of a new heaven and a new earth[83] is to fail to be faithful to Scripture. On the global scene, the renewal of creation is often perceived to assume greater urgency than the conversion of a few.

Such theologizing inevitably leads us to the importance of the church, which is the community of believers, the harbinger and showcase of the kingdom and the foretaste of the new creation. Again, it is the big picture that needs to be borne in mind. The current Western quest for authentic community by a lonely postmodern generation will be part of this, but it will work out differently in different areas of the world where "community" is still more in evidence than in the West. Giving attention to the church does not mean we serve the often petty, self-serving or self-preserving agendas of current institutions. Two thousand years of church history cannot be swept away and we must engage with what we have inherited, but we dare not be trapped by it. Theologians have the responsibility to call God's people back to clear principles about the nature and purpose of church and to release people from their ecclesiastical prisons. Our desire should be

---

79. Matt 13:52.
80. Cited by Olson, *Reformed*, 56.
81. Col 1:20.
82. 1 Cor 15:20–28.
83. 2 Pet 3:11–13; Rev 21:1—22:5.

to construct contemporary forms of authentic church[84] and to use all our power to release the resources of the past for the mission of the present.

A preoccupation with the gospel leads to a consideration of ethics, as Stanley Grenz knew well. Paul's ethical teaching, just to illustrate from one part of Scripture, is nothing other than an unfolding of the implications of the gospel and time and again he draws people back to first principles as the basis for building a case for behaving in a certain way. Whether the issue is "the collection," unity in the church, sexual behavior, reaction to idols, or the practice of worship, Paul draws people back time and again to the meaning of the gospel.[85]

Preoccupation with the gospel will also lead to a consideration of mission, the DNA of evangelicalism. All too often, however, mission has been handled in a purely pragmatic or commercial way, disconnected from theological considerations with the result that its method has jarred with its message. As evangelicals confessed at Lausanne (1974), what has been exported has often been a Western culture rather than a multi-cultured gospel, but that confession has not always led to reformation of practice. Sometimes the reason for the disconnection lies with evangelical theologians who have shown no interest in mission, sometimes it lies with the activists, who are too impatient to get on with the job. Both need to feed each other.

It Should Be Contextual in Character

Whatever their particular branch of theology may be, whether biblical, systematic, historical, or pastoral,[86] evangelical theologians will use the past to serve the present. If they do not do so, in what sense can they be called evangelical?

Therein lies the challenge. History gives us a sense of perspective that we otherwise lack when we are seeking to make sense of the context in which we find ourselves. Theology is a high wire art in which it is all too easy to fall off the rope one side, or the other. On one side we have the danger of accommodating too much and becoming so immersed in contemporary culture that we have no message to bring to it. We fail to maintain any distance from contemporary society and are so concerned with relevance that we

---

84. The word "authentic" is deliberately included to distance myself from the idea that any group of people meeting together to discuss religion or express some form of self-centered spirituality is church.

85. Thompson, *Pastoral Ministry According to Paul*.

86. Pastoral theology tends to suffer from the opposite error to the other disciplines in being only concerned with the contemporary to its detriment, as Oden in *Care of Souls*, and elsewhere, has rightly argued.

forget that the most relevant word of all is what God has done in Christ. The danger in our seeking to build a bridge to contemporary culture, as William Willimon has put it, is that "the traffic [moves] only in one direction," with the modern world "rummaging about in Scripture" and jettisoning what seems impractical or it cannot make sense of. But, "The point is not to *speak* to the culture; the point is to *change* it."[87]

There is ample evidence that too great a closeness to contemporary culture ends up silencing the Christian gospel, even where it is motivated by a genuine missionary desire.[88] Dean Kelly has demonstrated this in relation to mainline American denominations and, in spite of many attempts to draw different conclusions from his research than those he does, the main thrust of his argument seems hard to counter. Peter Berger has provided us with the theoretical understanding of why this should be so.[89] Unless Christians provide an overarching meaning system that is distinct from all the other smaller meaning systems on offer, why would anyone bother with the church (unless, of course, they have some cultural fascination with its musical tradition!)? "The question," Berger rightly claimed, "about any symbolic representation of the faith is not whether it is old or new, 'backward' or avant-garde, but whether it brings us any closer to the transcendent reality to which it refers."[90]

On the other hand, there is the danger of insulating ourselves from the contemporary world and becoming unable to communicate with it— the mistake of fundamentalism.[91] Christian Smith's research has shown that maintaining the right distance between the church and society is what lends the church vitality. We need to be engaged, yet challenging, picking our battles wisely in every culture.[92]

Many theological debates will continue to revolve around the question of distance from contemporary culture. That has been the case in most of the areas of dispute among evangelical theologians in recent days. Such disputes call for us to listen to each other, and not rush to premature judgments.

87. Willimon, "The Culture is Overrated," 31.

88. Bruce, *Firm in the Faith,* 65–94, illustrates this in his account of the demise of Student Christian Movement (SCM) and rise of Inter-Varsity Fellowship (IVF) in Britain in the mid- to late-twentieth century. See Kelly, *Why Conservative Churches are Growing.*

89. Berger, *Sacred Canopy.*

90. Berger, "Prologue: Bestrangement in Stockholm," 186.

91. Smith, *American Evangelicalism.* Curiously fundamentalism was not distant from mainline society in every respect, as its thriving in the southern states of the USA, the home of the oil industry and of geological research, indicates.

92. Smith, *American Evangelicalism.*

But it was ever thus. I wonder whether contemporaries of Daniel, Meshach, and Abednego would have held them in the honor we do. Would not some have argued that they had sold out and become "liberal"—too left wing, too postconservative—because they accepted education in Nebuchadnezzar's University, while others would have regarded them as ill-advised fundamentalists—too right wing, too conservative—in drawing the line at eating the king's food. Daniel 1 serves as a paradigm for evangelical theologians.

The ever-changing cultural dimension means that evangelical theologians will always be in transition and face a developing agenda. The global context raises new questions and in answering them we need to maintain the same uncomfortable position between distance and engagement with African, Asian, and Latin American cultures as evangelicalism has demonstrated at its best in the West. As James Nkansah-Obrempong recognized: "The dilemma African Evangelicals are facing is to develop an African Christianity that is authentically African and truly biblical. The concern to relate theology to culture without accommodating or losing the essential core of evangelical theology can be a challenge."[93] Challenge it is, but theology must direct its energies towards producing, in the words of the Lausanne Covenant, "churches that are deeply rooted in Christ and closely related to their culture."[94] Theology holds in tension God's eternal revelation with our human wrestling with how to express it for today.

It Should Be Gracious in Style

The character of evangelical theology should be shaped by the central commitments of evangelical spirituality, so it can never be an academic exercise divorced from godliness and prayerfulness. To engage in theology requires us to engage in worship, first and foremost as disciples of Jesus who are submitted to God. It is not an act of assertive human independence or academic speculation. Research and debate is carried out under the watchful eye of God, and needs to be conducted in a way that pleases him. This calls for conviction about his revelation and confidence in his truth to be infused by humility and grace. The core of the gospel is God's grace, arising from his gracious character,[95] and consequently our debates should be marked by the same graciousness.

---

93. Nkansah-Orempong, "Evangelical Theology in Africa," 298.

94. Clause 10. This clause remains one of the finest, succinct expressions of the ideal relationship between the church and culture yet written.

95. Exod 34:6–7.

Our holding of strong convictions has sometimes led us to be ungracious in our debates. We have not always modelled the love that Paul commended in 1 Cor 13 as one of the prime Christian virtues. We may have spoken with the tongues of acute intellectualism or as champions of evangelical tradition, but we have not always been patient, or kind, or kept no record of wrongs. Rather than protecting, we have exposed; rather than trusting we have been suspicious; rather than hoping we have written others off; rather than persevering we have excluded people from our circles. Our failure to engage with each other in love unconsciously betrays more about what we really believe about the Bible's authority than all our neat formulations about it. *If evangelical theology does not speak in an evangelical tone, it ceases to be evangelical.*

Sadly, that has not always been the case. Recent years have been marked by a series of sharp debates that have "exposed the fragility of the evangelical theological consensus."[96] They have concerned, in no particular order, open theism, the New Perspectives on Paul and the Reformation view of justification, theories of the atonement, sexual ethics, universalism, and the nature of the Bible's authority. Stanley Grenz himself suffered from ungracious words. When genuinely attempting to construct an evangelical theology for our own time, whether successfully or not, some wrote his method off as "not 'evangelical' in any useful sense."[97] More recently still, some evangelicals have fed suspicions about the authenticity of Tom Wright's commitment to evangelicalism, because in searching for what he believes to be a more genuine interpretation of the meaning of justification he is not prepared to stick with the mere repetition of reformation formulae.[98] In the debate about whether women should occupy teaching and leadership roles in the church, some have questioned the evangelical integrity of those with whom they disagree, not because their opponents in any way question the authority of Scripture but because they dare to interpret the Bible differently.[99] On most issues, I veer to the conservative end of the spectrum (not all, women in leadership is a case in point) but I lament the lack of grace many of my fellow believers demonstrate in the dealings with one another, and believe it seriously undermines the authenticity of our evangelical position. Adopting a fortress or defensive mentality that simply seeks to preserve or

96. Hutchinson and Wolffe, *Short History,* 266–67. And Olson, *Reformed,* 74–75.

97. These examples and numerous others could be documented but in order to avoid falling into the very trap which is being condemned here, I decline to do so.

98. See the hurt tone in Wright, *Justification,* vii–xi. Yet see the charitable and gracious interaction with Wright in Schreiner, "Justification: The Saving Righteousness of God in Christ," 19–34.

99. Smith, *God's Good Design,* 13, 42.

justify the received evangelical tradition is unnecessary and, ironically, untrue to the evangelical tradition. To be evangelical is to graciously engage in re-expressing God's eternal word for today's context.

If we need grace in our dealings with each other when debating with those who come from within our culture, we will need it even more when the cross-cultural dimension of theology becomes even more significant. The generous orthodoxy for which Grenz pleaded will become even more vital and in it all we must ensure we keep both in balance—generosity *and* orthodoxy.[100]

Both generosity and orthodoxy are crucial. If evangelicalism is to have any coherent meaning, boundaries certainly have to be drawn and orthodoxy upheld. But some have drawn very narrow boundaries, which not insignificantly often demonstrate a very selective view of evangelical history, and too readily expel those who do not conform in order to maintain the purity of the movement. Some streams within evangelicalism are anxious to define things more and more precisely in a way that would have been little understood by our predecessors. Their view of "orthodoxy" is the "orthodoxy" of one strand of evangelicalism, often preserved in historic aspic, rather than of the richer tradition of the historic church. Yet, theology, by its nature, is necessarily a living, creative discipline that seeks to restate the same Scripture for an ever-changing context, and it therefore requires us to be patient with one another. As is evident, this is certainly not to argue that "anything goes." It is to argue that in discerning "what goes" we do so by listening carefully to each other, putting the most charitable construction on each others' views, truly bringing our debates back to Scripture and not to any one contextually-locked interpretation of Scripture, and discussing our disagreements with grace.[101]

Conclusion

Apart from having the genuine gift of prophecy predicting the future is an impossible task. Our world is much more open than we often think and events happen that change the world in a single day. But evangelical theology in the future is likely to be affected by the shape of the evangelical

---

100. Grenz, *Renewing the Center,* 325–51.

101. I would commend the approach of Millard Erickson who, while clearly holding his own views, and not always accurately understanding those he reviews, helpfully evaluates them by identifying their positive contribution before setting out the negative and problematic aspects he perceives (e.g., *The Evangelical Left* and *Postmodernizing the Faith*).

movement, as it has been in the past. This means that, while continuing to wrestle with the issues of Western culture, it will increasingly be shaped by the growth of evangelicalism in the Global South that will raise new questions about the Bible and its interpretation, and the gospel and its application. Evangelical theologians, while remaining true both to core evangelical doctrines[102] and characteristics, will increasingly have to broaden their lenses to take the wider global horizon of the evangelical movement into account. But that is as it should be, since we believe in a living God whose trustworthy "word is not chained"[103] to any one area of the world or one form of culture, or even to one greatly-valued historical expression of the faith. God calls us ever forward in our vocation of combining faithfulness to his word with creativity in our handling of it, until the day when he will reign "all in all."[104]

Bibliography

Beale, G. K. *A New Testament Biblical Theology: The Unfolding of the Old Testament in the New*. Grand Rapids: Baker, 2011.
Bebbington, David W. "About the Definition of Evangelicalism . . . ." *Evangelical Studies Bulletin* 83 (Fall 2012) 1–6.
———. *Evangelicalism in Modern Britain: A History from the 1730s to the 1980s*. London: Unwin Hyman, 1989.
Bell, Rob. *Love Wins*. London: Collins, 2011.
Berkhof, Louis. *Principles of Biblical Interpretation*. Grand Rapids: Baker, 1950
Berger, Peter L. "Prologue: Bestrangement in Stockholm." In *Facing Up to Modernity: Excursions in Society, Politics and Religion*, edited by Peter Berger, 145–47. New York: Basic, 1977.
———. *The Sacred Canopy*. New York: Doubleday, 1967.
Bruce, Steve. *Firm in the Faith*. Aldershot, UK: Gower, 1984.
Carson, D. A. "Domesticating the Gospel: A Review of Grenz's *Renewing the Center*." In *Reclaiming the Center*, edited by Millard J. Erickson et al., 33–55. Wheaton, IL: Crossway, 2004.
———. *The Gagging of God: Christianity Confronts Pluralism*. Leicester, UK: Apollos, 1996.
Catto, Rebecca. "Reverse Mission: From the Global South to Mainline Churches." In *Church Growth in Britain: 1980 to the Present*, edited by David Goodhew, 91–103. Farnham, UK: Ashgate, 2012.
Chalke, Steve, and Alan Mann. *The Lost Message of Christ*. Grand Rapids: Zondervan, 2003.
Erickson, Millard J. *The Evangelical Left*. Grand Rapids: Baker, 1997

102. The discussion about diversity does not mean to say there is no consensus to evangelical belief. See Packer and Oden, *One Faith*, and the proposal by Allison in ch. 16 of the present volume.

103. 2 Tim 2:9.

104. 1 Cor 15:28.

———. *Postmodernizing the Faith: Evangelical Responses to the Challenge of Postmodernism*. Grand Rapids: Baker, 1998.
Franke, John R. *The Character of Theology: An Introduction to its Nature, Task and Purpose*. Grand Rapids: Baker, 2005.
Green, Joel B., and Mark D. Baker. *Recovering the Scandal of the Cross: Atonement in New Testament and Contemporary Contexts*. Downers Grove, IL: InterVarsity, 2000.
Henry, Carl F. H. *The Uneasy Conscience of Modern Fundamentalism*. Grand Rapids: Eerdmans, 1947.
Henry, Carl F. H., and Kenneth Kantzer. *Evangelical Affirmations*. Grand Rapids: Zondervan, 1990.
Hutchinson, M., and John Wolffe. *A Short History of Global Evangelicalism*. Cambridge: Cambridge University Press, 2012.
Jenkins, Philip. *The Next Christendom*. Oxford: Oxford University Press, 2002.
Kelly, Dean M. *Why Conservative Churches are Growing: A Study in the Sociology of Religion*. New York: Harper and Row, 1977.
Larsen, Timothy, and Daniel J. Treier, eds. *The Cambridge Companion to Evangelical Theology*. Cambridge: Cambridge University Press, 2007.
Lausanne Covenant, 1974. www.lausanne.org/en/documents/all.html.
Lewis, Donald M., ed. *Christianity Reborn: The Global Expansion of Evangelicalism in the Twentieth Century*. Studies in the History of Christian Mission. Grand Rapids, Eerdmans, 2004.
Lindbeck, George A. *The Nature of Doctrine*. Philadelphia: Westminster, 1984.
Lindsell, Harold. *The Battle for the Bible*. Grand Rapids: Zondervan, 1976
Manley, G. T., ed. *The New Bible Handbook*. London: Inter-Varsity Fellowship, 1947.
Marsden, George M. *Reforming Fundamentalism: Fuller Seminary and the New Evangelicalism*. Grand Rapids: Eerdmans, 1987.
———. *Understanding Fundamentalism and Evangelicalism*. Grand Rapids: Eerdmans, 1991.
Marsden, George M., ed. *Evangelicalism and Modern America*. Grand Rapids: Eerdmans, 1984.
MacDonald, Gregory. *The Evangelical Universalist*. Eugene, OR: Cascade, 2006.
McDermott, Gerald. "Evangelicals Divided: The Battle between Meliorists and Traditionalists to Define Evangelicalism." *First Things* (April 2011). www.firstthings.com/article/2011/03/evangelicals-divided.
McLeod, H. "Being a Christian at the End of the Twentieth Century." In *World Christianities, c. 1914–2000*, edited by H. McLeod, 636–47. Cambridge History of Christianity, Vol. IX. Cambridge: Cambridge University Press, 2006.
Micklethwait, John, and Adrian Wooldridge. *God is Back: How the Global Rise of Faith is Changing the World*. New York: Lane, 2009.
McGrath, Alister E. "Evangelical Theological Method: The State of the Art." In *Evangelical Futures: A Conversation on Theological Method*, edited by John G. Stackhouse, 15–37. Grand Rapids: Baker, 2000.
———. *A Passion for Truth: The Intellectual Coherence of Evangelicalism*. Leicester, UK: Apollos, 1996.
———. "Theology and the Futures of Evangelicalism." In *The Futures of Evangelicalism: Issues and Prospects*, edited by Craig Bartholomew, Robin Parry, and Andrew West, 15–39. Leicester, UK: Inter-Varsity, 2003.

Naselli, Andrew David, and Collin Hansen, eds. *Four Views on the Spectrum of Evangelicalism*. Grand Rapids: Zondervan, 2011.
Nkansah-Obrempong, James. "Evangelical Theology in Africa: Ways, Perspectives, and Dilemmas." *Evangelical Review of Theology* 34/4 (2010) 293–99.
Noll, Mark A., *Between Faith and Criticism: Evangelicals, Scholarship and the Bible*. Grand Rapids: Baker, 1991.
———. *The Scandal of the Evangelical Mind*. Grand Rapids: Eerdmans, 1994.
Oden, Thomas C. *Care of Souls in the Classic Tradition*. Theology and Pastoral Care. Philadelphia: Fortress, 1984.
Olson, Roger E., *Reformed and Always Reforming: The Postconservative Approach to Evangelical Theology*. Grand Rapids: Baker, 2007.
———. "Stanley J. Grenz's Contribution to Evangelical Theology." *Princeton Theological Review* 12/1 (2006) 27–28, 40.
Packer, J. I., and Thomas C. Oden. *One Faith: The Evangelical Consensus*. Downers Grove, IL: InterVarsity, 2004.
Ramm, Bernard L. *Protestant Biblical Interpretation*. 1950. Reprint. Grand Rapids: Baker, 1970.
Rosenau, Pauline Marie. *Post-modernism and the Social Sciences: Insights, Inroads and Intrusions*. Princeton: Princeton University Press, 1992.
Schreiner, Thomas R. "Justification: The Saving Righteousness of God in Christ." *Journal of the Evangelical Theological Society* 54/1 (2011) 19–34.
Sexton, Jason S. *The Trinitarian Theology of Stanley J. Grenz*. London: T. & T. Clark, 2013.
Smith, Christian, *American Evangelicalism: Embattled and Thriving*. Chicago: Chicago University Press, 1998.
Smith, Claire. *God's Good Design: What the Bible Really Says about Men and Women*. Kingsford, Australia: Matthias Media, 2012.
Stackhouse, John G., Jr., ed. *Evangelical Futures: A Conversation on Theological Method*. Grand Rapids: Baker, 2000.
———. *Evangelical Landscapes: Facing Critical Issues of the Day*. Grand Rapids: Baker, 2002.
———. "Evangelical Theology Should Be Evangelical." In *Evangelical Futures: A Conversation on Theological Method*, edited by John G. Stackhouse, Jr., 39–58. Grand Rapids: Baker, 2000.
Stibbs, Alan M. *Understanding God's Word*. London: Inter-Varsity Fellowship, 1950.
Thiselton, A. C. *The Two Horizons: New Testament Hermeneutics and Philosophical Description*. Grand Rapids: Eerdmans, 1980.
Tiénou, Tite. "Evangelical Theology in African Contexts.'" In *The Cambridge Companion to Evangelical Theology*, edited by Timothy Larsen and Daniel J. Treier, 213–24. Cambridge: Cambridge University Press, 2007.
Tomlinson, Dave. *The Post-Evangelical*. London: SPCK, 1995.
Thompson, James W. *Pastoral Ministry According to Paul: A Biblical Vision*. Grand Rapids: Baker, 2006.
Vanhoozer, Kevin J. *The Drama of Doctrine: A Canonical-Linguistic Approach to Christian Doctrine*. Louisville: Westminster John Knox, 2005.
———. *Is There a Meaning in this Text? The Bible, the Reader and the Morality of Literary Knowledge*. Leicester, UK: Apollos, 1998.

———. "The Voice and the Actor: A Dramatic Proposals about the Ministry and Minstrelsy of Theology." In *Evangelical Futures: A Conversation on Theological Method*, edited by John G. Stackhouse, Jr., 61–106. Grand Rapids: Baker, 2000.

Vondey, Wolfgang. *Beyond Pentecostalism: The Crisis of Global Christianity and the Renewal of the Theological Agenda*. Grand Rapids: Eerdmans, 2010.

Warner, Rob. *Reinventing English Evangelicalism 1966–2001: A Theological and Sociological Study*. Studies in Evangelical History and Thought. Milton Keynes, UK: Paternoster, 2007.

Wells, David F. *Above All Earthly Pow'rs: Christ in a Postmodern World*. Grand Rapids: Eerdmans, 2005.

Willimon, William H. "The Culture is Overrated." *Leadership Journal* (Winter 1997) 29–31.

Wright, Christopher, J. H. "Future Trends in Mission." In *The Futures of Evangelicalism: Issues and Prospects*, edited by Craig Bartholomew, Robin Parry, and Andrew West, 149–63. Leicester, UK: InterVarsity, 2003.

Wright, Nigel. *The Radical Evangelical: Seeking a Place to Stand*. London: SPCK, 1996.

Wright, Tom. *Justification: God's Plan and Paul's Vision*. London: SPCK, 2009.

———. *Surprised by Hope*. London: SPCK, 2007.

Memorial Sermon

BRUCE MILNE

Meditation on the Word, given by Dr. Bruce Milne at the Memorial Service for Dr. Stanley J. Grenz, March 20, 2005, First Baptist Church, Vancouver, BC

FOR OVER A DECADE it was my privilege to serve Dr. Stanley Grenz and his family in this church as their pastor; a privilege which I treasure immensely this afternoon, and will do for the rest of my life. Edna, Joel, Jen, Corina, Chris and Annika, the Lord bless you, and abound to you, in love, peace, and courage, now, and in all the future.

On one occasion, a few years ago, Stan and Edna were talking, and Stan mentioned the, then wholly unforeseen, circumstance of his early death, and said, were that to happen, he would like Bruce to preach the biblical message at the Memorial Service. He also told her what the theme should be: the resurrection. So, Stan, my friend, here it is, as best I can do it.

For the basis of our thought this afternoon, we will look, appropriately, at what is widely accepted as the profoundest theological discussion of the resurrection in the New Testament, 1 Corinthians, chapter 15. The passage is focused in the words in verses 3 and 4: "*I delivered to you as of the very first importance that Christ died for our sins according to the Scriptures, that he was buried, and that he was raised on the third day according to the Scriptures, and he appeared . . . .*"

There are two questions every thoughtful congregation addresses to the Christian preacher when he or she stands before them with the Word of God. The first question is, if you like, the "*What?*" question. *What* does this ancient text mean? When properly interpreted and set in its context, *what* is it saying? The second question, which comes on its heels, and which is also critically important, is the *"So what?"* question: *so what* does this ancient text say to us as we gather on this occasion, in this place? What are the implications of this God-inspired truth for my life, right now, as I sit before you in the pew? We'll follow that framework in these moments, and so first ask of the resurrection the "What?" question. What was it?

Well, Paul would say to us, clearly it was *an event*. He dates it, *"on the third day,"* something that actually happened in our space and time. Further, it was an *anticipated* event, it happened *"according to the Scriptures."* The resurrection of Jesus did not fall like a meteor from the heavens; it was part of a plan from the beginning, slotting into the whole developing purpose of our Sovereign God. Again it was a *foundational* event—it is *"of the first importance"* that Christ died and was buried and was raised again. And that preeminence is fully borne out as we read our New Testament. There wasn't a Christian sermon preached in these first days that didn't take its inspiration and motivation from the resurrection of Jesus. There wasn't an act of Christian evangelism that didn't have the resurrection as its master spring. Indeed, there was not a single word, never mind a sentence, of the New Testament which was penned, whether in the Gospels or Acts, or the Letters, or Revelation, but which was written in the conviction that he of whom they wrote had conquered death and was alive forevermore. As N. T. Wright notes: "There is simply no evidence for a form of early Christianity in which the resurrection was not a central belief." James Denney was right: "The resurrection of Jesus is the first, and last, and dominating element in the Christian consciousness of the New Testament."

Again, the resurrection was a *bodily* event, *"he was crucified . . . he was buried . . . he was raised"*—the identical subject each time, and therefore events which concerned the identical object. The Jesus who died upon the cross in his full, embodied humanity, who was laid in the tomb, *he* was raised: *bodily resurrection!* Paul stands here in 1 Corinthians in foursquare agreement with the narratives in the Gospels. The tomb was empty. He, the crucified one, was raised.

I still recall a conversation with my doctoral supervisor in Edinburgh, Professor T. F. Torrance, in which he recounted his final conversation with Karl Barth, shortly before the latter's death. The resurrection had just come into their conversation, when Barth leaned over, and said with considerable force—*"Wohlverstanden, liebliche Auferstehung!"*—("note well: *bodily* resurrection!"). Frankly, the Bible, from Genesis to Revelation, does not know any other kind of resurrection than that.

Then again, it was *provable*, the resurrection event. "'Provable," that is, in the normal sense required by historians: overwhelmingly attested by the evidence. And isn't that precisely what Paul's about in this passage as he continues with a litany of *"he appeareds"*: *"He appeared"* to individuals, like Peter, or Paul himself; *"he appeared"* to groups, like the twelve; and *"he appeared"* in the end to a crowd of five hundred at the same time. Surely he's saying: "Look, if you doubt this thing, ask the folk who were there, who were eyewitnesses, there's plenty of them around, and they can be questioned any time you run across them."

Indeed, in a very real, further sense, we ourselves are part of the evidence, right here in First Baptist this afternoon. For apart from any other consideration, if Jesus had not been truly, verifiably raised from the dead there would simply never have been a Christian mission, and therefore no Christian church to span the ages and embrace us right here this afternoon. In that sense the resurrection is as sure, and as physically intrusive, as these hard pews that you're sitting on as you listen to me right now! Furthermore it is as tangible and tactile as the second part of that hard-covered book sitting there within touching distance in the pews. To quote Denney again— "The existence of the Christian Church, the existence of the New Testament: these incomparable phenomena in human history are left without adequate or convincing explanation if the resurrection of Jesus be denied"—a *provable* event!

And one final feature, as Paul continues his exposition in the central section of this chapter from verse 20 onwards, the resurrection of Jesus from the dead was world-changing in its implications—a *cosmic* event. As far as God's universe is concerned, the resurrection is the anticipation of the future in-breaking of God's rule and kingdom, dreamed of in the Old Testament, fulfilled now in Jesus. It was nothing less than the arrival of the End; tomorrow's world today! The resurrection of Jesus Christ is the promise of that future day when all God's enemies are put down, and God, as verse 28 has it here, is "all in all"—*cosmic* implications for God!

But also, in verses 20–49, *cosmic* implications as far as God's people are concerned. They are two in number, and we have only time to state their glorious essence: first, *our conquest of death*: *"in Christ all will be made alive"* (verse 22); and second, and amazingly, *our transformation into the wholeness of the image of God*, an image finally embodied in Jesus himself. So incredibly, as verse 49 has it, *"we will bear the very image of that man from heaven, Jesus Christ."* Cosmic implications!

So, *what* is the resurrection?—*an event, anticipated, foundational, bodily, provable, cosmic.* Maybe the best bit of all—also *true*! *"But Christ has indeed been raised from the dead!"* (verse 20). It's true! Whatever moods of doubt, or cynical sophistication may assault it, it stands unshaken. It is true! He is Risen! Blessed be God!

Well, that's what Stan asks us to focus on in this service: the resurrection of Jesus Christ from the dead. "*On the third day He rose again.*"

But let's move on to the "So what?" question for the remaining moments. "Christ is risen . . . ." God has acted . . . ; everything is different because of that . . . . So what? What are the implications? From the many possibilities in the chapter, let me draw on just two: the *pastoral* and the *practical*.

First, the *pastoral*. It has been hopefully encouraging to remind one another in the last moments of the reality of the resurrection of Jesus and all its dimensions, but unless we're very careful at this point we can lose contact with the poignant, heartrending reason for our being here this afternoon. For we are met today, because at the human level a great tragedy has occurred. We are here because Dr. Stanley Grenz is dead; and we need, right now, to reconnect with the stark, earthly reality of this service. Putting it another way, there is no road to a legitimate celebration of resurrection this afternoon that does not first pass through the valley of the shadow of death.

So let's be quieter for a moment, and feel the deep, deep sadness of all this. We are gathered today to remember a very special person who has been abruptly snatched from our midst. Yes, and even more poignantly, actually torn from the very sight and side of his beloved wife in the fullness of his life, at the height of his powers; a husband with so many years still to share, a father with so much more to give, an "*Opa*" grand-dad, only newly entered upon the delights of that relationship. Family-member, teacher, mentor, colleague, theologian, author, musician, friend, brother in Christ, disciple of Christ, lover of God . . . our Stan has died. And though we may know the medical "why?" we have little or no sense yet of any spiritual "why?" Frankly it is dark.

So beyond those walls that cozily encircle us this afternoon, we cannot altogether silence the searching questions of the world out there, whether it be dismissive, atheistic modernism as it demands: "So, where is your so-called sovereign God of love in all this?" or critical, deconstructive postmodernism: "Surely now you guys get it, the sheer, downright arbitrariness of life, the pointless illegitimacy of trying to construct any kind of all-embracing explanation, any *meta-narrative*, of our finally ironic existence."

And what do we reply? What do we say to that? Well, this is what we say: "On the third day Jesus Christ rose from the dead!" In other words, we go back to our basics; we kneel in the shadows of Calvary, and gaze, and gaze, and gaze again at a love that has not, cannot, and will not let us go. We linger with the women, these courageous women, around the tomb, and hear the angel invitation: "Come, see the place where he was laid."

We stand gazing into that tomb, when suddenly we become conscious of a rustle of a cloak, and a presence nearby. We turn. No gardener this! ... "Mary," "Edna," "Joel," "Corina," "Jen," "Chris," "Annika" ... yes, and "Bruce," and "Margaret," "Tom," "Alice," "Roger," "Brian," "Sheila" ... and every one of us—because we're all important, we're all precious, we're all loved; He names us all.

What does it mean, as we hear the risen Jesus utter our name? It means this—that Stanley Grenz will live again! Not enclosed, as we now experience our human existence, hampered by earthly limitations, like that earthly body through which we related to him and knew him, for part at least, of his all too brief fifty-five years. But clothed anew in a heavenly, or what Paul calls in verse 44, a *"spiritual body."* We will meet him again, on that coming day, *"when the trumpet shall sound and the dead shall be raised incorruptible and we shall be changed"* (verse 52).

Until then, Stan is *"sleeping"* to use the euphemism of verses 20 and 51. But biblical sleep was regularly a highly significant experience—just talk to either of the two Josephs of the Bible! So, a form of existence, possibly not wholly unaware of things earthly, but resting *"with Christ,"* to use Paul's marvelous phrase to the Philippians—surrounded as never before by the limitless love of God from which death is powerless to separate us. Arguably, part of a new time-order, and yet, if the writer to the Hebrews is to be believed, in some strange and yet real sense, present among us as we gather week by week in worship, *"with the spirits of all the righteous made perfect."*

But through it all, waiting ... waiting, just as we in the church of God on earth wait—waiting for the trumpet call of heaven, that final glorious flowering of all the redeeming purposes of God; the new world, *"the heaven and earth of righteousness"*; where we will meet a new re-embodied Stan, resplendent now in the very likeness of his Lord. A Stan who will walk again, and talk again, and smile and laugh again, and tell jokes again, and play, and make music and dance and celebrate, and worship. Yes, and ask questions, and maybe even write more books! And where too, he will love again and be loved again, and embrace and be embraced, in the land of the Trinity forevermore, and evermore. "Christ was raised on the third day." The resurrection—so what? On a pastoral level, that's what!

But what of the interval, the here and now; what of the long years that stretch ahead before that final day? Which brings us in closing to the *practical* application. And that's verse 58: *"Therefore dear brothers and sisters, stand firm. Let nothing move you. Always give yourself fully to the work of the Lord, because you know that your labor in the Lord is not in vain."* And I want, as it were, in these final moments to simply put these words into Stan's mouth. "Stan, what do you want to say to us as we meet here in First Baptist sanctuary this afternoon, and as we bid you farewell for the present? What should we be doing, and being in the light of all this that's happened?"

First, Stan would say to us, *cherish community*. *"Therefore my dear brothers and sisters . . ."* Paul writes. Paul, what *are* you saying!? These Corinthians!—*"dear brothers and sisters"*! But Paul . . . surely you know—their theology's all over the place, the behavior of some of them is frankly unacceptable, and on so many points they directly oppose you—"dear, beloved *Corinthians"*? But you see Paul has been caught up in the previous verses in the glory and wonder of resurrection, and from that perspective of course there can be no final division or lasting separation; so he embraces them, even them, in his love: "One body in Christ," "members together," "raised with Christ," part of his indestructible and indivisible reality. And Stan, of course, wrote and taught so much about this very thing. Of the God who in the inner life of the Trinity, is himself community, creating and re-creating us in his image necessarily as *communal beings*, who find themselves ultimately in communion with him and with one another. So, as Stan takes his leave of us, like his Master, among his final words to us are these: "A commandment I give you: that you love one another." Forgive the hurts of the years, the failures that haunt us, the shadows of yesterday. See one another "in Christ." Love, love, love, and love again—*cherish community*!

Second, *exhibit stability*. *"Stand firm,"* says the text; *"let nothing move you."* Not least, this is a call to "stand firm" in face of the mystery, darkness, and pain of Stan's passing from us. Karl Barth, in one place, defines faith as "holding to the Word and promise of God in spite of all that stands against it." Happily in our lives, much of the time, we believe "because . . . ." But to every one of us there come moments when we are called to believe "in spite of . . . ." And this is such a moment. And so, Stan says to us, right now, today . . . in *this* circumstance of my home-call, "Stand firm!"

But this is also a call to engage in that endless challenge in the church, which Stan himself so tirelessly modeled, to remain firm and faithful to the changeless core of the Christian message "once for all delivered to the saints" and, at the same time, to be flexible enough in our telling of it to make it relevant to each passing age.

We do not know today what moods, or movements, or new cultural styles, or powerful, threatening social forces, lie out there in the future; but the signs are certainly not lacking that loyalty to the Bible's once-for-all message may become extremely costly in the decades ahead. So, Stan would nerve us for these coming challenges. Listen as he speaks: *"Stand firm, let nothing move you."*

So . . . *cherish community, exhibit stability*. Thirdly, *fulfill ministry*! *"Always give yourselves fully to the work of the Lord."* We've been faced today with the model of a man whose life was given up to ministry, from the day of his conversion right through to his final breath. Stan summons us to it again. *"The work of the Lord," "give yourselves fully"* to it, he urges us. What work? The New Testament answers that for us—evangelism, discipling, teaching, preaching, praying, caring, supporting, encouraging—living Christianly in our daily vocations, speaking up for justice, caring for the needy, looking after the children, and the vulnerable of every age, stewarding our resources, and sharing daily cups of cold water, and also struggling at times with difficult relationships, and against stubborn addictions within us, and above all else, seeking his glory in all things. *"The work of the Lord,"* give yourselves to it. And why so?—because it is so utterly worth it—*"your labor in the Lord is not in vain."* J. B. Phillips splendidly puts that: "Know that nothing you do for God is ever lost or ever wasted." Why? *Because Jesus Christ is risen from the dead,* and since he truly rose, all that is done in his name shares in his indestructibility. It is part of the permanent; part therefore of that which we will lay at his feet in tribute when he comes.

Can I make one closing application of this third point in the light of Paul's, and Stan's, summons to ministry. John Bunyan in his *Pilgrim's Progress* puts these words into the mouth of Mr. Valiant for Truth as he comes to cross the river of death into the celestial city. *"I am going now to my Father's, my sword I give to him that shall succeed me in my pilgrimage, and my courage and skill to him that can get it."* "And so he passed over to the other side." My friends, on this communion table before me, just in front of all Stan's books lying there, in a very real sense there lies a sword. Can you see it? It's the sword that Stan wielded, so conscientiously, so well through his ministry. But he has had to lay it down in the midst of his years. I wonder, is there someone here today, perhaps a number of us, whom God is calling right now to pick up that sword? It's the call of God to wrestle to articulate God's truth in this day and time, to teach, to write, to preach, to witness, to inspire the people of God, to build the church of Jesus Christ in this generation. Stan can wield that sword no more, but there's still so much to be done. Do you hear God's call today? Will *you* respond? *"Always give yourselves fully to the work of the Lord."*

So . . . *community*, and *stability*, and *ministry*, and finally, just in a sentence, *doxology*. That's verse 57: *"Thanks be to God who gives us the victory through our Lord Jesus Christ."* Here is the necessary climax of Paul's whole exposition of the resurrection. Paul, as the great theologian he was, knew that all theology culminates finally in worship. So he falls on his knees at the end. *"Thanks be to God!"* And that surely Stan urges us finally to echo: *"Thanks be to God!"* Of course, because in the end it's all from God, it's all his doing, it's all of his grace, it's all of his mercy, it's all his victory. And so, Stan would surely want us to end looking at God himself, the Father, the Son, the Spirit, the ever-blessed Trinity; the God of resurrection; the God who is here among us now. Stan would say to us, "worship him, thank him, extol him, love him, praise him, obey him, live for him, serve him"—until that day when this great God in the person of his eternal Son Jesus, risen and exalted, will come beating on the gates of time, and the everlasting doors will swing wide to admit him, and we'll see him upon his throne, and we'll fall before him in adoring, awe-filled worship. And then *with Stan* and all the saints, we will be "together forever with the Lord."

Thanks, thanks, thanks be to God! But you know that phrase in its Hebrew form—"Hallelujah!"

"Christ died for our sins, he was buried, he was raised on the third day." He will reign forever. Hallelujah! And again, Hallelujah!

Amen.

Select Bibliography of the Words of Stanley J. Grenz

Grenz Books

Isaac Backus—Puritan and Baptist. NABPR Dissertation Series 4. Macon, GA: Mercer University Press, 1983.
The Baptist Congregation. Valley Forge, PA: Judson, 1985. Reprint. Vancouver, BC: Regent College, 2002.
Prayer: The Cry for the Kingdom. Peabody, MA: Hendrickson, 1988. Revised, Grand Rapids: Eerdmans, 2005.
AIDS: Ministry in the Midst of an Epidemic. Coauthored with Wendell Hoffman. Grand Rapids: Baker, 1990.
Sexual Ethics: An Evangelical Perspective. Dallas: Word, 1990. Revised, Louisville: Westminster John Knox, 1997.
Reason for Hope: The Systematic Theology of Wolfhart Pannenberg. Oxford: Oxford University Press, 1990. Revised, Grand Rapids: Eerdmans, 2005.
Twentieth-Century Theology: God and the World in a Transitional Age. Coauthored with Roger E. Olson. Downers Grove, IL: InterVarsity, 1992.
The Millennial Maze: Sorting Out Evangelical Options. Downers Grove, IL: InterVarsity, 1992.
Revisioning Evangelical Theology. Downers Grove, IL: InterVarsity, 1993.
Theology for the Community of God. Nashville: Broadman and Holman, 1994. 2nd ed., Grand Rapids: Eerdmans, 2000.
Women in the Church: A Biblical Theology of Women in Ministry. Coauthored with Denise Muir Kjesbo. Downers Grove, IL: InterVarsity, 1995.
Betrayal of Trust: Confronting and Preventing Clergy Sexual Misconduct. Coauthored with Roy D. Bell. Downers Grove, IL: InterVarsity, 1995. 2nd ed., Grand Rapids: Baker, 2001.
A Primer on Postmodernism. Grand Rapids: Eerdmans, 1996.
Created for Community: Connecting Christian Belief with Christian Living. Wheaton: Victor/BridgePoint, 1996. 2nd ed., Grand Rapids: Baker, 1998.
Who Needs Theology? An Invitation to the Study of God. Coauthored with Roger E. Olson. Downers Grove, IL: InterVarsity, 1996.
The Moral Quest: Foundations of Christian Ethics. Downers Grove, IL: InterVarsity, 1997.
What Christians Really Believe—and Why. Louisville: Westminster John Knox, 1998.
The Fortress Introduction to Contemporary Theologies. Coauthored with Ed L. Miller. Minneapolis: Fortress, 1998.

Welcoming But Not Affirming: An Evangelical Response to Homosexuality. Louisville: Westminster John Knox, 1998.
Pocket Dictionary of Theological Terms. Coauthored with David Guretzki and Cherith Fee Nordling. Downers Grove, IL: InterVarsity, 1999.
Renewing the Center: Evangelical Theology in a Post-theological Era. Grand Rapids: Baker, 2000. 2nd ed., Grand Rapids: Baker, 2006.
Beyond Foundationalism: Shaping Theology in a Postmodern Context. Coauthored with John R. Franke. Louisville: Westminster John Knox, 2001.
The Social God and the Relational Self: A Trinitarian Theology of the Imago Dei. The Matrix of Christian Theology, Vol. 1. Louisville: Westminster John Knox, 2001.
Pocket Dictionary of Ethics. Coauthored with Jay T. Smith. Downers Grove, IL: InterVarsity, 2003.
Rediscovering the Triune God: The Trinity in Contemporary Theology. Minneapolis: Fortress, 2004.
The Named God and the Question of Being: A Trinitarian Theo-Ontology. The Matrix of Christian Theology, Vol. 2. Louisville: Westminster John Knox, 2005.

Grenz Edited Works

Christian Freedom: Essays in Honor of Vernon Grounds. Edited by Stanley J. Grenz and Kenneth W. M. Wozniak. Lanham, MD: University Press of America, 1986.
Perspectives on Theology in the Contemporary World: Essays in Honor of Bernard Ramm. Edited by Stanley J. Grenz. Macon, GA: Mercer University Press, 1990.

Grenz Essays in Works

"The Flight from God: Kierkegaard's *Fear and Trembling* and Universal Ethical Systems." In *Christian Freedom: Essays in Honor of Vernon Grounds,* edited by Kenneth W. M. Wozniak and Stanley J. Grenz, 69–85. Lanham, MD: University Press of America, 1986.
"The Appraisal of Pannenberg: A Survey of the Literature." In *The Theology of Wolfhart Pannenberg: Twelve American Critiques,* edited by Carl E. Braaten and Philip Clayton, 19–52. Minneapolis: Augsburg, 1988.
"Isaac Backus." In *Baptist Theologians,* edited by Timothy George and David Dockery, 102–20. Nashville: Broadman and Holman, 1990
"Star Trek and the Next Generation: Postmodernism and the Future of Evangelical Theology." In *The Challenge of Postmodernism: An Evangelical Engagement,* edited by David S. Dockery, 89–103. Wheaton: Victor/BridgePoint, 1994.
"The AIDS Epidemic and Sin." In *Baptist Faith and Witness: The Papers of the Study and Research Division of the Baptist World Alliance 1990–1995,* edited by William H. Brackney and L. A. (Tony) Cupit, 185–89. McLean, VA: Baptist World Alliance, 1995.
"Toward a Comprehensive Christian Ethic of Love." In *Christian Character, Virtue and Bioethics,* edited by Edwin C. Hui, 179–98. Vancouver, BC: Regent College, 1996.

Select Bibliography of the Words of Stanley J. Grenz

"Christian Integrity in a Postmodern World." In *New Dimensions in Evangelical Thought: Essays in Honor of Millard J. Erickson*, edited by David S. Dockery, 394–410. Downers Grove, IL: InterVarsity, 1998.

"Fideistic Revelationalism: Donald Bloesch's Antirationalist Theological Method." In *Evangelical Theology in Transition: Theologians in Dialogue with Donald Bloesch*, edited by Elmer M. Colyer, 35–60. Downers Grove, IL: InterVarsity, 1999.

"The Christian Vision of the Moral Life." In *Baptist Faith and Witness Book 2: The Papers of the Study and Research Division of the Baptist World Alliance 1995–2000*, edited by L. A. (Tony) Cupit, n.p. McLean, VA: Baptist World Alliance, 1999.

"Post-feminism and a New Gender Covenant: A Response to Elizabeth Fox-Genovese." In *Women and the Future of the Family*, edited by James W. Skillen and Michelle N. Voll, 46–56. Grand Rapids: Baker, 2000.

"'Genesis and the Millennium' and the Challenge of Pluralism." In *Genesis and the Millennium: An Essay on Religious Pluralism in the 21st Century by Bill Moyers*, edited by Derek H. Davis, 35–42. Waco, TX: J. M. Dawson Institute of Church-State Studies, 2000.

"Articulating the Christian Belief-Mosaic: Theological Method after the Demise of Foundationalism." In *Evangelical Futures: A Conversation on Theological Method*, edited by John G. Stackhouse, Jr., 107–36. Grand Rapids: Baker, 2000.

"Wolfhart Pannenberg." *The Oxford Companion to Christian Thought*, edited by Adrian Hastings, Alistair Mason, and Hugh Pyper, 509–10. Oxford: Oxford University Press, 2000.

"Is God Sexual? Human Embodiment and the Christian Conception of God." In *This Is My Name Forever: The Trinity and Gender Language for God*, edited by Alvin F. Kimel, Jr., 190–212. Downers Grove, IL: InterVarsity, 2001.

"The Universality of the 'Jesus-Story' and the 'Incredulity Toward Metanarratives.'" In *No Other Gods Before Me? Evangelicals and the Challenge of World Religions*, edited by John G. Stackhouse, Jr., 85–111. Grand Rapids: Baker, 2001.

"Toward a Nonfoundationalist Understanding of the Role of Tradition in Theology." Coauthored with John R. Franke. In *Ancient and Postmodern Christianity: Essays in Honor of Thomas C. Oden*, edited by Kenneth Tanner and Christopher A. Hall, 215–39. Downers Grove, IL: InterVarsity, 2002.

"Restoring a Trinitarian Understanding of the Church in Practice." In *Evangelicalism and the Stone-Campbell Movement*, edited by William R. Baker, 228–43. Downers Grove, IL: InterVarsity, 2002.

"The Social *Imago*: The Image of God and the Postmodern (Loss of) Self." In *The Papers of the Henry Luce III Fellows in Theology*, Vol. 6, edited by Christopher I. Wilkins, 49–78. Pittsburgh: Association of Theological Schools, 2003.

"How Do We Know What to Believe: Revelation and Authority." In *Essentials of Christian Theology*, edited by William C. Placher, 20–33. Louisville: Westminster John Knox, 2003.

"Ecclesiology." In *The Cambridge Companion to Postmodern Theology*, edited by Kevin J. Vanhoozer, 252–68. Cambridge: Cambridge University Press, 2003.

"Celebrating Eternity: Christian Worship as a Foretaste of Participation in the Triune God." In *Semper Reformandum: Studies in Honour of Clark H. Pinnock*, edited by Anthony R. Cross and Stanley E. Porter, 378–91. Carlisle, UK: Paternoster, 2003.

"Baptism and the Lord's Supper as Community Acts: Toward a Sacramental Understanding of the Ordinances." In *Baptist Sacramentalism*, edited by Anthony R. Cross and Philip E. Thompson, 76–95. Carlisle, UK: Paternoster, 2003.

"When Do Christians Think the End Times Will Happen? A Comparative Theologies Discussion of the Second Coming." In *Rapture, Revelation, and the End Times: Exploring the Left Behind Series*, edited by Bruce David Forbes and Jeanne Halgren Kilde, 99–130. New York: Palgrave Macmillan, 2004.

"Nurturing the Soul, Informing the Mind: The Genesis of the Evangelical Scripture Principle." In *Evangelicals and Scripture*, edited by Vincent Bacote, Laura C. Miguelez and Dennis L. Okholm, 21–41. Downers Grove, IL: InterVarsity, 2004.

"Biblical Priesthood and Women in Ministry." In *Discovering Biblical Equality: Complementarity without Hierarchy*, edited by Ronald W. Pierce, Rebecca Merrill Groothuis, and Gordon D. Fee, 272–86. Downers Grove, IL: InterVarsity, 2004.

"Community, Interpretative." In *Dictionary for Theological Interpretation of the Bible*, edited by Kevin J. Vanhoozer et al., 128–29. Grand Rapids: Baker, 2005.

"The Social God and the Relational Self: Toward a Trinitarian Theology of the *Imago Dei*." In *Trinitarian Soundings in Systematic Theology*, edited by Paul Louis Metzger, 87–100. London: T. & T. Clark, 2006.

Grenz Essays in Journals

"Church and State: The Legacy of Isaac Backus." *Center Journal* 2/2 (1983) 73–94.

"Isaac Backus and the English Baptist Tradition." *The Baptist Quarterly* 30/5 (1984) 221–31.

"A Theology for the Future." *American Baptist Quarterly* 4/3 (1985) 257–67.

"Reconsecrating the Naked Public Square." *Fides et Historia* 18/2 (1986) 65–75.

"Isaac Backus: Eighteenth-Century Light on the Contemporary School Prayer Issue." *Fides et Historia* 18/3 (1986) 5–14.

"The Sanctuary Trial and Religious Liberty." *Pacific Theological Review* 20/2 (1987) 21–31.

"The Flight from God: Kierkegaard's *Fear and Trembling* and Universal Ethical Systems." *Perspectives in Religious Studies* 14/2 (1987) 147–60.

"Commitment and Dialogue: Pannenberg on Christianity and the Religions." *Journal of Ecumenical Studies* 26/1 (1989) 196–210.

"Secular Saints: Civil Religion in America." *Baptist Quarterly* 33/5 (1990) 238–43.

"The Purpose of Sex: Toward a Theological Understanding of Human Sexuality." *Crux* 26/2 (1990) 27–34.

"Sacramental Spirituality, Ecumenism, and Mission to the World: Foundational Motifs of Pannenberg's Ecclesiology." *Mid-stream* 30/1 (1991) 20–34.

"Maintaining the Balanced Life: The Baptist Vision of Spirituality." *Perspectives in Religious Studies* 18/1 (1991) 59–68.

"Pannenberg and Evangelical Theology: Sympathy and Caution." *Christian Scholars' Review* 20/3 (1991) 272–85.

"Wolfhart Pannenberg: Reason, Hope and Transcendence." *The Asbury Theological Journal* 46/2 (1991) 73–90.

"The Community of God: A Vision of the Church in the Postmodern Age." *Crux* 28/2 (1992) 19–26.

"'Community' as a Theological Motif for the Western Church in an Era of Globalization." *Crux* 28/3 (1992) 10–19.

"The Irrelevancy of Theology: Pannenberg and the Quest for Truth." *Calvin Theological Journal* 27/2 (1992) 307-11.
"The Deeper Significance of the Millennium Debate." *Southwestern Journal of Theology* 36/2 (1994) 14-21.
"Star Trek and the Next Generation: Postmodernism and the Future of Evangelical Theology." *Crux* 30/1 (1994) 24-32.
"The Gospel and the Contemporary Pursuit of Spirituality." *Touchstone* 12/2 (1994) 32-36.
"Toward an Evangelical Theology of the Religions." *Journal of Ecumenical Studies* 31/1-2 (1994) 49-65.
"When the Pastor Fails: Sexual Misconduct as a Betrayal of Trust." *Crux* 31/2 (1995) 23-30.
"Anticipating God's New Community: Theological Foundations for Women in Ministry." *Journal of the Evangelical Theological Society* 38/4 (1995) 595-611.
"The Holy Spirit: Divine Love Guiding Us Home." *Ex Auditu* 12 (1996) 1-13.
"Response to Terry Muck, 'Constructing the Religious Self.'" *Insights* 113/1 (1997) 29-32.
"Christian Integrity in a Postmodern World," The Laing Lecture for 1997, *Vox Evangelica*, 27 (1997) 7-26.
"An Agenda for Evangelical Theology in the Postmodern Context." *Didaskalia* 9/2 (1998) 1-16
"Is God Sexual? Human Embodiment and the Christian Conception of God." *Christian Scholar's Review* 28/1 (1998) 24-41.
"Theological Foundations for Male-Female Relationships." *Journal of the Evangelical Theological Society* 41/4 (1998) 615-30.
"'Scientific' Theology/'Theological' Science: Pannenberg and the Dialogue between Theology and Science." *Zygon* 34/1 (1999) 159-66.
"God's Business: A Foundation for Christian Mission in the Marketplace." *Crux* 35/1 (1999) 19-25.
"The Imago Dei and the Dissipation of the Self." *Dialog* 38/3 (1999) 182-87.
"From Liberalism to Post-liberalism: Theology in the Twentieth Century." *Review and Expositor* 96/3 (1999) 385-404.
"Belonging to God: The Quest for a Communal Spirituality in the Postmodern World." *The Asbury Theological Journal* 54/2 (1999) 41-52.
"Burn Out: The Cause and the Cure for a Christian Malady." *Currents in Theology and Mission* 26/6 (1999) 425-30.
"Conversing in Christian Style: Toward a Baptist Theological Method for the Postmodern Context." *Baptist History and Heritage* 35/1 (2000) 82-103.
"Postmodern Canada: Characteristics of a Nation in Transition." *Touchstone* 18/1 (2000) 21-35.
"Why Do Theologians Need to Be Scientists?" *Zygon* 35/2 (2000) 331-56.
"What Does Hollywood Have to Do with Wheaton?" *Journal of the Evangelical Theological Society* 43/2 (2000) 303-14.
"Eschatological Theology: Contours of a Postmodern Theology of Hope." *Review and Expositor* 97/3 (2000) 339-54.
"The Hopeful Pessimist: Christian Pastoral Theology in a Pessimistic Context." *Journal of Pastoral Care* 54/2 (2000) 297-311.

"Beyond Foundationalism: Is a Nonfoundationalist Evangelical Theology Possible?" *Christian Scholars Review* 30/1 (2000) 57–82.
"The Spirit and the Word: The World-Creating Function of the Text." *Theology Today* 57/3 (2000) 357–74.
"Culture and Spirit: The Role of Cultural Context in Theological Reflection." *The Asbury Theological Journal* 55/2 (2000) 37–51.
"Deconstructing Epistemological Certainty in Theology: An Engagement with William J. Abraham's *Criterion in Christian Theology*." *Wesleyan Theological Journal* 36/2 (2001) 37–45.
"Christian Spirituality and the Quest for Identity: Toward a Spiritual-Theological Understanding of Life in Christ." *Baptist History and Heritage* 37/2 (2002) 87–105.
"Die Begrenzte Gemeinschaft (the Boundaried People) and the Character of Evangelical Theology." *Journal of the Evangelical Theological Society* 45/2 (2002) 301–16.
"The Social God and the Relational Self: Toward a Theology of the *Imago Dei* in the Postmodern Context." *Horizons in Biblical Theology* 24/1 (2002) 33–57.
"Concerns of a Pietist with a Ph.D." *Wesleyan Theological Journal* 37/2 (2002) 58–76.
"The Divine Fugue: Robert Jenson's Renewed Trinitarianism." *Perspectives in Religious Studies* 30/2 (2003) 211–16.
"Stanley Hauerwas, the Grain of the Universe, and the Most 'Natural' Natural Theology." *Scottish Journal of Theology* 56/3 (2003) 381–86.
"Toward an Undomesticated Gospel: A Response to D. A. Carson." *Perspectives in Religious Studies* 30/4 (2003) 455–61.
"Participating in What Frees: The Concept of Truth in the Postmodern Context." *Review and Expositor* 100/4 (2003) 687–93.
"The Doctrine of the Trinity: Luxuriant Meadow or Theological Terminus?" *Crux* 39/4 (2003) 15–18.
"Jesus as Symbol: Robert Neville's Christology and the Neo-Liberal Theological Project." *Modern Theology* 20/3 (2004) 467–73.
"The Virtue of Ambiguity: A Response to Archie Spencer." *Scottish Journal of Theology* 57/3 (2004) 361–65.
"(Pop) Culture: Playground of the Spirit or Diabolical Device?" *Cultural Encounters: A Journal for the Theology of Culture* 1/1 (2004) 7–25.
"Jesus as the *Imago Dei*: Image-of-God Christology and the Non-Linear Linearity of Theology." *Journal of the Evangelical Theological Society* 47/4 (2004) 617–28.

Grenz Essays in Other Periodicals

"Listen America!: A Theological and Ethical Assessment." *Foundations* 25/2 (1982) 188–97.
"Abortion: A Christian Response." *Conrad Grebel Review* 2/1 (1984) 21–30.
"Pannenberg on Marxism." *Christian Century* 104/27 (1987) 824–26.
"German Scholar Faults Marxism as Liberation Theology's Basis." *Christianity Today* 31 (15 May 1987) 44.
"What Is Sex For?" *Christianity Today* 31/9 (12 June 1987) 22–23.
"Elder Rule: A Threat to Congregationalism?" *Christianity Today* 31/9 (10 July 1987) 48–50.

"Beyond the Wall: Where the church suffers, there is God." *Christianity Today* 32 (19 February 1988) 21–22.
"Reasonable Christianity: Wolfhart Pannenberg Turns 60." *Christianity Today* 32 (2 September 1988) 22–24.
"Wolfhart Pannenberg's Quest for Ultimate Truth." *Christian Century* 105 (14 September 1988) 795–98.
"The 'Amen' Rebellion." *Christianity Today* 35/11 (7 October 1991) 24–25.
"Family Planning and the Plan of God." *Christianity Today* 35/13 (11 November 1991) 35–38.
"The Garden of Hope." *Christianity Today* 36/4 (6 April 1992) 20–21.
"Don't Take the Bait!" *Discipleship Journal* 72 (November 1992) 41–43.
"The 1,000-year Question." *Christianity Today* 37/3 (8 March 1993) 34–35.
"Predator, Wanderer, or Lover." Coauthored with Roy D. Bell. *Leadership* 16/3 (Summer 1995) 35.
"The Holy Spirit in the Old Testament." *Discipleship Journal* 16/1 (January–February 1996) 45.
"Is Hell Forever?" *Christianity Today* (5 October 1998) 92.
"Drive-Through Christmas." *Christianity Today* 43/14 (6 December 1999) 74.
"But We Are Baptized: Baptism as the Motivation for Holy Living." *Preaching* 16/6 (May–June 2001) 19–24.
"Where Judgment Begins: Sorting the Tangled Elements of Ethics and Integrity." A "Leadership Forum" featuring Mark Beeson, Stanley Grenz, David Handley and Erwin Lutzer. *Leadership* 24/2 (Winter 2003) 26–31, 35, 41, 51.
"Our Last and Only Hope: A Lesson in Trust from a Grounded Crow." *Christianity Today* 48/2 (February 2004) 81–82.
"We Dare Not Fall: Dealing with the Peril of Clergy Sexual Misconduct." *Enrichment: A Journal for Pentecostal Ministry* 9/4 (2004) 38–51.
"What (If Anything) Has Changed? The Postmodern Condition as Deconstruction and Reconstruction." *Enrichment: A Journal for Pentecostal Ministry* 10/1 (2005) 116–19.
"Does Evidence Still Demand a Verdict?" *Enrichment: A Journal for Pentecostal Ministry* 10/2 (2005) 104–7.
"What Does it Really Mean to be Postmodern?" *Enrichment: A Journal for Pentecostal Ministry* 10/3 (2005) 112–14.
"Being There for Each Other: The Church as Genuine Community?" *Enrichment: A Journal for Pentecostal Ministry* 10/4 (2005) 124–26.
"Truth in a Postmodern World." *Catalyst GroupZine* 1/1 (2006) 222–25.

Grenz Book Reviews

Review of *American Christianity: A Case Approach*, edited by Ronald C. White, Jr., et al., and *Less Than Conquerors: How Evangelicals Entered the Twentieth Century*, by Douglas W. Frank. *Baptist Quarterly* 33/2 (1989) 93–95.
Review of *Systematische Theologie*, Vol. 1., by Wolfhart Pannenberg. *Scottish Journal of Theology* 42/3 (1989) 401–3.
Review of *Confessing One Faith—The Origins, Meaning, and Use of the Nicene Creed: Grounds for a Common Witness. Journal of Ecumenical Studies* 26/1 (1989) 222–23.

Review of *Your Word is Truth: A Project of Evangelicals and Catholics Together*, edited by Charles Colson and Richard John Neuhaus, and *The Free Church and the Early Church: Bridging the Historical and Theological Divide*, edited by D. H. Williams. *Christian Century* 119/22 (23 October–5 November 2002) 42–43.
Review of *The Last Word and the Word After That*, by Brian D. McLaren. *The Journal of the Evangelical Theological Society* 52/3 (2009) 663–65.

Grenz Lectures

"What Does it Mean to be Trinitarians? The Role of the Doctrine of the Trinity in Christian Teaching and Practice." Paper presented at the 2004 Baptist World Alliance Meeting, Seoul, South Korea, and available as the electronic file "Trinity.bwa.essay.wpd" at the John Richard Allison Library.
"What Does it Mean to be Trinitarians?" Bible and Theology Lectureship. Assemblies of God Theological Seminary. Springfield, MO. January 18–20, 2005. Video files available at http://www.agts.edu/continuing_education/ministry_resources/order.html (accessed 20 November 2012).
"What Does it Mean to be Trinitarians? The Role of the Doctrine of the Trinity in Christian Teaching and Life." http://archives.allelon.org/articles/article.cfm?id=57 (accessed 27 March 2009).

Grenz Interviews

"Emergent Theologian: The Late Stan Grenz." Interview with Dick Staub. *The Kindlings Muse*. http://www.thekindlings.com/index.php?s=Emergent+Theologian%3A+The+Late+Stan+Grenz+Podcast%3A+Journeys+Interview+&sbutt=Go (accessed 8 April 2009).
"Community and Relationships: A Theological Take. An Interview with Stanley Grenz." Interview with Stephen Ibbotson. *Talk: The Mainstream Magazine* 1/3 (2002) 12–14.
"Next Wave Interview with Stanley J. Grenz." Carey/Regent College, Vancouver, BC, 20 April 1999. http://www.next wave.org/may99/SG.htm.

PhD Theses and Dissertations on Grenz

Berry, Chauncey Everett. "Revising Evangelical Theological Method in the Postmodern Context: Stanley J. Grenz and Kevin J. Vanhoozer as Test Cases." PhD diss., The Southern Baptist Theological Seminary, 2003.
DeFranza, Megan K. "Intersex and the *Imago*: Sex, Gender, and Sexuality in Postmodern Theological Anthropology." PhD diss., Marquette University, 2011.
Harris, Brian S. "Revisioning Evangelical Theology: An Exploration, Evaluation and Extension of the Theological Method of Stanley J. Grenz." PhD thesis, University of Auckland, 2007.

Hoke, James D. "Examining the Concept of Truth in Stanley Grenz's Theology: Assessing Its Influence on Emerging Evangelicals." PhD diss., Trinity Theological Seminary, 2008.
Knowles, Steven Denis. "Postmodernism and Evangelical Theological Methodology with Particular Reference to Stanley J. Grenz." PhD thesis, University of Liverpool, 2007.
Lenow, Evan C. "Community in Ethics: A Comparative Analysis of the Work of Thomas Aquinas and Stanley J. Grenz." PhD diss., Southeastern Baptist Theological Seminary, 2010.
Magnuson, Daniel K. "Postconservative Evangelical Theology in a Postmodern Context: Three Proposals." PhD diss., Luther Seminary, 2010.
Mellinger, Laurie A. "Teaching Theology as a Christian Spiritual Practice: The Example of Stanley J. Grenz." PhD diss., Catholic University of America, 2010.
Robertson, Jay T. "Evangelicalism's Appropriation of Nonfoundational Epistemology as Reflected in the Theology of Stanley J. Grenz." PhD diss., Mid-American Baptist Theological Seminary, 2002.
Sexton, Jason S. "The Role of the Doctrine of the Trinity in the Theology of Stanley J. Grenz." PhD thesis, University of St. Andrews, 2012.
Smith, Jay T. "A Generous Theology: Reinterpreting Convertive Piety as Trinitarian Participation in the Work of Stanley J. Grenz." PhD diss., Trinity College-University of Bristol, 2013.

Subject Index

angels, 324, 330–32
anthropology, 33, 259–60, 262, 266–68, 271, 274–75
  cosmic, 169
  cultural, 69
  in Grenz, 196
  not as focus of *imago dei*, 20
  Pauline, 92
  relational, 48
apocalypse of Jesus, 161–63, 165f.
apocalyptic,
  as resource for ministry, 165
  as resource for mission, 158–59, 167
  in NT, 158
  misappropiation of, 165–66
  rehabilitation of, 158f.
apocalyptic theology, 159–62, 165–67
apocryphal books, 241
Aquinas, Thomas, 35–36, 127, 331
Augustine, 84
  on God, 149
  on Psalm 22, 226n9
authority, 304, 307, 313
  theological, 48–49
  of church, 240, 323
  of Scripture, 237, 240, 244–46, 250, 255, 323–236, 328, 330–32, 335, 337, 413, 415, 427
  presumptive, 320, 325f.
Ayres, Lewis, 35

Backus, Isaac, 5, 9–10, 12
Balthasar, Hans Urs von, 162, 179–81, 392, 401
baptism, 113–14
Barth, Karl, 87, 88, 90
  and liberalism, 320

  and politics, 349–53
  as incoherent universalist, 181f.
  christocentrism of, 352
  on church, 188–91
  on election, 176f., 192
  on God, 351–52
  on metaphysics, 184
  on Scripture, 269
  on the Trinity, 32, 37, 45, 51, 86
Bavinck, Herman, 38–39, 44, 52, 237, 246, 247
Berger, Peter, 67, 69, 425
Berkouwer, G.C., 179–81, 327
Boff, Leonardo, 63, 100, 102–6. 109, 115–16, 137, 143
Briggs, Richard, 255–56, 264–66, 272, 277

Calvin, John, 229, 237, 244–46,
canon, 59, 70, 239–42, 271, 279
  interpretation of, 259–61, 264. 266–67, 416
catholic church,
  as universal church, 103, 106, 324,
Catholic Church,
  Roman,
    on canon, 241–42
    on authority, 326
    on tradition, 336–37, 382
    on sources of theology, 382, 395
Chalcedon,
  Council of, 251,
  theology of, 84, 89, 307, 330
character, 267–68
  of God, *see* God, character of
  and scripture, 272f.
christocentrism, 148. 161, 385

Subject Index

Christology
  in 1 John, 307
  in contemporary church, 330
church, *see* ecclesiology
colonization, 59-61, 75
communicative action, 51-53
communion theology, 47, 63 136-39, 141-42, 410
Congregation for the Doctrine of the Faith, 100f.
consummation, 53
  as end 51, 212
corpus theologicum, 319-38
  potential objections to, 333
cultural anthropology, 69
covenantal communion, 53
covenant lordship, 42, 45, 51
creedalism, 298, *see also* Chalcedon *and* Nicene Creed
creator/creature,
  distinction, 91-92
  relationality, 82, 85
Crisp, Oliver, 182
crucifixion, 162, 164, 200, 209, 226, 230, 239

demons, 330-32
Derrida, Jacques, 139-40
diakonia, 101
dictation theory, 239
dogmatics, 188-93
doubt, 219-21

ecclesiology, 18, 112-13, *see also* local church
  and Trinity, 41
  as disputed doctrine, 80
  communion, 97f.
  of story, 110
election, 87, *see also* Barth, on election
  divine self-, 86-87
Emery, Gilles, 36
episkope, 101-2
epistemology, 55, 237, 248, 250, 255, 268, 303f.
  reformed, 258-59
  virtue, 262, 267
  of Grenz, 24-25

eucharist, 98, 101-2, 109-11, 114, 116-17, 271, 308-9, 371
evangelicalism, 408-29
  characteristics of, 420f.
  disagreements within, 426-28
  future of, 413f.
  postconservative, xiii, xv, 5, 408, 413, 426
  progressive, xiii, xiv
  problem of, 311
experience, 293-94, 289, 296-300
  as theological source, 249, 256, 305, 414-15, 418-19

feeling, 37, 285-86, 290, 297
fellowship, 41, 64-65, 72, 90, 98-99, 105-7, 115, 141, 150, 207, 209-10, 213
formal principle, 47-48, 51, 53f. 324, 335
Frame, John, 43-45, 51
foundationalism, 306-7, 312f.
fundamentalism, xiv-v, 255, 256, 291, 330, 334, 362, 371, 407, 409, 421, 425
  post-, 14-15,
futurist theology, 13

Geertz, Clifford, 65, 68
Gnosticism, 200
God,
  character of, 63, 71, 198, 42, 268
  self-determination of, 37, 86, 87-89
  substance of, 137-38
Gregory of Nazianzen, 82
Gregory of Nyssa, 34, 162

hardening of heart, 275-26
harmony of Gospels, 70
heterosexuality, 125, 133, 253
historical Jesus, 103
homoousion, 34, 40, 84, 89, 201
homosexuality, 122-23, 125, 130-21, 295
hypostatic union, 82-83, 89

idolatry, 275
ignorance 266-68, 275

Subject Index   453

illumination, 243, 250, 295, 416–17
image of God, 36, 71, 89, 196, 200, 208,
    see also imago Dei
imago Dei, 20, 24, 47–48, 52–53, 82,
    89, 136, 195–98, 202, 212, 385
immutability, 88
imperative, 197–99, 206–8, 210
imperialism, 61, 75
incarnation, 38, 80, 82–84, 89–90
indicative, 197–99, 206–7
Jesus as, 206
individualism, 142
indigenizing principle, 74

Kasper, Walter, 99f.
Käsemann, Ernst, 207
kingdom of God as integrative motif,
    18, 417–18

language, 65
    in developing culture, 65f.
liberalism, 334, 345, 346n13, 350–51
liberation theology, 136, 144
local church, 120f.
Luther, Martin, 107, 139, 241, 384, 389

MacIntyre, Alistair, 262, 310, 344
McLaren, Brian, 4, 253–54, 383
metanarrative, 261, 272
material principle, 47–48, 51–53
McCormack, Bruce, 178, 184f.
Möltmann, Jurgen, 41–2, 63, 138, 141,
    143, 150
Moses, 202–3, 275–76

mutual indwelling, 81

neutrality, 267–68, 370
    inability of, 309
Nicaea, 34–35
Nicene Creed, 25, 307, 321, 409
Noll, Mark, 362, 372, 376
non-identical repition, 393f.

occasionalism, 270–71
openness theory, 85

Pannenberg, Wolfhart, 4f.

participation,
    in God, 35, 40, 47, 53, 72, 79, 84,
        91–92, 97–99, 107, 117–18, 150,
        161, 163, 166, 209–10, 264,
    in redemption, 199
    in social community, 66–67
    in the kingdom, 166, 168–69, 199,
        206–7
patristics, 34–35, 310
    contribution of, 34
Pentecost 104
    as "inner beginning" of church,
        110f.
pelagianism, 132
perichoresis, 44, 79f., 80f., 116
    in the church, 41, 47, 111, 113, 115,
        118
    in Trinity, 42, 64, 82–83, 117, 142
    as theology, 84–85
personal relationship, 289, 296,
    389–90
pietism,
    and evangelicalism, 14–15
    diffusion of, 288f.
    in Schleiermacher and Grenz, 283f.
    tethered, 286, 300
pilgrim principle, 74
plurality
    -in-unity, 64–65, 70–71
    and diversity, 70
pneumatological approach to scripture, 236–38, 244, 248–49, 252
politics, 343f.
postmodernity, 63, 303–4, 315–17,
    407
    turn to, 307–10, 312
    and theology
pre-existence, 111f.
    of the church, 112–17

queer theory, 124–27

Ratzinger, Joseph Cardinal, 99f.
religion in humans 363f.
revelation
    and the church, 385, 397–98
    and the drama/theatre analogy 384f.

Satan, 324, 329–31
Scripture
  Grenz's doctrine of, 416
  as norming norm, 48, 249, 251, 306, 311–13, 315–16
  pneumatological doctrine of, 238
sexuality, human, 121–34
sola scriptura, 217, 311, 313, 324, 335
  ghost of, 382–83

theatre, 384f.
theatrical company, 387f.
theodrama, 50–55
theology,
  apocalyptic see apocalyptic, theology
  black, 145–46
  gospel-centered, 422f.
  iconoclastic, 363, 369, 373, 374fig5, 375–79
  linguistic turn in, 65, 66, 68
  pro-Nicene, 35
  sacerdotal, 363, 365fig1, 367, 369f.
  scientific, 40f.
  Trinitarian systematic, 31, 35

theosis, 92
Torrance, T. F., 39, 40, 186, 187, 434

transformation principle, 74
Trinitarianism, *passim*
  weak, 32f.
  radical 32–33,
  strong, 33f.
Trinity
  and *missio Dei*, 72
  economic, 32n5, 52, 53, 55
  immanent, 36, 40, 52, 53, 55, 80
  meaning of, 46
triperspectivalism, 43f.

unity-in-diversity, 39, 44
unity-in-plurality, 64–65

Van Til, Cornelius, 44, 181–82
virgin birth of Jesus, 324, 330
virtue
  as goal of reading 264
  in hermeneutics, 259, 261f.
  in epistemology, 259, 262, 267
Volf, Miroslav, 41–42, 52

Walls, Andrew, 73
Warfield, B.B., 38–39, 246–47
Wesleyan Quadrilateral, 249, 252, 254
Wittgenstein, Ludwig, 66, 316

Scripture Index

Genesis

1	201, 272, 89
1:26f	89
1:26–27	196, 196n4, 197
1:27f	82
2	272
3	261, 268, 272
11:4	261
12:3	232
16:3	145

Exodus

3:14	83, 86
7–14	275
19:6	203
33:12–16	203
34:6–7	426
40:34–35	203

Leviticus

26:12	52

Numbers

6:24–26	44

Deuteronomy

3:24	205
4:34	205
29:4	274
29:10	274

2 Samuel

17:3	91
23:1–2	238

1 Kings

8:10–11	203

Psalms

1:1	218
1:2	219
2	219
3:2	219, 220
6	224
6:3	218
6:5	232
7	226
9	219, 226
10	218
10:4	219, 220, 229
11	218
12	218
13	224, 226
13:1–2	218
14	219
14:1	219, 229
14:53	219
17:9	218
18	219
19:7–8	203
22	218–19, 224–26
22:1	228n11
22:1–5	227–28

22:1–21a	227	65:6			205	
22:2	228	67			219	
22:6–8	227–28	69			224	
22:6	228	69:8			218	
22:7	218, 228	69:9			219	
22:8	228–29	70:1			218	
22:9–11	227, 229	70:3			219, 220	
22:12	218	71			224	
22:12–21a	230	71:11			219	
22:12–21	227	72			219	
22:14	230	74			218, 224	
22:15	230	74:9			218	
22:16	230	74:10			218	
22:17	231	78			219	
22:18	226, 230	78:38			224	
22:20	231	79			218, 219	
22:21b–26	227, 231	79:5			218	
22:22	231	80			224	
22:27	226	80:4			218	
22:27–8	232	82			219	
22:27–31	227, 232	85:3			224	
22:30	232	85:5			224	
22:30–31	233	86			219	
25	218	86:15			224	
30:5	224	88			218	
31	218	88:10			233	
31:11	218	88:17			218	
35	224	89:1			225	
35:17	218	89:46			218	
35:21	220	90			218, 224	
38	218	90:13			218	
38:11	218	94			224	
40	218	94:3			218	
42	218	96			219	
42:3	219, 220	98			219	
42:10	219, 220	102			219	
43	218, 224	102:8			xx	
44	218	103:8–9			224	
44:13	218	107:24			205	
46	219	108			219	
47	219	109			224	
49:5	218	115			203, 218	
51	218	115:17			233	
53	219	117			219	
53:1	219	118:11–12			218	
55	218	121:4			229	
57	219	126			219	
59:7	219	135			203	

137:3	219
140:9	218
141	220
145:8	224

Isaiah

1:4–5	205
2–4	224
2:2–4	232
6:9–10	203, 273
7:14	330
9:2–7	204
35:1–7	204
32:15	204
41:16–17	204
42:19	203–4
43:8	274
43:19–20	204
44:1–5	204
49:15	91
49:18	91
52–53	202
52:13—53:12	204
53:3	48n72
59:21	204
61:1	243
61:1–3	204
62:5	91
66:17–19	204

Jeremiah

5:21ff	274
31:33	204

Ezekiel

10:4–5	204
10:18–19	204
12:2	274
36	204
36:26–27	204
37	204
37:14	204
37:26–27	204
47:9–10	205

Daniel

1	426

Joel

2:28–29	204
3:18	205

Amos

9:13	205

Jonah

4:2b	224

Zechariah

7:11–12	274

Matthew

1:18–25	330
1:26	80
4:23–24	206
5:8	166
11:26	80
13:14–15	274
13:52	423n79
13:55	330n40
19:10	133n32
22:37–39	205
27:43	229
27:46	228n11
28:18	90
28:18–20	168

Mark

1:32–34	206
1:44–45	231
4:12	274
6:3	330n40
7:36	231
8:18	274
12:10	240
13:11	244

Luke

1:26–38	330
2:8–11	59
3:16	205
3:21–22	205
4:1–21	205
4:16–21	139
4:18–19	243
4:21	240, 260
4:22	330n40
4:40–43	206
5:14–15	231
8:10	274
9:1	206
9:1–10	206
10:1	206
10:20	206
10:10	206
11:13	198
19:42	274
20:36	198
24:27	240
24:44–45	242
24:47	260

John

1:1–18	80
1:14	208
3:16	388
3:18	211
3:29	91
5:24	211
6	308
8:28	81
8:43–44	274
9:39–41	274
10:30	64
10:33	207
10:38	64
12:40	274
13:18	240
14–17	80
14:6	354
14:11	81
15:34	48n72
15:1–17	81
15:17	206
16:13	54
16:14–15	54
16:15	81
17	80n3, 92
17:12	240
17:21	81
17:24	296
19:24	240
19:28	240
19:36–37	240
20:21	72

Acts

1:15–17	238
2	100, 104, 109–10, 112, 114
2:22–36	205
3:21	179
4:8–12	205
4:31	243
10:34	146
10:38	200
15	73
16:6–8	244

Romans

1:18f	82
1:18–24	274
1:20	81
7:7–25	169n28
8	170
8:1	211
8:18–23	211
8:23	199
8:29	197
8:38–39	212
10:16	274
11:8	274
14:17	172
15:19	244

1 Corinthians

1:21–22	378
1:25	235

2:11–14	242
7	130
7:9	134n33
11:27	271, 179
12	395
12–14	389
13	427
13:10	211
15	92, 165, 211, 433
15:20–28	423n82
15:25–28	211
15:28	429

2 Corinthians

2:14–17	279
3:12—4:6	275
4:3–4	275
13:14	44

Galatians

1:6–9	161
4	100, 110
4:4	330n40
4:26	109–10, 112–14

Ephesians

1:3–4	177
1:4	192
1:4–5	211
1:10	211
4	165
5:22–32	91

Philippians

2:6–11	201–2, 205

Colossians

1:15	82, 89, 211
1:16	83
1:20	423n80
1:27	82
2	105

1 Thessalonians

2:13	244

2 Timothy

3:16–17	238
2:9	429n103
4:4	274

Hebrews

1:14	331
2:3–18	205
2:5–10	211
2:9	211
2:11	211
2:17–18	202
4:12	266
4:15	202
5:1	274
12:22–23	105, 112

1 Peter

2:9	48

2 Peter

1	165
1:4	81
1:20–21	239
3:11–13	423n83
3:15–16	240

1 John

1:2	213
1:3	98
2:2	187, 191
2:3	210n33
2:5c	210n33
2:6	198, 206, 210n34
2:28	210
3:1–2	211
3:10	210, 210n33
3:14–18	210–11
3:16	210, 210n33

3:19	210n33	5:11	207
3:24	207, 210n33		
4:2	208, 210n33		
4:8	64, 81	Jude	
4:9	210n33	3	320
4:10	210n33		
4:12–16	210		
4:13	210, 210n33	Revelation	
4:16	81, 210	1:3	199
4:16b–19	210	7:9	47
4:17	197–98, 210n33	19:7	91
5:2	210, 210n33	21:1—22:5	423n83
5:10b	207	21:9	91

www.ingramcontent.com/pod-product-compliance
Lightning Source LLC
Chambersburg PA
CBHW021231300426
44111CB00007B/496